The Routledge Handbook of Contemporary Feminism

Feminism as a method, a movement, a critique, and an identity has been the subject of debates, contestations, and revisions in recent years, yet contemporary global developments and political upheavals have again refocused feminism's collective force. What is feminism now? How do scholars and activists employ contemporary feminism? What feminist traditions endure? Which are no longer relevant in addressing contemporary global conditions?

In this interdisciplinary collection, scholars reflect on how contemporary feminism has shaped their thinking and their field as they interrogate its uses, limits, and reinventions. Organized as a set of questions over definition, everyday life, critical intervention, and political activism, the *Handbook* takes on a broad set of issues and points of view to consider what feminism is today and what current forces shape its future development. It also includes an extended conversation among major feminist thinkers about the future of feminist scholarship and activism.

The scholars gathered here address a wide variety of topics and contexts: activism from post-Soviet collectives to the Arab spring, to the #MeToo movement, sexual harassment, feminist art, film and digital culture, education, technology, policy, sexual practices, and gender identity. Indispensable for scholars and undergraduate and postgraduate students in women, gender, and sexuality, the collection offers a multidimensional picture of the diversity and utility of feminist thought in an age of multiple uncertainties.

Tasha Oren is Associate Professor in the Film and Media Studies Program and the Department of Theatre, Dance and Performance Studies at Tufts University. She has held faculty positions at the University of Pennsylvania and at the University of Wisconsin–Milwaukee where she directed the Film, Media and Digital Studies Program. Oren's books and co-edited collections include *Demon in the Box: Jews, Arabs, Politics and Culture in the Making of Israeli Television; Global Currents: Media and Technology Now; East Main Street: Asian American Popular Culture; Global Asian American Cultures; Global Television Formats – Understanding Television Across Borders*; and the forthcoming *Food TV: On Eating Media.*

Andrea L. Press is currently William R. Kenan Jr. Professor of Media Studies and Sociology at the University of Virginia. A founding Chair of the Department of Media Studies and former Executive Director of the Virginia Film Festival, Press has held faculty appointments at the University of Michigan, the University of Illinois Urbana/Champaign, the London School of Economics, and Hebrew University. Press has authored, co-authored, and co-edited several books including *Women Watching Television; Speaking of Abortion; The New Media Environment; Media and Class; Feminist Reception Studies in a Post-Audience Age; The New Feminist Television Studies*; and the forthcoming *Media-Ready Feminism and Everyday Sexism.* She co-edits the *Communication Review.* Professor Press is incoming Vice-Chair of the Feminist Scholarship Division of the International Communication Association.

Routledge International Handbooks

ROUTLEDGE INTERNATIONAL HANDBOOK OF SEX INDUSTRY RESEARCH
Edited by Susan Dewey, Isabel Crowhurst, and Chimaraoke Izugbara

ROUTLEDGE HANDBOOK OF CULTURAL SOCIOLOGY 2E
Edited by Laura Grindstaff, Ming-Cheng Lo, John R. Hall

THE ROUTLEDGE HANDBOOK OF LATIN AMERICAN DEVELOPMENT
Edited by Julie Cupples, Marcela Palomina-Schalscha and Manuel Prieto

THE ROUTLEDGE INTERNATIONAL HANDBOOK OF EMBODIED PERSPECTIVES IN PSYCHOTHERAPY: APPROACHES FROM DANCE MOVEMENT AND BODY PSYCHOTHERAPIES
Edited by Helen Payne, Sabine Koch, Jennifer Tantia and Thomas Fuchs

THE ROUTLEDGE HANDBOOK OF TEACHING LANDSCAPE
Edited by Elke Mertens, Nilgül Karadeniz, Karsten Jørgensen, Richard Stiles

THE ROUTLEDGE INTERNATIONAL HANDBOOK OF SPIRITUALITY IN SOCIETY AND THE PROFESSIONS
Edited by Laszlo Flanagan and Bernadette Flanagan

THE ROUTLEDGE INTERNATIONAL HANDBOOK OF LANGUAGE EDUCATION POLICY IN ASIA
Edited by Andy Kirkpatrick and Anthony J. Liddicoat

ROUTLEDGE INTERNATIONAL HANDBOOK OF MIGRATION STUDIES 2E
Edited by Steven J. Gold and Stephanie J. Nawyn

ROUTLEDGE HANDBOOK OF CONTEMPORARY FEMINISM
Edited by Tasha Oren and Andrea L. Press

ROUTLEDGE HANDBOOK OF THE BELT AND ROAD
Edited by Cai Fang and Peter Nolan

ROUTLEDGE HANDBOOK OF LANGUAGE ACQUISITION
Edited by Jessica S. Horst and Janne von Koss Torkildsen

ROUTLEDGE HANDBOOK OF IDENTITY STUDIES, 2E
Edited by Anthony Elliott

For more information about this series, please visit: www.routledge.com/Routledge-International-Handbooks/book-series/RIHAND

The Routledge Handbook of Contemporary Feminism

Edited by Tasha Oren and Andrea L. Press

LONDON AND NEW YORK

First published 2019
by Routledge

2 Park Square, Milton Park, Abingdon, Oxfordshire OX14 4RN
52 Vanderbilt Avenue, New York, NY 10017

Routledge is an imprint of the Taylor & Francis Group, an informa business

First issued in paperback 2020

British Library Cataloguing-in-Publication Data
A catalogue record for this book is available from the British Library

Library of Congress Cataloging-in-Publication Data
Names: Oren, Tasha G., editor. | Press, Andrea Lee, editor.
Title: Routledge handbook of contemporary feminism / edited by Tasha Oren and Andrea L. Press.
Description: Abingdon, Oxon ; New York, NY : Routledge, 2019.
Identifiers: LCCN 2018058931 | ISBN 9781138845114 (hardback) | ISBN 9781315728346 (ebook)
Subjects: LCSH: Feminism.
Classification: LCC HQ1155 .R688 2019 | DDC 305.42—dc23
LC record available at https://lccn.loc.gov/2018058931

ISBN: 978-1-138-84511-4 (hbk)
ISBN: 978-0-367-67058-0 (pbk)

Typeset in Bembo
by Apex CoVantage, LLC

Contents

Figures

Tables

Notes on contributors

Linda Blum, Professor of Sociology at Northeastern University (Boston), is the author of *Between Feminism and Labor: The Significance of the Comparable Worth Movement* (1991); *At the Breast: Ideologies of Breastfeeding and Motherhood in the Contemporary United States* (1999); and *Raising Generation Rx: Mothering Kids with Invisible Disabilities in an Age of Inequality* (2015), the 2016 Outstanding Publication of the Disability and Society Section of the American Sociological Association.

Vanda Černohorská is a PhD candidate at the Department of Sociology at the Masaryk University in Brno, Czech Republic. She was awarded a Fulbright grant to spend academic year 2015–2016 as a Visiting Assistant in Research at the Yale Center for Cultural Sociology. In her research, she is focusing on the topic of new media activism as a contemporary feminist strategy.

Mia Consalvo is Professor and Canada Research Chair in Game Studies and Design at Concordia University in Montreal. She is the co-author of *Players and their Pets*, co-editor of *Sports Videogames*, and author of *Cheating: Gaining Advantage in Videogames*. She has most recently published the book *Atari to Zelda: Japan's Videogames in Global Context*, about Japan's influence on the video gamegame industry and game culture.

Tressie McMillan Cottom is an award-winning sociology professor, author and sought-after public speaker on race, higher education, technology, and culture. Her work has been featured by the *Washington Post*, NPR's *Fresh Air, The Daily Show*, the *New York Times, Slate*, and *The Atlantic*, among others. She is the author of *Lower Ed: The Troubling Rise of For-Profit Colleges in the New Economy* (The New Press) and lives in Richmond, Virginia.

Susan Fraiman is Professor of English at the University of Virginia, specializing in gender and sexuality studies. Her most recent book, *Extreme Domesticity: A View from the Margins* (2017), takes unconventional and precarious homemakers as the basis for a new feminist theory of domesticity. Other books include *Cool Men and the Second Sex* (2003) and *Unbecoming Women: British Women Writers and the Novel of Development* (1993).

Jennifer A. Fredricks is the Dean of Academic Departments and Programs and Professor of Psychology at Union College. She has published over 50 journal articles and book chapters on student engagement, family socialization, adolescent development, and extracurricular participation. Jennifer has received funding from the National Science Foundation, Spencer Foundation, American Educational Research Association, and Institute for Educational Studies to support her research. Jennifer is author of *Eight Myths of Student Engagement: Creating Classrooms of Deep*

Learning (Corwin Press), and is co-editing the *Handbook of Student Engagement Interventions: Working With Disengaged Youth* (Elsevier Press).

Rosalind Gill is Professor of Social and Cultural Analysis at City University of London and a Professorial Fellow at University of Newcastle, New South Wales. She is author of several books including most recently *Mediated Intimacy: Sex Advice in Media Culture* (Polity, 2018, with Meg-John Barker and Laura Harvey) and is currently completing a book for Duke with Shani Orgad to be titled *The ConfidenceCult(ure)* and published in 2019.

Jack Halberstam is Professor of Gender Studies and English at Columbia University. Halberstam is the author of six books including *Skin Shows: Gothic Horror and the Technology of Monsters* (Duke UP, 1995); *Female Masculinity* (Duke UP, 1998); *In a Queer Time and Place* (NYU Press, 2005); *The Queer Art of Failure* (Duke UP, 2011); *Gaga Feminism: Sex, Gender, and the End of Normal* (Beacon Press, 2012); and, most recently, a short book titled *Trans*: A Quick and Quirky Account of Gender Variance* (University of California Press). Halberstam is currently working on several projects including a book titled *Wild Thing: Queer Theory after Nature* on queer anarchy, performance and protest culture, and the intersections between animality, the human, and the environment.

Rachael Haynes is an artist and academic currently based in Australia. Rachael is a Lecturer in Visual Arts in the Creative Industries Faculty at Queensland University of Technology UT, where she teaches in the Open Studio program. Her research investigates feminist ethics, language and voice through solo, collaborative and curatorial projects. Rachael is also the Director of Boxcopy Contemporary Art Space and was a founding member of the feminist art collective LEVEL.

Sally Hines is Professor of Sociology and Gender Identities at the University of Leeds. She works in the areas of gender, sexuality, intimacy, and the body, particularly addressing transformations in these identity practices and looking at how these shifts feed into theoretical debates around citizenship, recognition, and social movements. Sally has published widely in these areas. Her sole authored books include *TransForming Gender: Transgender Practices of Identity, Intimacy and* Care" (Policy Press, 2007); *Gender Diversity, Recognition and Citizenship: Towards a Politics of* Difference" (Palgrave Macmillan, 2013); and *Is Gender Fluid?* (Thames and Hudson, 2018). Sally is currently working on two Economic and Social Research Council (ESRC) funded projects: the first looks at the experiences of trans men who become pregnant, and the second explores how gender is understood and practiced by young people in the contemporary UK.

Susan Kerns is a filmmaker, Assistant Professor of Cinema and Television Arts at Columbia College Chicago, and Co-founder and Co-director of the Chicago Feminist Film Festival. She has published articles in *Nip/Tuck: Television that Gets Under Your Skin, Journal of Graphic Novels and Comics*, and *Comunicazioni Sociali*. She also produced the documentary *Manlife*, wrote the screenplay for *Little Red*, and produced or directed numerous short films. She holds a PhD from the University of Wisconsin–Milwaukee.

Sahar Khamis is an Associate Professor of Communication and an Affiliate Professor of Women's Studies at the University of Maryland, College Park. Her area of expertise is Arab and Muslim media, with a special focus on cyberactivism and gender activism. Her latest co-edited book is titled *Arab Women's Activism and Socio-Political Transformation: Unfinished Gendered Revolutions*. She is also the co-author of the books *Islam Dot Com: Contemporary Islamic Discourses in Cyberspace* and *Egyptian Revolution 2.0: Political Blogging, Civic Engagement and Citizen Journalism.*

Mimi Marinucci, Professor of both Philosophy and Women's & Gender Studies at Eastern Washington University, is the author of *Feminism Is Queer: The Intimate Connection Between Queer and Feminist Theory* (Zed Books, 2010, 2016). Marinucci's teaching and research address the production of knowledge, particularly social knowledge regarding gender, sex, and sexuality.

Alice E. Marwick (PhD, New York University) is Assistant Professor of Communication at the University of North Carolina, Chapel Hill, and Faculty Affiliate on the Media Manipulation Initiative at the Data & Society Research Institute. She studies the social and cultural implications of social media and is the author of *Status Update: Celebrity, Publicity and Branding in the Social Media Age* (Yale 2013) and co-editor of *The Sage Handbook of Social Media* (2017).

Ethel Mickey (Ph.D., 2018, Northeastern University) is a Visiting Lecturer of Sociology at Wellesley College. Her research engages the sociology of gender, work and organizations, and critical feminist studies of technology. Her dissertation, Networks of Exclusion in a Gendered Organization in the High-Tech Industry, examines the relational mechanisms undergirding gender, race, and class dynamics in the technology sector. Her work has appeared in the Journal of Contemporary Ethnography; Feminist Formations; and Gender & Society (forthcoming).

Sarojini Nadar, PhD, is a Full Professor at the University of the Western Cape where she also holds the Desmond Tutu Research Chair. The chair focuses on developing and supporting advanced research in the area of religion and social justice. Her research is broadly located at the intersections of gender studies and religion, including gender-based violence, sexual and reproductive health, and most recently critical pedagogy in higher education. As an activist-academic she is committed to transdisciplinary socially engaged scholarship.

Kathleen M. de Onís is an Assistant Professor in Willamette University's Department of Civic Communication and Media in Salem, Oregon. Her teaching and research focus on rhetorical studies, energy colonialism, reproductive and environmental justice, and coalitional politics. Her essays appear in *Communication Monographs, Communication Theory, Environmental Communication: A Journal of Nature and Culture, Women's Studies in Communication*, and *Women & Language*, as well as in several edited collections.

Sherry B. Ortner is Distinguished Professor of Anthropology at UCLA. She received her AB from Bryn Mawr College and her PhD from the University of Chicago. She has done extensive ethnographic and historical research with the Sherpas of Nepal and in the United States. She also publishes regularly in the areas of cultural theory and feminist theory. Her most recent book is *Not Hollywood: Independent Film at the Twilight of the American Dream.*

Joseph Padgett is a PhD candidate in the Department of Sociology at University of South Carolina. Utilizing both survey and experimental methods, he applies a social psychological approach to studying sexual behavior, including the impact of social power on how people perceive others' sexual intentions. Joseph has also examined predictors of selection into hookup, date, and relationship sex; partner meeting context and risk-taking sexual behavior; and variance in college student date and hookup sexual encounters.

Courtney Pedersen is the Academic Program Director for the School of Creative Practice and a Senior Lecturer in Art History/Theory at QUT, Brisbane, Australia. She was previously the Head of Discipline for Visual Arts at the same institution. Courtney writes and teaches about modern and contemporary art, gender studies, and experimental practice. She has also been an artist for 25 years.

Jessica Pressman is Associate Professor of English and Comparative Literature at San Diego State University. She is the author of *Digital Modernism: Making It New in New Media* (Oxford University Press, 2014), co-author, with Mark C. Marino and Jeremy Douglass, of *Reading Project: A Collaborative Analysis of William Poundstone's Project for Tachistoscope {Bottomless Pit}* (University of Iowa Press, 2015), and co-editor of two other volumes. Her full CV is available at www.jessicapressman.com.

Carrie Rentschler's research examines feminist activism, media making, gender violence, and the politics of witnessing. She is author of *Second Wounds: Victims' Rights and the Media in the U.S.* and co-editor of *Girls and the Politics of Place*, and is currently writing a history of contemporary bystander culture. She teaches in the Department of Art History and Communication Studies and is associate faculty in the Institute for Gender, Sexuality, and Feminist Studies at McGill University.

Lisa Wade is a Professor at Occidental College in Los Angeles. She earned an MA in Human Sexuality from New York University and an MS and PhD in Sociology from the University of Wisconsin–Madison. She is the author of *American Hookup: The New Culture of Sex on Campus* and *Gender: Ideas, Interactions, Institutions*, and is co-editor of *Assigned: Life with Gender.*

Alison Winch's book, *Girlfriends and Postfeminist Sisterhood* (Palgrave 2014), won a Choice's Outstanding Academic Titles Award. She recently co-edited a special issue on "Intergenerational Feminism" for *Feminist Media Studies*, as well as "Mediated Intimacies" for *Journal of Gender Studies*. Her new co-authored book on the *New Patriarchs of Digital Capitalism* is forthcoming.

Marina Yusupova is a postdoctoral researcher at Newcastle University Business School. She is currently involved in research on women in top leadership roles and explores such topics as gendered aspects of competition, ambition, and friendship at work. Marina has been a Fulbright Researcher at SUNY Stony Brook, has recently co-edited the volume *Gender and Choice After Socialism* (2018, Palgrave Macmillan), and published widely on topics of gender, masculinity, identity, and post-Soviet transformations.

Contemporary feminism

Editors' introduction

Tasha Oren and Andrea L. Press

What is contemporary feminism? When we first set out to contemplate this question in early 2016, feminism as a core principle faced an uncertain future: academically dismantled, intellectually deconstructed, politically dwarfed, and culturally suspect, it seemed destined to be surrounded by qualifiers, hyphens, and "posts." *How is feminism still relevant for activists and academics?* we wanted to ask; what does it mean now? Can we still invoke the term as a unified concept? How, we wondered, is feminism useful, not only as a perspective but also as a methodology, a tradition, a subject, and a bridge to connect academic, political, social, and cultural perspectives and shore up their work in fortifying ways? In much academic work, we observed, feminism has made its way from title, to subtitle, to body text, to footnotes; it had been absorbed and in the process had lost its position as subject. In conversations with potential contributors, we learned that many felt ambivalent about using the term, not for its connotations of struggle or its political demands but rather for its sense of rigidity, perceived lack of inclusivity, air of privilege, ill fit of universal claims, and a sense that other, more urgent politics have pressed for alternative allegiances.

As we set to work on a volume of contemporary, globally relevant feminism – while based, as we were, in the United States – we also wondered whether it was possible to assemble such a collection without conceding that the term, as singular, could no longer stand.

Then, a stunning election season in the United States saw a candidate flaunt his history of sexual assault as he synthesized racist, xenophobic, and misogynist thuggery to win an election against a female opponent. The Women's Marches, the largest protest in US history, followed, drawing millions both in the United States and around the world with the call "women's rights are human rights" and gathering demands for social, racial, sexual, labor, immigrant, and reproductive justice under the banner of feminism. Then came published and verified reports on a decades-long practice of sexual assault and rape by a powerful Hollywood producer – and details as to how such conduct was sustained by a machinery of corporate power. Then other revelations tumbled out at a breathless pace, and at first it was as if the cultural sphere was doing the work of (and penance for) the political realm, as countless directors, actors, producers, hosts, and film and media executives were accused and swiftly removed and disowned by the same corporate entities that fostered their behavior for years. For many, the moment felt dizzying and even exhilarating (as Sherry Ortner describes in our conversation in this volume). Soon, other business figures, celebrity chefs, artists, professors, and even some politicians followed in what seemed like a mad dash to set one corner of the universe in long-overdue balance, just as elsewhere, news of racial, ethnic, sexual, and economic violence emanated in equal parts from the streets and the most rarified hallways of democratic institutions. As 2017 came to a close, Merriam-Webster declared "feminism" the top lookup word of the year. In these same months, "metoo," first used by activist Tarana Burke in 2006 to describe supportive empathy among women of color who recounted their sexual abuse, reemerged as #MeToo and, by 2018, came to signify not only the practice of public accusation of sexual misconduct (among known, ordinary, and anonymous accusers alike) but a larger feminist cultural upheaval and a reckoning.

It was in this phase of reclaiming feminism and the possibilities of its political future that we completed this collection, making it both a text of, and witness to, a transition in feminisms' status, deployment, and life. While it is tempting from this temporal vantage point to declare that feminism as an urgent social force is "back," it's important that we interrogate this narrative of exile and return as itself an instructive part of feminism's limitations and potential. This quick turn of events also reminds us of how circular and volatile these discourses are. What about feminism's stress on gender parity and critiques of patriarchy writ large? Can the reparative notion of intersectionality hold feminism together after this red-hot moment dissipates?

How contemporary feminism has developed and deployed as a series of exchanges, challenges, ideas, critiques, strategies, and debates is the basis for this volume as it examines whether and how feminism is useful within various aspects of public, institutional, cultural, and private life. We challenge accepted categories for thinking about feminism and propose some new ways forward based on the diverse, global entity feminism has become.

Feminist intellectual traditions: an overview

Historically, overviews of feminism in academic and activist context are often conceived as a series of waves, particularly when scholars analyze the history of US and Western feminism, though globally the history of feminism is not always synonymous with the wave metaphors commonly used in the West (Narayan 1997); we have tried to honor this distinction in choosing essays for this book. Wave metaphors emerged at the dawn of the "women's liberation movement," after Marsha Lear coined both the phrases "first-wave feminism" and "second-wave feminism," writing in the *New York Times Magazine* in 1968 about a newly emerged incarnation of the feminist movement. The distinction is undoubtedly familiar to most readers of this volume. Feminism's first wave is identified with the suffragette movement and often dated to the 19th and early 20th centuries, the period of the main struggles for women's suffrage. The "second wave's" point of origin is most often identified with Simone de Beauvoir's *The Second Sex* and the 1963 publication of Betty Friedan's formative work, *The Feminine Mystique*. These texts and much of what followed in this period focused on the problems of white, affluent women, which remained the primary constituency of second-wave feminism until widespread challenges forced a broadening of its perspective beginning in the 1980s.

During the era of second-wave feminism, which extended from about 1963 to 1980, feminist scholarship became ensconced in American universities for the first time. A generative era for scholarship, it gave rise to a series of fundamental terms still used today, though continually interrogated. This same period also saw a series of foundational debates over feminism – its subject, aims, and definitions – which remain unresolved and continue to animate academic and activist feminism. Early second-wave feminism was home to a liberal feminist movement that emphasized the need for legislating gender *equality*, focusing on parity of pay in the workplace and equality of (unpaid) labor at home, such as housework and childcare. This became a primary focus for political feminist activist institutions like the National Organization for

Women (NOW). Thus the fight for reproductive freedom, and NOW's other foci, were also structured around the central notion of equality and applied to arguments over access, control, protection, and compensation.

In opposition to liberal feminism's formulation of equality of the sexes within existing institutional structures as its mission, radical and socialist feminism emerged to challenge this vision in both structure and scope. Radical feminism, also a movement arising within the second wave, turned the reality of sexual inequality on its head by arguing for the essential *superiority* of women's nature, identifying their generally less violent behavior, historic lack of support for war, and oft-noted greater selflessness, compassion, and concern for the welfare of others. This initiated a debate among feminist theorists and activists about the very notion of a gendered "essential" nature. And while contemporary feminist scholars and activists have mostly argued for a more fluid, changeable notion of gender and away from a rigid binary of a two-gender system, the debate has reemerged in often surprising ways – as a few of our contributors will discuss.

Connected to the notion of women's "essential" nature is the tradition of feminist scholarship about women's unique "standpoint" (Hartsock 1983). Standpoint theory challenged the idea that most scholarship prior to the feminist era was "objective" by identifying the ways in which women, as both object and subject of this scholarship, were often omitted by mainstream Western scholarship both as research subjects and as researchers with a particular set of experiences that gave rise to specific framing questions and interests. This highlighted the importance of women's perspectives or standpoints and opened the way for research from a number of other standpoints in the US context.

In addition, standpoint theory suggested a distinct feminist position for African Americans, non-Westerners, non-heterosexuals, and non-cisgendered individuals. Work on Black feminist epistemology – in both the US and African contexts – in this volume connects directly with this diverse tradition and its contemporary legacy. Indeed, standpoint theory has made a major contribution to academic research, which had ensconced the perspective of white men as the *only* perspective. It enabled many research questions to be framed entirely differently in ways that would enrich and expand our knowledge base. Standpoint theory also opened the way for scholars to realize the importance of diverse research samples, as many samples had consisted entirely of white males and results had been universally generalized from this population. Arguably, it was standpoint theory that provided scholars and administrators with a concrete argument for the value of diversity within the population of researchers themselves, and facilitated organized efforts to diversify institutions at large.

In the decades of feminism's so-called second wave, Socialist/Marxist feminism was another vital locus of transformative feminist work in a number of disciplines. Heidi Hartman's studies of women's labor in relation to both patriarchal and Marxist analyses of the labor process are foundational: they challenged the unpaid labor women perform in the home and the unequal compensation they receive in the labor force (1976, 1979, 1981). Zillah Eisenstein (1978) summarized this field in her early work, which interrogated the distinction between the capitalist and patriarchal systems of oppression and their interconnections. Judith Stacey (1983) examined the case study of China, in which patriarchy remained a vital force even as socialism replaced feudalist modes of labor and social organization. As our conversation participants discuss in the coda section of this volume, this rich and politically vital intellectual tradition has had a lasting influence on how many thinkers frame feminist critiques of labor within the power relations of patriarchy – a critique that has had particular currency in our recent political climate.

These traditions have each influenced work in a variety of academic disciplines at the same time that each tradition generated active political movements of its own. Radical feminism's standpoint theory, for one, particularly influenced scholars working in the disciplines of political theory and philosophy, who often turned inwards to dismantle formative male-centered perspectives within scientific and humanistic academic disciplines. In the areas of so-called hard scientific research, work by Evelyn Fox Keller (1984) interrogated the development of scientific concepts in biology with standpoint theory to identify reigning "masculinist" concepts in biology. In political science, Nancy Fraser's (1985, 2004, 2008) work challenged the fundamental divide between the public sphere, identified with men, and the private sphere, traditionally identified with women, by demonstrating the realms' interconnectedness. This influential work set the stage for scholars such as Seyla Benhabib (1992), a democratic theorist whose work focuses on issues "minority" groups face in seeking democratic process within a majoritarian culture; and Sally Haslanger (2000), a philosopher of metaphysics who joins the "ideological" with philosophic traditions in her quest to interrogate both racial and gender biases in her field and in the social sciences generally. The work of feminist activism and scholarship toward ensuring equality of entry into institutional structures of power, knowledge, and culture – STEM (science, technology, engineering, and mathematics) education, museums, filmmaking, and technology work – is highlighted in the "ways in" section of this collection.

Political theorists have also contributed to this tradition of feminist interrogation of the mainstream of their discipline. Iris Marion Young (1990) argued for a notion of "structural injustice," challenging liberal philosophers who advocated procedural equality by pointing out that it did not address structural inequities among groups. Linda Zerilli (2005), a feminist political theorist, also treated issues of plurality in liberal societies and the problems they pose for the operation of democracy. The work of noted female political theorist Hannah Arendt has been central for Zerilli's work. Other feminist political theorists, such as Mary Dietz, have uncovered the work of overlooked female theorists – in her case, Simone Weil – arguing for resurrecting their centrality to the discipline (Dietz 1988). All have been crucial for creating a subfield of feminist political philosophy, which has now broadened to include axes of oppression other than gender.

Feminist perspectives revolutionized other disciplines as well. The field of history – and the practice of academic feminism – was never the same after feminist historians such as Joan Scott (1986) began to challenge the ahistoricity of feminists' own use of the analytic term "gender" while maintaining it as a primary access of domination throughout history. This tradition is well reflected in contributions to the "everyday" section of this volume.

Anthropology, too, was changed with the work of feminists such as Sherry Ortner, who continues her leading role in feminist anthropology with her essay on postfeminism in this volume. Her field-defining piece "Is Female to Male as Nature is to Culture?," published at the height of the second wave in 1972, influenced the categorical status of these distinctions in anthropology, opening the way for a more serious study of women's importance in the cultural life of societies. Other feminist anthropologists followed in her wake, ultimately transforming a discipline that already (and unusually) saw female scholars in leading roles since its inception.

The field of sociology too has been influenced by the work of the many feminist sociologists who have gained prominence in the field. Andrea L. Press's own mentors, Arlie Hochschild and Nancy Chodorow, have played a leading role in this process. Hochschild's development of a "sociology of emotion" subfield (2012) has opened up a key aspect of life – the emotional – to sociological reflection and analysis. This can be seen as a process of beginning to take seriously an area of social life previously thought of as "female" and therefore unworthy of sociological analysis – a trend critiqued by Judith Stacey and Barrie Thorne's 1985 call for the "missing feminist revolution" in the field.

Sexuality studies as well have legitimated an area of study previously thought to be simply governed by nature and therefore not amenable to sociological scrutiny. Radical feminist and legal scholar Catharine MacKinnon has put forth perhaps the most famous set of arguments asserting that heterosexuality is inherently about gender domination (1978), though this was argued by a spate of radical feminists at the same time, among them Andrea Dworkin (1987). The work of feminist sociologists such as Paula England and Sut Jhally (2011) is particularly relevant in this exploration of "hookup culture" and its underlying assumption. The second wave's sexual revolution has still not guaranteed women freedom of sexual expression and sexual gratification, as we see in this important study. Feminist sociologist Judith Stacey's (2012) work extends the study of sexuality to the study of non-traditional families, looking at the impact of non-normative sexualities on their children and alleviating cultural fears that such families negatively impact children.

An interdisciplinary academic and practitioner field known as psychoanalytic feminism also arose in the wake of the feminist academic revolution. Kicked off by Juliet Mitchell's feminist reading of Freud (1975), the work of feminist sociologist and psychoanalyst Nancy Chodorow was also notable in this area, and she is often identified as the founder of "feminist psychoanalytic sociology." Chodorow's extension of the notion of "work" to the process of "mothering" in her celebrated *The Reproduction of Mothering* (1978) opened up a previously taken-for-granted aspect of human life to sociological scrutiny and explanation. Chodorow challenged the "essential nature" of the almost universal phenomenon of mothering and its assumptive power about women's "natural" capacity and paved the way toward egalitarian models of parenting.

Socialist/Marxist feminism has been similarly generative for a spectrum of feminist work across sociology, economics, history, and many other disciplines. Following the tradition of Hartmann and Eisenstein, scholars have continued exploring the varied dimensions of paid and unpaid labor women perform, examining how their roles, compensation, and workplace environment differ from those of men. Intersectionality is a concept developed by Kimberle Crenshaw (1997; see also Crenshaw et al. 1996) and bell hooks (2014) to describe how interlocking systems of power affect each of these factors for society's most marginal members. It has been useful in feminist theory to articulate that the notion that gender cannot always be considered as the *primary* mode of oppression (hooks 2014). The idea of intersectionality became crucial to this area of study, as sociologists explored the double and triple jeopardy, and the penalties and hazards, experienced by workers who were both female *and* held various minority status, whether racial, sexual, non-Western, or a combination. Work in this area includes Kathleen Gerson's studies of women's "hard choices" between prioritizing work and family (2011), Linda Blum's study of the comparable worth movement (1991), and Ruth Milkman's historical work on women in the US labor movement (2016), among many others.

As we've described in some detail here, an early moment of reckoning in feminist scholarship exposed that much foundational thinking within the academy was based solely on men's experience. It further changed course for research questions in the realms of private and domestic life – identified as the lesser status of "women's domains." This revolution affected most fundamental scholarly disciplines in virtually every field. Yet the reach of these theoretical ideas, collectively known as the "second wave," extends well beyond the academy, but its adoption into political discourse has also opened feminism up to new critical self-assessment that found it too insular, elitist, White, Western, cisgendered, and upper-middle class in its orientation and vision. Feminism's developing intersectional perspective provided a clear perch for such a critique, as it offered a complex positionality that accounted for the interactions of oppression. In this sense, feminism's new center was itself a critique of feminism's cohesive centrality.

The intersectionality critique is responsible in part for the rise of what has become known as "third-wave" feminism. Rebecca Walker coined the term "third-wave feminism" in 2003 to differentiate a feminism more global, multiracial, less class specific, less heterosexual, and more gender diffuse than the more narrow focus of the second wave. Generally, the "third wave" is thought to refer to the feminism of the 1980s and 1990s. More recently, some (Baumgardner 2011;

Cochrane 2013) have talked of "fourth-wave feminism," generally defined as more psychological and spiritual than the feminisms which came before (Diamond 2009). As several authors in this volume will argue in a variety of contexts, much of contemporary feminism today struggles with difference, fought on the terrain of this "wave-based" legacy.

Telling this most visible history of feminist thought through the notion of waves has long ceased to be a mere metaphor for gathering forces that ebb, flow, and replace each other. It has become the method by which we tell this story of mainstream feminism, now characterized as a series of reactions, critiques, and counters. Rather than illuminating particular perspectives in contexts, wave theory emphasizes irreconcilability within feminism. What's more, this conflict model has mass media appeal and has often worked to divert attention from feminism's power and subject, as several of the final pieces in the volume explore. In organizing the contributions detailed below, we endeavored to avoid organization based on chronology, identity, location, or tradition. Instead, we offer the collected pieces under four questions of scope: how feminist critique interrogates its founding principles, how it theorizes everyday life and experience, how it interacts with institutions, and how it defines itself as a political force.

The *Handbook*: structure and sections

The contributions in this volume are organized by sections, each taking up feminism through different scales or types of questions. In the first section, *Ways of Being*, authors consider feminism philosophically and categorically as they examine notions of gender, essentialism, identity, epistemology, and political terminology and interrogate feminism's encounter with definitions. Next, *Ways of Living* examines feminism as a lived, everyday practice. Here, contemporary life – especially as experienced within an environment dense with digital tools and practices – is analyzed in a variety of contexts and feminist implications. The third section, *Ways In*, thinks through feminism as means of access to, and entry into, mainstream institutions. Essays in this section critically engage with feminist strategies of inclusion, change, and transformation within educational, industrial, and cultural institutions. The final essay section, *Ways of Contesting*, arrives at feminism as a global political movement. Here authors take up feminism as organized politics, charting contemporary and historical case studies that analyze the success and failures of feminism as activist ethos. In the final coda section, we engage in a conversation about the status, methodology, limits, and future potentialities of feminism with three notable feminist critics: Sherry Ortner, Jack Halberstam, and Tressie McMillan Cottom.

Section I: ways of being

Are categories useful? If thinking about difference is at the core of contemporary feminism, what set of unified terms, methodologies or definitions are still at play? Which distinctions remain or become vital? Which central notions require troubling? We begin with categories of gender, identity, and the fraught notion of essentialism. Feminism's complex relationship with essentialism has been brought to the fore yet again in recent years. In "Taking Exceptions Seriously: Essentialism, Constructionism, and the Proliferation of Particularities," philosopher Mimi Marinucci revisits the contested concept as a vital arena for feminism's engagement with categories such as sexuality, gender, and sex. Feminist critiques and rejection of essentialism have been a common element in so-called third-wave feminism and remain a troubling taxonomy – a notion that perceives gender as a biological and "natural" category of difference. However, essentialism (both strategic and "real") has also been enormously useful as a category that mobilized feminist legal and political arguments. In contemporary thought, gender as a constructed concept (arbitrary and non-empirical) and notions of gender fluidity coexist (in various degrees of comfort) alongside arguments for "true" gender identity mobilized by trans activists (among others) against gender border policing by conservative political antagonists. Similarly, arguments about sexuality have also deployed categories of "natural kind" as important political tools. In these arguments, the deployment of cisgendered biology as a source of gender or sexuality is rejected and replaced by different essential taxonomy (inherent gender identity or natural sexuality).

In this context, Marinucci thinks through the case for social construction and for our various attempts to make systematic sense of the various charged categorical deployments of gender, sex, and sexuality. This, in a moment where investment in a form of essentialism (take for example the rights of transgendered people to use bathrooms corresponding to their actual lived gender identity, or the rights of gays and lesbians to define their lives not as "lifestyle choice" but as a product of their inherent selves) is experienced as both politically progressive and fundamentally "true." Addressing this impasse, Marinucci formulates an argument for categories of sex and sexualities that are *made*, yet importantly are neither arbitrary nor outside empirical observation. In this sense, her formulation does not make sexuality and gender identity any less "real," while keeping the notion that taxonomies are constructed systems and alternatives are always, necessarily, available.

Alternative feminist systems of knowledge are at the heart of gender and religion scholar Sarojini Nadar's essay. "'Stories Are Data with Soul': Lessons from Black Feminist Epistemology" addresses a question central to feminist epistemology since the early days of feminism in the academy: is there a specifically "feminist" methodology that is more useful for feminist research, and for research about women? Nadar begins with distinguishing feminist research from research about or by women yet goes on to argue that even newer intersectionally driven research about women, much like the African-based scholarship she highlights, needs to draw from the main wells of feminist theory about research, position, and perspective. Nadar turns to the tradition of black feminism to extract a series of tenets about feminist methodology, which for her are useful specifically for research about African women. Basing her discussion on the long and distinguished traditions of black and African feminist theorists, Nadar draws out important commonalities between historical tenets of feminist methodology and traditions within African culture to stress the power of narrative and storytelling for the production of feminist modes of knowledge. Stories yield emotional and personal data, which are often discounted by the modes of judgment dominant in the academy. However, she argues, these modes of account and retelling, especially in the African context, are precisely called for in feminist research projects and offer unique knowledge for progress toward gender equality. Nadar's argument now works back to resonate with the unfolding project of #MeToo, as it also gained power through stories. In the #MeToo context, generating feminist knowledge is illustrated by the insistence on personal accounts and the outpouring of emotional knowledge as generative work in archiving, recording, and combating gender inequality and sexual abuse.

Nadar's work importantly highlights how traditions of feminist thought can be relevant across and with specificity of experience, location, and culture – a notion that later essays in the collection challenge. In this section, however, the question of persistent and new categories within feminist thought turns again to relevance, but from place to time. In "'Does Feminism Have a Generation Gap?' Blogging, Millennials, and the Hip Hop Generation," media scholar Alison Winch examines how contemporary feminism has been shaped by the notion of a generational divide and suggests important implications for the stubborn persistence of the "wave" metaphor.

Winch discusses the ways in which generational metaphors have dominated historical accounts of feminism and points to important continuities between the feminism of "our mothers'" generation and current feminist activities. Analyzing contemporary feminist blogs (the UK-based

Vagenda, the US-based *Crunk Feminist Collective*, and the *UK Feminist Times*), Winch highlights similarities between their approach to feminism and those of past generations, demonstrating how these "new" practices by young feminists are linked to, and continuous with, a tradition of alternative feminist publishing. Feminism's so-called generation gap is central here to understating the dominating logic of "waves" in feminist history and to the narrative of each new "wave" as a historical counter-response. This "conflict" discussion is often seized upon by the mass media and dominates its portrayal of feminisms. For Winch, thinking in these terms promotes a vision of feminism as harboring an inherent generational conflict that is neither accurate nor useful. Instead, she invokes Braidotti's notion of "zigzagging" as a more useful metaphor than generational progress or conflict. This moves away from reaction, counters, and discontinuities, and allows for a more productive narrative of feminism's history and ongoing project, as it stresses dynamic continuity. The approach advocated by Winch resists the logic of historical irrelevance and with it, of course, the notion of "postfeminism." As the feminist anthropologist Sherry Ortner argues in "Too Soon for Postfeminism: The Ongoing Life of Patriarchy in Neoliberal America," the notion that feminism's relevance remained fixed in a "past" historical point has gained prominence in steady parallel to the development of a feminist paradigm in the late 1980s. Arguing against postfeminism as a framework, Ortner notes that there is a persistent need to understand and employ the central feminist concept of "patriarchy" in order to make sense of the continued and possibly growing sexism in a variety of arenas in contemporary society. Accounting for a range of postfeminist theory and its uses, Ortner reads a series of recent popular films as ideological "illustrations" for feminist theory's explanatory power within contemporary global politics. As she emphasizes, it is patriarchy, not feminism, which has thrived under neoliberal capitalism, making postfeminism's claim for historical reframing both misguided and dangerous. Ortner's argument, written before the recent resurgence in feminist identification and the concomitant attention to widespread sexism in the workplace, is particularly instructive for our current moment, as she reflects in our interview in the book's final section.

The recent resurgence of feminist activism and critiques of patriarchy, paired with new attention to intersectionality, have reignited discussions about feminist practice, focus, and politics but have also posed new challenges for feminist identity and the question of "who is" or "who counts" as a feminist. It is this central question of category admission that the last two essays in this section address, from two very different vantage points. In "Lost in Translation: Challenging (White, Monolingual Feminism's) <Choice> with *Justicia Reproductiva*," civic communication and Latina/o/x scholar Kathleen M. de Onís presents a case study for the challenges of integrating an intersectional perspective to definitions of feminist politics and identity. De Onís traces the history of reproductive choice activism in the United States, so central to second-wave feminism, and illustrates how it has simply ignored or spoken past the concerns of many in the Latina and immigrant population. As De Onís argues, terminology and language can either forge an inclusive movement or fortify borders in place of shared concerns and alliances. Focusing in particular on discursive strategies, and the centrality of the word "choice" in the history of feminist reproductive politics, she points out how the term itself alienates and marginalizes those who espouse a "family first" identity, so central to many women in Latina culture. Here language and emphasis come to stand for the "whole" of feminism, as language itself confines Latina women to the "borders" of the reproductive rights movement and marks feminist identities as synonymous with the priorities of privileged, white, mainstream actors. To counter this exclusion, a Latina feminist activist group, the National Latina Institute for Reproductive Health, has coined the term "reproductive justice" (*justicia reproductiva*) to replace what they argue is the more selectively applicable term "choice," coined and used primarily in white-dominated feminist activist groups.

The author urges a closer communication between the political pro-choice movement, which tends to be white- and privilege-centered, and representatives of active Latina-based feminist movements, who are also concerned about reproductive rights but cannot fully take on the identity of those in the mainstream movement given the marginalizing nature of the latter's language and priorities. The piece ends with an anticipated meeting between the president of NOW and representatives of the *justicia reproductiva*/reproductive justice group. With this, it imagines a more unified future for a feminist movement that can think and speak priorities across racial, cultural, and class-based differences.

The challenges of inclusion, identification, and boundary-drawing within feminism – as well as the issue of whom feminism serves within a larger political order – are also central concerns for closing the section as it circles back to the question of essentialism, which opened the collection. Who counts as feminism's subject? Despite the emergence of pluralist feminism, critiques of feminism's conventional erasure of difference around issues of race, class, poststructuralist critiques of the fixity of sex and gender in the '90s, and debates over gender identity as a feminist category, all remain stress points. The site of the body, as we've seen with several of the preceding essays, is central to feminist intervention (health care, sexual violence, pregnancy, abortion, etc.) and forms a particularly charged place for feminist politics. In "The Feminist Frontier: On Trans and Feminism," transgender studies researcher Sally Hines examines disputes over who can take up an identity as a feminist and highlights a key area of contestation over "gendered authenticity" within the politics of who and what constitutes women within feminism. Hines's analysis of the fury over the invitation of a transwoman to speak at *Dykes March London*, and debates over toilet use and safe spaces, reveal the anxiety of "takeover" and erasure that link trans people with patriarchy, misogyny, and potential violence. As she notes, feminist texts that linked biology to sexuality laid the groundwork for these ideas as early as 1979, and disputes over gender identity and biology have persisted for at least five decades of feminist thought and practice. However, as the trans rights movement has gained visibility in recent years, these antagonisms have grown (especially in the UK), are virulently played out in social media, and for Hines, offer dangerous points of co-option of feminism into broader conservative political practices.

As Hines shows, surprisingly common anti-trans arguments from prominent feminists mirror conservative (and anti-gay) rhetoric that has also characterized the "bathroom debates" in both the US and the UK contexts (although Hines limits her discussion to the UK). These debates, in turn, are braided into larger feminist discussions of safety, identity, and free speech that have particular resonance in this current moment of #MeToo, with its emphasis on the need to attend to and believe women's accounts of their experience. This current emphasis pointedly contradicts the essay's focus on panic over "gender fraud" and the anti-trans feminist practice of discounting and disbelieving transwomen's own accounts of their sexuality and gender identity. As Hines concludes, anti-trans feminists may not represent the majority feminist position yet they enjoy an outsized presence in social media and cultural politics. Importantly, these boundary-policing discourses and reductive definitions of gender are deployed in the name of female safety and feminist truth-claims that produce trans bodies as feared others and belie everyday, embodied gendered experience.

Section II: ways of living

In this section, authors consider women's everyday experience, particularly in our contemporary digitally dense environment with feminist history or as an emergent social history. If the first section's emphasis was on identity, authors in the following section focus on feminism's encounter with everyday activity and ways of "doing." In this, the authors also stress the private and domestic realms where women have traditionally been located in theory, if not in reality. One of feminism's earliest interventions, of course, was to reintegrate the domestic and everyday life of women into political and economic discourses of power and labor. As such, the notion of a gendered "everyday life" or "women's private sphere," long overlooked by much historical and literary scholarship, has been a central theme in feminist historical and literary studies.

In "Everyday Life Studies and Feminism," literary scholar Susan Fraiman provides a theoretical overview of the emergence of "everyday life" or the quotidian as a locus for theoretical investigation. In her essay Fraiman argues for the re-evaluation of early feminist writers Simone de Beauvoir and Luce Giard, who she notes are often cited but rarely acknowledged for their contributions as pioneering theorists of everyday life. Fraiman analyzes how these texts theorize the place of domesticity and the repetitive, everyday actions involved in domestic labor, which decades of feminist theory have equated with women and femininity. Through her analysis, Fraiman illustrates how feminist work on the everyday has cleaved into "critique" and "appreciation" in parallel with notions of "difference" and "equality" feminism. These two competing tendencies, she argues, continue to give shape to feminist work on the domestic and everyday practices and, in large part, form an ongoing core tension within feminism itself. In linking an historical analysis of literary texts to contemporary feminist activism, Fraiman illustrates the importance of the politics of the everyday to conceptualizing just what feminism is, and demonstrates how this far-reaching question is far from settled.

How to account and theorize ordinary feminist practices in terms of feminist traditions and activism? How do we understand feminism as ways of making things in contemporary culture? These are the questions that guide feminist media scholar Carrie Rentschler as she takes on women craft, zine, and media makers as feminist practice within a contemporary makers' culture. In "Making Culture and Doing Feminism," Rentschler examines how material practices by girls and women constitute "acts of feminist making" that create not only objects but also a set of feminist attachments. This "we-ness" approaches feminist making as an often collaborative and network-based set of practices emerging from relations between friends, family members, colleagues, mentors, students, fellow activists, and other makers. An attentive analysis of these networked practices speaks directly to the broader definitional issue of how feminist identities are made in discourse and through material production and exchange – in short, how they are lived. As Rentschler argues, such maker practices are important (but often undervalued) sites of feminist work and material agency that function not only as culture-making but as critiques of labor, race, and class politics. Moreover, as an expansive theory of "doing" and "making" can challenge and enrich our conceptions of fabrication, it also enhances our grasp of what it means to "do feminism."

While Rentschler stresses agency and connected labor within contemporary digital culture, sociologist Rosalind Gill follows a starkly different aspect of contemporary digital labor, that of cultural practices of self and peer surveillance. In "Surveillance is a Feminist Issue," Gill considers the central role of surveillance through a host of popular practices and digital tools – from beauty apps to social media hubs and self-trackers – as she traces recent work that links surveillance and the production of selfhood with feminist theory. Paradoxically, for contemporary feminists the growing regulation of bodies, activities, and essential ways of being in the world often originate with women themselves. In examining this contemporary mode of peer and self-surveillance, Gill positions it as operating within the specific logic of postfeminism and neoliberalism. She rejects a top-down model of surveillance and argues that digital and media cultures and postfeminist modalities of subjecthood are coming together as "neoliberal optics" to produce a novel and extraordinarily powerful regulatory gaze on women. As her essay suggests, this contemporary era of surveillance, while located in the self, is facilitated and largely practiced through digital tools.

How everyday practices and conventions have formed, changed, and transformed with the use of digital tools in a densely connected, always-on digital environment has been a major line of inquiry for feminist scholarship across disciplines – and for many in this collection. One common, much discussed but as yet understudied contemporary practice is that of intimate sexual behavior and the casual culture of "hooking up," made easier by traditional social media and dedicated apps such as Tinder, Grindr, Blendr, Feeld, Bumble, and more recent variations. Women's sexual behavior and the gendered quality of erotic pleasure have animated and divided feminist theory and continue to ignite debate about the meeting place of sexuality and power. And while relatively new digital tools have often been the focus of cultural discourse around contemporary sexuality, their use has not so much changed sexual behavior as it has highlighted more fundamental shifts in some sexual mores and practices – especially among young women whose sexuality formed within such "new" norms.

Recent interest and increased publicity about the alleged epidemic of sexual assault on college campuses, paired with the pervasive casual sexuality of swipes and hookups, has raised new questions about feminist responses to hookup culture as a commonplace practice on contemporary college campuses. In "Hookup Culture and Higher Education," social researchers Joseph Padgett and Lisa Wade set out to provide a kind of primer for what we know about hookup culture. They begin with a historical overview of sexual practices and norms among straight undergraduates from the rise of the fraternity in the early turn of the 20th century, the transition from courtship to dating in the 1930s, and the emergence of "partying" culture in the 1960s as precursors to current practices. As the authors show, while male interests and sexual pleasure were certainly at the center and evolution of such practices, the women's movement and the sexual revolution played an important role in reframing many women's participation in such sexual practices on campus, emphasizing partying and casual sex as a right and granting an access to fun and pleasure once reserved only for men. The authors further account for the demise of dating and the rise of "hookup culture" on campus as they collect and synthesize how recent research accounts for and explains this phenomenon as a new cultural norm. Important for a feminist perspective are the notions of both harm and agency in such sexual practices and the difficulties inherent in fully accounting for young women's sexual freedom and desire while also attending to a host of problematic power imbalances and potential violence in such situations – the latter is addressed specifically in later sections and at length in the coda section of this collection. Here again, the tensions between "difference" and "equality" that opened this section also emerge as we consider how feminist approaches have historically framed sexual practices and their cultural significance.

We conclude the section on everyday, seemingly banal practices with an essay that considers feminist theory as an interventionist strategy into how such mundane activities are framed and represented in digital art. This final essay builds on the notions of labor, domesticity, and culture-making already explored by Fraiman and Rentschler and brings together material and digital culture. It also lays the groundwork for the next section by juxtaposing this research with contemporary feminist philosophy and art making as a critical (and institutional) practice. Through an analysis of *Circles*, an interactive, augmented reality digital work by Canadian artist Caitlin Fisher, comparative literature scholar Jessica Pressman explores how feminist critique serves as an important corrective to contemporary philosophical approaches to both materialism and the digital. Pressman's essay, "Circling Back: Electronic Literature and Material Feminism," offers a remarkably lucid introduction to the philosophical foundations of materiality and object-oriented ontology (OOO), a discussion of its potential, and a reflection on how feminist intervention in this context reaffirms the vitality of feminist thought as it insists on embodiment, situated context, historical specificity, and felt power relations.

Circles is a work of digital storytelling that combines interactive digital tools and small, ordinary feminine objects (which readers are invited to handle) to tell "small" domestic, interconnected stories about women's lives that emerge as fundamentally relational. Reading the work as a disruption, a feminist reworking of how digital aesthetics are commonly used, Pressman employs it as a tutor text to illustrate how feminist critique, feminist digital theory, and feminist philosophy have productively intervened in emerging theories of matter and digital theory. In Pressman's reading of the work and its feminist ethos, the sense of self and the process of its formation is one of mediation – social and technological – where subjects and objects are inseparable. Pressman's method of reading *Circles*' own style as argument identifies the aesthetics of "cute," long associated with femininity and devalued aesthetics, and "glitch," an intentional interruption in the smooth digital flow of operation. In the context of an intellectual history of "error" and "glitch feminism," the work becomes an ongoing feminist exploration into making art, making theory, and making sense of the physical and the digital.

Section III: ways in

This section considers feminist interventions into mainstream structures of knowledge and cultural production. Feminist critique has long functioned to point to, push against, and analyze how mainstream institutions maintain and delimit power through exclusion. How institutions deal with such critiques, create their own protocols for admission, access, or change (or entrenchment) form an important context for feminism's continuous engagement with what we think of as "mainstream" and how we imagine its future shape and function.

The essays collected in this section interrogate notions of inclusion and participation in educational institutions, the art world, filmmaking and exhibition, and developing digital technologies. As these analyses make clear, barriers to gender – and proposed solutions for inclusion – must account for multiple axes of oppression while contending with complex questions of what various visions of inclusion might practically look like.

Much recent literature about gender in education has posed a variety of questions about the progress women have made, the specific problems they encounter in STEM fields, and the crisis boys are experiencing in progressing through K-12 educational institutions. While other essays in our collection analyze inequities in gender achievement and participation in STEM fields, science education specialist Jennifer A. Fredericks's essay, "Gender and Schooling: Progress, Persistent Inequalities, and Possible Solutions" addresses the question of whether there is a crisis for girls in early K-12 education. To do this, she summarizes and analyzes a wide swath of studies addressing gender inequality in education.

Existing data on women's success or failure in STEM fields suggests systematic disadvantages for women's educational and professional advancement in these areas. And despite an increasing number of programs targeted at improving their progress, little concrete success is shown for women entering these fields. Perplexingly, women have achieved greater in-school success in the field of math. However, this has not translated into broader success and representation in STEM careers in later life. Moreover, while boys have slightly lower test scores on average, they outperform girls on post-school options, employment, and other economic indicators. Although the focus on achievement measures that show girls' advantage simply fails to capture the full range of inequalities in school, it is similarly unable to measure how gender is both constructed and reinforced in the classroom. Fredricks's essay provides important insights into such systemic classroom practices (both cultural and practical) as she points out mismatches between research and implementation and suggests strategies for educators and administrators involved at the K-12 level.

As Fredricks's research underscores, the continuing underrepresentation of women in STEM fields has stymied the most dedicated feminist researchers, educators, administrators, and policy-makers. How can feminist theory more effectively intervene and address the persistent lack of women in these fields – in both academia and in industry – accounting for a variety of complex structural and cultural conditions?

For women working in technology, corporate culture is most often a primary obstacle for advancement and success. These challenges are all the more magnified in the videogame industry, where under-the-hood technological skill is so commonly associated with a (hyper)male cultural practice. Feminist engagement with videogames has more traditionally concerned their textual manifestation – specifically, representation of women. More recently, girl and women players have also garnered some much-needed attention as an understudied (and rapidly growing) part of gaming culture. Reflecting on her own work and on feminist game studies as a burgeoning discipline, game studies scholar Mia Consalvo argues for the necessary extension of game studies beyond the symbolic world of games to analysis of the industry of game-making and the cultural field that encircles it. In "Why We Need Feminist Games Studies," the work of developers, marketers, critics, reviewers, gamers and their social media sites, as well as the academic discipline of game studies are all (and together) crucial arenas for feminist intervention in scholarly and institutional terms. In her expansive account, Consalvo begins with the experiences of female game designers, critics, and scholars (herself included) who found themselves targets of a virulent misogynist strand within gamer culture. This culture came to light most powerfully in what has since been called "Gamergate." Consalvo breaks down "Gamergate" as a long-brewing cultural process with deep roots that entangle and link certain corners of game-player culture, gaming publications, and long-entrenched industry practices. Approaching "Gamergate" not as an unprecedented and isolated explosion of venom but rather as part of an ongoing practice of exclusion and retaliation against women, people of color and other minorities, Consalvo reads it in relation to what she calls the "feminization of social, mobile and casual games" as both a counter-force and a phenomenon that stokes the ongoing cultural war over gaming.

In tracing these tensions further, Consalvo documents efforts by female game developers to bring working conditions and sexist exclusionary practices within their own industries to light. Resonating powerfully with recent revelations and the #MeToo movement, these practices are most pernicious not in public moments of acute and shocking bad behavior (by a few powerful men) but in their revelation of a system all but designed for persistent exclusion and disregard. As Consalvo shows, feminist analysis has been crucial in tracing how the gaming industry actively and tacitly guards long-cherished structural inequalities in mainstream gamer culture, even as it works to market to a female consumer. The next two essays examine how feminist production can be organized and disseminated while negotiating similar institutional dynamics in the field of culture.

In "Acting Out: Performing Feminisms in the Contemporary Art Museum," feminist artist Rachael Hynes and educator/curator Courtney Pedersen interrogate the label "feminist art" and its relationship to contemporary museum exhibition. "Feminist art," they observe, can easily become a label that at once valorizes and archives work, marking it part of a historical movement rather than a timely set of attitudes or strategies. How to keep such a category alive and vital? How to process feminist art's inclusion in mainstream art institutions without losing its political urgency? The authors offer an answer using the LEVEL feminist collective public programming around the Yoko Ono show *WAR IS OVER (IF YOU WANT IT)* at the Museum of Contemporary Art Australia (MCA). Through an overview of curatorial strategies of feminist work and performance, the authors introduce the challenges (and past failures) in exhibiting feminist art work and the difficulties in avoiding a "fixing effect" that renders them static, isolated, and stripped of their charge. As they review prominent critiques they also reveal how, in terms of ongoing political relevance, canonization can often be the flipside of non-inclusion, especially in light of the persistent underrepresentation of women artists at all levels of mainstream exhibition. What's more, they question the very possibility of mainstream inclusion in museums, contemporary institutions that, more than ever, depend on corporate support and the economic and political status quo. The design and work of the LEVEL collective in conjunction with Ono's exhibit is here explored as a series of activities and decisions that considered such challenges and worked to position the events not as mere confrontation and critique but as progressive solution and alternative visions that refuse the line between artists and viewers, history and present, and the sanctioned museum space and its "outside."

As other contributors in the volume suggest, the line between "feminist" and "woman" cultural practices and production is an important – and often productive – point for interrogation. Cultural work by women is not, of course, inherently feminist. But structural practice around the project, as well as its focus and means of production, can often infuse a work with feminist urgency as vital as their content and political impetus. In her essay "Can't I Just Be a Filmmaker? Women's and Feminist Film Festivals' Resurgence in a Postfeminist World," scholar and co-founder/co-director of the Chicago Feminist Film Festival Susan Kerns considers the recent resurgence of women's and feminist film festivals, their evolving mission and growing popularity. How do festivals take part in debates surrounding the purpose of such mission-specific endeavors? How have current women- and feminist-centered festivals found new success after being dismissed as "retrograde" nearly two decades ago? Kerns positions film festivals' history within both the film industry at large and the festivals' own evolving role from alternative showcase to a full participant in a competitive mainstream international film industry. The reemergence of women's and feminist film festivals, Kerns argues, is fundamentally linked to this history and the changing status of the film festival as cultural event. Film festivals are now a thick and highly hierarchical network of "tiered" showcases and exhibition organizations. Within them, women, queer, and feminist festivals have similarly multiplied and have staked out particular mission statements that reflect their own negotiation among the push and pull of artistic investment, activist outreach, and industry participation.

Kerns considers debates about what qualifies as a "feminist" or "women's" film in terms of various festival models. How such categories of films and filmmakers are defined, she finds, is largely shaped by the festival's purposes, its perceived mission, and how it constructs and addresses its public. In tandem, Kerns addresses the role of "general" film festivals in perpetuating underrepresentation of women filmmakers and feminist themes while decrying the absence of women as a problem.

Section IV: ways of contesting

In this section, we turn to feminist organizing and political activism. In a series of historical case studies from Russia, Egypt, the United States, and Slovakia, the authors here sketch out specific feminist action and stress the importance of context, distinct shared experience, access, and address for successful feminist intervention. Sociologists Linda Blum and Ethel Mickey open the section with an important early US-based case study of organizing around prevention of sexual harassment. In "Women Organized against Sexual Harassment: Protesting Sexual Violence on Campus, Then and Now," Blum and Mickey relate and analyze an early example of sexual harassment activism by tracing the history of a pioneering sexual harassment activist group formed in Berkeley in 1978. The notion of "sexual harassment" itself, its definition, and the argument that this structural gender hostility was a major factor keeping women from advancing in a variety of workplace settings were both novel notions, introduced by Lin Farley in 1975. "Women Organized Against Sexual Harassment" (WOASH) was formed at the University of California three years later and, as the authors argue, while short-lived, WOASH played an important role in the diffusion of a then new feminist critique. Coming on the heels of early women's movement organizing of the late '60 and '70s, WOASH was a part of a more widespread proliferation of so-called second-wave activist groups and women's communities at the end of an era, just before the Reagan landslide and years of conservative backlash.

Drawing on recently archived WOASH papers (now in the Bunting Library) to detail the events and discourses involving WOASH, the essay brings to light the obstacles to effectively addressing the structural issue of sexual harassment; the process of developing procedures for reporting and adjudicating complaints; tensions in the group's formation and activism and its work to manage media coverage of its aims and work. These insights are particularly valuable to contemporary work on renewed public discourse about and coverage of harassment – of which the #MeToo movement is only the most recent and visible example.

Vanda Černohorská charts the history of another historically significant collective, that of the prominent Slovak feminism collective ASPEKT, from its post-communist founding to its migration into digital space. As her chapter "Online Feminism: Global Phenomenon, Local Perspective" argues, the organization's eventual use of digital technologies emerged directly from its particular historical conditions, beginning with its struggle to undo lingering notions of feminism as a bourgeois ideology and the communist party's strained relationship to women's labor and social role. In approaching digital technologies not as tools but as sites of culture, Černohorská shows how ASPEKT's investment in its past history, its founders' experience with a communist regime skilled in erasing and rewriting history, and its engagement with international organizations largely shaped how ASPEKT envisioned its digital presence. As she writes, ASPEKT "embraced new technologies in order to preserve old heritage."

Highlighting an important theme in this section, Černohorská argues that while feminism and digital technologies can be easily imagined as "global," each of these (and their relationship to each other) must be understood with an emphasis on their specificity of place, history, sociopolitical experience, and cultural context – in other words, what can easily look like a familiar trajectory of development emerges as deeply and instructively singular. Like feminism, digital technologies themselves are conceived as transnational forces yet have distinct impact on a variety of scales from global organizational practices to individual and very private realms. In this sense, tracing particular digital feminisms works not only as feminist history but also as an important corrective to a tendency to think of feminism (and digital technology) as homogeneous. The tension that structures connective digital technologies as potentially global while simultaneously specific and culturally particular, their function for feminist activism, and the parallels they offer to feminism as theory and practice continue to serve as the theme to the next essay in this section.

In "Arab Women's Feminism(s), Resistance(s), and Activism(s) within and beyond the 'Arab Spring': Potentials, Limitations, and Future Prospects," Sahar Khamis sets out to analyze the development of cross-national Arab gender politics and activism forged within multiple invisibilities (media, economic, and academic), oppressive regimes of political and cultural power, and beside Western feminism – which until recently has had little to say to or about Arab and Muslim women. Arab feminist activism may have been gathering force before the events of 2011, but the eruption of the Arab Spring provided new momentum as many young women took up leadership positions in the uprising and took to social media to organize and publicize their struggle. While crucial for communication and organization in an environment of restrictive control of space and the threat of violence, a reliance on social media also left activists vulnerable to surveillance, misinformation campaigns, and direct state retaliation. Equally pernicious was a rapid loss of momentum due to media fatigue and empty gestures of "clicktivism," leaving activists demoralized. As Khamis notes, social media tools were uniquely suited to amplify moments of solidarity but were equally powerful in deepening divisions and fragmenting the burgeoning movement.

Arab women's feminist struggle remains, as Khamis concludes, an "unfinished revolution," and deeply entwined with larger struggles over the political future of the Arab world. But the analysis here illuminates both the built-in paradoxes of social media as political force and, more importantly, the necessity for understanding modern and indigenous feminisms not as "versions" of, or in comparisons to, Western feminist traditions but as complex, multifaceted, and particular movements emerging from women's lived experience.

Marina Yusupova's follow-up essay also takes on feminism in a particular national context, but with a sobering reversal: what if a practice is celebrated as feminist resistance *outside* of its own national contexts but is met largely with incomprehension within its local culture? "Pussy Riot: A Feminist Band Lost in History and Translation" proposes the example of the celebrated band as a "rootless" feminist practice and a case study of a "failure of feminism" in the region. Using the band's arrest as well as its contradictory reception in the West and in Russia, the author investigates the status of feminism in Russia and finds a disheartening picture. In stark contrast to the embrace of Pussy Riot as feminist icons in the West, the band's performance, politics, and celebrity were met with general bafflement or dismissal within Russia, even among liberal and anti-Putin critics. Yusupova finds this response consistent with diminishing interest or even recognition of feminism as a social movement that promises benefits to women – a trend she attributes to a growing informational isolation of Putin's Russia and a steady increase in support for traditional values and gender roles. Why, asks Yusupova, despite feminist activities and writing, has no home-grown feminist movement emerged in Russia? "Why has one of the most subversive ideologies of the twentieth and twenty-first centuries lost its revolutionary potential in Russia?" Yusupova's analysis highlights how the band's own words and performances highlighted feminism as a foreign gesture; notions of feminism's universal appeal, she warns, may well serve as barriers for local feminist voices.

As so many of the authors collected here note – and as the current moment in which we write attests – feminist social media is no longer a singular sphere of activity or a mode for feminist expression and organization but a complex and dispersed lived environment where multiplicities of elements continuously vacillate, diverge, and coalesce. Yet as Alice E. Marwick examines, in her concluding essay for this section, the history of how we got here and how such histories are understood and organized are crucial to understanding where we are and the challenges ahead.

In "None of This Is New (Media): Feminisms in the Social Media Age," Marwick excavates a largely North American prehistory of feminist social media through the hidden history of online feminism (from early LISTSERVs and Usenets to the "cyberfeminism" of the '90s, homepages, e-zines, and more), linking these to more contemporary, US-centered social media practice on Twitter and Tumblr like "hashtag feminism." For the latter analysis, she takes the infamous Gamergate controversy and feminist debates over intersectionality as case studies. As she finds, much is to be celebrated about this history, and the proliferation of feminist social media spaces "normalizes a feminist gaze on the world," yet peer content also starkly reflects the structural power relations among users. Thus a history of a "feminist internet" is as much a history of racial, ethnic, and economic division within a narrative of sharing and collaborative politics. Marwick's two case studies further illustrate how connected media simultaneously foster collaboration and conflict not only across seemingly opposing "sides" but within understandings and deployment of feminism itself. What's more, these two controversies offer concentrated examples of the two problems that continue to dog feminist activism at large: male harassment and White normativity. As this last essay observes, some of the challenges inherent in various conflicts among feminists – especially as correctives against privilege, assumption, and normativity – also demonstrate feminism's possibilities as conversations expand, voices and perspectives multiply, and new experiences shape priorities for the way forward.

Throughout this introduction, we have consciously avoided using the multiple "feminisms" to connote diversities of voices, perspectives, and priorities. We did so as the collection endeavors to investigate whether "contemporary feminism" remains a useful notion in the singular. Taken together, the articles collected here – most written specifically for the volume at our invitation to consider feminism as both methodology and subject – suggest that feminism's ethical charge is inseparable from its internally contested state. In this sense, arguing about feminism is important, indeed necessary, feminist work.

In this spirit, we offer the coda section of the collection, a conversation among leading contemporary feminist thinkers. For this unconventional conclusion, we chose three prominent feminist scholars, from three different disciplines and intellectual traditions, and invited them for an informal joint conversation on current and future directions for feminist scholarship and activism: anthropologist Sherry Ortner, whose celebrated scholarship on the cultural dimensions of gender and societal transformation have inspired us (as they have many scholars and readers); literary scholar Jack Halberstam, whose influential work in gender studies and popular culture offers an exciting working model for feminism's productive encounter with queer theory and the emerging field of trans studies; and sociologist Tressie McMillan Cottom, whose scholarship and popular media contributions to debates over feminism, race, and digital culture demonstrate how feminist public intellectuals can simultaneously impact and analyze contemporary discourse.

In the conversation that followed (reproduced almost entirely in the coda), we asked these scholars to comment on where feminism is now and what each perceived as feminism's future, limitations, and most promising potential. Each offered rich personal narratives of their intellectual development, feminism's role in their scholarship, and their hopes and concerns for the future. Our conversation covered feminism's scholarly tradition, Black feminism's rich intellectual legacy, queer critiques of feminist identity, #MeToo and its aftermath, the limitations of administrative and legislative powers for feminist ends, practical intersectionality, academic feminism and popular culture, and why the future belong to young queer BlackLivesMatter activists.

Publication notes

A version of Linda Blum and Ethel Mickey's "Women Organized against Sexual Harassment: Protesting Sexual Violence on Campus, Then and Now" is forthcoming in *Feminist Formations*.

Sarojini Nadar's "Stories Are Data with Soul: Lessons from Black Feminist Epistemology" first appeared in *Agenda*.

Alison Winch's "'Does Feminism Have a Generation Gap?' Blogging, Millennials, and the Hip Hop Generation" was first published in *Angelaki*.

Kathleen M. de Onís's "Lost in Translation: Challenging (White, Monolingual Feminism's) <Choice> with *Justicia Reproductiva*" first appeared in *Women's Studies in Communication*.

Sally Hines's "The Feminist Frontier: On Trans and Feminism" was first published in *Journal of Gender Studies*.

Marina Yusupova's "Pussy Riot: A Feminist Band Lost in History and Translation" was first published in *Nationalities Papers*.

Rachael Haynes and Courtney Pedersen's "Acting Out: Performing Feminisms in the Contemporary Art Museum" was first published in *Journal of Australian Studies*.

Bibliography

Baumgardner, J. 2011. Is there a fourth wave? Does it matter. *Feminist.com*. https://www.feminist.com/resources/artspeech/genwom/baumgardner2011.html Retrieved 21 April 2016.

Benhabib, S. 1992. *Situating the Self: Gender, Community and Postmodernism in Contemporary Ethics*. Routledge, London.

Blum, L. 1991. *Between Feminism and Labor: The Significance of the Comparable Worth Movement*. University of California Press, Berkeley and Los Angeles.

Chodorow, N. 1978. *The Reproduction of Mothering: Psychoanalysis and the Sociology of Gender*. University of California Press, Berkeley and Los Angeles.

Cochrane, K. 2013. *All the Rebel Women: The Rise of the Fourth Wave of Feminism*. Guardian Books, London.

Crenshaw, K. 1997. Intersectionality and identity politics: Learning from violence against women of color. In: M. L. Shanley and U. Narayan, editors. *Reconstructing Political Theory: Feminist Perspectives*. Pennsylvania State University Press, State College.

Crenshaw, K., Gotanda, H., Peller, G. and Thomas, K. 1996. *Critical Race Theory*. New Press, New York.

Diamond, D. 2009. The Fourth Wave of Feminism: Psychoanalytic Perspectives. *Studies in Gender and Sexuality* 10(4): 213-223,

Dietz, M. 1988. *Between the Human and the Divine: The Political Thought of Simone Weil*. Rowman and Littlefield, New York.

Dworkin, A. 1987. *Intercourse*. Free Press, New York.

Eisenstein, Z. 1978. *Capitalist Patriarchy and the Case for Socialist Feminism*. Monthly Review Press, New York.

England, P. and Jhally, S. 2011. *Understanding Hookup Culture: What Is Really Happening on College Campuses*. Media Education Foundation, Northampton, MA.Fraser, N. 1985. What's critical about critical theory? The case of Habermas and gender. *New German Critique* 35: 97–131.

Fraser, N. 2004. *Redistribution or Recognition? A Political-Philosophical Exchange*. Verso, London.

Fraser, N. 2008. *Unruly Practices: Power, Discourse, and Gender in Contemporary Social Theory*. University of Minnesota Press, Minneapolis.

Gerson, K. 2011. *The Unfinished Revolution: Coming of Age in a New Era of Gender, Work and Family*. Oxford University Press, Oxford.

Hartmann, H. 1976. Capitalism, patriarchy, and job segregation by sex. *Signs* 1: 137–169.

Hartmann, H. 1979. The unhappy marriage of Marxism and Feminism: Towards a more progressive union. *Capital and Class* 8(Summer): 1–33.

Hartmann, H. 1981. The family as the locus of gender, class, and political struggle: The example of housework. *Signs* 6: 166–194.

Hartsock, N. 1983. The feminist standpoint: Developing the ground for a specifically feminist historical materialism. In: S. Harding and M. B. Hintikka, editors. *Discovering Reality*. Springer, Dordrecht.

Haslanger, S. 2000. Feminism in metaphysics: Negotiating the natural. In: M. Fricker and J. Hornsby, editors. *The Cambridge Companion to Feminism in Philosophy*. Cambridge University Press, Cambridge.

Hochschild, A. 2012. *The Managed Heart: The Commercialization of Human Feeling*. University of California Press, Berkeley and Los Angeles.

hooks, bell. 2014. *Feminist Theory: From Margin to Center*. Routledge, New York.

Keller, E. F. 1984. *A Feeling for the Organism, 10th Anniversary Edition: The Life and Work of Barbara McClintock*. Times Books, New York.

Lear, M.W. 1968. The second feminist wave. *New York Times Magazine*.

MacKinnon, Catharine A. 1991. *Toward a Feminist Theory of the State*. Cambridge, MA: Harvard University Press.

Milkman, R. 2016. *On Gender, Labor, and Inequality*. University of Illinois Press, Urbana.

Mitchell, J. 1975. *Psychoanalysis and Feminism*. Vintage, New York.

Narayan, U. 1997. Contesting cultures: "Westernization," respecting cultures, and third world feminists. In: L. Nicholson, editor. *The Second Wave: A Reader in Feminist Theory*. Routledge, New York and London.

Ortner, S. 1972. Is Female to Male as Nature is to Culture? *Feminist Studies* 1(2): 5–31.

Scott, J. 1986. Gender: A useful category of historical analysis. *American Historical Review* 91(5): 1053–1075.

Stacey, J. 1983. *Patriarchy and socialist revolution in China.* University of California Press, Berkeley and Los Angeles.

Stacey, J. 2012. *Unhitched: Love, Marriage and Family Values From Western Hollywood to Western China.* New York University Press, New York.

Stacey, J. and Thorne, B. 1985. The missing feminist revolution in sociology. *Social Problems* 32(4): 301–316.

Walker, R. 2003. *Becoming Third Wave.* Heathengrrl's Blog, February 28, 2007. https://heathengrrl.blogspot.com/2007/02/becoming-third-wave-by-rebecca-walker.html Accessed March 28, 2019.

Young, I. M. 1990. *Throwing Like a Girl and Other Essays in Feminist Philosophy and Social Theory.* Indiana University Press, Bloomington.

Zerilli, L. 2005. *Feminism and the Abyss of Freedom.* University of Chicago Press, Chicago.

Section I
Ways of being

1

Taking exceptions seriously

Essentialism, constructionism, and the proliferation of particularities

Mimi Marinucci

Taking exceptions seriously

Essentialism is a concept that can be applied to just about any category to indicate that the various members of that category all share specific properties that unite them with one another, while simultaneously differentiating them from everything else. Additionally, essentialism suggests that the basis for determining which things belong to which categories is something that people discover rather than something they create. According to this account, the boundaries between and among categories do not themselves change, even if social and scientific beliefs about those boundaries is subject to revision. In other words, while we might be ignorant of, or mistaken about, what the categories are, essentialism is nevertheless committed to the belief that there are some things that are intrinsically and fundamentally the same, and some things that are intrinsically and fundamentally different. According to essentialism, the world divides naturally into distinct categories, or natural kinds, which exist independently of our ability to recognize these natural divisions. Indeed, the idea that science aims to "carve nature at its joints," which dates at least as far back as Plato (Phaedrus, 265d–266a), is representative of the long-held and widespread belief that the world divides innately into natural groupings, and that these natural groupings would exist even if they remained unknown to us. According to this belief, individuals are members of the same species, for example, because they bear a relationship to one another that purports to identify something fundamental about the structure of the natural world.

Someone who is focused on dietary matters might be tempted to associate cashews very closely with peanuts but not very closely with mangoes or poison ivy. As members of the Anacardiaceae family, however, cashews, mangoes, and poison ivy are close botanical relatives, whereas peanuts belong to the Fabaceae family along with other legumes such as lentils, chickpeas, green beans, and even licorice – which is not botanically related to star anise or fennel despite having a similar aroma and flavor. Whatever practical benefit might come from knowing the culinary properties of various species, those who endorse essentialism about species would likely regard such details as secondary to the more fundamental relationship that species bear to one another in virtue of their evolutionary proximity. Endorsing essentialism about biological categories, however, does not necessarily mean endorsing all of the details associated with any given taxonomy. In 1735, Carl Linnaeus published *Systema Naturae* (Linnaeus, 1964), which cataloged thousands of living things and assigned each one to a specific kingdom, phylum, class, order, family, genus, and species. Linnaeus, who is often credited as the founder of modern taxonomy, based this system of organization on outwardly observable similarities among members of the different categories without presuming to thereby capture any inherent order, instead regarding the system as more practical than natural (Quammen, 2007). The publication of Charles Darwin's *The Origin of Species* in 1859 (Darwin, 1999) signaled a shift away from the use of observable similarities in favor of the use of evolutionary proximity, or phylogeny, as the organizing principle. With this shift came a radical rethinking of the Linnaean taxonomy. For example, the first division Linnaeus articulated was into three kingdoms; namely animal, vegetable, and mineral. Notably, the focus on evolution led to the removal of categories (notably mineral) and the addition of others (such as fungi and protista). This shift was marked by confidence regarding the ability of a revised taxonomy to identify innate categories into which the world naturally divides. Despite this confidence, however, the taxonomy is generally regarded as a work in progress, subject to revision as knowledge of genetics improves, as evidenced by the use of a five-kingdom system in some current textbooks and a six-kingdom system in others. Indeed, the belief in natural kinds is not necessarily incompatible with what Colin McGinn (1989, 350) refers to as cognitive closure, which is the belief that there are some things we are simply ill-equipped to figure out. While it is possible to be an essentialist who is simultaneously pessimistic about our ability to delineate the boundaries between and among natural kinds, those who are committed to the existence of natural kinds are more commonly optimistic about the aptness of human sensory and cognitive apparatus for detecting natural kinds. Quine (1969), for example, offers successful evolution as evidence that we are attuned to which kinds of similarities are relevant in identifying natural kinds. Kornblith (1993, 35–57), Boyd (1999), and others make similar points, but they conceive of natural kinds not merely as collections of similarities but rather as clusters of properties that all stem from a single, causal mechanism. Evolution, for example, is offered as the causal mechanism underlying the division of life into the natural kinds represented by various species. Despite such optimism about our ability to recognize natural kinds, there is often much confusion and controversy when the boundaries between categories are called into question.

An analysis of essentialism is crucial to a rigorous exploration of feminism, particularly insofar as it is applied to concepts of sex, gender, and sexuality. Grosz notes that, unfortunately, essentialism "is rarely defined or explained explicitly in feminist contexts" (1990, 334).

> Essentialism entails that those characteristics defined as women's essence are shared in common by all women at all times. It implies a limit of the variations and possibilities of change. It is not possible for a subject to act in a manner contrary to her essence. Essentialism thus refers to the existence of fixed characteristics, given attributes, and ahistorical functions that limit the possibilities of change and thus of social reorganization.
>
> *(Grosz, 1990, 334)*

It is worth noting that while essentialism about what it means to be a woman is often grounded in biology, it is sometimes more closely associated with psychology or disposition (Grosz, 1990; Heyes, 1997; Stone, 2007). Feminism has a complex relationship with essentialism:

> Anti-essentialists of the third wave repeatedly argued that such universalizing claims bout women are always false, and function oppressively to normalize particular – socially and culturally privileged – forms of feminine experience. The widespread rejection of essentialism by feminism's third wave generated problems in turn. Ontologically, the critique of essentialism appeared to imply that women do not exist at all as a distinct social group;

> and, politically, this critique seemed to undercut the possibility of feminist activism, by denying women the shared identity or characteristics that might motivate them to engage in collective action.
>
> *(Stone, 2007, 16)*

Additional complications emerge in connection with the fairly recent suggestion, at least within contemporary Western culture, that intersex is a sex category distinct from both female and male. The term "intersexual" was used at least as early as 1917 (Goldschmidt, 1917), but it was not until the 1950s that it became its own research topic, particularly with the creation at Johns Hopkins Medical Center of a multidisciplinary team focused on intersexuality. An essentialist interpretation of sex categories allows for only three possibilities regarding the ontological status of intersexuality. One possibility is that there are still only the same two-sex categories, female and male, that were acknowledged in the past, and that the people who do not fit readily into either category are actually imperfect members (but members nonetheless) of one category or the other. Given this interpretation, female and male are natural kind categories, and intersex refers not to yet another natural kind but to females and males who are not readily recognizable as such due to a medical problem. This is the interpretation that seems to underlie the actions of many of the medical professionals, both past and present, responsible for performing surgeries on children with ambiguous genitalia to make them more perfectly and recognizably female or male. Indeed, this sort of medical intervention is often discussed in terms of "correcting" genital abnormalities (Dreger, 1998). In such cases, the thinking seems to be that, even when not easily identifiable as female or male, all people are in fact female or male. According to this thinking, correcting a genital abnormality is comparable to removing a growth or fitting someone with a cosmetic prosthesis. We do not generally regard people with large moles or missing limbs as constituting a distinct natural kind; according to this logic, nor should we regard people with genital abnormalities as a distinct kind.

Essentialism does not necessarily deny the integrity of intersex as a third sex category, however. A second possibility, on an essentialist understanding of sex categories, is that intersex is now, and therefore always has been, a natural kind, albeit one whose existence has been discovered only fairly recently. This suggestion is consistent with the opposition expressed by the Intersex Society of North America to the imposition of medically unnecessary genital surgery on infants and children for the sake of correction (www.isna.org). According to essentialism, if there really are three-sex categories now, then there really always have been three-sex categories; if there really were just two-sex categories in the past, then there still really are just two-sex categories today. The problem with genital surgery, on this interpretation, is not just that medical professionals sometimes make the wrong choice about whether to assign a child as female or male. While this is certainly a problem, particularly for those who are subjected to genital surgery before they are old enough to have any input into the process, it is not a problem that challenges the two-sex taxonomy. The concern that medical professionals may occasionally miscategorize a female infant as male, or vice versa, does not challenge the belief that everyone is either female or male. What does challenge this belief is the suggestion that there are some people who are properly categorized as neither female nor male but rather as members of a wholly distinct natural kind.

A third and final possibility, which also challenges the belief that everyone is either female or male, is the suggestion that there are indeed essential sex categories, but they are represented accurately neither by the two-sex system, which acknowledges only female and male, nor by the three-sex system, which acknowledges both female and male as well as intersex. The significance of this account is its suggestion that what we now recognize as female and male, as well as what we now recognize as intersex, would be more suitably categorized according to some different, as yet unknown or unaccepted sex taxonomy. This is the interpretation often applied to Anne Fausto-Sterling's five-sex model (1993), which posits not two, not three, but five biological sexes, including females (those with ovaries and no male genitalia), males (those with testes and no female genitalia), herms (those with both a testis and an ovary), ferms (those with ovaries and some sort of male or masculine genitalia), and merms (those with testes and some sort of female or feminine genitalia). While this analysis would be an excellent example of an essentialist approach that denies the validity of both the two-sex model and the three-sex model, it is not clear that this was actually Fausto-Sterling's intention. Several years after introducing the five-sex model, Fausto-Sterling indicated that it was "intended to be provocative" and referred to it as a "thought experiment" rather than a serious proposal (2000, 19).

In philosophy, thought experiments are used to explain or explore conceptual possibilities. A thought experiment describes a situation, sometimes one that is unlikely or even impossible, either as a means of demonstrating an idea that might otherwise be difficult to explain or to accept, or as a means of gauging intuitions regarding some philosophical question. For example, consider the scenario, presented by Emile Borel (1913), which suggests that any particular combination of letters and symbols, including the entire works of William Shakespeare, would almost certainly be among those eventually produced by a monkey randomly striking the keys of a typewriter for an infinite length of time. Variations of this thought experiment have been used to explicate the nature of both infinity and probability. For some, it supplies a means of challenging the claim that the complexity and beauty of the natural world are evidence that the universe could only have been created by a divine architect, or God.

Understood as a thought experiment, rather than as a revision or correction to the two-sex model, Fausto-Sterling's five-sex model is less about establishing the epistemic superiority of one essentialist taxonomy over another and more about exploring the possibility that epistemic factors alone may be insufficient to establish the superiority of any one taxonomy over another. Understood in this manner, the five-sex model threatens not just the two-sex model but also the very idea that physiological differences are sufficient to recommend one system of classification over other potential alternatives. In other words, the five-sex model does more to challenge essentialism about sex categories than it does to support it. Thus in addition to the three possibilities outlined above, each of which preserves essentialism in responding to examples of nonconforming individuals, there is yet a fourth possibility, which is to abandon essentialism in favor of the idea that categories are created rather than discovered.

These same four possibilities apply to other categories as well. Closely related to biological sex categories (such as female, male, and intersex) are gender categories (such as feminine and masculine, or women and men) as well as sexuality categories (such as heterosexual and homosexual). Some believe that gender and sexuality are straightforwardly derivative of sex, particularly on the two-sex model, with female and male characterized in complementary opposition to one another. Included in this understanding of female and male as natural kinds is the belief that membership in either category provides the foundation for feminine gender expression in women and masculine gender expression in men, along with sexuality in each sex oriented toward members of the opposite sex, as dictated by nature for the sake of sexual reproduction. Those who do not conform to this model in their gender presentation or sexual orientation are sometimes thought of as damaged, defective, or deviant, as exemplified by the existence of sexual orientation conversion programs that attempt, though largely unsuccessfully (American Psychological Association, 2009), to bring the sexuality of nonconforming individuals into alignment with their sex category. Others, however, regard the existence of people whose gender and sexuality disrupt established beliefs about biological sex categories as evidence that gender and sexuality constitute natural kinds apart from sex. This makes sense of the notion, for example, in the case of transgender people, that a person biologically identified as female might nevertheless "really" be a man, or that someone biologically identified as male might "really" be a woman. It is also consistent with the commonly held belief that homosexuality is a natural form of sexual expression rather than a deviation or defect.

The suggestion that sexuality consists of two natural kinds, namely homosexual and heterosexual, accommodates some examples in which people do not conform to the definitions associated with the two-sex dichotomy, but it in turn creates a problematic dichotomy of its own. Just as some people resist categorization as either female or male, there are people who resist categorization as either homosexual or heterosexual. Just as intersexuality can be construed as an intermediate between female and male, constituting a legitimate third natural kind category, bisexuality likewise can be construed as an intermediate between homosexual and heterosexual, constituting a legitimate third natural kind category. Similarly, however, just as there is room for the suggestion that female, male, and intersex do not exhaust the possibilities with regard to sex, there likewise is room for the suggestion that homosexual, heterosexual, and bisexual do not exhaust the possibilities with regard to sexuality. Consider the increasingly common use of the abbreviation LGBT (for lesbian, gay, bisexual, and transgender) followed by the plus symbol (+) as a way of acknowledging that there may be additional categories that are not yet widely acknowledged.

While the growing trend of including transgender when addressing lesbian, gay, and bisexual identities is arguably misleading, in that transgender refers to a category of gender rather than to a category of sexuality, the ontological status of transgender identity depends largely on the extent to which gender and sexuality are understood, in keeping with the traditional two-sex model, as the natural consequence of sex. Where gender presentation and sexual orientation are included in the definition of what it means to participate in either of two natural sex categories, transgender individuals, like intersex and homosexual individuals, represent exceptions to the taxonomy. The suggestion that the gender categories (women and men) are distinct from the sex categories (female and male), however, renders meaningful the suggestion that some women are biologically identifiable as male and some men are biologically identifiable as female. This suggestion maintains the notion that there is an essence of femininity and masculinity, or of womanhood and manhood, without thereby disregarding transgender individuals as deviant, damaged, or diseased. What this suggestion does not do, however, is accommodate the entire range of established and emerging gender categories. In addition to people who identify as women and men, regardless of which biological sex category they are associated with, there are also people who identify as *hijra*, two-spirit, *mahu*, genderqueer, nonbinary, gender fluid, androgynous, agender, and so on.

Some of these categories, such as two-spirit, *hijra*, and *mahu*, have a long tradition within specific cultures, while others, such as genderqueer and nonbinary, have come into use more recently. In Native American cultures, two-spirit refers to those, such as the *lhamana* among the Zuni (Roscoe, 1991) or *nádleehí* among the Navajo (*Two-Spirits*, 2009), who occupy an intermediate gender category. In Hawaii, *mahu* refers to those who are both male and female in spirit (*Kuma Hina*, 2015). In India, *hijra* refers to those who reject a male designation by undergoing surgical castration, dressing as women, and occupying an intermediate gender category. More recently, genderqueer, nonbinary, gender fluid, and so forth are emerging as terms of reference for various, and subtly distinct, ways of experiencing and expressing gender. Just as Fausto-Sterling's five-sex model challenges the assumption that everyone is either female or male (as well as the slightly less restrictive assumption that everyone is female, male, or intersex), such examples of alternative gender and sexuality categories likewise challenge the interconnected binary (twofold) and trinary (threefold) systems of sex, gender, and sexuality.

The proliferation of particularities

As outlined earlier, there is a limited range of potential ways to conceive of people who do not seem to fit the established binary categories of sex, gender, and sexuality. These different conceptions can be articulated more succinctly as follows:

Essentialist binarism: The binary taxonomy (regarding sex, gender, and/or sexuality) is accurate and adequate, representing the full range of real kinds that exist independently of our knowledge of them; individuals who do not fit this taxonomy are actually damaged or defective members of one natural kind category or the other.

Essentialist trinarism: The binary taxonomy (regarding sex, gender, and/or sexuality) is inadequate, representing only a portion of the range of real kinds that exist independently of our knowledge of them; individuals who do not fit this taxonomy are actually members of an intermediate third natural kind category.

Essentialist pluralism: The binary and trinary taxonomies (regarding sex, gender, and/or sexuality) are inaccurate, misrepresenting the range of real kinds that exist independently of our knowledge of them; individuals who do not fit this taxonomy, as well as some who do, are actually members of various other natural kind categories.

To a greater or lesser extent, these three ways of thinking respond to apparent exceptions to the binary taxonomy while simultaneously maintaining an essentialist account of sex, gender, and sexuality. A fourth option, however, abandons essentialism altogether:

Constructionist pluralism: The binary, trinary, and pluralist taxonomies (regarding sex, gender, and/or sexuality) are merely provisional, as there are no real kinds that exist independently of our knowledge of them; because the only categories that exist are the ones we create, any taxonomy will inevitably leave behind at least some individuals who do not fit.

Exceptions to existing binary, trinary, and pluralist models expose the limitations of the existing models. For example, the existence of intersex people challenges the sex binary, the existence of transgender people challenges the gender binary, and the existence of bisexual people challenges the sexuality binary. Tempting as it might be to assume that trinary models which include the third categories (intersex, trans, and bi) will resolve the problem of exceptions, the existence of people still not acknowledged even by these new categories – such as someone who is nonbinary, transgender, aromantic, and pansexual – suggests that the binary models and trinary models may both be inadequate. Tempting as it might be to assume that pluralist models that simply add enough new categories will eventually resolve the problem of exceptions, this has not been the result as of yet. The list that includes lesbian and gay was expanded to include bisexual, then transgender, and eventually asexual, polyamorous, pansexual, asexual, aromantic, and others. That the list continues to grow suggests that the existing inventory of sexuality categories is not inherently superior to some other as yet unknown set of categories. This suggestion not does not necessarily challenge essentialism, however, as it is consistent with essentialist pluralism, as described above, which maintains that there is a correct taxonomy of real kinds, even if it has not yet been discovered. The ongoing emergence of exceptions and alternatives to existing categories, however, also issues an invitation to entertain what is sometimes referred to as underdetermination (Quine, 1951), which is the belief that empirical evidence is insufficient to select from among the various taxonomies that have been or could be developed. In other words, the ongoing emergence of exceptions and alternatives to existing categories issues an invitation to entertain the constructionist version of pluralism, as described above.

There are some feminist positions that lean toward essentialism. Consider, for example, that transgender women have been excluded from spaces and events reserved for women, such as the Michigan Womyn's Music Festival, precisely because some believe biological assignment from birth to be a deciding factor in such discussions. Nevertheless, feminism is more commonly associated with the idea that gender is socially constructed. Indeed, feminist theorists were among the first to introduce the distinction between sex and gender, specifically as a means of articulating the notion that there are more differences between women and men that are attributable to socialization or gender than to biology or sex. This idea that at least some, perhaps even most, of the differences between women and men are the result of socialization is now widespread and largely uncontroversial. It is hardly controversial, particularly among feminists, to suggest that the fairly predictable differences commonly found in the habits of grooming and dress between women and men have more to do with what we have been taught than with intrinsic differences in our fundamental nature.

Ask just about any student who has attended the first class meeting of an introductory women's studies course to describe the experience, and there is a pretty good chance that the report will make mention of two columns on the board, one labeled "sex" and the other labeled "gender," with students suggesting items to be added to each list. Suggestions like "wears short hair" and "has polished fingernails" might appear as examples of gendered characteristics, with "penis," "ovaries," and other biological features offered as examples of features associated with sex. There are, of course, some traits commonly associated with gender, such as the assumption that men are generally better at quantitative reasoning than women, or that women display more nurturing tendencies than men, that invite more discussion and disagreement. While the notion that gender is socially constructed is not altogether uncontroversial, it is less controversial than the suggestion that not only is gender socially constructed, but sex and sexuality are socially constructed as well. It is more controversial to suggest that not just some, or even most, of the differences between women and men are socially constructed, but rather that such concepts as women and men, and even heterosexuality and homosexuality, are socially constructed. As early as 1960 there were at least some sociologists claiming that homosexuality is a "social role" (McIntosh, 1960), and there are at least some sociologists today claiming that "the male/female dichotomy is a social construction" (Palmer, 2016).

Perhaps it is worth asking precisely what it is that renders social construction so controversial. After all, even if the recent and ongoing proliferation of exceptions to the binary and trinary models does not entirely close the door on essentialism, it does open a window, at least a crack, to the possibility of social construction. The peremptory dismissal of that possibility seems epistemically arbitrary at best and irresponsible at worst. What follows, then, is not so much an attempt to provide an incontrovertible case in favor of social construction but rather to mitigate at least some of the concerns that recommend against it, thereby keeping the window open to the possibility of social construction. The following are examples of the sorts of comments that are offered in an effort to close that window:

1 How could sex be socially constructed? A vagina is a vagina. A penis is a penis. Ovaries and testes are real. People are categorized as female or male (or perhaps intersex) because of the bodies they have, not the other way around!

2 How could sexuality be socially constructed? Heterosexual sex acts are heterosexual sex acts. Homosexual sex acts are homosexual sex acts. People are categorized as straight or gay (or perhaps bi) because of who they perform those sex acts with, not the other way around!
3 How could sex and sexuality be socially constructed? If being female or male (or even intersex) and straight or gay (or even bi) were completely arbitrary, how could our decisions about which categories people belong to be as consistent as they are?
4 How could sex and sexuality be socially constructed? If being female or male (or even intersex) and straight or gay (or even bi) were completely arbitrary, why would our membership in these categories seem so real?
5 How could sex and sexuality be socially constructed? If being female or male (or even intersex) and straight or gay (or even bi) were completely arbitrary, why would our membership in these categories feel so natural?

As expressed in the first two examples above, a common concern about social construction is its apparent disregard for the empirical evidence used to determine category membership, such as the observable physical features of human bodies. This concern for empirical evidence, particularly evidence pertaining to human bodies, may help to explain why the social construction of gender, which tends to be defined in behavioral rather than bodily terms, is more readily accepted than the social construction of sex, which tends to be defined bodily, and why resistance to the social construction of sexuality, which is usually defined in both bodily and behavioral terms, falls somewhere in between. A closely related concern about social construction, as expressed in the last three examples, is its alleged assertion that the boundaries between categories are arbitrary. This concern is often accompanied by the corresponding belief that, if it can be demonstrated that the relevant taxonomy is not arbitrary, it thereby will be demonstrated that the categories identified within that taxonomy represent natural kinds.

In order to understand how a system of categorization can be socially constructed without disregarding empirical evidence and without being arbitrary, consider the following scenario, offered as a thought experiment. Imagine that the physical world is a mess and that, like the physical world in general, your living space in particular is also a mess. Focusing specifically on the portions of your world that house your personal effects, suppose you are in the process of making a transition from a larger closet to a smaller one or vice versa, from a shared residence to your own place or vice versa, from a car to a house or vice versa, or from permanent to temporary quarters or vice versa. All of your clothing and accessories are in a pile on the floor, and you confront the task of getting organized. For the sake of discussion, suppose you are attempting to organize your things to fit into a four-drawer dresser. One way to begin might be to divide the pile of clothing and accessories into smaller piles. While you could certainly toss things haphazardly into any random number of piles, this method would be of little practical benefit. If there are four drawers, then you will likely want to organize things into four piles, with the ultimate goal of transferring each of the four piles to one of the four drawers. If you hope eventually to be able find what you are searching for on a daily basis, the items should be sorted according to some set of criteria.

There is no shortage of criteria upon which you might base decisions about which things to put into which drawers. You might decide to arrange things based on their function, or perhaps by color, season, or fabric. Some systems have more practical value than others. For example, while a system in which things are organized by fabric content would be easy enough to understand and follow, it is not obvious how this would serve your daily interests, unless perhaps the fabric content had some impact on the amount of time or effort associated with laundry and related chores. There are obvious benefits to implementing a system that promises to reduce the time and effort needed to access articles of clothing when you need or want them. Even with convenience in mind, however, there are multiple possibilities of comparable merit. You might choose to devote one drawer to business attire, a second to fitness attire, a third to casual attire, and the fourth to undergarments worn with any or all of the other categories. You might instead choose to devote one drawer to summer attire, and the others to autumn, winter, and spring. Or you might devote separate drawers to T-shirts, long-sleeved shirts, shorts, and jeans.

Each of these systems of organization takes empirical evidence into account. When you examine a dress shirt and decide it belongs with business attire, or that a pair of yoga pants goes in the drawer designated for workout clothes, these decisions are by no means random or arbitrary. That shorts and jeans differ in length is not imaginary. Even so, none of these systems of organization was selected of necessity as the only possible system capable of accounting for the empirical features of the items to be organized. Furthermore, while some systems may have more practical advantages than others, none of them is perfect. Any system implemented is likely to leave you guessing about the best place for various items, especially as you add new types of clothing to your wardrobe. After putting the yoga pants with your workout gear, you might later reconsider upon admitting that you watch television in them more often than you actually do yoga in them. Do tank tops and camisoles belong with T-shirts or with undergarments? Does a black-and-white striped shirt belong with light or dark clothes? Do leg warmers and boot toppers belong with socks, or should they be considered outerwear and left out of the dresser altogether? Even if you had multiple dressers and the ability to add as many drawers as needed to accommodate an unlimited number of categories, it seems unlikely that you would ever stop encountering new items that just do not fit any of the categories you are already using. If you did manage to settle into a successful system, however, the relative success of your chosen system would not preclude the possibility of other successful systems, nor would it transform your *decisions* about what categories to use into *discoveries* about what categories are real. Even after implementing a more or less successful system to organize all of your clothes and accessories according to the type of weather in which they are worn, for example, you might nevertheless retain the ability to conceptualize the possibility of reorganizing those same clothes and accessories according to color or texture.

If you never had any reason to question your relatively successful system of categorization, perhaps because you learned it from your family and grew up using it, it might be more difficult for you to imagine developing and implementing an alternative system. A deeply ingrained system would likely feel more real and more natural than a newer one. After changing your system, perhaps by moving your socks and underwear into the top drawer together, you might spend a few days, maybe even a few weeks, reaching habitually for them in the lower drawer they once occupied. Unless there were something especially inconvenient or counterintuitive about the new location, however, with familiarity it would eventually feel just as natural as the old one.

Perhaps organizing the human world into sex, gender, and sexuality categories is not completely unlike organizing that pile of clothes on the floor. There may be other ways of categorizing people that are no more arbitrary and no less real or natural than the familiar binary model or the slightly less familiar trinary model. Indeed, it is quite possible that this familiarity is what makes the binary categories feel so real and so natural. Additionally, it is worth noting that the binary categories likely feel less real and less natural to those who do not fit comfortably within them. For someone whose assignment as female or male is uncomplicated, it might be difficult to imagine making sense out of some other set of sex categories. Someone whose relationship to the available categories is more complicated, however, might not experience those categories as real and natural. Finally, as long as those who fit neatly into the existing taxonomies are not displaced by an alternative category, it may just be a matter of getting accustomed to the change in order for new taxonomies to feel just as real and natural as more familiar ones.

Although it does not prove the claim that categories associated with sex, gender, and sexuality are socially constructed, the preceding thought experiment does respond to some concerns that might otherwise seem to caution against social construction. There is little to lose in terms of empirical adequacy and epistemic success by suggesting that neither the binary model nor the trinary model, nor even an alternative pluralist model, is capable of providing a comprehensive inventory of natural kinds, precisely because there are no natural kinds. There is, however, something of value to be gained as a result of rejecting essentialism. Not only does it offer the advantage of taking seriously the experiences of people who have been oppressed by the taxonomies developed under the ideology of essentialism, but it also renders the proliferation of new categories unproblematic. Removing the presumption that our categories aim to identify natural kinds thereby removes the corresponding presumption that this achievement could be made by only one system of categorization. Finally, despite having had a very long time to iron them out, essentialist models of sex, gender, and sexuality still have plenty of wrinkles, an obvious example of which is the many people who are not accounted for by these models. It therefore seems appropriate to revoke the conceptual priority that has long been granted to essentialist taxonomies.

References

American Psychological Association. *Report of the American Psychological Association Task Force on Appropriate Therapeutic Responses to Sexual Orientation*, 2009. www.apa.org/pi/lgbc/publications/therapeutic-resp.html

Borel, Émile. "Mécanique Statistique et Irréversibilité." *Journal de Physique*. 5e série 3 (1913): 189–196.

Boyd, Richard. "Homeostasis, Species, and Higher Taxa." In *Species: New Interdisciplinary Essays*, edited by Robert A. Wilson, 141–186. Cambridge, MA: MIT Press, 1999.

Darwin, Charles. *The Origin of Species*. New York: Bantam, 1999.

Dreger, Alice Domurat. "'Ambiguous Sex' – Or Ambivalent Medicine?" *The Hastings Center Report*. 28(3) (1998): 24–35.

Fausto-Sterling, Anne. "The Five Sexes: Why Male and Female Are Not Enough." *The Sciences*. 33(2) (1993): 20–25.

Fausto-Sterling, Anne. "The Five Sexes, Revisited." *The Sciences*. 40(4) (2000): 18–23.

Goldschmidt, Richard. "Intersexuality and the Endocrine Aspect of Sex." *Endocrinology*. 1(4) (1917): 433–456.

Grosz, Elizabeth. "Contemporary Theories of Power and Subjectivity." In *Feminist Knowledge: Critique and Construct*, edited by Sneja Gunew, 332–344. New York: Routledge, 2013.

Heyes, Cressida. "Anti-Essentialism in Practice: Carol Gilligan and Feminist Philosophy." *Hypatia*. 12(3) (1997): 142–163.

Intersex Society of North America. *Frequently Asked Questions*, n.d. www.isna.org/faq/patient-centered

Kuma Hina. Directed by Dean Hamer and Joe Wilson. United States: Independent Lens, 2015. DVD..

Kornblith, Hilary. *Inductive Inference and Its Natural Ground: An Essay in Naturalistic Epistemology*. Cambridge, MA: MIT Press, 1993.

Linnaeus, Carl. *Systema Naturae 1735: Facsimile of the First Edition*. Nieuwkoop: De Graaf, 1964.

McGinn, Colin. "Can We Solve the Mind-Body Problem?" *Mind*. 98(391) (1989): 349–366.

McIntosh, Mary. "The Homosexual Role." *Social Problems*. 16(2) (1968): 182–192.

Palmer, Nathan. "Sex Is a Social Construction, Even If the Olympics Pretends It's Not." *Sociology in Focus*, 2016. http://sociologyinfocus.com/2016/08/sex-is-a-social-construction-even-if-the-olympics-pretends-its-not

Plato. *Phaedrus*. Translated by Alexander Nehamas and Paul Woodruff. Indianapolis: Hackett, 1995.

Quammen, David. "A Passion for Order." *National Geographic*. 211(6) (2007): 72–87.

Quine, Willard Van Orman. "Two Dogmas of Empiricism." In *From a Logical Point of View*, 20–46. Cambridge, MA: Harvard University Press, 1951.

Quine, Willard Van Orman. "Natural Kinds." In *Ontological Relativity and Other Essays*, 114–138. New York: Columbia University Press, 1969.
Roscoe, Will. *The Zuni Man-Woman*. Albuquerque: University of New Mexico Press, 1991.
Stone, Alison. "On the Genealogy of Women: A Defence of Anti-Essentialism." In *Third Wave Feminism: A Critical Exploration*, edited by Stacy Gillis, Gillian Howie, and Rebecca Munford, 16–29. New York: Palgrave, 2007.
Two-Spirits. Directed by Lydia Nibley. United States: Independent Lens, 2009. DVD.

UNISA | university of south africa PRESS

2

"Stories are data with soul"[1]

Lessons from black[2] feminist epistemology

Sarojini Nadar

Introduction

In an op-ed piece in the *Mail and Guardian* newspaper in 2008[3] I told the story of driving behind an Ethekwini Municipality bus and being taken aback by the advertisement on the back of the bus which declared the municipality's support for the 16 Days of Activism Against Gender Violence. I was taken aback not by the support of the municipality for the campaign – but by the slogan which the municipality utilised to show their support: "Defending the weak!" In South Africa every year August is set aside as Women's Month. The 9th of August in particular is set aside to commemorate the day that 20,000 women from different race groups marched to the Union Buildings in Pretoria to protest against the unjust Pass Law which restricted the movement of black people. They chanted the slogan "*Wathinta bafazi wathinta imbokodo*," which has been loosely and popularly translated as "Strike a woman, strike a rock!"

I began to wonder how the nation had moved from the very powerful slogan "*Wathinta bafazi wathinta imbokodo*" to "Defending the weak"? This is a prime example of how the intentions behind August being set aside as Women's Month in South Africa, or the 16 Days of Activism Against Gender Violence, can so easily be co-opted by the very conservatism which such events are meant to oppose, resulting in these awareness days (which are indeed days meant to reconfigure society) becoming what bell hooks (1989) refers to as "commodity" and "spectacle."

These are the concerns that plagued me as I prepared for the occasion at which this paper was first presented, as a keynote address at the University of South Africa Annual Women in Research Lecture. During the weeks leading up to the lecture I agonised over what to say. Why was I so uncomfortable with this phrase "women in research," or the very occasion? Perhaps it was feelings of guilt at being given preferential treatment as women? Such a thought would invoke an immediate backlash of justifications: women have been denied a voice for so long; men get acknowledged every day so acknowledging women on special days is important and necessary. Most would say this lecture is to acknowledge the "special" role which women play in research – "special" never being fully or appropriately defined.

In the final analysis, many of the justifications for this initiative are based on the notion that basically women have been denied a voice in the research academy, so this is a space that has been created to reclaim and celebrate that voice. While women finding their voices in the academy is indeed a matter of celebration, an observation which bell hooks (1989) makes in her book *Talking back: Thinking feminist, Thinking Black*, is probably where the source of my discomfort lay. She says:

> The idea of finding a voice risks being trivialized or romanticized in the rhetoric of those who advocate a shallow feminist politic which privileges *acts of speaking* over the *content of speech*. Such rhetoric often turns the voices and beings of non-white women into commodity, spectacle. In a white-supremacist, capitalist, patriarchal state where the mechanisms of co-optation are so advanced, much that is radical is undermined, turned into commodity, fashionable speech as in 'black women writers are in now.'
>
> *(hooks, 1989: 14) [emphasis mine]*

Hence it is not enough to have the presence of women in the academy while gendered structural inequalities remain. It is not enough to have women present in the academy when their roles become an extension of their perceived domestic roles and they are encouraged and profiled as teachers (read: nurturers) more than as researchers. It is not enough to have the presence of women in the academy when universities remain largely patriarchal and untransformed (Mama & Barnes, 2007).

> This is a prime example of how the intentions behind August being set aside as Women's Month in South Africa, or the 16 Days of Activism Against Gender Violence, can so easily be co-opted by the very conservatism which such events are meant to oppose

bell hooks' comments regarding acts of speaking versus the content of the speech resonates with Amina Mama, who when doing an audit of women and gender studies units in South Africa found that:

> In terms of intellectual content . . . much of the teaching and research being undertaken by the existing units reflected an integrative 'women in development (WID)' industry approach rather than a critical feminist perspective.
>
> *(Mama 2011: e6)*

When *presence* ("women in research") becomes a replacement for *perspective* (critical feminism), then potentially radical spaces such as the Women in Research initiative can simply become what bell hooks calls commodity and spectacle – embracing and promoting a descriptive rather than an analytical approach.

Hence, to prevent the paternalism that can so easily emanate from events which acknowledge the "voices" of women in research, it is necessary to pay attention not just to the "acts of speaking" but to the "content of speech," as bell hooks asserts.

In order to do this, the discourse would have to move, I suggest, from the feminine to the feminist. Not all research done by women is feminist, and a good many men use the values and principles of feminist research in their scholarship. So the central question I raise in this article is: What are the values and lessons that can be learned from feminist ways of doing research (such as narrative research), and what difference does this make in African contexts? How can decades of feminist epistemology and more recently Black feminist epistemology and research practice enhance research practice in general and not just the practices of those who self-identify as feminists?

Black and African feminism

Before I begin the discussion regarding feminist research, it is first helpful to define how I am using the term "feminist" here. There are as many definitions of feminism as there are feminists. I use the term feminist being fully aware of the reluctance of many African women to identify with this term. While I understand and identify with the political objection to the term feminist in terms of its apparent exclusion of discourses of race and class,[4] I am also aware that many of these objections hide other biases, such as an unwillingness to recognise that gender equality can and must be part of African cultures too. Much has been documented about the reluctance of African women scholars to self-identify as feminists.[5] I do not wish to engage those debates here, except to quote from the African Feminist Charter of Principles which was born in Accra, Ghana, in November 2006 under the auspices of the African Women's Development Fund. Women from all parts of Africa boldly declare in the Charter:

> As African feminists, we are also part of a global feminist movement against patriarchal oppression in all its manifestations. Our experiences are linked to that of women in other parts of the world with whom we have shared solidarity and support over the years. As we assert our space as African feminists, we also draw inspiration from our feminist ancestors who blazed the trail and made it possible to affirm the rights of African women. As we invoke the memory of those women whose names are hardly ever recorded in any history books, we insist that it is a profound insult to claim that feminism was imported into Africa from the West. We reclaim and assert the long and rich tradition of African women's resistance to patriarchy in Africa. We henceforth claim the right to theorize for ourselves, write for ourselves, strategise for ourselves and speak for ourselves as African feminists.[6]

It is from this deep well of theorising, writing, strategising and speaking for ourselves as African feminists that I wish to draw some values for enhanced research practice. I want to turn the spotlight on Black feminist ways of knowing – our conceptions of knowledge production and dissemination; in a word, our epistemologies.

Obioma Nnaemeka, who has made famous the term nego-feminism,[7] asserts the following regarding feminist epistemology:

> Like other so-called marginal discourses, feminist discourse raises crucial questions about knowledge not only as being but as becoming, not only as a construct but as a construction, not only as a product but as a process. In other words, knowledge as a process is a crucial part of knowledge as a product. By injecting issues of subjectivity and location into epistemological debates, feminist scholarship seeks, as it were, to put a human face on what is called a body of knowledge and in the process unmasks this presumably faceless body. By focusing on methodology (and sometimes intent), feminist scholarship brings up for scrutiny the human agency implicated in knowledge formation and information management.
>
> *(Nnaemeka, 2003: 363)*

At least three crucial points regarding the contribution of feminist epistemology to research practice can be gleaned from Nnaemeka's statement above. One is that the *process* of research is as important as the *product* of research. Two, that the identity of the researcher is as important as the participants in the research. And three, as Nnaemeka so aptly states, feminism helps us "To put a human face on what is called a body of knowledge, and in the process unmasks this presumably faceless body." This is one of the most profound ways of describing the value that feminist discourse has injected into research and knowledge production.

What does it mean to put a human face to research? There are a number of research methods that have been developed within feminist scholarship, but one of the most profound ways in which research has been given a "human face" is through narrative research – basically story research. Feminists boldly declare that story is a legitimate and scientific part of research – the telling of stories, the listening to stories, the construction of stories in a narrative in order to represent research findings – all of these processes are counted as legitimate components of the research process and an essential part of feminist epistemology. And nowhere does this notion of narrative research cohere more than in Africa.

Narrative research within African feminist scholarship

While narrative research is becoming an increasingly popular research method (see Lieblich, Tuval-Mashiach & Zilber, 1998), this does not mean that narrative research or inquiry is simply accepted within the predominantly White and male research academy as legitimate or scientific. In fact in many quarters it is still regarded as "soft" research. The gendered and positivist bias against narrative research is best illustrated by the following story. My colleague Isabel Phiri and I have taught a course called African Women's Theologies over many years. Because so much of African Women's Theologies is derived from narratives of real "flesh and blood" African women – personal and sourced – we spend the first seminar simply asking the class to share their personal life-narratives or their theological journeys. This was clearly an attack on the academic sensibilities of one of our German exchange students, who declared to another student "In that class they don't study theology – they just drink tea and tell personal stories!" (see Nadar 2009a: 9–24 for a more detailed description of the context of this statement).

Stories, whether used within teaching or research (as part of data collection, analysis or dissemination) are considered essentially "feminine" and "soft", as Silvia Gherhardi and Barry Turner argue most poignantly in their chapter "Real men don't collect soft data" (2002: 81–100). They assert that:

> A common usage in discussion of Social Science links quantitative styles of inquiry and data collection with a 'hard' view of the world, and qualitative approaches with a 'soft' view . . . the connotations of these terms are to suggest that 'hard' social science is masculine and to be respected, whilst 'soft' social science is feminine and of a lower order of activity.
>
> *(Ghehardi & Turner 2002: 83)*

As a feminist researcher I have felt the brunt of these distinctions often. There are two ways that one can approach this perceptual problem of "soft" and "hard" science. Firstly, one can argue against the distinction, contending that it is a false dichotomy, particularly when the dichotomy is drawn from masculine and feminine stereotypes and moreover because this reduces the debate to biological essentialism.[8] The alternative, I would suggest, is that we view narrative research not as soft and feminine research but as an epistemological value of feminist thinking, particularly Black feminist thinking, from which other researchers can learn.

Epistemology is intricately linked with research methods and methodology. In other words, for Black feminist researchers it is important to know the factors that influence how knowledge is created, by whom and for whom. However, as Patricia Hill Collins (2000: 297) says: "Nothing in a research methodology is inherently White or Black, male or female. Certain methodologies can become coded as white/and or male and thus work to disadvantage Black women." So instead of viewing narrative knowledge as "women's knowledge," it is more helpful to see that what Black feminist scholarship has done through facilitating knowledge by means of narrative inquiry, is that it has called into question the purported "scientific" methods of data collection which claim to be value-free, emotion-less and objective. More importantly, what is significant is not just *what* knowledge is obtained, but the *way* in which such knowledge is obtained.

Brene Brown, a qualitative researcher in Social Work, also highlights the ways in which her use of narrative in the research academy raises questions, causing her to be wary of the labels that get attached to her work. She explains it as follows in her famous YouTube video on "The Power of Vulnerability":

> *A couple years ago, an event planner called me because I was going to do a speaking event. And she called, and she said, "I'm really struggling with how to write about you on the little flier."*
> *And I thought, "Well, what's the struggle?"*
> *And she said, "Well, I saw you speak, and I'm going to call you a researcher, I think, but I'm afraid if I call you a researcher no one will come, because they'll think you're boring and irrelevant."*
> *Okay.*
> *And she said, "But the thing I liked about your talk is you're a storyteller.*
> *So I think what I'll do is just call you a storyteller."*
> *And of course the academic, insecure part of me was like, "You're going to call me a what?"*
> *And she said, "I'm going to call you a storyteller."*
> *And I was like, "Why not magic pixie?"*
> *I was like, "Let me think about this for a second."*
> *I tried to call deep on my courage.*
> *And I thought, I am a storyteller.*
> *I'm a qualitative researcher.*
> *I collect stories; that's what I do.*
> *And maybe stories are just data with a soul. . .*[9]

Figure 2.1 Brene Brown talking at a TED conference in 2012

Source: © TED

While Brene Brown recognises that stories may simply be "data with soul," the epistemological foundations of African and Black intellectualism have always been based on narrative. Drawing on Barbara Christian's work on the "race for theory," Nnaemeka argues that Christian brought up for scrutiny the link between identity positions and feminist theory by insisting that people of colour have always theorised but differently:

> I am inclined to say that our theorizing (and I intentionally use the verb rather than the noun) is often in narrative forms, in the stories we create, in the riddles and proverbs, in the play with language, since dynamic rather than fixed ideas seem more to our liking.
>
> At issue here is the personalisation of theory formation in the West (Cartesian, for example) as opposed to the anonymity of a communal voice that articulates knowledge claims in African narrative forms and proverbs (which in Igboland are often preceded by '*ndi banyi si*/our people said').
>
> *(Nnaemeka 2003: 365)*

The problem is that like with the experience of feminist scholars within the academy, Black scholars too have had to fight for a space within the predominantly white and male academy for such forms of knowledge to be regarded as legitimate. Recently in South Africa there has been a drive by the National Research Foundation and other such research bodies to recognise and affirm what is termed "indigenous knowledge systems." While it may be legitimate to name storytelling as part of the indigenous knowledge systems of Africa, sometimes naming it as such has the opposite effect – that is, it ghettoises narrative research and distinguishes it from "mainstream" scientific research. The assertion that "maybe stories are just data with soul" is where feminist scholarship and African scholarship interrupts and interrogates the foundations of scientific research practice. However, narrative research must do more than interrupt and interrogate – it must also craft a legitimate space for itself in the academy, and it must enhance existing research practices, while redefining the academy.

So, how can the use of story or narrative research, an essentially Black and feminist way of doing research – enhance general research practice? I suggest five ways, and then discuss each in turn. Firstly, stories can be used to engender suspicion of master narratives. Secondly, stories are a tool of knowledge gathering as well as knowledge sharing. Thirdly, stories by their very nature object to objectivity by privileging subjectivity. Fourthly, stories make us reflexive as researchers, and finally stories engender a yearning for change that can be translated into a working for social transformation:

- Suspicion of master narratives of knowledge
- Tool of knowledge gathering as well as knowledge sharing
- Objecting to objectivity by privileging subjectivity
- Reflexive of our positioning as researchers
- Yearning for and working for change.

Suspicion of master narratives of knowledge

When I was doing my PhD we used to hold regular "work in progress" seminars. My PhD was based on the biblical book of Esther. The main research question was "To what extent can critical-literary-womanist readings of biblical texts be taken up by communities of faith to encourage gender-social transformation?" Having just completed my first five chapters of the critical-literary-womanist reading of the text, my sixth chapter, which I was presenting at this seminar, was a detailed description of the South African Indian Pentecostal community with whom I was going to read the text. When I had finished presenting, I was quite taken aback by one of the comments made by a professor who was very supportive of my critical hermeneutical work on the text, but whose "academic sensibilities" were "assaulted" by this chapter, which he claimed was rather "wishy-washy" compared to my thorough academic work done in the preceding chapters. His objection had to do with what he termed my lack of "critical distance." I interpreted his objection as him wanting me to create a scholarship around the "native people" in the same way that White Western anthropologists had done. The personal voice that was inserted into this master narrative of academia and scholarship was not acceptable.

In an article called "When counter narratives meet master narratives in the journal editorial-review process" Christine Stanley (2007: 14) describes a master narrative as follows:

> There is a master narrative operating in academia that often defines and limits what is valued as scholarship and who is entitled to create scholarship. This is problematic, because the dominant group in academia writes most research and, more often than not, they are White men. Members of marginalized groups, such as women and people of color, have had little or no input into the shaping of this master narrative.

Black feminist scholarship has attempted to disrupt this master narrative with counter-narratives, as I attempted to do in my PhD. These counter-narratives derive from our experiences both within and outside of the academy. However, even in so-called liberal scholarship the assumption is that the academic who is writing is a white male subject speaking to other white male subjects in the academy, often about poor, marginalized "others" outside of the academy. But what happens when the "poor and marginalised" are part of the academy? What happens when the "poor and marginalised" woman has risen through the ranks and is now a professorial colleague?

Brene Brown, in her talk referred to above on the power of vulnerability, shares the advice that her advisor of her doctoral thesis gave her: "If you can't measure it, it doesn't exist." This is the master narrative that the academy crafts, and that so many researchers get pulled into. Feminists have critiqued what they have largely termed "mindless quantification" practices in research, because these practices fail to recognise the "human face" of knowledge.[10] So while the master narrative claims to construct facts – ostensibly the "what" of human behaviour, narrative research has been cautious about promoting the idea that only asking "what" can answer all questions. Narrative research compels us to ask why and how.

Tool of knowledge gathering as well as knowledge sharing

The second contribution that narrative research methods have made to knowledge production within the academy is that it has been used both as a tool of knowledge gathering as well as knowledge sharing. Narrative research focuses on both phenomenon and method – that is to say narrative can be researched itself, or narrative can be used as a research method to produce data.[11]

One of the most valuable means of producing data in my own research has not been interviews or questionnaires, but biblical narratives in the context of a focus group-like discussion. I have used and developed a method which originated in Latin America called Contextual Bible Study which I have defined as follows (Nadar 2009b: 390):

> Contextual Bible Study is an interactive study of particular texts in the bible, which brings the perspectives of both the context of the reader and the context of the bible into critical dialogue, for the purpose of raising awareness and promoting transformation.

As is clear from the definition, initially the method was not designed as a tool of data collection, but as a means of conscientisation – using the bible for raising awareness and transformation. However, during the process of a research project conducted with Isabel Phiri in 2010, we learned how valuable this method of data production was.

Our research was premised on the fact that "A great deal of research on the continent of Africa has made direct links between cultural practices and HIV, arguing that patriarchy is a root cause of practices which promote HIV." We argued that "such research tends to portray African indigenous cultures and religions as generally unhelpful in the struggle against the virus" (Phiri & Nadar, 2010: 9). However, we were intrigued by the following possibility, and it is this that we set out to research: "What if indigenous cultures have inherent resources which can speak to contemporary challenges such as HIV?" (Phiri & Nadar, 2010: 9–10).

The most obvious way to answer our question, we presumed, was to hear from those who are the custodians of indigenous knowledge – traditional healers – so we embarked on a research project with traditional healers in rural Inanda and KwaNcgolosi in KwaZulu-Natal. The central question for the first focus group discussion was: "What is the creation story in your culture, and how does that construct your understanding of manhood and womanhood?." The participants related that in the Zulu creation myth[12] men, women, children, domestic animals and even farming tools all emerged together from a hole in a bed of reeds. That was the beginning of creation. Having listened to this story it became clear to us that the indigenous creation myth had much potential for gender equity, given that no hierarchy of creation exists in this myth – everyone, including the children and animals, are created together. However, the participants were not keen to apply this interpretation; instead, when encouraged to reflect on gender relations and how this creation myth can be used for gender equality, they began to argue for gender hierarchy using the creation myths from the bible as evidence! This surprised us as researchers in search of indigenous knowledge, because the participants were using the bible as an authority regarding gender relations, whereas since they were indigenous healers we expected that they would explain gender inequality using indigenous sources. Instead they asserted that a man is superior to a woman and a woman must respect a man because that is what the bible says and that is how God created humankind to live. It was at this point that they made a request for a bible study on creation to prove to us that their understanding of womanhood and manhood was contained in the bible and was therefore "fact".

We took up their challenge, and as a Hebrew bible scholar I decided to offer them a bible study based on both creation narratives found in Genesis 1 and 2. The participants were deliberately taken to the account of creation found in Genesis 1:27–28 as opposed to the account found in Genesis 2, as the account in Genesis 1 is arguably more egalitarian and less narrative. However, the participants saw immediately that this text was far too egalitarian compared to the one they were used to, and one of the men declared "In Genesis 2:21–22, the bible says that Adam was made from the soil and Eve was made from a little rib." He further explained that man is therefore original to the earth while woman is derivative from a man, hence the gender hierarchy that is "God-ordained". The conversations which this narrative opened up were far more rich and illuminating than any interviews we could have engaged with in this group. The power of narrative research was certainly proven through this exercise.

Donald Polkinghorne's (2007: 479) thoughts on narrative as a research tool capture this well:

> In the main, narrative researchers assemble storied texts that they analyze for the meaning they express. Evidence in the form of storied texts differs in kind from evidence in the form of scores or public observations. On the one hand, this difference is the strength of narrative evidence because it allows for the presentation of the meaning life events have for people.

> On the other hand, this difference lends support for conclusions in a different manner than scores. Storied evidence is gathered not to determine if events actually happened but about the meaning experienced by people whether or not the events are accurately described. The 'truths' sought by narrative researchers are 'narrative truths', not 'historical truths'.

Objecting to objectivity by privileging subjectivity

"Until lions have their own historians, tales of the hunt will always glorify the hunter." This African proverb, the origins of which are attributed to Ghana and other West African societies, is the foundation of the objection to so-called value-free or value-neutral scholarship. Patricia Hill Collins (2000: 257) highlights that positivist science has long claimed that absolute truths exist and that the task of scholarship is to develop objective, unbiased tools of science to measure these truths. According to this positivistic approach, true or correct knowledge is possible when the observer is neutral, the tools which the observer uses are "unbiased," and personal emotions, ethics and values do not creep into the research; or where the bias of the researcher is "controlled for."

How does one "control" for the bias of a researcher? If one is researching the subject of evolution, and one believes in creationism, how does one "control" for that? Rather than "controlling" for this bias, feminist narrative scholarship brings this bias into dialogue in the research, so that knowledge is acquired not through adversarial means but through dialogue. So instead of a white researcher claiming "not to see colour" in a research project with predominantly black participants, in narrative research the ways in which the researcher and the participants "see colour" are brought into dialogue. Gherhardi and Turner (2002: 83) describe this process very aptly: "As always we find that social reality confounds our armchair theorizing; it is more messy, more convoluted and more surprising than we thought it would be."

In a discipline such as mine (biblical hermeneutics) subjectivity in interpretation is frowned upon. I remember interviewing for a job at a South African university a few years ago when I was asked why my work was so "contextual" and "personal," and how I would insert myself into a department that was more "academically rigorous." Unfortunately, the assumption is that any claim to subjectivity in research renders it less academically rigorous.

Reflexivity of our positioning as researchers

In 2006, when I was invited to contribute an article to a book commissioned by the Human Sciences Research Council (HSRC) on the Jacob Zuma rape trial, I was cautioned by a male colleague not to get "too emotional" as there was a bigger political picture which I needed to understand. In the paper that eventually got published in a journal (the HSRC book never came to fruition) I made a disclaimer, which I quote at length here to make the point about reflexivity:

> As a survivor of rape, I cannot but think emotionally about this issue. Khwezi's story *is my* story, is the story of countless other women in this country. The facts of the story may differ, but the same elements re-surface over and over again in rape trials. Being accused of "playing with" the family friend who raped me (at the grand old age of 10), I cannot but get emotional when survivors are accused of "seducing" their rapists through for example wearing a "kanga." Having all the notes from my psycho-therapy sessions being requested by the defence, to prove something about my sexual history (again at the grand old age of 10) in my rape trial, could not but elicit emotions when I saw the same thing happening to Khwezi, when detail after detail of her sexual abuse as a child was presented as her

"sexual history," – information gleaned unscrupulously from her personal memoirs. Having to contend with a series of different prosecutors who do not argue strongly enough against private documents being made available for public scrutiny, elicit at the very least emotions, if not downright anger. So, this *is* an emotional issue and as a feminist who subscribes to the principles of womanism and African feminism I admit that my reflections here are tinged with emotionalism and make this admission unapologetically. Notwithstanding how "emotional" I feel about this issue, I also bring my analytical skills and tools from the discipline of gender studies and feminist theology to bear on this trial. The postmodern perspective which interrogates all analyses for objectivity (not just feminist) applies in the analysis of this case study too.

(Nadar 2009c: 91)

While positivist research argues for the "invisible" researcher, feminist narrative research calls us to be reflexive about our positioning. Rather than bracketing our emotions and our ethics from the process, we embrace them as part of the process. Being reflexive means that one recognises that the *process* of research is as important as the *product* (see Phiri & Nadar, 2010: 8–24). Emotion and intellect find a meeting space in narrative research. In fact, Patricia Hill Collins (2000: 265) sees emotion as an indicator of the validity and credibility of an argument. She shares a wonderful story about an undergraduate class who refuse to evaluate a prominent Black male scholar's views on Black feminism, in the absence of knowledge of his personal biography:

They were especially interested in the personal details of his life, such as his relationships with Black women, his marital status, and his social class background. By requesting data on dimensions of his personal life routinely excluded in positivist approaches to knowledge validation, they invoked lived experience as a criterion of meaning.

(Collins, 2000: 265)

Narrative research helps researchers to insert the "I" back into research – "lived experience as a criterion of meaning." So instead of presuming this omniscient, omnipotent invisible researcher, one gets a glimpse of the flesh and blood researcher. Nnaemeka (2003: 361) too makes a plea for recognising positionality as an important part of the research process:

This process will entail a constant interrogation of one's positionality at all levels – from the social and personal to the intellectual and political – as an active subject location of shifting reciprocity where meaning is made and not an essentialized location where meaning is discovered.

Yearning for and working for change and transformation

Finally, through the power of narrative research, the researcher, the participants in the research and those who consume the findings of the research are invited to be transformed at some level. Stories are not just told for the sake of telling a story, but for their power to invite us all to call deep on our courage to transform. The research we do is never solely for the sake of theory building but for the sake of community-building.

Quoting Richard Sklar, Nnaemeka (2003: 362) argues that "In African studies, as in other branches of humanistic and social research, the subordination of human and social problems to disciplinary trends has pronounced negative effects that undermine the integrity and social utility of scholarship." Patricia Hill Collins (2000: 265) calls researchers to an "ethic of personal accountability." Traditional research practices almost require a denial of moral and ethical accountability, whereas narrative research demands it. African feminisms do not only challenge conventional positivist scholarship but also some Western feminisms. As Nnaemeka (2003: 361) asserts:

> African feminisms bring up for scrutiny the relationship with and resistance to the endemic feminist politics and theorizing that inaugurate social irrelevance and forestall true engagement – from feminist social and epistemological exclusions to feminist scholarship's disconnection from social utility.

Conclusion

I began by invoking the F word, feminism, into the conversation on women in research. I asked us to consider that the spaces that are created to celebrate women in research do not become a commodity – or the politically correct thing to do – but a transformative space. I then moved on to explore some of the many links between Black and feminist epistemologies – ways of knowing, or coming to knowledge. While there are many ways of knowing or coming to know, in research one way that has consistently been put forward is narrative methods of research – story research. Narrative research has much to teach the academy about being accountable in our theories of research and practice, and I outlined five ways in which it does so.

Narrative research indeed invites us to consider that stories may simply be "data with soul." By employing narrative research so poignantly, Black feminist epistemology combines the science of knowing with the art of knowing.

Notes

1 This quote is taken from an online video by Brene Brown, 'The Power of Vulnerability', www.ted.com/talks/brene_brown_on_vulnerability.html, accessed November 13, 2013. Thanks to my friend Eliza Getman for her adeptness at finding the best online resources.

2 I am here invoking Biko's Black Consciousness use of the term Black, which understands Black to be inclusive and furthermore to be more than a matter of skin pigmentation but to be a reflection of mental attitude (Biko, 1978a, 1978b).

3 http://mg.co.za/article/2008-08-04-when-did-the-rock-become-weak, accessed 14 November 2013.

4 In my earlier works I too preferred the term womanist to feminist. For example, in my doctoral work I chose the African American term 'womanist', arguing that womanism rather than feminism addresses the pervasive realities of race and class (Nadar, 2003).

5 See, for example, Phiri and Nadar (2007). In addition, the three special issues of *Agenda* with the theme 'African Feminisms and the special issue of *QUEST: An African Journal of Philosophy / Revue Africaine de Philosophie* (2008) are helpful.

6 Charter of Feminist Principles for African Feminists, www.africanfeministforum.com/the-charter-of-feminist-principles-for-african-feminists/, accessed 14 November 2013.

7 This is defined as "the feminism of negotiation; second, nego-feminism stands for 'no ego' feminism. In the foundation of shared values in many African cultures are the principles of negotiation, give and take, compromise, and balance. Here, negotiation has the double meaning of 'give and take/exchange' and 'cope with successfully/go around.' African feminism (or feminism as I have seen it practised in Africa) challenges through negotiations and compromise. It knows when, where, and how to detonate patriarchal land mines; it also knows when, where, and how to go around patriarchal land mines. In other words, it knows when, where, and how to negotiate with or negotiate around patriarchy in different contexts. For African women, feminism is an act that evokes the dynamism and shifts of a process as opposed to the stability and reification of a construct, a framework" (Nnaemeka, 2003: 377–378).

8 A helpful definition of biological essentialism is offered by Lynda Birke (2000) who observes that "Feminist critics have noted how biologically essentialist ideas typically support the status quo – examples include the idea that male aggression or domination depends upon male hormones, or that women's biology or the biology of Black people makes them less suitable for certain jobs. So, in general, biological

essentialism is anti-feminist and racist." For instance in 1994, the influential *Time* magazine featured on its cover a story called 'Our Cheating Hearts' on infidelity, offering an evolutionary explanation for why men cheat on partners.

9 http://dotsub.com/view/a51d0f78-3541-4262-b032-5d7e0438ac22/viewTranscript/eng?timed=true, accessed 14 November 2013.

10 See Nicole Westmarland (2001) for more on the dichotomy set up between quantitative and qualitative research, in 'The Quantitative/Qualitative Debate and Feminist Research: A Subjective View of Objectivity', Forum Qualitative Sozialforschung / Forum: Qualitative Social Research, North America, available at www.qualitative-research.net/index.php/fqs/article/view/974, site accessed 14 November 2013.

11 Rachel Redwood makes a helpful distinction between story and narrative: "Although narrative can be regarded as both phenomenon and method, the term 'story' is usually used to describe what the actor tells and the 'narrative' is the researcher's account" (Redwood, 1999: 674).

12 This myth is re-enacted in two ways: first, when a baby is born, the hut in which the baby is born is fenced with reeds. Second, the *Umhlanga* or 'Reed Dance' is an annual ceremony in which maidens pay homage to the Zulu King and Queen Mother.

References

Biko S (1978a) *I Write What I Like*, London: Bowerdean Press.

Biko S (1978b) *Black Consciousness in South Africa*, New York: Random House.

Birke L (2000) 'Biological Essentialism', in Code L (ed.), *The Encyclopaedia of Feminist Theories*, London: Routledge, 46–47.

Gherhardi S & Turner B (2002) 'Real Men Don't Collect Soft Data', in Huberman MA & Miles MB (eds) *The Qualitative Researcher's Companion*, London: Sage Publications, 81–100.

Hill Collins P (2000) *Black Feminist Thought: Knowledge, Consciousness, and the Politics of Empowerment* (2nd ed.), New York: Routledge: 297.

hooks b (1989) *Talking Back: Thinking Feminist, Thinking Black*, Boston, MA: South End Press.

Lieblich A, Tuval-Mashiach R & Zilber T (eds) (1998). 'Narrative Research: Reading, Analysis and Interpretation', in *Applied Social Research Methods*, vol. 47, Thousand Oaks, CA: Sage Publications.

Mama A (2011) 'What Does It Mean to Do Feminist Research in African Contexts?' in *Feminist Review*, 0141–7789/11 www.feminist-review.com (e4–e20). doi:10.1057/fr.2011.22

Mama A & Barnes T (eds) (2007) *Feminist Africa 8: Rethinking Universities*, Cape Town: African Gender Institute.

Nadar S (2003) 'Gender, Power, Ideology and Interpretation/s: Womanist and Literary Interpretations of the Book of Esther', unpublished PhD dissertation, University of Natal, 2003.

Nadar S (2009a) 'Sacred Stories as Theological Pedagogy' in *Journal of Constructive Theology*, 14(2) & 15 (2), 9–24.

Nadar S (2009b) 'Beyond the "Ordinary Reader" and the "Invisible Intellectual": Shifting Contextual Bible Study From Liberation Discourse to Liberation Pedagogy', in *Old Testament Essays*, 22(2), 384–403.

Nadar S (2009c). 'Toward a Feminist Missiological Agenda: A Case Study of the Jacob Zuma Rape Trial', in *Missionalia*, 37(1), 85–102.

Nnaemeka O (2003) 'Nego-Feminism: Theorizing, Practicing, and Pruning Africa's Way', in *Journal of Women in Culture and Society*, 29(2), 357–385. doi:10.1086/378553

Phiri I & Nadar S (2007) 'What's in a Name? Forging a Theoretical Framework for African Women's Theologies', *Journal of Constructive Theology*, 12(2), 5–23.

Phiri I & Nadar S (2010) 'Talking Back to Religion and HIV & AIDS Using an African Feminist Missiological Framework: Sketching the Contours of the Conversation', in *Journal of Constructive Theology: Gender, Religion and Theology in Africa*, 16(2), 8–24.

Polkinghorne D (2007) 'Validity Issues in Narrative Research', *Qualitative Inquiry*, 13, 4. doi:10.1177/1077800406297670

Redwood R (1999) 'Information Point: Narrative and Narrative Analysis', in *Journal of Clinical Nursing*, 8, 663–674. doi:10.1046/j.1365–2702.1999.00292.x

Stanley C (2007) 'When Counter Narratives Meet Master Narratives in the Journal Editorial-review Process', in *Educational Researcher*, 36(1), 14–24. doi:10.3102/0013189X06298008

3

"Does feminism have a generation gap?"

Blogging, millennials and the hip hop generation

Alison Winch

This article explores a number of instances when generation is invoked and discussed in three feminist blogs: the UK *The Vagenda* (2012–), the US-based *Crunk Feminist Collective* (2010), and the UK *Feminist Times* (2013–14).[1] More specifically, it examines how generation is discussed in terms of a feminist identity, especially in relation to intergenerational conflict. I contextualize a textual analysis of these blogs within a conjunctural and intersectional understanding of generation. That is, I look at how these narratives of intergenerational feminism are produced or emerge from specific UK and US historical conditions, and the organization of social forces within them. I also look at how they map on to popular media discourses about generation. In addition, this article explores the ways in which generational identity intersects with categories of race, gender, class, sexuality and place.

I have chosen these three blogs because they usefully intervene in and illustrate key concerns around generation, intersectionality, and coming of age in the neoliberal conjuncture. Significantly, none of these sites are funded through advertising or brand sponsorship, and in this way their online practice is coterminous with their feminist politics. However, the obstacles that online feminist writers and editors face in corporate-run digital spaces are part of the subject of this article. *The Vagenda* blog is pertinent because the editors are white, heterosexual "millennials" who articulate a new brand of feminism that is distinct from what they characterize as a privileged (and implicitly white) previous wave. Located in London, UK (although not originally from there), they partly speak to and against a popular feminine metropolitan culture. In contrast, *Crunk Feminist Collective* are US-based and define themselves as belonging to the "Hip Hop generation." They are part of a growing network of feminists of colour who advocate for and develop intersectional theory by blogging, including *Colorlines, The Feminist Wire, Racialicious, Black Girl Dangerous* and *Janet Mock's Blog* (see Collins and Bilge 106). *Crunk Feminist Collective* situate their feminist politics within the context of a white supremacist neoliberal landscape, and the representation of their generational identities explicitly intersects with other axes of oppression. For these reasons, this blog is a productive case study in relation to *The Vagenda*, whose generational identities are articulated quite differently. Finally, *Feminist Times*, which I focus on to a lesser extent than the other two blogs, presents itself more as an online magazine. It ran for less than a year but is worthy of analysis because, as a feminist enterprise which pays its contributors, it could not compete financially within branded and corporate-run digital spaces.

Why generation?

Generation is a slippery concept. It is used by politicians and policy makers, as well as the mainstream media, to decentre issues such as class and race. For example, the characters of the millennial and the baby-boomer circulate in the mainstream media, particularly in the United States and the United Kingdom, in order to personify certain ideologically driven anxieties about contemporary culture (Little). Those who were born on or before 1980 and are coming of age in the neoliberal era are conventionally known as Generation Y, or the millennials. They are often constructed as narcissists who are pathologically obsessed with social media and high-end brands. Simultaneously they are represented as suffering from the selfishness of the post-war baby-boomer generation who have apparently contributed to rising house prices, job scarcity, and other socio-economic obstacles that hamper young people's trajectory into adulthood. This is evident in such inflammatory book titles as David Willetts' *The Pinch: How the Baby Boomers Took Their Children's Future – And Why They Should Give it Back* (2010) and Neil Boorman's *It's All Their Fault* (2010). Generation is also employed to scaffold inaccurate and often politically charged historical narratives. This is evident, for example, in the framing of feminist history as an evolutionary series of waves (Hemmings). Furthermore, within feminist contexts, it can invoke sameness. In other words, a blanket theory of generation assumes that feminists born around the same date have similar experiences of gendered oppression, regardless of race, class, sexuality, place or disability.

Despite these critiques, this article also argues for the productivity of thinking through and with the category of generation. In other words, it is useful to examine the various ways in which generation is talked about and deployed, particularly in the media. Furthermore, I want to suggest that generation can be a powerful analytical and intersectional tool. This is especially the case when we use the concept of generation alongside the framework of the conjuncture. Thinking about generation within what Doreen Massey – following Antonio Gramsci – calls a "conjunctural analysis" is fruitful, because it locates generational identities within the context of wider, and often contradictory, social and historical forces. In Massey's words, "A conjunctural approach leads us to examine the movements of the different instances in a social formation" (Massey 102). The conjuncture is partly about periodization, but it also understands historical change as contingent, conflicting and partial. Because of this, a conjunctural analysis does not frame history as evolutionary or predetermined. This renders the framework useful when applied to narratives about feminist generations as it understands history as being open to political actors, thus offering opportunities for intervention.

This conjunctural analysis of feminist generations is located within an intersectional understanding of identity. In other words, the concept of generation has explanatory force when making sense of identity categories, but it only does so when read alongside other vectors of oppression such as race, class, sexuality, place, and disability. For example, much of the mainstream media discourse about baby-boomers and millennials focuses on white middle-class generational identities which are located primarily in the United States and the United Kingdom. This has the effect of erasing experiences of, for example, working-class young people or young people of colour who do not fit in to the mainstream media characterization of the millennial. Simultaneously, generational location can intensify someone's experience of other intersecting forms of oppression: *when* you're born does matter. As Patricia Hill Collins and

Sirma Bilge argue, "Race, class, gender, and citizenship categories disadvantage many groups under neoliberal policies, yet, because age straddles all of these categories, young people's experiences of social problems are more intensified" (Collins and Bilge 117). Collins and Bilge focus on age rather than generation because they are discussing the contemporary neoliberal moment. As I discuss towards the end of this article, age and generation can be thought of as different but related categories.

In addition, I locate the textual analysis of these blogs within the discipline of women's writing, and note the affordances as well as the misunderstandings that can occur when writing feminism online. Digital feminisms are sometimes framed as radically different from previous generational articulations of feminism. However, as Jessalynn Keller argues in the context of girl blogging in the United States, online activist blogging is part of a lengthy tradition of feminist media production (Keller 2). Even though the networked site of the blog, as well as the fact that it is in constant process, forges a distinct type of feminist conversation and politics, there are still continuities as well as conversations with earlier feminist writing; although this might depend on how the bloggers forge and represent their generational identities. In addition, the writers and editors of these online sites practise their feminisms in online and offline spaces so I am keen not to offer a reductive analysis which celebrates a new kind of online feminism, one which is ontologically distinct from what can only be an imagined narrative of a coherent feminist past.

Rosi Braidotti's description of feminist timelines as "zigzagging" is pertinent here as I am also critical of using linearity as conceptual tool to define intergenerational feminisms (Braidotti 4). Nevertheless, this article argues that the relative newness of these media platforms for feminist activism and consciousness-raising raises fascinating questions. How does participating within what critics call the networked society enable, transform, inflect or circumscribe the ways in which feminists can write to and about each other? How does the platform of the blog or online magazine affect the kinds of dialogues that feminists can have? How do feminists write in tension with pervasive branded cultures? This article explores conversations that these feminists hold around generation, it locates digital feminist writing as both a continuation of and as distinct from other modes of writing feminism, and it examines the productivity of looking at how historical periods shape one's feminist politics and what effect this might have on intergenerational dialogue.

Feminist generations

Feminism is frequently talked about in terms of generation, both by feminists and the mainstream media. It is often framed as intergenerational conflict by deploying the familial metaphors of mothers and daughters – or more recently grandmothers (Walker; Henry). The wave metaphor is sometimes invoked in order to distinguish different generations of feminists: from the suffragettes, through the "second-wave" Women's Liberation movement in the 1970s, to the "third wave" in the 1990s, culminating in the contemporary resurgence in feminist activism, which has been called by some commentators the "fourth wave" (Cochrane). However, the use of waves to describe the multiplicity of feminist activism through history has been critiqued. Erin Sanders McDonagh and Elena Vacchelli argue that the "concept of temporal 'waves' of feminism serves to create a version of feminist activity that is presented as monolithic, and neatly ensconced in a clearly defined and delineated period of time." They maintain that temporal metaphors should be replaced by "a more geographic understanding of feminist activism" (Sanders McDonagh and Vacchelli).

The wave metaphor is also viewed problematically by Kimberly Springer ("Third Wave") who asserts that the wave analogy is untenable when thinking about black feminist activism; it obscures the historical role of race in women's organizing during the antebellum and abolitionist periods, as well as in the civil rights movement. Springer suggests that for black feminists, "The recuperation of the self in a racist and sexist society is a political enterprise and a Black feminist one that deprioritizes generational differences in the interest of historical, activist continuity" (Springer, "Third Wave" 1061). Moreover, the narrative of waves has functioned to whitewash feminist histories. Within a queer feminist context, Jack Halberstam argues that casting conflict "in the mother–daughter bond" is "transhistorical, transcultural, universal," and that it ignores "the instability of gender norms, the precarious condition of the family itself" as well as "the many challenges made to generational logics within a recent wave of queer theory on temporality" (Halberstam). In her interviews with self-defined radical feminists, Finn McKay argues that because women of different ages identify with radical feminism so conflicts between feminists should be discussed in terms of political differences rather than generational ones, and Rosalind Gill argues that framing feminism in generational terms seems "to risk pulling us back into polarized positions characterized by mistrust and suspicion on both sides (and why are there always only two sides, rather than three or four generations?)" (Gill 612).

When feminists criticize each other using generation, these instances are often picked up in the mainstream media and exploited. For example, the media report and foreground moments when feminists disparage each other, homing in on instances of generational hostility in order to amplify them. Using the trope of the catfight between women of different ages is a key way in which feminism is depicted as it is effective in locating feminism in the past, as no longer relevant, while simultaneously framing differences between activists as insurmountable (McRobbie). This has the function of personalizing feminist politics, locating it in the private sphere. Moreover, domesticating feminism in this way means that political difference is recast as a bicker or a row, rather than the performance of adversarial politics; adversarial politics being (still) a legitimate male performance. This is not to say that feminists themselves do not use generation as a call to arms. Indeed, generation is debated in different ways in all three blogs that I am looking at here.

The vagenda and millennial feminism

The UK blog *The Vagenda* (hereafter referenced as TV) is run by two friends in their twenties, Holly Baxter and Rhiannon Lucy Coslett, who work out of their kitchens. *The Vagenda* is a satirical take on women's magazines, an industry where both Baxter and Coslett have interned. The tagline for their blog is "King Lear for girls" and in their editorial they state that

> It is not, as the tagline says, like King Lear for girls (that is just a quote we nicked from Grazia that was so CRINGE – as they'd put it – that we totes had to use it, tbh). What the Vagenda is is a big "we call bullshit" on the mainstream women's press.
>
> *(TV, "A Letter from the Editor")*

They appropriate the hyperbolic language of postfeminism as circulated in women's magazines in order to critique and disrupt the power of the magazines themselves, as well as the branded landscape of the neoliberal girl and its feminine constructions (Negra; Winch). But what they call their "sweary" feminism is also part of a counter-discursive "loud, proud, sarcastic" feminist sensibility used by young online feminists (see Keller 76). *The Vagenda* writes about issues as diverse as female Shakespeare characters, through to marriage and abortion, but its main source of material is popular culture, and more specifically magazines targeting a female demographic.

Internships, working out of the kitchen, feminist blogging and the postfeminist media landscape are typical of what the mainstream media represent as the millennial experience, and this precarity is key to *The Vagenda*'s articulation of a new kind of feminism that is distinct from that practised by "our elders" (TV, "Girl Trouble"). The period that partly enabled the conditions of UK and US feminism in the 1960s onwards was defined by the welfare state, public ownership and wealth distribution through taxes. Those born in the United Kingdom and the United States after the Second World War – particularly if they were white and middle class – had more political representation in mainstream politics, partly because of the demographic bulge at this time but also because of the influence of the 1960s countercultural movement, as well as the supportive framework of the social democratic conjuncture. In contrast to this, young people forming their political consciousness under neoliberalism are alienated from the political process and tend not to vote, with the result being that the government can ignore them in terms of state aid, thus alienating them still further. The terrain where the so-called millennial generation forges their feminism is influenced by these contradictions. For example, in the United Kingdom these young people are witnessing the breakdown of the NHS, dwindling and insecure pensions, the withdrawal of state aid in the form of higher tuition fees, the imposition of bedroom tax, decreased levels of housing benefit and the withdrawal of Education Maintenance Allowances. At the same time they are caught up in circuits of debt and what David Graeber calls "bullshit jobs." *The Vagenda*'s depiction of precarious working lives, as well as its resentment towards older feminists, is partly a result of being young in this neoliberal conjuncture.

The Vagenda asks: "Does feminism have a generation gap? And is that a problem?" (TV, "Girl Trouble"). It explicitly locates itself as a "new wave" and it pits this against a more austere one:

> One of the things I love (and I mean LOVE) about this new wave of feminism, is that it features a range of women campaigning on different, varied issues. A war on many fronts, if you will. I see it as progress, as the feminist movement moving on from a time where you were essentially supposed to sign up to some kind of bullshit feminist charter in order to join the club.
>
> *(TV, "I am Sexy")*

Feminism is cast here teleologically, moving from a "bullshit feminist charter" and exclusive "club" to a freer, wittier and more plural feminism. The editors note that as young women they experience generational hostility from older feminists: "As writers of *The Vagenda* book, we (and from what our friends/colleagues say, young feminists in particular) have come to see being criticised by our elders as an occupational hazard when writing about women's issues" (TV, "Girl Trouble"). One contributor to *The Vagenda* with the initials "VH" (*The Vagenda* does not credit its authors with full names) writes in another post:

> Here's a manifesto I can get on board with: feminism isn't a sliding scale. You don't get rated out of 10 or have to sit an oral exam at the end of it. So just do whatever the fuck in your noble quest for gender equality, and don't attack other ~~women~~ people for doing the same.
>
> *(TV, "How to Tell")*

In *The Vagenda* blog we can see how wider historical shifts, which are personified in the mainstream media by the characters of the baby-boomer and the millennial, are mapped on to feminist generations. More specifically, the so-called second-wave feminist is framed as coterminous with the apparently privileged and selfish post-war baby-boomer. Significantly, *The Vagenda* pits its "new" feminism against one that is imbued with class privilege and as benefiting from a more robust public sector:

> Much of this criticism (well, what which [*sic*] didn't come from journalists who completely coincidentally ALSO WRITE FOR WOMEN'S MAGAZINES) came from middle class

> women in their late middle age who were lucky enough to have benefited from much feminist consciousness-raising when they were attending their progressive Russell Group Universities – talk to a state school educated girl who grew up in the feminist vacuum of the nineties (hiya!) and it is, of course, a different story.
>
> *(TV, "On Bikini Body Bullshit")*

Second-wave feminism is located in a distinctly different and more fortunate era and is being produced and performed in the spaces of elite universities. These opportunities are framed as being denied to young feminists today. Significantly, a conjunctural analysis can productively excavate the antagonism that is being enacted here. It can widen the field of vision so that the conflict does not have to be between older and younger feminists but can be seen as part of a larger shift in social and historical forces. Indeed, this characterization of the old and young feminist in conflict dovetails with popular media discourses about the selfish baby-boomer generation, the prudish second-wave feminist, and the betrayal of one generation by another. It glosses over specific and often contradictory historical conditions, and how they impact differently on different people, thus deflecting from an effective critique of patriarchal power structures.

Blogging poetics

Random House published *The Vagenda: A Zero Tolerance Guide to the Media* in 2014, and it received unfavourable reviews in the mainstream press. (The front cover sports a supportive tagline from Jeanette Winterson which demonstrates that not all "elders" turned against Baxter and Coslett.) In fact, the book's reviewers – typically it was women who were tasked with doing the write-ups – were of different ages. However, and significantly, Germaine Greer condemned the book in the *New Statesman*, casting its writers as "two young experts" who "yelp" their hyperbole but who reveal "a level of ignorance that is positively medieval" (Greer). Asking Greer to review the book could have been a tactical manoeuvre by the magazine's online editors as she is frequently used to invoke a nostalgic feminism. Moreover, she can be relied upon to critique other feminists, thereby depicting both herself and those under attack as ridiculous. Because she has come to stand in for second-wave feminism – a clearly ahistorical positioning – she is symbolically harnessed as a divisive means to mock the feminist movement.

Part of the problem that *The Vagenda* faced when its book was reviewed, and which was not foregrounded, was that its writing originated in the blogosphere and its popularity sprang from a connection with this digital genre. Despite this, its publication was put under the journalistic scrutiny usually given to a traditional book, and which did not pay attention to the ways in which a blog – unlike the relatively static medium of the book – can become untethered from its host website and flow through social media networks. *The Vagenda*, like all blogs, is networked; it is in constant process. Its content is frequently updated, amended, commented upon, reworked. Furthermore, the design, layout, embedded links, and comments are intrinsic to the ways in which digital feminisms are read, as well as influencing how they are written. A blog can function as a hub and in this way can facilitate dialogue between multiple sites. Indeed, *The Vagenda*'s writing is specific to a "networked counterpublic" of feminist activists, and this is quite a different form of communication from journalism, essay-writing, nonfiction or even a feminist newsletter (Keller).

Hosted by the free platform Wordpress, the editors upload posts which are later archived and still accessible. Simultaneously they micro-blog on feminist issues using Twitter. They have a comment function which is open to all so that there are loops of feedback which in turn affect the activism they practise; their writing is part of a larger digital feminist conversation. Their language is the brash, sarcastic and "sweary" language of some digital feminisms that talk back to postfeminist popular culture by using and amplifying its tone, partly to render the object of their critique absurd. It also creates affective links between feminists who are both beguiled but also oppressed by the power of women's magazines. Their blog needs to be understood as part of the online feminist "phatic economy" (Miller). That is, a networked feminist consciousness is performed online through such contentless activity as the "like" button and pokes, as well as retweeting, links, memes, giffs; the objective is to be social as well as to share information. Furthermore, as women in their twenties, Baxter and Coslett are also operating in a precarious labour market where they must continuously promote themselves to garner attention and receive freelance paid work. In a creative economy, labour is largely dependent upon using strategies of self-branding, and blogging is a way to cultivate recognition from potential employers. Indeed, *The Vagenda* attributes its subsequent work for the mainstream press, television and other media outlets directly to its blog.

These are all partly generational issues as younger feminists are more likely to develop their feminist consciousness online through blogs and social media. This is not to say that older feminists do not converse or strategize digitally, but they are more likely to have forged their feminist consciousness in a considerably different media environment. Significantly, coming of age in a new conjuncture – including its mediated landscape – does impact upon one's political identity, but in uneven and heterogeneous ways. Andra Siibak and Nicoletta Vittadini, following the sociologist Karl Mannheim, theorize the process of "generationing." They argue that generationing is

> founded on historical events and the socio-techno-cultural milieu experienced in the formative years, as well as the development of the narrative of collective memories and frames of interpretation of "times"; and rituals and habits developed during the following stages of life.
>
> *(Siibak and Vittadini 3)*

It is important to note that this process of generationing is not homogeneous. That is, not all young people coming of age in the neoliberal conjuncture harness the same collective memories or even have the same access to media. Because of this, understanding feminist identities in terms of generation has its limitations; that is unless we intersect the category of generation with other vectors of oppression. In addition, using digital media is often overemphasized in discussions of feminist generations. It is important to keep in mind that there are continuities in modes of feminist media production through different conjunctures; that feminist activism takes place in both online and offline contexts; and that there are differences in contemporary online participation among generational peers. The discussion of Hip Hop generation feminism below is an attempt to illuminate these synchronic generational differences.

Crunk feminist collective and hip hop generation feminism

Crunk Feminist Collective (hereafter referenced as CFC) is a resource "for hip hop generation feminists of color, queer and straight, in the academy and without." Its members aim to create

> a community of scholars–activists from varied professions, who share our intellectual work in online blog communities, at conferences, through activist organizations, and in print publications and who share our commitment to nurturing and sustaining one another through progressive feminist visions.
>
> *(CFC, "Mission Statement")*

A hub for social justice organizing, *Crunk Feminist Collective*'s members explicitly define themselves generationally, rather than in waves. This is in order to ally themselves with the Hip Hop generation of social justice activists, as well as being an implicit rejection of the narrative of feminist waves. Situated within the Hip Hop generation, *Crunk Feminist Collective*'s members assert their intersectional politics and identities as feminists of colour, as well as noting how they have "come of age" in the neoliberal era: "our connection to Hip Hop links us to a set of generational concerns, and a community of women, locally, nationally, and globally" (CFC, "Hip Hop Generation Feminism").

In her discussion of youth of colour and activism, Adreana Clay explores the various ways in which Hip Hop is a key component in the development of young people's political consciousness, noting that it is an organizing tool and an important cultural art form. Moreover, Clay identifies some of the crises and contradictions that young people coming of age in the Hip Hop era face, and distinguishes these from those shaping the historical and political terrain inhabited by a previous generation of activists. These contemporary contradictions include the fact that the legislative gains of the civil rights movement are set against the persistence of racial segregation and discrimination. White supremacist power structures are evident, for example, in the extreme violence of police surveillance as well as the prison industrial complex, not to speak of the vast discrepancies in wages and employment opportunities between youth of colour and white young people. Another generational issue facing Hip Hop generation activists is that they must mobilize "*in the shadow* of previous social movement activists" (Clay 7; author's emphasis), and that this "shadow" includes the mass commodification of the representations of these activists, such as T-shirts embossed with the face of Angela Davis. This "shadow" is evident in one of the discussions of intergenerational feminism in the *Crunk Feminist Collective* blog which I discuss below.

In contrast to *The Vagenda, Crunk Feminist Collective*'s writers define themselves most succinctly in relation to a feminist history. In their manifesto, they invoke their "feminist big sister Joan Morgan" who invited us to "fill in the breaks, provide the remixes, and rework the chorus," but maintain:

> While our declaration of feminism pays homage to our feminist foremothers and big sisters, Hip Hop generation feminism is not just a remix but also a remake that builds on the beats and rhythms from the tracks already laid down, but with a decidedly new sound, for a new era. This, in other words, ain't ya mama's feminism. This is next generation feminism, standing up, standing tall, and proclaiming like Celie, that we are indeed Here. We are the ones we have been waiting for.
>
> *(CFC, "Hip Hop Generation Feminism")*

Significantly, the time in which they were born – which signifies their feminist identity by generation rather than wave – is crucial to the political thrust of *Crunk Feminist Collective*. Their concerns are specific to their generation and being women of colour in America:

> We are members of the Hip Hop Generation because we came of age in one of the decades, the 1990s, that can be considered post-Soul and post-Civil Rights. Our political realities have been profoundly shaped by a systematic rollback of the gains of the Civil Rights era with regard to affirmative action policies, reproductive justice policies, the massive deindustrialization of urban areas, the rise and ravages of the drug economy within urban, semi-urban, and rural communities of color, and the full-scale assault on women's lives through the AIDS epidemic. We have come of age in the era that has witnessed a past-in-present assault on

> our identities as women of color, one that harkens back to earlier assaults on our virtue and value during enslavement and imperialism.
>
> *(Ibid.)*

The members of *Crunk Feminist Collective* define themselves and their politics as part of a specific historical moment. Their feminism is exhilaratingly marked against the neoliberal white supremacist and patriarchal "past-in-present."

Crunk Feminist Collective's articulation of feminist generational difference can be understood in relation to the larger shifts taking place in some social justice activism among people of colour in the United States, particularly in relation to Black Lives Matter. In her article "Black Lives on Campuses Matter: The Rise of the New Black Student Movement" Khadija White discusses the ways in which Black Lives Matter is distinct "from previous iterations of Black activist periods, most notably the modern civil rights movement" (White 88). One of these differences is that Black Lives Matter is a network rather than a movement. This is key when thinking about blogging as feminist activism; the blog is always connected and in process rather than being a static entity. White argues that there are continuities with previous black activist movements but that Black Lives Matter is defined by a radical self-care as well as "strong female leadership, an insistence on inclusion, and, among some parts of the network, a repulsion of the 'respectability' politics that had been a core feature of civil rights organising" (89). In their ethnographic work on social justice work, generation and black women, Carolyn D. Love, Lize A. E. Booysen and Philomena Essed note how younger women whom they interviewed in Colorado, whom they term "Millennials," were much more open to working with LGBTQ communities than the "Gen-Xers and Baby Boomers" (Love, Booysen, and Essed 12). This is also something that is key to *Crunk Feminist Collective*'s political organizing. As one blogpost maintains: "Heterosexism is a structural impediment. Patriarchy is a structural impediment. Cissexism is a structural impediment" (CFC, "Say No to Noteps").

The writers for *Crunk Feminist Collective* practise their feminism offline and online; they give talks, participate in protests, teach in universities, speak in churches, make films, among other political activities. Significantly, and unusually, there are no advertisements, pop-ups or brands sponsoring the site. This is a blog devoted to feminist activism without the compromises that inevitably come from having to refrain from talking about certain topics – sex, race and politics – in order to conform to the dictates of advertising companies. *Crunk Feminist Collective*'s site is maintained by donations (there is a click button for potential donors) and it is sponsored by Media Equity Collaborative. It is also crucial to locate the blog within a wider context of feminists of colour working towards social justice. *Crunk Feminist Collective*'s website has embedded links to Hip Hop artists, locating its feminist project within a broader generational culture that is not necessarily feminist but which shapes and reshapes feminist practice. By integrating links to Hip Hop artists, *Crunk Feminist Collective*'s members forge direct connections between the cultural forms that define their generational identity, as well as their writing. In addition, their content is inflected with Hip Hop – in its rhythms, lyrics, frequent intertextual allusions, and the socio-economic and generational terrain that is held in common. In their "Mission Statement" they define "crunk": "As part of a larger women-of-color feminist politic, crunkness, in its insistence on the primacy of the beat, contains a notion of movement, timing, and of meaning making through sound, that is especially productive for our work together" (CFC, "Mission Statement").

Participating in the online discussion around bell hooks calling Beyoncé a "terrorist," the black feminist theorist Brittney Cooper, writing for *Crunk Feminist Collective* as "Crunktastic," invokes the complexities of generational difference to explain her mixed response:

> [bell hooks and Cornel West] both make our work possible. But if the rhetoric continues, the two of them may also become a cautionary tale in what it means for revolutionaries not to age well. (Yeah, I said it.) And with regard to their speaker's fees, "I ain't sayin they golddiggers, but. . ." (And check it: I think they should make their paper, because I don't believe revolutionaries should live in poverty.) Anyway, we are all just trying to find our way here. My generation of intellectuals definitely could benefit from a more radical edge to our critique. But if the argument is that we have to violently mow down our icons, leaving a trail of their blood on the way to this new "radicalism," then you can keep it. Because something about that sounds alarmingly like the patriarchal, black male-centered, radical Black radicalism of old.
>
> *(CFC, "On bell, Beyoncé and Bullshit")*

The writing delineates its contradictory responses: it is a homage to bell hooks; an allegiance to Beyoncé as black female cultural icon; a critique of the hierarchy of black academics indicated through their fees, gender and age; anxiety over "my generation's" radical politics; a treatise against neoliberalism, among other insights. Cooper reveals the structures of her intellectual and emotional working through of a painful intergenerational moment. The invoking of Black Southern culture, Hip Hop references, brackets, asides, interwoven with the language of academia, layer the palimpsest of this particular online black feminist rhetoric. Feminist generations are positioned as contradictory, shaped through miscommunication and difference, but also in process and open to conversation – both because they are networked and also because Cooper's response, which exposes its own paradoxes, is not closed.

Blogs are usually intensely personal and written in the first person. This mode of writing is amenable to black feminist autobiographical poetics as well as an intellectual politics that is grounded in experience. As Patricia Hill Collins argues, black feminist writing is less about mastering white male epistemologies than about "resisting the hegemonic nature of these patterns of thought in order to see, value, and use existing alternative Afrocentric feminist ways of knowing" (Collins 267–68). Cooper, writing for and with *Crunk Feminist Collective*, forges her own feminist writing located within the Hip Hop generation. Denied a consistent and prominent voice in the mainstream media, this is an example of radically networked media production.

Digital feminist burnout

The founder of *Feminist Times* (hereafter referenced as FemT), Charlotte Raven, was born in 1969 and therefore would be understood in the mainstream media's framing of generation as a "Gen-Xer." This term was coined by Douglas Coupland in his book *Generation X: Tales for an Accelerated Culture* (1991). This generation is demographically smaller than the millennials and the baby-boomers – the two generations it is represented as being sandwiched between – and consequently attracts less coverage in the media. However, as with the categories of baby-boomer and millennial this particular generational grouping is problematic, not least because the dating of generational cohorts is inconsistent. Moreover, *Feminist Times* does not define itself generationally as its writers are of diverse ages and from different generational categories. *Feminist Times* offers a "pluralist platform for the stories and women often sidelined by the major magazines and newspapers" (FemT, "About Us"). The online magazine has an art director and the website is professionally and colourfully designed. Like *Crunk Feminist Collective* and *The Vagenda*, it is a brand-free space; its tagline is "life not lifestyle." It aims to address issues of age, generation, race, disability, sexuality, trans identity, among others, while seeking (and paying) feminists with a multiplicity of identity formations to write for them.

Pertinent to this article, and in particular to the intergenerational antagonisms invoked by Greer and *The Vagenda*, is a piece by Lynne Segal on ageing feminists. Segal notes how feminist movements have always alienated older women:

> In this country the Older Feminist Network was founded in 1982 by feminists, who felt that the women's liberation movement took little notice of them or the challenges they faced as women in an ageist culture (including, so it seemed, the women's movement itself).
>
> *(Segal, "Who's Afraid of Old Age?")*

Age can be a structure of oppression in a different way from generation. In other words, whereas being born in the United Kingdom or United States after 1980 means that – dependent on social class and other intersecting factors – one has less state support than those born before, women born post-war must contend with ageism in the workplace and the fetishization of youth as beauty. Even if some of them might hold a relatively fortunate position in relation to pensions or home ownership, they still face public erasure. Segal argues, in relation to ageing women, that these "frightening figures are not incidentally female, but quintessentially so, seen as monstrous because of the combination of age and gender" (ibid.).

Feminist Times was embroiled in what might seem like an intergenerational conflict. Raven wanted to revitalize the feminist magazine *Spare Rib* (1972–93) by appropriating its name. However, this resulted in a legal dispute with *Spare Rib*'s founders, Marsha Rowe and Rosie Boycott. Reading Rowe's and Boycott's position in *The Guardian* and in their blog, alongside Raven's narrative of the case, it seems that the conflict was not so much about generation as about misunderstandings, missed communications and miscommunication. It is pertinent to note, however, the different ways in which *Spare Rib* and *Feminist Times* were funded, and how this links to a conjunctural analysis of generation. *Spare Rib* (which is now available through the British Library's digital archives) was partly funded by the Greater London Council. It also had a price tag for each issue. That is, it was not free or expected to be free because it was a print magazine, competing in the print magazine market. Furthermore, it was able to exist because of the counter-hegemonic project of municipal socialism. *Feminist Times*, however, exists in the corporate spaces of digital culture where the assumption is that things are free. Of course, like much offline writing, online content is not free. Google's and Facebook's shareholders must be paid with users' content and users' data which are sold on to third-party organizations.

Branded spaces benefit from the unpaid labour of users who participate in the creation of content, as well as offering up lucrative data (Taylor). This inevitably feeds into issues of funding and ethical dilemmas about how to sustain a website and forge feminist connections while being dependent on business and advertisers. Feminists campaign against the ways in which corporations exploit people and land for profit, so how can they rely on these companies to fund their projects? *Feminist Times* (which, like *The Vagenda*, was kitchen based) funded itself through crowdfunding and a membership policy which was generated through direct debits. Importantly, it was committed to paying contributors. However, because it refused to compromise its politics, it was forced to "put the project on ice." It was not able to continue the project while being "both ethical and sustainable" (FemT, "Feminist Times: My Feminist Times 'Journey'").

Similarly, in July 2015 *The Vagenda* posted that it was having a "summer hiatus," and there have been no blogs since then, although the website is still live. It is noteworthy that *The Vagenda* is open to contributors but, partly because it is not funded by public- or third-sector bodies or by advertising, does not offer money or employment. *The Vagenda*'s editors cite the fact that "it's a lot of work. It's a full-time job, actually, and one that we're not actually paid for. And that is part of the problem – the amount of time this blog needs is not time that either of the two of us can afford." Situating themselves within a community of "feminist labour" they state that "you're in it for love, not for money":

> And we are tired. We are ever so, ever so tired, and in order to prevent the burnout that afflicts so many feminist writers and to quote our mothers: we need a lie down.
>
> *(TV, 'We Need a Lie Down")*

Inevitably feminist writing takes place online and offline and there needs to be a funding infrastructure so that feminists can be paid to write, as well as do the inevitable administration involved in sustaining a website. These case studies are evidence that sustainable and ethical models of online publishing that do not rely on corporate sponsorship, PR, or advertising revenue, and where work is remunerated, are essential. In the neoliberal conjuncture there is an ideological belief that not-for-profit political organizations and collectives should give away their labour without a fee, while corporations' bottom line is to make profit, in this case from the networked society's participatory culture. Nevertheless, the writers of the blogs discussed here are not remunerated for their blogging labour. This is clearly an untenable situation leading to frequent online feminist burnout (Martin and Valenti; Loza). Interestingly, both *Feminist Times* and *The Vagenda* participated in *Elle* magazine's feminist rebranding exercise for *Elle*'s November 2013 issue. Working with advertising companies as well as *Elle*, both blogs created brief campaign logos designed to flow through social media. For Baxter and Coslett this was a positive experience. However, Raven found this a deeply uncomfortable exercise that revealed how far magazines like *Elle* were circumscribed and held to account by commercial enterprises. For Raven it demonstrated how far brand domination inevitably stifles politics and creativity.

Another crucial issue facing digital feminisms is archival. Feminist writing is part of the creation of feminism; it constructs, in Kimberly Springer's words, "*our* reality" (Springer, "Radical Archives"; author's emphasis). Springer argues, in relation to her worries about leaving the preservation of activist material to corporations like Facebook: "This shaping and documenting of *our* reality means that activists are building a foundation *today* that will allow future organizers to not have to reinvent the wheel" (ibid.; author's emphasis). Working towards a more ethical way of hosting and enabling online feminist writing is also a means to preserve memory for future activists. Protecting feminist archives is fundamental because they have the valuable potential to run counter to the mainstream media's one-dimensional and divisive feminist narrative. They would allow for the plurality of feminist collective writing to be accessible. Claire Colebrook maintains that "any feminist claim in our present is in harmony and dissonance with a choir of past voices" and we read a feminist text "not according to the time within which it occurred but to a time it might enable" (Colebrook 14, 13). It is for this reason, and not because we should reify an imagined past feminist history that we are indebted to, that paying attention to and discovering ways of archiving online feminist writing is vital.

Conclusion

The term "generation" can fit neatly into pervasive discourses of nostalgia or fear of the new. In other words, anxieties over a neoliberal networked society and the commodification of women by brands can be easily projected on to younger feminists who practise their politics online and who operate within (and against) the discourses of popular culture. Similarly, worries about the authenticity of one's feminism or one's authority as a feminist might be glossed over by blaming those who formed their feminism in a conjuncture with more resources and more political optimism. In other words, behind antagonistic narratives about "older" and "younger" feminists could lie tensions engendered by shifts in historical and social forces. Moving the focus away from the age differences of the feminists involved and looking at the broader political contradictions at work allows for a more nuanced understanding of patriarchy and the way it functions, particularly within online branded spaces.

Generational categories – personified by the baby-boomer, Gen-Xer and the millennial – are not homogeneous. The socio-economic and cultural location of today's young people is dependent on vectors of gender, race, ethnicity, disability, sexuality, religion, place. Ken Roberts argues that working-class young people in the United Kingdom experienced the devastating impact of neoliberal policies before those protected by their middle-class status. Diane Negra and Yvonne Tasker maintain that although the recession has been branded a "mancession" it has disproportionately affected women. In their manifesto – and throughout their content – *Crunk Feminist Collective*'s members articulate how the present neoliberal moment in the United States is experienced differently by women of colour because the socio-economic, cultural and legislative forms of white supremacist patriarchy intersect to impact disproportionately on them. Thinking about generation within the context of contradictory and specific historical conditions, as well as thinking about it in relation to other vectors of identity such as race and place, can be useful in understanding bloggers' experiences and political motivations. It is through this understanding that intergenerational dialogue – including antagonistic dialogue – can progress.

Disclosure statement

No potential conflict of interest was reported by the author.

Note

1 In November 2016, after this article was accepted, *Feminist Times* was relaunched as an online monthly magazine via the digital publishing site "issuu." Significantly, it has rejected some of the affordances of the blog format. There are no comment functions and the magazine will be issued on a monthly basis rather than being continually updated. Raven frames this as an intergenerational feminist strategy by stating:

> Our new incarnation is tethered to the past because we want to receive something from feminism's golden age. We owe it to those who came before us to get this right so instead of being updated daily, like a blog, we will be producing monthly issues. This will give us plenty of time to reflect on the content and work constructively with our writers rather than hit them with idea-sapping deadlines. *(FEM 001 5)*

In addition, Raven aims to counteract the burnout experienced by feminist bloggers, as discussed above. We can see a deep concern around connecting to previous feminist publishing incarnations in *Feminist Times*' attempt to connect with "our foremothers": "Tethered proudly to the past, we are walking in the footsteps of our foremothers, respectful of their legacy" (FEM 001 3). Raven points out that there are no comment boards on the site as "I want to encourage a different kind of debate where there is time to reflect rather than fire off responses a mile a minute." Instead, she offers an e-mail address and promises to reply "and, who knows, you could even become one of our contributors" (FEM 001 5).

Bibliography

Baxter, Holly, and Rhiannon Coslett. *The Vagenda: A Zero Tolerance Guide to the Media*. London: Random, 2014. Print.

Boorman, Neil. *It's All Their Fault*. London: HarperCollins, 2010. Print.

Braidotti, Rosi. "Introduction." *Australian Feminist Studies* 24.59 (2009): 3–9. Print.

Clay, Adreana. *The Hip-Hop Generation Fights Back: Youth, Activism, and Post-Civil Rights Politics*. New York: New York UP, 2012. Print.

Cochrane, Kira. "The Fourth Wave of Feminism: Meet the Rebel Women." *The Guardian* 10 Dec. 2013. Web. 4 Apr. 2016. <www.theguardian.com/world/2013/dec/10/fourth-wave-feminism-rebel-women>.

Colebrook, Claire. "Stratigraphic Time, Women's Time." *Australian Feminist Studies* 24.59 (2009): 11–16. Print.

Collins, Patricia Hill. *Black Feminist Thought: Knowledge, Consciousness and the Politics of Empowerment*. London and New York: Routledge, 1990. Print.

Collins, Patricia Hill, and Sirma Bilge. *Intersectionality*. Cambridge: Polity, 2016. Print.

Coupland, Douglas. *Generation X: Tales for an Accelerated Culture*. New York: St. Martin's, 1991. Print.

Crunk Feminist Collective. "Hip Hop Generation Feminism: A Manifesto." 1 Mar. 2010. Web blog post. 14 Feb. 2016. <www.crunkfeministcollective.com/2010/03/01/hip-hop-generation-feminism-a-manifesto/>.

Crunk Feminist Collective. "Mission Statement." N.d. Web blog post. 14 Feb. 2016. <www.crunkfeminist collective.com/about/>.

Crunk Feminist Collective. "On bell, Beyoncé and Bullshit." 20 May 2014. Web blog post. 14 Feb. 2016. <www.crunkfeministcollective.com/2014/05/20/on-bell-beyonce-and-bullshit/>.

Crunk Feminist Collective. "Say No to Noteps and Straight Black Pride." 15 Jul. 2015. Web blog post. 14 Feb. 2016. <www.crunkfeministcollective.com/2015/07/15/say-no-to-noteps-and-straight-black-pride/>.

Feminist Times. "About Us." Web blog post. 14 Aug. 2014. Web. 4 Apr. 2016. <www.feministtimes.com/about/>. [Note that this URL is no longer active. Material will be available shortly via the *Feminist Times* archive at <www.feministtimes.com>.]

Gill, Rosalind. "Post-Postfeminism? New Feminist Visibilities in Postfeminist Times." *Feminist Media Studies* 16.4 (2016): 610–30. Print.

Graeber, David. "On the Phenomenon of Bullshit Jobs." *STRIKE! Magazine* 17 Aug. 2013. Web. 4 Apr. 2016. <strikemag.org/bullshit-jobs/>.

Greer, Germaine. "The Failures of New Feminism." *New Statesman* 14 May 2014. Web. 4 Apr. 2016. <www.newstatesman.com/culture/2014/05/germaine-greer-failures-new-feminism>.

Halberstam, Jack. "Justifiable Matricide: Backlashing Faludi." *Bullybloggers*. 19 Oct. 2010. Web blog post. 30 Sept. 2014. <https://bullybloggers.wordpress.com/2010/10/19/justifiable-matricide-backlashing-faludi-by-jack-halberstam/>.

Hemmings, Clare. *Why Stories Matter: The Political Grammar of Feminist Theory*. Durham, NC: Duke UP, 2011. Print.

Henry, Astrid. *Not My Mother's Sister: Generational Conflict and Third-Wave Feminism*. Bloomington: Indiana UP, 2004. Print.

Keller, Jessalynn. *Girls' Feminist Blogging in a Postfeminist Age*. London and New York: Routledge, 2015. Print.

Little, Ben. "A Growing Discontent: Class and Generation under Neoliberalism." *Soundings* 56 (2014): 27–40. Print.

Love, Carolyn D., Lize A. E. Booysen, and Philomena Essed. "An Exploration of the Intersection of Race, Gender and Generation in African American Women Doing Social Justice Work." *Gender, Work and Organization* (2015). Web. 16 Aug. 2016. doi:10.1111/gwao.12095.

Loza, S. "Hashtag Feminism, #SolidarityIsForWhiteWomen, and the other #FemFuture." *Ada: A Journal of Gender, New Media, and Technology* 5 (2014). doi:10.7264/N337770V.

Martin, Courtney E., and Vanessa Valenti. "#Femfuture: Online Revolution." Barnard Center for Research on Women. Vol. 8 (2012). Web. 16 Feb. 2016. <bcrw.barnard.edu/publications/femfuture-online-revolution/>.

Massey, Doreen. "Ideology and Economics in the Present Moment." *The Neoliberal Crisis*. Ed. Sally Davison and Katherine Harris. London: Lawrence, 2015. 102–12. Print.

McKay, Finn. "Political Not Generational: Getting Real About Contemporary UK Radical Feminism." *Social Movement Studies* 14.4 (2015): 427–42. Print.

McRobbie, Angela. *The Aftermath of Feminism: Gender, Culture and Social Change*. London: Sage, 2009. Print.

Miller, Vincent. *Understanding Digital Culture*. London: Sage, 2011. Print.

Negra, Diane. *What a Girl Wants? Fantasizing the Reclamation of Self in Postfeminism*. London and New York: Routledge, 2009. Print.

Negra, Diane, and Yvonne Tasker. *Gendering the Recession: Media and Culture in an Age of Austerity*. Durham, NC: Duke UP, 2014. Print.

Raven, Charlotte. "Feminist Times: My Feminist Times 'Journey.'" Web blog post. 16 July 2014. Web. 4 Apr. 2016. <www.feministtimes.com/category/charlottes-editorial/>. [Note that this URL is no longer active. Material will be available shortly via the *Feminist Times* archive at <www.feministtimes.com>.]

Roberts, Ken. "The End of the Long Baby-Boomer Generation." *Journal of Youth Studies* 15.4 (2012): 479–97. Print.

Sanders McDonagh, Erin, and Elena Vacchelli. "The Rebirth of Feminism? Situating Feminism in the Popular Imaginary." Part of "The Rebirth of Feminism?" symposium at Middlesex University. 30 Oct. 2013.

Segal, Lynne. "Who's Afraid of Old Age?" *Feminist Times* 6 Nov. 2013. Web blog post. 30 Sept. 2014. Web. 4 Apr. 2016. <www.feministtimes.com/whos-afraid-of-oldage/>. [Note that this URL is no longer active. Material will be available shortly via the *Feminist Times* archive at <www.feministtimes.com>.]

Siibak, Andra, and Nicoletta Vittadini. "Introducing Four Empirical Examples of the 'Generationing' Process." *Cyberpsychology: Journal of Psychosocial Research on Cyberspace* 6.2 (2012): 1–10. Print.

Springer, Kimberly. "Radical Archives and the New Cycles of Contention." *Viewpoint Magazine* 5 (2015). Web. 16 Feb. 2016. <viewpointmag.com/2015/11/02/issue-5-social-reproduction/>.

Springer, Kimberly. "Third Wave Black Feminism?" *Signs* 27.4 (2002): 1059–82. Print.

Taylor, Astra. *The People's Platform: Taking Back Power and Culture in the Digital Age*. New York: Fourth Estate, 2014. Print.

The Vagenda. "Girl Trouble: What is Everyone's Deal with Young Women?" 11 June 2014. Web blog post. 14 July 2015. <vagendamagazine.com/2014/06/girl-trouble-what-is-everyones-deal-with-young-women/>.

The Vagenda. "How to Tell if You're Feminist Enough." 11 Sept. 2014. Web blog post. 14 July 2015. <vagendamagazine.com/2014/09/how-to-tell-if-youre-feminist-enough/>.

The Vagenda. "I am Sexy, I am Funny, I am a Fucking Feminist." 28 Feb. 2013. Web blog post. 14 July 2015. <vagendamagazine.com/2013/02/i-am-sexy-i-am-funny-i-am-a-fucking-feminist/>.

The Vagenda. "A Letter from the Editor." 19 Jan. 2012. Web blog post. 14 July 2015. <vagendamagazine.com/2012/01/a-letter-from-the-editor/>.

The Vagenda. "On Bikini Body Bullshit." 24 June 2014. Web blog post. 14 July 2015. <vagendamagazine.com/2014/06/on-bikini-body-bullshit/>.

The Vagenda. "We Need a Lie Down." 3 July 2015. Web blog post. 14 July 2016. <vagendamagazine.com/2015/07/we-need-a-lie-down-2/>.

Walker, Rebecca. *Baby Love: Choosing Motherhood After a Lifetime of Ambivalence*. London: Souvenir, 2008. Print.

White, Khadijah. "Black Lives on Campuses Matter: The Rise of the New Black Student Movement." *Soundings* 63 (2016): 86–97. Print.

Willetts, David. *The Pinch: How the Baby Boomers Took Their Children's Future – And Why They Should Give it Back*. London: Atlantic, 2010. Print.

Winch, Alison. *Girlfriends and Postfeminist Sisterhood*. Basingstoke: Palgrave, 2013. Print.

4

Too soon for post-feminism

The ongoing life of patriarchy in neoliberal America

Sherry B. Ortner

Feminism can be seen as one of the great resistance movements of the twentieth century. It was tremendously successful, both in the sense of achieving many of its goals and in the sense of attaining a virtually global reach. Now, however, feminism appears to be in a state of crisis. Young women are said to be "post-feminist," while those who identify as feminists are under attack as handmaidens of neocolonialism and neoliberalism.

But patriarchy is still with us—"us," for purposes of this paper, being the USA in the early twenty-first century—in many spheres of life. I emphasize the issue of patriarchy as a particular way of focusing feminist theory and politics. Most people think of feminism as being about "women," and of course that is true, but it is only part of the story. In addition, many people think of feminism as being about "gender," about the cultural division of the world into male and female persons, and—here linking up with queer theory—about other forms of gendered identities (Ortner and Whitehead 1981; Butler 1990). Of course that is true too, but again it is only part of the story. For both "women" and "gender" exist, at least in the modern world, only as elements of a larger formation of power called patriarchy, and that will be the focus of this paper.

Again this paper is confined to patriarchal formations in the USA in the twentieth and twenty-first centuries. While arguably patriarchy is a global, or near-global, phenomenon, its significance in other parts of the world is the subject of intense debate, as will be discussed briefly later in this paper.

Patriarchy in the USA today is more fragmented than it once was, less monolithic and homogeneous, as a result of a century or so, on and off, of feminist activism. Yet it continues to play an often invisible, but highly damaging, role in contemporary social life. The main point of this paper, then, is to try to bring patriarchy back into focus in ways that will make sense to, and perhaps have a galvanizing effect on, a twenty-first century audience. In the first part of the paper, I will discuss an expanded version of the idea of post-feminism. In the second part of the paper, I will try to show how patriarchy persists quite vigorously in contemporary society, not only as a thing in itself, but also as a form of power that organizes and shapes major institutions of twenty-first century capitalism: the industrial production site, the military, and the corporation. The intertwining of patriarchy with other forms of power and dominance is the other key point of the paper. I see this intertwining as a kind of macro-version of Kimberlé Crenshaw's very productive concept of "intersectionality" ([1991] 2007), in which various forms of power cross-cut, cross-fertilize, and amplify one another.

Varieties of post-feminism

Starting in the late 1980s, feminist scholars began identifying a condition they called "post-feminism" (Rosenfelt and Stacey 1987; Traube 1994; Tasker and Negra 2007; McRobbie 2009; for summary, see Ortner 2013, Ch. 6). Originally it was meant to describe a new consciousness among younger generations of women. The argument was that younger women today have both incorporated the fruits of the earlier ("second-wave") feminist movement and rejected the idea of, or the necessity for, continuing to pursue feminist goals. Put more strongly, younger women are said to view that earlier movement as embodying and advocating a style of femininity/femaleness with which they do not want to be associated: "[P]ostfeminism signals more than a simple evolutionary process whereby aspects of feminism have been incorporated into popular culture . . . It also simultaneously involves an 'othering' of feminism. . ., its construction as extreme, difficult, and unpleasurable" (Tasker and Negra 2007, 4). Although we have little solid data, ethnographic or otherwise, on what "young women today" are actually thinking, and although we do not even know which "young women today" are in question, in terms of class, race, age, etc., two things seem fairly clear: that even if younger women have not completely rejected feminism, they are extremely ambivalent about it (see Aronson 2007; Ortner 2013);[1] and that most younger women find the label itself extremely problematic. For one small example of the latter point, in a recent interview with the American Idol (talent show) winner Kelly Clarkson (b. 1982), Clarkson was asked whether she viewed herself as a feminist. "No," she replied, "I wouldn't say feminist—that's too strong. I think when people hear *feminist*, it's like, 'Get out of my way, I don't need anyone'" (*Time*, 11 November 2013, 60).

But here let me expand the scope of the idea of "post-feminism". At the same time that younger generations of women are said to be distancing themselves from feminist ideals, or simply from the feminist label, there are challenges coming from other directions as well. The first of these stems from long-standing tensions between "Western feminism" and scholars of gender in other parts of the world, going back at least to Chandra Talpade Mohanty's path-breaking essay, "Under Western Eyes: Feminist Scholarship and Colonial Discourse" (1984). The issues here, to condense severely, include the idea that Western feminism is excessively focused on female autonomy, which is not necessarily seen as a desirable goal by women/feminists in the global south; and that Western feminism is excessively focused on challenging "patriarchy," when other issues, such as poverty, have greater priority for many women/feminists in the global south (see, e.g., Abu-Lughod 2002, 2013).

These concerns have played a major role in shaping several influential recent ethnographic studies (Ong 2003; Abu-Lughod 2005; Mahmood 2005). These studies prominently critique "feminism" in some form as seeking to impose anti-patriarchalism, as well as Western and/or middle class and/or "liberal" values of personal autonomy, on non-Western women and communities. These critiques may well be quite justified in their specific contexts, and in any event the issues behind the post-colonial critique of feminism are intellectually, ethically, and politically very complex. Space forbids engaging with them substantively here; what I point to with these examples is not the substance of their arguments, but their *effect*: another kind of post-feminism.[2]

Finally, and most recently, we have Nancy Fraser's attack on feminism as having become "a handmaiden of neoliberal capitalism" (2013). Fraser provides an interesting capsule summary of second-wave feminism as promising "two different possible futures," one in which "gender emancipation went hand in hand with participatory democracy and social solidarity," and the other in which "it promised a new form of liberalism, able to grant women as well as men the goods of individual autonomy, increased choice, and meritocratic advancement" (p. 2 of printout). Now, however, "feminism's ambivalence has been resolved in favour of (neo)liberal individualism" (p. 3 of printout). The poster child for this shift seems to be corporate executive and billionaire Sheryl Sandberg whose best-selling book *Lean In: Women, Work, and the Will to Lead* (2013) focuses on what women need to do to get ahead in the corporate world. I agree with Fraser that both tendencies were present in second-wave feminism, although unlike Fraser, I think they are both still actively in play. But again, this is not the place to engage substantively with these issues. Rather I introduce Fraser's argument as one more version of, and contributor to, the broader post-feminist climate.

Looking at these diverse, partially converging, and apparently intensifying aspects of what amounts to not only a post-feminist condition but also a post-feminist movement, one wonders whether the idea, and/or the label, of "feminism" is so fatally tainted by now that it could not or should not be revived. Feminism seems to have become what Erving Goffman once famously called a "spoiled identity," which many are evidently eager to reject.[3] And yet the original *raison d'etre* of the feminist movement, the gender inequalities produced and reproduced within a particular formation of power called "patriarchy," lives on. Indeed I argue that it is patriarchy and not feminism that, *pace* Fraser, thrives under neoliberal capitalism. This brings us to the rest of this paper.

Patriarchy as a system of power

One of the successes of the earlier feminist movement was to put the idea of male dominance and/or patriarchal power on the table, and to argue that gender inequality worked in much the same way as racial inequality: one group (people of color, or women) was considered in some way to be essentially and fundamentally inferior, and thus open to control and domination, or discrimination and exclusion, by the other group (white people, or men). The original feminist political project then was to work towards a state of gender equality in which neither sex was considered superior/inferior, and in which neither sex had the right to dominate or discriminate against the other. But the American feminist movement has gone through many changes since that time, under the impact of challenges from minority, queer, and (as just discussed) third-world women. One way to summarize these changes is to say that the issue of male dominance or patriarchy has become on the one hand more muted, and on the other hand more complicated, more intertwined with other forms of inequality like race, class, and sexuality. This intertwining, which Crenshaw ([1991] 2007) called "intersectionality," is a critical characteristic of all contemporary forms of inequality and it will be central to the present paper as well.[4]

I begin with a few definitions and clarifications. First, I have so far been using the term "patriarchy" very loosely, as an umbrella term to cover the whole range of ideas subsumed within phrases like "male dominance," "male superiority," "sexism," and so forth. Technically, patriarchy is only one form of male dominance, lodged in the figure of the father, and often enveloped in an ideology of protection and benevolence as well as domination and control. But the other terms have their own problems, and I choose "patriarchy" as having the particular virtue of evoking the idea of a social and political formation, rather than the image of a cave man with a club.

Second, while issues of patriarchy may seem irrelevant or of secondary importance to some groups, sectors, and classes of women, for a wide variety of reasons, I will argue later in this paper that the global macro-structure, the overarching system of states, corporations, and military organizations, remains a massive patriarchal system, and has to be addressed as such. That is, many women may feel that they experience little patriarchal oppression in their personal lives; many other women may feel that a patriarchal family and kinship system offers more benefits than costs in the modern world; in both cases—and others—there may be a sense that the important political struggles lie elsewhere. My point, however, will be that that "elsewhere" is itself organized on complex patriarchal as well as political–economic principles that need to be identified and challenged.

At this point, then, I need to focus down on the classic definition of the term, which literally means the rule of the father. Within this definition, patriarchy can be seen as having a particular structure, a particular organization of relations of power that involves not only men over women, but also men over other men. Furthermore, while one can think about patriarchy in pure form—and many all-male institutions approximate that form—in general it is always intertwined with other structures of power: colonialism, capitalism, imperialism, racism, and so forth.

I begin by sketching out a model of patriarchy assembled from a variety of scholarly and popular representations, everything from Freudian theory and feminist theory to ethnography, myth, and movies. I do not try to provide a systematic genealogy of the concept here, as it would take us much too far afield. I simply seek to expose a model or structure that is common to all the representations. In the present section, I will present the basic architecture of the model. In a later section, I will look at three films to consider a variety of elaborations, extensions, and nuances of the basic model, as it plays out in different contexts.

Although patriarchy is a system of social power, it is also a system of cultural categories and personal identities. As a system of cultural categories, it is grounded in a conceptual division of the world into two (and only two) kinds of gendered persons, "women" and "men," defined as both different and unequal. "Women" and "men" are shown in quotes, highlighting the culturally constructed, and normatively imposed, nature of these categories (Ortner and Whitehead 1981). Furthermore, the categories, which are defined as fundamentally and essentially heterosexual, function as both classifiers and identities. It is through the play of life by real people within patriarchal social formations that those categories/identities are reproduced.

Patriarchy as a formation is very old, but probably not (as Freud would have it [1950]) primordial. While pre-state societies probably had varying forms and degrees of male dominance, from virtually egalitarian to highly unequal (Ortner 1996), patriarchy as defined here—minimally as organized around the power of a father-like figure—probably emerges as part of the origins of the state in prehistory (Ortner 1996). If one were going back to nineteenth-century theory on the subject, the relevant theorist would be Engels ([1942] 1972) as much as Freud, although both of them are quite far from contemporary understandings.

Most contemporary societies are not patriarchal from top to bottom, if they ever were. Most are more complex, with multiple arrangements of gendered power, as a result of both the fragmenting forces of modernity and the recurrent cycles of feminist politics. But one does not have to look far to find very clear-cut examples of patriarchal structures of power at work *within* virtually every society in the world today, as it remains a formidable way of organizing not only gender relations, but also other major forms of power and domination.

Patriarchy is a "structure" in the technical sense; it is a set of relations between relations.[5] It is organized around three dyads and their many kinds of interaction: (1) the relationship between a patriarchal figure of some sort and other men; (2) the many homosocial but heterosexual relationships among the men themselves; and (3) the relationships between men and women. In the most classic form of the patriarchal structure, there is a leader who both rewards and punishes the men; there is a body of men who compete among themselves for status and power within the group and in the eyes of the leader; and there are relationships and non-relationships with women, who are either excluded from the group, or included on condition of being subordinated and controlled.

The ethos of different patriarchal structures can vary a great deal. A Buddhist monastery is a patriarchal structure in all the ways just described, but it is (meant to be) productive of peace and spirituality. An elite all-male college is a patriarchal structure, but the emphasis is on the production of a kind of genteel upper class masculinity. In many cases, however, patriarchal organization is mobilized in the service of producing a kind of aggressive masculinity, capitalizing on and intensifying the competitiveness endemic to the male group in these formations. In such cases, the exclusion of women tends to be more absolute, and the boundaries between "men" and "women," "masculinity" and "femininity," tend to be more heavily patrolled. Any breach of these boundaries, like the entry of women into all-male occupations, or into the military, tends to provoke very strong reactions.

The question of breaching social boundaries will be central to several of the film interpretations to follow, and needs a few words here. The issue was very powerfully theorized by Mary Douglas, whose book *Purity and Danger* came out in 1966 but remains relevant and useful to this day. Building on an earlier work by Arnold van Gennep (1960), Douglas argued that the breaching of social boundaries creates "pollution," a state or condition in which the integrity of the group has been weakened or degraded. The underlying model here is the body, which is vulnerable to both the entry of potentially dangerous matter from the outside (food, poison, etc.), and the loss of vital matter from the inside (blood, semen, etc.). From this perspective, the borders of certain kinds of strongly bounded groups, and strongly fortified identities, are similarly fraught with danger; violation of those boundaries will tend to provoke strong, and sometimes, violent reactions. The relevance of this will be clear shortly.

Brief detour: films as multi-purpose texts

In the next few sections, I will be using films as texts that tell us something real about patriarchy in the contemporary USA. Two of the films are documentaries, and one is a feature film based on a true story. I will be using the films primarily as ethnographic and/or cultural texts, that is, as in one way or another displaying the patriarchal dynamics just described. This requires some explanation, although I will have to be very brief.

I have recently completed a study of the world of American independent film, devoted to making films that stands outside of the Hollywood mainstream (Ortner 2013). As I discuss at length in the book, independent film people see themselves as trying to tell the truth about the world today, as opposed to (stereotypical) Hollywood, which is invested in fantasy and illusion for the sake of "entertainment." The world of independent film includes both features (fiction) and documentary, although even with features there is a commitment to an ethic and aesthetic of realism. As several observers have remarked, there is a kind of documentary impulse throughout much of independent film, across the feature/documentary divide.

As in much of film studies, one could approach these films by, in a broad sense, deconstructing them—taking them apart for their ideological biases, for their modes of subjectivation of viewers, and so forth. Even documentaries, which claim to be factual, have been the subject of this kind of deconstructive work; in fact they make especially inviting targets for ideology critique. In response to this, however, there is a very interesting literature in film studies about the truth and reality claims of documentaries: On the one hand, scholars agree that documentaries are constructed and manipulated like all (filmic) texts; on the other hand, scholars also agree that documentaries must be understood as pursuing a truth-telling agenda in ways that are different from other kinds of film, and must be interpreted at least in part from that point of view (Nichols 1991; Williams 1998).

Following this latter line of thinking, then, I will treat the films as critical realist accounts of the world we live in. This approach has a number of different components. First, I treat some of the films as "ethnographic," as describing some social and cultural reality (in this case patriarchy), represented at least in part from the point of view of those who inhabit that reality. Second, I treat one of the films as a cultural text, that is, a text not explicitly about patriarchy, but revealing it upon interpretation.

At the same time, all films must be seen as interventions in the public culture, that is, as representations within a space of other representations, aligning with some and contesting others (Appadurai and Breckenridge 1988). Thus I treat the films not only as realist accounts, but also as critical realist accounts, taking a position vis-à-vis both the object being described and the other representations with which they are in conversation. A dimension of this critical stance applies specifically to political films, mostly but not entirely documentaries: the films are meant to provoke action, either in the sense of getting people politically activated, or in the sense of having some kind of impact on policy, or both (Nichols 1991; Gaines 1999).

All of these functions of film, and especially of the kinds of realist films characteristic of American independent cinema, will be visible at one point or another in the discussions that follow. I will sometimes treat the films as descriptive ethnography, sometimes as texts requiring interpretation, and eventually as political interventions in American public culture on the subject of patriarchy today.

Patriarchy in neoliberal America

I turn now to three films in order to make a number of points. I want to show first that, unfortunately, patriarchy is alive and well in the USA today and still doing a lot of damage. Second, I will use the films to look at variations in the basic model, and to bring out more clearly the variety of harms a patriarchal order inflicts, not only on women, but also on many men, and on persons who do not neatly fit the gender categories. Finally, I want to show how the model or structure plays out both in itself and in parasitic ("intersectional") relationships with other forms of power in an advanced capitalist society: the class structure, the military, and the predatory neoliberal economy.[6]

North Country (Caro 2005)

North Country is a fictionalized account of a true story (Bingham and Gansler 2002) about a woman, called Josie Aimes in the film, who leaves a physically abusive husband and takes a job in the iron mines of Minnesota. The year is 1989, with still only a handful of women working in the mines. The male miners are misogynist in the extreme, but when Josie (Charlize Theron) complains about this to her higher ups, they try to shut her down. After endless and violent harassment, she finally quits, but hires a lawyer and brings a class action suit against the mine owners. The suit succeeds, and establishes one among several legal precedents for all subsequent sexual harassments suits in the USA.

The film is recognizably "feminist" in the classic sense, telling a story of a woman's struggle against discrimination, not as some autonomous neoliberal agent, but on behalf of the working women in general. Again I will return to the overt politics of this and the other films in the conclusions. Here I want to use the film as an ethnographic text, providing a virtual textbook illustration of a well-developed patriarchal order. I said above that a basic patriarchal structure has three intersecting components: the relationship of the patriarchal figure to the group, defined as a group of heterosexual men; the organization of relations among the men, bonded but also competitive among themselves; and the exclusion of women or their inclusion only under male control. Let us then start with the patriarchal figures, the "fathers".

The film is full of fathers, literal and metaphoric, and indeed has a hierarchy of fathers, all of whom are problematic vis-à-vis Josie. After being beaten by her husband, Josie returns to her parents' house. Her own father (Richard Jenkins) looks at her bruised face, seemingly with concern, but then says, "So . . . Did he catch you with another man?" We understand immediately that the father, who is a miner himself, is with the men. Next, after being both harassed and threatened by the men in the mine, Josie complains to her immediate boss, who gives her no sympathy and tells her she must learn to take it. This is the second father who sides with the men and will not help. Finally, after further and more severe harassment, Josie plucks up her courage and decides to call on the owner of the mine, who had led her to believe she could come to him with her problems. But when she gets there, he is surrounded by men, including her boss, and is told that she must either learn to get along or quit. The mine owner is of course the father of fathers, the boss of the boss; further both the owner and the boss are the bosses of her own father, and all of them have power over Josie.

Now let us look at the group of men, in this case the miners. They appear in the extreme form of the homosocial/heterosexual male group: highly misogynistic, solidary among themselves, and hostile to Josie and the handful of other women miners. They harass the women at work in the most extreme ways short of raping them. There is also a meeting at which they curse the women with vile language, yell with rage, stamp their feet, and altogether seem like a mob about to lose control. Here I want to make two different points.

First, the forms of harassment at work fit Douglas's model of pollution sketched briefly above. There is a virtually visible boundary around the male group and its territory; the women have breached the boundary, and the men respond by mobilizing the material signs of pollution: faeces are smeared on the walls of the women's locker room; someone masturbates on an article of clothing in one of the women's lockers when she is not there, leaving a pool of semen; a woman is locked into a portable toilet, which is rocked back and forth as she screams for help, and then finally turned over, covering her with shit.[7]

But the second point to be made about the men's behavior is historical. As noted above, patriarchal male groups, although always to some degree misogynistic, are not always and necessarily violent. In this case, however, two forms of pressure have been put on the whole arrangement, as both a patriarchal and a capitalist structure. In terms of the patriarchy, we learn at the beginning of the film that the first woman had taken a job in the iron mines in 1975, clearly an effect of the feminist movement of that era. The film is set in 1989, and we understand that Josie is only the most recent in a line of intrusions by women into this male territory, threatening the men in terms of their masculine identities. But the 1989 date is also relevant for the men as workers. The 80s are the time in which the American industrial economy is beginning to collapse, with the closing of factories and other industrial facilities (such as mines) becoming a regular occurrence (as summarized in Ortner 2013, 17, with references). The men then are doubly threatened, as both men and workers; they close ranks and react in ways predicted by Douglas's model.

And finally, what about the women? Within the family we see Josie's mother (Sissy Spacek) as a traditional wife, accepting of the husband's authority. She initially does nothing to contradict or undermine the father's hostile treatment of Josie, and in the early part of the film actively supports the idea that Josie should try to patch things up with the abusive husband. At the mine, as already discussed, we see women excluded from the male group of miners. Those who are "inside" are clearly irritants to the men, and have adopted various adaptive strategies so as not to rock the boat and to avoid retribution. From the women's point of view, Josie is a problem, and they do not support her. But this being the late twentieth century, we also have a third type of woman in the form of Josie, the woman who rocks the boat and threatens to undermine the structure.

In the end, the women miners and the mother come around (as does the father, but that is a different part of the story); Josie becomes part of a legal "class"; the class action suit is successful;

and a piece of feminist history is made. But my point here is not to follow the narrative of the film or the real-world history. Rather I have been using the film to show a patriarchal structure at work in a major sector of contemporary American society, both in relatively pure form and as it is intertwined with capitalist relations of power. We saw this intertwining on the dimension of the "fathers," where there is a kind of slippage between Josie's father of kinship, the boss at the mine, and the owner of the capitalist enterprise, all of whom say and do virtually the same thing vis-à-vis Josie, up and down the line. And we saw this slippage at the level of the group of miners, who are threatened as both men and workers, or in other words in terms of both their masculine identities and their material livelihoods, without a clear distinction between the two.

The Invisible War (Dick 2012)

The Invisible War is an award-winning documentary film by Kirby Dick on the subject of rape in the military. In the film, Dick provides both statistical data and the personal testimony of victims to show that the rape of women soldiers in the military is extremely widespread. According to a statistic provided in the film, over 20% of women veterans have been sexually assaulted while on active duty. (The figure for men is a little over 1%; more on male-on-male rape later in this paper.) Some of the more psychologically inclined commentators in the film tend to emphasize that the rapists are "predators," and no doubt some are; one title panel tells us that "15% of incoming recruits attempted or committed rape before entering the military—twice the percentage of the equivalent civilian population." But Dick keeps his eye on the big picture: the patriarchal structure of the military (though he never uses the terms "patriarchal" or "structure"), the ways in which it fosters this behavior, and the fact that the military seems either unwilling or unable to clean it up. Here again I want to show the workings of patriarchy as we see it in the film, within the very particular context of the armed forces.

Let us look first at the "fathers." Once again the film is full of fathers, layer upon layer of patriarchal authority, from lower ranking to higher-ranking officers, what is called in the military "the chain of command." Military commanders at all levels have what one commentator in the film called "an unbelievable amount of power." Their authority over their unit is virtually absolute, and there is almost no way to go outside, around, or over them. Specifically with respect to sexual assault, they can decide whether to believe the victim and take the complaint seriously enough to forward it for investigation or not; in the vast majority of cases, they do not. They either cast doubt on the woman's story, or they tell her it is her own fault, and either way she is urged or even commanded to get over it and get back in line. In some cases, the officers actually turn around and bring legal charges against the women. Many women in the film said the only thing worse than the rape was the commanding officers telling them it was their own fault, refusing to report the rape, and covering up the story. Thus as in *North Country*, we see that patriarchy is not simply the violence of individual men against individual women. On the dimension of the "fathers," here the military officers, it is a hierarchy of power and authority in which superior officers support lower level officers, and all of them support the men.

Now let us look at the relations among the men. In the model I am forwarding here, patriarchy is not just about the authority of the patriarch(s) but about the solidarity of the homosocial/heterosexual group of men. The solidarity of the military unit is an ultimate ideal and value; the men often describe themselves as a "band of brothers" who must be able to depend on one another without question. In 1979, the entrance requirements for women and men in the military were equalized and, except for being banned from combat, women began to enter on the same footing as men (Wikipedia, "Women in Combat"). The date is significant, once again suggesting an effect of the feminist movement of that period. The entry of women into the military appears to have had an effect similar to what we have seen in *North Country*: it violated an invisible boundary and destabilized a central feature of the patriarchal order, the solidarity of the male group. The rapes in turn appear in this context as at once punishments for this act, attempts to expel the intruders, and/or attempts to forcefully establish that if the women are to be "inside the boundary," they must be dominated and controlled. The Douglasian logic, in which the problem is violation of social boundaries, still holds.

Assuming this is correct, one may ask why the retaliation takes the form of rape, rather than the kinds of things we saw in *North Country*. I would suggest that this relates to the specific ethos of the military, which is—unlike the ethos of, say, an iron mine—explicitly an ethos of violence and domination. We see some of this in the film, including an extremely violent recruitment ad for the Marines, and some footage of brutal basic training. Even here, however, we may perhaps see a more specific aspect of the pollution logic at work. After all, rapes are not merely violent assaults on the victim's person, but specifically involve (violently) penetrating the bodily boundary.

The interpretation in terms of boundary violation may also help us think about the relatively high incidence of male–male rape in the military. As noted earlier, male–male rape in the military is also very common; although the film is mainly focused on the women, it also brings this out very clearly. According to one account, men actually make up a larger percentage of sexual assault victims than women—53% to 47% (*The Washington Times*, 20 May 2013). In addition, because of the gender imbalance in the military, the absolute number of men who are sexually assaulted is higher than the number of women. The *proportion* of women raped is much higher than the proportion of men (20% vs. 1%), but it is nonetheless clear that male-on-male rapes represent a significant part of the story.

The issues here are complex in relation to standard American assumptions about heterosexuality and homosexuality. As there does not seem to be any data on the sexual orientations of victims and perpetrators, we can only discuss this question hypothetically. For example, if it is assumed that the victims are homosexual, then the interpretation would be similar to that concerning the rape of women: that they are being punished for intruding in, and polluting, the homosocial/heterosexual group. And in fact they are actually more polluting to the male group than the women, as they have not only violated the social boundaries of the group, but have also challenged the gender binary that is at the basis of the group's identity.

According to one commentator in the film, however, most of the perpetrators and victims are at least nominally heterosexual. In this case, then, we must resort to the more straightforward account of the kinds of relationships involved in any band of brothers: the endless competitive jockeying for status, power, and authority that goes on in tandem with the claims of, and often subjective experience of, solidarity. As one (female) marine officer says in the film, "This is not an issue of sexual orientation, this is simply a matter of power and violence." In other words, the male–male rapes make sense simply as extreme versions of the direct domination of one man over another, regardless of sexual orientation, that is a standard part of the male group within a patriarchal order. Although such domination does not normally take the form of rape in ordinary life, the ethos of violence that is endemic to the army (or prisons) both feeds, and feeds on, the more basic state of endless competition for relative power and status within the male group.

And finally, what about the women? By definition, and in keeping with the basic patriarchal model, women were entirely excluded from the military, except in supporting roles, until recently. Once women began entering the military, it is clear that they have tried to keep their heads down, fit in, and not rock the boat. Along these lines, some of the more depressing parts of an already depressing film are segments involving the women who have headed up something called the Sexual Assault Prevention and Response Office (SAPRO), which was created in response to Congressional pressure to do something about the endless series of sex scandals in the military, the rape epidemic being only the most recent.

SAPRO seems at first to be a step forward, potentially offering the rape victims an alternative to the dead end (or worse) of reporting to their own commanding officers. It turns out, however, that this is not part of its mandate, and that it has no power whatsoever to make the military do anything at all; it can only "strongly suggest." Instead it puts all the emphasis (and, as one commentator wryly remarked, most of its budget) on the "prevention" part of its mandate, for example by producing posters and other kinds of publicity advising women to take precautions so they do not leave themselves open to rape. One ad they produced emphasizes the importance for women of always walking with a buddy after dark, thereby both blaming the victim and normalizing rape in one fell swoop.

This programme has been headed by women since its inception. The first director, a Dr. Kaye Whitley, PhD, talks on screen about the posters and the prevention campaign, but is unable to answer any other questions at all, and comes across as both ignorant and not quite in touch with reality. She is later replaced by a military officer, Major General Mary Kay Hertog, who praises Whitley and says she intends to carry on her work. The effectiveness of the work of this unit may be judged by the fact that, among other things, the head of the Air Force wing of this programme was himself arrested on charges of sexual assault (*Huffington Post*, 16 May 2013).

But the film having been made in 2012, there are several progressive women in the story who in fact are trying to bring about changes. We meet a Captain Anu Bhagwati (ret.), who is the director of the Service Women's Action Network of the US Marine Corps, who clearly takes this very seriously and is trying to make something happen. We also meet Susan Burke, a lawyer and the daughter of a military family, who brought together several of the victims in a lawsuit against the military. The case failed but Burke plans to continue working on this problem.[8]

The military appears as an almost pure patriarchal structure, a system for the production of violent masculinity, supported by a hierarchy of patriarchal authority, and deployed against any enemy within or without. A military entity has no inherent mission and can be put in the service of any group, nation, or cause. The mission of the American military is to defend the American nation, and the American nation's interests, but that of course brings us back to the connection with capitalism; for the American "nation's interests" are to a great degree the interests of capital, and that brings us to our final film.

Enron: The Smartest Guys in the Room (Gibney 2005)

With this film we leave the grime of the iron mines and the physical violence of the military and enter the world of money and ideas. No locker room will be smeared with faeces, and nobody will be raped. Yet we will see once again the basic outlines of a patriarchal structure, and a different kind of brutality that it can produce.

Enron: The Smartest Guys in the Room is based on a book by the same name by two senior writers for *Fortune* magazine, Bethany McLean and Peter Elkind (2004). It is the story of the rise and fall of the Enron Corporation, a company that dealt in gas and electric power, which was at one time the seventh largest corporation in America. It is specifically the story of a corporation that was organized as much as possible to pursue profit at all costs in an ideally deregulated, free-market neoliberal economy. But the company systematically engaged in accounting and other business practices that ranged from merely questionable to highly unethical to completely illegal, all designed to make the company appear to be in a better financial condition than it was. The point of all this was to keep the price of the stock constantly rising, since most of the wealth of the executives was in Enron stock options. But as various reporters (like McLean) began probing into Enron's finances, the investment banks eventually became less willing to prop the company up with loans, the market analysts eventually became less willing to promote the stock, and the whole thing collapsed.

The culture of the corporation was completely dog-eat-dog, both internally and with respect to their customers and clients. As one trader said on screen, "If I was going to see my boss about my compensation, and I knew that if I stepped on somebody's throat along the way my compensation would be doubled, of course I would do it." Those who did well within the company were richly rewarded with large bonuses, and many individuals became enormously wealthy in the process. At the same time, something like 20,000 employees, who had been encouraged (or in some cases forced) to put all their pension funds in Enron stock, lost not only their jobs and their medical insurance but also all of their retirement savings when the company went broke.

Now let us look at the question of Enron and patriarchy. The story here will be different from those in the films discussed earlier. This is not primarily a story about how women were marginalized or harassed (although they were). In fact women play a relatively small (although ultimately very important) role in the story and I will discuss them first. As usual in a patriarchal structure, there were relatively few women inside the boundaries, except those in supporting roles. Almost all of those who made it to higher levels seem to have slept with their bosses or colleagues, which in general did no harm to the male party's reputation but undermined the credibility of the female party. The most successful of the women executives, one Rebecca Mark, seems to have been as aggressive as many of the men, and was several times listed as "one of *Fortune*'s 50 most powerful women in business" (McLean and Elkind 2004, 253). Mark made a lot of deals, and made a lot of money, but she nonetheless kept running afoul of one or another of the top men, and was not only eventually fired but also blamed by some for the bankrupting of Enron.

The heroines of the story are once again the boat rockers, an executive of one of the dirtiest of the subsidiaries, and an accountant by trade, called Sherron Watkins, who blew the whistle on some key illegal practices (Swartz and Watkins 2004), and the *Wall Street Journal* reporter, Bethany McLean, who wrote one of the earliest critical pieces, declaring Enron stock to be overvalued in relation to the actual worth of the company, and thus opening the company to scrutiny.

Now let us look at the "fathers." The founder, Chairman, and Chief Executive Officer (CEO) of the corporation was a rather affable man called Ken Lay. The President and Chief Operating Officer (COO), and also by all accounts the villain of the piece, was a brilliant and ruthless man called Jeff Skilling. These and others at the top were important not only as a patriarchal hierarchy of fathers/bosses/officers who kept the women and the lesser men down, but also in establishing what can only be described as the violent ethos of the corporation. Lay preached the religion of the neoliberal free market, unencumbered by any human considerations other than the brainpower to make it work and the millions to be made from it. Skilling shared this vision, but conjoined it with a culture of extreme machismo. Among other things he periodically took some favoured male executives and friends of the corporation on dangerous, long-distance, overland motorcycle trips. In the world of Jeff Skilling, to be a successful Enron executive or trader you needed to have both a brilliant mind and (as one executive was said to have) "balls of steel" (McLean and Elkind 2004, 46). Skilling himself said he liked to hire "guys with spikes" (McLean and Elkind 2004, 55).

This brings us to the traders. When Skilling came aboard, Enron was a relatively staid company that owned natural gas production facilities and pipelines, and transacted the movement of physical gas from Point A to Point B. Skilling's "big idea" (and he very much believed in the "big idea") was to turn Enron into something like a financial market in gas products, in which value was determined not by actual supply and demand in real time, but by gambling on supply and demand under future, and thus not fully knowable, conditions. With this transformation, Enron became something like a stock exchange in gas and other forms of energy, and as a result hired large numbers of traders to engage in the trading of the "stock." The trading operation in turn became the biggest and most profitable part of Enron, and the traders ultimately came to wield a great deal of collective power. As the authors say, "They were like a powerful high school clique that terrorizes even the principal." And as one executive says, "They didn't appear menacing . . . but they were a mob" (McLean and Elkind 2004, 213). Towards the end of the book, Skilling says, "The traders have taken over. These guys have gotten so powerful that I can't control them any more." (McLean and Elkind 2004, 335)

With the traders then we meet once again the virtually all-male, homosocial/heterosexual group, here with an ethos of both great solidarity and tremendous, cutthroat competition. Their immediate leader was a former army tank captain by the name of Greg Whalley, described by one of the traders as a "screaming stud" (McLean and Elkind 2004, 214). Here is one account of life among the Enron traders:

> [One trader said,] "We were very competitive, and we just didn't feel that we could fail a lot." An executive named Bill Butler used to stalk the floor with an eight-foot-long black bullwhip, jokingly threatening traders who didn't seem to be spending enough time on the phone. Their esprit was such that the traders took great pleasure in outsmarting other parts of Enron, and they didn't show much mercy for one another, either. "If you showed any weakness, the antibodies would attack," says a former trader. "Life at Enron," says another, "was the purest form of balls-out guerrilla warfare".
>
> *(McLean and Elkind 2004, 217)*

As we can see from all the language and stories thus far, we are already well into the jungle—that is to say, the culture of the workplace—in which patriarchy and capitalism are deeply feeding off one another at Enron. Now let us look at how this works out when Enron does business with its customers in the outside world. Here the traders will appear less like the military band of brothers on the home front, threatened by the intrusion of polluting others, and more like the military in action, a group of men whipped up by their leaders and turned loose on the enemy with orders to take no prisoners. This is what happened most famously when Enron entered the electricity market of the State of California.

Enron had been involved, through lobbying, in promoting the deregulation of gas and electricity in California. Eventually the state was partially but not totally deregulated, leaving a situation where the rules were extremely complicated and unclear. It became a particular point of pleasure for the Enron traders to game the system and to make in the process an enormous amount of profit for the company and themselves. As part of subsequent investigations, audio tapes of conversations between traders about the California situation were recovered, and this is where we come back to the synergy between the patriarchal and capitalist mentalities in play. One of the traders' "games" (their term) called Ricochet involved exporting power out of the state when the price was low and then bringing it back when demand rose and prices soared. In one conversation we hear one of the traders say, "So we fuckin' export like a motherfucker." Another says, "Gettin' rich?" and the first says, "Tryin' to." Another strategy involved asking local power stations to go offline "for maintenance" in the middle of the shortage, again pushing the prices up. We actually hear two conversations in which a trader speaks to a man at a local plant asking him to go offline for a while, and the man readily agrees to do it. In yet another conversation, someone in California tells a trader in Houston that there is a fire under a major power line, causing further disruption. The trader is heard to say, "Burn, baby, burn! That's a beautiful thing!"

Even when there was no sexual language, there seemed to be a rape-like quality to the whole thing, a kind of violent and gleeful ravishing of a helpless victim. Nor was I the only one who heard it this way. At one point in this segment of the film, journalist Bethany McLean says, "The Enron traders never step back and say, 'Is it in our long term interest if we totally rape California like this?'" And then we hear the following conversation. The first trader says, "All that money you guys stole from those poor grandmothers in California." And the second trader says, "Now she wants her fucking money back for all the power you've charged her up her ass."

As with the other two films, the playing out of the patriarchal structure is clear, as are the ways in which the wielding of corporate economic power intersects and is infused with the sexuality and aggression of patriarchal relations. Now it is time to pull this all together.

Conclusions

I began this paper with a discussion of several forms of post-feminism, including the ambivalence of younger women about identifying with the feminist label; the negative representations of feminism in some important recent monographs coming from a broadly defined post-colonial perspective; and most recently the charge that feminism has become complicit with neoliberal capitalism. I presented these points not to discuss them substantively—impossible in the present paper—but simply to draw attention to the multiple, and seemingly proliferating, vectors of "post-feminism."

Insofar as feminism has survived as a scholarly and/or political project, it is almost entirely concerned with women and/or gender. What has largely disappeared is a concern with patriarchal power, a concern that was so central to early feminist work. Yet in the course of watching a large number of American independent films, as part of a different research project, I was struck by the degree to which patriarchy is still virtually everywhere. The first point of this paper, then, was to try to make patriarchy visible (again) and to show that it is something we cannot afford to dismiss or ignore. While it can appear in a relatively benign form (though always grounded in an assumption of male superiority and female inferiority), it is often the basis of aggression and violence. Using some of the films as ethnographic and/or cultural texts, I presented three examples of patriarchy in action: the extreme harassment of women in an industrial workplace; the rape of both women and men in the US military; and the ruthless internal competition and predatory business practices of a corporation. In all cases, I showed not only how patriarchy works as a specific arrangement of power relations in its own right, but also how it is deeply enmeshed with other systems of power in this advanced capitalist society. We could clearly see in the examples how the different forms of domination blurred into one another, or fed off one another, each intensifying the effects of the other.

One subtext, or in some cases the explicit text, of some of the post-feminist literature, is a growing sense that other political agendas have become more urgent. Neoliberal capitalism, environmental degradation, American militarism, and more have begun to capture intellectual and political attention on an ever-growing scale. I share a sense of the tremendous urgency of these issues, which I have written about at length elsewhere (Ortner 2013). My concern, however, is that the momentum of the new movements may completely push a feminist agenda off the table. There is a way in which feminism and anti-neoliberal capitalism (or anti-US militarism, or pro-environmentalism—name your issue) are being set up in some contexts as either-or propositions. But my examples in this paper have shown not only, as I said earlier, that patriarchy is alive and well in neoliberal America, but also that it is inextricably and aggressively intertwined with so much else that is bad in the contemporary world.

As a final point, however, we must return to the films, not as texts for our ethnographic or interpretive use, but as political interventions in American public culture. *North Country* and *The Invisible War* explicitly challenge patriarchal violence and injustice, and the anti-patriarchal subtext of *Enron* is very close to the surface as well. The films may be seen then as implicitly talking back to the post-feminist tendencies I emphasized in the earlier part of this paper. Made in a period when feminism in its classic form seems to be over, and made by men as well as women, they are perhaps harbingers of a new anti-patriarchal politics, for which we do not yet have a name.

Acknowledgments

Deepest thanks as always to those special friends and colleagues who shared with me their sharp critical insights and their wisdom, and (tried to) save me from my worst mistakes: Jessica Cattelino, Gwendolyn Kelly, Abigail Stewart, and Timothy D. Taylor. I am grateful as well to Laura Ahearn, who shared some of her unpublished work with me, and who has always been a valued interlocutor. Thanks too to issue editor Dimitrios Theodossopoulos, issue mate Jacqueline Urla, and the two anonymous journal readers for their very helpful comments. Finally thanks to audiences at the University of California, Riverside (Anthropology), and at the University of California, Los Angeles (Sociology), who pushed me very hard in their respective Q&As.

Notes

1 In an earlier work (Ortner 2006), I discussed the factor of ambivalence in resistance movements. The ambivalence we see in post-feminism is thus not new, but where it was recessive at the height of second wave feminism, it is apparently dominant today.

2 Another aspect of post-feminism in anthropology can be seen in the declining number of journal articles on subjects related to women and gender. I had a discussion of this point in an earlier draft but had to cut it for reasons of space. The discussion was based on Laura Ahearn's article on keywords in *American Ethnologist* (2014).

3 But see a very important project coming out of the University of Michigan that has attempted to rethink the feminist agenda in a global perspective, in response to the post-colonial critique: Lal et al. (2010) and Stewart et al. (2011). I regret not having the space to discuss this work in this paper.

4 An earlier version of this insistence on the intertwining of gender and other forms of inequality came from the work of so-called Marxist-feminists in the 1970s, who emphasized the linkages between gender and class under capitalism. See especially Eisenstein (1979).

5 The only recent work to explore the question of patriarchy as a "structure" in some sense is Pierre Bourdieu's *Masculine Domination* (2001). But Bourdieu spends a great deal of time on the question of "symbolic domination", that is, of the degree to which women internalize patriarchy as habitus, rather than on patriarchy as a system of social power, which is the primary focus of the present paper.

6 In Crenshaw's original discussion of intersectionality, race was a central component. In the three films that follow, however, racial difference is held constant (that is, everyone is white), thereby highlighting the patriarchy factor. Thanks to Abigail Stewart for emphasizing this point.

7 One of the elements of the film that I do not have time/space to discuss is that the events in the film are set during the Anita Hill sexual harassment hearings, and we see Hill on television in the background in several scenes. One detail of Hill's allegations, which for some reason always stuck in my mind as strange, was that Clarence Thomas left a can of Coke on Hill's desk with a pubic hair on top. Thinking about it in the context of the present discussion, it makes sense as another material sign of pollution.

8 Another female boat-rocker, not in the film, is Senator Kirsten Gillibrand who, according to a *New Yorker* article, was inspired by the film to develop legislation to address the epidemic of rape in the military (Osnos 2013). The legislation failed but Gillibrand has continued to press the issue.

References

Abu-Lughod, Lila. 2002. "Do Muslim Women Really Need Saving? Anthropological Reflections on Cultural Relativism and Its Others." *American Anthropologist* 104 (3): 783–790.

Abu-Lughod, Lila. 2005. *Dramas of Nationhood: The Politics of Television in Egypt.* Chicago, IL: University of Chicago Press.

Abu-Lughod, Lila. 2013. *Do Muslim Women Need Saving?* Cambridge, MA: Harvard University Press.

Ahearn, Laura M. 2014. "Detecting Research Patterns and Paratextual Features in *AE* Word Counts, Keywords, and Titles." *American Ethnologist* 41 (1): 17–30.

Appadurai, Arjun, and Carol Breckenridge. 1988. "Why Public Culture?" *Public Culture* 1 (1, Fall): 5–9.

Aronson, Pamela. 2007. "Feminists or 'Postfeminists'? Young Women's Attitudes Toward Feminism and Gender Relations." In *Feminist Frontiers*, edited by V. Taylor, N. Whittier, and L. J. Rupp, 7th ed., 519–531. Boston, MA: McGraw Hill.

Bingham, Clara and Laura Leedy Gansler. 2002. *Class Action: The Story of Lois Jensen and the Landmark Case that Changed Sexual Harassment Law.* New York: Doubleday.

Bourdieu, Pierre. 2001. *Masculine Domination.* Translated by Richard Nice. Stanford, CA: Stanford University Press.

Butler, Judith. 1990. *Gender Trouble: Feminism and the Subversion of Identity.* New York: Routledge.

Caro, Niki, dir. 2005. *North Country.* Produced by Nick Wechsler.

Crenshaw, Kimberlé. [1991] 2007. "Mapping the Margins: Intersectionality, Identity Politics, and Violence Against Women of Color." In *Feminist Frontiers*, edited by V. Taylor, N. Whittier, and L. J. Rupp, 7th ed., 431–440. Boston, MA: McGraw Hill.

Dick, Kirby, dir. 2012. *The Invisible War.* Produced by Tanner King Barklow and Amy Ziering.

Douglas, Mary. 1966. *Purity and Danger: An Analysis of Concepts of Pollution and Taboo.* London: Routledge and Kegan Paul.

Eisenstein, Zillah R., ed. 1979. *Capitalist Patriarchy and the Case for Socialist Feminism.* New York: Monthly Review Press.

Engels, Friedrich. [1942] 1972. *The Origin of the Family, Private Property, and the State*, edited by Eleanor Leacock. New York: International Publishers.

Fraser, Nancy. 2013. "How Feminism Became Capitalism's Handmaiden—and How to Reclaim it." *The Guardian*, Sunday October 13. Accessed March 17, 2014. www.theguardian.com/commentisfree

Freud, Sigmund. 1950. *Totem and Taboo: Some Points of Agreement between the Mental Lives of Savages and Neurotics.* Translated by James Strachey. New York: W. W. Norton and Company.

Gaines, Jane M. 1999. "Political Mimesis." In *Collecting Visible Evidence*, edited by J. M. Gaines and M. Renov, 84–103. Minneapolis, MN: University of Minnesota Press.

van Gennep, Arnold. 1960. *Rites of Passage.* Translated by M. B. Vizedom and G. L. Caffee. Chicago, IL: University of Chicago Press.

Gibney, Alex, dir. 2005. *Enron: The Smartest Guys in the Room.* Produced by Alison Ellwood, Alex Gibney, Jason Kliot, and Susan Motamed.

Lal, Jayati, Kristin McGuire, Abigail J. Stewart, Magdalena Zaborowska, and Justine M. Pas. 2010. "Recasting Global Feminisms: Toward a Comparative Historical Approach to Women's Activism and Feminist Scholarship." *Feminist Studies* 36 (1, Spring): 13–39.

Mahmood, Saba. 2005. *Politics of Piety: The Islamic Revival and the Feminist Subject.* Princeton, NJ: Princeton University Press.

McLean, Bethany, and Peter Elkind. 2004. *Enron: The Smartest Guys in the Room.* New York: Portfolio (Penguin).

McRobbie, Angela. 2009. *The Aftermath of Feminism: Gender, Culture, and Social Change.* London: Sage.

Mohanty, Chandra Talpade. 1984. "Under Western Eyes: Feminist Scholarship and Colonial Discourses." *Boundary 2* 12(no. 3)/13(no. 1) (spring/fall): 338–358.

Nichols, Bill. 1991. *Representing Reality: Issues and Concepts in Documentary.* Bloomington, IN: University of Indiana Press.

Ong, Aihwa. 2003. *Buddha is Hiding: Refugees, Citizenship, The New America.* Berkeley, CA: University of California Press.

Ortner, Sherry B. 1996. "The Virgin and the State." In *Making Gender: The Politics and Erotics of Culture*, edited by S. B. Ortner, 43–58. Boston, MA: Beacon Press.

Ortner, Sherry B. 2006. "Resistance and the Problem of Ethnographic Refusal." In *Anthropology and Social Theory: Culture, Power, and the Acting Subject*, edited by S. B. Ortner, 42–62. Durham, NC: Duke University Press.

Ortner, Sherry B. 2013. *Not Hollywood: Independent Film at the Twilight of the American Dream.* Durham, NC: Duke University Press.

Ortner, Sherry B., and Harriet Whitehead. 1981. "Introduction: Accounting for Sexual Meanings." In *Sexual Meanings: The Cultural Construction of Gender and Sexuality*, edited by S. B. Ortner and H. Whitehead, 1–27. Cambridge, England: Cambridge University Press.

Osnos, Evan. 2013. "Strong Vanilla: The Relentless Rise of Kirsten Gillibrand." *The New Yorker*, December 16: 40–46.

Rosenfelt, Deborah, and Judith Stacey. 1987. "Second Thoughts on the Second Wave." *Feminist Studies* 13 (2): 341–361.

Sandberg, Sheryl with Nell Scovell. 2013. *Lean In: Women, Work, and the Will to Lead.* New York: Knopf.

Stewart, Abigail J., Jayati Lal, and Kristin McGuire. 2011. "Expanding the Archives of Global Feminisms: Narratives of Feminism and Activism." *Signs: Journal of Women in Culture and Society* 36 (4): 889–914.

Swartz, Mimi with Sherron Watkins. 2004. *Power Failure: The Inside Story of the Collapse of Enron.* New York: Currency (Doubleday).

Tasker, Yvonne, and Diane Negra, eds. 2007. *Interrogating Post-Feminism: Gender and the Politics of Popular Culture.* Durham, NC: Duke University Press.

Traube, Elizabeth. 1994. "Family Matters: Postfeminist Constructions of a Contested Site." In *Visualizing Theory: Selected Essays from Visual Anthropology Review*, edited by L. Taylor, 301–321. New York and London: Routledge.

Williams, Linda. 1998. "Mirrors without Memories: Truth, History, and *The Thin Blue Line*." In *Documenting the Documentary: Close Readings of Documentary Film and Video*, edited by B. K. Grant and J. Sloniowski, 379–396. Detroit, MI: Wayne State University Press.

5

Lost in translation

Challenging (white, monolingual feminism's) <choice> with *justicia reproductiva*

Kathleen M. de Onís

On July 28, 2014, the *New York Times* published an article reporting that U.S. reproductive rights advocates are increasingly avoiding the phrase "pro-choice" in their messaging. This shift, according to the report, emerged around 2010 in response to younger activists' dislike of "political labels" and the term's narrow association with abortion (Calmes, 2014, para. 3). The article credited Planned Parenthood with leading the charge to "Shun 'Pro-Choice.'" What the *Times* piece failed to note was that Women of Color and their low-income allies have been problematizing "choice" for decades (Gerber Fried, 1990; Palczewski, 2010). In 1994, U.S. Black feminist activists fused reproductive rights with social justice to establish a reproductive justice framework to provide a lens for communicating the intersecting inequalities encountered by precarious communities. This new orientation offered an alternative to narrow legal conceptions of abortion <choice>. Given these important movement-building contributions and their elision in the news story, many reproductive justice activists expressed disgust with the article's "egregious and unforgivable re-write of history" and its persistent reliance on quotations from White women (Bayetti Flores, 2014, para. 7; Pérez, 2014).[1] As Verónica Bayetti Flores, the National Latina Institute for Reproductive Health's former policy analyst, opined in her rejoinder on *Feministing*, since the story's publication "women of color in the reproductive justice movement have been hollering a collective WTF" (2014, para. 1).

The *Times* article's erasure of other positionalities and perspectives resurrects and reinvigorates language contestations that have engendered fissures among diverse reproductive rights activists and scholars for decades (Condit, 1990; de Onís, 2012; Fixmer-Oraiz, 2010, 2013; Gerber Fried, 1990; Hayden, 2009; Palczewski, 2010; Silliman, Gerber Fried, Ross, & Gutiérrez, 2004; Solinger, 2005). Various iterations of this controversy animate extant women's studies communication scholarship, which offers important insights for historicizing and examining the language deployed in U.S. reproductive rights movements. Celeste Condit (1984, 1990) and Sara Hayden (2009) maintain that <choice>[2] encapsulates a broadening social justice perspective capable of addressing the needs of all women. They support this position by documenting various discourses recounting reproductive health experiences and events (e.g., the 2004 March for Women's Lives).

However, Hayden and O'Brien Hallstein (2010, p. xxviii) recognize that although the United States is currently characterized and shaped by "an era of 'choice,'" the term is fraught and contested. For example, Natalie Fixmer-Oraiz (2010, 2013, p. 150) argues in her work on emergency contraception and surrogacy that <choice> "mask[s] reproductive injustice." Catherine Palczewski (2010) offers a similar critique in her exploration of counterpublics via Women of Color's *reproductive freedom* advocacy.[3] Fixmer-Oraiz and Palczewski provide key contributions for better understanding the problematics of <choice>; however, detailed analysis of why the ideograph fails to translate culturally and linguistically remains underexplored in the literature in communication studies. This essay seeks to fill this lacuna.

Diverging from other ideographic analyses advocating for <choice>, I explore Spanish-speaking, migrant Latin@[4] realities by observing the interplay of cultural and linguistic difference, ideology, and language in the discourse of the National Latina Institute for Reproductive Health (or the Latina Institute/NLIRH) and the stakes of the group's appeals. As a women's rights advocacy group, the Latina Institute

> is the only national reproductive justice organization dedicated to advancing health, dignity, and justice for the 26 million Latinas, their families, and communities in the United States. . . .NLIRH uses policy change, culture shift, relationship building, and leadership development to advance a reproductive justice agenda informed by the priorities and experiences of activists on the ground.
>
> *(NLIRH, n.d., para. 1)*

These efforts, guided by the group's slogan, "salud, dignidad y justicia" ("health, dignity, and justice"), are rooted in two central concerns: abortion and migrant rights (J. González-Rojas, personal communication, August 3, 2010).[5]

This article's engagement with Latina Institute rhetoric is informed by scholarship on framing and social movements. Robert Benford and David Snow (2000, p. 631) find that "the extent to which they [political opportunities] constrain or facilitate collective action is partly contingent on how they are framed by movement actors as well as others." Furthermore, they assert, "The concept of resonance is relevant to the issue of the effectiveness or mobilizing potency of proffered framings, thereby attending to the question of why some framings seem to be effective or 'resonate' while others do not" (p. 619). Insofar as these outcomes can be measured, ideographs—the "building blocks of ideology"—and other key terms are inextricably linked with the efficacy of efforts committed to social change and human dignity (McGee, 1980, p. 7).[6] While a language term may maintain a particular meaning grounded in its diachronic dimension, it may also evolve as it expands, contracts, and clashes with other slogans synchronically (Condit, 1990; Hayden, 2009). Accordingly, discourse suggesting the limits of <choice> reveals an exigency that enjoins us to consider the implications of these appeals. By critiquing a term positioned as an ideograph, the Latina Institute calls attention to *bordering*, a discursive apparatus that dehumanizes People of Color and other "suspect" individuals via exclusionary, disciplining language inscribed on precarious bodies (DeChaine, 2012).

This study offers two key claims to contribute to conversations on *bordering* (Chávez, 2012; DeChaine, 2012; Hasian & McHendry, 2012; Ono & Sloop, 2002), *disidentifications* (Morrissey, 2013; Muñoz, 1999), and *ideographs* (Condit Railsback, 1984; Condit, 1990; Hayden, 2009; Palczewski, 2010). My first argument engages mutability concerns surrounding the ideographic weight of <choice>. In reviewing Latina Institute rhetoric, I find that the term engenders bordering effects and delimited elasticity because of the cultural and linguistic translation problems posed for Spanish-speaking, migrant Latin@ communities. This troubling outcome might be mitigated by engaging in disidentificatory practices and other techniques committed to differential coalitional politics via an alternative term and framework: *reproductive justice* (or *justicia reproductiva* in Spanish). My second claim calls for communication scholars to be more cognizant of U.S. monoculturalism and English monolingualism, which circumscribe the possibilities of communication scholarship. I suggest that engaging cultural and linguistic differences is paramount in studies documenting the interconnections of ideology and language to illustrate how this linkage enables and constrains (in)justice. This interest is especially important given growing coalitional efforts to achieve global change at the local level, which I have discussed elsewhere (de Onís, 2012).

To support these aforementioned arguments, this essay develops in three parts. First, I briefly historicize the evolution of <choice> and *justicia reproductiva/reproductive justice* and contextualize migrant Latin@ experiences in the United States. Second, I describe the reviewed texts and offer my analysis; I situate discussions of bordering, disidentifications, and ideographs in this section to evince how these concepts both inform and are shaped by my analysis of Latina Institute rhetoric. Finally, I examine the implications of my analysis for coalition building and communication scholarship by elucidating the potential of language terms to unite, divide, and/or elide diverse voices, bodies, and histories. In this final section, I discuss negotiating the fragmentation caused by disputes over the malleability of <choice> and issue a call for heightened reflexivity about the role of language, culture, and translation in scholarly work. I begin by briefly contextualizing <choice>, *justicia reproductiva/reproductive justice*, and Latin@ reproductive rights realities in the United States.

On language framing and living Latin@

U.S. reproductive rights movements have been and continue to be composed of diverse participants (Silliman et al., 2004).[7] During the decade preceding the 1973 *Roe v. Wade* ruling, <discrimination> was increasingly deployed to describe the injustice faced by low-income women due to legislative abortion barriers (Condit Railsback, 1984; Condit, 1990; Hayden, 2009; Palczewski, 2010). As feminists joined the ranks of those struggling for abortion rights in the mid-1960s, <choice>—a term used to resonate with libertarian appeals—permeated the scene. This slogan would leave an indelible and in some ways debilitating mark on reproductive rights discourse (Fixmer-Oraiz, 2010, 2013; Hayden, 2009; Palczewski, 2010).

Contesting the mainstream U.S. feminist movement's reliance on <choice>, the *justicia reproductiva/reproductive justice* framework seeks to address women's diverse, intersectional positionalities and their struggle for reproductive rights via a social justice commitment. This movement is indebted to Black feminist thought, especially scholarship by Kimberlé Crenshaw (1989) and Patricia Hill Collins (2000). Over the years, *justicia reproductiva/reproductive justice* also has been profoundly shaped by Asian, Latin@, and Indigenous women. This framework extends beyond "a narrower focus on legal access and individual choice to a broader analysis of racial, economic, cultural, and structural constraints on our [women's] power" (SisterSong, n.d., para. 5). Many U.S. Third-World feminists maintain that in carrying privileged assumptions, pro-<choice> framing further disadvantages women who confront systemic barriers inhibiting unrestricted, desirable <choices> (Gerber Fried, 1990; Roberts, Ross, & Kuumba, 2005; Silliman et al., 2004; Smith, 2005). These obstacles include but are not limited to poverty, racism, xenophobia, English monolingualism, lack of health insurance and access to care, sexism, heterosexism, undocumented legal status, and environmental and climate injustice (Chávez, 2013; Collins, 2000; Crenshaw, 1989; de Onís, 2012; Palczewski, 2010; Pezzullo, 2007).

Justicia reproductiva/reproductive justice supports women who wish to be childless as well as those who desire childbearing and motherhood. The framework also insists that necessary resources for effective parenting and attainment of quality health care for women and children be accessible and affordable (Hayden, 2009). This "right to mother and to mother well" is especially significant given historic coercive sterilization violence experienced by Women of Color and Indigenous women (Gutiérrez, 2008; Palczewski, 2010, p. 81). Accordingly, for communities living at the intersection of multiple oppressions, their daily struggle is rooted first and foremost in surviving.

Latin@ realities of reproductive health and well-being merit discussion to contextualize and respond to Latina Institute discourse. Migrant Latin@ women have the highest birthrate of any U.S. group. This rate is associated with a lack of contraceptive access and sexual education, as well as strong commitments to *familia* and *familismo*, whereby reverence for familial connections and childbearing is paramount (Aguirre-Molina & Molina, 2003; Flores & Holling, 1999; Holling, 2006; NLIRH, 2005). Latin@ women also experience about 20% of reported U.S. abortions and are disproportionately likely to seek out dangerous means for pregnancy termination (NLIRH, 2005). English monolingualism, a lack of culturally sensitive medical care, and inhumane detention and deportation policies (due to exposure of "undocumented" or "illegal" status) substantially limit access to safe abortions and other reproductive health services.

Migrant Latin@s encounter dehumanizing ideologies from politicians and the nation's citizenry. Their "[s]uspect bodies carry the border on them . . . [and] are susceptible targets" because of how they look and speak (Flores, 2003, p. 381; Zentella, 2007). This othering foments reproductive injustice, xenophobia, coloniality, and racism, which is especially acute for female bodies that are read as "always already reproductive" (Luibhéid, 2013, p. 194). Latina Institute members uncover and resist these intersecting oppressions in their discourse.

Texts and theory: engaging with Latina Institute rhetoric

This essay's focus on Latina Institute texts emerges from my interest in examining discourses alluding to the problematics of pro-<choice> terminology.[8] The selected documents were published in January 2010, amid a milieu of antimigrant and anti-woman sentiment and just before the ubiquitous catchphrase "the war on women" vigorously resurfaced. The first text, "Securing Real Choices Means Going Beyond 'Choice,'" appeared on the Latina Institute's *Nuestra Vida, Nuestra Voz* blog and on the *Reproductive Health (RH) Reality Check* Web site in commemoration of the 37th anniversary of *Roe v. Wade*.[9] The second document, "Advancing Reproductive Justice in Immigrant Communities," is a handbook available in both English and Spanish; it describes the Latina Institute's methodology for approaching *justicia reproductiva/reproductive justice* in migrant Latin@ communities.[10] In what follows, I analyze how the organization deploys <choice> and *justicia reproductiva/reproductive justice*, as well as how bordering, disidentifications, and ideographs serve as instructive, interconnected lenses for exploring the group's discourse.

<Choice>: a term for the privileged

The Latina Institute maintains that <choice> fails to encompass the lived realities of Latin@s because of complex reproductive health concerns (e.g., transportation, economic burdens, documentation status). The term's lack of resonance reflects *bordering*, as <choice> is unable to convey Latin@ reproductive health intricacies and barriers to well-being, including and especially abortion rights broadly construed.

Bordering calls attention to the dynamic dimension of how border rhetorics and those implicated in these discussions are actively and continually (re)constructed and relegated to the margins (DeChaine, 2012). The rhetoricity of the border signifies a troubling insider/outsider binary. This division is discursively seized upon by nativist and other like-minded rhetors who seek to delimit the rights and agency of migrant Latin@s (DeChaine, 2012; Ono & Sloop, 2002). Studying this disciplining function reveals the dual character of borders:

> On the one hand, the border is a material place of danger, hostility, and death—in a sense real. On the other hand, borders are rhetorical in the ways that we decide to epistemically map this ontological reality. The ways that we configure these borders as adequately guarded or unguarded, porous or contained, impacts the ways that we think about cultural relationships, global conditions, work situations, and imaginary communities.
>
> *(Hasian & McHendry, 2012, p. 107)*

Through these configurations, migrants and suspect (usually non-White) bodies confront discrimination, ostracism, and all too often death (DeChaine, 2012; Ono & Sloop, 2002; Park & Pellow, 2011). The Latina Institute and its constituency are well accustomed to these bordering effects, which the organization resists by critiquing <choice>. While this section centers on bordering in terms of socioeconomic and other related privileges, later in this essay I outline how <choice> carries cultural and linguistic translation constraints as well.

According to the organization, "[I]n 2010 as we in the United States commemorate the 37th anniversary of *Roe vs. Wade* 'choice' does not encompass the reproductive health decisions that low-income Latinas are making every day. The term pro-choice does not describe the complexity of our lives that leads to the need to consider abortion" (Henríquez, 2010, para. 3). This argument maintains that <choice> fails to reflect the realities of low-income Latin@s who cannot make unfettered decisions because of financial and other intersecting barriers. This acknowledgment suggests that their socioeconomic status "leads to the need to consider abortion" because many Latin@ women feel they have no <choice> but to terminate their pregnancies without a financial situation conducive to parenting and parenting well. Echoing long-standing critiques by *justicia reproductiva/reproductive justice* advocates, it seems unrestricted <choice> is obtainable only after economic and other inequities are mitigated for diverse, marginalized women. These constraints, which in many ways are abetted by persistent reliance on <choice>, reflect bordering language that threatens migrant Latin@ survival.

The Latina Institute also outlines other obstructions to women's *justicia reproductiva/reproductive justice* that are interlinked with poverty. Isolation caused by transportation and xenophobia eclipses <choice> to reveal the rhetorical materiality of bordering.

> If the closest family planning clinic is located miles away, if public transportation is lacking or dangerous, if anti-immigrant rhetoric instills fear both for immigrants and native-born members of a household, if politicians ban abortion funding for the poorest among us, the concept of "choice" is more of a privilege than a rallying cry. How these issues intersect make it complicated and difficult for us to have just one unified way of addressing abortion rights.
>
> *(Henríquez, 2010, para. 4)*

This excerpt further illuminates the precarity of migrant Latin@ women's positions. The Latina Institute suggests that <choice> and its privileged assumptions are incompatible with realities shaped by multiple systemic barriers and thus cannot rally those who are denied desirable options from which to choose. Furthermore, and because these positions can only be viewed intersectionally, there is no universal, prescribed approach for advancing abortion rights; mobilization efforts must retain flexibility when responding to varying contexts, exigencies, and experiences. This understanding is especially important for "[b]uilding bridges and intersecting reproductive health care with other progressive movements"—an effort predicated on necessity, not <choice>, and an expansive social justice framework (Henríquez, 2010, para. 5).

One means for "building bridges" involves recognizing and appropriating the bordering apparatus of <choice> to challenge normative assumptions about women's reproductive health and well-being. In this case, the Latina Institute participates in a mainstream reproductive rights Web site event that touts the importance of <choice> despite the group's commitment to problematizing the term. This resistive tactic reflects *disidentifications*, a hermeneutic that "refers to working simultaneously on and against norms in order to create social change" (Morrissey, 2013, p. 146). José Esteban Muñoz (1999, p. 161) asserts that disidentifications "come into discourse as a response to ideologies that discriminate against, demean, and attempt to destroy components of subjectivity that do not conform or respond to narratives of universalization and normalization."

Exemplifying a disidentificatory response, the Latina Institute relies on the very language it disavows by presenting its oppositional claims in a *Roe v. Wade* anniversary forum celebrating <choice>. The organization's commitment to repurposing the ideograph elucidates resistance to and appropriation of bordering, as the group effectively critiques the term's limitations and points to the slogan's normative, narrow abortion logics, thus exposing readers to an alternative ideology. This disidentification works with and challenges extant conceptions of abortion, citizenship, gender, maternity, and reproduction. It also reveals Latina Institute efforts to belong and participate with other reproductive rights groups despite its antiassimilationist rhetoric.

As evidenced in this section, the linkages between ideographs, bordering, and disidentifications are central in evincing and resisting poverty, xenophobia, racism, transportation restrictions, and other oppressions confronting migrant Latin@s. To better nuance how these and other intersecting forms of marginalization function with the aforementioned theories, I continue my analysis by discussing complex cultural considerations.

<Choice>: a term eliding cultural difference

The Latina Institute challenges common assumptions about reproductive rights language and advocacy by uncovering the ideological cultural limits of pro-<choice> terminology in Spanish-speaking, migrant Latin@ communities. The organization contends:

> En el trabajo de NLIRH con las mujeres latinas inmigrantes, hemos encontrado que, contrario a los mitos que presentan a estas mujeres como fieles partidarias del movimiento en contra de la libre elección al derecho del aborto, sus puntos de vista se encuentran ubicados a lo largo de un amplio espectro. El término "pro-elección" (proveniente del término pro-choice en inglés) o derecho a decidir es un término del idioma inglés definido dentro de un reducido contexto de los EE.UU. y por lo tanto no funciona en las comunidades inmigrantes. Así que, aunque una mujer inmigrante nunca se identifique como "pro-elección", sus valores fundamentales y opiniones políticas acerca de la salud sexual y los derechos reproductivos están realmente en línea con los valores del movimiento de la justicia reproductiva.
>
> *(Pérez, Fuentes, & Henríquez, 2010, p. 6)*[11]

As this statement makes evident, many migrant Latin@s neither hold anti-<choice> beliefs nor identify as pro-<choice>.[12]

Given its groundings in U.S. culture and the English language, the Latina Institute evinces that <choice> fails to resonate and risks bordering Latin@s. This incompatibility may be attributed to the linkage of <choice> with resource acquisition in the United States and pro-<choice> advocates' persistent association of the ideograph with privacy and decision-making (J. González-Rojas, personal communication, August 3, 2010; Silliman et al., 2004; Solinger, 2001). Spanish-speaking, migrant Latin@s might also be hesitant to discuss abortion <choice> because of the high cultural value placed on women's familial commitments via childbearing and -rearing in Latin American–influenced communities. Furthermore, the U.S. abortion-rights debate remains at a stalemate between the <choice> and <life> binary, which positions abortion as an isolated procedure. Accordingly, <choice> carries a stigma because of its taboo, narrow articulations (Aguirre-Molina & Molina, 2003; J. González-Rojas, personal communication, August 3, 2010; Pérez et al., 2010). Rather than being confined by a <choice>/<life> dualism and a myopic procedural perspective on abortion, migrant Latina@ views and values reside on a different, "broad spectrum" (Pérez et al., 2010, p. 6). Their social commitments are more intricate than those animating mainstream pro-<choice> discourse and the aforementioned U.S. ideological cultural milieu. After all, Latin@ belief systems are shaped by transnational, liminal subject positions that reflect differing experiences and epistemologies.

In contrast to <choice>, *justicia reproductiva/reproductive justice* offers an intersectional, culturally resonant framework for approaching reproductive health and well-being concerns. The Latina Institute explains:

> En efecto, el marco conceptual de la justicia reproductiva despolariza el debate de la libre elección y permite que el aborto deje de ser un asunto blanco y negro y se convierta en un tema que permita más matices y puntos de vista diferentes. La despolarización del aborto fue más evidente en la Conferencia Anual de Promotores/as. Esta conferencia reunió a un diverso grupo de trabajadoras(es) comunitarios de la salud. Muchas(os) de ellas(os) nunca habían discutido abiertamente el tema del aborto y tenían muchas dudas acerca de participar en una discusión al respecto. Sin embargo, por medio de la perspectiva de la justicia reproductiva y nuevos puntos de partida, fue posible para los participantes discutir los aspectos legales, clínicos y sociales del aborto—no el aspecto político—junto con otros temas críticos de la salud reproductiva.
>
> *(Pérez et al., 2010, p. 7)*[13]

The organization asserts that *justicia reproductiva/reproductive justice* offers Latin@ community health workers a compatible vocabulary and framework for discussing abortion rights. The term's capacity for cultural complexity facilitates conversations inclusive of perspectives that might otherwise be hidden or ignored due to anxieties over deviating from familial expectations and discussing the taboo procedure. When connected with other issues via *justicia reproductiva/reproductive justice*, restricted access to abortion services is incorporated into an ample context of intersecting issues, including "legal, clinical, and social aspects." Consequently, abortion ceases to be an isolated <choice> rooted in whether to undergo the procedure. Instead, it marks one decision amid a confluence of several other factors, which may or may not lead a woman to (try to) terminate her pregnancy.

The Latina Institute's rhetoric is instructive for apprehending the function of ideographs and other key terms in aggravating and assuaging injustice rooted in cultural difference. Unlike <choice>, *justicia reproductiva/reproductive justice* resonates with migrant Latin@ cultural ideologies and, in so doing, exposes and engages—rather than elides and erases—the challenges of their quotidian realities, particularly in relation to reproductive rights. The Latina Institute insists that <choice> does not resonate with its constituency because migrant Latin@s hold cultural understandings distinct from dominant U.S. ideology. Because "[i]deographs are culture-bound," the organization's position raises significant questions about the mutability and ideographic weight of <choice> (McGee, 2005, p. 463). While I have presented cultural translation (in)compatibilities as central to studying the troubling bordering effects of <choice> and the possibilities of *justicia reproductiva/reproductive justice*, a related argument can be made regarding linguistic concerns.

<Choice>: a transcreation, not a direct translation

In addition to cultural considerations for <choice> and *justicia reproductiva/reproductive justice*, the linguistic translation dimension of these terms is also important.[14] According to the Latina Institute, "the term 'pro-choice' does not even have a direct translation in the Spanish language" (Henríquez, 2009, para. 5). While "libre-elección," "pro-elección," "derecho a eligir," and "derecho a decidir" are transcreations (as evidenced in the Spanish excerpts in the previous section), these attempted equivalents fail to carry the same meaning and ideology as English's pro-<choice> (J. González-Rojas, personal communication, August 3, 2010).[15] These transcreations are forced, invented phrases and may mark a cultural boundary between English and Spanish speakers. This incompatibility exemplifies bordering in that it includes/excludes along particular lines.

In contrast, *reproductive justice* easily translates to *justicia reproductiva*, which features the concept of <justicia>, a familiar ideograph in the Spanish language and in Spanish-speaking cultures. Because Latin America and the Caribbean have endured dictatorships and colonialism—often facilitated by corrupt, U.S.-backed regimes—pursuing social <justice> is a well-accepted imperative and motivation (Carruthers, 2008; Grandin & Joseph, 2010; Grosfoguel, 2003; Maier & Lebon, 2010). Thus, it is unsurprising that the Latina Institute and migrant Latin@s, especially Spanish speakers, are drawn to the term.

The translation constraints for making a language term or framework feel present for Spanish-speaking, migrant Latin@s extends beyond reproductive rights terminology. For example, <la raza> is another ideograph that evinces linguistic and cultural differences between Spanish and English. "While the term literally translates as 'the race,' it is culturally interpreted as 'the people'" (Delgado, 1995, p. 452). An additional though less ideologically imbued illustration is the term "grassroot(s) organization," which lacks a direct translation in Spanish, as I discovered while doing fieldwork in Puerto Rico. "Organización de base" serves as an attempted transcreation, but it fails to carry the same significance as its English counterpart. The terms discussed in this section are just a few of innumerable instances that reveal the ways in which language carries particular cultural and linguistic understandings and ideologies that must be illuminated rather than eclipsed.

Linguistic translation shapes who and what is included/excluded and displayed/hidden in discourses impacting migrant Latin@ health and well-being. Attending to this function of language is crucial for intervening in the deeply troubling racist and xenophobic discursive milieu characterizing contemporary U.S. life. Efforts to communicate the limits of particular terms and the implications of English monolingualism's imposed transcreations take an important step forward in the quest for *justicia reproductiva/reproductive justice.*

From <choice> to justicia reproductiva

A primary aim of this essay is to explore Spanish-speaking, migrant Latin@ realities by analyzing the interaction of cultural and linguistic difference, ideology, and language. <Choice> is an assimilationist term that advances White, monolingual feminism, while eliding and often erasing the experiences, bodies, and voices of women inhabiting more precarious positionalities. Accordingly, attending to cultural and linguistic concerns profoundly problematizes the continued use of <choice> in reproductive rights discourses. I have illustrated why the rhetorical weight of this slogan must be understood in relation to its bordering, disidentificatory, and ideographic functions and how *justicia reproductiva/reproductive justice* provides a framework for attending to alternatives offered by Latina Institute rhetoric. Studying the operations of, and relations between, these discourses helps to inform and intervene in coalitional challenges and seeks to alter scholarly perceptions and practices.

Coalitional considerations

Ideographs and other key slogans mold understandings about the reproductive rights realities confronting diverse communities. They also shape the ways in which movement actors respond to various exigencies and experiences. While this essay echoes many long-standing and ongoing critiques of <choice> by Women of Color and other marginalized groups, it also introduces new questions and concerns regarding cultural and linguistic translation. These perspectives urge U.S. reproductive rights advocates to (re)consider the underlying terms, ideologies, and frameworks shaping movement discourses. After all, "although ideographs unite, they also divide" (Stassen & Bates, 2010, p. 2).

Latina Institute discourse reveals that <choice> lacks mutability in con/texts relating to the needs and experiences of Spanish-speaking, migrant Latin@s. Because <choice> has traditionally been associated with privilege, resource acquisition, and a narrow abortion myopia (Solinger, 2001, 2005), the term's history appears to influence the Latina Institute's view on the ideograph. In contrast, the organization demonstrates how *justicia reproductiva/reproductive justice* continues to expand. Synchronically, the ever-increasing number of present-day concerns implicating health and well-being necessitate a broad social justice frame, which resonates well with *justicia reproductiva/reproductive justice*. For example, in a different essay, I have argued that the term offers opportunities for coalition building with the climate justice movement (de Onís, 2012). Transnationality and the imperative to consider cultural and linguistic translation (in)compatibilities further suggest that <choice> may, in many reproductive rights con/texts, "go bad" (Morrissey, 2010, p. 336). By considering these dimensions, this essay simultaneously complicates and clarifies the "synchronic ideological conflict" between <choice> and *justicia reproductiva/reproductive justice* (McGee, 2005, p. 461).

Hegemonic terminology enacts a rhetorical boundary, as Spanish-speaking, migrant Latin@s encounter exclusion and erasure from many reproductive rights discourses. I argue that the bordering effects of <choice> might be resisted via disidentificatory practices. Some Latin@s, including Latina Institute members, appropriate bordering by engaging with and resisting dominant culture. Examining negotiations of borderlands consciousness and language's marginalizing effects reveals a site of oppression and resistance that is always already fluid and interactive. Adela Licona terms this site a *third space* that signals "both location and practice" (2012, p. 105).[16] She writes, "Third space is a site where things are articulated and disarticulated, and a practice that offers the opportunity to reflect on and revision the ways in which discourses have been used to erase, obscure, or exclude" (2012, p. 13).

Privileging mainstream U.S. culture and English by bordering other belief systems, experiences, and positionalities is debilitating for coalitional politics. Drawing on Chela Sandoval's *differential consciousness* and Amy Carrillo Rowe's (2008) *differential belonging*, Karma Chávez (2013) offers *differential vision* as a way of becoming political with others through coalition.

This collaborative effort is useful for considering the implications of Latina Institute discourse. According to Chávez (2013, pp. 46–47),

> A differential vision reflects an impure orientation, committed to a politics of relation with others that may differ in their approach . . . but that share a commitment to resisting hegemonic systems of power, even as they might understand that system differently. A differential vision can aid in creating, and perhaps sustaining, coalitional subjectivities and coalitions of resistance with both those who share the vision and those who may share only particular goals. This is because differential visions are multifaceted in how they present politics, and they also provide numerous opportunities for people to see their issues as inextricably connected.

Scholarship on differential organizing acknowledges that working together in coalition is "no easy task" (Chávez, 2010, p. 151). If individuals and groups do not deploy terms sufficiently mutable for resonating with different perspectives, then certainly this makes coalitional gestures even more difficult. While these collaborative efforts have been explored in communication scholarship about migrant and LGBTQ mobilizing (Chávez, 2013; Morrissey, 2013), the present case study offers additional opportunities for understanding and enacting differential vision from the lens of *justicia reproductiva/reproductive justice.*

The Latina Institute's reliance on a wide-reaching frame appeals to the diverse justice-based advocacy groups with which it seeks coalitions. The organization actively collaborates with Unid@s and other LGBTQ groups, as well as the National Coalition for Immigrant Women's Rights, the National Council of La Raza, and several Women of Color and mainstream feminist organizations. Initially, some of these groups might appear to embrace disparate goals; however, despite some agenda-setting and experiential differences, these organizations tend to share an ideological commitment rooted in resisting oppressive structures. Latin@ groups like La Raza, that advocate for migrant rights, are not typically drawn to pro-<choice> language and the polarizing, taboo abortion debate associated with the term (J. González-Rojas, personal communication, August 3, 2010). Meanwhile, longtime pro-<choice> groups (e.g., Planned Parenthood, the National Organization for Women, NARAL Pro-Choice America) do not place migrant rights at the nexus of their organizing, although in recent years the social justice issue has garnered greater attention. As a result of these differential orientations and commitments, the Latina Institute confronts the difficult task of ensuring its discourse resonates with pro-<choice>, LGBTQ, migrant, Latin@, and other groups. Reliance on *justicia reproductiva/reproductive justice* helps navigate the differences and commonalities characterizing these organizations, thus facilitating the development of both more and less obvious coalitions.

Despite the appeals of *justicia reproductiva/reproductive justice*, seeking a terminological panacea capable of conveying the same ideology and meaning for every human being committed to health, dignity, and justice would not be in keeping with the possibilities of differential vision. Given the increasingly diverse cultural and linguistic composition of the United States, as well as transnational coalitions, I am unconvinced that a "one-size fits all" term exists. Categories of race, ethnicity, country of origin, and language preference make such an ideograph or language term unlikely. Furthermore, uprooting <choice> completely from the vernacular is improbable, as this ideograph has a substantial discursive history and deep associations with U.S. cultural values rooted in neoliberal ideology. I suspect that <choice> will continue to have some influence on the struggle for reproductive rights in significant, though perhaps less prominent, ways for years to come. Given the absence of one perfect and universal term and the persistence of <choice>,

I find that *justicia reproductiva/reproductive justice* plays a vital role in expressing the lived realities of Spanish-speaking, migrant Latin@s. While this observation is key for coalitional politics, it is also worthwhile for communication scholarship.

Implications for communication studies

The inclusion of Latina Institute rhetoric in Spanish, with the English equivalents placed as footnotes, may have been initially jarring. This strategic move serves as a necessary intervention to counter monolingual logics and trouble discourses that present English-language preeminence as commonsense. In so doing, it offers a model from which others can draw when working with translation and non-English/multilingual con/texts to challenge normative ideologies. As María Lugones (2014, p. 77) explains,

> Resistance is in part constituted by different knowledges. Monoculturalism and monolingualism express the Eurocentrism that has accompanied the history of Western colonialism. Colonial power has attempted to either appropriate or erase all knowledges it encountered.

Recuperating the "knowledges" eclipsed by U.S. monoculturalism and English monolingualism requires communication scholars to challenge commonplace logics by confronting the cultural and linguistic translation problems of ideographs and other key terms. Such a commitment helps uncover the ways in which translation considerations contribute to and complicate ideographic inquiry.

Translation scholars and translators recognize multiple linguistic "knowledges" and the intricacies and politics of translation (see the *Translation Studies* journal; Allen & Bernofsky, 2013; Grossman, 2010). The discipline of communication studies, however, lags behind in this area. Translation is far more than merely changing the language of a word and (as anyone who has engaged in this activity can attest) requires a substantial amount of effort, time, and proficiency or fluency in more than one language. Unless one is reading scholarship in the fields of Latin@, Asian/Pacific American, or international and intercultural communication studies, translation tends to be overlooked or approached simplistically without acknowledging the complexities I outline above. This essay seeks to complicate these assumptions by insisting that translation differences merit increased attention and legitimacy in *all* fields. Ample opportunities remain for continued scholarship in this area, including research that moves beyond English and Spanish to foreground other languages and cultures.[17]

This essay also invites reflection on *what* language terms communication scholars study and *how*. While it stands to reason that pervasive, commonly used ideographs (e.g., <choice>) require analysis to observe their influence on social commitments, this practice is not unproblematic. Chávez (2012, p. 48) warns, "If scholars use the state's conservative ideographs—their ideological building blocks—to talk about matters of public interest . . . conservative ideology continues to frame the broader debate in people's minds." While <choice>, as studied in this essay, is not a "conservative ideograph," its effective co-optation in antiabortion rights discourse (e.g., "I am not a <choice>" or "<Life>, what a beautiful <choice>") and its dialectical positioning with <life> has proven troublesome, if not insurmountable, for the pro-<choice> movement (Fixmer-Oraiz, 2010; Hayden, 2009). Accordingly, heightened scholarly reflexivity about how terminology uncovers or obscures ideological, cultural, and linguistic differences is necessary for mitigating the precarity of marginalized communities. After all, "discourse can be both an instrument and an effect of power, but also a hindrance, a stumbling block, a point of resistance and a starting point for an opposing strategy" (Foucault, 1990, p. 101). This essay has sought to highlight how ideographs and other terms constrain and enable such processes in the quest for a more "livable life" (Butler, 2004, p. 1).

Pa'lante/forward: toward a coalitional present and future

On August 5, 2014, SisterSong executive director Monica Simpson published "Reproductive Justice and 'Choice': An Open Letter to Planned Parenthood" in response to the *Times* article about the supposed origins of the "shunning" of <choice>. Presented as a "collective endeavor," the open letter appeared on *RH Reality Check* and was endorsed by 38 organizations, including the Latina Institute, and 25 individuals, many of whom are professors. The letter offered "a few examples of the successes of the RJ [reproductive justice] movement as well as some examples where RJ organizations have taken a leadership role in promoting reproductive health and rights in our communities" (Simpson, 2014, para. 5).[18]

The letter also highlighted the importance of working together with Planned Parenthood and "other mainstream organizations" (Simpson, 2014, para. 17). In addition, it observed some missed opportunities, such as a 2011 voter rights setback in Mississippi, when a *justicia reproductiva/reproductive justice* framework should have been used. The text explained that "when urged to see the connection between reproductive health rights and voting rights, PPFA [Planned Parenthood Federation of America] rejected the notion" (Simpson, 2014, para. 8). In the spirit of coalition and frustrated by the *Times* article controversy, Simpson and the letter's cosigners asked Planned Parenthood to convene with Women of Color organizations to discuss how to better collaborate and recognize the contributions of various groups, communities, and histories.[19] A few hours after the article's release, Planned Parenthood president Cecile Richards (2014) responded by expressing her interest in the proposed meeting.

The conversations resulting from this unfolding controversy—though painful and uncomfortable for many—are paramount for addressing past and present injustices and for galvanizing a broad support base to overcome manifold reproductive rights and other related, interlocking injustices. This recognition moves us to consider: What are women's rights issues? What are migrant rights issues? What concerns can and should be included within the *justicia reproductiva/reproductive justice* frame, and what are the possibilities and limits of this growing movement for achieving short- and long-term goals? These are the difficult queries at the heart of the concept of differential vision.

As we strive for a day when *justicia reproductiva/reproductive justice* is experienced by *all* people, we must attend to the role of ideology, language, and translation in shaping societies and cultures. Despite persistent attempts to perpetuate the precarity of those living on the margins, disidentifications and other tactics offer us new coalitional pathways that challenge bordering and its narrow, hegemonic U.S. monoculturalism and English monolingualism. Recent efforts by mainstream feminist organizations to critique pro-<choice> language is, in some ways, encouraging; however, these endeavors must be approached with an awareness of our common and disparate histories; a willingness to share the important contributions of diverse reproductive rights advocates; and a commitment to uncovering and foregrounding cultural and linguistic concerns. The stakes are too high for these urgent matters to be lost in translation.

Acknowledgments

The author sincerely thanks the *Women's Studies in Communication* editor, the editorial assistants, and the two anonymous reviewers for their time, guidance, and detailed critique during the review process. Thank you, too, to Phaedra C. Pezzullo, Joshua Trey Barnett, and especially Sara

Hayden for their helpful comments on earlier drafts of this essay. A portion of this article was presented at the 2013 National Communication Association convention in Washington, DC, USA.

Funding

Thanks to the Organization for Research on Women and Communication for providing a research grant to fund the archival work informing this article.

Notes

1. To maintain consistency and facilitate locatability, I place accents on author names only when they are included in publications. These marks are sometimes absent due to preference or inadvertent omission.
2. I distinguish <choice> using carets to signal the term's ideographic stature and dominant role in shaping US discourses of reproductive health and well-being (Condit, 1990; Hayden, 2009).
3. Because *reproductive freedom* and *reproductive justice* lack the ideographic standing of <choice>, I italicize these terms to highlight their counterhegemonic relationship to the ideograph (Palczewski, 2010). Both *reproductive freedom* and *reproductive justice* are committed to an intersectional paradigm. Accordingly, scholarship tends to treat the terms synonymously (Fixmer-Oraiz, 2010, 2013; Gerber Fried, 1990; Palczewski, 2010; Silliman et al., 2004). I stray from this proclivity because it elides the cultural and linguistic differences and dimensions of these language terms.
4. I use "Latin@" in lieu of "Latina/o" in this essay. This former construction seeks to undo the troubling, rigid, normative binaries demarcating sexuality and gender and to illustrate that reproductive health and survivability are not insular, solely individual issues but rather are deeply entangled with communities, family, and intersecting oppressions (Holling & Calafell, 2011; Licona & Maldonado, 2014). However, Latinas endure greater precarity than their cisgender, heterosexual male counterparts, and in most cases, my use of Latin@ refers to women.
5. I use *migrant* for referencing refugees and immigrants regardless of documentation status (Chávez, 2013; Luibhéid, 2005, 2013). While the Latina Institute deploys "immigrant"/"inmigrante" in its rhetoric, I resist this language, given its use in hegemonic, xenophobic discourses that ignore intersectionality, perpetuate exclusion, and criminalize human beings.
6. Ideographs encapsulate a dominant collective commitment by exposing the "relationship between the 'power' of a state and the consciousness of its people" (McGee, 2005, p. 462). These abstract terms serve as influential argumentative warrants (Hasian, 2005).
7. Chela Sandoval (2000) offers a compelling history of US Third-World feminist organizing in the second half of the 20th century. She highlights the troubling practices and assumptions of US middle class, White feminists, whereby the oppressive problematics of patriarchy and domination were often replicated.
8. During my visit at the Latina Institute headquarters in New York City, interviewees frequently commented that <choice> lacked resonance in their communities. Intrigued by this claim, I combed the group's archives for similar assertions.
9. This piece is accompanied by 18 other articles on the *RH Reality Check* blog. The contributions reflect a blend of personal experiences, reflections on *Roe v. Wade,* and present-day legal challenges to women's reproductive health and well-being.
10. The audiences for these texts are diverse, as individual activists, *reproductive justice* and traditional feminist groups, and migrant and Latin@ organizations encounter Latina Institute rhetoric. The group's discourse circulates via e-mail and Web site posts, as well as at local, state, and national conferences, rallies, and planning events (J. González-Rojas, personal communication, August 3, 2010).
11. The Latina Institute's English translation: "In NLIRH's work with Latina immigrant women, we have found that, contrary to myths portraying these women as staunchly anti-choice, their views lie on a broad spectrum. The label of 'pro-choice' is an English term defined within a narrow US context and therefore often does not resonate with immigrant communities. So although an immigrant woman may never identify as 'pro-choice,' her core values and politics around sexual and reproductive health and rights are actually aligned with the values of the reproductive justice movement" (Pérez et al., 2010, p. 6). In this passage, <choice> is referred to inconsistently as "la libre elección," "pro-elección," or "derecho a decidir." These translation differences and their implications are discussed in the following section.

12 This passage erodes the popular myth that all Latin@s are conservative and anti-<choice>. This stereotype ignores cultural and individual differences. Polling results conducted in 2012 report that nearly 75% of registered US Latin@ voters believe abortion should be available without government meddling (Lopez, 2012).

13 The Latina Institute's English translation: "In effect, the reproductive justice framework de-polarizes the choice debate and moves abortion away from being a black and white issue to one allowing more nuances. The de-polarization of abortion was further evidenced at the Annual Conference of Promotoras/es. This conference brought together a diverse group of community health workers. Many of them had never openly discussed the issue of abortion and were very hesitant to engage in discussion on this issue. However, by using a reproductive justice perspective and new points of entry, it allowed participants to discuss the legal, clinical, and social aspects of abortion—not the political aspect—along with other critical reproductive health topics" (Pérez et al., 2010, pp. 6–7).

14 Communication scholarship on translation and reproductive rights is limited. The following studies provide an important base for continued scholarship: Chan (1990) discusses translation and language incompatibilities when describing the abortion rights of Asian migrant women. Similarly, Palczewski (2010) and I also mention language barriers briefly for this demographic (de Onís, 2012). Hayden (2009), meanwhile, includes the rhetoric of a Latina Institute member in her study, who petitions for the right to healthcarehealth care in one's preferred language. Given the complexity and depth of linguistic translation differences, more communication research is needed in this area.

15 While gathering Latina Institute texts, I perused the Spanish section of the organization's Web site. When I entered "pro-elección" as a search term, which is arguably the closest transcreation of <choice>, it yielded no results. In contrast, a search for *justicia reproductiva* found numerous texts.

16 Licona (2012, p. 12) draws on Gloria Anzaldúa's mestiza consciousness, "Chela Sandoval's differential consciousness and Emma Perez's decolonial imaginary," to theorize her conception of third space.

17 For instance, studying Hindi, Mandarin, and Vietnamese translation concerns might help intervene in various injustices confronting migrant Asian communities in the United States.

18 When outlining past successes, Simpson describes "Responding to Environmental Violence" as a key contribution made by the Native Youth Sexual Health Network and highlights the links between extractive industries and detrimental human health effects. These connections evince the ways in which environmental, climate, and reproductive injustices are entangled and must be countered simultaneously, as they stem from shared logics of coloniality, domination, and disposability (de Onís, 2012; Endres, 2009; Pezzullo, 2007, 2014). Recognizing these linkages, though not always immediately obvious or easy, is key for cultivating a more robust support base committed to a differential vision.

19 The letter also asks Planned Parenthood to mention *reproductive justice* groups in future media interviews about the movement and requests that the organization examine how its affiliates are working with Women of Color groups "in supporting or obstructing effective RJ organizing in their states and communities" (Simpson, 2014, para. 23).

References

Aguirre-Molina, M., & Molina, C. W. (2003). *Latina health in the United States: A public health reader.* San Francisco, CA: Jossey-Bass.

Allen, E., & Bernofsky, S. (2013). *In translation: Translators on their work and what it means.* New York, NY: Columbia University Press.

Anzaldúa, G. (1987). *Borderlands/La frontera: The new Mestiza.* San Francisco, CA: Aunt Lute.

Bayetti Flores, V. (2014, July 31). #KnowYourHistory: Women of color have been moving beyond 'pro-choice' for decades. *Feministing.* Retrieved from http://feministing.com/2014/07/31/knowyourhistory-women-of-color-have-been-moving-beyond-pro-choice-for-decades/

Benford, R. D., & Snow, D. A. (2000). Framing processes and social movements: An overview and assessment. *Annual Review of Sociology, 26,* 611–639. doi: 10.1146/annurev.soc.26.1.611

Butler, J. (2004). *Undoing gender.* New York, NY: Routledge.

Calmes, J. (2014, July 28). Advocates shun 'pro-choice' to expand message. *New York Times.* Retrieved from www.nytimes.com/2014/07/29/us/politics/advocates-shun-pro-choice-to-expand-message.html?_r=4

Carrillo Rowe, A. (2008). *Power lines: On the subject of feminist alliances.* Durham, NC: Duke University Press.

Carruthers, D. V. (Ed.). (2008). *Environmental justice in Latin America: Problems, promise, and practice.* Cambridge, MA: MIT Press.

Chan, C. S. (1990). Reproductive issues are essential survival issues for the Asian-American communities. In M. Gerber Fried (Ed.), *From abortion to reproductive freedom: Transforming a movement* (pp. 175–178). Boston, MA: South End Press.

Chávez, K. (2010). Border (in)securities: Normative and differential belonging in LGBTQ and immigrant rights discourse. *Communication and Critical/Cultural Studies*, 7(2), 136–155. doi: 10.1080/14791421003763291

Chávez, K. (2012). Border interventions: The need to shift from a rhetoric of security to a rhetoric of militarization. In D. R. DeChaine (Ed.), *Border rhetorics: Citizenship and identity on the US–Mexico frontier* (pp. 48–62). Tuscaloosa: University of Alabama Press.

Chávez, K. (2013). *Queer migration politics: Activist rhetoric and coalitional possibilities*. Urbana: University of Illinois Press.

Collins, P. H. (2000). *Black feminist thought: Knowledge, consciousness, and the politics of empowerment*. New York, NY: Routledge.

Condit, C. M. (1990). *Decoding abortion rhetoric: Communicating social change*. Urbana, IL: University of Illinois Press.

Condit Railsback, C. M. (1984). The contemporary American abortion controversy: Stages in the argument. *Quarterly Journal of Speech*, *20*, 411–442. doi: 10.1080/00335638409383707

Crenshaw, K. (1989). Demarginalizing the intersection of race and sex: A Black feminist critique of antidiscrimination doctrine, feminist theory, and antiracist politics. *University of Chicago Legal Forum*, 139–167.

DeChaine, D. R. (2012). *Border rhetorics: Citizenship and identity on the US – Mexico frontier*. Tuscaloosa: University of Alabama Press.

Delgado, F. P. (1995). Chicano movement rhetoric: An ideographic interpretation. *Communication Quarterly*, *43*(4), 446–454. doi: 10.1080/01463379509369991

de Onís, K. M. (2012). "Looking both ways": Metaphor and the rhetorical alignment of intersectional climate justice and reproductive justice concerns. *Environmental Communication*, *6*(3), 308–327. doi: 10.1080/17524032.2012.690092

Endres, D. (2009). The rhetoric of nuclear colonialism: Rhetorical exclusion of American Indian arguments in the Yucca Mountain nuclear waste siting decision. *Communication and Critical/Cultural Studies*, *6*(1), 39–60. doi: 10.1080/14791420802632103

Fixmer-Oraiz, N. (2010). No exception postprevention: "Differential biopolitics" on the morning after. In S. Hayden & D. L. O'Brien-Hallstein (Eds.), *Contemplating maternity in the era of choice: Reproduction and discourses of maternity* (pp. 27–48). Lanham, MD: Lexington.

Fixmer-Oraiz, N. (2013). Speaking of solidarity: Transnational gestational surrogacy and the rhetorics of reproductive (in)justice. *Frontiers*, *34*(3), 126–163. doi: 10.5250/fronjwomestud.34.3.0126

Flores, L. A. (2003). Constructing rhetorical borders: Peons, illegal aliens, and competing narratives of immigration. *Critical Studies in Media Communication*, *20*(4), 362–387. doi: 10.1080/0739318032000142025

Flores, L. A., & Holling, M. A. (1999). Las familias y las latinas: Mediated representations of gendered roles. In M. J. Meyers (Ed.), *Mediated women: Representations in popular culture* (pp. 339–354). Cresskill, NJ: Hampton.

Foucault, M. (1990). *The history of sexuality*. New York, NY: Pantheon Books.

Gerber Fried, M. (Ed.). (1990). *From abortion to reproductive freedom: Transforming a movement*. Boston, MA: South End Press.

Grandin, G., & Joseph, G. M. (2010). *A century of revolution: Insurgent and counterinsurgent violence during Latin America's long Cold War*. Durham, NC: Duke University Press.

Grosfoguel, R. (2003). *Colonial subjects: Puerto Ricans in a global perspective*. Berkeley, CA: University of California Press.

Grossman, E. (2010). *Why translation matters*. New Haven, CT: Yale University Press.

Gutiérrez, E. R. (2008). *Fertile matters: The politics of Mexican-origin women's reproduction*. Austin, TX: University of Texas Press.

Hasian, M. (2005). *In the name of necessity: Military tribunals and the loss of American civil liberties*. Tuscaloosa, AL: University of Alabama Press.

Hasian, M., & McHendry, G. F. (2012). The attempted legitimation of the vigilante civil border patrols, the militarization of the Mexican–US border, and the law of unintended consequences. In D. R. DeChaine (Ed.), *Border rhetorics: Citizenship and identity on the US–Mexico frontier* (pp. 103–116). Tuscaloosa, AL: University of Alabama Press.

Hayden, S. (2009). Revitalizing the debate between <life> and <choice>: The 2004 March for Women's Lives. *Communication and Critical/Cultural Studies*, *6*(2), 111–131. doi: 10.1080/14791420902833189

Hayden, S., & O'Brien Hallstein, D. L. (Eds.). (2010). *Contemplating maternity in an era of choice: Explorations into discourses of reproduction.* Lanham, MD: Lexington Books.

Henríquez, S. (2009, August 6). Sotomayor, *Roe v. Wade*, and the right to privacy. *NLIRH: In the News.* Retrieved from http://latinainstitute.org/

Henríquez, S. (2010). *Securing real choices means going beyond "choice." RH Reality Check.* Retrieved from www.rhrealitycheck.org/

Holling, M. A. (2006). El simpático boxer: Underpinning Chicano masculinity in with a rhetoric of familia in Resurrection Blvd. *Western Journal of Communication, 70*(2), 91–114. doi: 10.1080/10570310600709994

Holling, M. A., & Calafell, B. M. (2011). Tracing the emergence of Latina/o vernaculars in studies of Latin@ communication. In M. A. Holling & B. M. Calafell (Eds.), *Latina/o discourse in vernacular spaces: Somos de una voz?* (pp. 17–29). Lanham, MD: Lexington Press.

Licona, A. C. (2012). *Zines in third space: Radical cooperation and borderlands rhetoric.* Albany: State University of New York Press.

Licona, A. C., & Maldonado, M. (2014). The social production of Latin@ visibilities and invisibilities: Geographies of power in small town America. *Antipode, 46*(2), 517–536. doi: 10.1111/anti.12049

Lopez, A. (2012, January 20). Poll: Majority of Latina/o population supports reproductive rights. *The American Independent.* Retrieved from http://americanindependent.com/

Lugones, M. (2014). Radical multiculturalism and women of color feminisms. *Journal for Cultural and Religious Theory, 13*(1), 68–80. Retrieved from www.jcrt.org/archives/13.1/lugones.pdf

Luibhéid, E. (2005). *Entry denied: Controlling sexuality at the border.* Minneapolis, MN: University of Minnesota Press.

Luibhéid, E. (2013). *Pregnant on arrival: Making the illegal immigrant.* Minneapolis, MN: University of Minnesota Press.

Maier, E., & Lebon, N. (2010). *Women's activism in Latin America and the Caribbean: Engendering social justice, democratizing citizenship.* New Brunswick, NJ: Rutgers University Press.

McGee, M. C. (1980). The "ideograph": A link between rhetoric and ideology. *Quarterly Journal of Speech, 66,* 1–16. doi: 10.1080/00335638009383499

McGee, M. C. (2005). The "ideograph": A link between rhetoric and ideology. In C. R. Burgchardt (Ed.), *Readings in rhetorical criticism* (pp. 452–463). State College, PA: Strata.

Morrissey, M. E. (2010). Equality as an ideograph: The gay rights movement and proposition 8. *Proceedings from Alta Conference on Argumentation,* 331–337.

Morrissey, M. E. (2013). A DREAM disrupted: Undocumented migrant youths disidentifications from US citizenship. *Journal of International and Intercultural Communication, 6*(2). doi:10.1080/17513057.2013.774041

Muñoz, J. E. (1999). *Disidentifications: Queers of color and the performance of politics.* Minneapolis, MN: University of Minnesota Press.

National Latina Institute for Reproductive Health. (2005). *Latina immigrants and abortion: Fact sheet.* Retrieved from http://latinainstitute.org/

National Latina Institute for Reproductive Health. (n.d.). *Who we are.* Retrieved from http://latinainstitute.org/

Ono, K. A., & Sloop, J. M. (2002). *Shifting borders: Rhetoric, immigration, and California's Proposition 187.* Philadelphia, PA: Temple University Press.

Palczewski, C. (2010). Reproductive freedom transforming discourses of choice. In S. Hayden & D. L. O'Brien-Hallstein (Eds.), *Contemplating maternity in the era of choice: Reproduction and discourses of maternity* (pp. 73–94). Lanham, MD: Lexington.

Park, L. S., & Pellow, D. (2011). *The slums of Aspen: Immigrants vs. the environment in America's Eden.* New York, NY: New York University Press.

Pérez, M. Z. (2014, July 31). An open letter to the *New York Times*: Race and the reproductive rights movement. *Colorlines.* Retrieved from http://colorlines.com/archives/2014/07/an_open_letter_to_the_new_york_times_race_and_the_reproductive_rights_movement.html

Pérez, M. E., Fuentes, L., & Henríquez, S. (2010). *Advancing reproductive justice in immigrant communities: Promotoras/es de salud as a model.* New York, NY: NLIRH.

Pezzullo, P. C. (2007). *Toxic tourism.* Tuscaloosa, AL: University of Alabama Press.

Pezzullo, P. C. (2014). Contaminated children: Debating the banality, precarity, and futurity of chemical safety. *Resilience: A Journal of the Environmental Humanities, 1*(2). Retrieved from www.jstor.org/stable/10.5250/resilience.1.2.004

Richards, C. (2014, August 5). A response to an open letter on reproductive justice and 'choice'. *RH Reality Check.* Retrieved from http://rhrealitycheck.org/article/2014/08/05/response-open-letter-reproductive-justice-choice/

Roberts, L., Ross, L., & Kuumba, M. B. (2005). The reproductive health and sexual rights of women of color: Still building a movement. *NWSA Journal, 17*(1), 93–98.

Sandoval, C. (2000). *Methodology of the oppressed*. Minneapolis, MN: University of Minnesota Press.

Silliman, J., Gerber Fried, M., Ross, L., & Gutiérrez, E. R. (2004). *Undivided rights: Women of color organize for reproductive justice*. Cambridge, MA: South End Press.

Simpson, M. (2014, August 5). Reproductive justice and 'choice': An open letter to Planned Parenthood. *RH Reality Check*. Retrieved from http://rhrealitycheck.org/article/2014/08/05/reproductive-justice-choice-open-letter-planned-parenthood/

SisterSong. (n.d.). *What is reproductive justice?* Retrieved from www.sistersong.net/

Smith, A. (2005). Beyond pro-choice versus pro-life: Women of color and reproductive justice. *NWSA Journal 17*(1), 119–140. Retrieved from http://web.clark.edu/ssendak/ws%20web%20stuff/readings/beyond%20pro-choice%20versus%20pro-life.pdf

Solinger, R. (2001). *Beggars and choosers: How the politics of choice shapes adoption, abortion, and welfare in the United States*. New York, NY: Hill and Wang.

Solinger, R. (2005). *Pregnancy and power: A short history of reproductive politics in America*. New York, NY: New York University Press.

Stassen, H., & Bates, B. (2010). Constructing marriage: Exploring marriage as an ideograph. *Qualitative Research Reports in Communication, 11*(1), 1–5. doi: 10.1080/17459430903412848

Zentella, A. C. (2007). "Dime con quién hablas, y te diré quién eres": Linguistic (in)security and Latina/o unity. In J. Flores & R. Rosaldo (Eds.), *The Blackwell companion to Latino studies* (pp. 25–39). Malden, MA: Blackwell.

6

The feminist frontier

On trans and feminism

Sally Hines

Introduction

In "I am a feminist but: Transgender, Men, Women and Feminism" (Hines, 2005), I examined the relationship between trans masculinity, femininity and feminism. Drawing on empirical research conducted between 2000–2004,[1] the paper considered how trans[2] men and women articulated their experiences of second-wave[3] feminism and explored their relationship to contemporary feminist communities. The majority of trans male participants spoke about their involvement in feminist and/or lesbian communities and, particularly, within queer subcultures, before and/or during transition. Yet they largely viewed feminist communities of the 1980s and 1990s as socially and politically problematic; speaking of instances where their masculine identities were challenged. These men spoke of their continued involvement within feminist politics and queer communities, and located contemporary feminism (now of a more than decade ago) as a less hostile personal and political space. Many of the trans women interviewed also found themselves rejected by feminist communities during the 1980s and 1990s, which refused to accept their female identity. Nonetheless, most of these women aligned themselves with feminist politics and sought to construct gendered expressions in contrast to stereotypical models of femininity. I concluded the paper by suggesting that feminism was highly relevant for an understanding of gender dynamics as illuminated by the stories of trans people and argued for a comprehensive incorporation of trans experiences into future gendered analyses.

Over the last decade, however, the optimism of this piece may be questioned by sustained antagonism from sections of feminism towards trans people, and, especially, towards trans women. I suggest that related factors in what, arguably, are an increasingly hostile relationship, connect to the growing visibility of trans movements, a strengthened framework of rights for trans people, prominent positions in media and culture now enjoyed by some feminists with anti-trans perspectives, and the ever-more central role of social media within social movements. With these points in mind, this paper explores the present relationship between feminist and trans theory and activism, focusing particularly on the role of social media in these disputes.

The paper begins by exploring distinct feminist perspectives on transgender; mapping out the key area of contention as that of gendered authenticity, or the question of what, or who, constitutes "woman." Here, I also consider the emergence, meanings and contestations of the term "trans exclusionary radical feminism" (TERF), which, since its inception in 2008, has become an established yet controversial part of the lexicon of feminist and trans movements. The next section sets out its means of data collection and analysis, and addresses the use of digital methodologies. Subsequent parts of the paper address central areas of debate between feminism and transgender through case study material. The case studies focus on events that have occurred since the millennium and are used to highlight particular epistemological and political tensions. In conclusion, the paper stresses the importance of rejecting trans-exclusionary feminism and foregrounding the links between feminism and transgender as a key social justice project of our time.

What makes a woman?

The relationship between feminist theory and transgender has a complex history. Illustrating the intersections of feminist theory, politics and community space, the place of trans people within feminism has long been disputed. The stance of what has recently become to be known as a "TERF" (trans-exclusionary radical feminist) perspective is evident in the much cited 1979 book by Janice Raymond, *The Transsexual Empire*. Raymond's claim is that gender is an expression of biological sex, the latter of which is chromosomally dependent. Moreover, she stresses the impossibility of changing chromosomal sex. From this premise, gender and sex are locked into each other and secured at birth. This leaves Raymond to read gender transition from male to female[4] as a male practice, devised by a patriarchal medical system in order to construct subservient women. From Raymond's position, trans women are not, nor can they ever become, women.

As I have argued elsewhere (2005, 2014), Raymond's work crafted a specific feminist perspective on trans femininity that has been extremely difficult to dispel in both feminist writing and activism. Moreover, as the case studies explored later in the paper indicate, questions about gendered authenticity, or "realness" remain at the hub of feminist debates around transgender. Within the academy, feminist academic Shelia Jeffreys (6, 2014) continues to reinforce Raymond's position about the fixity of sex and gender, fiercely denying the gender identities and expressions of trans women and men. Similarly, Germaine Greer (1994) has written from a feminist perspective on the intrinsic relationship between biology and womanhood and, as will be explored later in the paper, continues to challenge trans women's self identities from this perspective. Trans scholars and activists including Carol Riddell (1996), Sandy Stone (1996) and Julia Serano (2007, 2013), amongst others, have written on the ways in which Raymond's book impacted on feminist communities in the 1970s and 1980s, creating divisions that have been hard to heal. Moreover, these writers have spoken about the personal impact of *The Transsexual Empire* as it impeded their personal safety, damaged their careers and split communities. Central to these conflicts is the notion of authenticity – of who is, or can be, considered to be a "woman." From a feminist position such as Raymond's, one cannot *become* a woman, since the characteristics of womanhood are fixed at birth (through chromosomes) and strengthened by life experience (through gender socialization and experiences of gender discrimination). Raymond is overt: "the man who undergoes sex conversion is *not* female" (Raymond, 1979, p. 10 italics in original).

I do not wish to suggest that Raymond was the initiator of feminist hostility to trans women. As Sandy Stone (1996) has described, much of Raymond's text came out of, and focused upon, existing debates about the presence of trans women in "women's" spaces – in this instance, of Stone herself as sound engineer in the 1970s Californian women's music collective "Olivia Records." Founded in 1973, the collective made and promoted women's music. Living together and pooling money, the collective established itself as a central figure in lesbian feminist 1970s US culture. As Carol Riddell suggests, "Raymond's book did not 'invent' anti-transsexual prejudice, but it did more to justify and perpetuate it than perhaps any other book ever written" (1996, p. 131). Illustrating the divisive effects of Raymond's work on feminist communities in the 1970s, trans researcher and activist Cristan Williams writes:

> I've done several interviews around the trans caricatures Janice Raymond created for the TERF community to go after. [. . .] These radical feminist institutions – the 73 Conference, Olivia Records – they were trans-inclusive [. . .]. Thus far TERFs like Raymond have gotten away with creating this false narrative about how their Radical Feminist spaces were being invaded by violent trans women and it's just not the case.
>
> *(Williams, 2014)*

What is interesting in this narrative is not only further contextualization of early anti-transgender feminism, but Williams' point that many of these feminist spaces were *not* hostile towards trans women. Williams' narrative indicates not only the long-held tensions between sections of feminist and trans communities, but concurrent histories of solidarity. In a recent interview with the online journal *Transadvocate* titled "TERF hate and Sandy Stone," Stone uses the term "TERF" as she recalls the meeting that prompted her to leave the Olivia Records collective after protest about her presence from other feminists: "The TERFs refused to stop disrupting the meeting unless I left the room." I wish to depart from the content of Stone's narrative – the context and the politics of the hostility – to address her employment of "TERF." Stone uses the term once towards the end of the interview. In contrast, her interviewer, Cristan Williams, uses the term in their opening question: "Can you tell me how you first became aware of the TERF movement?" (Williams, 2014) and utilizes it in numerous subsequent questions. I suggest that culturally for Williams – a trans activist and researcher from an earlier generation to Stone – "TERF" is a customary expression. My conjecture here is not that Williams uses the term to problematically lead Stone but, rather, that Stone takes up the word because it maps so closely onto her experience to enable a strong linguistic fit. Ontologically and epistemologically it works to narrate the power relations at stake produced through discursive struggles around gendered authenticity and the tenure of feminism.

As suggested in an interview between two feminist activists for online news journal *Trans-Advocate*, the term "TERF" appears to have been first used in a US-based feminist blog in 2008:

> C.W: From what I can see, yours is the earliest use [. . .]
>
> T: L [. . .] and I are pretty sure that we started using trans-exclusionary radfem (TERF) activists as a descriptive term in our own chats a while before I used it in that post.
>
> *(Williams, 2014)*

The term "TERF" quickly spread to other trans and feminist blogs (Williams, 2014) and now is established in everyday feminist speech. Other feminists, however, have contested the term, viewing it as "hyperbolic, misleading, and ultimately defamatory" (Williams, 2014). Still, the first user is clear that this was not the case: "It was not meant to be insulting. It was meant to be a deliberately technically neutral description of an activist grouping" (Williams, 2014). Moreover, the original user sought to distinguish between strands of radical feminism in terms of their views on transgender:

> We wanted a way to distinguish TERFs from other radfems with whom we engaged who were trans-positive/neutral, because we had several years of history of engaging productively/

> substantively with non-TERF radfems, and then suddenly TERF comments/posts seemed to be erupting in RadFem spaces where they threadjacked dozens of discussions, and there was a great deal of general frustration about that.
>
> *(Williams, 2014)*

"TERF" developed to delineate current political battles around gendered self-determination. In addition to describing a particular feminist perspective, the term works to attach this perspective to a distinct branch of radical feminism. As illustrated in the earlier quote from Stone, however, the term is not only used in the present tense; there "TERF" is used to decode power relations in past feminist cultures.

The positioning of "woman" at the nexus of the feminist project enabled second-wave feminism to define its political goals and demarcate its political community. Following the theorization of gender roles as hierarchical, feminist cultures emerged as sites of resistance. A universal understanding of "woman" (as distinct from "man") was soon to fracture, however, as the constitution of the feminist subject was called into question. Working-class and black feminists, in particular, challenged the capabilities of a largely middle class, white movement to articulate and organize around their interests. The recognition of "difference," for example, in relation to race, class, sexuality, age and embodiment, thus led to the development of more complex models of feminist analysis throughout the 1990s (Hines, 2014). Here, we can see the emergence of conceptual critiques of an anti-transgender feminist perspective, which bonded gender and sex. By focusing on "difference" as politically productive, feminist scholars such as Amber Hollibaugh (1989), Gayle Rubin (1989) and Carol Vance (1984) wrote against a biologically determined model of gender and sexuality. The theorization of difference was also at the heart of strands of feminist theory that were influenced by post-structuralist thought. Reflecting an increasingly plural feminism, Jane Flax for example, argued that "none of us can speak for 'woman' because no such person exists except within a specific set of (already gendered) relations-to 'man' and to many concrete and different women" (Flax, 1997, p. 178). Most notably, Judith Butler's critique of a sex/gender model provided feminist theory with further tools through which to analyze not only the socially constructed basis of gender, but that of sex itself:

> The presumption of a binary gender system implicitly retains the belief in a mimetic relation of gender to sex whereby gender mirrors sex or is otherwise restricted by it. When the constructed status of gender is theorized as radically independent of sex, gender itself becomes a free-floating artifice, with the consequence that *man* and *masculine* might just as easily signify a female body as a male one, and *woman* and *feminine* a male body as easily as a female one.
>
> *(Butler, 1990, p. 6, italics in original)*

Multiple gendered identities and experiences were thus addressed by feminist scholars throughout the 1990s. The writing of trans activists, of course, was also central to challenging anti-transgender feminism. During the 1990s, Leslie Feinberg (1996), Henry Ruben (1996), Sandy Stone (1996), Jack Halberstam (1998) and Susan Stryker (1998) and, in the millennium, Emi Koyami (2003) and Julia Sorano (2007, 2013), offered direct critiques of the rejection of trans people from feminism. This work was also important in drawing out intersecting areas of concern between trans theory and feminism, particularly around issues of the body.

An understanding of the body as central to second-wave feminism, for example, around health and reproductive rights and sexual harassment and violence, meant that the female body became not just a political issue, but a site of feminist politics in and of itself. While during the 1970s and 1980s, the insistence that one must have a female body to be a feminist was employed to dispute the position of cis[5] men within feminism, more recently it has been used to question the place of trans people, and especially trans women, within feminist communities. This led to trans activist and academic Stephen Whittle's line of questioning: "How can feminism accept men with women's bodies (or is that women with men's bodies)?" (Whittle, 1996). Here, Henry Rubin's work his helpful to consider a feminist identity that is unfixed to the body. Rubin proposes an "action paradigm" in which feminist identity arises out of political commitment rather than embodiment: "Womanhood" is no longer a necessary, nor sufficient qualification for feminist identity. A feminist is one who acts in concert with feminist ideals' (Rubin, 1989, p. 308). Subsequently, analyses of embodiment may be developed without essentialist connotations. Rubin illustrates how embodiment may be employed dialectically to enable a feminist approach that can take account of "differently located bodies which appear similar in form" (Rubin, 1989, p. 308). This may allow, for example, "a way of knowing that can provide me(n) with a feminist viewpoint, and that is not generated to out of a woman's experience of her body. Instead, it is generated out of subjectively located struggle" (Rubin, 1989, p. 308). Nevertheless, almost a decade on, Whittle's question continues to haunt the relationship between feminism and transgender.

Conflicts around how a woman's body are constituted, or who has the authority to take up the identity of feminist, work their way to and fro, across and between, at least five decades of feminist thought and practice. Debates around community belonging – about inclusion and exclusion – have thus been ever-present since feminism's second wave. From the conflicts at *Olivia Records* in the 1970s, through to clashes about the presence of trans women at *Michigan Womyn's Music Festival* in the 1990s, to tensions about the role of trans women in feminist spaces in the 2000s, ontological disputes have cut through feminist cultures. In the present, these exertions are articulated through the language of "TERF," though, as I have sought to address in this section of the paper, their epistemological effects have a long precedence. At both theoretical and political levels, anti-transgender feminism has never gone unchallenged. Yet neither has it ever departed these spheres. What is more, as the case studies in the following sections of the paper indicate, hostility to the self-determination of gender identity appears to strengthen as trans people gain increased citizenship rights. Additionally, as I also move on to examine, feminist hostility towards trans women is particularly evident, in the UK, amongst feminist writers with a strong profile and is made ever more virulent through the use of social media.

Digital methodology

Though acknowledging the importance of the digital to identity formation and expression, it has been suggested that sociologists have been relatively slow to engage with digital media for research purposes (Daniels and Feagin, 2011; Lupton, 2012). Social media tools are particularly relevant for research exploring issues of identity and community as these mediums are widely used by individuals and community activists from minority groups (Stryker, 2013). Whittle foregrounds social media as a significant resource for trans community-building, suggesting that the development of home computers and the growth of the internet have brought dramatic shifts to transgender communities; bringing together what was previously a "[. . .] geographically dispersed, diverse trans community [. . .]" (Whittle 1996, p. xii).

There now exists a wealth of web-based material on trans mailing lists, discussion forums, chat rooms and individual vlogs and blogs, which detail opinions and experiences of trans people globally. Individually and collectively, trans people also have a high profile on social networking sites. In their paper, "Trans Media Moments" Marty Fink and Quinn Miller present findings from their two-year study of trans people's use of the social media platform Tumblr, suggesting that "for transgender, transsexual, genderqueer, and gender nonconforming people, emergent media technologies offer new outlets for self-representation" (2014, p. 611).

Analyzing social media for this project enabled access to significant and topical debate within feminist and trans communities. This allowed the consideration of the collective voices of trans people, and the analysis of issues of importance to trans individuals and members of trans social movements in the UK over a selected time period. A mapping exercise was conducted across different social media including *Facebook, Myspace, Reddit, Tumblr, Twitter and Whatsapp*. This focused on the frequency of related posts and the amount of subsequent traffic generated, the number of posts relating to feminist debates about transgender and vice versa, and the extent to which these posts attracted responses. The search terms "feminism," "feminist," "terf," "trans," "trans women," "transgender," "transition" and "transsexual" were used to measure traffic. Across the social media platforms, approximately 50 accounts were followed for a six-month period and around 1000 posts analyzed from these.

As Carolin Gerlitz and Bernhard Rieder suggest, social media platforms "broaden the grammars of action" (2013, p. 347) for social researchers. Social media offers not only text "but links, follows, mentions, likes, tags and retweets, which broaden material and activities available for analysis" (Thielmann, et al., 2012). Subsequently, an additional range of digital media, such as vlogs and blogs, were also analyzed, as were comment sections of online news and discussion sites. This gave access to more in-depth discussion on relevant debates and enabled links to offline media such as print or broadcast journalism. This was important since debate frequently arose as a result of commentary from high profile feminist writers or journalists in both on and offline media, meaning that debate in on and offline spaces, or social and traditional media, was not so clearly delineated. Resonating with of scholars such as Katie Davis, (2012), Jessica Ringrose et al. (2013) and Danah Boyd (2014) I found that there was much slippage between on and offline media. Moreover, as is evident in the case studies, key players are often the same people in both "new" and "traditional" media. Content analysis was applied to digital materials in order to focus on patterns and flow of, and responses to, communication (Krippendorff, 2004).

Subsequent parts of the paper explore debates about feminism and transgender through case studies. Case studies very usefully show repeat practices and the formulation of broader phenomenon (Platt, 1992; Roseneil and Budgeon, 2004; Hines, 2006). Each of the case studies in this paper marks a moment since the millennium when issues of debate were of particular significance in terms of the amount of coverage generated on social media, and, often, subsequent coverage in national media.

The Paranoia of gender deception: *Dyke March* London

The first case study relates to an event that occurred on the 21st of June 2014. Initial analysis is taken from a blog written by the central figure four days after the event. A prominent trans activist accepted an invitation to speak at *Dyke March* London, an event to increase lesbian visibility that is held each year in a number of countries world-wide. As the speaker took the stage, a group of anti-trans feminist activists began to shout to drown out her speech. They held banners titled "Why Should Lesbians Worship the Penis?," "We Know Male Violence When We See It" and "No Platform to Misogyny," and handed out leaflets to the assembled marchers. The leaflet begins with the word "Sisters" in large bold text followed by an exclamation mark. The speaker, the leaflet declares, is "a trans activist who identifies as a lesbian." The leaflet, addressed to the event organizers reads:

> By inviting a misogynist, ant-feminist, lesbian-hating man to speak for us, Dyke March London is contributing to lesbian invisibility, the taking over by men of lesbian spaces, creating a March hostile to lesbians, enforcing the idea that penis is female and that lesbians should accept it, demonising women who stand up to it

Some social media activity against the choice of speaker was evident in the days leading up to the event. A Twitter post on 18th June 2014, read: "expressing my support of protest against #dykemarchlondon male speakers." The next day a post from another tweeter read: "[. . .] Anyone would think they had an aversion to actual dykes #dykemarchlondon #dykemarch" followed minutes later with a post from a new poster: "Why for 3 years now has #dykemarchlondon had male keynote speakers? this is erasure and its infuriating." On the morning of the March, a post read: "#Solidarity with all dykes at #DykeMarchLondon today A bittersweet event for female-loving-females as it's being colonised by men #DykeMarch." Also on the 21st June, @WomenCanSee posted a meme.[6] The text "#DykeMarchLondon Brought to you by men: Authorised by men: Spoken by men" was surrounded by men's symbols, with a woman's symbol placed next to the text marked through with a large red cross. Both the organizers of the March and members of trans and allied communities kept a low social media presence on the hashtag DykeMarchLondon, though on the day of the event, the speaker posted a link to her speech on Twitter; a section of which I quote below:

> [. . .] It's amazing to be here, to be surrounded by so many inspirational women. Being invited to speak here is extremely humbling, and I'm a bit nervous, so I hope you'll bear with me. [. . .] There are those who hold the view that because of certain aspects of my biology, I do not, and can never, truly qualify as a lesbian. There are those who feel this very strongly. Some of them are active in lesbian and queer women's spaces.

Here, the speaker directly addresses the issue of contestation as discussed throughout this paper – the refutation of her gender by other members of feminist and lesbian communities. Moreover, the denial of her gendered identity dovetails into the denial of her sexual identity: if she is not seen as a woman, she cannot be seen as a lesbian.

In organizing through the name "Actual Dykes," the group opposed to the choice of speaker, positioned themselves counter to her lesbian identity. The notion of "deception" has long run through feminist denouncements of transgender. If female self-identity is dismissed, one must be "pretending" to be a woman. This maps on to an alarming pattern of what are referred to in the media as cases of gender "fraud" in the UK,[7] where people have been convicted of concealing their gender from lovers (see Sharpe, 2015; Whittle, 2013). According to Elisabeth Gross, in such instances, the law does not seek "not to protect sexual autonomy against fraudulent solicitation of sex, but rather to protect gender norms and compulsory heterosexuality" (2009, p. 165). These matters are not purely didactic; rather they bring the significant material effects of imprisonment. Moreover, the protection of gender and sexual norms that fuel the panic of "gender fraud," can, literally, be a matter of life and death. In her memoir *Trans*, Juliet Jacques (2016) speaks of a wave of violence and murder facing trans women, and particularly trans women of colour: "I saw," she writes, "that for many people around the world expressing themselves as they wished meant risking death" (2016, p. 63). As the next section of the paper indicates, challenges to the gender identities of trans women and pronouncements of gender deception are ever-more present in debates about public toilet use and notions of "safe-space."

Debating safe-space: from *toiletgate* to *no unexpected penises*

The second case study relates to an event that took place at *Pride London*[8] in June 2008. Initial analysis of the case is gathered from a blog account written by the central figure the following day. Whilst on the March, a trans woman went to the designated Pride toilets at Trafalgar Square. A Pride steward informed her that she could not use the women's toilets and that she, and other trans women, should use the disabled toilets. On her blog, the woman says, "we made a collective fuss" (Nicholls, 2008). The steward, she writes, used their radio to inform a colleague "we're being attacked by a mob of trannies." A police officer, who was also a LGBT liaison officer, told the woman that if she wanted to use the woman's toilet, she needed to show her Gender Recognition Certificate.[9] The woman, who had actually been involved in the drafting of the Gender Recognition Act (GRA), told the officer that toilet use did not feature in the GRA: "it did not take away the rights that had been there before." Still, the woman was denied access to the female toilet.

The problematic of gendered public toilets is not restricted to this instance. As Dara Blumenthal suggests: "Public toilets are places where individual identity is put to the test through experiences of fear, anxiety, shame, and embarrassment, yet also places where we shore up, confirm, and check the status of our gendered identities" (2014, p. 1). In the UK, the "toilet issue" is debated in relation to equalities and diversity policy; the NUS, for example, has argued successfully for gender-neutral facilities on campuses, while the House of Commons Speaker, John Bercow is currently consulting on how to make the newly refurbished Commons a more "gender-neutral space," with toilet facilities key to recommendations. In the US, the "bathroom problem" is debated by State and frequently proves contentious; thus *Time Magazine* recently covered the issue, describing it as "the latest civil rights fight" (Steinmetz, 2015). Recalling the struggles of civil rights, disability and women's movements around segregation of, and access to, public space, Steinmetz quotes prominent US trans campaigner Janet Mock as stating that public toilet use is "the great equalizer for all of us" (Steinmetz, 2015). These questions indicate how gendered identity and embodiment are managed, negotiated and resisted through the ongoing mundane processes and everyday spaces of life.

The right of trans women to use women's public toilets has been at the centre of feminist debate around transgender, bringing issues of everyday gendered embodied experience and regulation to the fore. As well as the Pride incident discussed above, this is further highlighted through an analysis of the 2014 *Twitter* hashtag #NoUnexpectedPenises. The hashtag first appeared on *Twitter* in June 2014 amidst ongoing debate within feminist communities about the place of trans women in female toilets, as well as spaces such as women's refuges', health services and prisons. Talking to other people on *Twitter* about women-only spaces, UK journalist and high profile feminist activist Sarah Ditum posted of the: "necessity of excluding penised individuals from some women-only spaces" (3 June 2014). In reply, another UK feminist with a strong media profile tweeted: '@Sarah Ditum I love you and agree with you. It is my right NOT to have penises around me if I choose #NoUnexpectedPenises. The hashtag was subsequently used 2046 times over three days by feminist activists to reinforce Ditum's original statement. Moreover, there was a proliferation of supporting posts from feminists who did not use this specific hashtag. The hashtag quickly became a forum whereby women posted experiences of sexual harassment or assault in public places, such as on the street, in swimming pools or toilets, thereby repeatedly drawing a correlation between the use of public space by trans women and sexual violence. The presence of trans women in "women's" spaces is thus aligned with violence against women, and, moreover, as Alison Phipps argues, with rape:

> The penis is the key object here, 'stuck' to trans women through an invasive and violent obsession with their surgical status, but also imagined as a separate entity which is itself responsible for sexual violence rather than being, as Serano reminds us, merely someone's genital organ (2013, p. 31).
>
> *(Phipps, 2016, p. 311)*

As discussed in earlier parts of this paper, feminist refusal to acknowledge trans women as women is not restricted to public toilet space. Nor is it a recent occurrence, as the aforementioned instances of trans exclusion in feminist cultural spaces in the decades of the 1970s and 1980s indicate. Rather, sections of feminism have sustained their rejection of the self-identities of trans women. In 1996, for example, prominent feminist writer and academic Germaine Greer publically opposed a trans woman's membership of an all women's college at Cambridge University where she taught. Greer's anti-feminist rhetoric has continued. In a chapter titled "Pantomime Dames" in her book *Whole Woman*, Greer addresses the debate about the place of trans women in women's spaces as such: "When he forces his way into the few private spaces women may enjoy and shouts down their objections, and bombards the women who will not accept him with threats and hate mail, he does as rapists have always done." (Greer, 1994, p. 102). Here, trans women are not only misrepresented as men,[10] but are aligned with the very worst of men. The threat of violence against women is enacted through "gender fraud." As Phipps states, "this politics of fear uses the language of victimisation and emotional triggers to great effect [. . .]" (Phipps, 2016, p. 312).

Over the last decade Greer has been unrelenting in her standpoint. In a speech at Cambridge University in 2015, Greer asserted that trans women are not women because they do not have vaginas. Her statement led to a petition by Cardiff University's Women's Officer when she was invited to speak later that year. In turn, this snowballed in traditional and social media. Tweets both supporting and refuting Cardiff University's petition against Greer's talk were in the thousands and most UK broadsheet newspaper covered the story. When asked to qualify her views in an interview with presenter Kirsty Walk on BBC *Newsnight*, Greer repeated her earlier sentiments, stating that "[. . .] I think that a great many women don't think that post-operative MtF transsexual people look like or sound like or behave like women but they daren't say so." This is one example of the ways in which anti-transgender feminism has moved from a marginal sub-cultural position to enter a more mainstream and high profile feminist constituent. Similarly, writing in *The Times* Jenni Murray, presenter on the BBC Radio Four programme "Woman's Hour" has challenged the identities of trans women as "real women" (2017). Author and journalist Julie Bindel offers another instance of a high profile feminist who has continued to deny the identities of trans women and who has continually positioned trans women as potential perpetuators of violence against women:

> A trans-sexual 'woman' will always be a biological male. A male-to-female transsexual serving a prison sentence for manslaughter and rape won the right to be relocated to a women's jail. Her lawyers argued that her rights were being violated by being unable to live in her role as a woman in a men's jail. Large numbers of female prisoners have experienced childhood abuse and rape and will fail to appreciate the reasons behind a biological man living among them, particularly one who still has the penis with which he raped a woman.
>
> *(Bindel, 2009)*

Bindel's line of thought mirrors that of the protagonists in the case studies discussed previously and has been defended by other celebrated feminist writers and journalists. In her article "Julie Bindel's Dangerous Transphobia," in *The Guardian*, C. L. Minou brings to light the ways in which Bindel's thinking stands counter to the feminist analysis she applies to all other topics. For Bindel, in other aspects, gender is malleable and socially constructed, biology is unfixed, the struggle for bodily autonomy is key for all women, and misogyny is a central feminist issue (Minou, 2010). Minou continues:

> Indeed, what is astonishing about Bindel's writing on transsexuals [. . .] is how often it resembles the diatribes of anti-gay bigots: the disregard of our own voices, the disbelief that transness is anything but a degeneracy, and the general air of condescension and paternalism. Gays and lesbians have long known that such diatribes are not merely 'offensive,' but dangerous – as is transphobic writing like Bindel's, and for the same reason: they support social attitudes that have often proven deadly for trans people.
>
> *(Minou, 2010)*

Thus, Bindel's public platform, like that of Greer's, has been contested by other feminists and trans people. Her nomination for "Journalist of the Year" by LGBT[11] organisation *Stonewall* in 2008, for example, led to protests and, as the next section of the paper will explore, she has since been included in the National Union of Students (NUS) "No Platforming" policy.

The politics of speech: *no-platforming*

In recent years, feminist debates about transgender have affected broader political and media discussions through which notions of "safety," "free speech" and "censorship" are counter posed in discussions about "no-platforming." The term "no platform" can be traced back to Left politics in the 1970s when Left affiliated groups sought to prevent far-right groups, such as "The National Front," from organizing in public spaces. The NUS similarly developed its no-platform policy in 1974 to prevent far-right groups demonstrating on campuses. It stated that "individuals or members of organisations or groups identified by the Democratic Procedures Committee as holding racist or fascist views may stand for election to any NUS position, or attend or speak at any NUS function or conference. Furthermore, officers, committee members, or trustees may not share a platform with any racist or fascist." Within feminist debates about transgender, the term "no platforming" has become commonplace in recent years. In 2011, the NUS GLBT conference voted to extend the NUS policy to include Julie Bindel. Germaine Greer has also been included in NUS no-platform policy. Such decisions are upheld on grounds of protecting students from emotional harm, in line with NUS "safe space" policy. Bindle's views, the conference argued, could incite hatred towards and exclusion of our trans students. In response, Bindle, like Greer, used her access to mainstream media to denounce the decision, arguing that she had been censored and that her right of "free speech" had been violated. No-platforming in these instances is frequently pitted against the democratic practice of "debate." Writing in support of Bindel, *Guardian* and *New Statesman* writer Sarah Ditum thus states: "A tool that was once intended to protect democracy from undemocratic movements has become a weapon used by the undemocratic against democracy" (Ditum, 2014). Yet, as Ahmed's (2012) work shows, it is those who have the greatest levels of cultural and material capital who have the highest access to public platforms. Still, the language of censorship is invoked; an invocation that obscures levels of structural power (Ahmed, 2012; Phipps, 2016).

Like Greer, Bindle repeatedly heightens public controversy in defending her original position, which, in turn, leads to further media coverage. Talking to online current affairs magazine *Spiked*, for example, Bindel stated: "I'm transphobic, of course, because I suggest that men with beards and penises shouting 'shut up, you transphobe' at women, 'you've misgendered[12] me', might be a bit *Nineteen Eighty-Four*" (Hulme, 2015). Thus, Bindel's rhetoric is explicit in accomplishing exactly that which she has been critiqued for. Similarly, in talking about US celebratory Caitlyn Jenner on BBC's *Newnight*, Greer stated: "Just because you lop off your dick and where a dress, it doesn't make you a woman" (Greer, *Newsnight*, 2015). Later the same week, Greer intensified her point when speaking to Victoria Derbyshire from the BBC; saying: "I've asked my doctor to give me long ears and liver spots and I'm going to wear a brown coat but that won't turn me into a fucking cocker spanie." Greer's comments led to a flurry of activity on traditional and social media both in condemnation and support. In terms of the latter, Greer's comments were honed in on by social media posts which overlaid the text "I am a woman" on a range of inanimate objects, thus mocking the identities of trans women. Such instances seamlessly illustrate the cyclical nature of social media debate and its intersecting relationship with offline events, as drawn out in this paper. On being interviewed on *BBC News* about Greer's comments, actress Rebecca Root remarked that this is "something I would expect from the gutter press not from someone with such an academic standing" (BBC, 2015). Root's point is significant in focusing attention on the social and cultural capital inhabited by high profile feminist academics and journalists who populate anti-transgender discourse as evidenced by each of the case studies in this paper.

Conclusions

This paper has drawn on virtual material to explore the contemporary relationship between feminism and transgender. It has considered the volatile temperament of feminist political discourse as it produces knowledge claims about who constitutes a female or feminist subject. I have argued that, despite links being forged between many sections of feminist and trans communities, there is a strong branch of anti-transgender sentiment running through contemporary feminist discourse. Moreover, this strain of feminism is particularly reflected in the work of leading feminist journalists writing for Left-leaning media, and amplified through the use of social media. While anti-transgender feminists may be in a minority, they have a high level of social, cultural and economic capital. It is, I believe, vital to counter this tendency in order to avoid the continuation of narratives in which, as Cressida Heyes writes, "transliberation" and "feminism" have often been cast as opposing movements (2003, p. 1095)

As the first section of this paper has addressed, anti-transgender feminism has a long history of denying the identities of trans women through recourse to the fixity of biological sex. However, a different, though no less problematic, slant on the sex/gender distinction is currently in play. In recent years, the language of anti-transgender feminism is articulated through a distinction between "female" and "woman." In contrast to the direct rejection of trans women of traditional anti-transgender feminism, many current feminist commentators separate these concepts in refuting gendered authenticity. The argument is as follows: trans women may be "women" because they occupy that social role, however, they are not "female" as they do not have the requisite chromosomal make-up. Thus, whilst nodding to self-definition and maintaining the feminist analysis of "gender" as socially constructed, "sex" is deferentially positioned to regulate gendered belonging. The challenge to the sex/gender binary as developed by numerous feminist and trans scholars, which was addressed in the first section of this paper, is negated in the current feminist narration of biological "fact." Ignored too is the stress placed on the organic diversity of "sex" in the work of feminist biologists such as Anne Fausto Sterling (1985, 2000, 2012) and Joan Roughgarden (2004). Rather than engaging with the productive diversity of nature, or heeding Roughgarden's creative call to "affirm diversity as one of our nation's defining principles" (2004, p. 1), many liberal feminist writers and activists offer a reductive model of biology. This enacts a regressive nature/culture divide to position trans women outside of feminist concerns and distance them from feminist cultures and spaces.

At a time when trans people are gaining increased legal rights and social visibility, cultures of trans exclusionary feminism appear to be strident. As indicated through the case study material in this paper, an area of acute disquiet concerns the place of trans women within "women's" spaces. Long inscribed feminist treatises of bodily autonomy are forsaken as feminists query other women's genitals and rebuff their hormonal and chromosomal make-up in the policing of feminist space. Moreover, reductive models of biology and restrictive understandings of the sex/gender distinction are articulated in defence of this feminist position. Such conduct is defended through recourse to women's "safety" and proclamations of censorship are declared when these views are challenged.

My analysis suggests that the surveillance and the regulation of the female body through the notion of female authenticity is intensifying in present times These exclusionary practices have profound material impact. In addition to working to philosophically Other, a social group, these "other" bodies become bodies to fear. Further, as Sara Ahmed (2012) suggests, it is bodies who may well "pass" that become *the* bodies that are fetishized as bodies of fear. As the case study analysis for this paper suggests, an emphasis on the link between the "sexed" body and the identity and experience of "woman," not only continues to be reinstated in attempts to regulate the boundaries of feminism, but is routinely recalled to reinstate the trans body as the body of fear.

The separation of bodies in public space is the cornerstone of segregation policy and has long been practiced to regulate bodies in relation to race, especially, but also gender, age, class disability and sexuality. These practices have been vehemently challenged by social justice movements. Moreover, public scrutiny of the bodies of black women, women athletes and of intersex people through "sex verification" practices has a long history, which feminist writers and activists have importantly challenged. I suggest, however, that a current wave of embodied segregation and sex verification is in operation as some feminists police the bodies of others in their movements. While this may sound hyperbolic, it is important to remember the role of first wave white middle-class feminists in eugenic movements (Mancel and Hibberd, 1998; Moss et al., 2015). The search for embodied "purity," then, has deep and unpleasant roots within feminism. Trans and feminist activists and writers, and their allies, have countered anti-transgender feminism through public debate, scholarship and policy recommendations. Nevertheless, the views of anti-transgender feminists have become further entrenched and the public airing of trans-exclusionary discourse more widespread. At the end of a recent BBC *Newsnight* programme "Is transgender the new civil rights frontier?," featuring Sarah Ditum and activist, musician and writer CN Lester, Emily Maitlis turned to Sarah Ditum and said: "There is a danger isn't there, that you will look back and say a revolution was happening and you were on the wrong side, that you didn't realize that this was a civil rights movement? [. . .]" (Mailtlis, 2016). I concur that bodily autonomy and self-determination of gender are, indeed, basic civil rights.

In exploring how issues of identity and embodiment have played out within feminism in recent years, this paper has highlighted the influential role of social media in contemporary political debate. Online dynamics often heighten tensions that are then debated offline, leading to further media coverage and entrenchment of position both on and offline. Online abuse is now receiving significant social and political attention following threats against high profile female commentators such as academic Mary Beard, feminist writer and activist Caroline Criado-Perez, MP Stella Creasy, and, indeed, Sarah Ditum herself. As Emma A. Jane (2012) argues, however, the impact of online abuse, which she terms "e-bile," has often been negated in academic circles. In an important appeal for scholarship to take online misogyny seriously, Jane points to the ways in which abuse is disproportionately targeted at women. Additionally, the nature of abuse targeted at women, she argues, is different: it is often focused on the victim's appearance and is highly sexualized. As this paper has illustrated, trans women are frequently the victims of such misogynic on and off – line abuse. Moreover, as I have examined, the focus and tone of the abuse is focused on the body, with its affects intrinsically embodied. Yet, the perpetuators are frequently not only women themselves, but women who are also victims of misogynist online abuse. To stress: not only is gendered, sexual and embodied abuse against trans women not taken seriously within high profile sections of feminist cultures, high profile feminists themselves often propagate the abuse. Ruminating on this paradox leads back to the question of gendered authenticity and the "sexed" body – to the question of who is (or is not) a woman? To be blunt, the abuse of trans women is not considered to be a feminist issue within some sections of feminism because trans women are not considered to be women.

The tensions between feminism and transgender discussed in this paper run through Jacqueline's Rose's (2016) deliberation on trans narrative, "Who do you think you are?." Though the strains on managing "livable lives" (Butler, 2006) for trans people are at the fore of the piece, Rose manages to close on a hopeful note: "Perhaps, even though it doesn't always look this way on the ground, trans activists will also – just – be in a position to advance what so often seems impossible: a political movement that tells it how it uniquely is, without separating one struggle for equality and human dignity from all the rest" (2016, p. 13).[13] While Rose's vision is inspiring, I add a caveat–that anti-transgender feminism be explicitly recognized by social justice movements as a discursive and material practice that is in breach of the goals of equality and dignity. Indeed, one that runs counter to the ability to fulfil a livable life or, often, a life at all.

Disclosure statement

No potential conflict of interest was reported by the author.

Notes on contributor

Sally Hines is Professor of Sociology and Gender in the School of Sociology and Social Policy at the University of Leeds. She has published widely in the areas of transgender, gender, sexuality, intimacy, citizenship and recognition, the body and feminist politics and theory, and is co-editor of the Routledge Book Series "Advances in Critical Diversities." Sally is currently PI on two major ESRC funded awards: "Pregnant Men: An International Exploration of Trans Male Practices and Experiences of Reproduction" and "Living Gender in Diverse Times: Young People's Understandings and Practices of Gender in the Contemporary UK."

Notes

1 The term "transgender" is used in this paper to address a range of gender diverse identities and practices including, though not limited to, trans men, trans women and non-binary people.
2 The term "trans" is used as shorthand for "transgender" and covers a range of gender identities under this umbrella.
3 I use this term in relation to feminist politics from 1960s–1990s, though I recognize the problematic of using the metaphor of waves to discuss feminism – see Hemmings, 2011.

4 Though Jeffrey's (1997) feminist critique of transgender includes trans men, in the main, feminist critiques have addressed trans women.
5 The term "cis" is short for "cisgender,", a term that describes people whose gender corresponds with the sex that they were assigned at birth. People who do not identify as trans are cis.
6 A "meme" is a catchphrase, concept or idea which spreads from person to person on the internet.
7 Since 2012 four people in the UK have been convicted of sexual assault under the Sexual Offences Act (2013) in relation to cases of "gender fraud.".
8 "Pride London" is the UKs largest annual lesbian, gay, bisexual and transgender gathering.
9 In 2004, The UK "Gender Recognition Act" (GRA) enabled some trans people to change their birth certificates and to marry in their acquired gender. A "Gender Recognition Certificate" (GRC) is granted to people who are successfully approved by a "Gender Recognition Panel" (GRP). The current process has been subject to much critique from trans organizations (seeSee Author, 2013) and is under review.
10 Known as "misgendering.".
11 "LGBT" is the acronym for Lesbian, Gay, Bisexual and Transgender.
12 To "misgender" is use incorrect gendered pronouns.
13 Since the publication of Rose's (2016) essay, letters of reply to LRB have been published by leading feminist writers and activists that reinstate an anti-transgender position of denying the identities of trans women as women – and so the chain of controversy begins anew.

References

Ahmed, S. (2012). *The cultural politics of emotion*. London: Routledge.

Bindel, J. (2009). My sexual revolution. *The Guardian*.

Blumenthal, D. (2014). *Little vast rooms of doing: Exploring identity and embodiment through public toilet spaces*. Lanham, MD: Rowman & Littlefield International.

Boyd, D. (2014). *It's complicated: The social lives of networked teens*. New Haven, CT: Yale University Press.

Butler, J. (1990). *Gender trouble: Feminism and the subversion of identity*. New York: Routledge.

Butler, J. (2006). *Precarious life: The powers of mourning and violence*. London and New York: Verso.

Daniels, J., & Feagin, J. R. (2011). The (Coming) social media revolution in the academy. *Fast Capitalism*, *8*, 2.

Davis, K. (2012). Tensions of identity in a networked era: Young people's perspectives on the risks and rewards of online self-expression. *New Media & Society*, *14*(4), 634–651.

Ditum, S. (2014). 'No platform' was once reserved for violent fascists. Now it's being used to silence debate. *NewStatesman*.

Fausto Sterling, A. (1985). *Myths of gender: Biological theories about men and women*. New York, NY: Basic Books.

Fausto Sterling, A. (2000). *Sexing the body: Gender politics and the construction of sexuality*. New York, NY: Basic Books.

Fausto Sterling, A. (2012). *Sex/gender: Biology in a social world (the Routledge series integrating science and culture*. London and New York: Routledge.

Feinberg, L. (1996). *Transgender warriors: Making history From Joan of Arc to Dennis Rodman*. Boston, MA: Beacon Press.

Fink, M., & Muller, Q. (2014). 'Trans media moments: Tumblr 2011–2013.' *New Media and Society*, *15*, 7.

Flax, J. (1997). Postmodernism & gender relations in feminist theory. In S. Kemp & J. Squire (Eds.), *Feminisms* (pp. 170–179). Oxford: Oxford University Press.

Gerlitz, C., & Rieder, B. (2013). Mining one percent of twitter: Collections, baselines, sampling. *M/C A Journal of Media and Culture*, *16*, 2.

Greer, G. (1994). *The whole woman*. London: Black Swan, 74.

Gross, E. (2009). Gender outlaws before the law: The courts of the borderlands. *Harvard Journal of Law & Gender*, *32*, 165–231.

Halberstam, J. (1998). *Female masculinity*. Durham, NC: Duke University Press.

Hemmings, C. (2011). *Why stories matter: The political grammar of feminist theory*. Durham, NC: Duke University Press.

Heyes, C. J. (2003). Feminist solidarity after queer theory: The case of transgender. *Signs: Journal of Women in Culture and Society*, *28*(4) (Summer 2003), 1093–1120

Hines. (2005). 'I am a feminist but . . .': Transgender men, women and feminism. In J. Reger (Ed.), *Different wavelengths: Studies of the Contemporary women's movement*. London and New York: Routledge.

Hines, S. (2006). What's the difference?: Bringing particularity to queer studies of transgender. *Journal of Gender Studies, 15*, 1.

Hines, S. (2013). *Gender diversity, recognition and citizenship: Towards a politics of difference, Palgrave.* Basingstoke: Palgrave Macmillan.

Hines, S. (2014). *Gender diversity, recognition and citizenship: Towards a politics of difference.* Basingstoke: Palgrave Macmillan.

Hollibaugh, A. (1989). Desire for the future: Radical hope in passion and pleasure. In C. Vance (Ed.), *Pleasure and danger: Exploring female sexuality* (pp. 403–404). London: Pandora.

Jacques, J. (2016). *Trans: A Memoir.* London: Verso.

Jane, E. A. (2012). 'You're a ugly, whorish, slut' understanding E-bile. *Feminist Media Studies, 14*(4), 531–546.

Jeffreys, S. (1997). Transgender activism: A feminist perspective. *The Journal of Lesbian Studies, 1*, 55–74.

Jeffreys, S. (2014). *Gender hurts: A feminist analysis of the politics of transgenderism.* London and New York: Routledge.

Koyami, E. (2003). Transfeminist manifesto. In R. Dicker, & A. Piepmeier (Eds.), *Catching a wave: Reclaiming feminism for the 21st century* (pp. 244–263). Boston: Northeastern Press.

Krippendorff, K. (2004). *Content analysis: An introduction to its methodology* (2nd ed.). Thousand Oaks, CA: Sage.

Lupton, D. (2012). *Digital sociology: An introduction.* Department of Sociology and Social Policy, University of Sydney. Retrieved August, 2012, from www.academia.edu/1830701/Digital_Sociology_An_Introduction

Maitlis, E. (2016). *Newsnight.* Retrieved from www.youtube.com/watch?v=Mnui7OqawSM

Mancel, D., & Hibberd, J. (1998). 'We picked the wrong one to sterilise': The role of nursing in the eugenics movement in Alberta, 1920–1940. *University National Library of Medicine, 3*(4), 4–11.

Minou, C. L. (2010, Feburary 1st). Julie Bindel's dangerous transphobia. *The Guardian.*

Moss, E. L., Henderikus, S., Kattevilder, D. (2015). From suffrage to sterilization: Eugenics and the women's movement in 20th century Alberta. *Canadian Psychology/Psychologiecanadienne, 54*(2), 105–114.

Murray, J. (2017, March 5). Trans women shouldn't call themselves 'real women'. *The Guardian.*

Nicholls, J. (2008). *The angels: Activism news.* Retrieved from http://theangels.co.uk/2008/07/trans-problem-at-london-pride/

Phipps, A. (2016). Whose personal is more political? Experience in contemporary feminist politics. *Feminist Theory, 17*(3), 303–321.

Platt, J. (1992). "Case study" in American methodological thought. *Current Sociology, 40*, 17–48.

Raymond, J. (1979). *The transsexual empire.* London: The Women's Press.

Riddell, C. (1996) 'Divided sisterhood: A critical review of Janice Raymond's *The Transsexual Empire*', R. Ekins & D. King (Eds)., *Blending genders: Social aspects of cross-dressing*, London: Routledge.

Ringrose, J., Harvey, L., Gill, R., & Livingstone, S. (2013). Teen girls, sexual double standards and 'sexting': Gendered value in digital image exchange. *Feminist Theory*, 2 'Special Issue: Feminisms, 'sexualisation' and contemporary girlhoods', *14*: 3.

Rose, J. (2016). Who do you think you are? *London Review of Books, 38*(9), 3–13

Roseneil, S., & Budgeon, S. (2004). Beyond the conventional family: Intimacy, care and community in the 21st century. *Current Sociology, 52*, 2.

Roughgarden, J. (2004). *Nature's rainbow: Diversity, gender, and sexuality in nature and people.* Berkeley, CA: University of California Press.

Ruben, H. (1996). Do you believe in gender? *Sojourner, 21*, 6.

Rubin, G. (1989). Thinking sex: Notes for a radical theory of the politics of sexuality. In C. Vance (Ed.), *Pleasure and danger: Exploring female sexuality* (pp. 267–293). London: Pandora.

Serano, J. (2007). *Whipping girl: A transsexual woman on sexism and the scapegoating of femininity.* Boston, MA: De Cappo Press.

Serona, J. (2013). *Excluded: Making feminist and queer movements more inclusive.* New York, NY: Avalon Publishing Group.

Sharpe, A. (2015, December 16). The dark truth behind the convictions of gender fraud. *The NewStatesman.*

Steinmetz. (2015). Laverne Cox talks to TIME about the transgender movement. *Time Magazine.* Retrieved from http://time.com/132769/transgender-orange-is-the-new-black-laverne-cox-interview/

Stone, S. (1996). The empire strikes back: A posttransexual manifesto. *Camera Obscura, 10*(2:29), 150–176.

Stryker, S. (1998). The transgender issue: An introduction. *GLQ, 4*, 2.

Stryker, S. (2013). *The transgender studies reader 2.* New York, NY: Routledge.

Thielmann, T., Van der Velden, L., Fischer, F., & Vogler, R. (2012). Dwelling in the web: Towards a googlization of space. *SSRN: Social Science Research Network.* Retrieved from http://papers.ssrn.com/sol3/papers.cfm?abstract_id=2151949.

Vance, C. (Ed.). (1984). *Pleasure and danger: Exploring female sexuality.* New York, NY: Routledge.
Whittle, S. (1996). Gender fucking or fucking gender? Current cultural contributions to theories of gender blending. In R. Ekins & D. King (Eds.), *Blending genders: Social aspects of cross – Dressing and sex – Changing* (pp. 196–215). London: Routledge.
Williams, C. (2014). TERF hate and Sandy Stone. *The Trans Advocate.* Retrieved from www.transadvocate.com/terf-violence-and-sandy-stone_n_14360.htm

Section II
Ways of living

7

Everyday life studies and feminism

Susan Fraiman

In the 1980s, as women's studies was gaining a foothold in the US academy, feminist theorists commonly made a distinction between "equality" and "difference" approaches to the project of unseating patriarchy.[1] Generally speaking, the first pursues equal access to traditionally male institutions and prerogatives, while the second recognizes the specificity of women's lives and redeems qualities traditionally denigrated as "feminine." In these terms, looking back at 19th-century issues, we can recognize suffrage as an equality campaign; by contrast, laws protecting women from hazardous working conditions may be seen as reflecting a difference strategy. We find a similar split in feminist emphases today between, for example, "leaning in" (equality) and providing for nursing mothers (difference). Positions falling into one of these two camps recur and occasionally rival one another throughout the history of Western feminist thinking. When Mary Wollstonecraft argued the cause of women's education in *A Vindication of the Rights of Woman* (1792), she took an equality tack. When Virginia Woolf touted books about women's feelings as no less important than books about war in *A Room of One's Own* (1929), she was elaborating a difference argument. As theoretical and tactical approaches, "equality" and "difference" have each made huge contributions, yet each also has attendant risks. "Equality" may urge uncritical assimilation to male-dominated hierarchies (corporate, military, etc.), upholding their authority; "difference," even when clearly framed in social rather than biological terms, may reinforce notions of women as essentially distinct from men (more nurturing, emotional, etc.). Further, by pivoting on the sole binary of gender, both approaches risk inattention to other structures of inequality. Responding to this limitation, feminist scholars in the 1990s would proceed to theorize identity and injustice in newly complex and fluid ways – as constituted by the intersecting axes of race, class, sexuality, and nation as well as gender.[2]

Why preface my remarks on feminist theories of everyday life with this backward look? I do so because my essay sets out to accomplish three things: to show how feminist interventions serve to reorient the field of everyday life studies; to recover the feminist contributions made to this field by two women – one well-known, the other neglected, and both overshadowed by male colleagues; and to demonstrate the continued explanatory value of "equality versus difference" in parsing feminist approaches.

What is everyday life studies?

Emergent in the wake of industrialization, studies of everyday life endeavor to bring into visibility and somehow make sense of our humble, taken-for-granted, seemingly unremarkable experience of the quotidian. The project has meant subjecting modern Western individuals to the kind of anthropological scrutiny more often reserved for non-Western peoples. The goal has been to explore patterns of behavior not because they are foreign but because they are so familiar as to fall beneath our notice. Artists as well as social theorists in this tradition set out to register and evaluate the neglected minutiae of our daily lives: the ways we sleep and ambulate, ingest and eliminate, work and recreate, care for ourselves and others, slip in and out of self-awareness, and interact with people, objects, and our surroundings. Generally speaking, everyday life studies is a science of the "small." Though usually framed in relation to larger social structures, the objects of attention are micro-moments and micro-actions – turning a street corner, stirring a pot, feeding an infant. They are actions that take place without rising to the status of "event." They are moments in time that leave no historical mark (at least as "history" has traditionally been understood). As these examples suggest, such practices are "everyday" not only because they are "ordinary" but also because they typically occur *every day*, perhaps even every few hours. Whether tied to bodily rhythms or the rigors of wage work, the non-events of everyday life are almost always characterized by patterns of repetition.[3]

There is one more point to be made as I conclude this brief overview. Theorists of the everyday, focusing on the effects of modernity, have taken various stances on the political implications of our daily routines. Some have tied their repetitive nature to the mechanization and alienation of labor in a capitalist society. For Michel Foucault, domination is not restricted to the factory floor; the workings of power are more diffuse and insidious than this, operating in the very interstices of our seemingly private lives. Michel de Certeau (one of the field's most influential figures, along with Henri Lefebvre) describes his own approach to everyday life as both "analogous and contrary" to Foucault's:

> If it is true that the grid of "discipline" is everywhere becoming clearer and more extensive, it is all the more urgent to discover how an entire society resists being reduced to it, what popular procedures (also "miniscule" and quotidian) manipulate the mechanisms of discipline and conform to them only in order to evade them.[4]

For Certeau, the quotidian is a site not of forcible conformity but of micro-opportunities to defy the dominant order. Other everyday life theorists incline toward one of these two positions (with pessimists, by my count, edging out optimists) – but a significant number describe the politics of our personal routines as changeable and contingent. Our daily practices may, in this view, indicate compliance, resistance, or a combination of both, depending on the circumstances. Indeed, according to Ben Highmore, contradiction is at the heart of our day-to-day experiences. Turning specifically to the domestic realms of cooking and childcare, Highmore makes a case for "the central ambiguity of routine, its characteristically dual nature of comfort and constraint."[5]

Women in and as the quotidian

What does all of this have to do with women and gender? Why should we as feminists care about the quotidian, and what is at stake in querying how it has been framed? How might a feminist perspective shed light both on the meanings of everyday life itself and on the area of everyday life studies? In pursuing these questions, we should first admit that no one can escape the everyday.

The mighty as well as the meek have their rituals of self-care, their share of small tasks accomplished on autopilot, their habitual ways of slip-sliding along. It is thus not entirely logical that the rhythms of ordinary life have been most strongly identified with "ordinary" people. More often than not, "low" behaviors have been studied in relation to those of low status – the manners of staff in a hotel kitchen, for example, or the wearing of hats by migrants arriving in Britain – with the distinct advantage, it must be said, of shedding valuable light on common lives.[6] Within this tradition, no single figure has been seen as so plainly coextensive with everyday life as a woman caught up in cycles of cooking, cleaning, and caring for family. In an oft-cited passage, Lefebvre asserts that "everyday life weighs heaviest on women," and no space so readily evokes the quotidian as a kitchen piled with vegetables to be peeled and dishes to be washed. When George Eliot wished to conjure "monotonous homely existence," she turned naturally to images of manual labor, especially in a domestic context: "those old women scraping carrots with their work-worn hands . . . those homes with their tin pans, their brown pitchers, their rough curs, and their clusters of onions."[7]

If women are, in fact, tasked with an inordinate share of repetitive, everyday labor, it is primarily because they so often feed, clothe, and otherwise tend not only their own bodies but also the bodies of one or more others. This is arguably true even of a well-off woman relative to her male counterpart (especially when we include customary emotional work), and the household work she declines is inevitably ceded to a woman further down the status ladder. In addition to women's lived experience of shouldering domestic duties, there is also the cultural construction of femininity itself as banal, beholden to biological rhythms, limited in mobility, and lacking in originality. The everyday is therefore a distinctly feminized category for two reasons: first, because women have been, in a literal sense, disproportionately responsible for activities regarded as "everyday" in lieu of activities regarded as "eventful"; and second, because women have been taken to *represent* the everyday. To be a woman is to be a walking emblem of the minute, repetitive, and unremarkable.

Given the double (symbolic as well as practical) identification of everyday life with women, demeaning views of the latter are central to negative views of the former. As Rita Felski observes, "The modernist horror of routine has much to do with its feminine connotations, even as the disdain for the everyday as it is conventionally lived often relies on a disparagement of domestic activities and skills associated with women." Traces of gendered disdain persist, Felski argues, even among those who redeem everyday life but do so only by re-making it as less banal.[8] Following Felski's lead, a feminist approach to everyday life studies begins by recognizing the feminization of everyday life as well as the resulting misogynist logic of looking askance at daily routines. In opposition to this construct, feminist writers over the years have generally favored one of two approaches. You will notice they map quite neatly onto the equality and difference strategies with which I began. The first approach attacks the presumed connection between women and everyday domestic practices. Those in this camp argue that females are no more naturally or inevitably enmeshed in daily routines than males are. Protesting women's restriction to domestic spaces and activities, they demand equal access to the public sphere and full participation in the properly "historical" work of creating rather than maintaining. This feminist perspective wants nothing to do with "everyday life" and decries the chaining of women to endless rounds of housework and childcare. The second approach focuses more on the construct's misogynist corollary. Those in this camp also deny that women are hard-wired to be the everyday sex. Instead of fleeing domestic routines, however, they go on to affirm the value of these practices. They do so by asserting the importance – indeed, the necessity – of producing the physical and emotional space we call "home." Recognizing the unwaged labor that goes into social reproduction, they give due credit to the women who customarily perform it. Those who take this approach may also cite the comforting aspects of routine and celebrate the value of daily care work. Finally, while defending the repetitive, they trouble the opposition between repetition and invention by pointing to the deviations, innovations, and extraordinary moments that are, in fact, closely interwoven with the familiar and expected.

As in everyday life studies generally speaking, feminist commentators are thus divided between negative and positive emphases. Focusing (as I will be doing) on women's particular tie to domestic routines, they disagree as to whether these suppress or express female agency. In what remains of this essay, I will consider texts illustrating each of these two positions, the first corresponding to my description of equality feminism, the second to difference feminism. Along the way, I will also have cause to cite my own recent work in everyday studies. While I see anti- and pro-domesticity arguments as equally indispensable to a robust feminist analysis, it will be clear that my work aligns more closely with the difference project of recuperating domestic knowledge and concerns.

My two exemplary texts, both written by women, would seem to contradict Lefebvre's insulting and illogical assertion that women's immersion in everyday life precludes their ability to comprehend it.[9] To me, it is hardly surprising that women's long-standing, practical intimacy with domestic routines should conduce to a heightened understanding of them. And don't women have, if anything, a heightened stake in analyzing a discourse for which the category "woman" does so much symbolic work? Yet Lorraine Sim is correct to observe that the history of everyday life studies has too often been mapped as if female thinkers had little to contribute. Noting that "theory" as a field has favored male figures, Sim suggests looking elsewhere for female perspectives on everyday life – in particular, to works of literary and visual art. Though I take Sim's point, my project here is to feature two *theorists* – Simone de Beauvoir and Luce Giard – whose works are sometimes cited but rarely given the credit they deserve in accounts of everyday life studies.[10]

The everyday as oppression: Simone de Beauvoir

Simone de Beauvoir (1908–1986) has been both a celebrated figure among contemporary feminists and a problematic one. As author of *The Second Sex* (along with other works in multiple genres), she is more frequently cited than actually taught in feminist theory courses, and for those who know her work, she has seemed an anomalous if not controversial thinker (see note 21). There are arguably several reasons for this. Translated into English in 1953 (after debuting in French in 1949), *The Second Sex* appeared in the lonely lull between the first and second waves of the women's movement – after suffrage had finally been won and before the renewal of feminist activism in the late 1960s.[11] If it has seemed a chronological outlier relative to "wave" accounts of Western feminism, it is also something of an intellectual outlier – more in dialog with predecessors like G.W.F. Hegel than Mary Wollstonecraft. True that Beauvoir's theorizing of man as normative Subject and woman as Other would resonate with subsequent feminist critiques, as would her emphasis on femininity as a social construct. Yet 1980s feminists would also be dismayed by her negative view of women's bodies and insistence on women's complicity with their oppression – the latter reflecting existentialist views of individual freedom and ultimate responsibility for one's own fate. Beauvoir's ties to French existentialist Jean-Paul Sartre and his circle, in addition to influencing her work, have distorted as well as enhanced her reputation. Her intellectual partnership with Sartre has tended to obscure her originality as a philosopher, and their open sexual relationship has put the focus on her personal life. A final hindrance has been the 1953 translation by H. M. Parshley. Though much faulted, it remained the only English-language edition of *The Second Sex* until finally superseded by Constance Borde and Sheila Malovany-Chevallier's more faithful and complete translation in 2011. In the end, Parshley's errors actually did Beauvoir a service: the critical furor they provoked contributed to what was, by the end of the century, a renewed, more philosophically attuned, and appreciative surge of interest in her most famous publication.[12]

Of those calling for a new appreciation as well as rendering of this text, the most vocal has been Toril Moi, who also speaks to my own project of recovering Beauvoir as a theorist of everyday life. Noting the connection between style and philosophical project, Moi comments on Beauvoir's comfortable use of the first person: "By placing her own everyday 'I' on the philosophical scene, Beauvoir indicates that she thinks of the ordinary and the everyday as integral to her philosophical project of analyzing women's situation." The same is suggested, Moi adds, by the philosopher's willingness to call on everyday sources, from "gossip and hearsay" to "ephemeral student publications."[13] In the reading that follows, I consider everydayness in Beauvoir not in relation to her writing style or source materials but rather as a topic of discussion – in particular, as the topic of an extensive section devoted to women's daily lives as homemakers. As we will see, instead of signifying a woman writer's confident, theorizing "I," here the everyday is synonymous with women's collective experience of servitude and stagnation.

Beauvoir is best known for her ringing declaration that "one is not born, but rather becomes, woman."[14] In Volume I, "Facts and Myths," she bears this out with a masterful account of ideological forces and material conditions accumulating over centuries to produce woman as man's subordinate "Other." Volume II, "Lived Experience," turns to the poor creature produced thereby – by history writ large but also by each individual's passage from girlhood to a womanhood conventionally defined by marriage and maternity. An introduction to this section reminds us, "When I use the word 'woman' or 'feminine,' I obviously refer to no archetype, to no immutable essence; 'in the present state of education and customs' must be understood to follow most of my affirmations" (*SS*, 279). In Beauvoir's view, the result of these present circumstances is that "women in general *are* today inferior to men; that is, their situation provides them with fewer possibilities" (*SS*, 12–13). At the heart of their limiting and debasing situation is women's relegation, day after day, to the care of home and family.

Beauvoir's critique of domestic routines develops over the space of almost 20 pages, pausing to cite passages drawn from a range of literary sources.[15] In the end, however, her case against homemaking for its subjugating effects may be said to rest on the following three points. First and foremost is its circumscription of women's lives within four walls. As Beauvoir explains, by cruel contrast with a girlhood spent close to nature, once married, a woman finds herself a prisoner behind closed doors (*SS*, 470). Yet instead of clamoring to escape, the protagonist of Beauvoir's account attempts, tragically, to find liberty in her confinement. By reducing her reality to the domestic realm, she gains a sense of ownership, control, and even authority: "By renouncing the world, she means to conquer a world" (*SS*, 470). Especially at night, "when the shutters are closed, woman feels like a queen . . . she is no longer dispossessed, because she does away with that which she does not possess . . . nothing else exists" (*SS*, 471). According to Beauvoir, the woman's efforts to beautify her home are part of this desperate fantasy. Furniture and "knick-knacks" give her an illusion of aesthetic agency and selfhood: "It is she who has chosen, made, 'hunted down' . . . who has aesthetically arranged them" (*SS*, 471). Even the vagrant's wife adorns her shanty with rugs and curtains – an effort all the more futile in a space with no windows (*SS*, 470). Trapped inside, the housewife replaces activity in the outside world with things. As Beauvoir concludes, "because she *does* nothing, she avidly seeks herself in what she *has*" (*SS*, 471).

Beauvoir's second point concerns the unending, embittering nature of domestic work. The housewife's labor might seem to contradict the previous assertion about *doing nothing*. According to Beauvoir's "existentialist morality" (*SS*, 16), however, "doing" requires expressing one's freedom through discovery and invention, taking actions that improve society, transcending oneself and the mere "facticity" of one's present moment. Such actions – enabled by and definitive of conventional masculinity – are all but precluded by conventional femininity. As Beauvoir laments, "the wife is not called to build a better world" (*SS*, 476). Instead, she is stuck in cycles of housework, doggedly maintaining the status quo, sentenced to stagnation, held back from transcendence, doomed to immanence.[16] "Few tasks," Beauvoir writes,

> are more similar to the torment of Sisyphus than those of the housewife; day after day, one must wash dishes, dust furniture, mend clothes that will be dirty, dusty, and torn again. The housewife wears herself out running on the spot: she does nothing; she only perpetuates the present.
>
> *(SS, 474)*

Beauvoir admits that some have praised "the poetry of housework" and concedes that "numerous women writers have lovingly spoken of freshly ironed linens" (*SS*, 472). The problem, as she sees it, is the *negative* as well as interminable nature of the housewife's war against dirt – the devotion to eliminating rather than creating, to fighting a presumed evil rather than forwarding a good. Beauvoir appears to make a qualified exception for cooking, which she describes as "more positive work and often more enjoyable than cleaning" (*SS*, 478). Indeed, anticipating my second text, she describes marketing rather rapturously as a chance to socialize and pursue ripe cheeses at a good price (*SS*, 479). On cooking as "mystery, magic, spell," she cites a long passage by Colette (*SS*, 479). "Women writers," she further allows, "have particularly celebrated the poetry of making preserves." The housewife with her bubbling jars "has captured the passage of time in the snare of sugar" (*SS*, 480). All of this lyricism serves only, however, to delay Beauvoir's ultimate verdict – for as with housework, "repetition soon dispels these pleasures" (*SS*, 481). At its best, she adds, a meal is never an end in itself; it means nothing unless consumed by an approving male, enabling his pursuit of larger goals. "Home and food are useful for life," she writes, "but do not confer any meaning on it: the housekeeper's immediate goals are only means, not real ends" (*SS*, 481). According to Beauvoir, the housewife labors only to abet another's transcendence, and does so at the expense of her own.

We have seen that Beauvoir decries the thankless, negative tenor of the housewife's struggle: "She attacks the dust, stains, mud, and filth; she fights sin, she fights with Satan" (*SS*, 476). In a third strike against domestic routines, however, Beauvoir turns this metaphor upside down by turning to the housewife whose battle with dirt has become pathological. In Beauvoir's depiction, this maddened housewife is herself a Satanic figure, at war with whatever lives and breathes: "Whenever a living being enters her sphere, her eye shines with a wicked fire" (*SS*, 476). Once tyrannized, the maniacal housewife is now the tyrant. Ordering family members to wipe their feet, she sees their every gesture as threats to her regime of cleanliness. Ominously, "she would like to stop everyone from breathing" (*SS*, 476). Turning against breath, sunlight, and joy, by the end of this paragraph Beauvoir's housewife has become a veritable monster. A final sentence invokes the infamous case of the Papin sisters, two servants who killed and gouged out the eyes of their mistress and her daughter in 1933. Surprisingly, Beauvoir does not condemn the murders. On the contrary, linking the victims to bourgeois housewives whose "hatred of dirt was inseparable from their hatred of servants, of the world, and of each other" (*SS*, 477), Beauvoir portrays the crime as fully justified. While we may grasp the class logic of this move, the swerve away from interrogating gender injustice is jarring. (Had the *master* been murdered, the story might have had more resonance – but he, of course, was away from home at the time.) As I see it, the disconcerting upshot of this whole account is to reframe the housewife, however victimized, as only getting what she deserves.[17]

If the parable of the Papin sisters strikes me as missing its political mark, I am nevertheless grateful to Beauvoir for what is, overall, a scathing and discerning critique of women's domestic servitude. Joining writers from Charlotte Brontë to Charlotte Perkins Gilman, Beauvoir produced what was undoubtedly the most fully historicized, complexly theorized, and psychologically probing analysis to date of women's confinement by marital norms.[18] Beauvoir is especially persuasive on the way domestic concerns can eat up women's lives, excluding all else. Those who exalt housework, she observes, are those who dip into it briefly before resuming their more "essential" work – for many women, by contrast, housework has become the whole of their existence (*SS*, 481). Readers must keep in mind that Beauvoir's "woman" is a being defined and deformed by conventions of male superiority; time and again she stresses that women are not innately inferior but rendered so by social mores. Despite this emphasis, however, I remain troubled by Beauvoir's reliance on extreme, drawn-out portraits of women stunted by their situation and often responding with their own forms of aggression. The effect of these two-dimensional figures is, first of all, to collapse women into "woman," overlooking the diverse forms of agency, creativity, and resistance women actually muster despite constraints. In addition, the fact that Beauvoir's maniacal housekeepers – "frigid or frustrated women, old maids, desperate housewives" (*SS*, 477), as she also calls them – are portrayed with such fervor and emphasis seems to place them beyond all hope of reform. Despite Beauvoir's claims to the contrary, they threaten to become, as the cumulative effect of intensive description, archetypes after all.[19] As such, they risk reinforcing many of the most damaging stereotypes of women (as frigid, hysterical, castrating, etc.). Insisting on the housewife's pathology may even, as we saw above, cast middle-class homemakers as the prime oppressors of family and servants alike – women whose murder is cause for celebration.[20]

Before leaving Beauvoir, I would note still one more troubling implication of so passionately denouncing housework as repetitive, negative, and "inessential" – as holding those who do it captive in a state of immanence. Much as I appreciate Beauvoir's petition for all humans to share in the prerogatives of freedom and mobility, I think she goes too far in devaluing the skill, creativity, and compassion demanded by domestic practices. It is also the case that *someone* needs to feed and clothe us; to clean up the messes we make as embodied creatures in a physical world; to care for us when we are young, sick, old, and dying. In an ideal world, these jobs would be valued, shared, and well-remunerated. As it is, they are allocated to women and low-status men for little or no pay; to shun such mundane tasks is effectively to leave them for unnamed others to do. In the end, Beauvoir's rejection of labor that is manual and quotidian hints at an aversion to the needy body as well as disdain for the female and feminized workers who cater to it.[21]

The everyday as invention: Luce Giard

We have seen how, at a key moment in Beauvoir's account of everyday life, the housewife imprisoned by marital norms and domestic labor is recast as the crazed, bourgeois mistress responsible not only for family misery but also for class oppression. In *Extreme Domesticity: A View from the Margins* (2017), I document a similar logic at work in humanities scholarship today: in areas from American to Victorian studies, the domestic woman is often viewed with neither sympathy nor regard but taken instead as a ready symbol for everything deplorably heteronormative and bourgeois.[22] Certainly I am grateful for studies critical of domesticity as a specific ideology, emergent in the 19th century and bent on producing female propriety as a sign of middle-class supremacy. In this most recent book, I myself am out to reject this ideology along with those households committed to its values. What I resist is scholarship reducing *all* housewives to emblems of these values, repudiating domesticity tout court, and thus overlooking the diversity of actual homemakers, many of whom are unable or unwilling to comply with normative standards. My goal in *Extreme Domesticity* is to sever domestic practices from a *necessary* tie to traditional "family values" and class complacency. I do so by aligning them instead with masculine women, feminist beliefs, working-class communities, self-sufficient divorcées, the hybridity of immigrant households, and the desperate improvisations of women and men without reliable shelter. One of my book's assumptions is that the politics of domestic gestures – dressing a child, slicing an onion, sweeping a floor – may be conservative, progressive, or both at once, depending on the context.[23] But while seeing domesticity as complex and variable, I am interested above all in challenging received views with an appreciative analysis of homemakers and housekeeping. Like everyday theorist Certeau – you will recall his political optimism relative to Foucault – I see in everyday activities the potential for micro-acts of creative disobedience. Like Felski and Highmore, I am willing to claim the comfort and stability of familiar routines, especially for those recently dislocated or suffering from chronic insecurity. But the scholar to whom I am most indebted for her lyrical evocation and defense of women's domestic practices is Certeau's brilliant but woefully neglected collaborator, Luce Giard. The following discussion of Giard is drawn from the introduction to my study of domesticity from the margins.

A historian and philosopher of science, Giard collaborated closely with Certeau throughout the 1970s. Yet many of those who celebrate Certeau's *The Practice of Everyday Life* are unaware of (or have nothing to say about) *The Practice of Everyday Life, Volume 2: Living and Cooking*, which Giard co-authored along with Pierre Mayol. While Certeau's name is synonymous with everyday life studies, Giard's feminist contribution – her homage to French homemakers in "Doing-Cooking" – has gained her scarcely more than a footnote in the field.[24] Ironically, her very closeness to Certeau is partly responsible for this oversight. As executor of his literary estate, she is known primarily as the posthumous editor of his work. Though somewhat more visible in the area of food studies, her own writing has been almost entirely subsumed by Certeau's. One of my goals here and in my book is to give Giard's study of women's domestic labor the recognition it deserves.

Both volumes of *The Practice of Everyday Life* came out in French in 1980. But though an English translation of volume 1 followed just four years later, it would take until 1998 for volume 2 to become available in English, a delay reflecting and adding to its relative obscurity. According to Giard, the US publisher of volume 1 had rejected the second as too narrowly "French" (see *LC*, ix).[25] Yet it's hardly a stretch to suggest that doubts about the work's "universality" may have had as much to do with gender as nationality. It was, indeed, precisely the neglect of women's everyday lives that drove Giard to produce "Doing-Cooking" in the first place. As she recalls, "I made a remark that women were strangely absent. . . . I protested, I argued (it was the time of feminist awareness), and I did so well that we decided to remedy this serious gap" (*LC*, xxviii). The woman-centered work that resulted, constituting the latter half of volume 2, sets out to refute the view so vividly set out by Beauvoir: that women's daily kitchen labor is intrinsically boring and conservative. It is, Giard admits, a view that she herself once held: "For a long time, I still regarded as elementary, conventional, and pedestrian (and therefore a bit stupid) the feminine savoir faire that presided over buying food, preparing it, and organizing meals" (*LC*, 152). Her study, drawing on in-depth interviews as well as her own experience, would redress the general tendency to demean, along with these practices, the generations of French women who have honed and transmitted them. Her goal is to honor "these non-illustrious women (no one knows their names, strength, or courage anymore)"; to document their "basic gestures always strung together and necessitated by the interminable repetition of household tasks performed in the succession of meals and days, with attention given to the body of others" (*LC*, 154); to celebrate the rich subculture she titles the Kitchen Women Nation (*le peuple féminin des cuisines*) (*LC*, 155).

There is, Giard observes, a contradiction in France between respect for food and disrespect for domestic food preparation, a female occupation judged, as we have seen, to be "repetitive and monotonous, devoid of intelligence and imagination" (*LC*, 156). "Doing-Cooking" endeavors to show not just the time-consuming labor but the modes of intelligence and creativity needed to conjure a series of dishes for multiple palates, three times a day, every day of the year. Cooking, Giard argues, "is just as mental as it is manual; all the resources of intelligence and memory are thus mobilized. One has to organize, decide, and anticipate . . . take into consideration Aunt Germaine's likes and little Francois's dislikes" (*LC*, 200). "One has to calculate," she continues,

> both time and money, not go beyond the budget, not overestimate one's own work speed, not make the schoolboy late. One has to evaluate in the twinkling of an eye what will be the most cost-effective in terms of price, preparation, and flavor.
>
> (*LC*, *200*)

Where Beauvoir saw futile repetition, Giard sees women with the stamina and know-how to execute a precisely choreographed sequence of steps – women, we might say, who have mastered a specific set of techniques.

It is also the case, as Giard explains, that while recipes may be repeated, the outcome is never exactly the same. Cooks must continually adapt to a changing set of circumstances. Leftovers must be incorporated, a stew stretched to accommodate one more, substitutions made for ingredients that have spoiled (see *LC*, 200). The daughter updates her mother's recipe to suit prepackaged foods and modern appliances (see *LC*, 208–211). As a result, Giard asserts, "one has to know how to improvise with panache" (*LC*, 200). Revised for practical reasons, recipes are further individualized as a matter of personal style and taste, so that cooking is revealed to be a space not only of repetition but also of creative deviation and reconfiguration: "Style affirms itself, taste distinguishes itself, imagination frees itself, and the recipe itself loses significance, becoming little more than an occasion for a free invention . . . a subtle game of substitutions, abandonments, additions, and borrowings" (*LC*, 201). In keeping with Certeau's vision, Giard's cook finds tactical opportunities to heed some directions while ignoring others, to invent shortcuts and veer from customary paths. We recall that Beauvoir conceded the pleasure of selecting cheeses and cabbages; in another memorable passage, Giard lays out the micropolitics of buying food at a traditional market. No passive act of consumption, marketing emerges here, in more than one respect, as a sophisticated art. Multiple senses are brought into play – the discerning touch, practiced eye, and discriminating nose.

> The outstretched index finger lightly touched the flesh of fruits to determine their degree of ripeness . . . a circumspect glance detected the presence of bruises on the apples, one smelled the scent of melons at length as well as the odor of chèvre cheeses. . . . All of this involved actualizing a certain competence.
>
> (*LC*, *205*)

If there is an art to picking melons, there is also an artfulness to getting a bargain. "Each purchase," Giard explains, "was a chance for the buyer to use trickery with the vendor's trickery" (*LC*, 205).[26] Thanks to her cunning, an experienced shopper may gain the subtlest of victories.

She may enjoy a brief triumph not over the vendor – herself a mere co-actor in what Giard calls the "innocent theater of the poor" (*LC*, 205) – but over the larger workings of power.

The whole back and forth of choosing and bargaining amounts, Giard says admiringly, to a "marvelous gestural ballet" (*LC*, 205). It is one of several places she compares the ordinary art of cooking to one that is nominally "higher." Take, for example, her lovely description of sifting flour the old-fashioned way:

> Wide-open hands held the fragile wooden circle of the sifter at two diametrically opposite points and shook it with a light tapping of the fingers. . . . A tender complicity was established with this volatile and precious flour . . . this gesture was done gently and in a measured fashion, restrained and silky like the touch of certain pianists.
>
> *(LC, 204–205)*

Elsewhere, she compares culinary invention to composing in other media:

> I learned the tranquil joy of anticipated hospitality, when one prepares a meal to share with friends in the same way in which one composes a party tune or draws: with moving hands, careful fingers, the whole body inhabited with the rhythm of working, and the mind awakening.
>
> *(LC, 153)*

In each of these cases, adding to the mental and "tactical" aspects of putting meals on the table, Giard points to cooking as an embodied aesthetic practice. Before concluding my discussion of Giard, I would note two things about the latter passage. There is, first of all, her sense of domestic life as expressing and producing sociality – a meal prepared and shared as a fundamental rite of friendship. More important, I take from this scene of *learning* to cook for *friends* an implied alternative to notions of women laboring in obedience to "natural" marital and maternal imperatives. As Giard explains in her opening paragraph,

> What follows very much involves the (privileged?) role of women in the preparation of meals eaten at home. But this is not to say that I believe in an immanent and stable feminine nature that dooms women to housework and gives them a monopoly over both the kitchen and the tasks of interior organization.
>
> *(LC, 151)*

The allocation of housework to women in modern France reflects, she continues, a set of political and material conditions that are by no means fixed and universal. And so she repeats Beauvoir's mantra: "I do not see the manifestation of a feminine essence here" (*LC*, 151). Later Giard will go on to illustrate the role of such variables as poverty (see *LC*, 173–177), regional agricultures (see *LC*, 177–179), mechanization and commercialization (see *LC*, 208–211), and a host of other geographical and historical factors, all of which combine to form and transform local culinary practices.

In the de-naturalizing view I share with Giard, not only the gendered division of domestic labor but every aspect of domesticity answers to a shifting context of layered climatic, material, technical, social, and economic forces (see *LC*, 171–173). Varying by place and time, domesticity is also, I have argued, uneven in its gender politics – capable of cutting both ways. Feminists analyzing housework must grapple with two interrelated tensions. The first involves stressing women's long-standing tie to domesticity while denying it originates in some kind of feminine "essence." Here Giard arguably does better than Beauvoir in exploring cooking as a gendered practice while never losing sight of its status as a cultural artifact. The other tension, reflected by the structure of my essay, is that between asserting the value of domestic cultures, while also acknowledging the undeniably oppressive aspects of domestic labor, especially when imposed on women to the virtual exclusion of all else. This is, I have argued, a good example of the tension between difference feminism (with its emphasis on appreciation) and equality feminism (with its tendency toward critique). Giard's emphasis, needless to say, is on the positive aspects of domesticity. As she declares in her introduction, "With their high degree of ritualization and their strong affective investment, culinary activities are for many women of all ages a place of happiness, pleasure, and discovery" (*LC*, 151). Yet by referencing *many* rather than *all* women, Giard carefully leaves room for those who may feel, along with Beauvoir, stifled rather than inspired by household routines.

I will close by reiterating Giard's gesture: I believe we need all the tools in our feminist toolkit, critique as well as appreciation, if we wish to take the measure of women's disparate everyday lives. Granting the merit of both my feminist thinkers does not, however, mean they are the same. To make a case for the continued explanatory value of "equality-difference" is, among other things, to recognize the reality of persistent disagreements within feminism. As feminists in the 21st century, do we lobby for servicewomen's inclusion on the frontlines of battle (equality) or for shifting monies from defense to education (difference)? Do we dignify the readers and writers of "chick lit" (difference) or fight for a piece of the sci-fi market (equality)? Acknowledging this recurrent divide need not blind us to other divisions among women, nor does it doom us to infighting. Rather, as Ann Snitow's overview of equality-difference concludes, "The electricity of its internal disagreements is part of feminism's continuing power to shock and involve large numbers of people in public conversation."[27] Let us hope the divergent views in this essay will be a spur to that conversation.

Notes

1 For a thorough consideration of the equality-difference split (and related oppositions within feminist thinking) see Ann Snitow, "A Gender Diary," in *Conflicts in Feminism*, ed. Marianne Hirsch and Evelyn Fox Keller (New York: Routledge, 1990), 9–43. Snitow sees these not as mutually exclusive positions but as tendencies crisscrossing one another; most women, she suggests, "live in a complex relation to this central feminist divide" (9).

2 For the founding text of intersectional analysis, see Kimberlé Crenshaw, "Mapping the Margins: Intersectionality, Identity Politics, and Violence Against Women of Color," *Stanford Law Review* 43, no. 6 (1991):): 1241–99. For models of identity complicating a single focus on gender, see Susan Stanford Friedman, "'Beyond' Gender: The New Geography of Identity and the Future of Feminist Criticism," in *Mappings: Feminism and the Cultural Geographies of Encounter* (Princeton: Princeton University Press, 1998), 17–35.

3 On repetition as a defining characteristic of everyday life, see especially Rita Felski, "The Invention of Everyday Life," in *Doing Time: Feminist Theory and Postmodern Culture* (New York: New York University Press, 2000), 81–5; and Ben Highmore, "Homework: Routine, Social Aesthetics and the Ambiguity of Everyday Life," *Cultural Studies* 18, no. 2/3 (2004): 322–25. Citing Henri Lefebvre on everyday time as cyclical, Felski goes on to note the association of repetition with women, to see its negative valence as distinctively modern, to defend the value of routine, and to question the usual opposition between repetition and innovation. Highmore also invokes Lefebvre to claim cyclical, bodily rhythms; as Highmore explains, these are not erased by but continue to influence and limit the linear routines dictated by modernity. Felski and Highmore have both been key to my own understanding of this and other aspects of the everyday.

4 Michel de Certeau, *The Practice of Everyday Life*, trans. Steven Rendall (Berkeley: University of California Press), xiv, xix. Certeau's reference is to Michel Foucault, *Discipline and Punish: The Birth of the Prison*, trans. Alan Sheridan (New York: Vintage Books, 1995), 26. Whereas Foucault theorizes "a micro-physics

of power," effected via "dispositions, manoeuvres, tactics, techniques, functionings" operating within a "network of relations," Certeau will extend/counter this view with his notion of *oppositional* tactics, noting that "many everyday practices (talking, reading, moving about, shopping, cooking, etc.) are tactical in character. And so are, more generally, many 'ways of operating': victories of the 'weak' over the 'strong' (whether the strength be that of powerful people or the violence of things or of an imposed order, etc.)."

5 Highmore, "Homework," 308.

6 See Erving Goffman's *The Presentation of Self in Everyday Life* (Harmondsworth: Penguin, 1959) on hotel staff in the Shetland Islands, excerpted as "Front and Back Regions of Everyday Life," in *The Everyday Life Reader*, ed. Ben Highmore (London: Routledge, 2002), 50–7. Illustrating what Goffman sees as shifts in decorum and self-presentation according to social context, workers conform to mainstream mores in front of guests, while reverting to "island" manners in such "backstage" regions as the kitchen. On photos of black British immigrants, newly arrived from the Caribbean, see Stuart Hall, "Reconstruction Work: Images of Post War Black Settlement" (1984), in *The Everyday Life Reader*, 251–61. For Hall, jauntily angled hats and stylish dress suggest the swagger, determination, and innocence of people in transition to a cold climate and unfamiliar culture.

7 Henri Lefebvre, *Everyday Life in the Modern World* (New York: Transaction, 1984), 73; George Eliot, *Adam Bede* (New York: Penguin Books, 1980), 223, 224.

8 Rita Felski, "Introduction: Special Issue on Everyday Life," *New Literary History* 33, no. 4 (2002), 612–13, 609–10.

9 Noting that women are the principal "subjects" and "victims" of everyday life, Lefebvre opines that "because of their ambiguous position . . . they are incapable of understanding it." Lefebvre, *Everyday Life in the Modern World*, 73.

10 Lorraine Sim, "Theorising the Everyday," *Australian Feminist Studies* 30, no. 84 (2015), 110–15. Exceptions include, of course, several important feminist commentaries. In addition to Sim, I have already had occasion to mention two essays by Felski, "The Invention of Everyday Life"; Introduction; an earlier precedent is the review-essay by Laurie Langbauer, "Cultural Studies and the Politics of the Everyday," *diacritics* 22, no. 1 (1992); 47–65. As Sim acknowledges, Highmore's *The Everyday Life Reader* includes a sizeable number of women; one of them is Giard, who goes on to play a prominent role in Highmore's "Homework"; Michael Sheringham's *Everyday Life: Theories and Practices from Surrealism to the Present* (Oxford: Oxford University Press, 2006) also devotes a subsection to Giard in a chapter on Certeau (237–47).

11 English and US women would gain the franchise in 1918 and 1920, respectively; French women would wait for the vote until 1944, just five years before Beauvoir published *Le Deuzième Sexe*.

12 Simone de Beauvoir, *The Second Sex*, ed. and trans. by H. M. Parshley (New York: Knopf, 1952); Simone de Beauvoir, *The Second Sex*, trans. by Constance Borde and Sheila Malovany-Chevallier (New York: Vintage Books, 2011). The Parshley edition was criticized primarily for its radical abridgment (made at the request of publisher Alfred Knopf and omitting as much as 15% of the original text); for translations that garbled or ignored Beauvoir's engagement with specific philosophical concepts and conversations; and for translations that misconstrued her analysis of gender. The result was to diminish her importance as a philosopher while also muddying the significance of her work for subsequent feminist theorists. Key essays on the failures of the Parshley edition are Margaret A. Simons, "The Silencing of Simone de Beauvoir: Guess What's Missing from *The Second Sex*," *Women's Studies International Forum* 6, no. 5 (1983): 559–64; and Toril Moi, "While We Wait: The English Translation of *The Second Sex*," *Signs* 27, no. 4 (2002): 1005–35. Ironically, the Borde and Malovany-Chevallier translation would be controversial in its own right, with Moi once again vociferous in her criticism. See Toril Moi, "The Adulteress Wife," *The London Review of Books* 32, no. 3 (February 11, 2010): 3–6, for her scathing (and much debated) review.

13 Toril Moi, *What Is a Woman? And Other Essays* (Oxford: Oxford University Press, 1999), 177.

14 Simone de Beauvoir, *The Second Sex*, trans. by Borde and Malovany-Chevallier, 283; hereafter abbreviated "*SS*."

15 Almost all of these were omitted by the Parshley edition, and the resulting text is both harsher in tone and less nuanced in its argument than that restored by Borde and Malovany-Chevallier. I might note that the overall effect of such omissions was to attenuate Beauvoir's participation not only in larger philosophical conversations but also in literary ones. On Parshley's deep cuts to this particular section, see Moi, "While We Wait," 1009–11.

16 The opposition between "transcendence" and "immanence" is central to existentialist philosophy. On the role of this dichotomy in Beauvoir's feminist critique of housekeeping, see Andrea Veltman, "The

Sisyphean Torture of Housework: Simone de Beauvoir and Inequitable Divisions of Domestic Work in Marriage," *Hypatia* 19, no. 3 (2004): 121–43, which brings Beauvoir's existentialist ethics to bear on women's continuing oppression by housework today, whether as exclusive duty or as "second shift."

17 In her 1960 autobiography, Beauvoir recalls having shared with Sartre precisely this belief. To them, the victims embodied "the sort of woman who would deduct the price of a broken plate from her maid's wages, and wear white gloves to hunt down the least grain of forgotten dust on the furniture: in our eyes such creatures deserved the death penalty a hundred times over." Note that "deserving the death penalty" goes beyond blaming the victims to putting *them* on trial. Later conceding the sisters' insanity, the philosophers would modify their view of the sisters as class revolutionaries, and Beauvoir now readily admits, "We were therefore wrong in regarding their excesses as being due to the hand of rough justice"; see Simone de Beauvoir, *The Prime of Life*, trans. by Peter Green (Middlesex: Penguin Books, 1965), 130, 131. Yet as we have seen, Beauvoir continued as late as 1949 to invoke the Papin sisters by way of vilifying the housewife.

18 On images of female confinement as a hallmark of women's writing in the 19th century, see Sandra Gilbert and Susan Gubar's classic study, *The Madwoman in the Attic: The Woman Writer and the Nineteenth-Century Literary Imagination* (New Haven: Yale University Press, 1979). The eponymous madwoman is Brontë's Bertha Mason, whose domestic prison offered a succinct trope for the plight of Victorian women. Gilman would not only echo this trope in "The Yellow Wallpaper" (1892) but also offer an antidote in non-fiction works proposing communal living and collective responsibility for cooking.

19 Toward the end of her book, Beauvoir treats three types of women who justify rather than change their oppressive circumstances: the narcissist, the woman in love, and the mystic. All represent ineffective strategies and inauthentic lives, and all are overdrawn in the manner of the maniacal housewife. The list of three, each headed by a definite article, suggests a quasi-scientific taxonomy, if not a set of archetypal figures. Meryl Altman, "Simone de Beauvoir and Lesbian Lived Experience," *Feminist Studies* 33, no. 1 (2007), 212, memorably describes such incongruous, essentialist elements as recurrent features of Beauvoir's constructionist text: "Many chapters and arguments in *The Second Sex* take the form of a sandwich, with problematically essentialist or essentializing filling enclosed between slices of social constructionist bread."

20 Mistresses do, of course, help to maintain class hierarchy in the workplace of the home, and it is part of Beauvoir's existentialist project to hold women accountable for failing to own their freedom. There is, however, a difference between noting female complicity of various kinds and positively demonizing the housewife. What I find more than once in this text is a slippage between viewing women as *complicit* and viewing them, far more punitively, as *guilty* (see note 17).

21 In Sonia Kruks's helpful overview of Beauvoir's shifting reception over the years, she lists a number of complaints voiced by 1980s feminist theorists, almost all of which resonate with my own reading. These include the tension between moments of essentialism and constructionism; the contradiction between seeing women as helpless and seeing them as responsible; the misogyny implicit in Beauvoir's "contempt for most women's lives"; and the promotion of "masculinist values as the norm to which women should aspire" – in particular, the norm of freely acting, autonomous selfhood; Sonia Kruks, "Beauvoir's Time/Our Time: The Renaissance in Simone de Beauvoir Studies," *Feminist Studies* 31, no. 2 (2005), 287–88. Kruks goes on to describe the "renaissance" in Beauvoir studies beginning in the 1990s, making available a wide range of more favorable views. These have been particularly illuminating on Beauvoir's philosophical influences and innovations but do not, in my opinion, wholly invalidate earlier critiques.

22 Susan Fraiman, *Extreme Domesticity: A View From the Margins* (New York: Columbia University Press, 2017).

23 Take, for example, the gestures involved in establishing privacy and storing possessions. Often linked only to gated communities and walk-in closets, security for one's person and things takes on an entirely different meaning and urgency in the context of homelessness; for those in makeshift quarters, setting up domestic boundaries offers protection from assault and theft as well as from well-meant interference.

24 Michel de Certeau, Luce Giard, and Pierre Mayol, *The Practice of Everyday Life, Volume 2: Living and Cooking*, trans. Timothy J. Tomasik (Minneapolis: University of Minnesota Press, 1998); hereafter abbreviated "*LC*." See note 10 for the handful of exceptional critics referencing Giard. She is nevertheless so unheralded that online searches net little biographical information apart from her collaboration with and commemoration of Certeau; even her birth date has eluded me.

25 Timothy J. Tomasik, eventual translator of volume 2, takes this rationale at face value, attributing the particular difficulty of translating Giard to the French concept of *terroir* (whose meaning he broadens to

include "discursive *terroir*," the regional specificity of texts as well as food). In addition to his translator's note, see Timothy J. Tomasik, "Certeau à la Carte: Translating Discursive *Terroir* in *The Practice of Everyday Life: Living and Cooking*," *South Atlantic Quarterly* 100, no. 2 (2001): 519–42.

26 Certeau, *The Practice of Everyday Life*, xix, cites shopping and cooking as examples of everyday practices that are "tactical in character" (see note 4). See also Daniel Miller, *A Theory of Shopping*, excerpted as "Making Love in Supermarkets" in *The Everyday Life Reader*, ed. Ben Highmore (London: Routledge, 2002), 342, on women's shopping for their families as "primarily an act of love, that in its daily conscientiousness becomes one of the primary means by which relationships of love and care are constituted by practice."

27 Snitow, "A Gender Diary," 30.

8

Making culture and doing feminism

Carrie Rentschler

> This book is an action. It was conceived, written, edited, copy-edited, proofread, designed, and illustrated by women.
>
> —*Robin Morgan (1970, xiii)*

Debates about the contemporary status of feminism have often centered around issues of whether, if, and how individuals identify as feminists. Toril Moi warned in 2006 that "we are witnessing the emergence of a whole new generation of women who are careful to preface every gender-related claim that just might come across as unconventional with 'I am not feminist, but . . .'" (1736). Moi and others mourned what they saw as a generational dis-identification with feminism among individuals born in the 1980s. And yet feminist print materials, mix tapes, cyber-feminist work, and female-centered music subcultures proliferated over the 1990s and 2000s – an era identified with what Ednie Kaeh Garrison (2000) called the "networked and tactical subjectivities" of DIY third-wave feminism.[1]

As social movement scholars suggest, young women's resistance to identify as feminist "reveals a disconnection between . . . 'doing activism' and 'being activist'" (Bobel 2007, 148). Chris Bobel's research suggests that "one can 'do activism' without 'being activist,'" creating "a more complicated picture of identity at the center of social movements" (2007, 140). Doing feminism and self-identifying as feminist, then, may not necessarily be coextensive or even desirable in some cases. Bobel's research demonstrates how the high expectations for what it means to be an activist in movement communities dissuades some people from identifying as one. In turn, some feminist scholarship increasingly prioritizes the question of what it means to do feminism over that of what it means to be feminist (see Keller, Mendes, and Ringrose 2016 for one example of recent work), including my own.

This chapter examines recent studies of contemporary feminism as something one does and performs via practices of making. It begins from the presumption that doing feminism and being feminist are not the same thing. I bracket the latter in order to analyze how feminist scholars conceptualize contemporary feminisms as ways of doing things in the process of making culture. This chapter draws a distinction between feminist doing and feminist activism to suggest that making feminism is not necessarily a form of activism, at least not explicitly so. Feminist making, however, may transform notions of feminist activism. But in order to conceive of feminist making *as* activism, activism itself must also be substantially redefined in the process. If we look to 1960s models of protest cultures in practices of contemporary feminist making, Alison Piepmeier suggests we will be disappointed in things like third-wave feminist zines (2009, 160). But if we "come with different expectations of what political work and activism look like," if we can recognize other ways people become politicized via "modelling [feminist] process, active criticism, and imagination," (160) we can identify other relationships between making and doing feminism. In her own work, Piepmeier urges us to ask the question of what zines do in order to figure out the political work of which they might be a part (2009, 158).

I take up Piepmeier's suggestion in order to examine how the doing of feminism has been identified with cultures of making. I further conceptualize the relationship between feminist making and the recognition of that work as ways of doing feminism, examining how this relationship can value productivity and instrumentality in ways that also work against some feminist aims (see, e.g., Gajjala 2013). I define the relationship between making and doing feminism as the work of formulating, designing and creating media, technology, and other artifacts that both represents, and constitutes, what it is to practice feminism within, and as, sites of struggle. I examine how a core set of feminist texts – and texts approximate to feminism – articulate the relationship between feminist making and doing feminism in order to analyze how feminist scholarship conceives of personal and social transformation around the processes of transforming digital and other materials.

Today, feminists overwhelmingly locate the signs of social transformation in the transformation of material objects, as forms of making that register social change in particular communicative acts and their instruments of creation. When pundits say feminism is dead (see, e.g., Pozner 2003), feminists point to recorded and documented feminist practices that provide evidence otherwise; I include my own work here and the analysis I have done on feminist hashtag activism (Rentschler 2014a, 2014b, 2017). Hashtags become online aggregators of feminist expression and key spaces of feminist consciousness-raising (Gunn 2015; Kennedy 2007). Animated GIFs become moving picture carriers of political emotion (Miltner and Highfield 2017). YouTube videos become platforms of activist pedagogy. And zines become key tools of feminism by sustaining "the physical reality of protests, revolutions, and political expressions such as the Occupy Movement(s)" (Weida 2013). Media practices like these articulate feminism as a set of what Red Chidgey (and others) refer to as "do-it-together" acts of creation, aggregation, transmission/distribution, affective propagation, consciousness-raising, and teaching (see Chidgey 2013, 2015).

Rather than a study of these practices, this chapter analyzes how scholars and self-identified makers conceptualize the relationship between making cultural artifacts and doing feminism, where making trumps acts of consumption and revalues processes of production; where process is valued more than the artifacts that are made; and where ongoing inequalities and structures of oppression still value "maker" labor over the labors of caring, supporting, repairing, maintaining, and fixing things, and even consuming, all of which are inextricably tied to cultures of making digital culture and material craft culture (see, e.g., Duffy 2015; Jarrett 2014, 2016). Girl studies scholarship has long attended to girls' media making practices in order to carve out a conception of girls as makers and cultural producers, to disarticulate those durable ideological links between femininity and pop cultural consumption as signs of female passivity. When girls make things, as Anita Harris argues, it "signif[ies] a desire to be a cultural producer, that is, to actively engage in the construction of one's cultural world, rather than simply consume" (Harris 2008, 221).

In light of the large corpus of material on cultures of making and feminism, this chapter offers only a partial review of the literatures; it also analyzes a limited scope of feminist making around those literatures that have most explicitly, and extendedly, examined the relationship between making and doing feminism. It pays particular attention to texts that circulate around and about feminist making, maker culture, and crafting as practices of contemporary feminism, where making is understood as a way of doing feminism. In the process, this work often defines contemporary feminism around particular practices, and kinds, of cultural fabrication. As a result, other feminist practices often become less visible in the process, especially when they are not as easily represented in artifactual form.

This chapter tacks back and forth between discussion of feminist media making and feminist making more generally, referring to the latter when ideas of feminist making transcend the particular artifacts of feminist media and technology. I refer to feminist making to conceptualize feminism as forms of techné, a diverse set of processes people engage through digital and other tools of making in order to do feminism in certain ways (see Rentschler and Thrift 2015a; see also Balsamo 2011; Murphy 2012). The texts I draw from include work on zine making, meme propagation, hashtags, textile crafting, and, less centrally, music making. A significant body of scholarly work about making and doing feminism examines zine culture and the forms of feminism identified with third-wave practice over the 1990s and 2000s. Zines have been extensively studied as artifacts of feminist making, and they have thus been centered in feminist scholarship on gender and media making. This chapter draws most heavily on this body of work for its analysis of how feminist scholarship approaches the relationship between making and doing feminism. I do not, however, hold zines up as the *ur*-example of feminist making. Other texts explore blogging and social media making as practices of doing feminism. This is also the body of work in which feminists of color and anti-capitalist feminists address the significant issues of labor, employment, and attributions of authorship that structure practices of feminist making in relationship to media cultures and their industries. Rather than see participation in media making "as an obvious good," these authors illustrate how imperatives to participate "compel more work from any participants in online culture" (Driscoll and Gregg 2011, 567), reproducing deep inequalities that undergird calls to "be creative" for no money. How that work gets attributed and compensated also reveals racial, class, and gender relations of power within feminist movements and beyond them.

I also refer to a "we" in this chapter to locate myself within the field of scholarship on feminist media and making. Many of the texts examined here articulate acts of feminist making with the act of creating a "we," a set of feminist attachments that, as Sara Ahmed says, can connect "the 'we' with the 'I,' the feminist subject with the feminist collective" (2004, 188). This "weness" approaches feminist making as an often collaborative and network-based set of practices emerging from relations between friends, family members, colleagues, mentors, students, fellow activists, and other makers. This work is often done with other people, but at other times it is very consciously done alone, as musicians know all too well when it comes to practicing. The "we" is also an exclusive and excluding pronoun. In recognition of this, the chapter critiques how some forms of feminist making and some makers are overlooked, underrecognized, and often undercompensated and exploited in the process of their making. That the contributions by women of color, particularly around social media feminisms, are often not attributed, not cited, used non-consensually, and are often un- and undercompensated suggests that feminist making and doing is also tied to institutionalized forms of racial, colonial, and class exploitation (see, e.g., Nakamura 2014).

What is meant by doing feminism and what kinds of activities come to represent it, then, reveal some of the hierarchies of value and the unequal and uneven distributions of recognition and credit that certain forms of making, and certain makers, garner. This usually breaks down into valuations of men makers over women, and white women producers and makers over women of color. Additionally, when making becomes evidence for "actually existing feminism," forms of practice that are less overtly tied to the creation of material works – and some kinds of material works – become less visible and count less readily as proof of feminist process and practice. Some practices of making, for instance, may seem more concrete and "empirical" than the work of organizing, where the latter can be more difficult to materialize in objects and other made things, particularly in the form of things that are recognized as having artifactual value.

This chapter turns first to feminist articulations of what it means to make media and other things as feminists, to understand how making is understood as a feminist practice, a way of transforming the world in feminist terms in the process of fabricating objects. As I argue, making comes to matter because it embodies the physical transformation of things as simultaneously the social transformation of those who make them (see, e.g., Fotopoulou 2016). Theories of craft are central to this discussion as socially binding and embodied practices of making with others. I then turn to analysis of the gendering of makers in maker culture discourse and the ways feminist scholars reinterpret maker subjects in feminist terms around the feminist labors of physical making and craft and the labors of care, support, and pedagogy of which they are a part. At the same time, feminist maker discourse must grapple with contemporary realities of precarious and increasingly freelance-based employment in media, design, and other industries. I turn to the work of anti-capitalist feminists and feminists of color who most readily address the conditions of uncompensated creative and social media labor within these conversations. Using a framework on feminist labor, the last section of the chapter argues for a shift from ideas of feminist making back to talk of doing feminism to examine what forms of feminist action get left out of the recent focus on feminist making. I also suggest that a theory of articulation is needed in order to analyze whether and how the doing of feminist making connects to the doing of feminist activism in contemporary feminisms.

What is feminist making?

Feminists look to the ways people use and make media (and other objects and artifacts) in order to understand how they imagine (and do) social change in feminist terms. Feminist artifacts serve as evidence for the existence of feminism and its cultural labors, for the ways people "put their outrage into order" in the process of making, collecting, and archiving feminist materials (see Eichhorn 2013, 157; see also Piepmeier 2009; Rentschler 2017). Scholars study feminist artifacts in part to get at the cultures of production in which they are made and, in turn, to account for the experiences of co-making things that shape feminist consciousness, fellow feeling, and feminist knowledge. Scholars and makers alike approach cultures of production as the spaces in which people create and enact feminist processes out of which feminist materials are made. Much of the emphasis on feminist making rests on the ways collective practices of fabrication can build community and politicize people. What it means to "do feminism" and to "make feminist things," then, are closely linked.

In a lot of contemporary work on the subject of feminist making, making matters because of the roles it plays in establishing shared epistemologies, building collective consciousness, building community, and, in turn, ideally creating relationships of transformative solidarity. Maker work represents "epistemologies of doing" – ways of knowing the world by engaging in practices of making (see Gajjala, Rybas and Altman 2007). To do feminism, in this perspective, means both making things *as feminists* (through feminist processes engaged by feminist makers, or whose making associates makers with feminism) and making feminist *things* (e.g., feminist works). Making things as feminists refers to the feminist processes people engage in acts of fabrication. Feminist making, in other words, may or may not be done by self-identified feminist makers. The feminist content of their making is also not determined by whether or not makers are self-identified feminists. As I suggest, it is instead the work and the processes of making – the "feminist protocols," if you will (see Murphy 2012) – that shape feminist articulations of making and maker culture in terms more clearly identified with what it means to do feminism. Such protocols suggest, as well, that making can create conditions and sets of processes through which some people come to identify as and with feminisms. Making feminist things refers to both feminist processes and material feminist works – a feminist version of Hannah Arendt's (1958) sense of "homo faber" as the maker of public works in *The Human Condition*.[2]

Anna Feigenbaum, for instance, argues in her analysis of the Greenham Common Women's anti-nuclear peace encampment in the UK that "women's cultural artifacts and communication practices were the very means by which their politics garnered shape and meaning" (Feigenbaum 2013, 2). Activist artifacts such as songbooks, newsletters, and handicrafts embodied qualities of the politicizing labor that produced them, becoming carriers of activist thought and action. For Feigenbaum and others, making creates conditions in which people come to consciousness and can enact collective action, which Greenham women did by blockading the missile base, camping on the land around it, and cutting the fence, among other things. They were activists who came together and then made things collectively, the latter of which helped sustain their collective protest. Other artifacts, such as the lesbian feminist newsletters Cait McKinney (2015) analyzes from the 1970s, served to network otherwise disparate lesbian feminist researchers, activists, and writers in order to do the work of creating lesbian feminist histories. The network thinking and practice of newsletter producers represented "a critical idealism" that could "facilitate other kinds of collectivities from which to work collaboratively" (2015, 314) long before the internet.

In linking "doing feminism" and "making media," feminist scholars define what it is to do feminism in particular ways, in particular places, by particular subjects, and in particular struggles – some of which are internal to feminist movements. In the process, a certain set of practices easily come to define and stand in for feminism on a broader scale. Many feminist scholars are especially interested in the work of amateur makers rather than professionals. They often study forms of making identified with the "space of the amateur," in girls' bedrooms, home-based and school workshops, explicit maker spaces, or on easy-to-use mobile apps and other tools of mostly non-professional, non-compensated making (see Bratich and Brush 2011, 252; see also McRobbie and Garber 1991/1978; Kearney 2006).

One standout book, Alison Piepmeier's (2009) *Girl Zines: Making Media, Doing Feminism*, directly articulates this relationship by showing how grrrl zines document as well as make manifest third-wave feminisms, "becoming the mechanism that third wave feminists use to articulate theory and build community" (9). Her work and a larger body of scholarship in media studies of girls, sexuality, and feminism examines how (primarily) female-identified subjects make and re-make media and technologies as part of the process of doing feminism, and, for some, queering their lives (see, e.g., Driver 2007; Gray 2009). Other feminist scholarship is also directly titled around this conjuncture, including Mary Celeste-Kearney's (2006) *Girls Make Media*; Leslie Drake and Jennifer Heywood's (1997) edited collection, *Third Wave Agenda: Being Feminist, Doing Feminism*; and Elizabeth Groeneveld's (2016) *Making Feminist Media* on feminist print culture and third-wave feminism. From black feminist perspectives, online cultures of making and documentation speak to some of the contemporary practices of doing black feminism around the experience of women of color. As Suey Park and David Leonard assert:

> Viral black feminism has thus emerged as a powerful tool in spotlighting the injustices endured and the injustices that contributed to the illegibility of black female pain. It has become a space to theorize, articulate, and document a twenty first-century black feminism,

> one that remains focused on antiblack racism, persistent patriarchy, intersectionality, and reconceptualizing spaces of resistance to both hear and see black women's voices and experiences.
>
> *(2016, 210)*

How people do feminism emerges directly from lived experiences and the ways they organize around it. What doing feminism means and is depends not only on who is doing it and where, but also on what kinds of feminist work must be done in order to nurture one's political subjectivity in different conditions of intersecting oppressions and privileges, including relationships of domination within feminism, and by white feminism in particular. We see in different forms of feminist making different kinds of feminism, and different lived feminist realities. The action of doing feminism by making and distributing things through networks defines a number of contemporary feminisms, and relationships of power within feminist movements, over the past 20+ years.

In the preface to *Sisterhood Is Powerful*, Robin Morgan declared: "This book is an action. It was conceived, written, edited, copy-edited, proofread, designed, and illustrated by women" (1970, xiii). Morgan intimately links the doing of feminism to material and symbolic transformations of the world through practices of making (see also Rentschler and Thrift 2015a), as well as other forms of labor less represented by physical "works." She acknowledges the various labors that went into making the anthology and the people who worked on the project. She also goes a step further to conceptualize their work together as a form of feminist action (see Harker and Farr 2016), a struggle the various makers of *Sisterhood Is Powerful* differently addressed in the face of a number of barriers to its publication. These barriers included other forms of labor the books' feminist makers had to do in their lives over the course of the book's production, forms of labor tied to employment and social and familial care that are still too often not identified with the making and doing of feminism.

While not part of the book's production per se, Morgan recognized that women's other labors were connected to the labors of making the book, even as they necessarily slowed down the process of the book's publication. A book that offered feminist interpretations of some of the conditions of women's lives, then, became an opportunity to comment on the different forms of women's labor that go into, and happen alongside, that of book making. Morgan also suggested that before we look to the effects of media making and social responses to them for signs of their action in the world, we should first recognize action as something that is already constituted in feminist making. In this view, feminist cultural production is always already a form of action in the context of the other work women-identified people do (see also Gumbs 2008).

In contemporary maker discourse, making represents one of the key ways in which the action of fabrication reveals action – or doing – more generally. Yet making is but one part of the definition of doing; it is a *kind* of doing, "to produce (a material thing) through the combination of parts, or by giving a certain form to a portion of matter, to manufacture; to construct, assemble, frame, fashion," according to the Oxford English Dictionary. Among its more expansive meanings, the verb "to do" is defined as an action carried out onto or with a noun or pronoun. To do is "to perform, execute, achieve, carry out, effect, [or] bring to pass" something; it can also be "to produce, *make*, bring into existence" (emphasis added). Definitions of doing resonate with a range of reproductive and social labors as well as notions of "productive labor" tied to capitalism, such as bringing new life into existence, bringing a ritual to pass, performing care, and making things for oneself and others.

The low-power radio activists Christina Dunbar-Hester studied, for example, "vested DIY with emancipatory goals, believing if people 'can look under the hood,' take something apart, break it and repair it, this will have an effect on how agents understand themselves in society" (2017, 200). In their efforts to empower more women to work in radio and do the technological work of building low-power stations, activists saw technical know-how as "tools for social action" where "technical affinity was hailed as a potential way to reconfigure established patterns of masculinity and femininity" (Dunbar-Hester 2014, 55). While their attempts to reconfigure gender relations around radio activism often failed, activists' practice of making low-power radio technology was nonetheless understood as one of the main avenues for creating that change. Their do-it-yourself ethos represented "a mode of technical and political decision-making that rests on technological empowerment" (Dunbar-Hester 2017, 189). In this framework, making signifies a transfer of technical know-how via peer-to-peer education and co-working in the form of organized low-power radio barn-raisings and skill share workshops. Making does the work of consciousness-raising through the fabrication and soldering of electrical connections and the assembling of transmitters.

Across different maker-identified cultural practices, making is often understood to help people think critically and become more conscious. Matt Ratto (2011) coined the term "critical making" to capture the particular activist pedagogical mind-set of maker-based learning, where making is associated with critical changes of experiential and cognitive states, or what Garnet Hertz calls "the productive aspects of hands-on thinking through technology" (2015, 13). Notions of craft are central to this way of thinking about making as critical pedagogy. Richard Sennett, for instance, approaches craft work as "engaged material consciousness," the process of knowing by making in which understanding cannot be separated from doing (2008, 120). Makers, he suggests, "become particularly interested in things we can change" through processes of fabrication and other material transformations (120). For Sennett, craft work is highly experiential, constituting both states of feeling and ways of doing and enacting skill that shape this engaged material consciousness. His definition of craft retains the aesthetic, embodied, and deeply personal aspects of feeling that are bound up with know-how and the experience of making things.

While Sennett is less concerned with understanding craft as an essential element of activism, for Jack Bratich and Heidi Brush (2011) the work of doing crafts represents "the ability or capacity to act" and "a way of understanding current political possibilities" (234) in the context of social change. For them, crafting *crafts* the capacity to do feminism. Similarly, as Alison Piepmeier observes in her analysis of feminist zine culture, "materiality enables a special kind of community" where "the tangible object transforms an imagined relationship into an embodied one" (2009, 82). Bratich and Brush analyze the relationship between craft and activism through the lens of "fabriculture," the ways in which making concretizes political belief via gendered forms of making (2011, 246). Not only a representational medium, then, craft work can create binding practices that link structures of feeling to embodied ideologies and affective affinities. It "fastens the concrete and the abstract into a material symbol," which, as they suggest, "encourages us to think media outside of its representational quality, in its binding capacities, subjectivation processes, and social value" (Bratich and Brush 2011, 246).

For them, craft represents a "resurgent technology" that, in the process of making things, also makes social relationships. These relationships can be, but are not necessarily, politicized in the process. Bratich and Brush draw on articulation theory to argue that making connects embodied practice and political belief. As Stuart Hall put it, articulation is "a linkage which is not necessary, determined, absolute and essential for all time" (1986, 53; cited in Slack 1996, 115). To study how articulation works requires examination of "the mechanisms which connect dissimilar features" (Hall 1980, 325, cited in Slack 1996, 115). A key theoretical and methodological concept in cultural studies, articulation represents "a process of creating connections" (Slack 1996, 114), which in the context of maker cultures is often laid bare via the social processes of building and combining material things.

The capacity to make is therefore understood as a capacity to create change that is performed in concrete acts of making. The visibility, tactility, audibility, and otherwise experiential, sensorial characteristics of concrete making compellingly materializes the doing of feminism – not unlike a scientific demonstration aims to prove a theoretical hypothesis. Making demonstrates feminism is happening, is being done, in the process of materially fabricating culture. It concretes feminism in digital and other material forms. If we are not participants in the making, we may not witness the making being done, but we can pay witness to and lay hands on feminist works and materials as concrete embodiments of doing feminism.

This argument echoes David Gauntlett's (2011) celebratory thesis in *Making Is Connecting*, where the material creation of things builds social relationships around the capacity to *do* things. Capacities, however, represent potentials to act; they do not guarantee action. Additionally, craft is a contextualized set of practices that can, but does not necessarily, make connections between embodied making, political belief, and social action. In this way, craft and other kinds of making may materialize these connections in ways that are readily visible and audible, or it may not.

In our analysis of the 2012 Binders Full of Women (BFW) meme, Samantha Thrift and I approach making memes as a praxis of doing feminism which compares to other kinds of craft culture (2015b, 348). We argued that feminist meme propagators "do feminist cultural production in meme form 'as itself the medium of action'" (Rentschler and Thrift 2015b, 340), a mode of consciousness-raising via digital and physical making that breaks down online/offline distinctions of doing. By examining how some propagators made Halloween costumes as iterations of the BFW meme, we analyzed their practice as visceral forms of physical co-production, ways of physically doing feminism together that evidence a practice much more closely associated with making: sewing. Memes are not only craft-like, they *are* craft that inspires other kinds of making. In dialog with other feminist scholars and folks in meme studies, we argued that humor and having fun fuel memes as feminist community-building media (see, e.g., Reilly 2015; Miltner and Highfield 2017; Zuckerman 2014; Shifman 2015).

Not everyone likes memes, cares about their aesthetics and use, or "gets" them, though that breaks my heart a bit. But the same could be said for other crafts that constitute feminist making: they may not be to everyone's aesthetic. For some, the handmade quality of a feminist-made thing – let's say a zine or other do-it-yourself lo-fi cultural practice – bears heavily on its value (see Spencer 2005). As Piepmeier argued in *Girl Zines*, the intimate connections people can form with others through the materiality of the made objects determines their value, rather than aesthetic judgments over whether something is, say, beautiful. Zines, for instance, "leverage their materiality into a kind of surrogate physical interaction and offer mechanisms for creating meaningful relationships" (2009, 59). The development of feminist processes and forms of experience that can be felt via the embodied community of something like feminist zine cultures take more precedence than other kinds of aesthetic qualities zines may possess. Making matters to feminism because of the role it can play in consciousness-raising and the creation of felt collectivity, both of which can be located in processes of materialized making and the creation of digital artifacts.

Feminist making connects the labors of making things online with the labors of female craft culture, linking the technical practices of online communication and coding with the technical and creative know-how of traditional (read "feminine") arts and craft work.[3] As two zinesters explained to Red Chidgey, feminist making draws on longer feminist histories of "a politic that connects not just the personal to the political, but the critical to the creative" (Hoffman and Yudacufski quoted in Chidgey 2015, 105). Making things matters because it creates conditions in which people work together. And in working together, they articulate and address shared grievances and develop responses to collective problems (see Rosner and Fox 2016). In this framework, collectivity emerges out of doing things together, creating some of the conditions for doing feminism as a group rather than as individuals (see Bratich and Brush 2011, 234; see also Toupin 2014; Chidgey 2015; Henry 2014). In articulating these relations, feminists explicitly reclaim maker identities and women's craft cultures as valuable gendered forms of techné in a maker culture context that still overly identifies makers as male.

Women as makers: gendered individuation, paid work, and feminist labor in making

Who is recognized as a maker is intimately related to gendered understandings of different kinds of technological labor, what forms of techné are seen as valuable, and which makers are even recognized as such (see, e.g., Aires 2015; Balsamo 2011; Chachra 2015). Most maker discourse presumes a model of making that is based in practices traditionally gendered male and tied to tool making. Mainstream maker culture still often undervalues technologies such as textiles and sewing implements, while circuit boards, soldering irons and other kinds of tools are more valued. And while key practices in, say, electronic music making by women have recoded the circuit board and the synthesizer as feminist technologies (see, e.g., Rodgers 2010, 2015), these technologies are still overwhelmingly understood as the purview of male musicians. In this context, feminist making struggles against male-identified maker cultures and its valuation of some kinds of techné over others (see Rosner and Fox 2016; Sayers 2015).

In this context, feminist scholars reclaim histories of women's craft cultures against the overly male-identified stories being told about maker cultures, male tech geeks, and hacker cultures (see, e.g., Bratich and Brush 2011; Powell 2012; Rosner and Fox 2016; Sayers 2014). As scholar and feminist hacker Sophie Toupin argues, "feminist technologists have explicitly taken up the discourse of making in direct response to the hegemonic masculinity of hacker culture" (2014; quoted in Nguyen, Toupin and Bardzell 2016, n.p.), what Christina Dunbar-Hester (2010) also characterizes as a culture of "dudecore." Against "dude" and "brogrammer" culture, with all of its gender hostilities toward women (Banet-Weiser and Miltner 2015), scholars and practitioners of feminist making assert that feminist techné is about "the possibility of transformation through socio-technical practice" (Nguyen, Toupin and Bardzell 2016, n.p.), the materialized conditions that can create connections between embodied practice, political belief, and community formation. Rather than "reify the creation of new artifacts," feminist hacking, for instance, "presents itself primarily as a method for encounter and engagement," of doing feminism with others (Nguyen, Toupin and Bardzell 2016, n.p.; see also Haranalova 2014). Here a capacity to act collectively emerges from the combination of "intellectual inquiry, ethical enactment and socio-technical practices" that constitute feminist making (Nguyen, Toupin and Bardzell 2016).

As Evgeny Morozov explains, the maker movement is deeply imbedded with military money, corporate investments, and corporatized maker identities and cultures (see also Turner 2008). What makes it a movement is "the intellectual infrastructure that allows makers to reflect on what it means to be a maker" (Morozov 2014, n.p.) in terms that often ignore if not purposely discount issues of radically unequal and exploitative systems of employment. According to engineering professor Debbie Chachra, "Describing oneself as a maker – regardless of what one actually or mostly does – is a way of accruing to oneself the gendered, capitalist benefits of being a person who makes products" (Chachra 2015, n.p.).

Chachra identifies several problems with maker movement ideology, particularly the ways in which "the artifacts are important, the people are not" (2015, n.p.). What maker culture values is often male-identified, as histories of gender and technology more broadly have shown (e.g., Cowan 1988; Oldenziel 2002; Wajcman 2004). The cultural primacy of *making*, especially in tech culture – that it is intrinsically superior to not-making, to repair, analysis, and especially caregiving – is informed by the gendered history of who made things, and in particular, who made things that were shared with the world, not merely for hearth and home (Chachra 2015, n.p.; see also Bix 2009).

Relational forms of labor – "doing things for and with other people" – provide an alternative to that of homo faber's construction of public works. Chachra identifies this labor with "the barista, the Facebook community moderator" (who "keeps dick pics and beheadings out of your Facebook feed"; see Chen 2014), "the social worker," and "the surgeon" (2015, n.p.). For Chachra, teaching is a form of technological labor that is rarely recognized as such in the context of the maker movement. In feminist maker cultures, on the other hand, pedagogy and peer-to-peer learning take center stage. Feminist academic networks such as HASTAC, FEMTECHNET, and FEMBOT model this attention to pedagogy in their open access publishing, their support of digital and queer feminist digital humanities and tech cultures, and their innovations in online-distributed and collaborative courses on gender and technology.

Mainstream, mostly male-identified maker culture tends to bracket questions of labor and paid work in its approach to building knowledge. Making is generally approached as either an "exotic, specialized activity" that transforms individuals into critically conscious agents (Sengers 2015, 15), or as David Gauntlett describes, "an everyday form of creativity" that "creates something novel . . . in a process which evokes joy" (2011, 70). The former is based in cultures of expertise and the particular valuation of the maker in technology culture (see Chachra 2015). The latter appears most readily in amateur cultures of experimentation seemingly disconnected from cultures of work, employment, and often precarious labors. Gauntlett's reference to "sparking joy" echoes one of the key tests Japanese decluttering expert Marie Kondo (2014) suggests her clients use to decide whether a commodity in their lives is worth keeping. For Gauntlett and Kondo, then, the value of things is based in part on the affective response they can create in makers and users. This is an affective response not connected to collectivizing for social change, however. For Gauntlett, making creates good feelings in the context of capitalist systems.

Many feminists and anti-capitalists are highly skeptical of maker discourse because of its masculinism, its sexism, its investments in capitalist values of labor, and its affective commodity fetishism in addition to its masculinism and sexism. Most maker discourse also tends to elevate the individual freelancer as an ideal of neoliberal capitalist making. Questions of labor and paid work can distinguish feminist approaches to feminist making from other maker discourse if they account for the largely uncounted work and labor made invisible in these industries and platformed networks. They don't always do this work or see it as a priority.

Studies of feminist making draw from the ethos of do-it-yourself and do-it-together activities as well, and in these discussions making is also often separated from the work of supporting oneself. When scholars talk about feminists doing feminism in the process of making things, they are usually talking about people who do so voluntarily, in their free (or leisure) time, and without pay. This is important activity to account for, in part because it is not necessarily being done in order to create profits for others; it represents making for the pleasure of making. They often have in mind the hobbyist, the crafter, and the amateur who tinkers, where making is understood as different from what one does for a job. While we see in a lot of the feminist work I have discussed thus far a celebration of craft cultures and the revaluation of domestic arts like knitting, sewing, crocheting, macramé, and other textile and fabric arts, we find more attention to issues of labor and employment being addressed by scholars of color and those who study the links between gendered craft and industry.

Analysis of maker culture rarely links up to questions of paid and unpaid labor in the contexts of contemporary gig economies, underpaid and unpaid internships, freelance work, and other forms of precarious employment (see McRobbie 2015; Sengers 2015). Making is understood as "labor freely given," echoing the ways online labor and freelance economies rely on unpaid and underpaid workers who consent – in a coercive Gramscian sense – to do work for exposure or to get their name out there (see Duffy 2018; Terranova 2000; McRobbie 2015). As Garnet Hertz (2015) suggests too, the maker idealized in maker culture is often presumed to come from urban educated classes rather than those needing to make do or who fabricate things for a living.

Paid and unpaid work overlap in the world of craft and its histories of technology, exploiting the labors of indigenous women and women of color, often through outsourced labor operations. Tech industries have long depended on women's creative and craft labors for their design work and manufacturing. Lisa Nakamura's (2014) research on Navajo women's weaving examines how the intellectual property of their patterns was exploited in the design of silicon chips, while Cait McKinney's (forthcoming) research shows how the design of early punch card computers appropriated women's skills with knitting needles to explain how to use the machines. Key figures of maker culture will sometimes celebrate women's craft, for instance in books by Gauntlett (2011) and Sennett (2008; whose book is notably titled *The Craftsman*), while some practitioners trace genealogies of maker culture explicitly to women's craft in order to undermine the male dominance of the field (see Sayers 2014). These acknowledgments of women's craft labor rarely address the repetitiveness and injury that can arise from it (see McRobbie 2015), or what Marisol Sandoval (2015) calls the "hands and brains" doing dangerous manual labor to build the electronic materials making up digital culture's tools.

In some ways, feminist craft represents an effort to disrupt the fetishism of the commodity form, to return the sociality of making to the things being made. Some scholars and practitioners of feminist hacking, for instance, articulate anti-capitalist ways of collectivizing feminist maker cultures in direct response to male dominance in those spaces (see, e.g., Nguyen, Toupin and Bardzell 2016; Toupin 2014), drawing from longer histories of feminist protest actions that center collective making as processes of communal support and care, such as the Greenham Women's Peace Encampment (Feigenbaum 2015). Feminists also articulate making in terms that sometimes revalue women's reproductive and caring labors, and challenge the overemphasis on productive labor as making things to be sold (see, e.g., Sofia 2000; D'Ignazio et al. 2016; Haraway 1985).

But at the same time that craft and other forms of media making can express collective making, they are also forms of commerce that increasingly proliferate in contexts of neoliberal capitalism. Maker cultures do not circumvent the market; in fact, many individual makers actively seek out opportunities to merchandise and sell what they make, where the agency of making is directly tied to its commoditization. Women's craft work has witnessed a particular resurgence around online craft merchandising sites such as Etsy.com, where the unique and homemade stands out against the mass-produced and corporately branded. In this context, where a "neoliberal capitalist system [ ] has separated effort, affect and creativity from production . . . craft and DIY reappear as political acts, reclaiming the personal and communal" (Powell 2012, n.p.). Yet they do so in a thoroughly marketized and branded space that rarely accounts for conditions of work and employment, or poverty. As Angela McRobbie warns, those labors are also reappropriated into the new craft labor economies tied to the industries of fashion and design (see, e.g., McRobbie 2015; see also Duffy 2018). Understood as an "elite, affluent, leisure-time kind of activity," maker culture becomes something "that is very different from what poor people do with technology or in developing nations. It's removed from that and the politics of class and income" (Hertz 2015, 16).

The idea of making as a political act connects the entrepreneurial ideologies of maker space frameworks coming out of Silicon Valley to those notions of collective small-scale making coming out of histories of the counterculture – as Fred Turner's (2008) work has so aptly analyzed. Embodied by back-to-the-land New Communalists, members of the counterculture came to view social change as something one enacted through technology and the transformation of social consciousness rather than through political action (Turner 2008, 4). By "deploying small-scale technologies – ranging from axes and hoes to amplifiers, strobe lights, slide projectors, and LSD," small collectives through they could "bring people together and allow them to experience their common humanity" (4) in the form of communal living.

Alongside Turner's analysis of the countercultural roots to utopian thinking about cyberculture, Angela McRobbie "dissect[s] the incitement to 'be creative'" (McRobbie 2015, 17). Feminist makers are working in a context riven with economic uncertainties and precarities. The call to "be creative" is a pedagogical and an activist invitation to make the world around you by becoming a maker. That incitement to creativity can also become another form of social control within capitalist social relations – a way of valuing productivity over that of social care.

> Creativity becomes something inherent in personhood, which has the potential to be turned into a set of capacities. The resulting assemblage of "talent" can be subsequently unrolled in the labor market or "talent-led economy." The creativity *dispositif* comprises various instruments, guises, manuals, devices, toolkits, mentoring schemes, reports, TV programmes, and other forms of entertainment. I see these come together as a form of governmentality . . . with a wide population of young people in its embrace.
>
> *(McRobbie 2016, 15, emphasis in original)*

McRobbie further argues that the "imperative to 'be creative' . . . to discover one's own capabilities, to embark on a voyage of self-discovery" is "far removed from the hard facts of self-employment" (McRobbie 2015, 18). The relationship between making and doing feminism is therefore not divorced from the economic realities of increasingly freelance-based, precarious work in which many young people find themselves, many of whom work under conditions of what Brooke Erin Duffy calls "aspirational labour": "a mode of (mostly) uncompensated, independent work that is propelled by the much-venerated ideal of getting paid to do what you love," with the caveat that most people never end up getting paid (2018, 4).

Craft cultures and their markets come with no guarantees of political liberation or emancipation, for individuals or for collectives. We ought to take pause when the act of re-making the self by making media and doing craft is offered as the epitome of doing feminism. As Red Chidgey warns, "several trajectories of DIY are being mobilized in the current moment – from the grassroots and participatory to the neoliberal and conservative" where "self-described DIY projects . . . cannot necessarily guarantee liberating possibilities or outcomes by intention of declaration alone" (2015, 102). Any politics can be associated with do-it-yourself making. According to Sarah Banet-Weiser and Laura Portwood-Stacer, popular feminism celebrates the making of things and, in turn, making oneself, but not in ways that transform structures of privilege and oppression. They might transform structures of feeling, such that making becomes a way of soothing the self and reclaiming some sense of agency. As they suggest,

> Feminism has found its most visible popularity in the messages about self-making, self-love, and self-care that abound on social media and in corporate campaigns, messages mostly aimed at privileged white women and lacking a subtext of self-care as political warfare.
>
> *(2017, 884)*

What then could a different vision of feminist making as political work look like? Or might we ask instead what it might mean to do feminism otherwise?

From making back to doing feminism

The emphasis on the "doing" of feminism suggests that feminism is not only a set of beliefs, epistemologies, and texts (all of which require making and maintenance) but also sets of concrete practices and ways of doing things with media and other materials. Feminism is something people enact, perform, create, repair, and transform. It requires experimentation, and as Aristea Fotopoulou and Kate O'Riordan (2014) have argued, "Experiments of course need to be repeated if knowledge is to be produced through them." Repetition represents the doing of feminism around different forms of feminist praxis.

What we mean by doing feminism exceeds what we mean by making media and other forms of making. Deep into her book *Girl Zines*, Alison Piepmeier turns directly to the question of the work zines do, asking: "Why would anyone do this work – engage in protest, write a book, create a zine – if they didn't believe that the world could be a different place?" (2009, 156). For her and the zine makers she studied, zines do the work of political pedagogy by "teaching strategies for change." Their cultural work "does a new kind of political work" (159) centered around "small-scale acts of resistance . . . modeling process, active criticism, and imagination" that targets "late-capitalist cynical culture" (160). Drawing from Anita Harris's (2006) work on girl culture, Piepmeier argues that young women's zine making represents an active choice to disengage "from formal politics and its agendas" (161) to do politics otherwise. Politics represents, for Piepmeier, the acts of "drawing attention to what's wrong with the world, awakening their readers' outrage, and providing tools for challenging existing power structures" (162). To see this work as political "requires an altered understanding of what counts as political" so that we can see "what's happening now" (162). Pointing her readers to the "cultural, the local, and the quirky as real and meaningful sites of political intervention," she locates third-wave feminism in those practices that occur, in part, through the making of zine culture in the 1990s and 2000s (162). Similarly, in an online context Jessalynn Keller argues that blogs provide "spaces for girls to reframe feminist activism according to their own experiences" (2011, 435). This is a particular vision of activism that Fiona Hackney calls "quiet activism" counterposed to, say, the movement-based feminist tools of public amplification in Occupy (Radovac 2014; Costanza-Chock 2012), or the materials of feminist publicity, singing, and other kinds of eventfulness associated with protest camp–based movements (e.g., Feigenbaum 2013, 2014).

For Piepmeier and other scholars of feminist zine making, doing feminism is conceived as an act of maker-based agency, linking the making media/doing feminism conjuncture directly to other maker culture discourse and ideology. Like zine culture, the maker movement is also "about raising more personal awareness that things could be different, that you can lead your life or structure your life in a different kind of way if you take making as central instead of consuming as central" (Sengers 2015, 12). Phoebe Sengers's elevation of making echoes other critical maker discourse, such as that articulated by Alex Galloway (2015), who argues, "The problem is not in our imagination. The problem is in our activity" (Galloway 2015, 78). And yet, how do we open up our imaginations without experimenting with them in practice? As Jonathan Sterne suggests, "we cannot get pragmatic without doing a little dreaming. . . . Imagine how much better life would be if cultural practices did not need to be mapped onto a grid using a political compass" (2004, 99).

For Janice Radway, zine making represents a way of doing social relations performatively (2011, 147). Like Piepmeier, Radway's study of zines aims to understand the "process by which the sometimes small effects of prior practices live on in the desires, acts, and interventions constituting people's subsequent lives," producing "slow change, perhaps, but change nonetheless" (2011, 146). In this way of approaching girls and zine making, where making constitutes and maintains a set of social relations, Radway examines how "the small effects of prior practice live on in the desires, acts and interventions constituting people's subsequent lives" (2011, 146). Radway sees in zine making a gender potential that young women engage to shape their social lives, a form of social and affective techné they carry with them. As she suggests, "zines ought to be thought of not simply as texts to be read but also as acts to be engaged and passed on" (2011, 142), where the effects of their making and reading extend into the future in ways that cannot be known in advance.

Viewed from the vantage point of zine making, we might say that feminist making not only materializes feminist ways of knowing, it creates conditions of community and selfhood that are about making oneself and others, now and in the future. This notion of doing feminism via making media points to the qualities and kinds of action that constitute feminism as critical practices and works in the world. In Radway's framework, the politics of feminist making lies not in the making itself but instead emerges from the collective consciousness-making of people making things together, where feminism is lived and materialized. As Stephen Duncombe also argued about zine culture, "Individuals can and will be radicalized through underground culture, but they will have to make the step to political action themselves" (Duncombe 1997, 192, cited in Radway 2011, 143).

Duncombe summons a theory of articulation to make sense of the politics of zine culture, suggesting that political action is a kind of work people do together in addition to the process of making. What that work of change looks like exceeds practices of making. As makers, Richard Sennett suggests, "we become particularly interested in things we can change" through processes of fabrication and other material transformations (Sennett 2008, 120). But what kind of change do we dismiss when we fail to recognize some forms of making *as* making? What practices get left out of the category of feminist making also tells us something about what kinds of practices come to count as feminism and feminist activism. As Sarah Banet-Weiser and Laura Portwood-Stacer remind us, "The traffic in feminism does not guarantee us the political tools to neutralize the violence that erupts wherever popular feminism gains a foothold. It *does* give us the means to make hashtags and tshirts and brands and books," but "our popularity will not protect us" (2017, 887). Feminism is something that must be done, in concert with others, in ways that must radically exceed but are also bound up with the making of media, conditioned by but not at all guaranteed through those processes of making – particularly when making not only circulates in branded corporate culture but is also conditioned and enabled by it.

One way we understand making as a part of the process of making change is by approaching making as a political tool, a way to instrumentalize action through the making of actual instruments. Making media and other materials are part of the process of making change, but they are also much more and less than political tools. Musicians know that instruments enable you to do more than make sound. They enable you to make music, to move yourself and others in ways that can express political ideas but also create affective, embodied intensities through loudness and movement. Through practices of making, "Millions of people learn once again that everyday making has a beauty to it, and that everyday making is something done together, as a community and culture" (Powell 2012, n.p.).

I have analyzed here some of the ways that feminist techné, craft work, and networked action reframes the question of what it means to do feminism. Thinking through the relationship between making and doing feminism might begin to expand what we think constitutes making; it might also enable us to more closely scrutinize what forms of doing feminism we most readily pay attention to, and why. How might we also value other crucial forms of feminist labor that happen in and around feminist works but are not as easily accessible through them and are sometimes made invisible through them? A first step here is crediting originary makers of feminist artifacts and communication, those who conceptualize and first articulate a way of doing things, of expressing feminist ideas, and sharing them, from hashtags and key feminist concepts to key feminist texts (see, e.g., Loza 2014; Park and Leonard 2016). This is especially directed at "cultures of the grab" (Senft 2008) in white feminism and journalism when their practitioners fail to credit and cite the work of women of color.

It would also recognize forms of making that challenge typical conceptualizations of fabrication, to recognize the digital scanning, reassembling and digital sharing, for example, of out-of-print feminist texts like *This Bridge Called My Back* (see Adair and Nakamura 2017) as a key act of feminist making. The young people who do that work transformatively remake one of the most important texts of 20th-century feminism. This and other kinds of "doing" often fall out of the picture of what it means to do feminism when particular forms of feminist making become so centrally associated with feminist understandings of what it is to enact feminism. As sociologist Nancy Naples suggests, what we come to focus on most readily as feminist activism often marginalizes and makes other forms of feminist practice harder to see (2005, 216–217).

I suggest shifting the emphasis from the making of feminist things that might instrumentalize our conceptions of feminism into artifactual tools toward the doing of feminism as a capacious assemblage of actions, technologies, ideas, and people (see, e.g., Balsamo 2011, 31; see also Fotopoulou 2016). As a drummer, former martial artist and self-defense teacher, I am especially compelled by the conceptions of material agency articulated to doing and the deeply physical forms of social embodiment they foster. Feminism is, after all, physical (see McCaughey 1997; Rentschler 1999); it is something one does with others. For me, feminism signifies something one does rather than something one makes. We need artifacts, documents, and digital trails to make the doing of feminism knowable, to tell stories of feminism over time, and to organize those stories into bodies of knowledge. It is the doing itself that matters most, where the often ineffable, deeply felt qualities of enacting feminism exceed any artifacts that may attempt to represent it.

Drawing from a performance studies framework, the "crafted objects" and texts of feminism can be seen as "records of the of all the actions that took place over a given time, with the 'event' or act of making physically inscribed upon them" (Burisch 2016, 66). In decentering the artifactual nature of feminist craft in favor of seeing feminist making as sets of processes and performances – in "shifting from objects to actions" and their interrelationship, as performance artist Nicole Burisch puts it (216, 59) – the "crafted object" and its "objecthood" come instead to "serve . . . as a record of an event or process, a prop or tool, and in some cases [it] disappear[s] altogether" (Burisch 2016, 56, 57). In this way, following Anne Balsamo, I see feminist doing and making as a verb, rather than a noun (2011, 33). I'm interested in feminist practices that transform personal politics into collective ones, and that make feminism transmissible as ways of doing things. By "doing feminism," I have in mind the protocol feminism Michele Murphy details in her book about the women's reproductive self-help movement, where feminist self-help activists established "standardizable and transmissible components of feminist practices" around such things like vaginal and cervical self-examination (2012, 29).

As someone who co-founded a self-defense teaching collective and organized for a graduate employee union, I experienced firsthand the relationship between doing things together and making change. Many of the actions that made up those practices of doing feminism elude easy documentation and are hard to capture in the artifactual crafts and technologies of so much maker culture. Many of the things we make as organizers and activist teachers are also rarely seen or treated as feminist artifacts – the lesson plans, the binders full of paper masters for old handouts, the punching bags (yes, those too), the meeting agendas: those media that constitute the protocols and practices of doing feminism in different ways. We do not often recognize the organizational memos we write, the databases we created, and the speeches we gave to build movements and create new institutional formations as acts of making feminism.

But I want to suggest that it is precisely those analog and digital material artifacts that are evidence of feminist making – of making feminist organizations, institutions, and practices. As is often the case, those artifacts often disappear, which also presumes that they ever took artifactual form in the first place. Through the textual and artifactual traces of these kinds of feminist making practices, we can begin to define the actions and agencies of contemporary feminisms differently, through practices of making that are perhaps less centrally identified with craft and maker cultures and more closely tied to feminist protocols, modes of feminist performative "doing," and more ephemeral traces of feminist practices – like the handwritten notes one may have made for a public speech about the necessity of graduate student medical benefits for those of us living with chronic conditions. These artifacts will never be celebrated in maker culture. They will not be held up as feminist craft. They will never be sold on Etsy. And they don't have much aesthetic value as made things. But they begin to represent some of the ways many folks currently do and once did feminism with others in certain places and at certain times. I want to suggest that it is worth thinking about how our desires to witness feminism happening in the crafting of objects can be directed toward actions and ways of doing feminism that leave behind far less inviting, not nearly as pretty, and in some cases quite boring looking artifactual things in their organizing for workplace equity and a world free of gendered violence. We make feminisms in the process of embodying other kinds of feminist practices that leave gestural marks, faint paper trails and performative hauntings that may be hard to witness, but nonetheless have served, and continue to, as indexes of the works and labors of feminists.

Acknowledgments

Thanks to Anne Balsamo, Sarah Banet-Weiser, Darin Barney, Stefanie Duguay, Elizabeth Groeneveld, Kim Knight, Krista Geneviève Lynes, Cait McKinney, Maggie Mills, Jonathan Sterne, Michele White, the crew at the Feminist Media Studio at Concordia University, and audiences at the Feminist Research Collective at UT-Dallas and the Society for Cinema and Media Studies for crucial conversations and citation sharing on the topic of maker culture, media making, and doing feminism.

Notes

1 Alison Piepmeier discusses the third-wave feminist subjectivity that forms around grrrl zines, stating "the modes of thinking evident in many grrrrl zines demonstrate this sort of tactical subjectivity, not permanently grounded in particular identity configurations but mobile, flexible, and responsive to a culture of late capitalism and late modernity" (2009, 93).

2 See Mary Dietz (2002) for a feminist re-reframing of Arendt's concept of homo faber. Dietz reinterprets feminist readings of Arendt's *The Human Condition* in order to reconsider homo faber's actions of making in non-masculine terms. In essentially "de-gendering" Arendt's notion of homo faber as the maker of works, she critiques Arendt's theory of action for not going far enough, for stopping at "the action context of speaking" rather than continuing on to "the action context of doing" (138).

3 See Kylie Jarrett (2014) for an articulation of "women's work" vis-à-vis digital culture and feminist understandings of immaterial labor. Jarrett uses the term "consciously to underscore the importance of placing feminist critiques of the historical labor relations typically experienced by, and attributed to, women in the interrogation of digital media economics" (16).

Bibliography

Adair, Cassius and Lisa Nakamura (2017). "The Digital Afterlives of *This Bridge Called My Back:* Woman of Color Feminism, Digital Labor, and Networked Feminism" *American Literature* 89(2): 255–278.

Ahmed, Sara (2004). *The Cultural Politics of Emotion.* Edinburgh: University of Edinburgh Press.

Aires, Isadora Santiago (2015). *Women in the Making: Feminism Versus the Maker Culture.* Los Gatos, CA: Smashwords, 1–16.

Arendt, Hannah (1958). *The Human Condition.* Chicago, IL: University of Chicago Press.

Balsamo, Anne (2011). *Designing Culture: The Technological Imagination at Work.* Durham, NC: Duke University Press.

Banet-Weiser, Sarah and Kate M. Miltner (2015): "#MasculinitySoFragile: Culture, Structure, and Networked Misogyny" *Feminist Media Studies.* doi:10.1080/14680777.2016.1120490

Banet-Weiser, Sarah and Laura Portwood-Stacer (2017). "The Traffic in Feminism: An Introduction to the Commentary and Criticism in Popular Feminism" *Feminist Media Studies* 17(5): 884–888.

Bix, Amy (2009). "Chicks Who Fix: Women, Tool Knowledge, and Home Repair, 1920–2007" *Women's Studies Quarterly (WSQ)* 37(1 and 2): 38–60.

Bobel, Chris (2007). "'I'm Not an Activist, But I've Done a Lot of It': Doing Activism, Being Activist, and the 'Perfect Standard' in a Contemporary Movement" *Social Movement Studies: Journal of Social, Cultural and Political Protest* 6(2): 147–159.

Bratich, Jack and Heidi Brush (2011). "Fabricating Activism: Craft-Work, Popular Culture, Gender" *Utopian Studies* 22(2): 233–260.

Burisch, Nicole (2016). "From Objects to Actions and Back Again: The Politics of Dematerialized Craft and Performance Documentation" *TEXTILE: Cloth and Culture* 14(1): 54-73. https://doi.org/10.1080/14759756.2016.1142784

Chachra, Debbie (2015). "Why I Am Not a Maker" *The Atlantic,* January 23. Accessed July 26, 2017 at: www.theatlantic.com/technology/archive/2015/01/why-i-am-not-a-maker/384767/

Chen, Adrian (2014). "The Laborers Who Keep Dick Pics and Beheadings Out of Your Facebook Feed" *Wired,* October 23. Accessed August 5, 2017 at: www.wired.com/2014/10/content-moderation/

Chidgey, Red (2013). "Reassess Your Weapons: The Making of Feminist Memory in Young Women's Zines" *Women's History Review* 22(4): 658–672. doi:10.1080/09612025.2012.751773

Chidgey, Red (2015). "Developing Communities of Resistance? Maker Pedagogies, Do-It-Yourself Feminism and DIY Citizenship" in Matt Ratto and Megan Boler, eds. *DIY Citizenship: Critical Making and Social Media.* Cambridge, MA: MIT Press, 101–114.

Costanza-Chock, Sasha (2012) "Mic Check! Media Cultures and the Occupy Movement" *Social Movement Studies* 11(3/4): 375–385.

Cowan, Ruth (1983). *More Work for Mother: The Ironies of Household Technology from the Open Hearth to the Microwave.* New York, NY: Basic Books.

Dietz, Mary (2002). *Turning Operations: Feminism, Arendt, Politics.* New York, NY: Routledge.

D'Ignazio, Catherine, Alexis Hope, Alexandra Metral, Willow Brugh, David Raymond, Becky Michelson, Tal Achituv and Ethan Zuckerman (2015). "Towards a Feminist Hackathon: The 'Make the Breast Pump Not Suck!' Hackathon" *Journal of Peer Production* 8: n.p. Accessed August 5, 2017 at: http://peerproduction.net/issues/issue-8-feminism-and-unhacking/peer-reviewed-papers/towards-a-feminist-hackathon-the-make-the-breast-pump-not-suck/

Drake, Leslie and Jennifer Heywood, eds. (1997). *Third Wave Agenda: Being Feminist, Doing Feminism.* Minneapolis, MN: University of Minnesota Press.

Driscoll, Catherine and Melissa Gregg (2011). "Convergence Culture and the Legacy of Feminist Cultural Studies" *Cultural Studies* 25(4/5): 566–584.

Driver, Susan (2007). *Queer Girls and Popular Culture: Reading, Resisting and Creating Media.* New York, NY: Peter Lang.

Duffy, Brooke Erin (2015). "Gendering the Labor of Social Media Production" *Feminist Media Studies* 15(4): 710–714.

Duffy, Brooke Erin (2018). *(Not) Getting Paid to Do the Work You Love: Gender, Social Media and Aspirational Work.* New Haven, CT: Yale University Press.

Duncombe, Stephen (1997). *Notes From Underground: Zines and the Politics of Alternative Culture.* New York, NY: Verso.

Dunbar-Hester, Christina (2010). "Beyond 'Dudecore'? Challenging Gendered and Raced Technologies Through Media Activism" *Journal of Broadcasting & Electronic Media* 54(1): 121–135.

Dunbar-Hester, Christina (2014). *Low Power to the People: Pirates, Protest and Politics in FM Radio Activism.* Cambridge, MA: MIT Press.

Dunbar-Hester, Christina (2017). "Feminists, Geeks and Geek Feminists: Understanding Gender and Power in Technological Activism" in Victor Pickard and Guobin Yang, eds. *Media Activism in the Digital Age.* New York, NY: Routledge, 187–204.

Eichhorn, Kate (2013). *The Archival Turn in Feminism: Putting Our Outrage in Order.* Philadelphia, PA: Temple University Press.

Feigenbaum, Anna (2013). "Written in the Mud: (Proto-) Zine-Making and Autonomous Media at the Greenham Women's Peace Encampment" *Feminist Media Studies* 13(1): 1–13.

Feigenbaum, Anna (2014). "Resistant Matters: Tents, Tear Gas and the Other Media of Occupy" *Communication and Critical/Cultural Studies* 11(1): 15–24.

Feigenbaum, Anna (2015). "From Cyborg Feminism to Drone Feminism: Remembering Women's Anti-Nuclear Activisms" *Feminist Theory* 16(3): 265–288.

Fotopoulou, Aristea (2016). *Feminist Activism and Digital Networks: Between Empowerment and Vulnerability.* London, UK: Palgrave MacMillan.

Fotopoulou, Aristea and Kate O'Riordan (2014). "Introduction: Queer Feminist Media Praxis" *ADA: A Journal of Gender, New Media & Technology* 5. doi:10.7264/N3CN7263

Gajjala, Radhika (2013) "Use/Useless: Affect, Labor and Non-Materiality" *nomorepotlucks.* Accessed at: http://nomorepotlucks.org/site/useuse-less-affect-labor-and-nonmateriality-radhika-gajjala/

Gajjala, Radhika, Natalia Rybas, and Melissa Altman (2007). "Epistemologies of Doing: E-Merging Selves Online" *Feminist Media Studies* 7(2): 209–213.

Galloway, Alexander (2015). "Critique and Making" in Garnet Hertz, ed. *Conversations in Critical Making.* CTheory Books, 65–86.

Garrison, Ednie Kaeh (2000). "U.S. Feminism-Grrrl Style! Youth (Sub)Cultures and the Technologies of the Third Wave" *Feminist Studies* 26(1): 141–170.

Gauntlett, David (2011). *Making is Connecting: The Social Meaning of Creativity, From DIY and Knitting to YouTube and Web 2.0.* Cambridge: Polity Press.

Gray, Mary (2009). *Out in the Country: Youth, Media and Queer Visibility in Rural America.* New York, NY: New York University Press.

Groeneveld, Elizabeth (2016). *Making Feminist Media: Third-Wave Magazines on the Cusp of the Digital Age.* Wilfrid Laurier University Press.

Gumbs, Alexis Pauline (2008). "'We Can Learn to Mother Ourselves': A Dialogically Produced Audience and Black Feminist Publishing 1979 to the 'Present'." *Gender Forum*, no. 22. Accessed at: www.genderforum.org/issues/black-womens-writing-revisited/we-can-learn-to-mother-ourselves/

Gunn, Caitlin (2015). "Hashtagging From the Margins: Women of Color Engaged in Feminist Consciousness Raising on Twitter" in *Women of Color and Social Media Multitasking: Blogs, Timelines, Feeds and Community*, edited by Keisha Edwards Tassie and Sonia M. Brown Givens, 21–34. London, UK: Lexington Books.

Hackney, Fiona (2013). "Quiet Activism and the New Amateur: The Power of Home and Hobby Crafts" *Design and Culture* 5(2): 169–193.

Hall, Stuart (1980). "Race, Articulation and Societies Structured in Dominance" in *Sociological Theories: Race and Colonialism.* Paris: UNESCO, 305–345.

Hall, Stuart (1986). "On Postmodernism and Articulation: An Interview with Stuart Hall" edited by Larry Grossberg. *Journal of Communication Inquiry* 10(2): 45–60.

Haranalova, Christina (2014). "Hacktivism: The Art of Practicing Life and Computer Hacking for Feminist Activism" *Dpi* 27. Accessed October 3, 2017 at: https://dpi.studioxx.org/en/hacktivism-art-practicing-life-and-computer-hacking-feminist-activism.

Haraway, Donna (1985). "A Manifesto for Cyborgs: Science, Technology, and Socialist Feminism in the 1980s" *Socialist Review* 15(2): 65–107.

Harker, Jaime and Cecilia Conchar Farr, eds. (2016). *This Book Is an Action: Feminist Print Culture and Activist Aesthetics.* Urbana, IL: University of Illinois Press.

Harris, Anita (2008). "Young Women, Late Modern Politics, and the Participatory Possibilities of Online Cultures" *Journal of Youth Studies*, 11(5), 481–495.

Harris, Anita (2012). "Online Cultures and Future Girl Citizens" in Elke Zobl and Ricarda Drüeke, eds. *Feminist Media: Participatory Spaces, Networks and Cultural Spaces*. Bielefeld, DE: Transcript Verlag, 213–235.

Henry, Liz (2014). "The Rise of Feminist Hacker Spaces and How to Make Your Own: Building Community Spaces, a Brief History of Feminist Organization in Tech, and What Comes Next" *Model View Culture*, February 3. Available at: https://modelviewculture.com/pieces/the-rise-of-feminist-hackerspaces-and-how-to-make-your-own

Hertz, Garnet, ed. (2015). *Conversations in Critical Making*. Victoria, BC: CTheory Books.

Jarrett, Kylie (2014). "The Relevance of 'Women's Work': Social Reproduction and Immaterial Labour in Digital Media" *Television & New Media* 15(1): 14–29.

Jarrett, Kylie (2016). *Feminism, Labour and Digital Media: The Digital Housewife*. New York, NY: Routledge.

Kearney, Mary Celeste (2006). *Girls Make Media*. New York, NY: Routledge.

Keller, Jessalynn (2016). *Girls' Feminist Blogging in a Post-Feminist Age*. New York, NY: Routledge.

Keller, Jessalynn, Kaitlynn Mendes and Jessica Ringrose (2016). "Speaking Unspeakable Things: Documenting Digital Responses to Rape Culture" *Journal of Gender Studies* 27(1): 22–36. http://dx.doi.org/10.1080/09589236.2016.1211511

Kennedy, Tracy L.M. (2007). "The Personal Is Political: Feminist Blogging and Virtual Consciousness-raising" *The Scholar and Feminist Online* 5(2): n.p.

Kondo, Marie (2014). *The Life-Changing Magic of Tidying Up: The Japanese Art of Decluttering and Organizing*. Berkeley, CA: Ten Speed Press.

Loza, Susana (2014). "Hashtag Feminism, #SolidarityIsForWhiteWomen, and the Other #FemFuture" *Ada: A Journal of Gender, New Media and Technology* 5. http://adanewmedia.org/2014/07/issue5-loza/

McCaughey, Martha (1997). *Real Knockouts: The Physical Feminism of Women's Self-Defense*. New York: New York University Press.

McKinney, Cait (2015). "Newsletter Networks in the Feminist History and Archives Movement" *Feminist Theory* 16(3): 310–328.

McKinney, Cait (forthcoming). "The Knitting Needle Computer" in Phoebe Bronstein and Carol Stabile, eds. *Media Fails: What Flops, Fiascos, and Bungles Tell Us About Media History*. University of Illinois Press.

McRobbie, Angela (2015). *Be Creative: Making a Living in the New Culture Industries*. Cambridge, UK: Polity Press.

McRobbie, Angela and Jenny Garber (1991/1978). "Girls and Subcultures: An Exploration" in Tony Jefferson and Stuart Hall, eds. *Resistance Through Rituals: Youth Subcultures in Post-War Britain*. London: Routledge, 209–232.

Miltner, Kate and Tim Highfield (2017). "Never Gonna GIF You Up: Analyzing the Cultural Significance of the Animated GIF" *Social Media + Society*, July: 1–11.

Moi, Toril (2006). "'I Am Not a Feminist But': How Feminism Became the F-word" *PMLA* 121(5): 1735–1741.

Morgan, Robin, ed. (1970). *Sisterhood is Powerful: An Anthology of Writings from the Women's Liberation Movement*. New York, NY: Random House.

Morozov, Evgeny (2014). "Making It: Pick Up a Spotwelder and Let the Revolution Begin" *New Yorker*, January 13. Accessed July 26, 2017 at: www.newyorker.com/magazine/2014/01/13/making-it-2

Murphy, Michelle (2012). *Seizing the Means of Reproduction: Entanglements of Feminism, Health, and Technoscience*. Durham, NC: Duke University Press.

Nakamura, Lisa (2014). "Indigenous Circuits: Navajo Women and the Racialization of Early Electronics Manufacture" *American Quarterly* 66(4): 919–941.

Naples, Nancy A. (2005). "Confronting the Future, Learning from the Past: Feminist Praxis in the Twenty-First Century" in Jo Reger, ed. *Different Wavelengths: Studies of the Contemporary Women's Movement*. New York: Routledge, 215–235.

Nguyen, Lilly, Sophie Toupin and Shaowen Bardzell (2016). "Feminist Hacking/Making: Exploring New Gender Horizons of Possibility" *Journal of Peer Production* 8: n.p. Accessed 26 July 2017 at: http://peerproduction.net/issues/issue-8-feminism-and-unhacking/feminist-hackingmaking-exploring-new-gender-horizons-of-possibility/

Oldenziel, Ruth (2001). "Man the Maker, Woman the Consumer: The Consumption Junction Revisited" in Angela N. H. Creager, Elizabeth Lunbeck and Londa Schiebinger, eds. *Feminism in Twentieth-Century Science, Technology and Medicine*. Chicago, IL: University of Chicago Press, 128–148.

Park, Suey and David Leonard (2016). "Toxic or Intersectional? Challenges to (White) Feminist Hegemony Online" in Janell Hobson, ed. *Are All the Women Still White? Rethinking Race, Expanding Feminism*. Albany, NY: SUNY Press, 205–225.

Piepmeier, Alison (2009). *Girl Zines: Making Media, Doing Feminism.* New York: New York University Press.
Powell, Alison (2012). "Cultures of the 'Maker' Movement" blog post. Accessed at: www.alisonpowell.ca/?p=522
Pozner, Jennifer (2003). "The 'Big Lie': False Feminist Death Syndrome, Profit, and the Media" in Rory Dicker and Alison Piepmeier, eds. *Catching a Wave: Reclaiming Feminism for the 21st Century.* Boston, MA: Northeastern University Press, 31–56.
Radovac, Lilian (2014). "Mic Check: Occupy Wall Street and the Space of Audition" *Communication and Critical/Cultural Studies* 11(1): 34–41.
Radway, Janice (2011). "Zines, Half-Lives and Afterlives: On the Temporalities of Social and Political Change" *PMLA* 126(1): 140–150.
Ratto, Matt (2011). "Critical Making: Conceptual and Material Studies in Technology and Social Life" *The Information Society* 27(4): 252–260.
Ratto, Matt (2015). "Defining Critical Making" in Garnet Hertz, ed. *Conversations in Critical Making.* Victoria, BC: CTheory Books, 33–54.
Reilly, Ian (2015). "The Comedian, the Cat, and the Activist: The Politics of Light Seriousness and the (Un)serious Work of Contemporary Laughter" *Comedy Studies* 6(1): 49–62.
Rentschler, Carrie (1999). "Women's Self-Defense: Physical Education for Everyday Life" *Women's Studies Quarterly* 26(1): 152–161.
Rentschler, Carrie (2014a). "Rape Culture and the Feminist Politics of Social Media" *Girlhood Studies* 7(1): 65–83. http://dx.doi.org/10.3167/ghs.2014.070106.
Rentschler, Carrie (2014b). "#safetytipsforladies: Feminist Twitter Takedowns of Victim Blaming" *Feminist Media Studies* 15(2): 353–356.
Rentschler, Carrie (2017). "Bystander Intervention, Social Media Testimony and the Anti-Carceral Politics of Care" *Feminist Media Studies* 17(4): 565–584.
Rentschler, Carrie and Samantha Thrift (2015a). "Doing Feminism in the Network: Networked Laughter and the Binders Full of Women Meme" *Feminist Theory* 16(3): 329–359.
Rentschler, Carrie and Samantha Thrift (2015b). "Doing Feminism: Event, Archive, Techné" *Feminist Theory* 16(3): 239–249.
Rodgers, Tara (2010). *Pink Noises: Women on Electronic Music and Sound.* Durham, NC: Duke University Press.
Rodgers, Tara (2015). "Cultivating Activist Lives in Sound" *Leonardo Music Journal* 25: 75–83.
Rosner, Daniela and Sarah Fox (2016). "Legacies of Craft and the Centrality of Failure in Mother-Operated Hackerspace" *New Media & Society* 18(4): 558–580.
Sandoval, Marisol (2015). "The Hands and Brains of Digital Culture: Arguments for an Inclusive Approach to Cultural Labor" in Eran Fischer and Christian Fuchs, eds. *Reconsidering Value and Labour in the Digital Age.* Basingstoke, UK: Palgrave MacMillan, 42–59.
Sayers, Jentery (2014). "The Relevance of Remaking" blog post. Accessed at: http://maker.uvic.ca/remaking/
Sayers, Jentery (2015). "Humanities and Critical Approaches to Technology" in Garnet Hertz, ed. *Conversations in Critical Making.* Victoria, BC: CTheory Books.
Senft, Theresa (2008). *Camgirls: Celebrity and Community in the Age of Social Networks.* New York, NY: Lang.
Sengers, Phoebe (2015). "Critical Technical Practice" in Garnet Hertz, ed. *Conversations in Critical Making.* Victoria, BC: CTheory Books, 8–20.
Sennett, Richard (2008.) *The Craftsman.* New Haven, CT: Yale University Press.
Shifman, Limor (2014). *Memes in Digital Culture.* Cambridge, MA: MIT Press.
Slack, Jennifer Daryl (1996). "The Theory and Method of Articulation in Cultural Studies" in David Morley & Kuan-Hsing Chen, eds. *Stuart Hall: Critical Dialogues in Cultural Studies.* New York, NY: Routledge, 112–127.
Sofia, Zoe (2000). "Container Technologies" *Hypatia* 15(2): 181–201.
Sterne, Jonathan (2005). "The Burden of Culture" in Michael Bérubé, ed. *The Aesthetics of Cultural Studies.* Oxford: Blackwell Publishers, 80–102.
Terranova, Tiziana (2000). "Free Labor: Producing Culture for the Digital Economy" *Social Text* 18(2): 33–58.
Toupin, Sophie (2014). "Feminist Hacker Spaces: The Synthesis of Feminist and Hacker Cultures" *Journal of Peer Production* 5. Available at: http://peerproduction.net/editsuite/issues/issue-5-shared-machine-shops/peer-reviewed-articles/feminist-hackerspaces-the-synthesis-of-feminist-and-hacker-cultures/
Turner, Fred (2008). *From Counterculture to Cyberculture: Stewart Brand, The Whole Earth Network, and the Rise of Digital Utopianism.* Chicago: University of Chicago Press.

Wajcman, Judy (2004). *Technofeminism.* Cambridge: Polity Press.
Weida, Courtney (2013). "Feminist Zines: (Pre)Occupations of Gender, Politics, and D.I.Y. in a Digital Age" in K. Staikidis, ed. *The Journal of Social Theory in Art Education* 33: 67–85.
Zuckerman, Ethan (2014). "Cute Cats to the Rescue? Participatory Media and Political Expression" in Danielle Allen and Jennifer Light, eds. *From Voice to Influence: Understanding Citizenship in the Digital Age.* Chicago: University of Chicago Press, 131–150.

9

Surveillance is a feminist issue

Rosalind Gill

We are living in a moment of unprecedented surveillance: surveillance by the state, by corporations, by media, and by technology companies, the latter amassing an almost unimaginable amount of information about us from our "data trails." However, we are not only being watched, we also monitor ourselves and others, as a "surveillant imaginary" (Andrejevic, 2015) takes hold in contemporary culture. Most work on surveillance studies focuses on men, both as objects and actors – we need to think only of the anti-heroes Julian Assange ("WikiLeaks") and Edward Snowden (National Security Agency), celebrated for their role in "leaking" information in the public interest. Moreover, in academia, surveillance studies remain an especially male-dominated field within sociology, political science, and digital cultural studies.

In this chapter I will argue that surveillance is a feminist issue. I will contribute to the emerging field of feminist surveillance studies (Dubrofsky and Magnet, 2015), and I will further highlight research within feminist media studies that may contribute to this field but is not necessarily recognized as surveillance studies. This includes work on the male gaze and the politics of looking, female friendship, social media use, and the quantified self. In addition, my aims in this chapter are as follows: first, to move beyond top-down theorizations of surveillance in order to open up questions about peer surveillance and self-surveillance; second, to build a conceptual architecture to show the connections between postfeminist culture and surveillance; and third, to explore the links between neoliberalism and new practices of looking, which Mark Hayward (2013) dubs a "neoliberal optics." Overall, I will argue that digital and media cultures and postfeminist modalities of subjecthood are coming together to produce a novel and extraordinarily powerful regulatory gaze on women.

The chapter is divided into two broad parts. In part one I will offer a brief introduction to the study of surveillance, including emerging work in feminist surveillance studies, and will then introduce contemporary understandings of neoliberalism and postfeminism. The second part of the paper will look in detail at surveillance as a feminist issue. It will begin by outlining relatively conventional accounts of media surveillance of women (e.g., in advertising and celebrity culture). It will then turn to the participatory culture of postfeminism to examine peer surveillance, drawing on Alison Winch's (2015) work on the shift from a panopticon to a gynaeopticon. Finally, I will approach the diverse range of practices that might be characterized as self-surveillance, including the growing significance of self-tracking technologies, photographic filters, and beauty apps. The chapter concludes by asking whether we are seeing the emergence of a distinctively postfeminist and neoliberal gaze.

Surveillance studies

Surveillance studies has grown dramatically in recent years as an academic area of expertise – as well as a public topic of interest. David Lyons (2001:2) has proposed a widely accepted definition of surveillance which regards it as "any collection and processing of personal data, whether identifiable or not, for the purposes of influencing or managing those whose data have been garnered." Not surprisingly, the bulk of research focuses on the surveillance practices of the state, the military, the immigration apparatus, and more recently, corporate surveillance by companies like Google or Facebook. A growing interest in biometric surveillance is centered mostly on compelled forms of surveillance, showing how it works to "dismantle or disaggregate the coherent body bit by bit" (Ericson and Hagerty, 2006) so that a whole person becomes fragmented into a composite of data sets. As Lisa Nakamura (2015) has argued, these practices also re-make the body, "classifying some bodies as normative legal, and some as illegal and out of bounds."

Nakamura's work is part of an emergent field of feminist surveillance studies. As yet relatively new, it represents a much-needed challenge to mainstream surveillance studies which has not "placed a difference, gender and sexuality at the forefront of their enquiries" (Walby and Anais, 2015). In their important intervention into the field, Rachel Dubrofsky and Shoshana Amielle Magnet (2015) set out the commitment of feminist surveillance studies to critical projects that are intersectional, interventionist, and activist in their orientation – drawing as much from queer theory and critical race studies as from gender studies. To date, this work has largely focused on top-down forms of surveillance as they intersect with and constitute gendered, racist, and classed systems of colonialism, exclusion, wars on terror, drugs, and so forth. Airport scanners, reproductive technologies, the surveillance of sex workers and their clients, and even birth certificates have been examined – demonstrating how these practices authorize some bodies and not others, criminalizing and marginalizing people through seemingly neutral apparatuses – that are revealed as anything but. "There is no form of surveillance that is innocent"," as Nakamura (2015) says. My argument here is that media and cultural studies has much to contribute to this body of work.

One area of scholarship which has particular relevance to this project is the growing interest in self-tracking and self-monitoring (Nafus and Sherman, 2014; Lupton, 2014a; Rettberg, 2014), which has been understood as giving rise to a "quantified self" – a reflexively monitoring self who uses the affordances of digital technologies to collect, monitor, record – and potentially share – a range of information about her or himself. This is in part facilitated by the potentialities of mobile phones which now include as standard (i.e., in their factory settings) a variety of applications that allow users to self monitor a range of aspects of their lives: for example, to count their steps, record their weight, monitor their caloric intake, and measure and evaluate their sleep. Increasing numbers of people now routinely "track" several aspects of their everyday lives via their phones, and applications are proliferating at an extraordinary rate with multiplying health apps (blood pressure, glucose levels, medication records, etc), psycho apps (mood, relaxation, meditation, confidence), apps related to pregnancy (which now outnumber those available for any other health-related topic), apps to monitor work and productivity, apps to get organized, apps to monitor finance, and even those to track one's sex life.

Taken together these apps massively augment the possibilities for digital self-monitoring, reinforcing the rationality of relentless self-scrutiny, which is a feature of postfeminist and neoliberal culture. Lupton's (2014b) conceptualization foregrounds links between the quantified self and neoliberalism: "the very act of self tracking, or positioning oneself as a self tracker, is already a performance of a certain type of subject: the entrepreneurial, self optimising subject." They fit perfectly with a neoliberal society concerned to replace "critique with technique, judgment with measurement" (Davies, 2014:16) in such a way to efface power and displace it onto seemingly neutral or impersonal systems or algorithms that can govern "at a distance" (Latour, 1987). Governing thus becomes recast as a technical rather than political activity – one in which both "big data" and micro-measurement increasingly play a part (Ajana, 2013) – and is entangled with questions about ownership, privacy, "dataveillance" and so on.

Postfeminism and neoliberalism

The surveillance of women must be understood in relation to the profound grip of postfeminism and neoliberalism in contemporary culture. According to many scholars (Gill, 2007; McRobbie, 2009; Gill and Scharff, 2011; Henderson and Taylor, in press) there are strong links between neoliberal values and the postfeminist sensibility circulating in contemporary culture – to the extent to which postfeminism might be considered as the gendered version of neoliberalism (Gill, 2017). Neoliberalism has been broadly understood as a political and economic rationality characterized by privatization, a "rolling back" and withdrawal of the state from many areas of social provision alongside an emphasis "that human well-being can best be advanced by liberating individual entrepreneurial freedoms and skills within an institutional framework characterized by strong property rights, free markets and free trade" (Harvey, 2005:2). In neoliberal societies the enterprise form is extended to "all forms of conduct" (Burchell, 1993:275) and "interpellates individuals as entrepreneurial actors in every sphere of life" (Brown, 2005:42). Individuals are constituted as self-managing, autonomous and "responsibilised."

Extending critical writing on neoliberalism, feminist scholars have compellingly demonstrated its gendered politics. Both postfeminism and neoliberalism are structured by a grammar of individualism that has fulsomely displaced notions of the social or political, or any idea of individuals as subject to pressures, constraints, or even influence from the outside. Used as a critical term, postfeminism reflects upon how popular culture both takes feminism into account and also repudiates it (McRobbie, 2009). Angela McRobbie (2009) suggests that this "double entanglement" facilitates both a doing and an undoing of feminism in which young women are offered particular kinds of freedom, empowerment, and choice "in exchange for" or "as a kind of substitute for" feminist politics and transformation. McRobbie's work brings to the fore the importance of feminism in understanding the postfeminist moment – a point also emphasized by Yvonne Tasker and Diane Negra (2007:3), who argue that postfeminism has to do with the "pastness" of feminism "whether that pastness is merely noted, mourned or celebrated."

A specific theorization of *postfeminism as a sensibility* has become significant in the last decade. The idea of a postfeminist sensibility is designed to highlight a number of key points. First postfeminism used in this way refers to an *object of study* rather than a perspective, a historical period, or a backlash as in other formulations (see Gill, 2007b; Gill, 2016). That is, rather than *being* a postfeminist, I identify myself as an *analyst of postfeminist culture* interested in critically interrogating the ideas and discourses that comprise the common sense about gender in contemporary culture. Second, the term highlights the sense of the *patterned nature* of social life and the necessity of capturing the empirical regularities in contemporary discourses and representations of gender. "Sensibility" was chosen rather than other alternative lexical options such as "ideology" or "regime" in order to retain a fluidity, a sense of postfeminism as a cultural but also an affective and psychological phenomenon (see below and Gill, 2017 for longer discussion). A third key feature of this perspective is its *empirical value* – its usability in studies of contemporary culture.

Unpacking the postfeminist sensibility

A number of relatively stable features of this sensibility have been identified recurrently across studies and contexts. These stress the significance of the body in postfeminist culture; the emergence of "new femininities" that break with earlier significations in important ways; the prominence given to notions of choice, agency, autonomy, and empowerment as part of a shift toward entrepreneurial modes of selfhood (Banet-Weiser, 2012); the importance of makeover and self-transformation, linked to what we might understand as the "psychic life of neoliberalism and postfeminism" (Scharff, 2016; Gill, 2016); the distinctive affective tone of postfeminism, particularly its emphasis upon the upbeat and the positive, with the repudiation of pain, injury, insecurity, and anger (Scharff, 2016; Kanai, 2015; Gill and Orgad, 2017); and finally the importance of surveillance to neoliberal and postfeminist cultures. We explore these in turn.

First there is the pre-eminent emphasis upon *the body* as both the locus of womanhood, and the key site of women's value. Earlier constructions of femininity in Western culture highlighted other features – many of them problematic, for example, women's role as mothers, or as bearers of certain psychological characteristics such as compassion, or as occupiers of particular roles such as caring – but today the body is to the fore. As Alison Winch (2015) has put it, "managing the body is . . . the means by which women acquire and display their cultural capital." While the body has been argued to be a "project" for everyone in late modernity (Featherstone, 1999), for women the requirement to work on and perfect the body has reached such an intensity that it has been suggested that patriarchy has "reterritorialized" – albeit in obfuscated form – in the fashion and beauty complex (McRobbie, 2009). A key aspect of this is that such aesthetic labor must be regarded as freely chosen rather than culturally demanded – with the implication that in undertaking body and beauty practices women are simply "pleasing themselves" rather than being subject to external pressures. Linked to this the idea of makeover and self-transformation has become prominent in postfeminist culture.

More broadly, postfeminism is implicated in the emergence of a set of distinctive "*new femininities*" (Gill and Scharff, 2011), as constructions of gender identity undergo a shift. One example of this tendency is the change in the way that women's sexuality is represented. Scholars of media noted that representations of women in the 1970s and early 1980s largely centered around depicting women as weak, passive objects of a male gaze. They were often presented as unintelligent and as preoccupied with a narrow range of gender-stereotyped interests (see Gill, 2007 for discuission). In the sphere of intimacy, constructions often highlighted women's insecurity, lack of knowledge, and desire to be liked/loved. When represented sexually tropes of objectification dominated – as in the classic adverts in which women were shown draped over cars and so forth. In postfeminist media culture, a striking shift is the break with "traditional" forms of passive objectification, substituted by the construction of women as active, desiring sexual subjects. It may be that this is simply objectification in a new form (Gill, 2003), but nevertheless the shift is a significant one (see Barker et al., 2018)

Such "entrepreneurialism" is not limited to "sexiness" or to work to add value to or capitalize the body. In fact these examples are instances of a much wider trend toward *entrepreneurial selfhood* that is intimately related to neoliberalism. This is marked by injunctions to work on, discipline, improve, and maximize the self. As such women are hailed as active, bold, confident subjects who are empowered to write the stories of their own lives, who are, to put it another way, architects of their own destinies. In cultures marked by a postfeminist sensibility, notions of choice and agency are prominent and invoked repeatedly. One of the most profound consequences of this is the implication that women are no longer constrained by any inequalities or power relations that might hold them back: their lives are the outcome of their own choices. As such, languages for talking about structures and culture have been eviscerated. Any remaining power differences between women and men mostly presented as being self-chosen, not as the outcome of cultural forces or unfair structures, and inequalities have become increasingly "unspeakable" (Gill, 2014) both because they challenge the neoliberal hegemony and because of widespread "gender fatigue" (Kelan, 2009) – although this is currently challenged by the rise of popular feminism (but see Gill, 2016 on post-postfeminism).

Further it is clear that postfeminism has a "*psychic life*" similar to that of neoliberalism (Scharff, 2016; Brown, 2015). This draws our attention to the fact that the sensibility is not simply manifest in cultural products such as films or magazines but also acts to shape subjectivities. One aspect of this can be seen in the new significance accorded to notions of character and attitude in postfeminist culture (Allen and Bull, 2016). "Resilience," "happiness," "grit," and "confidence" are among the characteristics celebrated in postfeminist cultures – matching perfectly neoliberal capitalism's emphasis upon individualism and the need for subjects who embrace risk, take responsibility for themselves, and have the all-important quality of "bouncebackability" for when things go badly (Forkert, 2014; Neocleus, 2013) In research on contemporary imperatives to confidence (Banet-Weiser, 2015; Favaro, 2017; Gill and Orgad, 2015), the peculiarly gendered aspects of this can be seen clearly, as "low self-esteem" among girls and women becomes invoked as the cause of women's problems, with individual programs and strategies to develop confidence being heralded as the solutions. The solution becomes: work on your confidence, don't change the world. A confidence trick indeed!

Finally, the postfeminist sensibility is also marked by a distinctive *affective or tonal quality*. Writing in 2009, Angela McRobbie discussed what she saw as a postfeminist "melancholia" in contemporary culture as gender distress in the form of eating disorders, self-harm, and certain forms of addiction "came to be established as predictable, treatable, things to be managed medically rather than subjected to sustained social scrutiny" (2009:112). Importantly, McRobbie highlights the *normalization* of female distress against the backdrop of repeated injunctions to girls and women to recognize themselves as powerful, as successful, as winners in the new gender order – what Anita Harris (2014) calls "can do girls." Without any language (e.g., feminism) to understand their experiences of pain, suffering, or failure as structurally produced, she argues, a range of "postfeminist disorders" became vehicles for expressing young women's "illegible rage," effectively materializing agony that was "unspeakable" in political terms. However, alongside the outward expression of pain and distress as individual pathologies, it can also be argued that postfeminism is marked by other affects: defiance and "performative shamelessness" (Dobson, 2015), "warmly-couched hostility" (Elias and Gill, 2016), and languages of self-actualization and inspiration (Gill and Orgad, in press; Henderson and Taylor, in press) – seen in everything from self-help, to popular memes, to greetings cards that instruct to "live, love, laugh" or "dance like nobody is watching." The "feeling rules" (Hochschild, 1979) of postfeminism (Kanai, 2015) call forth a subject who is fun, resilient, positive, and relentlessly upbeat, such that particular affective states and ways of being are to be disavowed and repudiated – especially anger, which in turn has become associated with the "feminist killjoy" (Ahmed, 2010).

Surveillance is a feminist issue

Another key feature of postfeminist culture is surveillance. This will be my focus in the remainder of the chapter. Within media, cultural, and gender studies more broadly, surveillance of women's bodies and of their appearance are long-established topics of concern, though they may not previously have been apprehended through the explicit use of the term surveillance. Nevertheless, ideas such as "practices of looking" (Betterton, 1987), "ways of seeing" (Berger, 1972), the male gaze (Mulvey, 1975), and the female gaze (Gamman and Marshment, 1989; spectacular girls (Projansky, 2014) and ways of appearing (Conor, 2004) offer – amongst many other terms – compelling and important bodies of work on the way women become subject to particular kinds of observation and scrutiny in popular culture. Research on beauty practices and body image represents another large subfield of research which draws on feminist-Foucauldian approaches to argue that women's appearance is subject to profound discipline and regulation – even when beauty practices are seemingly freely chosen. As Sandra Lee Bartky (1990) has argued, women are "not marched off to electrolysis at gunpoint," nor are they passive in the extraordinary ingenuity they display in beauty rituals, yet "in so far as the disciplinary practices of femininity produced a 'subjected and practiced,' an inferiorized, body, they must be understood as aspects of far larger discipline, an oppressive and inegalitarian system of sexual subordination."

This chapter contributes to an understanding of surveillance as intensifying, extensifying, and moving into the realm of subjectivity or psychic life. It highlights the potentially injurious force of surveillance and its proliferating spheres, techniques, and practices. We begin with a relatively familiar site of surveillant practices: the media.

Media and surveillance

More than a decade ago, in my book *Gender and Media* (Gill, 2007), I argued that "surveillance of women's bodies . . . constitutes perhaps the largest type of media content across all genres and media forms" (2007b:149) – a trend that has been increasing exponentially. It is impossible to understand the heightened surveillance of women's appearance in contemporary culture without reference to celebrity culture with its circulating news articles, magazines, gossip sites, and social media. In tandem with new photographic technologies, it has helped to inaugurate a moment of 360-degree surveillance. Being "in the public eye" now also has an amplified meaning, as camera phones can be used to record and upload images and video within seconds, giving rise to hitherto unknown phenomena such as the ability to precisely locate the whereabouts of a celebrity from images uploaded to Twitter or Instagram. The dissemination and uptake of practices previously associated with the paparazzi such as "the upskirt" shot has generated discussion (Schwartz, 2008), as has the use of other covert filming techniques – frequently designed for the objectification of women (e.g., the scandal over the filming, then distribution, of images of women eating while on train journeys). This represents the domestication and mainstreaming of photographic practices once associated with professional media in a way that must be understood as part of the wider force of convergence culture, participatory media, and the breakdown of stable distinctions between producers and consumers. As Amielle Shoshana Magnet (2015) has argued, the *pleasures* of this kind of gaze need to be theorized; it represents perhaps a scopophilic surveillance. The *costs* of this also require urgent attention. As I argue below, it constitutes what Mark Andrejevic (2015) dubs the "vertiginous growth" of the "surveillant imaginary," and, importantly, the dispersal of this imaginary as a way of being in and apprehending the world.

Familiar and everyday forms of intensified surveilling of women's bodies are to be found in the gossip and celebrity magazines and websites whose content is dominated by forensic dissection of the cellulite, fat, blocked pores, undepilated hairs, wrinkles, blotches, contouring, and hairstyle/sartorial/cosmetic surgery (mis)adventures of women in the public eye. I hope that at some future point in history people will look back upon the preoccupations of this period with horror and incredulity. The sheer volume and intensity of this nano-surveillance (Elias, forthcoming) of female celebrity bodies represents in my mind a kind of madness and malaise at a cultural level. Red circles or other textual devices highlight close-ups of each and every "failing" bodily part in a context in which no aesthetic misdemeanor is too trivial to be microscopically "picked over and picked apart by paparazzi photographers and writers" (Gill, 2007b:149).

It is striking to note the extent to which the surveillant gaze is becoming more and more intense – operating at ever finer-grained levels and with a proliferating range of lenses that do not necessarily regard the outer membrane of the body (the skin) as their boundary. This intensified and increasingly forensic surveillance is seen repeatedly in contemporary advertising and beauty culture – with the recurrent emphasis upon microscopes, telescopic gunsights, peep holes, alarm clocks, calipers, and set squares. Images of cameras and of perfect "photo beauty" or of "HD-ready" skin also proliferate. Most common of all are the motifs of the tape measure (often around the upper thigh) – an image that is becoming almost ubiquitous in beauty salons – and the magnifying glass, used to scrutinize pores or to highlight blemish-free skin, but (more importantly at a meta-level) underscoring the idea of the female face and body as under constant (magnified) surveillance.

One case in point is Benefit's POREfection campaign (2015), which constructs facial beautification through an analogy with espionage rendering women as "spygals" (at a beauty counter near you). Likewise Estee Lauder's (2015) campaign for "little black primer" invites us to "spy" women's made-up eyes through a peephole. Perfumier Douglas also deploys the magnifying glass trope, repeatedly encouraging the audience for their brand messages to forensically analyze what is wrong with a face (our own or others') and how it can be improved (e.g., is it too "wide," "thin," "round," "square," is the nose too "broad" or "long"). These are just a few examples attesting to the way in which an ever-refined (and punitive) visual literacy of the female face is being normalized, and has intensified with the prevalence of high-definition digital photographic technologies.

As well of the ubiquity of media surveillance of the female body, its extensiveness across media sites, and its intensification to ever finer-grained micro-surveillance, it is also worth mentioning the way in which it is entangled with hostility toward women in general and feminists in particular. We need only think of the excoriating attacks on Hillary Clinton's body and fashion sense by the right-wing media, or of the way in which women who speak out about gender inequality can be subjected to the most vicious micro-surveillance and commentary on their appearance. Indeed one of the oldest and most well-established patterns of media representation of women is the move which *disentitles* someone from speaking on the grounds that she is ugly. Body shaming is a political tactic. In postfeminist media culture, this is given a new twist such that perceived attractiveness can also be grounds for attack. Furthermore, women who speak publicly – but particularly those who speak as feminists – can also find themselves being threatened or punished by "exposure" of various kinds. An example is actress Emma Watson, who was viciously trolled for publicly stating her support for the feminist He for She campaign, with the threat that if she did not "shut up," her private photographs would be published. What all these tendencies have in common is the way in which they connect scrutiny of women's appearance with the right to speak. It is clear that hostile surveillance of women's bodies in this way is intimately connected to their silencing. There is an important and growing body of research on hate speech, "e-bile," and popular misogyny (Jane, 2014; Banet-Weiser and Miltner, 2016), but as yet the ways in which its dynamics are implicated in surveillance of women have not been extensively explored.

Horizontal and peer surveillance

The topic of trolling brings us to the second mode of surveillance I want to discuss: horizontal surveillance. This is surveillance that operates laterally across society rather than in a top-down way. It is surveillance by peers rather than surveillance from above by the state, the military, employers, and so forth. The rapid proliferation of social media and Web 2.0 technologies have brought horizontal surveillance to attention, but arguably it existed as a phenomenon long before the internet, seen in practices of community social control, for example, or in the way that young women "police" each other's looks and behaviors – operating through what Alison Winch (2013) has called a "girlfriend gaze."

Winch's work has been important in theorizing different modalities of surveillance, tracking a shift from a panoptic to a gynaeoptic mode. The Panopticon was Jeremy Bentham's design for a prison in which a watchtower in the middle facilitated the possibility of the prisoners, in cells arranged around the outside, being under surveillance all the time. Those doing the surveillance could watch without themselves being seen, while inmates had to *assume that they were observable* at all times, even if this was not in fact the case. Michel Foucault used the panopticon as a metaphor to understand how subjects internalize disciplinary power. It captures vividly the notion of a surveillance society.

This version of surveillance was challenged by Thomas Mathieson (1997) who argued that in societies dominated by media rather than the many being under surveillance by the few, there is a reversal in which the few are watched by the many. He calls this idea the synopticon. It resonates with contemporary media culture and celebrity in which the "masses" follow an elite of models, actors, and musicians.

However, Alison Winch has argued that neither the panopticon nor the synopticon fully captures the nature of contemporary surveillance:

> The fragmentation of media audiences into niche markets and evolution of a web 2.0 world where women coproduce and participate in brand spreading, means that the image of the synopticon and panopticon needs development. In digital culture, the panopticon, the synopticon and the paradigms of the many watching the many women, work in harmony. The internalised gaze is honed, perfected and given the opportunity to indulge through synoptic practices such as celebrity scrutiny. This is then devolved among gendered networks through which women can relate and express intimacy. In the gynaeopticon they all turn their eyes on each other in tightly bound networks where they gaze and gazed upon.
>
> *(ms p. 5)*

Building on Winch's important intervention, I would argue that contemporary culture teaches practices of micro scrutiny and assessment – whether they are directed from "ordinary people" to celebrities or whether they are implicated in our looks between ourselves – Winch's (2013) "girlfriend gaze" or what we have called "peer surveillance" (Ringrose et al., 2012). Research by Ana Elias supports this notion of a homosocial gaze, characterized simultaneously by affection and by "normative cruelties" (Ringrose and Renold, 2010), and "warmly-couched hostility" (Elias and Gill, 2016). Young women in Elias's study in the UK and Portugal felt themselves to be subject to almost ubiquitous surveillance. Simone talked about feeling that on the (London) underground "everyone is scanning you, like everyone is measuring you, taking my measures." This experience offered few safe spaces – not even the changing rooms at the gym or pool. One woman described feeling that even in the most cursory "glance" she was being "x-rayed."

Another vividly expressed her experience of being subject to a "checklist" gaze – in which other women would sweep up and down her body "checking out" different features of her appearance:

> Adriana: "I experience it on a daily basis, I mean. . . . If I happen to be at any given place and even with people that know me well . . . I realise that they look at you very often from head to toe in order to grasp how you look and if there is anything different in the way you look, kind of 'ok, hold on, let me check you out!' I understand that it is not malicious, most of the time . . . but . . . it feels almost like a checklist kind of 'ok you are approved, move ahead'" [makes gesture as if on production line for robots]
>
> *(quoted in Elias, forthcoming)*

Such modes of apprehending one another as women also relate to what Terri Senft (2008) has called "the grab" as a characteristic form of attention in social media. In this postfeminist economy of visibility, men are frequently imagined as bearers of a more benign gaze, with women the ones who both appreciate and attack other women in a form of intimate homosocial policing (envy, appreciation). Heterosexual men, by contrast, are often depicted only as "admirers" of women, presented as "grateful" when any woman shows them attention or is sexually interested in them – a motif that runs throughout magazine sex advice (Gill, 2009; Barker et al., 2018). However, Rachel O'Neill's (2017) work on pickup culture challenges this view, showing vividly how men's looks at women can be hostile, evaluative, and vicious. Likewise Laura Thompson's (2018) work on heterosexual dating sites compellingly demonstrates how a common response among men to a rebuff – however gentle or polite (e.g., "Thanks but I'm seeing someone else now") – can provoke vitriolic abuse that is almost always centered on the woman's appearance (e.g., "I didn't like you anyway you fat bitch."). So common have these forms of abuse become that dedicated sites exist for women to post their experiences (Tinder Nightmares, Bye Felipe). "Selfie-hatred" sites are another arena which provide a vehicle for men to attack women's ugliness and narcisissism (Burns, 2015), part of a wider "networked misogyny" (Banet-Weiser and Miltner, 2016). These forms of horizontal surveillance, then, are not only "gynaeoptic" (among women) but circulate across gender lines, but with women as their primary object.

Self-surveillance

The final modality of surveillance I want to consider is self-surveillance, which sits alongside media surveillance and horizontal surveillance. In a moment in which practices of looking are so central to postfeminist culture, it would be surprising if this hadn't extended to the self. And indeed it has! Again it seems to play out in profoundly assymetrical ways, with women exhorted to relentless self-scrutiny and self-improvement, incited to see and apprehend themselves through what Susan Bordo (1997) called a "pedagogy of defect," which operates at ever finer levels. This is seen clearly in the extraordinarily rapid development of smartphone apps dedicated to the purpose. While many self-tracking and self-monitoring apps – for example those concerned with exercise, sleep, time management, or various health indicators (blood pressure, blood sugar, heart rate) are targeted and used across genders, a growing number of genres of apps focus preeminently upon women. These include "psycho-technology apps" (e.g., around developing mindfulness, positive thinking, happiness, and confidence/self-esteem); dieting apps that inform, evaluate, and track food intake; the enormous range of applications marketed to women around menstruation, conception, pregnancy, and parenting; and proliferating "beauty apps" – of which there are tens of thousands already. I consider these briefly here as one example of how the surveillant imaginary extends to the self.

Earlier I highlighted the proliferation of images of magnifying glasses, tape measures and high-definition imaging technologies as tropes in cosmetics advertising. A quantified/biometric rationality increasingly runs through contemporary beauty culture. This could be seen as a metricization of the postfeminist gaze, which subjects the female body to increasingly "scientific" and quantified forms of surveillance and judgment, which – as we have argued elsewhere (Elias and Gill, 2016) – now extends to trichological, glandular, dermatological, vascular, and genetic aesthetics, no longer even seeing the skin as a meaningful boundary. This is further underscored with the development of beauty pharmacology (e.g., tablets to promote healthy skin and nails, drinks to build collagen) as well as the contemporary force of the "clean eating" movement with its ideas of being "beautiful on the inside" (too). The apps that we consider below are usually free of charge or under a dollar and push the postfeminist surveillant beauty culture even further in this direction, with a focus on scanning and surveilling the self in evermore minute fashion.

It is possible to identify several distinct genres of self-surveilling beauty app. First and most ubiquitous are "filters" and "selfie-modification" apps which promise to edit and enhance photos ready for posting. Amy Slater from the Centre for Appearance Research in Bristol found in her research in seven European countries that 43% of young women routinely used filters and 74% agreed with the statement that "I would never publish a photo that I don't look my best in." The use of filters on selfies has become so commonplace that a filter has been built into the reverse photo function of most new phones since 2016, *automatically* enhancing selfies in a set number of highly predictable and formulaic ways.

The app versions of filters promise to help you more closely resemble ideals of normative femininity with capacities to lose weight, contour the face, "swipe to erase blemishes, whiten teeth, brighten dark circles and even reshape your facial structure" (Face Tune). They encode troubling racialized subtexts too, with popular features including eyelid reshaping, nose remodeling, or skin lightening in increasingly transnational circuits of beauty. As Ana Elias and I have argued elsewhere, selfie-modification apps "increase the extent to which the female body and face are rendered visible as a site of crisis and commodification." Increasingly they also produce feedback loops in which cosmetics (e.g., foundation, tightening serum) are claimed to reproduce on actual embodied faces the filter effects produced by these apps: a definite case of life being forced to imitate art(ifice). As with other types of beauty apps, they further intensify visual literacies of the face, feeding into the extent to which more and more products and practices become normatively demanded. MAC now has an eight-step routine for coloring the lips alone!

Pedagogic apps offer instructions and tutelage in techniques to enhance appearance, delivering it in the form of professional help from "your personal beauty advisor" on your phone. While there is much generic tutoring, similar to magazine's tips on "how to perfect smoky eyes" and so forth, what is striking is the extent to which camera phones have facilitated customizable "help." For example, many apps allow you to upload a photo so that they can advise on what colors look good, what hairstyle would suit, what foundation match is ideal, what your ideal brow arch would look like – and then on how to achieve and perfect the recommended looks. "Try-out" apps take this several steps further, allowing you to enact a "virtual makeover" of your face or body. "Do you sometimes wonder how you would look with whiter teeth and a brighter smile?" one app asks – and instantly shows you the made-over "you." Plastic Surgery Simulator Lite and many other apps ask people, "How would you look with a different nose, chin, breasts or buttocks, or with less weight?" Facetouchup promises, "We bring you the same digital imaging technology that surgeons use." Horizontal links to the plastic surgery industry are well-established, and increasingly these apps form a digital shop window for women considering cosmetic procedures – complete with GPS location-based "push notifications" with "reviews, special offers, etc."

A different type of beauty app takes self-surveillance to a whole new level by using the camera function of smartphones to scan the face or body for actual or potential damage: broken veins, sun damage, moles, and so forth. These "problems" may not be visible to the naked eye but can be predicted using apps such as UMSkinCheck or Smoking Time Machine, allowing users to engage in anticipatory labor to forestall or mitigate these risks. While some of these detect serious health conditions (e.g., indications of skin cancer), the vast majority are about aesthetic self-surveillance: no one dies of tiny broken capillaries or of cellulite on the upper arms!

Finally an enormous number of apps promise "aesthetic benchmarking." "Do you ever wonder if you are ugly and your friends just don't tell you? Ugly Meter, Face Meter, Golden Beauty Meter, and many other apps will offer you their (algorithmic) answers to these questions. You can also check out How Old Do I Look? How Hot Am I? and determine your degree of facial symmetry or how closely you resemble the golden ratio. In giving their feedback, there are no holds barred: "You're so ugly you could win a contest," along with products, labor, or cosmetic procedures that might help: eye bag removal, laser hair therapy, and so forth. Quite aside from the particularities of each of these popular apps, what they do collectively, in my view, is quite extraordinarily to intensify the surveillant gaze, inciting girls and women to self-surveill, to scan, to monitor, to submit to judgment, to consider themselves, above all, as flawed, defective and in need of forensic self-scrutiny and relentless aesthetic labor" (Elias et al., in press).

Conclusion: postfeminist looking and neoliberal optics

Forty years ago, the way that art, film, and television "looked at" and portrayed women was subject to animated discussion. John Berger (1972) wrote that women in art were continually presented as objects: "men look and women appear"," he argued; "men look at women and women watch themselves being looked at." Laura Mulvey (1975) discussed the cinematic gaze arguing that men were "bearers of the look" and women defined by their "to be looked-at-ness." Decades of discussion in feminist studies, queer theory, and black and anti-racist scholarship challenged this "monolithic" position with its tendency to deny female agency, to elevate gender above all other differences (e.g., class, race, age), to remain trapped in a heteronormative framing, and to "read off" meanings from studies of texts rather than examining the viewing practices of actual embodied viewers and audiences

Almost half a century on, what is clear is that these issues are not resolved, but more than this, that we urgently require a revitalization of the debates about ways of seeing, looking, gazing – at ourselves, at each other, and at those people elevated to hypervisibility in contemporary culture, whether our entertainment celebrities or our politicians. What I have sought to do in this chapter is to argue that surveillance is a feminist issue, and one to which media, film, and cultural studies scholars have much to contribute. It is of course not just an issue of gender, as surveillance plays out unevenly both within and across genders: trans rather than cisgendered people, disabled rather non-disabled people are far more subject to surveillance, which is also marked in classed and racialized ways.

In this chapter in foregrounding gender in relation to the politics of looking, I have not, however, posited a gender bifurcated gaze, a split between an assumed binary of men who look and women who appear. Rather I have sought to argue that there are multiple modalities of surveillance in operation, including media surveillance, peer surveillance, and self-surveillance. These are not neatly gendered in the way that Berger or Mulvey might have argued. Rather, they are shaped by distinctively postfeminist and neoliberal ways of seeing and apprehending the self and others, by a sensibility in which extracting and producing value from the body is central and an entrepreneurial ethic dominates. Is there, as Mark Hayward (2013) has argued, a neoliberal optics? Are we seeing the emergence of a "postfeminist gaze"? (Riley, Evans, & Mackiewicz, 2016). One thing is sure: while we are all implicated in the surveillant imaginary, the "work of being watched" remains disproportionately women's work in a way that requires our urgent attention.

Acknowledgments

I would like to thank Ana Elias for ongoing discussions that informed this paper, and Elektra Lapavitsas for her editorial assistance.

References

Ahmed, S. *The Promise of Happiness*. Durham: Duke University Press, 2010.

Ajana, B. *Governing Through Biometrics: The Biopolitics of Identity*. Basingstoke: Palgrave Macmillan, 2013.

Allen, K. and Bull, A. *Call for Papers: Grit, Governmentality and the Erasure of Inequality: The Curious Rise of Character Education Policy*, 2016. www.britsoc.co.uk/events/forthcoming-events.aspx

Andrejevic, M. "Foreword." In Dubrofsky, R. E. and Shoshana, A. M. (eds.) *Feminist Surveillance Studies*. Durham and London: Duke University Press, 2015.

Banet-Weiser, S. *AuthenticTM: The Politics of Ambivalence in a Brand Culture*. New York: New York University Press, 2012.

Banet-Weiser, S. "'Confidence You Can Carry!': Girls in Crisis and the Market for Girls' Empowerment Organizations." *Continuum* 29(2), 2015a: 182–193.

Banet-Weiser, S. and Miltner, K. M. "# MasculinitySoFragile: Culture, Structure, and Networked Misogyny." *Feminist Media Studies* 16(1), 2016: 171–174.

Barker, M.-J., Gill, R. and Harvey, L. *Mediated Intimacy: Sex Advice in Media Culture*. Cambridge: Polity, 2018.

Bartky, S. L. *Femininity and Domination: Studies in the Phenomenology of Oppression*. New York and Oxon: Routledge, 1990.

Berger, J. *Ways of Seeing*. London: Penguin, 1972.

Betterton, R. *Looking on Images of Femininity in the Visual Arts and Media*. London: Pandora Press,1987.

Bordo, S. "Braveheart, Babe and the Contemporary Body." In *Twilight Zones: The Hidden Life of Cultural Images from Plato to O.J.* London: University of California Press, 1997.

Brown, W. "Neoliberalism and the End of Liberal Democracy." In *Edgework: Critical Essays on Knowledge and Politics*. Woodstock, Oxfordshire: Princeton University Press, 2005.

Brown, Wendy. *Undoing the Demos: Neoliberalism's Stealth Revolution*. Cambridge, Mit Press, 2015.

Burchell, G. "Liberal Government and Techniques of the Self." *Economy and Society* 22(3), 1993: 267–282.

Burns, A. L. "Self (ie)-discipline: Social Regulation as Enacted Through the Discussion of Photographic Practice." *International Journal of Communication*, 9, 2015: 18, ISSN 1932-8036. Available at: <https://ijoc.org/index.php/ijoc/article/view/3138>. Date accessed: 24 February 2019.

Conor, L. *The Spectacular Modern Woman: Feminine Visibility in the 1920s*. Indiana: Indiana University Press, 2004.

Davies, W. *The Limits of Neoliberalism: Authority, Sovereignty and the Logic of Competition*. Thousand Oaks, CA: Sage, 2014.

Dobson, A. S. *Postfeminist Digital Cultures: Femininity, Social Media, and Self-representation*. London: Springer, 2015.

Dubrofsky, R. E. and Magnet, S. A. "Feminist Surveillance Studies: Critical Interventions." In Dubrofsky, R. E. and Magnet, S. A. (eds.) *Feminist Surveillance Studies*. Durham and London: Duke University Press, 2015.

Elias, A. *Beautiful Body, Confident Soul: Young Women and the Beauty Labour of Neoliberalism*. Unpublished PhD thesis, submitted to King's College London, in press.

Elias, A. and Gill, R. "Beauty Surveillance: The Digital Self-monitoring Cultures of Neoliberalism." *European Journal of Cultural Studies*, 2016, 21(1), 59–77.

Elias, A., Gill, R. and Scharff, C. (eds.). *Aesthetic Labour: Rethinking Beauty Politics in Neoliberalism*. Basingstoke: Palgrave Macmillan, 2016.

Ericson, R. & Haggerty, K. *The New Politics of Surveillance and Visibility*. Toronto: University of Toronto Press, 2006.

Favaro, L. "'Just Be Confident Girls!': Confidence Chic as Neoliberal Governmentality." In Elias, A. S., Gill, R. and Scharff, C. (eds.) *Aesthetic Labour: Rethinking Beauty Politics in Neoliberalism.* Basingstoke: Palgrave Macmillan, 2016.

Featherstone, M. "Body Modification: An Introduction." *Body & Society*, 5(2–3), 1999: 1–13.

Forkert, K. "The New Moralism: Austerity, Silencing and Debt Morality." *Soundings*, 56(56), 2014: 41–53.

Gamman, L. and Marshment, M. *The Female Gaze: Women as Viewers of Popular Culture.* London: Women's Press, 1989.

Gill, Rosalind. "From sexual objectification to sexual subjectification: The resexualisation of women's bodies in the media." *Feminist Media Studies*, 3(1), 2003: 100–106.

Gill, R. *Gender and the Media.* Cambridge: Polity, 2007a.

Gill, Rosalind. "Mediated intimacy and postfeminism: A discourse analytic examination of sex and relationships advice in a women's magazine." *Discourse & Communication*, 3.4, 2009: 345–369.

Gill, Rosalind. "Unspeakable inequalities: Post feminism, entrepreneurial subjectivity, and the repudiation of sexism among cultural workers." *Social Politics: International Studies in Gender, State & Society*, 21.4, 2014: 509–528.

Gill, R. "Post-postfeminism? New Feminist Visibilities in Postfeminist Times." *Feminist Media Studies*, 2016.

Gill, R. "The Affective, Cultural and Psychic Life of Postfeminism." *European Journal of Cultural Studies*, 2017.

Gill, R. and Orgad, S. "The Confidence Culture." *Australian Feminist Studies* 86, 2015, 324–344

Gill, R. and Orgad, S. "Confidence Culture and the Remaking of Feminism." *New Formations* 91, 2017, 16–34

Gill, R. and Scharff, C. (eds.) *New Femininities: Neoliberalism, Postfeminism and Subjectivity.* London: Palgrave, 2011.

Harris, A. *Future Girl: Young Women in the Twenty-first Century.* Psychology Press, 2004.

Harvey, D. *A Brief History of Neoliberalism.* New York: Oxford University Press, 2005.

Hayward, M. "ATMs, Teleprompters and Photobooths: A Short History of Neoliberal Optics." *New Formations* 80/81, 2013: 194–208.

Henderson, M. and Taylor, A. *Postfeminism Down Under: The Australian Postfeminist Mystique.* Routledge, in press.

Hochschild, A. "Emotion Work, Feeling Rules, and Social Structure." *American Journal of Sociology*, 1979: 551–575.

Jane, E. A. "'Your a Ugly, Whorish, Slut': Understanding E-bile." *Feminist Media Studies* 14(4), 2014: 531–546.

Kanai, A. "WhatShouldWeCallMe? Self-Branding, Individuality and Belonging in Youthful Femininities on Tumblr." *M/C Journal* 18(1), 2015.

Kelan, Elisabeth K. "Gender fatigue: The ideological dilemma of gender neutrality and discrimination in organizations." *Canadian Journal of Administrative Sciences/Revue Canadienne des Sciences de l'Administration*, 26.3, 2009: 197–210.

Latour, B. "The Politics of Explanation: An Alternative." *Knowledge and Reflexivity: New Frontiers in the Sociology of Knowledge* 10, 1988: 155–176.

Lupton, D. *Self-tracking Modes: Reflexive Self-Monitoring and Data Practices.* Paper presented at Imminent Citizenships: Personhood and Identity Politics in the Informatic Age' workshop, 27 August 2014, ANU, Canberra, 2014a.

Lupton, D. "Beyond the Quantified Self: The Reflexive Monitoring Self." *This Sociological Life*, 2014b. http://simplysociology.wordpress.com/2014/07/28/beyond-the-quantifiedself-the-reflexive-monitoring-self/

Lyon, D. *Surveillance Society: Monitoring Everyday Life.* Buckingham: Open University Press, 2001.

Magnet, A.S. *When Biometrics Fail: Gender, Race and the Technology of Identity.* Durham, NC: Duke University Press, 2011.

Mathieson, T. "The Viewer Society: Michel Foucault's Panopticon Revisited." *Theoretical Criminology* 1(2), 1997: 215–234.

McRobbie, A. *The Aftermath of Feminism: Gender, Culture and Social Change.* London: Sage, 2009.

Mulvey, L. "Visual Pleasure and Narrative Cinema." *Screen* 16(3), 1975.

Nafus, D. and Sherman, J. "This One Does Not Go Up to 11: The Quantified Self Movement as an Alternative Big Data Practice." *International Journal of Communication* 8, 2014: 1784–1794.

Nakamura, L. "Afterword. Blaming, Shaming and the Feminization of Social Media." In Dubrofsky, R. E. and Shoshana, A. M. (eds.) *Feminist Surveillance Studies.* Durham and London: Duke University Press, 2015.

Neocleous, M. "Resisting Resilience." *Radical Philosophy* 178(6), 2013.
O'Neill, R. "The Aesthetics of Sexual Discontent: Notes From the London 'Seduction Community'." In Elias, A., Gill, R. and Scharff, C. (eds.) *Aesthetic Labour: Rethinking Beauty Politics in Neoliberalism*. London: Palgrave, 2017.
Projansky, S. *Spectacular Girls: Media Fascination and Celebrity Culture.* New York: New York University Press, 2014.
Rettberg, J. W. *Seeing Ourselves Through Technology: How We Use Selfies, Blogs and Wearable Devices to See and Shape Ourselves.* Basingstoke: Palgrave Macmillan, 2014.
Riley, Sarah, Adrienne Evans, and Alison Mackiewicz. "It's just between girls: Negotiating the postfeminist gaze in women's 'looking talk'." *Feminism & Psychology*, 26(1), 2016: 94–113.
Ringrose, J., Harvey, L., Gill, R. and Livingstone, S. "Teen Girls, Sexual Double Standards and 'Sexting': Gendered Value in Digital Image Exchange." *Feminist Theory* 14(3), 2013: 305–323.
Ringrose, J. and Renold, E. "Normative Cruelties and Gender Deviants: The Performative Effects of Bully Discourses for Girls and Boys in School." *British Educational Research Journal* 36(4), 2010: 573–596.
Scharff, C. "The Psychic Life of Neoliberalism: Mapping the Contours of Entrepreneurial Subjectivity." *Theory, Culture & Society*, 2016: 1–16 (published online ahead of print).
Schwartz, M. "The Horror of Something to See: Celebrity 'Vaginas' as Prostheses." *Genders Online Journal* 48, 2008. www.atria.nl/ezines/IAV_606661/IAV_606661_2010_51/g48_schwartz.html
Senft, Theresa M. *Camgirls: Celebrity and Community in the Age of Social Networks.* Vol. 4. Peter Lang, 2008.
Slater, A. *Social Media and Appearance Concerns.* Paper presented at Nuffield Council of Bioethics meeting 22 June, London, 2016.
Tasker, Y. and Negra, D. (eds.). *Interrogating Postfeminism: Gender and the Politics of Popular Culture.* London: Duke University Press, 2007.
Thompson, Laura. ""I can be your Tinder nightmare": Harassment and misogyny in the online sexual marketplace." *Feminism & Psychology*, 28.1, 2018: 69–89.
Walby, K. and Anais, S. "Research Methods, Institutional Ethnography and Feminist Surveillance Syudies." In Dubrofsky, R. E. and Magnet, S. A. (eds.) *Feminist Surveillance Studies.* Durham: Duke, 2015.
Winch, A. *Girlfriends and Postfeminist Sisterhood.* Basingstoke: Palgrave Macmillan, 2013.
Winch, A. "Brand Intimacy, Female Friendship and Digital Surveillance Networks." *New Formations* 84 (84–85), 2015: 228–245.

10

Hookup culture and higher education

Joseph Padgett and Lisa Wade

Introduction

Over the past decade, the term "hookup culture" has come to be used to characterize the sexual culture that dominates residential college campuses. Hookup culture prescribes frequent sexual contact between multiple individuals, all of whom claim no romantic intent. These sexual encounters themselves are referred to as "hookups," and the act of engaging in such an encounter is described as "hooking up." For prior reviews, see Garcia, Reiber, Massey, and Merriwether (2012), Heldman and Wade (2010), Pham (2017), Stinson (2010), and Wood and Perlman (2016).

Scholars describe it as a hookup *culture* because casual sexual encounters have become normative among adults of both sexes to such a degree that those who do not personally wish to hook up face a dilemma in terms of locating partners willing to engage in alternative types of partnering practices (Bogle 2008; Wade 2017a). Dating occurs, but most students only date someone with whom they have already been hooking up, meaning hookups are now the primary route into relationships (Kalish 2014; Kuperberg and Padgett 2015; Monto and Carey 2014; Regnerus and Uecker 2011). Rising college students are socialized into collegiate hookup culture by the mass media and colleges themselves (Conklin 2008; Garcia et al. 2012; Hartley and Morphew 2008; Reynolds 2014). On campus, hooking up is ideologically dominant, enacted in practice, and institutionalized (Wade 2017b).

The study of hookup culture is important for contemporary feminist theory, as hookup culture itself is gendered. It has been enabled by recent historical changes in gender-based norms and practices, some of which are positive. It reflects, for example, the erosion of the value of virginity, the proscription against pre- and non-marital sex for women, and the gendered double standard for sexuality based in the erasure of female sexual desire. In hookup culture, women are freer to have sex, and to have sex with many partners, without censure or punishment, and they do so with fewer unintended pregnancies and early marriages.

Hookup culture, however, also reproduces both gender difference and inequality. Women are at higher risk of sexual assault and report less pleasure and fewer orgasms than men (Armstrong, England, and Fogarty 2012; Armstrong and Budnick 2015; Cantor et al. 2015; Fisher, Cullen, and Turner 2000; Flack et al. 2007; Kilpatrick, Resnick, Ruggiero, Conoscenti, and McCauley 2007;

Krebs, Lindquist, Warner, Fischer, and Martin 2007; Sinozich and Langton 2014; White House Task Force to Protect Students from Sexual Assault 2014). They also report higher rates of regret, distress, and lowered self-esteem, among other emotional and psychological harms (Bersamin et al. 2013; Eagan et al. 2014; Eshbaugh and Gute 2008; Fisher, Worth, Garcia, and Meredith 2012; Flack et al. 2007; Freitas 2008; Lewis, Granato, Blaney, Lostutter, and Kilmer 2012; Owen, Fincham, and Moore 2011; Paul and Hayes 2002; Smith, Kristofferson, Davidson, and Herzog 2011; Stepp 2007). Gender intersects with other student characteristics, structuring their experience along race, class, and other lines as well (Allison and Risman 2014; Armstrong and Hamilton 2013; Bogle 2008; Brimeyer and Smith 2014; Freitas 2008; Kuperberg and Padgett 2015, 2016; Owen et al. 2011; Rupp and Taylor 2013; Rupp, Taylor, Regev-Messalem, Fogarty, and England 2014; Spell 2016).

Hooking up is how young people on campus today explore sex and find love. It may be, in fact, how the majority of youth do so, both in and out of college and before and after enrollment. Like the sexual cultures that came before it, it creates gendered opportunities and constraints that shape men's and women's experiences in different and often unequal ways. Sexuality continues to be an arena of both feminist struggle and masculine domination in which new freedoms sometimes come alongside new forms of power and control. Understanding these dynamics is important to feminist theory and action. To this end, in this entry we offer historical context for understanding the emergence of hookup culture in higher education, review the basics of what we know, and make suggestions for future research.

Historical context for collegiate hookup culture

During the colonial era in the United States, most college students were -classmiddle- men training to become ministers (Bowman 2015; Brubacher and Rudy 1997; Rudolph 1962 [1990]; Thelin 2004). Curriculums were rigorous, schedules were rigid, and religious values were front and center. The idea that students should have fun was introduced by the sons of wealthy families, who began sending their children to college in the mid-1700s. These students resisted the religiosity of their instructors, the tedium of the curriculum, and the expected subordination to authority, kicking off 100 years of riots and rebellions on college campuses.

Some of these students consolidated their resistance into social fraternities. Beginning in 1825, against the better judgment and efforts of college presidents (Hitchcock 1863), these elite social groups sprang up on college campuses. In just a few decades, there were 299 chapters of 22 fraternities at 71 colleges (Syrett 2009). Fraternity men innovated the college lifestyle that we see on campuses today, prioritizing their social lives over their intellectual ones. By the early 1900s, wrote the historian Nicholas Syrett (2009: 146), it was "glaringly obvious" that, "for the most part, fraternity men did not study much, dedicating themselves instead to extracurricular activities, camaraderie, athletics, and having fun."

Fraternity men added the sexual conquest of women into their repertoire beginning in the early 1900s. Prior to that era, fraternity men primarily had sex with women who had substantially lower social and economic status: poor women, sex workers, and women they enslaved. Fraternity men enjoyed these activities, but they were not framed as a game. The economic and legal inequality between the men and the women involved gave women little power to negotiate sexual terms, so extracting sexual favors from them couldn't easily be defined as a "win."

By 1930, though, women made up 40% of the national collegiate population. Around this time, the wider sexual culture was transitioning from courtship to dating. Courtship was characterized by heavy familial involvement in, and direct monitoring of, the partnering process. Dating began supplanting courtship as Americans increasingly began living in cities with night lives. Partnering activities shifted from private family homes to the public sphere and became more peer-influenced. Dates commonly involved economic consumption, taking place in public venues such as soda parlors and theaters, but the contexts of dates remained intimate in the sense that a dating couple went out alone or with a small group of other dating pairs (Bailey 1989; England and Thomas 2007). While sex outside of marriage remained stigmatized, especially for women, the shift from courtship to dating began to separate marriage from sexual activity to some degree. It is noteworthy that, although dating retained the sexual exploration characteristic of the very latest stages of courtship, it emerged not only as a new pattern of sexual partnering but as a recreational activity.

On campus, with fraternity men's attention turned to women who were ostensibly their social and economic equals (in every way except for gender), college men reframed the extraction of sexual favors as competitive. If these women were supposed to say "no," had the power to do so, and much to lose if they did not, then men had to work hard to get them to say yes. Around this time fraternity men began measuring each other's status by their sexual exploits.

During the same decades, life on college campuses became an American cultural curiosity. The mass media began profiling college life and the "college novel," a new genre of fiction, started filling bookstores shelves (Hevel 2014; Syrett 2009). The fraternity man was centered in this coverage and came to stand in for what *Life* magazine called "youth culture" (Cosgrove 2013). The party lifestyle invented by fraternity men and incubated in their elite social clubs was held up as the model for how all members of an increasingly diverse population of young people pursuing higher education should "do" college.

By the 1960s, the baby boomers were chafing against in loco parentis and colleges increasingly decided to treat students like adults instead of children (Peril 2006). The 1978 movie *Animal House* quickly became a cultural touchstone for college life, continuing to shape students expectations today (Wasykiliw and Currie 2012). Responding to the popularity of the movie, the alcohol industry began marketing directly to college students, spending millions on collegiate advertising campaigns (Moffett 1989; Sperber 2000; Wechsler and Wuethrich 2002). When the drinking age was raised in all states from 18 to 21 between 1984 and 1987, the idea that some went to college to have fun was fully entrenched. Fraternity membership, which had decreased during the anti-institutional post-Vietnam era, again soared (Syrett 2009). With bars and clubs now checking IDs, staff policing residence halls, and sororities not allowed to throw parties with alcohol, fraternities and similar organizations became the last place on and around college campuses where students could party like they thought they should (Wade 2017a).

While partying in college – and the sexual conquest that had become central to it – had always been a male prerogative, the idea that women have a right to party and have sex like men was one outcome of the sexual revolution and women's movement. Though feminists of that era advocated for many changes, the one that most powerfully took hold was the idea that women should have access to parts of life once reserved for men. In the decades since, women have increasingly entered previously male-dominated occupations and leisure activities (Catalyst 2016). They have also increasingly adopted "masculine" personality traits (Risman 2018; Twenge 1997). Called the "stalled" or "unfinished" revolution (Davis, Winslow, and Maume 2017; Gerson 2011), this has not been matched by men's movement into female spheres or adoption of feminized traits. When young men and women arrive on college campuses today, then, they both tend to bring the idea that sexual activity should follow a stereotypically male model.

Scholars place the emergence of a hookup culture and decline of a dating culture on college campuses somewhere around the late 1980s or early 1990s (Bogle 2008; Downing-Matibag and Geisinger 2009; England, Shafer, and Fogarty 2007; Fielder and Carey 2010b; Heldman and Wade 2010). Inspired by the sexual revolutionaries in the 1960s and '70s, sexual norms began to shift more dramatically toward permissiveness. Young people began spending time in "party" atmospheres and engaging in casual sex with greater frequency. These highly social, large party settings replaced the smaller, more intimate gatherings which characterized dating. The casual sex encounters that began during such events are comparable to today's hookups, which entail individuals meeting at bars, clubs, music events, and other large parties, often for the first time, and engaging in a range of sexual activity

The children of people who grew up during the sexual revolution began arriving on campus in the late 1980s. This decade was characterized by a lengthening of education, delayed marriage, improved access to birth control methods and abortion, and rising individualism, androcentrism, neoliberalism, and post- or neoliberal feminism (Arnett 2006; Bay-Cheng and Goodkind 2015; Butler 2013; Hamilton and Armstrong 2009; Harden 2013; Laumann et al. 1994; Rottenberg 2017; Stinson 2010; Twenge 1997, 2009). As sexual culture shifted from courtship to dating to hooking up, Americans slowly disconnected sex from marital relationships. When sexual culture was characterized by courtship, sex, and marriage were nearly inextricable. After dating came to prominence, relationship requirements replaced the more prohibitive marital restriction. With hooking up, the distance between sex and commitment has become wider still, at least during young adulthood.

The college years, then – stereotypically a part of young adulthood, even if not in practice – are generally seen as a time to experiment sexually, with serious relationships often framed as time-consuming and emotionally distracting (Bogle 2008; Regnerus and Uecker 2011; Rosenfeld 2007; Rosin 2012; Vander Ven 2001; Wade 2017a). The campus environment concentrates students into an institutionally embedded, socially pre-selective context where students meet others who have similar worldviews and interests, leading to more compatible matches, while perceiving a degree of safety and shared identity (Kimmel 2008; Kuperberg and Padgett 2015; Laumann, Ellingson, Mahay, Paik, and Youm 2004). Hookups fit better than relationships with the rhythm and structure of campus life (Wade 2017b), such that it is now institutionalized. This institutionalization probably started at larger and more socially progressive institutions, spreading to smaller and more conservative institutions over time. Research conducted on various types of colleges and universities in the 2000s suggests it is now present on all or most residential campuses of all kinds, with the rare exception of ones dominated by an assertive, top-down sexual culture (e.g., evangelical and Mormon institutions). Today, living on campus usually means hookup culture becomes a part of one's life such that even students who are reluctant to hook up contend with the culture (Allison and Risman 2014; Armstrong and Hamilton 2013; Wade 2017a, 2017b).

Hooking up: the basics

In this section, we review the facts as we know them: who hooks up and with whom; with what frequency and sexual content; when, where, and how students hook up; and with what motivations and outcomes. We draw on existing research and also rely on data from the Online College Social Life Survey (OCSLS; N = 24,131). These data were collected by Paula England and collaborators between 2005 and 2011 from students at 22 institutions of higher learning across all regions of the United States, including 12 research universities, five comprehensive regional universities, four liberal arts colleges (two affiliated with a religion), and one community college. While the data are based on a convenience sample, mostly in large introductory sociology courses, and thus not fully representative of students nationally, the OCSLS is the largest, most comprehensive set of data available for analyzing college student hookup behaviors. Unless otherwise cited, the data is derived from our own analysis of the OCSLS.

Hooking up occurs on college campuses at moderate rates – with women reporting slightly fewer hookups than men

Researchers report variously that 60%–80% of college students have hooked up (see also Fielder and Carey 2010a; Kuperberg and Padgett 2015). On average, men report about 0.23 more hookups than female students – a small but statistically significant difference. Including abstainers, students report an average of eight hookups by their senior year. A minority of students – 14% – hook up ten times or more (Armstrong et al. 2010; Ford et al. 2015; England et al. 2007 Monto and Carey 2014). Other smaller quantitative studies of individual institutions report similar numbers (Abercrombie and Mays 2013; Fielder et al. 2013; Foxhall 2010; Grello, Welsh, and Harper 2006; Katz, Tirone, and van der Kloet 2012; Knox and Zusman 2009; Najmabadi 2012; Uecker, Pearce, and Andercheck 2015).

Differences in hookup culture participation exist by race, as well, intersecting with gender. The average number of hookups overall is 4.06, but black men (with an average of 6.03), white men (5.51), and white women (4.33) report higher average numbers of hookups than do black women (2.50) and Asian men (2.77). This may echo what Wade (2017a) refers to as a hierarchy of sexual desirability in the erotic marketplace, wherein white men and women and black men are at the top, making it easier for them to find willing partners.

Of the more than 24,000 OCSLS respondents, 36 self-identified as transgender (about 0.15%), and the average number of hookups among transgender respondents (4.56) was statistically the same as their cisgender peers (4.06), but more research is needed to confirm this finding. Likelihood of engagement in and frequency of hookups differ by sexual preference for men but not women. Kuperberg and Padgett (2016) found homosexual men to be more than twice as likely as their heterosexual counterparts to have hooked up since starting college, but found the likelihood of having engaged in hookups to be about the same for homosexual and heterosexual women. The average number of hookups for heterosexual and homosexual women responding to the OCSLS was the same (3.59); the average for heterosexual men was 4.88, compared to 6.80 for homosexual men.

Religiosity does not correlate with hookup participation, except in very specific ways (Kuperberg and Padgett 2016). Women who regularly attend religious services are less likely than other women to have hooked up, with women who attend religious services once or more per month having an average of 2.57 hookups, compared to 3.96 among women who attend religious services a few times per year and 4.03 among women who never attend religious services. Men who attend religious services once per month or more are less likely than other men to have hooked up and have a lower average number of hookups (3.75) than other men. However, men who attend religious services a few times per year are more likely to have hooked up and have a somewhat higher average number of hookups (5.58) than men who never attend religious services (5.13).

Fraternity and sorority membership also has an impact on engagement in hookup culture. Among fraternity and sorority members, the average number of hookups is 6.77, compared to 3.69 among non-members. Athletes are another group who are afforded status on college campuses; they hold a special place in hookup culture as well, being sought-after hookup partners for some (Wade 2017a). The percentage of OCSLS respondents who report having hooked up at least once is higher among athletes (72%) than non-athletes (61%), and the average number of hookups is also higher among athletes (5.64) than non-athletes (3.93).

The sexual content of hookups varies substantially – but women report less, and less orgasmic, sexual activity than men

Respondents to the OCSLS were asked about the sexual content of their most recent hookup. Based on their reports, only about 1% of students reported no sexual contact with the partner of their most recent hookup; 62% reported that either they manually stimulated their partner's genitals using their hand or vice versa; 39% reported receiving or performing oral sex; 41% reported engaging in vaginal sex; and about 2.5% engaged in anal sex. Overall, 42% of students report some type of penetrative sex during their most recent hookup encounter, and 13% report having had penetrative sex without the use of a condom.

The level of sexual activity reported by males relative to females is found to differ significantly, with males reporting more sexual activity of all types than females. Sixty-seven percent of males and 59% of females reported manual genital stimulation; 48% of males and 35% of females reported giving or receiving oral sex; 5% of males and 1% of females reported engaging in anal sex. The frequency of vaginal sex showed the smallest, yet still statistically significant, difference between males (42%) and females (40%) (Kuperberg and Padgett 2015).

While there is essentially no difference in the number of men (28%) and women (26%) who report performing oral sex on their hookup partner, far more men (42%) than women (22%) report receiving oral sex from their partner during their most recent hookup. Women who stimulate their own genitals during sexual activity increase their odds of orgasm (Armstrong et al. 2012), however this behavior is more prevalent during hookups for men (13%) than women (6%). Men generally report orgasm from hookups much more frequently than women (44% and 21%, respectively). Orgasm is more common when considering only those hookups that involve penetrative sex, but even in this case, men (78%) more frequently report orgasm than women (42%).

Hooking up is a scripted sexual activity – still reflecting a gendered active/passive binary

Most hookups, especially ones with a new partner, begin at a party on or near campus. About 30% of students report having met their most recent hookup partner in a bar or club, with other common meeting contexts being institutional settings, such as classes and study groups (30%) and dorms (18%). When respondents were asked where they and their partner were directly before their most recent hookup encounter, about 12% indicated a fraternity or sorority party, 6% a party at a dorm, 16% just hanging out in a dorm, 20% a party at an apartment or house where students live, and 13% at a bar or nightclub. Regarding where they actually went to hookup during their most recent encounter, 30% of students indicated their own room, 35% said in a partner's room, another 13% said a room that was not their or their partner's but was private, and 13% indicated that they hooked up in plain sight in a public place.

Reflecting historical power dynamics on college campuses, the party scene on most campuses is largely controlled by male students who throw parties. This party scene, where students commonly locate hookup partners, is characterized by socializing in large groups, drunkenness, loud music, and dancing (Allison and Risman 2014; Bogle 2008; Ford et al. 2015; Hollowell 2010; Kuperberg and Padgett 2015; Paul and Hayes 2002; Reid, Webber, and Elliot 2015; Russett 2008; Vander Ven 2011; Wade 2017a). Most hookups occur under the influence of alcohol because drunkenness is part of how students differentiate between casual versus non-casual sex (Wade 2017a). Men have consumed an average of six drinks and women an average of four (Ford et al. 2015, see also Barriger and Vélez-Blasini 2013). Reflecting the intersection of race and gender, white men consume the most alcohol (six drinks on average), followed by Hispanic men (five), Asian men and white women (four), black men and Asian and Hispanic women (three), and black women (two). The use of marijuana and other drugs accompanies hookups less frequently. About 11% of all OCSLS respondents report marijuana use during their most recent hookup, with rates being higher among males (15%) than females (9%). Only about 3%

of males and 1% of females reported having been under the influence of other drugs, such as methamphetamine or cocaine.

Most students, both men (48%) and women (52%), report that they mutually initiate hookups with their hookup partner. However, women are more frequently passive actors, with 39% of women indicating that their partner initiated their most recent hookup encounter, compared to only 25% of men. Twenty-six percent of men report initiating their most recent hookup, but only 9% of women report being the initiator. Many hookups begin with "grinding," or sexualized partner dancing (Ronen 2010). Grinding is usually initiated by a student approaching another on the dance floor from behind; in other-sex couplings, the man almost always approaches the woman. Students transition from grinding to hooking up if touching becomes intimate or the person in front turns around to allow kissing. If students hook up with the same person more than once, their sexual activity typically ascends according to a scripted erotic trajectory in which fellatio generally precedes either intercourse or cunnilingus (Ford et al. 2015).

Students generally enjoy their hookups – though women are especially likely to report harm

OCSLS respondents overwhelmingly enjoyed their hookups; about 48% said that overall they enjoyed their most recent encounter "very much," 37% indicated enjoying the encounter "somewhat," and 10% "very little." Only 5% indicated not enjoying the hookup at all, with no substantial difference in enjoyment by gender. Asked how they felt looking back on their most recent hookup encounter, 46% of were glad they hooked up, 40% had neutral feelings about it, and only 14% regretted doing so. In addition to viewing their hookups positively overall, students also enjoy the sex during their hookups. Nearly half reported enjoying the sex that took place in their most recent hookup "very much" – 52% of men and 48% of women.

Researchers have, however, found relationships between casual sex and lowered self-esteem, regret, distress among those who regret hookups, feelings of emotional detachment, and other emotional and psychological harms, with women possibly experiencing these things more so than men (Bersamin et al. 2013; Eagan et al. 2014; Eshbaugh and Gute 2008; Fisher et al. 2012; Flack et al. 2007; Freitas 2008; Lewis et al. 2012; Owen et al. 2011; Paul and Hayes 2002; Smith et al. 2011; Stepp 2007). In Uecker et al.'s (2015) study, "uninspireds" reported more regret than the average student and "uninhibiteds" reported less (see also Vrangalova and Ong 2014).

Sexual contact always carries the risk of sexually transmitted infection and unintended pregnancy. Among those reporting penetrative sex, about 32% do so without using a condom (see also Fielder and Carey 2010b), and drinking alcohol, sexual ambivalence, and casualness about sex are all associated with lesser likelihood of use (Downing-Matibag and Geisinger 2009; Kuperberg and Padgett 2017; Lewis et al. 2012; MacDonald and Hynie 2008; Paul, McManus, and Hayes 2000).

Approximately 1 in 5 women in college and 1 in 16 men will be the victim of sexual assault (Armstrong and Budnick 2015; Cantor et al. 2015; Fisher et al. 2000; Kilpatrick et al. 2007; Krebs et al. 2007; Sinozich and Langton 2014; White House Task Force to Protect Students from Sexual Assault 2014). The OCSLS asked respondents about sexual violence during their most recent hookup encounter: 3% of men and 5% of women report either rape, attempted rape, or having unwanted sex because they were too intoxicated to prevent it. Additionally, 1% of men and 2% of women report having been verbally pressured into sex they did not want during their last hookup. This gives some idea about the occurrence of unwanted sex during hookups, but overall rates of sexual victimization since starting college are more alarming. About 17% have been the victim of either rape, attempted rape, or unwanted sex while incapacitated at some point since starting college, but this is more common among women (19%) than men (12%). Five percent of men and 9% of women report having been verbally pressured into having unwanted sex since starting college.

Students hook up for many reasons – but both women and men desire romantic relationships

College students hookup for physical pleasure (Fielder and Carey 2010a), out of a desire for non-romantic emotional closeness (Wade and Heldman 2012), because of lack of availability of partners for long-term relationships with whom to have sex (Kuperberg and Padgett 2016), or simply to fit in (Bogle 2008; Wade 2017a). Another motivation for engaging in casual sex, one popularly attributed to men, is to bolster one's social status (England and Thomas 2007), though this may not be a strictly male motivation (Wade 2017a).

The most common reason students report hooking up, though, is to meet a romantic partner and begin a committed relationship. Uecker et al. (2015) asked over 500 students who had hooked up at least once whether they did it for excitement, for pleasure, to conform, because they were too busy for anything more, and/or in the hopes of forming a relationship. Four clusters of motivations emerged: 50% were "utilitarians" (student who were hooking up to find a partner), 27% were "uninhibiteds" (students who were doing it for the fun and excitement), and 19% were "uninspireds" (students who did not generally have a reason for hooking up). The motivations for the remaining 4% were unclear. Garcia and Reiber (2008) similarly report that half of the college students they surveyed ($N = 507$) hooked up with a partner with whom they hoped to start a romantic relationship. About 44% of OCSLS respondents had some interest in a relationship with their partner prior to hooking up with them and 64% were interested in a relationship with the partner after the hookup took place. Women (33%) tended to indicate a complete lack of romantic interest in their partners after hooking up, somewhat less frequently than men (42%). Other research also finds differences by gender and race, too (Kuperberg and Padgett 2016).

Though most hookups do not turn into relationships, most relationships do begin with hookups (Kalish 2014). Hookups sometimes turn into dating and dating sometimes turns into a relationship. If an initial date goes well, additional dates follow; continued dating signals mutually increasing levels of relationship interest (Bailey 1989; Rose and Frieze 1993). Students may pull back on sexual behavior and restart the script when they transition to dating (Reid et al. 2015). There is considerably less sexual activity during dates. Thirty-two percent reported manual genital stimulation during their most recent date; 21% gave or received oral sex; 21% engaged in vaginal sex; and about 2% had anal sex. Substantially more sexual activity of all types took place during students' hookups relative to dates. In fact, many college students believe an inverse relationship exists between eagerness to have sex during a date and the degree of romantic interest in the dating partner. That is, the more interested a person is in having a serious, long-term relationship with their dating partner, the more reluctant they may be to have sex, preferring instead to "take things slowly" once romantic interest is present (Reid, Elliot, and Webber 2011; Wade 2017a). This represents a substantial reversal of the traditional sequence of relationship building leading toward sex, if not a complete separation of sex and relationship formation. Whereas romantic interests and relationship building previously preceded sex, sex now occurs prior to relationship development or separate from it altogether.

Students generally have more experience with hooking up than dating and more experience with dating than committed relationships (only 11% abstained from all three and a quarter engaged in all three). Still, by their senior year students report an average of 1.83 relationships each (defined as a commitment lasting six months or more), with 66% of men and 74% of women reporting at least one (Ford et al. 2015). While women are not more likely than men to say that they are interested in a committed relationship, women in relationships are six times as likely to report having an orgasm during their last sexual encounter as are women who are hooking up with a first-time partner and twice as likely to report an orgasm as are women who have hooked up with their partner three times or more (Armstrong et al. 2012).

Gender and the culture of hooking up

Collegiate hookup culture is possible because of historical changes that have given women more control over their sexuality and lifted some of the stigma of female sexual behavior, but it does not yet offer men and women the equal playing field it seems to promise. Though ostensibly both men and women are invited to be casually sexually active, gender continues to shape students' experiences. Thanks to the persistence of male-dominated Greek life and the tradition of male-controlled partying even in the absence of fraternities, male students generally have more influence over students' social and sexual lives. Party culture, in response, tends to reflect the priorities of privileged men on campus, involving heterosexualized environments, hypersexualized themes that objectify women, and maximized opportunities for casual sexual encounters. Those encounters are generally initiated by men who choose among women who are positioned as objects of their desire. The sexual activities typical of hookup encounters result in orgasm for men more often than they do for women. In addition to these inequities, women report higher rates of emotional and psychological harm due to their hookup experiences. Women are more likely to feel disrespected by their hookup partners, and they are more likely than men to be victims of sexual battery and assault, whereas men are more likely to perpetrate such violence.

Directions for future research

Moving forward, research at both macro and micro levels will help improve our understanding. On the micro end is the process by which hookup culture is enacted by individuals in interaction. Research on hookup culture thus far has done a better job of documenting the who, what, when, where, why, and with what consequences, than the *how*. This is probably because answering this kind of question generally requires close observation, which raises ethical concerns (Weinberg and Newmahr 2015; Wiederman 2008). Methodological innovation is required to address these concerns so that scholars can thicken the description of how hookup culture happens in practice.

On the macro end, while the OCSLS has been a boon for scholars, it is a non-representative sample of students, collected from a limited number of institutions as many as 12 years ago with a survey instrument designed before a critical mass of research. Some researchers have tapped major research datasets, such as the General Social Survey, to investigate hookup culture (e.g., Monto and Carey 2014), but these lack hookup-specific measures. The literature on hookup culture would benefit from a new, nationally representative sample of students that would enable a more precise picture of college sexual cultures.

Such a study would also enable us to discover how college hookup culture varies across different institutions. The existing research that offers an answer to this question does not reveal significant differences, except on commuter campuses and ones that impose a faith-based sexual culture from the top-down (Bogle 2008; England, personal communication; Lovejoy 2012). Higher education is so diverse, however, that it seems unlikely that this finding will survive future research. In particular, some types of schools, like historically black colleges and universities, have been almost completely neglected (but see Hall, Lee, and Witherspoon 2014).

The literature on hooking up would also benefit from a better understanding of the emotional life of students in hookup culture. The existing scholarship is contradictory: students report that they enjoy hooking up but also that it is the source of emotional pain and trauma. Living in hookup culture is an emotionally fraught, high-stakes experience about which most students have great ambivalence. We still have a lot to learn about why and which students like hookup culture, the myriad (and especially non-acute) causes of pain and pleasure, and how students manage their ambivalence. Research on sociosexuality is promising (e.g., Uecker et al. 2015; Vrangalova and Ong 2014), and we should continue to look into different experiences by gender, gender identity, race, class, disability, sexual orientation, Greek affiliation, other socially meaningful statuses, and their intersections.

Kalish (2014) asked students if they thought hookup culture helped or harmed students' abilities to form and maintain committed romantic relationships, and they largely believed the culture was harmful. They argued that it trivialized both sex and emotional connection and hindered the development of relationship-building skills (like open communication and interpersonal vulnerability). A productive next step in the literature may be exploring whether and how hooking up, adopting hookup culture's ideological underpinnings, or simply living in the culture shapes one's future sexual and romantic relationships.

Technology is likely relevant to the investigation of both hooking up and relationship formation. Hookup culture preceded widespread use of cell phones and far preceded hookup apps like Grindr and Tinder. Such technologies are not necessary to facilitate hookups when students live in a hookup culture, but they almost undoubtedly shape cultures today. We have little understanding of how. This work may involve theorizing the difference between hooking up as a behavior, the hookup script, and hookup cultures. If hookup cultures are geographically localized, for example, hookup apps might be serving to export the hookup script out of localized cultures and into wider ones. While there is a great deal of moral panic around the apps and how it might be changing sexual and romantic relationships, we have little sense as to the extent that this might be happening.

Relatedly, we know next to nothing about the extent to which the ideologies that promote hooking up supportive attitudes and behaviors are now a part of American culture. Existing hookup research is squarely focused on college students and the campus environment. While there are reasons to believe the campus environment is uniquely suited to, and has contributed to the emergence of, hookup culture, hookups are not likely to be strictly the province of college students. Asking where else in American society we find hookup cultures and examining hookups and the existence of hookup culture among non-college emerging adults, and all adults 21 to 101, is an important piece of the sexual behavior puzzle that is currently missing, representing a rich opportunity for future research.

Finally, all existing research paints hookup culture with a broad brush, finding harm for substantial numbers of participants. It is possible, however, to imagine cultures of casual sex that differ from the picture we have painted in meaningful ways. Others may be harmful in different and possibly worse ways, but it is also possible that there exist hookup cultures that are more caring and conscientious, less based on status hierarchy, physically and emotionally safer, and characterized by equal relations. As we continue to examine hookup cultures in various locales – both across institutions of higher education, throughout the public sphere, and comparatively across history – we would be wise to stay attuned to such differences, eventually building a literature on hookup cultures in the plural that enables us to better theorize the many roles of so-called casual sex in individuals' lives, their relationships, and their societies.

References

Abercrombie, Chelsey and Stephen Mays. 2013. "Let's Talk About Sex: The Truth Behind the Myth of Hook-Up Culture at the University of Georgia." *The Red and Black*, October 31.

Allison, Rachel and Barbara J. Risman. 2014. "'It Goes Hand in Hand With the Parties': Race, Class, and Residence in College Student Negotiations of Hooking Up." *Sociological Perspectives*, 57(1): 102–23.

Armstrong, Elizabeth A., Laura Hamilton, and Paula England. 2010. "Is Hooking Up Bad for Young Women?" *Context.* Retrieved February 15, 2016 from https://contexts.org/articles/is-hooking-up-bad-for-young-women/.

Armstrong, Elizabeth A. and Jamie Budnick. 2015. "Sexual Assault on Campus." *Council on Contemporary Families*, April 20. Retrieved February 15, 2016 from https://contemporaryfamilies.org/assault-on-campus-brief-report/.

Armstrong, Elizabeth A., Paula England, and Alison C. K. Fogarty. 2012. "Accounting for Women's Orgasm and Sexual Enjoyment in College Hookups and Relationships." *American Sociological Review*, 77(3): 435–62.

Armstrong, Elizabeth A. and Laura Hamilton. 2013. *Paying for the Party: How College Maintains Inequality.* Cambridge, MA: Harvard University Press.

Arnett, Jeffrey. 2006. *Emerging Adulthood: The Winding Road From the Late Teens Through the Twenties.* Oxford: Oxford University Press.

Bailey, Beth L. 1989. *From Front Porch to Backseat: Courtship in Twentieth Century America.* Baltimore, MD: John Hopkins University Press.

Barriger, Megan and Carlos J. Vélez-Blasini. 2013. "Descriptive and Injunctive Social Norm Overestimation in Hooking Up and Their Role as Predictors of Hook-Up Activity in a College Student Sample." *Journal of Sex Research*, 50(1): 84–94.

Bay-Cheng, Laina and Sara Goodkind. 2015. "Sex and the Single (Neoliberal) Girl: Perspectives on Being Single Among Socioeconomically Diverse Young Women." *Sex Roles*, 73(11/12). Retrieved February 29, 2016 from www.springerprofessional.de/journal-11199-onlinefirst-articles/5748366.

Bersamin, Merlina, Byron L. Zamboanga, Seth J. Schwartz, M. Brent Donnnellan, Monika L. Hudson, Robert S. Weisskirch, Su Y. Kim, V. Bede Agocha, Susan Krauss Whitebourne, and S. Jean Caraway. 2013. "Risky Business: Is There an Association between Casual Sex and Mental Health among Emerging Adults?" *Journal of Sex Research*, 51(1): 43–51.

Bogle, Kathleen A. 2008. *Hooking Up: Sex, Dating, and Relationships on Campus.* New York, NY: New York University Press.

Bowman, Rex. 2015. *Rot, Riot, and Rebellion: Mr. Jefferson's Struggle to Save the University that Changed America.* Charlottesville, VA: University of Virginia Press.

Brimeyer, Ted and William Smith. 2014. "Religion, Race, Social Class, and Gender Differences in Dating and Hooking Up Among College Students." *Sociological Spectrum*, 32(5): 462–73.

Brubacher, John Seiler and Willis Rudy. 1997. *Higher Education in Transition: A History of American Colleges and Universities.* Piscataway, NJ: Transaction.

Butler, Jess. 2013. "For White Girls Only?: Postfeminism and the Politics of Inclusion." *Feminist Formations*, 25(1): 35–58.

Cantor, David, Bonnie Fisher, Susan Chibnall, Reanne Townsend, Hyunshik Lee, Carol Bruce, and Gail Thomas. 2015. "Report on the AAU Campus Climate Survey on Sexual Assault and Sexual Misconduct." *Association of American Universities.* Retrieved February 15, 2016 from www.aau.edu/registration/public/PAdocs/Survey_Communication_9-18/Final_Report_9-18-15.pdf.

Catalyst. 2016. *Women in the Workforce: United States.* New York: Catalyst. Retrieved July 25, 2017 from www.catalyst.org/knowledge/women-workforce-united-states.

Conklin, John. 2008. *Campus Life in the Movies: A Critical Survey from the Silent Era to the Present.* Jefferson, NC: McFarland.

Cosgrove, Ben. 2013. "The Invention of Teenagers: LIFE and the Triumph of Youth Culture." *TIME*, September 28.

Davis, Shannon, Sarah Winslow, and David Maume. 2017. *Gender in the Twenty-First Century: The Stalled Revolution and the Road to Equality.* Oakland, CA: University of California Press.

Downing-Matibag, Teresa M. and Brandi Geisinger. 2009. "Hooking Up and Sexual Risk Taking among College Students: A Health Belief Model Perspective." *Qualitative Health Research*, 19(9): 1196–209.

Eagan, Kevin, Ellem Stolzberg, Joseph Ramirez, Melissa Aragon, Maria Ramirez Suchard, and Sylvia Hurtado. 2014. *The American Freshman: National Norms Fall 2014.* Los Angeles, CA: Higher Education Research Institute, UCLA.

England, Paula, Emily Fitzgibbons Shafer, and Alison C. K. Fogarty. 2007. "Hooking Up and Forming Romantic Relationships on Today's College Campuses." Pp. 559–72 in *The Gendered Society Reader*, edited by M. S. Kimmel and A. Aronson. New York, NY: Oxford University Press.

England, Paula and Reuben Thomas. 2007. "The Decline of the Date and the Rise of the Hookup." In *Family in Transition*, edited by A. Skolnick and J. Skolnick. New York, NY: Pearson.

Eshbaugh, Elaine and Gary Gute. 2008. "Hookups and Sexual Regret Among College Women." *Journal of Social Psychology*, 148(1): 77–89.

Fielder, Robyn L. and Michael P. Carey. 2010a. "Predictors and Consequences of Sexual 'Hookups' among College Students: A Short-Term Prospective Study." *Archives of Sexual Behavior*, 39: 1105–19.

Fielder, Robyn L. and Michael P. Carey. 2010b. "Prevalence and Characteristics of Sexual Hookups Among First-Semester Female College Students." *Journal of Sex and Marital Therapy*, 36: 346–59.

Fielder, Robyn L., Jennifer L. Walsh, Kate B. Carey, and Michael P. Carey. 2013. "Predictors of Sexual Hookups: A Theory-Based, Prospective Study of First-Year College Women." *Archives of Sexual Behavior*, 42(8): 1425–1441.

Fisher, Bonnie, Francis Cullen, and Michael Turner. 2000. *The Sexual Victimization of College Women*. Washington, DC: National Institute of Justice and Bureau of Justice Statistics.

Fisher, Maryanne, Kerry Worth, Justin Garcia, and Tami Meredith. 2012. "Feelings of Regret Following Uncommitted Sexual Encounters in Canadian University Students." *Culture, Health and Sexuality*, 14(1): 45–57.

Flack, William, Kimberly Daubman, Marcia Caron, Jenica Asadorian, Nicole D'Aureli, Shannon Gigliotti, Anna Hall, Sarah Kiser, and Erin Stine. 2007. "Risk Factors and Consequences of Unwanted Sex among University Students – Hooking Up, Alcohol, and Stress Response." *Journal of Interpersonal Violence*, 22(2): 139–57.

Ford, Jessie, Paula England, and Jonathan Bearak. 2015. "The American College Hookup Scene: Findings from the Online College Social Life Survey." *TRAILS: Teaching Resources and Innovations Library for Sociology Published Online*.

Foxhall, Emily. 2010. "Yalies, Under the Covers." *Yale News*, February 8.

Freitas, Donna. 2008. *Sex and the Soul: Juggling Sexuality, Spirituality, Romance, and Religion on America's College Campuses*. Oxford: Oxford University Press.

Garcia, Justin R. and Chris Reiber. 2008. Hook-Up Behavior: A Biopsychosocial Perspective. *Journal of Social, Evolutionary, and Cultural Psychology*, 2(4): 192–208.

Garcia, Justin R., Chris Reiber, Sean G. Massey, and Ann M. Merriwether. 2012. "Sexual Hookup Culture: A Review." *Review of General Psychology*, 16(2): 161–76.

Gerson, Kathleen. 2011. *The Unfinished Revolution: Coming of Age in a New Era of Gender, Work, and Family*. Oxford and New York, NY: Oxford University Press.

Grello, Catherine M., Deborah P. Welsh, and Melinda S. Harper. 2006. "No Strings Attached: The Nature of Casual Sex in College Students." *Journal of Sex Research*, 43(3): 255–67.

Hall, Naomi, Anna Lee, and Daphne Witherspoon. 2014. "Factors Influencing Dating Experiences Among African American Emerging Adults." *Emerging Adulthood*, 2(3): 184–94.

Hamilton, Laura and Elizabeth A. Armstrong. 2009. "Gendered Sexuality in Young Adulthood: Double Binds and Flawed Options." *Gender & Society*, 23: 589–616.

Harden, Nathan. 2013. "Peter Pan Goes to College." *Society*, 50(3): 257–60.

Hartley, Matthew and Christopher Morphew. 2008. "What's Being Sold and To What End? A Content Analysis of College Viewbooks." *Journal of Higher Education*, 79(6): 671–91.

Heldman, Caroline and Lisa Wade. 2010. "Hook-Up Culture: Setting a New Research Agenda." *Sexual Research and Social Policy*, 7: 323–33.

Hevel, Michael. 2014. "Setting the Stage for Animal House: Student Drinking in College Novels, 1865–1933." *Journal of Higher Education*, 85(3): 370–401.

Hitchcock, Edward. 1863. *Reminiscences of Amherst College: Historical Scientific, Biographical and Autobiographical*. Carlisle, MA: Applewood Books.

Hollowell, Clare. 2010. *The Subject of Fun: Young Women, Freedom, and Feminism*. Ph.D. dissertation, Centre for Gender and Women's Studies, Lancaster University, Lancasert, UK.

Kalish, Rachel. 2014. *Sexual Decision Making in the Context of Hookup Culture: A Mixed-Method Examination*. Ph.D., Stony Brook University.

Katz, Jennifer, Vanessa Tirone, and Erika van der Kloet. 2012. "Moving In and Hooking Up: Women's and Men's Casual Sexual Experiences during the First Two Months of College." *Electronic Journal of Human Sexuality*, 15: 1.

Kilpatrick, Dean, Heidi Resnick, Kenneth Ruggiero, Lauren Conoscenti, and Janna McCauley. 2007. *Drug-Facilitated, Incapacitated, and Forcible Rape: A National Study*. National Crime Victims Research and Treatment Center. Retrieved February 15, 2016 from www.ncjrs.gov/pdffiles1/nij/grants/219181.pdf.

Kimmel, M. 2008. *Guyland: The Perilous World Where Boys Become Men*. New York, NY: Harper.

Knox, David and Marty Zusman. 2009. "Sexuality in Black and White: Data from 783 Undergraduates." *Electronic Journal of Human Sexuality*, 12: 1.

Krebs, Christopher, Christine Lindquist, Tara Warner, Bonnie Fischer, and Sandra Martin. 2007. *The Campus Sexual Assault Study*. National Institute of Justice. Retrieved February 15, 2016 from www.ncjrs.gov/pdffiles1/nij/grants/221153.pdf.

Kuperberg, Arielle and Joseph E. Padgett. 2015. "Dating and Hooking Up in College: Meeting Contexts, Sex, and Variation by Gender, Partner's Gender, and Class Standing." *Journal of Sex Research*, 52(5): 517–31.

Kuperberg, Arielle and Joseph E. Padgett. 2016. "The Role of Culture in Explaining College Students' Selection into Hookups, Dates, and Long-Term Romantic Relationships." *Journal of Social and Personal Relationships*, 33(8): 1070–96.

Kuperberg, Arielle and Joseph E. Padgett. 2017. "Partner Meeting Contexts and Risky Behavior in College Students' Other-Sex and Same-Sex Hookups." *Journal of Sex Research*, 54(1): 55–72.

Laumnan, Edward O., John H. Gagnon, Robert T. Michael, and Stuart Michaels. *The Social Organization of Sexuality: Sexual Practices in the United States*. Chicago: University of Chicago Press.

Laumann, Edward O., Stephen Ellingson, Jenna Mahay, Anthony Paik, and Yoosik Youm. 2004. *The Sexual Organization of the City*. Chicago, IL: University of Chicago Press.

Lewis, Melissa, Hollie Granato, Jessica Blaney, Ty Lostutter, and Jason Kilmer. 2012. "Predictors of Hooking Up Sexual Behavior and Emotional Reactions Among U.S. College Students." *Archives of Sexual Behavior*, 41(5): 1219–29.

Lovejoy, Meg. 2012. *Is Hooking Up Empowering for College Women? A Feminist Gramscian Perspective*. Ph.D., Braideis University.

MacDonald, Tara and Michaela Hynie. 2008. "Ambivalence and Unprotected Sex: Failure to Predict Sexual Activity and Decreased Condom Use." *Journal of Applied Social Psychology*, 38(4): 1092–107.

Moffett, Michael. 1989. *Coming of Age in New Jersey: College and American Culture*. New Brunswick and London: Rutgers University Press.

Monto, Martin A. and Anna G. Carey. 2014. "A New Standard of Sexual Behavior? Are Claims Associated with The 'Hookup Culture' Supported by General Social Survey Data?" *Journal of Sex Research*, 51(6): 605–15.

Najmabadi, Shannon. 2012 "Hookup: The Search for Satisfation." *Daily Californian*, June 11.

Owen, Jesse, Frank Fincham, and Jon Moore. 2011. "Short-term Prospective Study of Hooking Up among College Students." *Archives of Sexual Behavior*, 40: 331–41.

Paul, Elizabeth L. and Kristen A. Hayes. 2002. "The Casualties of 'Casual' Sex: A Qualitative Exploration of the Phenomenology of College Students' Hookups." *Journal of Social and Personal Relationships*, 19(5): 639–61.

Paul, Elizabeth L., Brian McManus, and Allison Hayes. 2000. "'Hookups': Characteristics and Correlates of College Students' Spontaneous and Anonymous Sexual Experiences." *Journal of Sex Research*, 37(1): 76–88.

Peril, Lynn. 2006. *College Girls: Bluestockings, Sex Kittens, and Coeds, Then and Now*. New York, NY: W. W. Norton.

Pham, Janelle M. 2017. "Beyond Hookup Culture: Current Trends in the Study of College Student Sex and Where to Next." *Sociology Compass*, 11(8): e12499.

Regnerus, Mark and Jeremy Uecker. 2011. *Premarital Sex in America*. New York, NY: Oxford University Press.

Reid, Julie A., Sinikka Elliott, and Gretchen R. Webber. 2011. "Casual Hookups to Formal Dates: Refining the Boundaries of the Sexual Double Standard." *Gender and Society*, 25(5): 545–68.

Reid, Julie A., Gretchen Webber, and Sinikka Elliot. 2015. "'It's Like Being in Church and Being on a Field Trip': The Date Versus Party Situation in College Students' Accounts of Hooking Up." *Symbolic Interaction*, 38(2): 175–94.

Reynolds, Pauline. 2014. "Representing 'U': Popular Culture, Media, and Higher Education." *ASHE Higher Education Report*, 41(4): 1–145.

Risman, Barbara. 2018. *Where Will the Millennials Take Us: A New Generation Wrestles with the Gender Structure*. Oxford and New York, NY: Oxford University Press.

Ronen, Shelly. 2010. "Grinding on the Dance Floor: Gendered Scripts and Sexualized Dancing at College Parties." *Gender & Society*, 24(3): 355–77.

Rose, Suzanna and Irene Hanson Frieze. 1993. "Young Singles' Contemporary Dating Scripts." *Sex Roles*, 28(9/10): 499–509.

Rosenfeld, Michale J. 2007. *The Age of Independence: Interracial Unions, Same-Sex Unions, and the Changing American Family*. Cambridge, MA: Harvard University Press.

Rosin, Hanna. 2012. *The End of Men: And the Rise of Women*. New York, NY: Riverhead.

Rottenberg, Catherine. 2017. "Neoliberal Feminism and the Future of Human Capital." *Signs*, 42(2): 329–48.

Rudolph, Frederick. 1962 [1990]. *The American College and University: A History*. Athens, GA: University of Georgia Press.

Rupp, Leila and Verta Taylor. 2013. "Queer Girls on Campus: New Intimacies and Sexual Identities." Pp. 82–97 in *Intimacies: A New World of Relational Life*, edited by Alan Frank, Patricia Clough, and Steven Seidman. New York, NY: Routledge.

Rupp, Leila, Verta Taylor, Shiri Regev-Messalem, Alison C. K. Fogarty, and Paula England. 2014. "Queer Women in the Hookup Scene: Beyond the Closet?" *Gender and Society*, 28(2): 212–35.

Russett, Jill. 2008. *Women's Perceptions of High-Risk Deinking: Understanding Binge Drinking in a Gender Biased Setting*. Ph.D. dissertation, Department of Education, The College of William and Mary in Virginia, Williamsburg, VA.

Sinozich, Sofi and Lynn Langton. 2014. *Rape and Sexual Assault Victimization Among College-Age Females, 1995–2013*. U.S. Department of Justice. Retrieved February 15, 2016 from www.bjs.gov/content/pub/pdf/rsavcaf9513.pdf.

Smith, Christian, Kari Kristofferson, Hillary Davidson, and Patricia Snell Herzog. 2011. *Lost in Transition: The Dark Side of Emerging Adulthood*. New York, NY: Oxford University Press.

Spell, Sarah. 2016. "Not Just Black and White: How Race/Ethnicity and Gender Intersect in Hookup Culture." *Sociology of Race and Ethnicity*, 3(2): 172–87.

Sperber, Murray. 2000. *Beer and Circus: How Big-Time College Sport Is Crippling Undergraduate Education*. New York, NY: Henry Holt.

Stepp, Laura Sessions. 2007. *Unhooked*. New York, NY: Penguin.

Stinson, Rebecca D. 2010. "Hooking Up in Young Adulthood: A Review of Factors Influencing the Sexual Behavior of College Students." *Journal of College Student Psychotherapy*, 24: 98–115.

Syrett, Nicholas. 2009. *The Company He Keeps: A History of White College Fraternities*. Chapel Hill, NC: University of North Carolina Press.

Thelin, John. 2004. *A History of American Higher Education*. Baltimore, MD: Johns Hopkins University Press.

Twenge, Jean M. 1997. "Changes in Masculine and Feminine Traits Over Time: A Meta-Analysis." *Sex Roles*, 36(5/6): 305–25.

Twenge, Jean M. 2009. "Status and Gender: The Paradox of Progress in an Age of Narcissism." *Sex Roles*, 61: 338–40.

Uecker, Jeremy, Lisa Pearce, and Brita Andercheck. 2015. "The Four U's: Latent Classes of Hookup Motivations Among College Students." *Social Currents*, 2(2): 163–81.

Vander Ven, Thomas. 2011. *Getting Wasted: Why College Students Drink Too Much and Party Too Hard*. New York, NY: New York University Press.

Vrangalova, Zhana and Anthony Ong. 2014. "Who Benefits from Casual Sex? The Moderating Role of Sociosexuality." *Social Psychological and Personality Science*, 5(8): 1–9.

Wade, Lisa. 2017a. *American Hookup: The New Culture of Sex on Campus*. New York, NY: W. W. Norton & Co.

Wade, Lisa. 2017b. "What's So Cultural About Hookup Culture?" *Contexts*, 16(1): 66–8.

Wade, Lisa and Caroline Heldman. 2012. "Hooking Up and Opting Out: Negotiating Sex in the First Year of College." Pp. 128–45 in *Sex for Life*, edited by L. Carpenter and J. D. DeLamater. New York, NY: New York University Press.

Wasylikiw, Louise and Michael Currie. 2012. "The Animal House Effect: How University-Themed Comedy Films Affect Students' Attitudes." *Social Psychology of Education*, 15: 25–40.

Wechsler, Henry and Bernice Wuethrich. 2002. *Dying to Drink: Confronting Binge Drinking on College Campuses*. Emmaus, PA: Rodale Books.

Weinberg, Martin and Staci Newmahr. 2015. *Selves, Symbols, and Sexualities: An Interactionist Anthology*. Thousand Oaks, CA: Sage.

White House Task Force to Protect Students from Sexual Assault. 2014. *Not Alone: The First Report of the White House Task Force to Protect Students From Sexual Assault*. Retrieved February 15, 2016 from www.whitehouse.gov/sites/default/files/docs/report_0.pdf.

Wiederman, Michael. 2008. "Methodological Issues in Studying Sexuality in Close Relationships." Pp. 31–56 in *The Handbook of Sexuality in Close Relationships*, edited by John Harvey, Amy Wenzel, and Susan Sprecher. New York, NY: Taylor & Francis.

Wood, C. and Perlman, D. 2016. "Hooking Up in the United States." In *The Wiley Blackwell Encyclopedia of Family Studies*, edited by Constance Shehan. Hoboken, NJ: Wiley.

11

Circling back

Electronic literature and material feminism

Jessica Pressman

Occulus Rift Virtual reality headgear is usually donned for video gameplay – to provide superhuman strength and far-off adventures, to kill dragons or soldiers, or to explore fantastic places – not to hold teacups and faded family photographs and to tell domestic tales. But Canadian digital artist Caitlin Fisher challenges such expectations, and the explicitly gendered associations of games and virtual reality (VR), by using this very technology for new modes of feminist storytelling. Fisher's *Circle* (2012) is a work of augmented reality storytelling that embeds Quick Response (QR) bar codes onto analog objects, little domestic treasures passed down among four generations of women. You read this work by selecting, holding, and even fondling these analog objects before you scan them with a digital device (in some versions of the work, you use Occulus Rift and in others an iPad); this action elicits a digital connection that plays the multimedia and multimodal story files to present an augmented or virtual reality experience in storytelling. Fisher inserts the domestic stories of women onto the very things they supposedly touched and shared, and she invites her readers to read by touching. The result is an affective experience that is both deeply embodied and complexly digital.

This essay reads *Circle* as turning attention to the materiality and relationality of objects, animate and inanimate, in ways that promote reflection on the meaningful relationships between them. Specifically, I will show that Fisher's *Circle* presents objects (animate and inanimate) as existing, always, in relational networks of meaning. The objects in *Circle* not only represent symbolic and familial networks of interpersonal relationships but also actually operate in a digital network of programmed code, software, and hardware. Understood this way, with a focus on media specificity, the work promotes attention to the contexts through which matter generates meaning and invites interpretation. *Circle* encourages a focus on situatedness and positionality, which is a central facet of feminism (Andersen, 2015).[1] It does so not only through a narrative about women's stories and histories but also through an aesthetic that puts the reader in the position of selecting, handling, and interacting with things within a very specific (and programmed) network. This work of digital literature is about objects and operates through them. It thus provides an opportunity to explore object-oriented inquiry while also critiquing the gendered presumptions and ideological undercurrents of its contemporary manifestation in the philosophical movement known as object-oriented ontology (OOO). Inspired by Fisher's digital literature, I pursue literary criticism's central practice of close reading to show how digital literature provides a platform from which to critique contemporary philosophical debates about materiality – the quality and characteristics of bodies (animate and inanimate) and the ways in which these things mean – in our digital age. Fusing literary criticism and feminist theory, I analyze *Circle* in order to argue that this work pursues aesthetics of "glitch" and "cute" in subversive ways that display and invite feminist practice and critique.

Material feminism

Materiality

"Material relationality" is a term most often associated with Bruno Latour's concept of actor-network theory (ANT), a way of understanding sociology "not as 'the science of the social,' but as the *tracings of associations*" (*Reassembling the Social*, 5, italics in original). This focus on associations and agents rather than actions and actors has inspired much recent interdisciplinary research that uses network theory to explore social and cultural situations. Latour's ANT has also helped to locate a growing awareness and critique of anthropocentricism, the default mode of centering all thinking and value around human beings. In a recent article titled "Agency at the Time of the Anthropocene," Latour writes, "To be a subject is not to act autonomously in front of an objective background, but *to share agency with other subjects that have also lost their autonomy*" (5, italics in original). Any sense of autonomy, individualism, and monadism is replaced by a focus on networked relations. This paradigmatic shift supports newfound attention to objects not just as part of an "objective background," a setting in which humans operate in the foreground, but as agents in and of themselves.

Object-oriented ontology (OOO) is a philosophical movement that emerges from and is inspired by the combination of Latour's ANT and Quentin Meillassoux's speculative realism.[2] OOO attempts to circumscribe, or downright reject, the historically central role of humans in ontology. Ian Bogost writes:

> Ontology is the philosophical study of existence. Object-oriented ontology ('OOO' for short) puts *things* at the center of this study. Its proponents contend that nothing has special status, but that everything exists equally – plumbers, cotton, bonobos, DVD players, and sandstone, for example.
>
> *(blog post, italics in original, Bogost, 2009)*[3]

Graham Harman, a leader in OOO, explains the intervention thusly: "The human/world relation is treated as extra special, different in kind from the relation of cotton and fire. This is the heritage that must be abandoned" (*Speculative Realism* 135). OOO asserts that real things exist distinctly from humans, and they can act distinctly from humans too. OOO challenges us to reconsider a philosophical tradition that is anthropocentric and to attempt to think, or rather, using the language of OOO, "to speculate" about objects without human subjects.

There is a lot to be excited about in OOO, specifically in its creative effort to retool traditional modes of thinking about objects through speculation and imaginative projection. What excites N. Katherine Hayles, she explains, is "the possibility that an object-oriented approach can be fleshed out through meticulous accounts of how nonhuman objects experience the world – or to put it in more general terms, the ways nonhuman objects have of being in the world" ("Speculative Aesthetics" 170) and the "insistence that objects resist us knowing them completely" (172). But, there is also a lot to be concerned about, and these concerns reverberate with central tenets of traditional feminist critique. Feminist theory argues for the importance of bodies as real, marked matter that is always constituted by material histories and actual situated contexts. Feminism teaches us to be wary of attempts to devalue or ignore the very real socioeconomic, historical, and ideological contexts that sustain power relations and hierarchies. Applying such attention to OOO, we find, as Caroline Bassett writes,

> The problems arising with OOO, for critical feminism at least, is not the rocks and the grease, and the way in which many of these ontographic collections (Bogost 2012) overwhelmingly consist of objects traditionally "gendered masculine" (Wajcman 1991), but the way in which the priorities they insist upon render irrelevant a series of questions concerning "humans,," their relationships with each other and with technologies, and how each of these is articulated and mediated by the other.
>
> *("Not Now: Feminism, Technology, Postdigital" 142)*

By divorcing matter from materiality, physicality from embodiment, and flesh from gender, OOO posits the consideration of objects without the human. This act also includes stripping away the humane and humanistic from such inquiry. Such extractions are, as Bassett points out, and I agree, more about hiding or privileging certain priorities over others than about actually thinking outside of the anthropocentric box.

Hayles seems to detect an aspect of subterfuge in OOO, describing it as intentionally working to hide or "black box" its operations. She writes,

> The effect of encapsulating relations *within* objects, as Harman does, is to mask the system's dynamics and make it difficult to think about the dynamics at all. The black boxing of relations obliterates the specificity of how complex systems work.
>
> *(Hayles, "Speculative Aesthetics" 176, emphasis added)*

The language of "black boxing" is relevant and instructive here because it comes from the world of computing. "Black box" describes a system or device that hides its operations from view. Think of the evolution of our laptops, from clunky computers whose screws and components were visible and thus able to be taken apart, to today's sleek MacBooks that hide internal components in smoothly brushed silver; as much art as tools, these machines present the computer as an aesthetically splendid black (or silver) box. The connection between OOO and computing is easy and necessary to make: easy because the name "object-oriented" is a type of computer programming, and necessary because the gendered-masculine associations of both inform each other. Though Hayles never uses the "f" word – "feminism" – in her discussion of OOO, her critique cuts that way. She takes Harman to task for presenting (even fetishizing) objects as thingy matter separate from specific contexts of materialism. Both Hayles and Bassett point out that OOO operates through black boxing, by hiding the gendered ideologies that undergird the operative theory. To address the gendered associations shared between OOO and computing, we now move to examine related efforts to employ feminist thinking to renovate object-oriented theory in ways that address gender politics – "the priorities" (to use Bassett's words) – that lurk beyond the supposed objectivity of OOO.

Feminism

Feminism holds that bodies matter, and material contexts affect experience; thus, that embodied, cultural contexts inform knowledge and value. In the age of "transcendental data," as Alan Liu calls the digital era, wherein information appears disembodied, feminist scholars have had to fight hard and articulately to identify where and how materiality matters. Theorists like N. Katherine Hayles, Donna Haraway, Wendy Chun, Sadie Plant, and Anne Balsamo have shown that digital technologies are neither disembodied nor value-neutral but always situated in historical, political, and ideological contexts.[4] As our computing technologies get smaller and more sophisticated, and its black boxes ever-more inaccessible, we need to further refine our thinking about the relationship between animate and inanimate bodies as well as about the porous boundaries between the real and the virtual.

Developments in biotechnology, computing, and posthumanism have afforded new perspectives on materiality and the relationship between animate and inanimate objects. Indeed, what counts as human is a subject of debate in our posthuman world (Hayles, 2012).[5] In their introduction to the recent volume, *New Materialisms: Ontology, Agency, and Politics*, Diana Coole and Samantha Frost write, "new ways of thinking about living matter are radically and rapidly reconfiguring our material world – both empirically and conceptually" ("Introducing the New Materialisms" 24). Let me introduce the term "New Materialism" here. Coined by Manuel DeLanda and Rosi Braidotti independently in the late 1990s, it was used to describe efforts to cut across or "transverse" humanistic disciplines in order to update materialist thinking to consider not just objects, settings, and actions but also their interactions (Dolphijn and van der Tuin, 2012).[6] Karen Barad introduced the term "intra-actions" to stand "(in contrast to the usual 'interaction,' which presumes the prior existence of independent entities/relata)" and which suggests that "relata do not preexist relations; rather, relata-within-phenomona emerge through specific intra-actions" ("Posthuman Performativity" 133). For Barad, entities do not and cannot exist separately from their relations. In this sense, all entities are made of their relationships or *intra-actions*. This terminological shift from *interaction* to *intra-action* represents a larger paradigmatic one: a shift in perspective from entities to emergence. All action is recognized as situational and relational.

The need for new ways of understanding the relational quality of materiality is central to recent movements in feminist theory. Stacy Alaimo and Susan Hekman, editors of *Material Feminisms*, argue that feminist theory must engage with materialism and New Materialism in order to get beyond "the impasse caused by the contemporary linguistic turn to feminist thought" ("Introduction: Emerging Models of Materiality in Feminist Theory" 1). Moving to overturn the emphasis on discursivity promoted by Judith Butler and postmodern feminist theory, these recent thinkers bring feminism to bear on New Materialism and vice versa. In contrast to OOO's speculation about objects as abstract and extracted, even disinfected, feminist materialists pursue the messy and "the mangle" (Andrew Pickering's word for the complex arrangements of technologies, theories, practices, and people that constitute and produce science). They engage the "vicious porousity," Nancy Tuana's phrase for "a conceptual metaphor" that denotes "the rich interactions between beings through which subjects are constituted out of relationality" ("Viscous Porousity: Witnessing Katrina" 188). Such a focus disallows, or at least seriously complicates, OOO's investment in arguing for the agency of objects. In a mangle model of relations, practices, and activities, separating distinct actors becomes challenging, as does assigning agency to any one thing.

New Materialism and material feminism pursue the local and specific contexts of emergence. There are political ramifications of this type of focus, and this fact is embraced rather than avoided by its practitioners. Far from the conceptual and speculative philosophy of OOO, Coole and Frost explain, "materialism means practical, politically engaged social theory, devoted to the critical analysis of actual conditions of existence and their inherent inequality" (24–25). Understanding that material feminism examines the specificities of systems and events, we can finally turn to our tutor text – a work of digital literature that operates through a programmed network of analog and digital, human and nonhuman, agents to present an object-based and gendered narrative in a very specific configuration of technological relations. We turn to *Circle* to see how material feminism is made manifest in art.

Caitlin Fisher's *Circle*

Circle is a work of born-digital electronic literature, which means that it is made on the computer and read through computational devices. It is, like other electronic literature, dependent upon a network of operations occurring across hardware, software, and programming code. Its computational processes and technological components are inseparable from its poetics. There is no linguistic "text" to analyze separately from the material – technological and artifactual – context that constitutes the work. The menagerie of little objects arranged on the tabletop, the digital devices, the narrative fragments, and the reading practices all participate collectively to produce the literary experience. Unlike many genres of electronic literature, including web-based hypertext and Flash poetry, *Circle* is generated through real-time interaction between the reader and the work's database, which includes both its archive of analog objects embedded with QR codes and available for handling as well as its digital database of sound and image files. *Circle* is interactive in that it requires input from the reader in order to produce its performance. It is also *intra-active* (Barad's term), for it uses augmented reality technology to create a situation wherein animate and inanimate objects collaborate to present an emergent aesthetic. Importantly, for my purposes here, it does all of this in ways that employ aesthetics that examine and critique object-oriented philosophy.

Fisher describes *Circle* as an "augmented reality tabletop theater piece" (Fisher, 2013)[7] because the work consists of a collection of small, personal, and domestic objects (a bracelet, a piece of stationary, family photographs, a doll's head, etc.) collected in a carrying box and arranged on a tea service tray on a tabletop. Each of these items contains a digitally encoded marker, a version of a QR bar code. The reader picks up an object, holds it in her hand, and turns her iPad (or, in versions in development, the VR headset) toward it to launch the software and *Circle*'s story. This narrative is not presented as text to be read; it is, instead, heard as a sound file, an oral telling. The narrator's voice speaks in a soft and gentle tone while old family photographs appear before the reader's eyes. The sensorial experience presents personal stories about the relationships between the narrator, her absent mother, her devoted grandmother "Jelly," and her baby daughter Harriet. This text is presented in fragments, literally discrete sound files that can be accessed in any order depending upon which analog object the reader selects and scans. Formally, the work is a hypertextual narrative, a network of vignettes that tells the stories of networked relationships between women and the things they touched, treasured, and built lives around.

At the center of *Circle* is a woman who gives voice, literally and figuratively, to the stories of the women in her life. Our narrator has recently become a mother and has acquired a newfound appreciation of the woman who raised her. The narrator uncovers the forgotten stories behind the things the reader holds, the objects revered by her beloved grandmother, Jelly. Fisher places the reader in the position of also holding and discovering the backstories of these things, stories which are literally attached to the things the reader holds. Fisher pairs advanced digital technology with a carefully curated collection of little objects to tell a rather simple domestic story. These kinds of stories aren't usually the content of augmented reality games and storytelling, but Fisher appropriates distinctly digital aesthetics to serve feminist purposes.

The objects that constitute *Circle* are all of a certain sort: small and holdable (able to fit in the palm of the hand), personal, and feminine. They are the stuff of homes and parlors, of make-up tables and jewelry boxes. *Circle* puts these objects on display and prompts the reader to interact with them in new ways through new media. The work makes us see these objects anew, along with the women who once held, owned, and gifted them. In short, I see Fisher's *Circle* as an artistic manifestation of "material feminism." The work provides an opportunity to consider and critique contemporary trends in thing theories that ignore embodiment and thus disregard feminism, including object-oriented ontology. *Circle* shows how literature, and digital literature in particular, provides a platform for reflecting on how we think about things.

Against OOO

Circle enacts relational storytelling. The narrative needs to be contextualized before it can be understood and made to cohere. For example, we learn that our narrator is a young mother to daughter Harriet and that she finds motherhood to be a time to reflect upon the woman who raised her (her beloved grandmother, "Jelly") as well as the woman who did not (her absent mother). The narrator divulges that Jelly raised her "since my parents went on holiday to Morocco in 1967 and didn't come back." In the tone of a grown woman gifted recently with newfound insights, she describes her own mother from a perspective of generosity but also, and importantly for understanding that this is a work about relational feminism, from a perspective attuned to the impact of historical contexts. The narrator's mother was a young mother in the 1960s, when women were exploring their sexuality (and the craft arts): "We have mothers who cry, sleep all day, weave curtains from beads we later choke on." These glorious days of social rebellion, sexual exploration, and macramé had an impact on others, particularly the little children left to be cared for by their grandmothers because such children had "Mothers we need to tuck in at night after parties, mothers we tell to please get more milk and who is sleeping in my bed." *Circle* shows that there are not only stories and backstories but also stories that connect characters (human and objects) into a web or network of relationships.

Circle is told circularly or, more accurately, recursively. The work's vignettes can be accessed in any order the reader chooses, depending on which objects she selects, so the stories build in a cumulative manner but also through repetition. Repetition and recursion are built into the narrative content. Our narrator tells us, "My grandmother was raised by her grandmother, too." This line encompasses the content of an entire vignette and sound file. It tells us that Jelly and the narrator share the trauma of an absent mother and suggests that this experience bonds them. The grammatical structure of the sentence also implies something subtle and poignant: that this repetition in narrative structure is not limited to the characters within this story but also represents how women's stories are often told in asides, in sentences that end with "too." This addendum is a connector, an add-on. Its grammatical structure links sentences and people into a relational network. This linkage is a hyperlink of sorts that serves, at the level of narrative and at the level of critical intervention that this work serves, as part of the point.

Circle is about objects, and it operates through them. Its narrative depicts key moments in the development of its human subjects but also in the histories of inanimate objects that trigger these memories. The work tells the stories of how these selected things arrived at a place where they could be held and touched by the reader and scanned by the digital apparatus. This scenario might be the perfect place to promote OOO's idea of object agency, for *Circle* attaches digital markers to objects, embedding them with stories that exist even if we do not read them. These objects exist in and of themselves; they are each an autonomous agent that contains (literally, for they are each encoded with) digital data. Yet, *Circle* depicts these objects, and human relationships to them, as existing in complicated contexts of mediation, symbolism, and emergence. The work thus challenges OOO's attribution of autonomy and agency to objects.

Take, for example, the golden bracelet, a central component of *Circle*'s object collection and its narrative. The narrator tells us that Jelly's mother "has a bad heart and dies when my grandmother is ten," leaving Jelly to be raised by her grandmother. Jelly (the narrator's grandmother) wears her mother's gold bracelet as a kind of personal memorial that marks her own body. The story presents this object as not just a figurative and personal metonym for a lost mother; it is more material than that. A psychic once told Jelly that the piece of jewelry actually contains the beating heart of her dead mother: "'Let me hold that,' the psychic says, 'whoever wore this has a bad heart – you can still hear it beating.' *Tha-thump, that-tha-thump.*" When we, the readers, hold the bracelet, we hear the story of the artifact and of Jelly's mother. We hold the heart of the story in our hands – the trauma of losing one's mother, a trauma that bonds Jelly and the narrator. Our hearts ache for these children even as the narrative shows that this central loss turns these women into loving women and caregivers. The transmission of this information – from mother's body to bracelet to child, and from diegetic character to bracelet to reader of the narrative – centers *Circle*, and this centering happens around a circular symbol for infinity and repetition. A bracelet's center is void, but, as *Circle* shows, emptiness and loss can serve as the cornerstone for love and growth.[8] The bracelet adorns the narrator's wrist and dangles in front of her own baby, Harriet, tantalizing the fourth generation of women to hear its hidden heartbeat and desire to know the story behind it. Harriet "grabs my bracelet with the hidden heartbeat. You can still hear it beating. *Tha-thump, that-tha-thump.*" We, the readers of *Circle* who now hold the bracelet in our hands, become part of this circle of women as we transmit their stories through intra-actions with their things.

We read *Circle* by entering and interacting with its relational network of things. We select, hold, and examine the objects before us; in the process we become aware of how these artifacts participate in a sophisticated technological apparatus that mediates our ability to access hidden family histories. The women's stories that *Circle* tells not only center around but also actually emerge out of interaction with these objects. It is through this network of analog objects, digital technologies, and programming that *Circle* presents a literary exploration of material relationality. The work thus suggests that materiality and meaning emerge through relations between animate and inanimate agents. *Circle* tells the stories of how these women became who they are, how they emerged and arrived in their current situations through networks of relations and interactions with animate and inanimate objects. In so doing, *Circle* invites us to consider the systems of mediation, both technological and social, which shape our own interactions, experiences, and selves.

Circle not only presents a context for humans and things to interact but also invites examination into how objects arrive at a certain moment wherein they *can* interact. The work suggests that these sedimented histories of arrival (histories of labor, movement, distribution, and sharing, etc.) inform that interaction and its interpretation. In an essay titled "Orientations Matter," Sara Ahmed argues "we touch things and are touched by things" not simply by virtue of being within the reach of objects but because "what is reachable is determined precisely by orientations we have already taken" (245). This means that immediate experience is always part of a longer history of interactions and situations. It also means that focusing on orientation – rather than just on actors, actions, and settings – allows us to see how, as Ahmed writes, "Orientations are about the direction we take that puts some things and not others in our reach" (245). Past orientation leads to present situation. This fact renders all artifacts, animate or inanimate, embedded with layers of experience that have meaningful impact on how they interact. Understood this way, objects are not isolated and discrete but interconnected. Ahmed states, "The materialization of subjects is hence inseparable from objects" (248–249). This view stands in opposition to OOO's effort to comprehend objects as distinct from subjects, but it is certainly proven true in *Circle*'s networked narrative.

Although *Circle* presents objects that seem to be autonomous agents, the stories that these things contain are actually histories of the object's materialization, its orientation and arrival, and these histories are imprinted by and inseparable from the human stories in *Circle*. The golden bracelet exemplifies this point, as it is said to contain the beating heart of a woman. *Circle* presents an object-centered aesthetic that animates the inseparability of subjects and objects while also drawing attention to the layers of mediation involved in enabling their interaction. In *Circle*, orientation is not only conceptual but also technological. For a reader approaching this work, reading requires getting oriented to a sophisticated technological apparatus: the reader must orient herself in very physical and embodied ways in order to focus her gaze (and the digital scanner) on a particular object (and its digital marker) so as to virtually touch that object and thereby elicit the text it contains. *Circle* makes it inescapably clear that our relationships with objects are always mediated and impacted by orientation and, often, by technologies.

Circle is part of Fisher's decades-long engagement in using augmented reality (AR) technologies for storytelling, specifically for telling stories about women from a feminist perspective. *Circle* is still in development. In fact, it might be more appropriate to call *Circle* "a working project" rather than "a work" because it has gone through multiple iterations and technological instantiations. The version exhibited in 2012 at the Electronic Literature Organization (ELO) conference at Morgantown, West Virginia, used paper to hold the digital markers, whereas the version I discuss here uses actual objects imprinted with QR codes and a tablet or VR headgear to scan these three-dimensional objects; this version was built later using the Unity game engine and Qualcomm's Vuforia Augmented Reality SDK.[9] Specific technological updates aside, however, *Circle*'s history of development is part of its argument about relationality and context-based meaning. This production history is also part of a larger story about the inseparability of content and format, of how an artist uses technological innovation to drive the production of new literary works and, conversely, of new augmented reality literature explores the same topic in different iterations. Fisher makes no effort to present *Circle* as autonomous and complete – quite the opposite. The messiness of creation is put on display. Its history is part of its project, available in every online exhibition and archive of the work. This information disables a progressive narrative of development and instead serves as a framing device for understanding that this work is not just a thing, object, or completed entity; it is a constellation of processes and contexts, a generative and generated experience. *Circle* exemplifies how Fisher's oeuvre demonstrates networks of animate and inanimate objects collaborating within a digital context to update literature – to make it *arrive* for readers who must themselves practice emergent readerly orientations.

Aesthetics

We finally arrive at the place in this essay where we can carefully examine the aesthetics and formal attributes of this compelling digital work and recognize how they serve a material feminist practice. I will focus on two aesthetics at work in *Circle*: glitch and cute. By "at work," I mean to suggest that this piece of literature employs these particular aesthetic tropes in order to pursue a strategic critical intervention. *Circle* uses an aesthetic of cute in order to promote critical deconstruction of the presumed binary and value hierarchy of beautiful/cute, high/low art or art/craft; and the work pursues an aesthetic of glitch in order to destabilize the dualism of normal and glitchy, correct and error. These deconstructive impulses depend not on linguistic and rhetorical turns (to which we have become accustomed in postmodern theory and about which we have seen material feminism respond) but on things. It is, in fact, impossible to read this work and ignore its thingy-ness. Though the work functions through a complex digital apparatus, its analog objects are central and real. You hold these things in your hands and fondle them in order to access a story that prompts you to reflect upon how women's stories are told – or not told. And all of these objects are of a particular variety and aesthetic: they are small, feminine, and cute.

Cute

Circle operates through an aesthetic of cute. "Cute" is a term usually used to discount a work of art – to signify that it is not serious, relevant, or all that good. But Sianne Ngai's *Our Aesthetic Categories: Zany, Cute, Interesting* offers a way of thinking critically about the aesthetic of cute, and I will rely upon this scholarly work to argue that *Circle* prompts us to reconsider cute as a means of challenging established aesthetic values and, specifically, their gendered biases. Ngai pursues a historical excavation and deconstruction of the category of "cute" that uncovers reasons why (and when) calling something "cute" denotes dismissal and, particularly relevant for my purposes, alignment with the feminine. Far from being the opposite of serious art, "cuteness" actually has an important presence in the 20th-century avant-garde, Ngai shows. Cuteness operates as smallness in canonical short poems like William Carlos Williams's super-cute "This Is Just to Say"; and, she argues, cute also serves to focus readerly attention on domesticity, as in Gertrude Stein's *Tender Buttons.* Ngai traces the history of cuteness as a negative aesthetic judgment to 19th-century America and the emergence of mass industrial culture in it, wherein "cute" came to express commodity fetishism and a desire to return "to a simpler, sensuous world of domestic use and consumption, populated exclusively by children and their guardians" (*Our Aesthetic Categories* 66). This is when "the value of cuteness seems to shift from unequivocally positive (charming socks) to negative or ambiguous (innocent boy)" (59). "Cute" came to designate the negative affects of smallness, vulnerability, and softness – qualities associated with women, children, and the domestic realm, all of which, due to industrialization, became further and further removed from that of physical labor and of men. This is the historical context in which "cute" takes on a negative tinge in the hierarchical registry of aesthetic judgments and thus becomes aligned with the feminine.

Ngai contrasts the cute and the beautiful: "cuteness contains none of beauty's oft-noted references to novelty, singularity, or what Adorno calls 'a sphere of untouchability'" (54). But in a brilliant act of deconstructive interpretation, Ngai shows that the opposition and dualism is not that simple. Cute is actually about power relations and gender differentials. Ngai writes, "in vivid contrast to beauty's continuing associations with fairness, symmetry, or proportion, the experience of cute depends entirely on the subject's affective response to a imbalance of power between herself and the object" (54). Cute objects demand to be held and squeezed; they thus exert power over the viewer by exploiting their position of powerlessness. "The cute commodity," Ngai explains, "for all of its pathos of powerlessness, is thus capable of making surprisingly powerful demands" (64). *Circle* demonstrates this idea; its cute objects induce us to hold them. The objects exert power over us and, certainly, over the narrative. The work displays an "aestheticization of powerlessness" (64), which Ngai argues is the paradoxical power of cute, and it programmatically positions the cute, little, femininized things in Fisher's tabletop menagerie so that they compel us to interact with them in certain ways. These cute little things are not only quite powerful but also capable of producing art. Cute becomes powerful in *Circle*'s feminist aesthetic practice.

Glitch

We read *Circle* by interacting with its cute analog objects, but *Circle* also makes inescapably clear that this interaction depends upon digital processes, devices, and networks. Reading this work requires that we focus the digital reading device on an object, wait for the digital connection, and hope for the best. The best is when the digital circuit seamlessly prompts an image or sound file to play so that we can hear the story and experience a sense of immediacy to our narrator and the women in her life. But what actually happens is quite different. Along with the narrative fragments presented in images and sounds, we get noise; we get glitch. Rather than immediacy, we get hypermediacy (Bolter and Grusin, 1999);[10] we become acutely aware of the technologies mediating our access to the personal stories and artifacts of female relationships.

According to the Shannon-Weaver communication model, which became the basis for information theory, noise is a by-product of information transmission. It is the supplemental aspect of communication that is added to the message as it is moves through a medium during the process of being transferred to the receiver. Noise is that which needs to be filtered out in order to leave the message.[11] The presence of noise thus indexically references the technology involved in enabling communication. In other words, noise draws our attention to the fact that technology mediates. *Circle* makes noise a central aspect of its aesthetic, using it in intentional and purposeful ways. Rather than "noise," then, a term that references the unwanted aspect of communication transmission, we might call *Circle*'s supplemental element "glitch." Glitch signifies differently than noise. It doesn't just register the presence and fact of mediation; it indexes a fault in the system. Unlike noise, which communication theorists understand to be an essential component of technological communication, glitch is a symptom of error. It turns our attention to the technological inner workings of mediation, to the operations and processes, not just their effects and end products. "A glitch is a mess that is a moment, a possibility to glance at software's inner structure," Olga Goriunova and Alezi Shulgin write, which is why "glitches are compelling for artists and designers as well as regular users" ("Glitch" 114 and 116, respectively). In her entry on "Glitch Aesthetics" for the *Johns Hopkins Guide to Digital Media,* Lori Emerson explains that glitch

> captures a moment in which an error in the computer system is made visible; it therefore exploits randomness and chance as a way to disrupt the digital ideal of a clean, frictionless, error-free environment in which the computer supposedly fades into the background.
>
> *(237)*

Circle uses glitch, that undesirable element of systems operation, for purposeful aesthetic purposes: to tell a story of women and illuminate the systems that render their stories legible or, often, not. Glitch reminds us that there are gaps and hidden histories, parts of the sound file that we cannot hear and stories about the women who we will never know.

Circle is intentionally glitchy. The digital markers are placed close together, often overlapping on the same object, making it hard for the software to smoothly process multiple markers at a time. The effect is confusing and messy. Multiple sound files open at once and speak over each other, creating repetitive echoes and eerie sounds. The glitches interrupt the narrator's human voice with unnerving technical sounds, forcing recognition that our engagement with these cute objects and the human tales tell is deeply remediated by digital technologies. In this way, *Circle* might be exemplary of what Legacy Russell calls "Glitch Feminism." Russell identifies glitch as a symbol for social revolution. Seeing glitch as a rupture that illuminates sexist injustice, particularly within the field of computing which is gendered masculine, Russell argues that glitch is "an error in a social system that has already been disturbed by economic, racial, social, sexual, and cultural stratification," so that the glitch serves not as "an *error* at all, but rather a much-needed erratum" (italics in original, 2012).[12] *Circle* uses glitch aesthetics to appropriate error for feminist purposes – to turn attention to the systems involved in mediating information transmission and to stimulate critique of how these systems operate.

Circle's use of glitch also suggests that women and their stories just might be glitches in computing. Caitlin Fisher could herself be seen as a glitch in this system. She is a female artist, scholar, and technological innovator honored by a Canada research chair and widespread international recognition. Her work consistently explores gendered dynamics and feminist theory: from her

2000 dissertation, *Building Feminist Theory: Hypertextual Heuristics*, which examined intersections between feminist and hypermedia theories; to her first digital novella, *These Waves of Girls* (2001), a web-based hypertext about emergent sexuality and lesbian identity; all the way to *Circle*. Fisher's work – and *Circle* is exemplary in this regard – uses new media technologies to challenge trends pervading contemporary computing culture and the critical trends it inspires, particularly those that focus on objects and information without caring about embodiment, materiality, or gender. Fisher, like her work *Circle*, employs the glitch as aesthetic feminist practice to challenge the status quo.

Conclusion: circling back around to circle the wagons

Caitlin Fisher's *Circle* uses cutting-edge technology to turn attention to the complexly mediated contexts that frame our interactions with even the simplest objects. The work prompts us to touch and hold artifacts culled from domestic life and to hear the women's stories they contain, all in the service of promoting consideration of how these interactions and *intra-actions* happen and how they mean. The cute little objects in *Circle* and the glitchy aesthetics they produce stimulate recognition that materiality is always dependent upon situated networks of emergence. These networks include animate and inanimate entities but are always encased in interpretative systems based in human contexts and biases. *Circle* is about relationality: relations between human readers and analog objects, between these objects and the digital devices that scan them, between this transmedial format and the literary performance that it produces. Presenting a reading experience of relationality, *Circle* demonstrates Barad's claim, "It is through specific agential intra-actions that the boundaries and properties of the 'components' of phenomena become determinate and that particular embodied concepts become meaningful" (133). Situatedness, that central component of feminism, and specifically of material feminism, is made manifest and aesthetic in this work of digital literature.

As an augmented reality work of literature, *Circle* exists at the interstice between virtual and real, and it uses this position of inbetweenness to enact Tuana's concept of "viscous porosity" and to insist upon the messy arrangement of contexts that enable embodiment, experience, and meaning. This is a work of feminist storytelling that invites feminist literary criticism to close-read its tangled web. *Circle* compels us to recognize that where feminist storytelling goes, so too should feminist literary criticism. When we do follow, we see how literary aesthetics can combat philosophical trends toward forgetting the ethics and politics of materiality in the pursuit of focusing on objects. *Circle* inspires us to see how experience, materiality, and indeed literature are emergent, relational, and embodied. Such work reminds us that we need not – and should not – forget that understanding what matter *is* does not foreclose remembering what matters.

Acknowledgment

I'd like to thank Melissa Sodeman, a dear friend in my personal network of feminist scholars, for helping me to realize the central points of this essay and, more importantly, why such thinking matters.

Notes

1 For more on the importance of situatedness and positionality to feminist epistemology, see Elizabeth Anderson's "Feminist Epistemology and Philosophy of Science", *The Stanford Encyclopedia of Philosophy* (Spring 2017 Edition), Edward N. Zalta (ed.). https://plato.stanford.edu/archives/spr2017/entries/feminism-epistemology/ (Accessed August 11, 2015).

2 See Quentin Meillassoux's *After Finitude: An Essay on the Necessity of Contingency* (New York: Bloomsbury Continuum International Publishing Group, 2008 [2006]).
3 The Comments section of this blog post are illuminating in that they display a communal thinking through of the very act of defining OOO and thus the challenge of defining OOO at all. http://bogost.com/writing/blog/what_is_objectoriented_ontolog/ (December 2009) (Accessed July 10, 2015).
4 These are just a sample of such scholars doing such important work, but see, in particular, N. Katherine Hayles's *How We Became Posthuman: Virtual Bodies in Cybernetics, Literature and Informatics* (Chicago: University of Chicago Press, *1999*), Donna Haraway's *Simians, Cyborgs and Women: The Reinvention of Nature* (New York: Routledge, 1991), Wendy Hui Kyong, *Control and Freedom: Power and Paranoia in the Age of Fiber Optics* (Cambridge, MA: MIT Press, 2006), Sadie Plant's *Zeroes + Ones: Digital Women and the New Technoculture* (New York: Doubleday, 1997), and Anne Balsamo's *Designing Culture: The Technological Imagination at Work* (Durham: Duke University Press, 2011).
5 For the defining scholarly intervention on the "posthuman," see. Katherine Hayles's *How We Became Posthuman: Virtual Bodies in Cybernetics, Literature and Informatics* (Chicago: University of Chicago Press, 1999).
6 See Rick Dolphijn and Iris van der Tuin's *New Materialism: Interviews & Cartographies,* University of Michigan, Open Humanities Press, 2012; see, in particular, section 5: "The Traversality of New Materialism," https://quod.lib.umich.edu/o/ohp/11515701.0001.001/1:5.2/--new-materialism-interviews-cartographies?rgn=div2;view=fulltext

Dolphijn and van der Tuin argue that "the immanent gesture of new materialism is transversal rather than dualist." http://quod.lib.umich.edu/o/ohp/11515701.0001.001/1:5.2. (Accessed August 11, 2015).
7 See a description and documentation of the work, at http://futurecinema.ca/arlab/.
8 Thanks to Melissa Sodeman for this insight.
9 The ELO conference website, along with the archived Media Arts show containing *Circle* is available here: http://el.eliterature.org/.
10 In *Remediation,* Jay David Bolter and Richard Grusin describe "immediacy" as experience of losing track of the technological mediation at work in creating an affective aesthetic experience, while "hypermediacy" is the flipside or "alter ego" of immediacy. This conceptual dualism works to for describing and understanding *Circle.*
11 See Claude E. Shannon and Warren Weaver, *The Mathematical Theory of Communication* (University of Illinois Press, 1949).
12 Online, http://thesocietypages.org/cyborgology/2012/12/10/digital-dualism-and-the-glitch-feminism-manifesto/ (Accessed June 17, 2015).

Bibliography

Ahmed, Sara. "Orientations Matter." In *New Materialisms: Ontology, Agency, and Politics*, eds. Diana Coole and Samantha Frost. Durham: Duke University Press, 2010: 234–257.

Alaimo, Stacy and Susan Hekman, eds. *Material Feminisms.* Bloomington: Indiana University Press, 2008.

———. "Introduction: Emerging Models of Materiality in Feminist Theory." In *Material Feminisms*, eds. Stacy Alaimo and Susan Hekman. Bloomington: Indiana University Press, 2008: 1–19.

Barad, Karen. "Posthuman Performativity." In *Material Feminisms*, eds. Stacy Alaimo and Susan Hekman. Bloomington: Indiana University Press, 2008: 120–154.

Bassett, Caroline. "Not Now: Feminism, Technology, Postdigital." In *Postdigital Aesthetics: Art, Computation and Design*, eds. David M. Berry and Michael Dieter. Basingstoke, UK, Palgrave Macmillan, 2015: 136–150.

Bogost, Ian. "Object-Oriented Ontology: A Definition for Ordinary Folks." Web blog post. Bogost.com. December 8, 2009. Accessed July 10, 2015 from http://bogost.com/writing/blog/what_is_objectoriented_ontolog/

——— *Alien Phenomenology, or What It's Like to Be a Thing.* Minnesota: University Of Minnesota Press, 2012.

Bolter, Jay David and Richard Grusin. *Remediation: Understanding the New Media.* Cambridge, MA: MIT Press, 1999.

Coole, Diana and Samantha Frost, eds. *New Materialisms: Ontology, Agency, and Politic.* Durham: Duke University Press, 2010.

———. "Introducing the New Materialism." In *New Materialisms: Ontology, Agency, and Politic.* Durham: Duke University Press, 2010: 1–43.

Dolphijn, Rick and Iris van der Tuin, eds. *New Materialism: Interviews & Cartographies.* Ann Arbor: University of Michigan Library, Open Humanities Press, 2012. Online. http://dx.doi.org/10.3998/ohp.11515701.0001.001

Donaldson, Jeffrey. "Glossing Over Thoughts on Glitch. A Poetry of Error." *ArtPulse Magazine* (online). Accessed from http://artpulsemagazine.com/glossing-over-thoughts-on-glitch-a-poetry-of-error [n.d.]

Emerson, Lori. "Glitch Aesthetics." In *The Johns Hopkins Guide to Digital Media*, eds. Marie-Laure Ryan, Lori Emerson, and Benjamin J. Robertson. Baltimore: The Johns Hopkins University Press, 2014: 235–237.

Fisher, Caitlin. *Circle* (Augmented Reality Installation, 2012). Documentation of the installation piece is available here: https://vimeo.com/64504258 and www.youtube.com/watch?v=Z9i9jRrolKk

Goriunova, Olga and Alexi Shulgin. "Glitch." In *Software Studies\A Lexicon*, ed. Matthew Fuller. Cambridge, MA: The MIT Press, 2008: 110–118.

Harman, Graham. "The Well-Wrought Broken Hammer: Object-Oriented Literary Criticism," *New Literary History*, vol. 43, no. 2 (Spring 2012): 183–203.

———. *Towards Speculative Realism: Essays and Lectures*. Winchester, UK: Zero Books, 2010.

Hayles, N. Katherine. *How We Think: Digital Media and Contemporary Technogenesis*. Chicago: Chicago University Press, 2012.

———. "Speculative Aesthetics and Object Oriented Inquiry (OOI)," *Speculations: A Journal of SpeculatiVe Realism* V (2014): 158–179.

Latour, Bruno. "Agency at the time of the Anthropocene," *New Literary History*, vol. 45, no. 1 (Winter 2014): 1–18

———. *Reassembling the Social: An Introduciton to Actor-Network-Theory*. Oxford: Oxford University Press, 2005.

Liu, Alan. "Transcendental Data: Toward a Cultural History and Aesthetics of the New Encoded Discourse." *Critical Inquiry*, vol. 31, no. 4, 2004 (Summer): 49–84.

Meillassoux, Quentin. After Finitude: An Essay on the Necessity of Contingency. Trans. Ray Brassier. New York: Bloomsbury, 2010.

Ngai, Sianne. *Our Aesthetic Categories: Zany, Cute, Interesting*. Cambridge, MA: Harvard University Press, 2012.

Pickering, Andrew. *The Mangle of Practice: Time, Agency, and Science*. Chicago: Unversity of Chicago Press, 1995.

Russell, Legacy. "Digital Dualism and the Glitch Feminism Manifesto." *The Society Pages* (online), December 12, 2012. Accessed from http://thesocietypages.org/cyborgology/2012/12/10/digital-dualism-and-the-glitch-feminism-manifesto/

Tuana, Nancy. "Viscous Porousity: Witnessing Katrina." In *New Materialisms: Ontology, Agency, and Politic*. Durham: Duke University Press, 2010: 188–213.

Wajcman, Judy. *Feminism Confronts Technology*. Pennsylvania: Penn State University Press, 1991

Section III
Ways in

12

Gender and schooling

Progress, persistent inequalities, and possible solutions

Jennifer A. Fredricks

Since the passage of Title IX in 1972, there has been significant progress in ensuring equal educational opportunities by gender and unprecedented changes in girls' achievement and educational participation. This has led some to change the rhetoric from a concern over how girls are disadvantaged in schools to a focus on boys' underachievement.[1] However, while girls have made remarkable progress in several areas, significant disparities in some educational and occupational outcomes continue to persist. Moreover, schools still expose young people to rigid conceptions of masculinity and femininity that serve to perpetuate traditional gender norms.

The goal of this chapter is to describe the contradictory findings regarding gender inequities in education, describe how gender is constructed in the classroom, and outline different approaches to improving girls' educational experience. Specifically, I critique claims regarding gender differences that either favor boys or girls by showing how these findings are shaped by the research question, theoretical perspective, and type of analysis. The chapter concludes with a discussion of feminist pedagogy, which is grounded in feminist theory, and how this perspective offers an alternative to current gender inequality research and practice and can be used to create more equitable environments that support learning for all students.

Are girls disadvantaged in schools?

The publication of a number of reports and popular books during the 1980s and 1990s led some to conclude there was a "girl crisis" in education.[2] The American Association of University Women garnered extensive media attention with the report *How Schools Short Change Girls*. Key conclusions of this report were that (1) girls have fewer interactions with teachers and are given less attention and opportunities than boys in the classroom; (2) girls have lower self-esteem; (3) girls' experiences and contributions are marginalized in both curriculum and pedagogy; and (4) girls are less likely than boys to take upper-level math and science courses and pursue technological careers.[3] The "girl crisis" movement was further reinforced by research by Gilligan and her colleagues, which suggested that early adolescent girls lose their voice as a result of a more complex notion of subjectivity and sense of self. Prior to adolescence, girls are clear about what they know and are able to express their opinions freely. With the onset of puberty, girls begin to experience a conflict between expressing their authentic self and the need to identify with the stereotype of a women who is quiet and assertive.[4] Popular books written during this period, including *Reviving Ophelia*,[5] *School Girls*,[6] and *Failing at Fairness*[7] further contributed to the belief that girls were experiencing psychological damage and educational neglect due to a "girl poisoning" culture.

The extent to which girls are truly disadvantaged in the educational system has been a subject of debate. Some recent research suggests that concerns about differential treatment in the classroom by gender have been overplayed. In a meta-analysis of studies on sex differences in classroom interactions from 1970 to 2000, researchers found that teachers did interact more with their male students than with their female students, but these interactions were primarily to reprimand or critique male performance. There was no evidence that teachers had more positive interactions with males than with their female students.[8] These findings suggest that both girls and boys are being shortchanged in classrooms. Girls are more likely to be ignored, while boys are more likely to receive negative attention related to disruptive behaviors.

The claim that early adolescent girls lose their voice and are constrained by femininity has also been the subject of dispute. For example, Sommers voiced concerns over the quality of the qualitative data Gilligan used to make her claims, suggesting that her work was more driven by ideology than objective data.[9] Furthermore, using quantitative data Harter and her colleagues failed to show an overall loss of voice among adolescent females, though they did show that a subset of females who did identify with the good women stereotype were more passive in public situations.[10] This finding suggests a modification of Gilligan's argument, in that it is not gender but gender orientation that predicts the loss of voice. Additionally, reviews of the literature have shown relatively small gender differences in self-esteem, raising questions about the claim of a dramatic decline in self-esteem for girls in adolescence.[11] Finally, Goodwin's ethnography of girls at play challenges the assumption of feminine passivity. Instead, she found that girls tended to assert themselves and often challenged boys in peer interactions and playground games.[12]

Gender and STEM

Science and technology are one area outlined in the AAUW report[13] where gender inequities continue to persist. In primary school, girls and boys take math and science courses in equal numbers and perform equally well in these domains.[14] However, despite the lack of gender differences in aptitude or course selection, females are less likely to pursue degrees and careers in some STEM fields, especially computer science, physics, and engineering.[15] The metaphor of a leaking pipeline has been used to explain why females are choosing to opt out of STEM courses, majors, and careers at various stages of their educational careers.[16] The underrepresentation of females is troubling because STEM careers tend to be higher paying and higher prestige occupations. Moreover, we are losing an important source of talent and have less diverse perspectives when fewer females pursue STEM careers.[17]

Motivational factors are one explanation for females' lower representation in some STEM fields and careers. Girls have been found to have lower perceptions of their abilities in math and lower interest in math than do boys.[18] Other studies find that girls have less positive attitudes toward science and are more likely to perceive science as an uninteresting and difficult domain.[19] From a young age, students report the stereotypic view of physical science topics being for "boys" and biological topics being for "girls."[20] These preferences impact on course-taking behavior; girls have been found to prefer courses in the biological sciences, whereas boys are more likely to choose courses in the physical sciences or have a broader range of preferences.[21] These gender-typed beliefs have been linked to gender-typed course enrollment decisions, college majors, and career aspirations.[22]

Other research has explored how individual beliefs about the malleability of ability influence motivation, achievement, and course-taking decisions. Individuals who believe ability is an innate stable trait are more likely to give up when a task is challenging and attribute failure to lack of talent. In contrast, students who view effort and hard work as the key to success have higher motivation and are more likely to persist when tasks are challenging.[23] Girls are more likely to endorse ability beliefs and be vulnerable to these beliefs, especially in math and science domains. For example, Dweck found that the combination of viewing math ability as a trait and believing that girls are less good at math resulted in girls having decreased motivation and interest in pursuing math careers.[24]

Occupational preferences and lifestyle values also play a role in the decision to pursue STEM-related careers. Women appear to be opting out of these careers at a higher rate than men because of preferences for careers that allow them to interact with and help people, which are seen as less characteristic of STEM fields.[25] Women also express greater concern that STEM careers are incompatible with achieving a work/family life balance.[26] Finally, some women may be reluctant to pursue scientific careers because they feel that their multifaceted identities are incompatible with a "scientific identity," which is often perceived as emphasizing masculine traits such as objectivity, rationality, and lack of emotions.[27]

Are schools disadvantaged against boys?

Outside of concerns over girls' underrepresentation in STEM careers, in the past 15 years the rhetoric over whether schools shortchange girls has shifted to a concern over "failing boys." One reason for this shift is statistics showing that boys are lagging behind girls on several achievement and educational attainment indicators in the elementary, middle, and high school years.[28] On average, girls get higher grades, have higher reading test scores, take more advanced courses, and have higher rates of participation in extracurricular activities.[29] Other studies find advantages for girls on indicators of student engagement (i.e., effort, attention, and classroom behavior), self-discipline, and social skills. In addition, boys have been found to have higher rates of school disciplinary sanctions and are overrepresented in populations of antisocial behavior, learning disabilities, and attention disorders.[30]

There also is a growing gender gap in college enrollment and completion rates. While the proportion of both male and female students attending college has increased since the 1970s, the percentage of women enrolled at both the undergraduate and graduate levels have increased at a much faster pace than the percentage of men. Women earn 58% of all bachelor degrees, 62% of masters, and 54% of doctoral degrees.[31] Women also have made progress in several postgraduate areas where they had traditionally been underrepresented. At least half of biology and chemistry majors are now women, though females are still largely underrepresented in engineering, physical sciences, and computer science majors.[32]

The framing of education as a concern for boys may also be a result of a resurgence of neoliberalism educational reforms, which emphasize privatization and accountability.[33] This has resulted in schools overvaluing achievement test scores because they need to compete with one another for students and limited funding. Another reason for this shift is a concern by some scholars that schools have become feminized as a result a teaching force that is primarily female and an assumption that schools tend to emphasize feminine ways of relating.[34]

Popular books and media-driven panic over school violence have also contributed to the shift to a focus on boys' issues. For example, in his book *Real Boys*, Pollack claims that boys have increasing rates of depression, violence, drug use, and academic failure because of a "boy culture" which emphasizes separation and toughness and makes it difficult for boys to experience emotional vulnerability and connection.[35] His solution is to allow boys to reject strict conceptions of masculinity and to strengthen their connection to parents and teachers.[36] Additionally, some scholars have expressed concerns that schools are not structured to meet boys' emotional needs because teachers are more likely to classify boys' behavior as a discipline problem rather than trying to understand their needs.[37] Finally, some have argued that the tendency toward more cooperative and progressive pedagogical approaches does not support biological based differences in ways of learning.[38] Supporters of this perspective argue that girls learn better when instruction emphasizes cooperation, while boys learn better in more structured and competitive-based environments.[39]

Some fear that the increased focus on boys in educational research, policy, and practice will hurt girls and take away some of the small educational gains that they have made.[40] There is also a worry that the emphasis on boys' underachievement will result in less research focused on girls and less funding for educational programs for girls.[41] Attempts to change curriculum and pedagogy to be more "boy-friendly" may also negatively impact on girls. For example, some have advocated aligning language arts curriculum and pedagogy more closely with boys' interests in adventures, mysteries, and humor, as a way to increase literacy scores.[42] These changes have the potential to hurt some girls whose interests may not align with boys' stereotypical preferences.[43]

Problems with framing education in terms of gender differences

Critiques of framing education either in terms of a "girl" or a "boy" crisis are numerous. One problem is that it compares "girls" as one unitary group, with "boys" as another, and neglects important variability in the experience of gender by socioeconomic status, ethnicity, and location. Research shows that African-American boys have a greater risk of special education placement, higher rates of school suspension, and higher rates of grade retention than their white counterparts.[44] Other research finds greater educational risks for low-income boys. Entwisle, Alexander, and Olson documented a larger gender gap in reading achievement for low-income boys than for their higher-income counterparts. This gender gap was explained by low-income boys having higher retention rates and teachers giving them lower ratings of classroom behavior than their more economically advantaged peers.[45] In an era of limited educational funding, it is important to determine which girls and boys are most at risk in educational settings so that resources can be targeted to those students with the greatest need.

Another concern is that on most attitudinal and achievement indicators boys and girls are more alike than they are different.[46] There is a significant overlap between the distribution for boys and girls on most variables, with individual differences being significantly large than mean gender differences.[47] There also is some evidence of greater variability in boys' achievement scores at the extremes, with more boys at both the bottoms and tops of the distributions.[48] Furthermore, even when there are areas where there are persistent gender differences, such as spatial abilities, these differences are related to experience and can be reduced through instruction.[49] Overinflated claims of gender differences serve to reify gender stereotypes and have the potential to limit females' education and occupational opportunities.[50]

The extent of gender differences also varies across dimensions. On some dimensions like literacy, boys are at a disadvantage. However, in other ways boys are benefitting from our current educational system, such as in involvement in higher-prestige STEM courses and involvement in the privileged world of sports.[51] Another problem is that by focusing on achievement measures other indicators of educational inequality have been neglected. For example, although boys on average have slightly lower test scores, they outperform girls on post-school options, employment, and other economic indicators.[52] Furthermore, this strategy fails to capture the full range of range of inequalities in school and how gender is both constructed and reinforced in the classroom.

How is gender constructed in the classroom?

One way that students observe gender norms is through the division of labor in schools. In 2011, 84% of teachers were female, up from 82% in 2005.[53] Females are also more likely to take on traditional feminine roles in schools such as caring for sick children and preparing food. In contrast, men are more likely to serve in administrative roles, coach sports, and fix things in school.[54] There are also gender differences in work specialization, with female teachers concentrated in languages and literature courses, and male teachers more likely to teach in sciences, mathematics, and industrial arts.[55]

Gender is also constructed through classroom materials. Although books are less gender biased than in the past, in children's literature books females are still more likely to be placed in stereotypical roles, such as a passive observer, while males are more likely to be portrayed as assertive and adventurous.[56] Textbooks also continue to perpetuate gender stereotypes, with females underrepresented in both the language and images of science textbooks.[57] Another concerns is that few texts include females' perspectives on key historical and social events.[58] Finally, the presentation of masculinity in historical textbooks serves to reinforce patriarchal assumptions about men's power.[59]

Teachers also hold gender-stereotypic views about children's abilities in different domains. Much of this research has focused on the stereotypes that teachers have about girls' abilities in math and science fields. Teachers are more likely to stereotype math as a masculine domain, believe that girls gain less from additional effort in math than do boys, and believe that math is more difficult for girls than for boys.[60] In a study of teachers' beliefs regarding gender and mathematics, Fennema, Peterson, Carpenter, and Lubiniski found that teachers thought their best students were male and reported that these male students were more competitive, more logical, more adventurous, and enjoyed mathematics more than their best female students. Additionally, teachers were more likely attribute girls' success in mathematics to hard work and boys' success to ability.[61]

Teachers' views about classroom behaviors are also gender stereotyped. Teachers tend to have more favorable attitudes toward students who are cooperative, compliant, and orderly. Given the nature of socialization, girls are more likely than boys to exhibit this type of behavior in the classroom.[62] Teachers also more likely to identify boys as underachievers and expect higher rates of misbehavior from their male students than their female students.[63] They also punish boys at higher rates than girls and are more likely to use punishment as a means of controlling gender (i.e., by shaming boys when they "act like a girl").[64] There is also evidence that teachers view classroom behaviors differently by gender. For example, lying and cheating are considered more serious negative behaviors for girls than for boys, while restlessness and disorderliness are more acceptable in boys than in girls.[65]

Much research has focused on the question of whether teachers' differential expectations act as self-fulfilling prophecies that affect children's later motivation and achievement. Although research shows that teacher expectancy effects are small, they have been found to have a cumulative negative effect over time, especially for youth from stigmatized groups (i.e., girls in math).[66] In fact, research shows that girls in mathematics are more negatively influenced by teacher expectancy than females in stereotypically "feminine" classes.[67]

Unfortunately, most teachers are not trained to recognize and prevent gender stereotyping in the classroom, and raising awareness is not necessarily enough to change behaviors.[68] Even when teachers are aware of gender stereotypes, they still may unwittingly perpetuate them. For example, in a study of three feminist elementary teachers, Resenbrink found that even with a knowledge of feminism, teachers still held some gendered expectations and produced behaviors that resulted in differential treatment for boys and girls.[69] Moreover, Spencer, Porche, and Tolman found that even in a school where teachers had a commitment to gender equity, there were noticeable differences in boys' and girls' experiences in the classroom. Girls felt greater pressure from their teachers and their peers to behave, be smart, and be nice to the boys. In contrast, boys got greater attention from their teachers because it was assumed that they would require more help.[70]

Single-sex education

Single-sex education has been suggested as a possible vehicle for improving girls' achievement, especially in STEM domains. As a result of changes to Title IX legislation, there has been a dramatic rise in the number of single-sex schools, though the effectiveness of this approach remains controversial.[71] On one side, proponents argue that single-sex classrooms (1) allow girls to focus on academics without distractions, (2) counter gender inequality by reducing sex biases in teacher interactions, (3) allow for greater sensitivity to biologically based differences and gendered ways of learning, (4) help girls to develop confidence and empower girls in traditionally "male-typed" domains, and (5) lower sexual distractions in the classroom.[72] On the other hand, critics of single-sex education have cited evidence of few differences between boys and girls in their capacities for learning[73] and a concern that separating by gender will actually increase gender stereotypes and legitimize institutional sexism.[74]

The research on the benefits of single-sex education has been mixed. Some studies show achievement benefits from single-sex education,[75] while others find few achievement benefits[76] and no advantage in terms of STEM-related course-taking and occupational choices.[77] One explanation for the different conclusions regarding the outcomes of single-sex education is that many studies have not controlled for differences in student, school, and teacher characteristics.[78] For example, girls who attend single-sex schools tend to enter school more academically advantaged, have more involved parents, and be from higher socioeconomic status families.[79] A recent meta-analysis of the literature comparing single-sex and co-educational schooling showed a small advantage for single-sex education in uncontrolled studies (i.e., no controls for demographic, individual, and family self-selection effects, no random assignment), but no difference between single-sex and coeducation in controlled studies (i.e., random assignment or control for selection effects).[80]

Feminist pedagogy

Rather than separating girls and boys in different classrooms, other scholars have argued that we can improve girls' experience in school by integrating feminist pedagogy and methodologies into classrooms. One of the key components of feminist pedagogy is the reformulation of the teacher-student relationship to equalized power relations and model democratic relationships between teachers and students.[81] In these classrooms, students assume more responsibility for teaching and teachers for learning. The reduction of teacher-student authority occurs through less teacher directed techniques, small group discussions, shared leadership, and collective decision-making about course content and grading.[82]

Attention to and validation of women's personal experience and voice is another central cornerstone of feminist pedagogy.[83] The goal of this pedagogy is to empower women to see themselves as authoritative constructors of knowledge.[84] Creating safe environments where all students feel free to collaborate, engage in dialogue, and share their experiences are key aspects of feminist classrooms. The importance of collaboration is based on the premise that females prefer shared and equalitarian modes of communication over competition, and this type of learning builds a sense of community and solidarity.[85] Finally, at the core, feminist pedagogy is concerned with social change. The goal of these classrooms is to challenge dominant patriarchal frameworks; make visible women's actions, achievements, and concerns; and help students to engage in political or activist work aimed at creating a more just society.[86]

Over the past two decades, there has been an increased focus on using feminist pedagogy, which grew out of women's studies departments, to reform science education and help make science more attractive for all students, but particularly for female and minority students.[87] The goal of feminist science pedagogy is to validate the voices and experiences of all students, especially female students; challenge existing practices in science as masculine in nature; place the teacher in the role as facilitator; and empower students to reconsider the role that science plays in their lives.[88]

A feminist pedagogy in science has been defined in a variety of ways including: "female friendly," "gender inclusive," "liberatory," and "transformative."[89] There have been two different ways of approaching feminist initiatives in science that differ in how they consider power relations. "Female friendly" and "gender inclusive" approaches have tried to equalize the opportunities in school by encouraging young women to go into math and science, by critiquing the gender representation in curriculum, and by analyzing school practices for stereotypes.[90] These approaches have tended not to challenge existing structures and instead have focused more on changing the curriculum and instruction to attract more women.[91] These approaches tend to emphasize the doing and knowing of science; grounding science in both genders' lived experience; and emphasizing active learning and participation, collaboration, and the societal values of sciences.[92]

In contrast, "liberatory" and "transformative" models emphasize the intersection of science and activism with the goal of examining the social, historical, and political contexts from which science is constructed.[93] These models are premised on the belief that science education has been traditionally a culture of exclusion which ignores the voices of subordinated groups. The goal of these approaches is to shift the focus in reforms to the discriminatory practices in science and education to help students to critique unequal power relations, why they exist, and what they can do about them. Moreover, the goal of these classrooms is to make explicit how, when, and why women's and minorities' work has been excluded in science and the impact of these exclusions on knowledge construction.[94]

Interestingly, there have been few empirical studies on the effectiveness of integrating feminist pedagogical principles in the classroom.[95] Feminist pedagogy also has its detractors and resisters, and even those who embrace the principles acknowledge the challenges of implementing these ideas on the classroom. For example, one concern raised is that the emphasis on personal experience has led some students to deny social facts that contradict their worldviews and refuse to consider alternative explanations.[96] In feminist classrooms, it is important to help students to move beyond moral dichotomies and be able to deconstruct women's personal experience in order to examine how these narratives are also selective and constructed in particular times and contexts.[97]

The claim that women's preferred way of learning is collaborative has also been critiqued by some for being essentialist and for overlooking the importance of collaboration and connection to other groups.[98] Finally, the assumption of equal power relations is difficult to achieve. Class, race, and heterosexism oppression still operate in many feminist classrooms, as white middle-class females' perspectives still tend to predominate. The reality is that students are only together in classrooms for a few hours per week, making it difficult to develop a safe space where some students' views do not feel marginalized, trivialized, or stereotyped.[99] One of the challenges feminist teachers face is how to create less hierarchical relations with their students, but at the same time still use their voice and authority in some situations to make sure that some women, especially those from traditionally underrepresented groups, are not silenced.

Future directions

In conclusion, the research to date provides a mixed view of girls' schooling experience. On the one hand, gaps in mathematics achievement have virtually disappeared and more girls are enrolled in higher education today than are boys.[100] On the other hand, girls still continue to be underrepresented in STEM courses and careers like engineering, physics, and computer science.[101] In addition, traditional notions of masculinity and femininity continue to be reproduced in the classroom through the division of labor, curricular materials, and teachers' gender ideological beliefs about what is appropriate and acceptable behavior for male and female students.[102]

The review also highlights limitations in current understanding of gender and education and fruitful areas of future research. One of the central themes is the need to move beyond research that focuses on gender dichotomies to consider the diversity of both females' and males' experience in the classroom. Future research needs to examine how gender interacts with race, class, culture, immigration, and sexuality, to impact on classroom experience and educational outcomes. It is also important to understand the experience of boys and girls who do not conform to traditional gender stereotypes. For example, studying girls who like and choose to participate in math and science can provide insight into gender and the complex process of identity formation.[103]

This review also illustrates disconnects between educational research and practice. Many schools have implemented programs and policies related to gender that have not been informed by research. One example is the proliferation of single-sex education programs, despite limited research on the effectiveness of programs.[104] Additionally, there been limited research on the effectiveness of curricular reforms to increase girls' representation in math and science, especially among girls from different ethnic and economic backgrounds,[105] as well as limited work on the efficacy of feminist pedagogical principles.[106] The reality is that most students are in coeducational environments. As a result, it is also important to develop curricular materials that simultaneously meet the needs of both boys and girls. A more systematic analysis of the efficacy of best practices and programs for educating both boys and girls is also needed.

Finally, developing more effective models of teacher education and professional development is a critical area of future work. Teacher education curricula related to gender and schooling are often shallow, superficial, and sometimes even inaccurate.[107] Feminist pedagogy offers an alternative to current teacher education around gender and provides a way of thinking about teaching and learning that can help guide the choice of content, classroom practices, and teacher-student relationships. Training teachers in feminist pedagogical principles can help to create more equitable school environments where hierarchical power relations are disrupted and all students' voices are heard.

Notes

1 Weaver-Hightower, "Boy Turn," 475–477.
2 Farady, "Girl Crisis," 44–45; Weaver-Hightower, "Boy Turn," 471–472.
3 American Association of University Women, *Shortchange Girls*, 2–5.
4 Brown and Gilligan, *Meeting at Crossroads*, 216.
5 Pipher, *Reviving Ophelia*, 44.
6 Ornstein, *School Girls*, 18–26.

7 Sadker and Sadker, *Failing at Fairness*, 6–14.
8 Jones and Dindia, "Sex-Equity in the Classroom," 455.
9 Sommers, *War Against Boys*, 122.
10 Harter, Waters, and Whitesell, "Lack of Voice as False Self-Behavior," 162–163.
11 Kleinfeld, *Myth Schools Shortchange Girls*, 63; Kling et al., "Gender Differences in Self-Esteem," 486; Hyde, "Gender Similarities," 589.
12 Goodwin, *Hidden Life of Girls*, 246–247.
13 American Association of University Women, *Shortchange Girls*, 4.
14 US Department of Education, *Gender Equity in Education*, 2–4.
15 National Science Board, *Science and Engineering*, Chapter 2, 5.
16 Blickenstaff, "Women and Science Careers," 369.
17 Ibid., 370.
18 Frenkel et al., "Development of Mathematics Interest," 525; Watt, "Development of Adolescents' Self-Perceptions," 1567.
19 Brotman and Moore, "Girls in Science," 978.
20 Andre et al., "Competence Beliefs," 741.
21 Brotman and Moore, "Girls in Science," 979.
22 Eccles, "Where Are All the Women?" 207–208; Wang and Degol, "Motivational Pathways to STEM," 307.
23 Dweck and Molden, "Self Theories," 123–125; Wang and Degol, "Motivational Pathways," 308.
24 Dweck, "Is Math a Gift?" 50.
25 Wang and Degol, "Motivational Pathways," 309–310.
26 Ibid., 310.
27 Blickenstaff, "Women and Science Careers," 382–383; Brotman and Moore, "Girls in Science," 987.
28 Buchmann, Diprite, and McDaniel, "Gender Inequalities in Education," 321–325; Weaver-Hightower, "Boy Turn," 474.
29 Buchmann, Diprite, and McDaniel, "Gender Inequalities," 320–323; Meece and Scantlebury, "Gender and Schooling," 204–285; US Department of Education, *Gender Equity*, 1–3.
30 Buchmann, Diprite, and McDaniel, "Gender Inequalities," 322.
31 Ibid., 325–326.
32 National Science Board, "*Science and Engineering*," Chapter 2, 14.
33 Weaver-Hightower, "Boy Turn," 476–477.
34 Connell, "Teaching the Boys," 213; Martino and Berrill, "Boys, Schools, and Masculinities," 101.
35 Pollack, *Real Boys*, 4–7.
36 Pollack, "The 'War for Boys'," " 194–195.
37 Fredricks, *Eight Myths of Student Disengagement: Creating Classrooms of Deep Learning*, 201–203.
38 Gurian, Henley, and Trueman, *Boys and Girls*, 17; Sommers, *The War Against Boys*, 169; Weaver-Hightower, "Boy Turn," 473.
39 Gurian, Henley, and Trueman, *Boys and Girls*, 20–25.
40 Weaver-Hightower, "Boy Turn," 486.
41 Ibid.
42 Fredricks, *Eight Myths*, 204–206.
43 Weaver-Hightower, "Boy Turn," 486.
44 Fredricks, *Eight Myths*, 201.
45 Entwisle, Alexander, and Olson, "Early Schooling," 127–128.
46 Kling et al., "Gender Difference in Self-Esteem," 486; Voyer and Voyer, "Gender Differences in Achievement," 1191.
47 Hyde and Lindberg, "Nature of Gender Differences," 21; Hyde, "Gender Similarities," 581–586.
48 Weaver-Hightower, "Boy Turn," 486.
49 Hyde and Lindberg, "Nature of Gender Differences," 23.
50 Hyde, "Gender Similarities," 589–590.
51 Weaver-Hightower, "Boy Turn," 486–487.
52 Ibid.
53 Feistritzer, *Profile of Teachers*, 12.
54 Meece and Scantlebury, "Gender and Schooling," 284.
55 Ibid.
56 Davis and McDaniel, "You've Come a Long Way," 533; Meece and Scantlebury, "Gender and Schooling," 284.

57 Bazler and Simonis, "High School Chemistry Textbooks," 360; Potter and Rosser, "Factors in Life Science Textbooks," 680.
58 Meece and Scantlebury, "Gender and Schooling," 284.
59 Kuzmic, "Textbooks, Knowledge, and Masculinity," 119–120.
60 Keller, "TeachersTeachers' Stereotyping,"171; Tiedmann, "Gender Beliefs of Teachers," 58.
61 Fenemma et al., "Teachers Attributions," 65–66.
62 Meece and Askew, "Gender, Motivation, and Educational Attainment," 150.
63 Jones and Myhill, "Seeing Things Differently," 541.
64 Connell, "Teaching the Boys," 217.
65 Borg, "Secondary School Teachers," 76.
66 Jussim and Harber, "Teacher Expectancies," 142–143.
67 McKown and Weinstein, "Children's Differential Response," 173.
68 Kenway et al., *Answering Back*, 203.
69 Resenbrink, *All Our Places*, 146.
70 Spencer, Porche, and Tolman, "We've Come a Long Way," 1797–1999.
71 Bigler and Signorella, "Single Sex Education," 660, 663–666.
72 Mael et al., *For and Against Single Sex-Schools*, 3–4; Pahlke, Hyde, and Alison, "Effects of Single-Sex," 1042–1043.
73 Hyde, "Gender Similarities," 589–590.
74 Halpern et al., "Single-Sex Schooling," 1706.
75 Cherney and Campbell, "A League of Their Own," 718; Streitmatter, *For Girls Only*, 35–39.
76 Halpern et al., "Single-Sex Schooling," 1706; Pahlke, Hyde, and Allison, "Effects of Single-Sex," 1064.
77 Cherney and Campbell, "A League of Their Own," 719–721; Feniger, "The Gender Gap," 677–678.
78 American Association of University Women, *Separated by Sex*, 14–15.
79 Ibid.
80 Pahlke, Hyde, and Allison, "Effects of Single-Sex," 1064.
81 Webb, Maria, and Walker, "Feminist Pedagogy," 68.
82 Manicom, "Transformations, Standpoints, and Politics," 380.
83 Ibid., 370–371.
84 Ibid., 380.
85 Webb, Maria, and Walker, "Feminist Pedagogy," 68–69.
86 Manicom, "Transformations, Standpoints, and Politics," 368; Weiner, "Out of the Ruins," 86.
87 Calbrese Barton, "Liberatory Science Education," 144–146; Capobianco, "Science Teachers Attempts," 2.
88 Mayberry and Rees, "Pedagogy, Practice, and Science Education," 194–195.
89 Capobianco, "Science Teachers Attempts," 3; Calbrese Barton, "Liberatory Science Education," 144; Roychoudhury, Tippins, and Nichols, "Gender-Inclusive Science Teaching," 899.
90 Rosser, *Female-Friendly Science*, 55–72; Roychoudhury, Tippins, and Nichols, "Gender-Inclusive Science Teaching," 899.
91 Capobianceo, "Science Teachers Attempts," 3.
92 Rosser, *Female Friendly Science*, 55–72.
93 Calbrese Barton, "Liberatory Science Education," 147–153; Mayberry and Rees, "Pedagogy, Praxis, and Education," 194–195.
94 Calbresse, Barton, "Liberatory Science Education," 147.
95 Weiner, "Out of the Ruins," 86.
96 Markowitz, "Unmasking Moral Dichotomies," 51–52; Weiner, "Out of the Ruins," 88.
97 Manicom, "Transformations, Standpoints, and Politics," 372.
98 Ibid., 375–376.
99 Ibid., 377–378.
100 Buchmann, Diprite, and McDaniel, "Gender Inequalities in Education," 321–325.
101 National Science Board, "Science and Engineering," Chapter 2, 14.
102 Meece and Scantleburry, "Gender and Schooling," 283–285: Spencer, Porche, and Tolman, "We've Come a Long Way," 1797.
103 Weaver-Hightower, "Boy Turn," 487.
104 Bigler and Signorella, "Single Sex Education," 660.
105 Brotman and Moore, "Girls in Science," 993; Meece and Scantleburry, "Gender and Schooling," 289.
106 Weaver-Hightower, "Boy Turn," 488; Weiner, "Out of the Ruins," 88.
107 Sadker and Zittleman, "Gender Equity in Teacher Education," 134.

References

American Association of University Women. *How Schools Shortchange Girls: A Study of Major Findings on Girls and Education: Executive Summary*. Washington, DC: Author, 1998.

American Association of University Women, Educational Foundation. *Separated by Sex: A Critical Look at Single Sex Education*. Washington, DC: Author, 1998.

Andre, Thomas, Myrna Whigham, Amy Hendrickson, and Sharon Chambers. "Competency Beliefs, Positive Affect, and Gender Stereotypes of Elementary Students and Their Parents About Science Versus Other School Subjects." *Journal of Research in Science Teaching* 36, no. 6 (2009): 719–747.

Bazler, Judith, and Doris Simonis. "Are High School Chemistry Textbooks Gender Fair?" *Journal of Research in Science Teaching* 28, no. 4 (1991): 353–362.

Bigler, Rebecca, and Margaret Signorella. "Single-Sex Education: New Perspectives and Evidence on a Continuing Controversy." *Sex Roles* 65 (2011): 659–669.

Blickenstaff, Jacob. "Women and Science Careers: Leaking Pipeline or Gender Filter." *Gender and Education* 17, no. 4 (2005): 369–386.

Borg, Mark. "Secondary School Teachers' Perceptions of Pupils' Undesirable Behaviours." *British Journal of Educational Psychology* 68 (1998): 67–79.

Brotman, Jennie, and Felicia Moore. "Girls and Science: A Review of Four Themes in the Science Education Literature." *Journal of Research in Science Teaching* 45, no. 9 (2008): 971–1002.

Brown, Lyn, and Carol Gilligan. *Meeting at the Crossroads*. Cambridge, MA: Harvard University Press, 1992.

Buchmann, Claudia, Thomas Diprete, and Anne McDaniel. "Gender Inequalities in Education." *Annual Review of Sociology* 34 (2008): 319–337.

Calabrese Barton, Angela. "Liberatory Science Education: Weaving Connections Between Feminist Theory and Science Education." *Curriculum Inquiry* 27, no. 2 (1997): 141–163.

Capobianco, Brenda. "Science Teachers Attempts at Integrating Feminist Pedagogy Through Collaborative Action Research." *Journal of Research on Science Teaching* 44, no. 1 (2007): 1–32.

Cherney, Isabelle, and Kate Campbell. "A League of Their Own: Do Single-Sex Schools Increase Girls' Participation in the Physical Sciences?" *Sex Roles* 65 (2011): 712–724.

Connell, Raewyn. "Teaching the Boys: New Research on Masculinity and Gender Strategies for Schools." *Teachers College Record* 98, no. 2 (1996): 206–235.

Davis, Anita, and Thomas McDainel. "You've Come a Long Way, Baby – or Have You? Research Evaluating Gender Portrayal in Recent Caldecott Winning Books." *Reading Teacher* 57, no. 5 (1999): 532–536.

Dweck, Carol. "Is Math a Gift? Beliefs That Put Females at Risk." In *Why Aren't More Women in Science? Top Researchers Debate Evidence*, edited by Stephen Ceci and Wendy Williams, 47–55. Washington, DC: American Psychological Association, 2007.

Dweck, Carol, and Daniel Molden. "Self Theories: Their Impact on Competence, Motivation, and Acquisition." In *Handbook of Competence and Motivation*, edited by Andrew Elliot and Carol Dweck, 22–40. New York: Guilford Press, 2005.

Eccles, Jacquelynne. "Where Are All the Women? Gender Differences in Participation in Physical Science and Engineering." In *Why Aren't More Women in Science? Top Researchers Debate Evidence*, edited by Stephen Ceci and Wendy Williams, 199–210. Washington, DC: American Psychological Association, 2007.

Entwisle, Doris, Karl Alexander, and Linda Olson. "Early Schooling: The Handicap of Being Poor and Male." *Sociology of Education* 80, no. 2 (2007): 114–138.

Farady, Michael. "The Girl-Crisis Movement: Evaluating the Foundation." *Review of General Psychology* 14, no. 1 (2010): 44–55.

Feistritzer, Emily. *Profile of Teachers in the United States, 2011*. Washington, DC: National Center for Educational Information, 2011. www.edweek.org/media/pot2011final-blog.pdf.

Feniger, Yarif. "The Gender Gap in Advanced Math and Science Course Taking: Does Same-Sex Education Make a Difference." *Sex Roles* 65 (2011): 670–679.

Fennema, Elizabeth, Penelope Peterson, Thomas Carpenter, and Cheryl, Lubinski. "Teacher's Attributions and Beliefs About Girls and Boys in Mathematics." *Educational Studies in Mathematics* 21, no. 1 (1990): 55–69.

Fredricks, Jennifer. *Eight Myths of Student Disengagement: Creating Classrooms of Deep Learning*. Thousand Oaks, CA: Sage Publicatins, 2014.

Frenkel, Anne, Thomas Goetz, Reinhard Perkun, and Helen Watt. "Development of Mathematics Interest in Adolescence: Influences of Gender, Family, and School Context." *Journal of Research on Adolescence* 20, no. 2 (2010): 507–537.

Goodwin, Marjorie. *Hidden Life of Girls: Games of Stance, Status, and Exclusion.* Malden, MA: Blackwell, 2006.

Gurian, Michael, Patricia Henley, and Terry Trueman. *Boys and Girls Learn Differently: A Guide for Teacher and Parents.* New York: Jossey Bass, 2001.

Halpern, Diane, Lise Eliot, Rebecca Bigler, Richard Fabes, Laura Hanish, Janet Hyde, Lynne Liben, and Carol Martin. "The Pseudoscience of Single-Sex Schooling." *Science Magazine* 33 (2011): 1706–1707.

Harter, Susan, Patricia Waters, and Nancy Whitesell. "Lack of Voice as a Manifestation of False Self-Behavior Among Adolescents. The School Setting as a Stage on Which the Drama of Authenticity is Enacted." *Educational Psychologist* 32, no. 3 (1997): 153–173.

Hyde, Janet. "The Gender Similarities Hypothesis." *American Psychologist* 60, no. 6 (2005): 581–592.

Hyde, Janet, and Sara Lindberg. "Facts and Assumptions About the Nature of Gender Differences and the Implications for Gender Equity." In *Handbook for Achieving Gender Equity Through Education*, 2nd Edition, edited by Susan Klein, 19–32. Mahwah, NJ: Lawrence Erlbaum, 2007.

Jones, Susan, and Kathryn Dindia. "A Meta-Analytic Perspective on Sex-Equity in the Classroom." *Review of Educational Research* 74, no. 4 (2004): 443–471.

Jones, Susan, and Debra Myhill. "Seeing Things Differently: Teachers Construction of Underachievement." *Gender and Education* 16, no. 4 (2003): 531–546.

Jussim, Lee, and Kent Harber. "Teacher Expectations and Self-Fulfilling Prophecies. Knowns, Unknowns, Resolved, and Unresolved Controversies." *Personality and Social Psychology Review* 9, no. 2 (2005): 131–155.

Keller, Carmen. "Effects of Teachers' Stereotyping of Mathematics as a Male Domain. *Journal of Social Psychology* 141, no. 2 (2001): 165–173.

Kenway, Jane, Sue Willis, Jill Blackmore, and Léonie Rennie. *Answering Back: Girls, Boys, Feminism in Schools.* New York: Routledge, 1998.

Kleinfield, Juidth. *The Myth that Schools Shortchange Girls: Social Science in the Art of Deception.* Washington, DC: Women's Freedom Network, 1998.

Kling, Kristin, Janet Hyde, Caroline Showers, and Brenda Buswell. "Gender Differences in Self-Esteem: A Meta-Analysis." *Psychological Bulletin* 125, no. 4 (1999): 470–500.

Kuzmic, Jeffrey. "Textbooks, Knowledge, and Masculinity. Examining Patriarchy From Within. In *Masculinities at School*, edited by Nancy Lesko. Thousand Oaks, CA: Sage, 2000.

Manicom, Ann. "Feminist Pedagogy, Transformations, Standpoints, and Politics." *Canadian Journal of Education* 17, (1992): 365–389.

Mael, Fred, Mark Smith, Alex Alonson, Kelly Rogers, and Doug Gibson. *Theoretical Arguments for and Against Single-Sex Schools: A Critical Analysis of the Explanations.* Washington, DC: American Institute for Research, 2004. www.air.org/sites/default/files/downloads/report/SSX_Explanatory_11-23-04_0.pdf

Markowitz, Linda. "Unmasking Moral Dichotomies: Can Feminist Pedagogy Overcome Student Resistance?" *Gender and Education* 17, no. 1 (2005): 39–55.

Martino, Wayne and Deborah Berrill. "Boys, Schooling, and Masculinities: Interrogating the 'Right' Way to Educate Boys. *Educational Review* 55, no. 2 (2003): 99–117.

Mayberry, Marlee, and Margaret Rees. "Feminist Pedagogy, Interdisciplinary Praxis, and Science Education." In *Meeting the Challenge: Innovative Feminist Pedagogy in Action* edited by Marlee Mayberry and Ellen Rose, 193–214. New York: Routledge, 1999.

McKown, Clark and Rhona Weinstein. "Modeling the Role of Child Ethnicity and Gender in Children's Differential Response to Teacher Expectations." *Journal of Applied Social Psychology* 32 (2002): 159–184.

Meece, Judith and Kathryn Askew. "Gender, Motivation, and Educational Attainment. In *APA Educational Psychology Handbook. Volume 2: Individual Differences and Cultural and Contextual Factors*, edited by Karen Harris, Sandra Graham and Tim Urdan, 139–160. Washington, DC: American Psychological Association, 2012.

Meece, Judith and Kathyrn Scantlebury. "Gender and Schooling: Progress and Persistent Barriers." In *Handbook of Girls and Women's Psychological Health*, edited by Carol Goodheart and Judith Worell, 283–291. New York: Oxford Press, 2006

National Science Board. *Science and Engineering Indicators, 2012.* Arlington, VA: National Science Foundation, 2012.

Orenstein, Peggy. *School Girls: Young Women, Self-Esteem, and the Confidence Gap.* New York: Doubleday, 1994.

Pahlke, Erin, Janet Hyde, and Carlie Allison. "The Effects of Single-Sex Compared with Coeducational Schooling on Students' Performance and Attitudes: A Meta-Analysis." *Psychological Bulletin* 140, no. 4 (2014): 1042–1072.

Pipher, Mary. *Reviving Ophelia: Saving the Selves of Adolescent Girls.* New York: Penguin Group, 1994.

Pollack, William. *Real Boys: Rescuing Our Sons from the Myths of Boyhood.* New York: Random House, 1999.

Pollack, William. "The 'War for Boys': Hearing 'Real Boys' Voices, Healing Their Pain." *Professional Psychology: Research and Practice* 37, no. 2 (2006): 190–195.

Potter, Ellen, and Sue Rosser. "Factors in Life Science Textbooks that May Deter Girls' Interest in Science." *Journal of Research in Science Teaching* 29 (1992): 669–686.

Resenbrink, Carla. *All in our Places: Feminist Challenges in Elementary School Classrooms.* Lanham, MD: Rowan and Littlefield, 2001.

Roychoudhury, Anita, Deborah Tippins, and Sharon Nichols. "Gender-Inclusive Science Teaching: A Feminist: Constructivist Approach." *Journal of Research in Science Teaching* 32, no. 9 (1995): 897–924.

Rosser, Sue. *Female Friendly Science: Applying Women's Studies Methods and Theories to Attract Students.* New York: Pergamon Press, 1990.

Sadker, David, and Myra Sadker. *Failing at Fairness: How America's Schools Cheat Girls.* New York: Scribner's Sons, 1994.

Sadker, David, and Karen Zittleman, "The Treatment of Gender Equity in Educaiton." In *Handbook for Achieving Gender Equity Through Education*, 2nd Edition, edited by Susan Klein, 131–149. Mahwah, NJ: Lawrence Erlbaum, 2007.

Sommers, Christine. *The War Against Boys: How Misguided Feminism is Harming Our Young Men.* New York: Simon and Schuster, 2000.

Spencer, Renne, Michelle Porche, and Deborah Tolman. "We've Come a Long Way-Maybe: New Challenges for Gender Equity in Education." *Teachers College Record* 105, no. 9 (2003): 1774–1807.

Strietmatter, Janie. *For Girls Only: Making a Case for Single-Sex Schools.* Albany, NY: SUNY Press, 1999.

Tiedemann, Joachim. "Teachers' Gender Stereotypes as Determinants of Teacher Perceptions in Elementary School Mathematics." *Educational Studies in Mathematics* 50, no. 1 (2002): 49–62.

U.S. Department of Education. *Gender Equity in Education: A Data Snapshot.* Washington, DC: Author, 2012. http://www2.ed.gov/about/offices/list/ocr/docs/gender-equity-in-education.pdf

Voyer, Daniel and Susan Voyer, "Gender Differences in Scholastic Achievement: A Meta-Analysis: *Psychological Bulletin* 140, no. 4 (2014): 1174–1204.

Wang, Ming-Te, and Jessica Degol. "Motivational Pathways to STEM Career Choices: Using Expectancy-Value Perspectives to Understand Individual and Gender Differences in STEM." *Developmental Review* 33 (2013): 304–340.

Watt, Helen. "Development of Adolescents' Self-Perceptions, Values, and Task Perceptions According to Gender and Domain in 7th Through 11th Grade Australian Students." *Child Development* 17, no. 5 (2004): 1556–1574.

Weaver-Highertower, Marcus. "The 'Boy Turn' on Research on Gender and Education." *Review of Educational Research* 73, no. 4 (2003): 471–498.

Webb, Lynne, Maria Allen, and Kandi Walker. Feminist Pedagogy: Identifying Principles. *Academic Educational Quarterly* 6 (2002): 67–72.

Weiner, Gaby. "Out of the Ruins: Feminist Pedagogy in Recovery." *The Sage Handbook of Gender and Education*, edited by Christine Skelton, Becky Francis, and Lisa Smulyan, 79–93. London: Sage, 2006.

13

Why we need feminist game studies

Mia Consalvo

The editors of this collection gave their authors a series of questions that this volume hopes to address. Among others, they include "Is foregrounding a gender-centered axis still relevant?" and "How does feminism invigorate academic research and politics?" If you are an academic who works in the area of game studies and you write about gender, or if you are simply a woman in this field, these questions remain all too relevant. The goal of my chapter is to explain why that is, as well as to argue for the consistent need for a strong feminist engagement with popular culture, and game culture in particular, in this contemporary period. Game studies has witnessed a growing engagement via feminist critiques of game content as they relate to representations of women and girls, but this chapter will also highlight how feminist scholars must both continue to analyze the larger games industry for its structures and practices, as well as the field of game studies itself, which – knowingly or not – often marginalizes games or game content that is deemed as "feminized" and therefore "not worthy" of sustained attention.

In 2012 I was invited to write a piece about video games for the first issue of *ADA: A Journal of Gender, New Media & Technology* (Consalvo, 2012). The challenge was to describe what I thought was an important issue or research area to address in the journal's forthcoming pages. Responding to events I had been following at the time, I titled the piece "Confronting Toxic Gamer Culture: A Challenge for Feminist Game Studies Scholars." My intent was to spur attention to and study of the increasingly poisonous atmosphere that women were facing online, particularly in relation to video games and online play. In the piece I picked a few of the most glaring and disheartening incidents that circulated in the games community, including the "Dickwolves" controversy that arose when the popular site Penny Arcade published a webcomic in 2010 satirizing the overuse of rape as well as collection quests in many online games. When some readers protested the casualization of rape that they felt the comic implied, the creators responded indifferently, initially refusing to apologize. Further protest led to real life rape threats against some of the women who spoke out, and the subsequent announcement by Penny Arcade writers that they were going to create "Team Dickwolves" T-shirts to have for sale at an upcoming expo event they were hosting (Consalvo, 2012). Another event precipitating even more long-lasting venom was the launch of Anita Sarkeesian's Kickstarter campaign in 2012 to help fund a series of YouTube videos she wanted to create that examined "five common and recurring stereotypes of female characters in video games" (Sarkeesian, 2012). Sarkeesian had created other critical videos about pop culture prior to this via her Feminist Frequency site, but the turn to video games brought on a wave of particularly gendered (as well as some racist) harassment and abuse that was unprecedented.

Other events I touched on included professional game writer Jennifer Hepler's abuse at the hands of (alleged) Bioware fans after she suggested that future games could give players the option of skipping battles and focus on stories instead. The response to Hepler's proposition included postings to forums calling her "the cancer that is killing Bioware" (Polo, 2012). In that essay I asked readers to consider such events in the context of structural forces such as sexism and homophobia as well as new media technologies that helped spread hateful messages easily. I also called for more research into the individuals and groups that engaged in those attacks and fostered a climate where such abuse would appear commonplace. So, for example, I suggested that "if game content is sexist or marketing materials feature booth babes, is it a surprise that male gamers feel entitled to echo sexist remarks in their own gameplay?" (Consalvo, 2012). Shortly after the publication of my essay, I became the target of similar attacks.

In the second half of 2014, the movement now known as "Gamergate" coalesced, forming in response to Eron Gjoni's lengthy blog post about his ex-girlfriend Zoe Quinn, the indie-game creator of mental health simulator *Depression Quest*. In the post, Gjoni accused Quinn of sleeping with multiple men while she was still in a relationship with him, and then using those men to gain favorable reviews for her game. But rather than see the blog post for what it was – sour grapes from a jilted former partner – certain quarters of the internet exploded, directing rage, rape, and death threats as well as doxxing attacks toward Quinn and those who were seen as helping her profit from her activities (despite the game being free to play) (Chess & Shaw, 2015).

In an effort to reposition itself publically as more socially acceptable, the movement was christened "GamerGate" by conservative actor Adam Baldwin, and those who began the attacks started arguing that their ire was actually directed toward ethical lapses in games journalism. In the ensuing storm, which continued across the internet for at least a year, game developers such as Brianna Wu, tech worker Randi Harper, and game critic Anita Sarkeesian received multiple death threats, and countless women journalists and academics were also held up for scrutiny, abuse, and attack (Mortensen, 2018). While I will address the movement and its aftermath at the end of this chapter, what I believe Gamergate demonstrates is not that such attacks are new and noteworthy, but as Jenson and de Castell point out, that they are only the latest in a long string of incidents that continually target women, people of color, and other minorities who dare to speak out. They write, "what is new with Gamergate and the ongoing sexism and misogyny that characterizes game cultures and industries is that *nothing is new*. . . . The real shock should be that it is "same ol' same ol'," and we need to name that significant fact" (Jenson & De Castell, 2016, p. 192). What I instead would like to do is use the movement as emblematic of our continued, urgent need for feminist critiques of games-related culture and the development of a strong and vibrant feminist game studies practice.

This chapter is therefore part personal reflection and part academic discussion, a call for explaining why we need feminist game studies projects now more than ever. We have always been in need of this work, but it has become more urgent as the threats against those who speak out become more vicious and sustained. Three main touch points form the focus for this essay: the evolution of the hashtag #1ReasonWhy; the feminization of social, mobile, and casual games; and the war over game culture that became mainstream news.

#1ReasonWhy

Many scholars, journalists, and game developers have written about the lack of women in the game industry, particularly in the fields of programming and design (Code, 2016; Consalvo, 2008). Part of that dearth can be explained by the shortage of a pipeline in technical fields, such that very few women major in areas such as computer science – and that number has dropped from 35% to 24% as of early 2017 (T. Williams, 2017). That results in fewer potential women hires made in those areas by game studios. Likewise, quality of life issues, as detailed by the International Game Developers Association (IGDA) in a report in 2005, play a large part in who continues to work in the industry after experiencing its brutal work schedules for even a few years. The report was pulled together in part due to the outcry raised by the now infamous (in the game industry) "EA_Spouse" blog post published in 2004, which claimed that as a company, EA engaged in systematic abuse of its workers, "comparing working at EA to being incarcerated, making note of time 'off for good behavior' and describing a typical workweek as stretching from 9 a.m. to 10 p.m., Monday through Saturday" (Surette, 2006). In response, the IGDA's report on industry practices highlighted an issue long considered a badly kept secret – a reliance by many studios on endemic "crunch" for employees (with work weeks that could be 80+ hours long for weeks or months at a time). Excessive crunching has been cited as a key reason for developer burnout, with women developers more likely to leave the field because of the problem (Consalvo, 2008). Compounding these issues is a studio structure that facilitates harassment and sexism, which has until quite recently has been left to flourish in many studios because of the vast gender imbalances that can be found in them. Such problems have until recently been mostly anecdotal, in part because many developers who have experienced such problems have been afraid to speak out, for (very real) fear of retaliation.

Yet this changed in November 2012, when game designer Luke Crane posed what he thought was an innocent question to Twitter, asking "why are there so few lady game creators?" A designer named Filamena Young quickly answered him, "you realize that's more complicated than a tweet can answer, I'm very sure." She then went on to create the hashtag #1Reason-Why, which other developers took up, responding with personal stories as to why they believed there were so few women in their industry. The hashtag exploded with thousands of tweets from women and allies that "detailed their own experiences with sexism in the field of game development along with other obstacles that prevent women from joining game development as a career" (Blodgett & Salter, 2014). As Blodgett and Salter write after an analysis of nearly 8,000 tweets from the hashtag, responses detailed personal stories of sexual harassment, rape, overt sexualization, harassment, silencing, and the pervasiveness of gendered assumptions about women's skills and interest (or lack thereof) relative to working in games. Examples of tweets from the hashtag included the following recounting of issues and problems:

> Not-to-be-missed, vital-for-networking after-parties thrown by big names at game dev conferences . . . that feature strippers. #1reasonwhy
>
> #1reasonwhy because when greeting a man visiting from another gaming studio he turned to my boss and exclaimed "She's cuter than ours"
>
> because I get mistaken for the receptionist or day-hire marketing at trade shows. #1reasonwhy

For anyone familiar with the industry (as well as the technology sector generally), such stories from women developers are not new, but the sustained chorus from the hashtag touched a collective nerve, demonstrating that sexism was not an aberration or individual problem, but instead a structural feature of such workplaces. As Blodgett and Salter explain, if the workplaces with such cultures either encourage or fail to stop such practices, efforts to attract more women into the field will likely fail. They write that even with the growth of incubators, programs, workshops, and special events that focus on teaching girls and women how to code, or cultivating their interest in making games, "these same girls are unlikely to sustain their interest when faced with systemic discrimination, constant microaggressions, and ever-present reminders from industry gatekeepers that this clubhouse still reads 'no girls allowed'" (2014).

What incidents such as the #1ReasonWhy hashtag demonstrate is the importance of workplace culture for all those who inhabit it. Even if a particular studio has no such problems, the climate or atmosphere that surrounds the game industry is one known increasingly as being toxic for women. Likewise, studios that do not expect crunch from workers (and they do exist) become the exception rather than the rule. For example, preliminary work by Olli Sotamaa about Finnish game studios reveals that due to national labor laws and workplace cultures, "crunch time" doesn't exist in those companies. He also points out that this doesn't mean those studios are at a disadvantage –rather they are competing very successfully, creating multimillion global hits like Rovio's *Angry Bird* franchise and Supercell's *Clash of Clans* and *Clash Royale* (Sotamaa, 2016). And crunch isn't just a women's issue. Even many male developers report wanting to leave the industry in significant numbers, in part due to the prevalence of crunch. Investigating the structures and practices that facilitate both crunch and sexism can improve the experiences of *all* game developers. Feminist game studies scholars need to investigate those studios that successfully balance work/life obligations as well as those that cultivate atmospheres where diversity and tolerance are expected.

The feminization of casual and social games

Some of my earliest work studying gameplay focused on women game players, investigating their particular play styles, how avidly or frequently they played, and how those findings differed or not compared with prior research on women and games (Royse, Lee, Undrahbuyan, Hopson, & Consalvo, 2007). More recently I have investigated how families play games together via Facebook (Boudreau & Consalvo, 2014; Consalvo & Vazquez, 2015; Vázquez & Consalvo, 2015) and also how predominantly women players challenged much of what we know about how and why women play, particularly in online casual games like the now defunct massively multiplayer online game (MMOG) *Faunasphere* (Consalvo & Begy, 2015). Such research has taken as a given that women play games, and they have multiple ways to engage in play and with other players – they are not interested solely in the "social" activity that early research claimed was their main objective as other scholars have also pointed out (Jenson & De Castell, 2008). Most of that earlier work has examined women's play in the context of reclaiming that practice as a valid and important element of game culture rather than something at the margins. This has often been in contrast to popular discourses about male players, who have been considered by most researchers as well as mainstream culture as the dominant, "normal" type of player for the same time period under study. More recently things have begun to change, although the games and spaces where women do play – such as *Candy Crush Saga* or *Kim Kardashian: Hollywood* – are again discursively being pigeonholed and re-marginalized, as places where "only women" might be found, in spaces that do not offer "real games" at all. Such rhetorical moves about "real" games or "real" players are of course "typically tied to the assumptions and cultural norms of a specific period of time and moment in play" (Consalvo & Paul, 2013). And this constant negotiation and re-negotiation of who "counts" or belongs of course has a long history, and other researchers have examined this trend too.

In the early 1990s a "games for girls" movement began with the creation of companies and games targeted at making games that girls would want to buy and play. Early scholars focused on efforts such as Brenda Laurel's company Purple Moon and its *Rockett* series of games, which were billed as "friendship adventures" rather than as games (Laurel, 2001). While some writers have praised such efforts and promoted research into the possible different interests that girls might have in games, others have argued that those types of efforts marginalize girls and impose on them very limiting ideas of what they might want to play (Brunner, Bennett, & Honey, 2000; Jenson & de Castell, 2011). Although Laurel's initial high profile efforts eventually ended (Purple Moon was bought by Mattel to curtail it as competition), other companies such as Her Interactive have continued to produce games that appeal strongly to girls (as well as women) over the years, such as the *Nancy Drew* series of adventure games.

More recently, with the advent of new game platforms that don't rely on a dedicated system such as a PlayStation 4 or Xbox One console (such as mobile phones and tablets), many new types of games and game formats have come into existence – spreading further than traditional gamer audiences. More specifically, the rise of casual games, and then mobile and social games, has been key to expanding the audience for who plays games. Yet rather than being positioned as expansions to the general marketplace, they are often marginalized and denigrated as "feminized" and as "not real" games by hardcore gamers and some in the enthusiast press, characterized as activities in which "real gamers" would not engage.

Feminist scholars have carefully documented this trend as well as how such games are sold to women in ways quite different from traditional game marketing campaigns. Important early work by Shira Chess focused on how Nintendo's advertising addressed to women for games on their Wii consoles and DS handheld systems positioned play for women as something that should be "productive" in some way, either as a launching point for successful family interactions, as a fitness experience to improve one's body, or as a way to facilitate general mental or cognitive improvements. By doing this, Chess argues that "video games are able to maintain status as masculine play spaces, reinforcing [the] subtext that women should only play in specific circumstances" (Chess, 2011, p. 235). Yet as Vanderhoef also points out, later ads by Nintendo for the DS system such as the 2008 "I play for me" campaign feature a number of popular Western actresses and feature no such purposefulness to the play being offered, instead emphasizing "everyday women having fun and kicking back with video game software, something almost unheard of in the popular imagination prior to the rise of the 'casual' genre" (Vanderhoef, 2013). Such a move is similar to the "just for me" time that Radway has remarked on about women romance readers – declaring an activity as well as the time and space associated with it for themselves is a way that women resist demands on their time in private, often home settings (Radway, 1984). Vanderhoef's point is not that we have progressed past a point where women's play is seen as problematic or in need of justification, however – it is instead to point to how a genre of games – casual and now social – has increasingly become "feminized" by association with women players and their "different" styles of play.

Should this "feminization" of a particular genre or platform necessarily be a problem? Shira Chess has analyzed many different games designed for female audiences and their dramatic evolution over a fairly short period of time. The games she has studied include those in the time management *Diner Dash* series (Chess, 2012), gothic themes and the use of romance in the popular hidden object/adventure series *Return to Ravenhearst* (Chess, 2014, 2015), and games that offer an "invest/express" mechanic, such as Zynga's successful games *Farmville* and *Castleville* and the more recently successful *Kim Kardashian: Hollywood* (Chess, 2018). Chess argues that the latest of these games "continue to produce low-risk, positive play styles, considered typical of casual games" (Chess, 2018, p. 119). More interestingly, however, she identifies in them a designed idea of "feminine leisure style" that relies on exploiting "interstitial pockets of time" – something she believes emulates "many of the real world perceptions of women's time" (p. 120). But Chess also points out that this newer form of design "has seeped into the larger cultural milieu" to appear in games for wider audiences as well, reconfiguring game design more broadly for everybody (p. 119).

Analyzing a nationally representative sample of Swedes, Lina Eklund similarly found that casual gaming was "equally engaged in by both men and women, contrary to the dominating ideology which connects women with casual gaming and men with hardcore" (Chess, 2018; Eklund, 2016). Eklund writes that this is nothing new, but rather history shows us

> how less valued culture became female and what was considered real became the domain of men; which is what we are seeing in contemporary game culture. Boundaries are enforced where authentic game culture is considered masculine and women involved in gaming are considered casuals – read mass culture gamers, of less value than real gamers.
>
> *(2016, p. 26)*

So even as designers are attempting to reach a broader audience that does exist, game culture itself attempts to redraw lines for participation – even if women do play, the reasoning goes, they don't necessarily play "real" games or play in hardcore ways. Yet that claim about hardcore playing has also been refuted, in part by a study of players of *EverQuest 2* (a MMOG), showing that among its players, women are often the hardest of the hardcore, playing for many more hours than male-identified players (D. Williams, Consalvo, Caplan, & Yee, 2009).

Looking beyond what popular discourse says about players as well as analyses of the games and those who play them, Anable makes an additional larger critique: she argues that while it is true that not all casual games are explicitly gendered,

> the extent to which casual games are perceived as in need of being rescued from feminized mass culture or preserved as a site where women are actually playing video games is less important than the fact that game studies tends to dismiss the entire category because these seemingly simple games do not fit neatly into an emerging field that privileges procedural complexity, expensive hardware, and graphic realism.
>
> *(Anable, 2013, n.p.)*

This call for a better understanding of casual – and now social – games is quite necessary for understanding the increasingly complex roles that games play in our lives. We have always had games that we move around with while playing, games that are casual (both in their roles and in how we play them), and games that are social or invite sociality. Certainly the effort to gender some games as feminine and others as masculine and then valorize one sort over the other is something that the game industry and some players have done quite well over the years. But we need game studies as a field to also stop doing the same thing – and to recognize the politics behind our own definitions and boundaries. There have been some attempts to do this: Jesper Juul's *A Casual Revolution* takes casual games seriously, pointing to their different approaches to game fictions as well as novel interface options like plastic guitars and microphones (Juul, 2010). But more than this, we need game studies to undertake broader analyses – examining more thoroughly different types of games and according *Kim Kardashian: Hollywood* and *Candy Crush Saga* as much serious attention as a *Skyrim* or *League of Legends*. A feminist game studies should not take at face value the labels for games assigned by the industry or even by players themselves – it also cannot escape the systems within which it finds funding and attention. But at least in making explicit how values get attached to games research – which games do we talk about in our research, which games are we tweeting about or discussing on Facebook – we can be more honest in our approaches, and build a more inclusive and comprehensive game studies practice.

The war over game culture: Gamergate

A growing tide of articles and essays have begun to appear analyzing the events and aftermath surrounding Gamergate, the event that began in summer 2014 that ostensibly focused on "ethics in games journalism" but became more popularly associated with its sexist and racist attacks on women game developers, game critics, and game studies academics (Chess & Shaw, 2015; Cross, 2016; Jenson & De Castell, 2016; Mortensen, 2018; Shaw & Chess, 2016). Reading through those pieces, one can clearly see a direct call in game studies for even more engaged feminist theory and feminist scholars, in order to better understand not just how such events precipitate but also their history, variously mediated forms, and multiple rhetorics. This is particularly pertinent, as such feminist scholars' own work can become the subject of attack by those opposed to any changes in "traditional" hardcore game design, marketing, and press.

Leading with some of the most self-reflective writing on the topic, Shira Chess and Adrienne Shaw recount events within Gamergate that led to attacks on themselves as well as other game studies academics for their/our[1] role in "a conspiracy to destroy video games and the video game industry" (Chess & Shaw, 2015, p. 208). Part of the reason for writing their essay was to create more detailed documentation of the pervasive "sexism, heterosexism and patriarchal undercurrents that seem to serve as a constant guidepost for the video game industry" (p. 208). Responding to the need for exploration of Gamergate's links to new forms of social media as well as historical expressions of misogyny, Mortensen's analysis of events makes links between Gamergate tactics and both the rise of "image board culture"[2] and the "leisure-centered aggression" of football hooligans (2018, pp. 794–796). With respect to image board culture, which played a key role in how Gamergate propagated information (as well as misinformation), Mortensen explains that

> the system [of image boards such as 4chan] serves to retain entertaining information that supports the agenda or drama, while the less entertaining facts will be lost. The selectively ephemeral nature of chans supports the attitudes and feelings of the members, rather than the boring or even unpleasant facts they might want to ignore, and the medium itself supports and strengthens any existing echo chamber effect in the community.
>
> *(p. 796)*

What makes her argument about image boards and their spread of disinformation particularly pertinent is her analysis of the dangerous ideologies they spread, and how Gamergate tactics could be compared with hooliganism's tactics. Mortensen points to how both hooligans' and Gamergate's "language was hypermasculinine, and they had little need for values seen as more feminine" (p. 796). In particular, she provides details on how Gamergaters' language for investigating academics such as Chess and Shaw was "aggressively defensive" and employed a "strong tone of machismo" (p. 796). She also makes the key point that while it was often men employing this rhetoric, women likewise participated – as they have in hooliganism. Thus "women in GG defended nudity, sexually explicit images, and aggression against women in games, and GG highlighted their female supporters, particularly the pornography workers" (p. 797). Her findings remind us that we need not only to understand how men might participate in sexist practices, but also how women can and do engage in – and occasionally benefit from – employing the same rhetorics.

Other academics approached Gamergate from slightly different angles, also acknowledging the sexism, but showing how elements of "gameness" or gamification might be applied to understanding various actions within the Gamergate sphere. For example, Katherine Cross makes an excellent case for seeing the actions of many Gamergaters as engaged in a form of gamification, writing that "what GamerGate presents us with is gamified activism – 'activism' understood here as organized political action to achieve certain goals" (Cross, 2016, p. 24). Gamergaters made various references to "enemies" and "final bosses" that needed to be "slayed" in order to be victorious, with Anita Sarkeesian and Leigh Alexander often identified in those ways. But as Cross points out, "seeing someone as a final boss, almost by definition, means you do not apprehend them as a person" (p. 26). Cross's argument is to remind us that "the Internet is a real place and that avatars are us" (p. 32) rather than simple abstractions or fictional constructions. Likewise, I have suggested another way to understand some of the activities of Gamergate is through their rhetorical deployment of gaming capital (Consalvo, 2015). Gaming capital (drawing from Bourdieu's original conception of cultural capital) is a concept I developed in *Cheating*, and it encompasses a wide range of skills, abilities, expertise, and authority that game players can gather and cultivate, usually focused on a particular game or game genre (Consalvo, 2007). Gaming capital includes the diversity of information a player might know about games, expertise gained not only through play but also through experimentation and the researching of various routes to advancement or knowledge of a particular games-related domain. Gaming capital is something players can then perform or display to gain credibility, to be considered an authority among other players.

The concept of gaming capital is useful in understanding both how Gamergate participants see *themselves* as possessing authentic gaming capital and their "enemies" (mostly women and minorities, as well as their allies, named social justice warriors or SJWs) as lacking such capital. This was obvious from the beginning, as Gamergate would attack particular individuals for a perceived lack of knowledge about particular games or game culture, or for not showing proper dedication to or participation in game culture as they defined it. In effect, they were determining what counted as gaming capital (interest in certain types of games, proficiency at those games, acceptance of sexist and racist norms in game culture and the industry) and using their own acceptance of such practices as a baseline from which to judge others (and usually find them wanting). Thus through their attacks on women journalists and claims that women developers like Zoe Quinn were not making "real games" or were writing about issues unimportant to "real gamers," Gamergate supporters asserted through their performances that they knew more about games, they had more history playing, and so they were the ones whose opinions should count.

Yet even if gender and game knowledge seem to be key elements to understanding Gamergate, I would argue that intersectional approaches to analysis are even more critically needed. For example, race and class were also key foci for Gamergate, as those arguing for more inclusive representations of racial and ethnic minorities in games were also met with attacks and abuse, just as were those agitating for more diverse portrayals of sexual minorities. Often this resulted in attacks that focused on gender and sexuality or race and gender in complicated ways. For example, in June 2015 the games critic and blogger Tauriq Moosa wrote an opinion piece for game site *Polygon* titled "Colorblind: On *The Witcher 3*, *Rust*, and gaming's race problem" (Moosa, 2015). In his essay, Moosa discussed different examples of games that have ignored race (*The Witcher 3*) or dealt with race in provocative ways (*Rust*), writing that many games fail to include people of color in their representations and instead assign the category of "race" to fantasy creatures such as elves and orcs, which is demeaning in that it "reinforces how dismissed we are – by not even being considered human" (2015). Moosa was attacked for his arguments, with the pro-Gamergate Encyclopedia Dramatica's entry for Moosa reducing his nuanced critique to the reductive taunt: "Tauriq whines about how there aren't any black people in 14th century Poland" ("Tauriq Moosa – Encyclopedia Dramatica," n.d.), as well as other attacks too racist to cite here. As a writer for the *Daily Vox* recounted, the attack on Moosa for this and other "transgressions" (such as approving of the appearance of gay relationships in Nintendo's newest *Fire Emblem* game in a tweet) ultimately became overwhelming, which led him to temporarily delete his Twitter account, unable to deal with the onslaught of abuse heaped on him for expressing his opinions about video games (The Daily Vox Team, 2015). Here we can see how even male privilege didn't save Moosa from harassment, as his views on race (and likely his own race) put him in Gamergate's sights, a new target to vilify – not simply for holding unacceptable views, but also for lacking gaming capital.

In addition to gender, Mortensen's critique of Gamergate also touches on class issues – another way that intersectionality is needed in understanding online hate and harassment. She writes that "one of the more interesting myths about the targets of GG was that they were wealthy" (Mortensen, 2018, p. 798). In addition to many complaints that Zoe Quinn was becoming wealthy from her game sales (for a free game, this would be remarkable), they especially zeroed in on Anita Sarkeesian, complaining that her Kickstarter was "overfunded" and that she "made money" from the abuse she received (p. 798).[3] Even though this is the business model that anyone launching a Kickstarter can benefit from, somehow Sarkeesian is a "scam" for engaging in it. But it isn't simply her gender that gets her into trouble: many attackers also target her ethnicity, which they often get wrong, assuming she is Jewish (oldwalmartfart, 2015). When corrected and told she is of Armenian descent, they simply switch gears and attack her for that instead (Feminist Frequency, 2015). Exposing and analyzing those elements of the attacks provides a more nuanced understanding of the abuse – demonstrating how elements of classism and racism as well as misogyny are a part of Gamergate's repertoire.

Finally, one of the most important avenues in need of an intersectional approach to understanding Gamergate is so far the least theorized – Gamergate's deployment of the "#notyourshield" campaign – a hashtag they started to counter the ploy of "SJWs" who were supposedly acting in the best interests of minorities and women. As Chess explains,

> the conceit of NYS is that those posting under its label were typically not white, cis-, heterosexual, men but composed of those who have been theoretically "othered" by the politics and culture surrounding the video game industry. Women, people of color, and those who were non-binary, often posted images of themselves holding signs proclaiming that so called "Social Justice Warriors" (SJWs) could not use their bodies as an excuse to attack the patriarchal structure of the video game industry. The use of photos (as opposed to word-only tweets) announced a kind of authenticity: these were not sock puppets but real people.
>
> *(Chess, 2016)*

Mortensen also commented on #notyourshield, pointing out that the hashtag had its origins on 4chan, where an African-American participant in the /v/ channel wanted to show "that female and non-White gamers did not want more diversity in games" (Mortensen, 2018, p. 796). Yet Mortensen also writes that the "design of this hashtag came with instructions concerning how White men could make non-White and female sock puppets" (p. 796). Identity does not always signify sympathy with a particular social or political position, but untangling the complicated history and deployment of the hashtag and its participants – both fake and authentic – is important work and would lead to a deeper understanding of how race, class, gender, sexuality, and other identity markers can be mobilized in contradictory ways, particularly in ways that work against social justice calls for inclusion based on such identity-based categories.

Conclusions

It was the goal of this chapter to demonstrate the continued need for a feminist game studies, and also to argue for more intersectional analyses of events surrounding games (as well as within games themselves). Over the past decade, a more diverse group of people has been playing and enjoying games, yet this has meant increasing backlash from more reactionary elements of both the game industry and game culture. Women who work as game developers still have their credibility questioned and often experience workplace harassment, as Cecilia D'Anastasio's 2018 investigation of the sexism endemic at Riot Games (maker of *League of Legends*) makes all too clear (2018). Entire categories of games have been branded as "not real games" because it is primarily (or presumably) women who play them. The culture surrounding games can be hostile to anyone who dares to critique the status quo of "traditional" gamer culture. Yet as Steinkuehler writes, "rhetorically, the presence, influence, and consumption of games by women have played a fundamental role in the slow and steady acceptance of videogames as a communicative medium in the United States" (Steinkuehler, 2016, p. 53). Just as feminist scholars and critiques are resisted and attacked, they also prove their necessity; we need this growing and diverse set of approaches to engage with an evolving and increasingly vital part of contemporary culture – video games.

Notes

1 I am one of the academics who took part in their "fishbowl" event and became another target due to that participation, the essay I wrote in 2012, and my role as president of the Digital Games Research Association at the time.
2 Image board culture encompasses sites such as 4chan, where discussions and replies often use GIFs and/or other visual materials that draw on memes to make their points.
3 This complaint is easily found across the internet. Shinryujin writes on GiantBomb that "Anita is a scam" because with her Kickstarter, "normally a producer pays a marketer to bring customers to him/her, essentially buying customers. Anita reverses this by making the customers pay her to bring themselves to her, thus making herself the producer and marketer, giving her all the benefits, and shouldering none of the cost" (Shinryujin, 2013).

References

Anable, A. (2013). Casual games, time management, and the work of affect. *Ada: A Journal of Gender, New Media, and Technology, 2*. Retrieved from http://adanewmedia.org/2013/06/issue2-anable/
Blodgett, B., & Salter, A. (2014). *#1ReasonWhy: Game Communities and the Invisible Woman. Paper presented at the Foundations of Digital Games conference*, Ft. Lauderdale, FL, April 3-7.
Boudreau, K., & Consalvo, M. (2014). Families and social network games. *Information, Communication & Society, 17*(9), 1118–1130. https://doi.org/10.1080/1369118X.2014.882964
Brunner, C., Bennett, D., & Honey, M. (2000). Girl games and technological desire. In J. Cassell & H. Jenkins (Eds.), *From Barbie to Mortal Kombat: Gender and computer games* (pp. 72–88). Cambridge, MA: MIT Press.
Chess, S. (2011). A 36–24–36 Cerebrum: Productivity, gender, and video game advertising. *Critical Studies in Media Communication, 28*(3), 230–252. https://doi.org/10.1080/15295036.2010.515234
Chess, S. (2012). Going with the flo. *Feminist Media Studies, 12*(1), 83–99. https://doi.org/10.1080/14680777.2011.558350
Chess, S. (2014). Strange bedfellows: Subjectivity, romance, and hidden object video games. *Games and Culture, 9*(6), 417–428. https://doi.org/10.1177/1555412014544904
Chess, S. (2015). Uncanny gaming. *Feminist Media Studies, 15*(3), 382–396. https://doi.org/10.1080/14680777.2014.930062
Chess, S. (2018). A time for play: Interstitial time, Invest/Express games, and feminine leisure style. *New Media & Society, 20*(1), 105–121. https://doi.org/10.1177/1461444816660729
Chess, S. (2016, August 30). *Whose shield is it anyway? Some thoughts on GamerGate and NotYourShield | In Media Res*. Retrieved February 19, 2017 from http://mediacommons.futureofthebook.org/imr/2016/08/30/whose-shield-it-anyway-some-thoughts-gamergate-and-notyourshield
Chess, S., & Shaw, A. (2015). a conspiracy of fishes, or, how we learned to stop worrying about #GamerGate and Embrace Hegemonic Masculinity. *Journal of Broadcasting & Electronic Media, 59*(1), 208–220. https://doi.org/10.1080/08838151.2014.999917

Code, B. (2016, November 7). *Video games are boring*. Retrieved February 15, 2017 from www.gamesindustry.biz/articles/2016-11-07-video-games-are-boring

Consalvo, M. (2007). *Cheating: Gaining advantage in videogames*. Cambridge, MA: MIT Press.

Consalvo, M. (2008). Crunched by passion: Women game developers and workplace challenges. In Y. B. Kafai, C. Heeter, J. Denner, & J. Sun (Eds.), *Beyond Barbie and Mortal Kombat: New perspectives on gender and gaming* (pp. 177–192). Cambridge, MA: MIT Press.

Consalvo, M. (2012). Confronting toxic gamer culture: A challenge for feminist game studies scholars. *Ada: A Journal of Gender, New Media, and Technology*, *1*(1). Retrieved from http://adanewmedia.org/2012/11/issue1-consalvo/

Consalvo, M. (2015). *Gamergate in 8*. Presented at the Canadian Game Studies Association, Ottawa, Canada.

Consalvo, M., & Begy, J. (2015). *Players and their pets: Gaming communities from Beta to Sunset*. Minneapolis, MS: University of Minnesota Press.

Consalvo, M., & Paul, C. A. (2013). Welcome to the discourse of the real: Constituting the boundaries of games and players. In *FDG* (pp. 55–62). Chania, Greece. Retrieved from https://pdfs.semanticscholar.org/39f8/02dc86888fdbc853a4acb54305679743f3e7.pdf

Consalvo, M., & Vazquez, I. S. (2015). Game platforms and the evolution of cheating practices: An exploratory study. *Journal of Gaming & Virtual Worlds*, 7(1), 3–19. https://doi.org/10.1386/jgvw.7.1.3_1

Cross, K. (2016). Press F to revolt: On the gamification of online activism. In Y. B. Kafai, B. M. Tynes, & G. T. Richard (Eds.), *Diversifying Barbie and Mortal Kombat: Intersectional perspectives and inclusive designs in gaming* (pp. 23–34). Pittsburgh, PA: ETC Press.

The Daily Vox Team. (2015, June 30). *Why gamergate hounded Tauriq Moosa off Twitter*. Retrieved from www.thedailyvox.co.za/why-tauriq-moosa-trended-this-weekend/

D'Anastasio, C. (2018, August 7). Inside the culture of sexism at Riot Games. *Kotaku*. Retrieved from https://kotaku.com/inside-the-culture-of-sexism-at-riot-games-1828165483.

Eklund, L. (2016). Who are the casual gamers? Gender tropes and tokenism in game culture. In M. Willson & T. Leaver (Eds.), *Social, casual and mobile games: The changing gaming landscape* (pp. 15–30). New York, NY: Bloomsbury.

Feminist Frequency. (2015, April 19). *Once harassers learn I'm not Jewish, their anti-semitism turns into anti-Armenian sentiment without skipping a beat.*pic.twitter.com/Y5pHfuRDTM [microblog]. Retrieved from https://twitter.com/femfreq/status/589586261523845120?lang=en

Jenson, J., & De Castell, S. (2008). Theorizing gender and digital gameplay: Oversights, accidents and surprises. *Eludamos. Journal for Computer Game Culture*, *2*(1), 15–25.

Jenson, J., & De Castell, S. (2011). Girls@Play: An ethnographic study of gender and digital gameplay. *Feminist Media Studies*, *11*(2), 167–179. https://doi.org/10.1080/14680777.2010.521625

Jenson, J., & De Castell, S. (2016). Gamer-Hate and the "problem" of women. In Y. B. Kafai, G. T. Richard, & B. M. Tynes (Eds.), *Diversifying Barbie and Mortal Kombat: Intersectional perspectives and inclusive designs in gaming* (pp. 186–199). Pittsburgh, PA: ETC Press.

Juul, J. (2010). *A casual revolution: Reinventing video games and their players*. Cambridge, MA: MIT Press.

Laurel, B. (2001). *Utopian Entrepreneur*. Cambridge, MA: MIT Press.

Moosa, T. (2015, June 3). *Colorblind: On the witcher 3, rust, and gaming's race problem*. Retrieved February 17, 2017 from www.polygon.com/2015/6/3/8719389/colorblind-on-witcher-3-rust-and-gamings-race-problem

Mortensen, T. E. (2018). Anger, fear, and games: The long event of #GamerGate. *Games and Culture (13)*8, 787-806. https://doi.org/10.1177/1555412016640408

oldwalmartfart. (2015, April 5). *Anita Sarkeesian is a Jew Hoe*! Retrieved February 19, 2017 from http://oldwalmartfart.deviantart.com/journal/Anita-Sarkeesian-is-a-Jew-Hoe-524905255

Polo, S. (2012, February 20). *Inclusion: What Jennifer Hepler's story is all about*. Retrieved from www.themarysue.com/inclusion-what-jennifer-heplers-story-is-all-about/,www.themarysue.com/inclusion-what-jennifer-heplers-story-is-all-about/

Radway, J. A. (1984). *Reading the romance: Women, patriarchy, and popular literature*. Chapel Hill, NC: University of North Carolina Press.

Royse, P., Lee, J., Undrahbuyan, B., Hopson, M., & Consalvo, M. (2007). Women and games: Technologies of the gendered self. *New Media & Society*, *9*(4), 555–576. https://doi.org/10.1177/1461444807080322

Sarkeesian, A. (2012). *Update 33: The future of Tropes vs Women; an end in sight · Tropes vs. Women in video games*. Retrieved February 15, 2017 from www.kickstarter.com/projects/566429325/tropes-vs-women-in-video-games/posts/1469466

Shaw, A., & Chess, S. (2016). Reflections on the casual games market in a post-GamerGate world. In M. Willson & T. Leaver (Eds.), *Social, casual and mobile games: The changing gaming landscape* (pp. 277–289). New York, NY: Bloomsbury.

Shinryujin. (2013, September 16). *The case against Anita Sarkeesian* (by Anonymous). Retrieved February 19, 2017 from www.giantbomb.com/profile/shinryujin/blog/the-case-against-anita-sarkeesian-by-anonymous/103108/

Sotamaa, O. (2016, April). *Studying game industries (plural).* Presentation given at Concordia University, Montreal, Canada.

Steinkuehler, C. (2016). Women in defense of videogames. In Y. B. Kafai, B. M. Tynes, & G. T. Richard (Eds.), *Diversifying Barbie and Mortal Kombat: Intersectional perspectives and inclusive designs in gaming* (pp. 48–56). Pittsburgh, PA: ETC Press.

Surette, T. (2006, April 26). *EA settles OT dispute, disgruntled "spouse" outed.* Retrieved February 15, 2017 from www.gamespot.com/articles/ea-settles-ot-dispute-disgruntled-spouse-outed/1100-6148369/

Tauriq Moosa – Encyclopedia Dramatica. (n.d.). Retrieved February 17, 2017 from https://encyclopediadramatica.se/Tauriq_Moosa#Fire_Emblem_Supports_Gay_Marriage.2C_Tauriq_Supports_It._Except_He_Don.27tVanderhoef, J. (2013). Casual threats: The feminization of casual video games. *Ada: A Journal of Gender, New Media, and Technology, 2.* Retrieved from http://adanewmedia.org/2013/06/issue2-vanderhoef/

Vázquez, I. S., & Consalvo, M. (2015). Cheating in social network games. *New Media & Society, 17*(6), 829–844.

Williams, D., Consalvo, M., Caplan, S., & Yee, N. (2009). Looking for gender: Gender roles and behaviors among online gamers. *Journal of Communication, 59*(4), 700–725. https://doi.org/10.1111/j.1460-2466.2009.01453.x

Williams, T. (2017, January 16). *What happened to women in computer science?* Retrieved from www.goodcall.com/news/women-in-computer-science-09821

14

Acting out

Performing feminisms in the contemporary art museum

Rachael Haynes and Courtney Pedersen

The position that feminist art holds within the art museum is complex and often contradictory. As Meaghan Morris pointed out, feminism "is not easily adapted to heroic progress narratives",[1] and there is a danger that when absorbed into museum exhibitions, feminist art can become part of another seductive, but false narrative – one where feminism is no longer necessary as a strategy in the visual arts. "Feminist art" can become a historicising category, a genre or period; framed as a singular movement locked into a fixed historical moment, rather than a dynamic set of strategies that are still potentially highly productive. This highlights the tension between archiving and valorising feminist artwork of previous generations on the one hand, and continuing the ongoing feminist work that is still required today. In 2013, LEVEL was commissioned to provide a public program as part of the *WAR IS OVER! (IF YOU WANT IT): YOKO ONO* exhibition held at the Museum of Contemporary Art Australia (MCA). The resulting work was part of a larger project, *We need to talk*, that utilises reflexive and discursive strategies to move beyond the script of feminism as a historical moment and back to the lived experience of feminist art as political understanding and social engagement. This paper reflects on the experiences with this artwork, from the perspective of two of its practitioner/participants, and provides the context and rationale for its design and eventual realisation. While advocating for change in the lives of contemporary women, this project rejects heroic narratives in three key ways. First, the work takes place on the threshold of the art museum, and by occupying this liminal space, it challenges easy categorisations of "artwork" or "public program." Second, by engaging conversation as a strategy to create art, *We need to talk* emphasises the open-ended and processual nature of negotiated discussions, and foregrounds diverse women's voices and desires. Third, as a continuing artwork that manifests in different contexts without appearing to tangibly move forward, *We need to talk* challenges narratives of progress. It is intended as both a convivial and provocative response to Luce Irigaray's controversial claim that science (and consequently, society) privileges that which goes faster over equally essential forces. Given the culturally determined nature of progress narratives, and the gendered nature of cultural determination, the work explores the potential for change beyond or outside of progress.

Yoko Ono represents a problematic and often contradictory example of an apparently rediscovered woman artist. Her works have retrospectively been interpreted through a feminist lens, specifically important early works such as her performance *Cut Piece*, but she did not identify as a specifically feminist artist at the time, nor was she considered part of the feminist art movement. However, the inclusion of *Cut Piece* and other film-based works in the blockbuster exhibition *WACK! Art and the Feminist Revolution* marked the beginning of the current repositioning of Ono in relation to a feminist art history. The feminist aspects of her practice were highlighted in both the conception and marketing of the MCA's survey exhibition. While exhibitions such as the Yoko Ono retrospective can be seen as revisionist attempts to assert a feminist canon of art, art historian Griselda Pollock has questioned whether this is possible without a radical critique of the canon structure itself. Jessica Sjöholm Skrubbe has noted an emerging "canon of feminist art," observing a tendency to privilege certain artists, artworks and themes in the recent flux of feminist exhibitions, publications and conferences that have occurred within contemporary institutions.[2] These exhibitions include the key international projects *WACK! Art and the Feminist Revolution* 2007 (MOCA in LA), *Global Feminisms* 2007 (Brooklyn Museum), and *elles@centrepompidou* 2009–2010 (in Paris), and, here in Australia, *A Different Temporality* 2011 (Monash Museum of Modern Art), and *Contemporary Australia: Women* 2012 (Queensland Art Gallery/Gallery of Modern Art in Brisbane). The recurrence of these sorts of projects highlights the currency of these debates and the necessity of examining the unfolding relationship between feminist art and the contemporary museum.

While in many cases these exhibitions facilitated the acquisition of significant works by women by museum collections, this was not always the case. Additionally, collecting itself can be a potentially problematic process. While the museum collection constitutes a crucial component of the knowledge that passes into the future, and therefore must be inclusive and representative, it also faces limitations in its ability to convey the processual and experiential aspects of feminist art practice. Therefore, the collected object cannot be relied on as the sole feminist voice in the museum. To recognise the different temporalities and polyphony of voices inherent to feminist art practice, a range of different engagements are required. Feminist artists were never unanimous regarding the desirability of retrospective insertion into existing museum collections, and the residue of this ambivalence is sometimes still evident. While some may have dreaded recuperation, there is also the possibility that "being 'recuperated' . . . may be the most efficient way of attaining one's objectives."[3] Regardless of this ambiguity, the fixing effect of recuperation into the museum can be quite confounding. In 1975, American artist Carolee Schneemann performed her work *Interior Scroll*, during which she unfolded a long strip of paper from her vagina and read the text inscribed on it. Kelly Phillips comments on the historicising transformation that takes place in the museological treatment of these artefacts "under glass" in her experience of *WACK! Art and the Feminist Revolution*:

> Nothing could have prepared me for the sight of Carolee Schneemann's accordian-folded script from *Interior Scroll* now enshrined in a Plexiglass vitrine, its tiny, handwritten type contributing to the mystification of the movement.[4]

The relics of this iconic and confrontational feminist performance by Schneemann in 1975 are now reinserted into the institutional frame forty years later. The limitation of these blockbusters, Phillips goes on to argue, is both the exclusion of significant feminist works, and "the recognition that feminism as an ongoing project is diminished."[5] The curators of *WACK!* acknowledged that feminist art practice's strength was its aesthetic and conceptual diversity, or what Catriona Moore has described as its "critical restlessness."[6] The significant risk of a major historical survey such as this was that it would allow for only certain types of diverse practice, fitting within the imaginary prescription of historically "feminist" art. Ruth Noack's close reading of Sanja Iveković's work *Triangle* reveals that while canonisation is initiated because of people's attachment and often sincere response to the work itself, its elevation to a significant moment in art history risks its false depiction as representative of a homogenous movement.[7] Noack quotes Iveković herself as identifying this tendency, and the inherent difficulties of the task: "I agree with Linda Nochlin that it is difficult (I would say almost impossible) to transform a life experience of feminism and feminist art practice into a historical text."[8]

As artists and educators both in studio practice and art history, we are concerned by the seductive nature of the categorisation of feminist art in a simplistic way. Students and young artists in general are tempted to see feminist practices as the quaint but archaic habits of an earlier generation. The museumification of feminist art practice can intensify this perception. As Pierre Bourdieu noted in the late 1960s, the art museum could be considered a reliquary where "bourgeois society deposited [items] inherited from a past that is not their own."[9] Some of the curatorial approaches in the exhibitions mentioned were more radical or challenging than others.

One of the more remarkable exhibitions was the *elles@centrepompidou* project in Paris. For this project, the curator, Camille Morineau, proposed that the museum show only artworks by women practitioners for an entire year. This was a particularly radical departure for a museum with one of the most significant collections of twentieth century artworks in the world – a museum that would be required to put away its Duchamps and Picassos for the duration. This is not an unproblematic approach, as it provokes the related issues of separatism and essentialism in relation to art made by women, particularly given feminist theory's longstanding critiques of the culturally determined category of "woman," and the potentially patronising hiving off of "women's" art as a subcategory of mainstream art production. While the gesture appeared radical, and the project significantly improved the museum's holdings of works by women in the collection, Morineau's subsequent experience of the museum's attitude towards women puts this radicality into doubt, and raises the question of the long-term impact of exhibitions such as *elles*. Rather than seeing this as an institutional achievement, it may be more fitting to see it as an anomalous moment of temporarily indulging the demands of women artists and curators, as well as capitalising on the fashionability of feminism at that moment in time. Indeed, Morineau has commented on the "guerrilla process" that was required in curating the exhibition, due to the reluctance of her male colleagues and superiors, and the institutional resistance to feminism and feminist goals in relation to the exhibition.[10] Therefore, while significant, projects such as *elles@centrepompidou* are, at best, an uneasy rapprochement between feminist agendas and those of the art museum. Griselda Pollock points out the following:

> What corporation would sponsor a feminist intervention which challenges the assumptions of class, race and gender that underpin the current social system despite gestures of inclusiveness and minor corrections to its histories of discrimination? The museum in contemporary society is increasingly bonded into the circuits of capital between entertainment, tourism, heritage, commercial sponsorship and investment.[11]

Jessica Sjöholm Skrubbe describes this as "alibi practice" by large museums, who seem to address these inequities within collecting and exhibiting practices through token acts, in order to resume "business as usual."[12]

This tokenism raises the question of whether long-term change is ever made possible through strategies of the all-women survey or feminist blockbuster exhibition. Do these exhibitions position feminism as a historical moment, simply in order that it may be deemed no longer relevant or at issue? Sjöholm Skrubbe argues that, while important, these events are also potentially "dangerous" and may in fact "function as hegemonic strategies that reinforce the status quo, whether deliberately or not."[13] These tokenistic acts on the behalf of the museum may simply be another example of the co-option and sanitisation of radical gestures in order to maintain established hierarchies and power dynamics. In response to this dilemma, Nancy Proctor calls for "truly radical practice that produces sustainable change in the structure of the museum and its systems of power."[14] It was in the context of these debates regarding feminist art's place in relation to the art museum that LEVEL began to design its museum-based chapter of the project *We need to talk*. The significant achievements of second-wave feminist artists and art workers form the crucial framework for both this project and for LEVEL as a whole. These practices were a powerful reaction to a set of conditions: women's exclusion and marginalisation within the art market, their omission from the established historical canon, and, as a consequence, their poor representation in the museum.

As Australian curator and art historian Janine Burke observed when she proposed the exhibition *Australian Women Artists 1840–1940* in Melbourne in the 1970s, the standard response was that it would be a very small exhibition indeed. Through the determined efforts of a number of feminist artists and art historians the "secret history" of women in art was slowly but surely pieced together. Established in 1975 in the wake of Lucy Lippard's visit to Australia, the feminist journal *LIP* featured numerous articles by and about Australian women artists, particularly discussing the previously overlooked heritage of women's craft. Frances (Budden) Phoenix, Vivienne Binns and Marie McMahon were important exponents of this rediscovery. In 1976, there was a significant protest regarding the absence of women in the Biennale of Sydney, and, after subsequent meetings in 1977 and 1978, Vivienne Binns and Virginia Coventry drafted a letter outlining concerns and strategies regarding the equitable inclusion of women artists.[15] In this country, much was also owed to the historian Joan Kerr, whose motivation drove the landmark publication *Heritage: The National Women's Art Book, 500 Works by 500 Australian Women Artists from Colonial times to 1955* and inspired numerous other women to expand on this work. On the international stage, Linda Nochlin's polemical text "Why Have There Been No Great Women Artists?" triggered a recognition of the role of institutional bias in sidelining female artists' work.[16] Debates over the poor representation of women in art museums reached fever pitch in the United States in the late 1980s when the activist collective the Guerilla Girls protested against the Whitney Museum Biennial for the lack of women artists in its curated program.[17] The Guerilla Girls' response was searing, but also playful, and they expanded on this activism by going on to produce a series of works that added up the numbers for museums and galleries. In their 1989 public poster work *Do women have to be naked to get into the Met. Museum?*, they observed that works by women made up less than five per cent of the works in the collection at New York's Metropolitan Museum of Art (the Met) but that eighty-five per cent of the nudes depicted were female. Since the height of this form of art activism in the 1980s and 1990s, many have assumed that the position of women in the art world has become easier. However, when the Guerilla Girls revisited the Met for more accounting in 2005, it was revealed that the percentage of works by women in the collection had actually decreased, and, in 2012, they once again discovered an alarming lack of improvement. At that point, only four per cent of works in the Met's contemporary art collection were by women. There were more male nudes, but they were not sure that this was an improvement.[18]

Sadly, the numbers for women in museums in Australia are often not much better. The *CoUNTess* website, which reports on the inequitable representation of women in galleries, museums and other major exhibitions, has identified a disturbingly familiar paucity of women in a range of venues. There were depressing statistics on the Queensland Art Gallery/Gallery of Modern Art survey exhibition *21st Century: Art in the First Decade* 2011, which featured sixty-eight male artists, twenty-eight female artists, and eight groups, and the even grimmer numbers reflected in the Kaldor Collection donated to the Art Gallery of New South Wales in 2010, which contained works by 194 male artists, seven collaborations, and only two female artists.[19]

LEVEL was initiated in February 2010 in reaction to the lack of opportunities and professional support for women artists.

As an artist-run initiative originally established by three artists – Courtney Coombs, Rachael Haynes and Alice Lang – and more recently expanded to include six co-directors, LEVEL is an evolving response to the need for recognition and support by making space for dialogue about gender and art practice. Largely inspired by the collective models of the second wave, LEVEL utilises strategies of collaboration and a commitment to critical engagement with ideas of gender. Taking heed of Sue Best's 1994 caution about the dangers of succumbing to a single feminist "style" of practice, the collective actively embraces a diversity of contemporary women's art.[20] The initiation of LEVEL in many ways paralleled the development of alternative studio and exhibition spaces for women artists in the 1970s. As Jenni Sorkin recently commented, these programs were formed in direct response to the absence of women artist's work in museums and public culture.[21] In 2010 and 2011, Courtney Coombs, Rachael Haynes and Alice Lang ran gallery and studio programs in Brisbane, with three galleries and ten artist studios. LEVEL was privileged to work with over a hundred women artists and curators from across Australia and internationally, building connections between early-career and more established practitioners. Since then, the collective has worked on a project basis and continued a residency program, which supports female artists in the development of new work for exhibition and provides ongoing feedback through studio visits and discussions. As a result of discussions and collective engagement with these projects over the last three years, the LEVEL professional relationship has developed to incorporate collaborative art practice. While LEVEL began as a physical artist-run exhibition space, its program always incorporated a dynamic emphasis on discussion, peer mentoring and support. In this way, LEVEL has developed as a discursive space, and these projects are focused on ways of opening up and sharing dialogues about feminism with other women artists, curators and thinkers. Creating collaborative artworks became a logical extension of this discursive activity.

LEVEL's first collaborative project, *Food for Thought*, was commissioned by the Next Wave Festival in Melbourne in 2012 as a response to Judy Chicago's iconic but controversial work, *The Dinner Party*, completed in 1979. *The Dinner Party* raises questions concerning the "collaborative" nature of art production and the use of central core imagery in women's art.[22] *Food for Thought* involved the bringing together of women around a dinner table for the sharing of food and ideas. Rather than reproducing Chicago's work, this project sought to engage directly with misconceptions of feminism as a rigid or dictatorial philosophical position, through the facilitation of conversations between Australian women artists, curators and thinkers in an open and exploratory way. The artwork was located in the practice of asking questions and allowing a diversity of answers to emerge. Fabric banners made during a series of workshops held in Brisbane and Melbourne were included in the *Food for Thought* installation. Participants in the banner workshops were encouraged to reflect on their own experiences as women and visually represent these personal statements and political ideas. In some ways, this approach knowingly invests in the broader strategy in 1970s feminist art to celebrate the undervalued contribution of women and "women's work" through domestic handicrafts, which historically were delegated a secondary role to that of fine art. As Lucy Lippard described in 1976, women were "shedding their shackles, proudly untying the apron strings—and in some cases, keeping the apron on, flaunting it, turning it into art."[23]

Following on from this, LEVEL hosted picnics and dinners in Tokyo, where the conversation extended beyond the local context. As the experience of each project shaped the next, it became clear that the reflexivity of a feminist methodology, in which the politics of subjective and collective positions were questioned and re-evaluated, was becoming increasingly visible and was moving the collective more and more towards a participatory field of practice of the kind associated with artists such as Suzanne Lacy. Lacy's particular approach to art making was informed by her involvement with the Feminist Art Program at CalArts in the early 1970s, where working with those from outside the professional arts community was seen as a necessary and radical rejection of cultural hierarchies. While she has consistently worked as an artist activist whose projects involve the broader community, her practice has appeared and then disappeared from the art discourse as tastes and fashion in art have changed.

The dynamics and politics of participatory art practices have been hotly debated for the past decade. This way of working enjoyed renewed critical prominence after the French curator Nicholas Bourriaud published his book on the topic towards the end of the 1990s, titled *Relational Aesthetics*. While Bourriaud described relational artworks as active engagements with the ethical negotiations of social relations within the designated spaces of art (museums and galleries), critics of this kind of art making have sometimes expressed their distrust of the museum's capacity to serve as a transformational social space. There is a lingering suspicion that participatory art (or social practice, as it is sometimes known) is simply providing an amenity for the museum (much like the bookshop or café), or that this type of work feeds into the contemporary consumer-driven demand for "experiences" rather than artefacts. Another potential challenge for this kind of work is that it can dictate the audience's participatory experience to such a degree that it becomes simply the acting out of a predetermined script.

What is often ignored in histories of participatory art, as the British artist/curator Liam Gillick, critic George Baker, and others have subsequently pointed out, is the strong influence of feminist precursors in the establishment of this way of working.[24] As Helena Reckitt argues, "the absence of feminism is especially problematic in this context given how closely Bourriaud's projects emulate forms of affective and immaterial work that have long been areas of female activity and feminist analysis."[25] This tendency to blatantly ignore the influence of feminist strategies in contemporary art is further highlighted by artist Tania Bruguera:

> why is it that most men think anything regarding feminist art is of no concern to them? Since so much contemporary art by men owes such a debt to feminist/women predecessors, in terms of content, form, and materiality, and so much now fashionable institutional critique has its roots in less fashionable feminist critiques of power, the question becomes ever more absurd.[26]

These feminist strategies include the use of collaboration and audience or community-based participation. As Mary Jo Aagerstoun and Elissa Auther assert, these strategies were utilised in order to "subvert the myth of individual artistic genius, use art as a teaching tool, mitigate the isolation of women artists in the art world, and uncover and underscore previously hidden aspects of women's lives."[27]

The potential for these kinds of practices in terms of opening up important dialogues for feminism and the museum is exemplified by Lacy's recent project, *Silver Power*, at the Tate Modern in London. Women who had been involved in second-wave feminist activism were invited into conversation with one another to discuss their experiences within the framework of the art museum. As part of this project, the participants attended a series of preliminary workshops before the performance, where over 400 women took part in the conversation. The work took place as a dialogic experience for both participants and audience members, with an equal emphasis on listening and empathising as much as speaking and organising. Catherine Elwes, in her position as both participant and critic, described the experience and its impact:

> The spectacle of the women talking and listening was enveloped in the thick hum of their massed voices, which provoked tears in Edie Kahler, Mo Throp's daughter, astonishment at the experience of "properly listening" in one transcriber, a hushed sense of veneration in many and in at least one young woman, a call to arms.[28]

In this way, the project sought to acknowledge the social and political changes brought about by these activist women by utilising conversation as a participatory form of engagement within the context of the art museum.

This particular intersection of discursive and participatory strategies was also the starting point for the project *We need to talk*. This project gradually developed into a potluck mass picnic on the lawn outside of the MCA in Sydney. Preceding the picnic, a public workshop was held to make the picnic rugs. In this workshop, attendees responded to the question of what their preferred future would look like. They drew up and cut out their desires as multi-coloured and multi-patterned letters that were then ironed onto fabric squares. The workshop allowed for the opening up of conversations between participants through a tactile engagement with materials and the playful exploration of language. This process had already begun earlier in Brisbane through the Q[ARI]: Queensland Artist Run Initiatives project, facilitated by curators Naomi Evans and Pia Robinson at Griffith University Art Gallery, where visitors to the gallery were invited to celebrate and/or protest by embellishing denim squares for integration into the final rugs. This dual response of celebration and acknowledgement of women's voices, alongside critical dissent and a call for action, spoke to the double complex of a contemporary feminist position in relation to its past.

LEVEL was asked to realise this project as part of the MCA's *Re-School* program, essentially the commissioning of public programs that also function as artworks. The project needed to stand alone, but also respond to a major exhibition of Yoko Ono's work. The "educational turn" in contemporary art and in museums became a crucial aspect of the context of this project. This tendency describes the use of educational formats, models and processes within contemporary art, and conceptualises curatorial and artistic production as "expanded educational praxes."[29] While the designer and cultural theorist Valerie Casey argues that "contemporary emphasis on 'edutainment' and immersive tourist experiences appear to be at the expense of aesthetic and intellectual encounters esteemed in the traditional museum,"[30] the involvement of artists as educators and facilitators in this program also opens up the potential for an exploration of radical pedagogy within the frame of the museum. While participatory strategies have perhaps been co-opted by the contemporary art museum for its own agenda – that is, as an exchange for capital in the experience economy – this project outlines a feminist reinvestment in these strategies, and a reinscribing of activism within its aims.

Yoko Ono's art practice, an ongoing investigation of gender, art and culture since the early 1960s, has often been overshadowed by her pop culture reputation. Regardless, her work throughout this period has remained overwhelmingly affirming, while engaging passionately with political and ecological issues. This positive pursuit of change was LEVEL's starting point when considering the structure of the picnic conversations. While previous dinner parties and picnics have revolved around women's difficulties and frustrations (operating as a form of contemporary consciousness raising), the collective agreed that in order to both reflect the spirit of Ono's work and a desire for the project to evolve meaningfully, the "conversation" needed to enter into a dialogue with the language of Ono herself.

LEVEL responded to Ono's invitation to a better world, "If You Want It," by inviting participants to express their own desires. Rather than challenging questions about experiences of discrimination, adversity and self-doubt, the work was framed as a collaboratively written charter of aspirations and demands. Participants were asked to complete cards for inclusion in a final series of poster placards and picnic rugs. In this way, *We need to talk* can be contextualised in relation to Grant Kester's conception of dialogic works in contemporary art that involve "open ended forms of participatory interaction."[31] Similarly, this project utilised the workshop as a framework for these actions, and a strategy of "tactical mobilisation of craft traditions."[32] What is at stake in this approach, as Kester articulates, is not only the aesthetic aspects of such engagements but also the ethical and activist dimension.

This project as a whole has been informed by the traditions and histories of feminist activist art. LEVEL has adopted Mary Jo Aagerstoun and Elissa Auther's characterisation of feminist activist art as "simultaneously critical, positive, and progressive."[33] Feminist activism has often been popularly perceived as primarily adversarial, aggressive or confrontational, but Aagerstoun and Auther's definition emphasises the optimistic and affirming aspects of activist art:

> By critical we mean work that seeks to expose underlying ideologies or existing structures that have a negative effect on women and their lives; by positive we mean work that takes a stand, expressing its maker's faith in achieving results or positing alternatives; by progressive we mean a belief in the feminist tenets of equality and inclusiveness, a better world free of sexism, racism, homophobia, economic inequality, and violence.[34]

By taking an activist approach in this manner, *We need to talk* moved from simple critique of the museum to an active pursuit of alternative visions and progressive solutions. By working with women from both within and beyond the art world, the separate sanctity of the museum (that Bourdieu recognised and took issue with in 1969) was rejected.

LEVEL was intrigued by the possibility that a work could both adapt itself to Yoko Ono's body of work and engage with current debates about the museum as a shifting, negotiated and discursive space. The picnic component of the project took place in the traditional threshold zone of the museum approach—in this case the carefully maintained lawn in front of the MCA, facing the dress circle view of Sydney's recognisable landmarks: Circular Quay, the Sydney Opera House and the Harbour Bridge. As analyses of Karl Friedrich Schinkel's early nineteenth-century design for the Altes Museum in Berlin have revealed, the space in front of the museum becomes as crucial to the authority of the institution as the building itself. This threshold and its attendant effect of physically distancing the viewer from everyday life has become a defining physical feature of the museum building, and Suzanne MacLeod has noted that the Altes model (particularly Schinkel's design for approaching steps) came to define the image of the art museum for at least a century.[35] Placing the work in this threshold space deliberately built a bridge between the internal activities of the museum and the social space of the world outside. Valerie Casey has analysed what she refers to as the three stages of the museum. The third of these is the performing museum as a site of historical re-enactment. It could be argued that today's museums, with their strong emphasis on public programs and participatory projects are fully immersed in this third "moment." This project was designed to exploit this enthusiasm while also engaging critically with the historical legacies of second-wave feminism and their meaning for contemporary women. A consideration for LEVEL in the design of this project was whether the collective and its guests would be simply re-performing the activist gestures of an earlier generation. This artwork forms an ongoing examination of the contemporary relevance of these strategies, and questions the assumption of a linear chronology of feminist art or any such "heroic progress narrative." In this way, the project also reflects on the challenge of Nancy Proctor's call for sustainable change in relation to the art museum by utilising feminist strategies for collective action through participatory and dialogic formats and through specific spatial interventions.[36]

In her article "Woman's Reappearance: Rethinking the Archive in Contemporary Art – Feminist Perspectives," Giovanna Zapperi proposes an embrace of "feminist time" as a strategy to avoid the entombing impulse of the museum. She describes this notion of temporality as one "that comprises returns, accelerations and discontinuities, where the subjective and collective dimensions are related to a number of historical, social and cultural conditions."[37] Zapperi suggests that by responding to Griselda Pollock's suggestion of an "elliptical traverse of time,"[38] women artists and curators can elude the teleological oblivion of timelines and their resultant effect of redundancy. Participants in the workshop and picnic at the MCA responded enthusiastically to this invitation to revisit the past and envisage the future as simultaneous events. From the older participants there was a sense that questions regarding the better world they wished for were unresolved and ever-present, while the younger women were encouraged to consider their current anxieties and aspirations in the context of longer and older discussions. The materialisation of this discussion in the form of banners and picnic rugs that occupied the entrance approach for the MCA emphasised the ambiguous and problematic position that contemporary feminism holds in both the museum and the art world more broadly. LEVEL's project, *We need to talk*, used the established feminist art methodology of opening up both literal and figurative space for dialogue, and, in doing so, invited participants to see feminist practice as a living continuum, with both cultural and personal relevance. Matthew Fuller's provocation that "it is perhaps those artists whose activity most profoundly breaks with the established currents of art practice and with the social normativity of the museum who can make most use of them"[39] in some part explains the fascination that the museum continues to hold for feminist art practice. By skirting around the edges of the museum's hierarchical structures, both literally and figuratively, *We need to talk* foregrounded the complex and often fraught relationship between feminism and the museum in a conversation without end.

Disclosure statement

No potential conflict of interest was reported by the authors.

Notes

1 Meaghan Morris, "Too Soon Too Late: Reading Claire Johnston 1970–81," in *Dissonance: Feminism and the Arts 1970–90*, ed. Catriona Moore (Sydney: Allen & Unwin, 1994), 126–38.
2 Angela Dimitrakaki and Lara Perry, "Constant Redistribution: A Roundtable on Feminism, Art and the Curatorial Field," *Journal of Curatorial Studies* 2, no. 2 (2013): 226.
3 Dario Gamboni, *The Destruction of Art: Iconoclasm and Vandalism Since the French Revolution* (London: Reaktion Books, 1997), 167.
4 Kelly Phillips, "Feminism Under Glass: WACK! Art and the Feminist Revolution," *FUSE* 32, no. 2 (March 2009): 36.
5 Ibid., 36.
6 Catriona Moore, "Review: WACK!: Art and the Feminist Revolution; Global Feminisms: New Directions in Contemporary Art," *Australian & New Zealand Journal of Art* 9, no. 1–2 (2008): 247.
7 Ruth Noack, *Sanja Iveković Triangle, One Work* (London: Afterall Books, 2013), 14.
8 Sanja Iveković in Noack, ibid., 13.
9 Pierre Bourdieu and Alain Darbel, *The Love of Art: European Art Museums and Their Public*, trans. C. Beattie and N. Merriman (Cambridge: Polity Press, 1991), 14.

10 Mira Schor, "MoMA Panel: Art Institutions and Feminist Politics Now," *A Year of Positive Thinking – Mira Schor*, http://ayearofpositivethinking.com/2010/05/23/moma-panel-art-institutions-and-feminist-politics-now/ (accessed September 1, 2014).
11 Griselda Pollock, *Encounters in the Virtual Feminist Museum: Time Space and the Archive* (London: Routledge, 2007), 10.
12 Dimitrakaki and Perry, "Constant Redistribution," 235.
13 Ibid., 235.
14 Ibid., 234.
15 Vivienne Binns, Ian Milliss and the Women's Art Group, "History/Herstory," in *Sydney Biennale: White Elephant or Red Herring? Comments From the Art Community Alexander Mackie College of Advanced Education.* Student Representative Council (Sydney: Union Media Services, 1979), www.ianmillis.com/documents/historyherstory.htm (accessed March 3, 2015).
16 Linda Nochlin, "Why Have There Been No Great Women Artists?" in *Woman, Art and Power: and Other Essays* (New York, NY: Westview Press, 1988), 145–76.
17 While revisionist art history in a Western context was established as a separate discipline in the 1970s and 1980s, it would take until the 1990s and 2000s for global women's art practices to be acknowledged, for example in museum publications such as the New Museum co-published *Talking Visions: Multicultural Feminism in a Transnational Age* edited by Ella Shohat, 1998 and exhibitions such as *Global Feminism* in 2007 (Brooklyn Museum).
18 Guerrilla Girls, "Guerrilla Girls: Naked Through the Ages," 2012, www.guerrillagirls.com/posters/nakedthroughtheages.shtml (accessed July 9, 2013).
19 "When Private Collections Go Public," *CoUNTess: Women Count in the Art World*, http://countesses.blogspot.com.au/2011/06/what-happens-when-private-collections.html (accessed July 8, 2013).
20 Susan Best, "This Style Which Is Not One," in *Dissonance: Feminism and the Arts 1970–90* (St Leonards, NSW: Allen & Unwin, 1994), 154–68.
21 Jenni Sorkin, "The Feminist Nomad: The All-Women Group Show," in *WACK! Art and the Feminist Revolution*, ed. Cornelia Butler and Lisa Gabrielle Mark (Los Angeles, CA: The Museum of Contemporary Art and The MIT Press, 2007), 460.
22 A notable example of this is the Australian artist Frances (Budden) Phoenix's account of her involvement in the production of Chicago's work, and the attempted insertion of the text "No Goddesses, No Mistresses", in *Our Story/Herstory? Working on – Judy Chicago's 'Dinner Party'* (Sydney, NSW: Phoenix Artwork, 1982).
23 Lucy Lippard, *From the Center: Feminist Essays on Women's Art* (New York, NY: Dutton, 1976), 57.
24 Helena Reckett, "Forgotten Relations: Feminist Artists and Relational Aesthetics," in *Politics in a Glass Case: Feminism, Exhibition Cultures and Curatorial Transgressions*, ed. Angela Dimitrakaki and Lara Perry (Liverpool: Liverpool University Press, 2013), 140.
25 Ibid., 138.
26 Schor, MoMA Panel.
27 Mary Jo Aagerstoun and Elissa Auther, "Considering Feminist Activist Art," *NWSA Journal* 1 (2006): viii.
28 Catherine Elwes, "Suzanne Lacy: Silver Action," *Moving Image Review & Art Journal* 2, no. 2 (October 2013): 297.
29 Mick Wilson and Paul O'Neill, "Curatorial Counter-rhetorics and the Educational Turn," *Journal of Visual Art Practice* 9, no. 2 (June 2010): 177.
30 Valerie Casey, "Staging Meaning: Performance in the Modern Museum," *TDR* 49, no. 3 (2005): 79–80.
31 Mick Wilson, "Autonomy, Agonism, and Activist Art: An Interview with Grant Kester," *Art Journal* 66, no. 3 (2007): 118.
32 Ibid., 118.
33 Aagerstoun and Auther, "Considering Feminist Activist Art," vii.
34 Ibid., vii.
35 Suzanne MacLeod, *Museum Architecture: A New Biography* (Hoboken, NJ: Taylor and Francis, 2013), 62.
36 Dimitrakaki and Perry, "Constant Redistribution," 234.
37 Giovanna Zapperi, "Woman's Reappearance: Rethinking the Archive in Contemporary Art – Feminist Perspectives," *Feminist Review* 105 (2013): 23.
38 Ibid., 25.
39 Matthew Fuller, "Breach the Pieces," *Intermedia Art: Tate*, 2000, www.2tate.org.uk/intermediaart/entry15470.shtm (accessed November 29, 2014).

15

Can't I just be a filmmaker? Women's and feminist film festivals' resurgence in a postfeminist world

Susan Kerns

> I don't know if that's our role. . . . We are not a film organization that funds movies.
>
> —*Lesli Klainberg, Executive Director of Film Society of Lincoln Center, which runs the New York Film Festival, when asked what role festivals play in overcoming gender disparity among film directors, 2016*[1]

> Nine out of forty-nine of the filmmakers [at the Festival de Cannes] are women. That's twenty percent of the selection. What percentage of filmmakers in the world are women? According to a recent report, it's seven percent. I've been saying this for four years now but what you see in Cannes is a consequence, not the cause. More needs to be done in the film schools, the universities and the production houses, to favour women, and then you would see results.
>
> —*Thierry Fremaux, Cannes Film Festival Director, responding to a question about why few female directors were in Official Selection, 2016*[2]

> Every film in our Official Selection (US), fiction and nonfiction, is directed or co-directed by a woman. . . . And they're all incredible movies. As an expression of tokenism usually reserved for women, I am bringing five films by American men in a sidebar called, "Men Make Movies – The Struggle Continues."
>
> —*Michael Moore, Founder and President, Traverse City Film Festival, 2016*[3]

Articles about the underrepresentation of women in above-the-line film production roles now appear regularly, yet crew statistics hold steady. Women make up 19% of directors, writers, producers, executive producers, editors, and cinematographers working on the top 250 domestic-grossing films, which is even with percentages from 2001 (Lauzen, "The Celluloid Ceiling," 2016, p. 1).[4] Women direct 9% of these films and fare best as producers (20%–26% between 1998 and 2015, though not in a successive increase). They fare worst as cinematographers (2%–6%) (Lauzen, "The Celluloid Ceiling," 2016, p. 2). These percentages increase slightly in independent films, where women are employed in 28% of these same roles (Lauzen, "Women in Independent Film," 2017, p. 4). Women direct 29% of films screening at the 23 "high profile" film festivals included in the study (Lauzen, "Women in Independent Film," 2017, p. 2). These numbers are higher in documentaries (31%) than in fictional narrative films (26%), and women again fare best as producers (32%) and worst as cinematographers (11%) (Lauzen, "Women in Independent Film," 2017, p. 5). The number of women working in these positions in independent film overall reached a current historic high in 2016–2017, and there has been at least a 7% increase in the number of women directors, writers, and executive producers since 2008 (Lauzen, "Women in Independent Film," 2017, p. 5). Yet only two of these areas are at historic highs – writers and executive producers – and the number of editors and producers has declined slightly (Lauzen, "Women in Independent Film," 2017, p. 5). The largest percentage point spread in any one area since 2008 is an 8-point non-successive spread of executive producers, whose numbers were at their lowest in 2015–2016 (Lauzen, "Women in Independent Film," 2017, p. 5). In other words, although some gains are being made, overall employment in these roles has remained essentially stagnant in the past decade. Headline responses to this year's study illustrate these confounding statistics, as *Deadline* proclaimed "Female Directors Gaining Ground at Major Film Festivals – Study" while the *New York Times* observed, "Women Face Long Odds at U.S. Film Festivals, Study Finds" (Robb, 2017; Goodman, 2017). Overcoming this widespread problem has been on the minds of journalists, yet film festivals, a key distribution outlet for emerging filmmakers, are less eager to enter the conversation. When asked, festival representatives often root these issues further back in the filmmaking process to suggest the industry's gender problems are to be found in film education and production; lack of distribution, they claim, is merely another effect of the system's inequities and does not have its own engrained biases.

The resurgence of women's and feminist film festivals has been one response to this inertia. Since there is a desire for women to be integrated into all areas of the film industry organically, film festivals dedicated to showcasing women's films, or even highlighting films with themes or production histories deemed "feminist," may be seen as encouraging a segregated industry. Yet supporting these initiatives helps increase the breadth of on-screen representations of women, bolster filmmakers' careers, and generally leverage the works included. The continued relevance of women's and feminist film festivals marks the importance of resisting the idea that these festivals are something society, or even the feminist movement itself, left behind – necessary once but no longer relevant. Of the 4,000 to 5,000 film festivals operating internationally, approximately 100 focus on films by women or foreground feminist film content.[5] The sheer number of these festivals illustrates a desire and perceived need for spaces to showcase films by and about people underrepresented in mainstream media. Women's film festivals typically limit themselves to showcasing films directed by women and, more recently, genderqueer individuals, but this is not always the case, as some women's film festivals simply require that women are at the center of a film's content. Feminist film festivals program films whose content or production can be seen as in some way "feminist." The Chicago Feminist Film Festival, of which I am the co-founder and co-director with Michelle Yates, allows for a wide interpretation of "feminism" in the hope that filmmakers will determine if they believe their films fit. However, films must meet at least one criterion: they must be created with an eye toward gender, sexuality, or social justice issues or by people underrepresented in the media field. In other words, they can be feminist in content or production history. Many are both. A multiplicity of films fit this bill, including fictional narratives, documentaries, and experimental films about any number of subjects or in various genres (horror, dance, environmental, etc.). Films might address historical incidents not widely discussed, critique mainstream media, or simply expand representations of women on screen. Since women's film festivals generally focus on production and crew roles for women, their ultimate goal might be to render themselves unnecessary as women gain increased access to funding and above-the-line positions within the film industry. Feminist film festivals, however, likely have a longer haul, as their aims include supporting gender and racial equity initiatives outside of just filmmaking and media representations.

Women's and feminist film festival "circuits": an overview

Skadi Loist outlines three historical periods of film festival "circuits": festivals as showcases for national cinemas (1930s to the 1960s); for agenda-oriented, cultural, or political cinemas (1960s to the 1980s); and currently as part of the filmmaking industry itself (1980s to the present). This third "circuit" came about as festivals became their own sort of distribution path and expanded to offer things like film funding and workshops rather than just exhibition opportunities. Loist explains, "Whereas the first phase was majorly influenced by national diplomatic strategies, and the second by new politics and social movements, this third era has been most impacted by a complex shift of several interlocking cultural and economic agendas" as culture "has increasingly turned into a value-generating creative industry" (Loist, 2016, p. 58). Patricia White notes, "the elite European film festivals established around World War II still confer the most prestige, even as the network has meaningfully diversified" (White, *Women's Cinema, World Cinema*, 2015, p. 29). Most of the prominent women's film festivals emerged during the second phase, as these specialty festivals sought to increase screening opportunities for contemporary women filmmakers, show forgotten films by women directors, raise consciousness about women's issues, and create spaces for dialogue. These festivals can be a vital part of a filmmaker's career, as they sometimes operate as a parallel distribution system and act as a career catalyst. Screening at these festivals increases filmmakers' access to audiences and industry professionals of all kinds, while filmmakers amass festival credits that can help them gain access to funding or other professional opportunities. Furthermore:

> Each struggle or movement used arts and culture as activist tools, where film screenings in community settings were part of general awareness-raising endeavors. All of these festivals were first established as safe spaces and gathering spots for identity issues, to constitute and consolidate communities with specific causes. While they continue to be community spaces, they have oftentimes also gradually grown to become alternative distribution networks and brokers for specific themes, representations, and filmmakers. (Loist, 2016, p. 57)

Women's and feminist film festivals become activist spaces through programming and exhibition practices that aim to leverage film content and networking opportunities. These festivals energize and rally feminists more largely, including the underrepresented filmmakers who screen and to some extent create their own festival "circuit."

Women's film festivals began in the early 1970s with the Women's Event at the Edinburgh Film Festival in 1972, followed by the First International Festival of Women's Films in New York (1972), Philadelphia's First International Festival of Films by Women (1972), the Toronto Women and Film Festival (1973), and Chicago Films by Women Festival (1974). These festivals laid the foundation for all that followed. B. Ruby Rich notes, "Instant success made for an immediate trend" (Rich, *Chick Flicks,* 1998, p. 30). However, by the late 1990s, gender-specific festivals were seen as retrograde and waning, as if their time and purpose had come and gone. Whereas in the 1970s, women's film festivals might be the only chance audiences had to see films by women, Rich wrote in 1998, "Today, when women routinely produce films . . . in great quantity . . . it's an effort to recall that once, not so terribly long ago, there was nothing at all routine about women setting out to make or exhibit films" (Rich, *Chick Flicks*, 1998, p. 29). This optimism was likely due to the surge in popularity of, and access to, American independent films and the visibility of directors like Penny Marshall, Barbra Streisand, Jane Campion, Kathryn Bigelow, Julie Dash, Allison Anders, and numerous others directing Hollywood-produced or independent films. In the 1970s, each festival "decision was ideologically charged" including programming criteria and goals, festival themes, and target audiences, whereas in 1998, "there's no lack of recognition of just how much times have changed and mutated, far away from the assumed activism of the period. Such rhetoric today would be unthinkable in the context of a program of films" (Rich, *Chick Flicks*, 1998, p. 31). "Such rhetoric," which Rich also calls "flashbacks," includes statements about transforming stereotypical portrayals of women on-screen, metamorphosing aesthetics to challenge the medium, and using film as a catalyst for consciousness-raising, even encouraging women to make their own films (Rich, *Chick Flicks*, 1998, pp. 32–33).

Certainly no one writing in the 1990s could have known that women's employment in Hollywood film production would grow only sluggishly for the next 20 years. Since home videos and cable were widely available at that time, it makes sense that people believed women would no longer need designated distribution outlets in order for their work to gain visibility. Furthermore, since technological developments like digital cameras and affordable editing software began allowing emerging filmmakers to produce films without the access to capital once needed, it seems logical that the number of women in film naturally would have substantially increased. Yet the potential "democratization" of filmmaking resulted only in a glut of content judged against high-end film aesthetics – often the aesthetics of well-funded male filmmakers. In other words, even if a wider variety of stories ended up in films created by a broader range of people, those filmmakers still struggled to show their work and find audiences. Since industry practices remained exclusionary in production and distribution, this third phase of film festivals – the shift to festivals as part of the industry – necessitates thinking across each circuit to better understand how "agenda-oriented, cultural, or political" programming philosophies might still be necessary within what Loist calls the "value-generating creative industry" so that there might be more opportunity for "alternative" and mainstream distribution networks, and their filmmakers, to converge. Furthermore, in the shift from festivals as safe spaces to alternative distribution networks, festivals have shifted from an embodiment of activism to a call for change in the industry. These festivals remain "safe spaces" for films, filmmakers, and audiences that share a certain politics, yet they also respond to labor practices. As long as the film industry continues privileging white cis-male-made or white cis-male-oriented films via funding, distribution, festival awards, and the like, specialty festivals like women's and feminist remain relevant not just as a response to the industry but also as a catalyst for change.

Many of the women's and feminist film festivals operating today were founded in the 2000s, suggesting that although the original women's film festivals faded, their undertakings had not been accomplished.[6] In 2006, film theorist Patricia White wrote, "I am not arguing that we should go back to organizing separate festivals or women's events at major festivals, but advocacy and critical attention are still needed" (White, "The Last Days of Women's Cinema," 2006, p. 149). Noting the low numbers of women directors at Sundance that year, White observed that although the "numbers game is of course not the most nuanced way to think about women's roles in cinema, . . . issues of basic equity are still so glaring that it seems a legitimate place to start" (White, "The Last Days of Women's Cinema," 2006, p. 149). When deliberating "feminist" programming, White mentions an interview with Cameron Bailey, then programmer and now artistic director at the Toronto International Film Festival (TIFF), who said that due to former TIFF programmer Kay Armitage's commitment to feminism, TIFF had been including women's films for years. Yet at the time of the interview, Bailey noted "feminism has faded from view generally" and it is "harder to find programmers who will 'out' themselves" as feminists (quoted in White, "The Last Days of Women's Cinema," 2006, p. 148). Invoking Angela McRobbie, White says feminism is "something 'taken into account' in other programming strategies" rather than "a conscious, quantitative effort" (White, "The Last Days of Women's Cinema," 2006, p. 148). Programmers then, as today, do not have quotas for women filmmakers. Yet "without efforts to shape reception discourses," according to White, the films' "divergent enunciative strategies and responses to transnational feminist practice tend to be evened out" in exhibition circuits (White, "The Last Days of Women's Cinema," 2006, p. 148). In other words, programming at major festivals boosts the visibility of these films, but they may simply become part of conventional "art house" fare and not necessarily activate consequential audience response. White has continued grappling with these issues in her recent book, *Women's Cinema, World Cinema*, which takes up the relationship between films by women directors, the festival and art house film circuits, and what she calls "middlebrow" aesthetics. She explains that she does not use the term "middlebrow" pejoratively but rather to distinguish between "high art" cinema and "mass culture" (White, *Women's Cinema, World Cinema* 2015, p. 215). In other words, "art house" cinema, where (international) women's films tend to be programmed, is seen as something in between – more accessible than "high art" cinema but potentially more challenging, even if only due to subtitles, than mainstream Hollywood cinema.

One might hope the proliferation of film festivals within the past ten years, since these statements were made, would have helped increase percentages of women breaking into the film industry via festivals if feminism is, indeed, intuitively "taken into account." However, festivals have become progressively more competitive as filmmaking costs decrease due to digital technologies. This does not mean there is no barrier to entry, but high-end cameras and post-production software once priced for professionals are now within consumer price ranges (hence the term "prosumer") and are much more user-friendly, requiring less professional training for use. The result is that in 2015, the Sundance Film Festival received 4,105 feature film submissions, of which they programmed 124 (Bernstein, 2015). For comparison, in 1993, 250 features were submitted and 141 screened (Sundance Institute, "33 Years," 2017). The short film statistics are even more competitive, as 8,061 were submitted in 2015, and only 60 were programmed (Bernstein, 2015). That submission number jumped to 8,985 in 2017. In 1996, the first year for which shorts submissions numbers are available, 1,200 shorts were entered (Sundance Institute, "33 Years," 2017). These are disheartening odds for anyone, and although Sundance's submission numbers are not broken down by gender identity or race, a study completed by Professor Stacy Smith and others found that women directed 32% of the short and mid-length films (60 minutes or fewer) screened at ten top film festivals (Smith, Pieper, Choueiti, and Case, 2015). This drops to 28% when limited to fictional narrative shorts, but increases to 37% of documentary directors. Animated shorts fall in the middle at 31% (Smith, Pieper, Choueiti, and Case, 2015). These numbers were consistent over the five years studied and indicate a decline in women's film employment when women attempt to move from short films into feature film work, as also evidenced by Martha Lauzen's studies. Even when women break into top-tier festivals like Sundance with short films, they continue struggling to access the funding, resources, and support necessary to make the leap to the next level. Although many festival programmers hope to move beyond organizing separate events or counting the number of women or other underrepresented directors screening at these major festivals, the fact remains that both are still necessary as long as men continue to have more access to opportunities and funding from film school to feature filmmaking.

Women's and feminist film festivals help keep makers and audiences committed to this struggle. Leshu Torchin, discussing human rights film festivals and activism, explains that festivals often are "places for renewal of commitment, where one sheds the yoke of cynicism by watching empowering stories and mingling with equally committed people" (Torchin, 2012, p. 6). This engagement operates differently than the "expectation of transformation" often purported to occur during festivals, or at times used as a critique of politically specific festivals (Torchin, 2012, p. 6). Instead they help filmmakers and activists form a "network" that encompasses vast and various connections that "become sites for all manner of alliance building" (Torchin, 2012, pp. 9–10). These alliance-building festivals often include what she terms "activist" films that "[function] as a truthful narration of a situation, presented with the intention of bringing about beneficial change" (Torchin, 2012, p. 2). Since these films denounce historical untruths or present inequities, they are often documentaries. She suggests "thinking of the film festival as a field of witnessing" (Torchin, 2012, p. 3), because these festivals and their films require examination of "the interface between the testimony or programmed films and the audiences hailed as witnessing publics, viewers who take responsibility for what they have seen" (Torchin, 2012, p. 2). Sonia Tascón argues that activist film festivals "'embrace' spectators differently" (Tascón and Wils, 2017, p. 32). Since "film screenings are part of a network of activities," audiences "are guided towards a life 'beyond the film,'" in part because activist film festivals perform "unruliness" via "the encouragement of an active, critical viewer, who disrupts the social order through 'the question'" (Tascón and Wils, 2017, p. 32) – in this case, the question of women creators and feminist perspectives within media itself. Even attending a screening at these types of festivals, then, is political action and potentially alliance-building for audiences and filmmakers. Additionally, screenings often are just one portion of women's, feminist, or other activist film festivals, as panels, workshops, other types of exhibits, installations, and virtual reality experiences often accompany screenings. The festival space, then, becomes one of engagement between the audience and the film but also between spectator, maker, and subject matter.

Despite engagement at several levels during alliance-building festivals, there remains a disconnection between activist film festivals and filmmakers and the film industry at large. In considering festivals "publics" and "counterpublics," Cindy Wong suggests, "if the major A-list festivals should be seen primarily as embodying the bourgeois public sphere, then alternative film festivals . . . should be examined as subaltern festivals" (Wong, 2016, p. 90). She further breaks down the idea that within A-list festivals, various sections:

> have different publics and impact compared to the main competition section. The very contradictory tendencies within film festivals can give rise to a better understanding of how different public spheres – bourgeois, counter, and subaltern – either complement each other or demand their own "spaces" within negotiated contestations. (Wong, 2016, p. 90)

White also discusses "counterpublics" and acknowledges the fact that she can access certain international women's films already speaks to inequities in the filmmaking system. Although the films she discusses in her book *Women's Cinema, World Cinema*

> are diverse and enabled by divergent meanings of feminism and different industrial formations in their countries of origin, most of them circulate through the same festival and art house networks. Their access to these networks is in turn determined by material questions like format and language as well as ideological judgments of value. (White, *Women's Cinema, World Cinema,* pp. 7–8)

The films that become popular via top-tier film festivals and art house distribution circuits, then, speak to the aesthetic tastes of prestige festival programmers – or, at a minimum, do not challenge them in uncomfortable ways. Ezra Winton and Svetla Turnin argue that festival programmers have "the power to shape the festival space as either one of circulation within an accepted capitalist framework, or a reconfigured space" of activism and dissension, and they put forth the idea that festivals can be reconceived as spaces that facilitate a less comfortable cultural politics (Winton and Turnin, 2017, pp. 91–92). Since the top-tier festivals tend to be festivals bustling with buyers and sellers, it makes sense that they would operate in the service of capitalistic gains. However, these aims also reinforce systems of inequity and White's aforementioned unchallenging "middlebrow" aesthetics.

One might suspect that since activist and other specialty festivals and their engagement opportunities speak across Loist's festival circuit waves, addressing industry issues would be embedded into festival programming, panels, and talkbacks. Yet within this parallel distribution circuit, addressing industry issues often are not included in festival activities, or they might be foregrounded in conjunction with the political aims of the festivals, but not necessarily in an industry context. Furthermore, Patricia White notes:

> Festivals established and programmed around identity and community . . . rarely function as launches for feature film releases and do not confer prestige or attract distributors and press attention in the way that the economics of feature film distribution and artists' livelihoods demand; their influence lies in the culture and community, not in the film world. (White, *Women's Cinema, World Cinema,* p. 77)

Incorporating networking opportunities for filmmakers attending activist festivals, or initiatives like festival mentorships for student or emerging filmmakers, forwards the larger cause of gender equality, thus moving beyond or augmenting alternative distribution outlets whose primary purpose is monetary gain or industry clout. However, in order to further bridge gaps between underrepresented filmmakers, the festival circuits that do embrace them, and the mainstream film industry, efforts either need to be made to bring more prestige to activist and other specialty film festivals, perhaps in the form of major cash awards, distribution opportunities, mainstream press coverage, or star backing (like Geena Davis's Bentonville Film Festival), or to incorporate additional initiatives to support underrepresented filmmakers in the prestige and wider audience-facing festivals.

The overlooked importance of mission statements

Film festival mission statements are one place to look for insight into what festivals profess to do and serve – industry, audience, or otherwise – how festivals negotiate whom they think their "publics" and "counterpublics" are, and how certain initiatives might be incorporated to overcome disparities within the film industry. Some festivals clearly identify their publics and their aims for interacting with them, while others strategically claim publics they may not reach. Mark Peranson delineates festivals as "business" or "audience" festivals – major international festivals with marketplaces versus smaller or regional festivals more concerned with pleasing audiences (Peranson, 2009, 27–28). Many also refer to festivals using a tiered system, with the top tier including the most celebrated international film festivals like Cannes, Berlin, Venice, Sundance, Toronto, and the like. These "business" festivals tend to have industry-focused missions, meaning they foreground their importance to the international film industry and their concern for maintaining quality. For example, the Berlin International Film Festival calls itself "a great cultural event and one of the most important dates for the international film industry" (Internationale Filmfestspiele Berlin, 2016). The Sundance Institute (which runs the Sundance Film Festival) is "a champion and curator of independent stories for the stage and screen," yet it also features a variety of initiatives like its Native American and Indigenous Film Program, Diversity Initiative, and Women Filmmakers Initiative, all of which support underrepresented filmmakers through screenings, labs, and grant programs with the goal of boosting the diversity of filmmakers in their festival (Sundance Institute, "Our Story," 2016). These programs reflect how Sundance has interrogated their programming in relationship to the larger filmmaking industry. They did not assume underrepresented filmmakers were doing something wrong; instead, they assumed that somewhere in the process, white cisgendered men gained an advantage.

Business festivals like Sundance and Berlin influence programming choices at "audience" festivals, which, according to Peranson, showcase and promote a specific type of filmmaking via a commitment to artistry. For example, the Big Sky Documentary Film Festival's mission "is to celebrate and promote the art of nonfiction filmmaking, and to encourage media literacy by fostering public understanding and appreciation of documentary film" (Big Sky Documentary Film Festival, "About," 2016). These audience-facing and appreciation-oriented statements omit information about the industry, and although some now include marketplaces, most focus on celebrating genres or aesthetics. Women's and feminist film festivals do not quite fit in here, as they generally hope to increase issue awareness or expand on-screen representations while also highlighting women and genderqueer filmmakers. Although they are audience festivals, politics are front and center in programming philosophies even if all films programmed are not overtly political. These aims are made clear in mission statements like the International Women's Film Festival of Créteil. Their mission is three-pronged to include expanding on-screen representations of women, doing "memory work" via retrospective screenings of women filmmakers, and "defending" women's cinema by promoting films directed by women while acknowledging the various facets that work against women filmmakers, like attaining artistic recognition and securing funding (International Women's Film Festival of Créteil, "About," 2017).[7] The Rocky Mountain Women's Film Festival shares a similar mission "to inspire community and elevate the voices of women through film" by "supporting women filmmakers, as well as promoting film as art and education" (Rocky Mountain Women's Film Festival, "Our Mission," 2016).

Indicating the crossover between specialty film festivals as part of political movements as well as part of the film distribution cycle, as earlier suggested by Loist, some women's film festivals are now building an industry focus into their mission. The Women's International Film & Arts Festival, which began in 2005 and takes place in Miami, aims to be "the premiere film festival in the world for women to screen and market their films, discuss new industry trends and opportunities, as well as connect and network with supportive audiences and industry professionals" (Women's International Film & Arts Festival, "Our Mission," 2017). Feminist film festivals often are differently activist-oriented due to the centrality of political film content. The Davis Feminist Film Festival, for example, "uses alternative media as a springboard for linking art to social issues. The goal of the festival is to showcase independent film . . . in order to explore perspectives often missing from mainstream media and culture" (Davis Feminist Film Festival, "About," 2016). At the Chicago Feminist Film Festival, our mission also incorporates programming films that emphasize "issues of gender, sexuality, race, and other forms of inequality" in inclusive screening spaces. However, we also aim to create a space for audiences and filmmakers to "forge connections between local, national, and international film" as well as each other (Chicago Feminist Film Festival, "About," 2017). Helping filmmakers network not only with one another but also with students and other audience members is key to how attendees feel the "embrace" of our festival. Networking within the framework of our more intimate "feminist" festival space allows students and audiences much easier access to filmmakers, who are not whisked away to a green room or out back exits, and the content of the films screened often lays the groundwork for discussions based in social issues awareness and activism. These mission statements indicate a useful bifurcation in the rationale behind continuing to operate both women's and feminist film festivals. Although all are audience facing and issue- or activist-oriented, they also look to industry practices not only to define themselves against exclusionary practices but also with an eye toward changing them. Filmmaker identity, issues of on-screen representations, and desires to counter the lack of women working in Hollywood come up frequently in these festivals' mission statements, though feminist film festivals in some cases may be more engaged with inspiring social action than industry response.

The most common type of film festival is the mid-tier audience festival where pleasing audiences is key. These festivals tend to showcase films that played other major film festivals but did not screen in local theaters, and most "international" film festivals named after a city or state fall into this category. These festivals do not have the industry clout of Sundance and Berlin, but more general audiences attend these festivals than any other festivals, which makes programming at this level especially important. Audience festivals tend to be risk averse precisely because they need to please audiences and funders through ticket sales and programming choices. As such, they are more likely to program "safe" films that will not radically unsettle festival audiences or their preexisting viewpoints. Yet audience film festival mission statements do tend to claim public service and educational outreach as central to their existence, rather than entertainment (though their marketing may suggest otherwise), so these festivals to some extent rely on Torchin's aforementioned "expectation of transformation," or the belief that audiences can be politically, socially, or otherwise altered by merely seeing a film. How this manifests itself in the general public is exceedingly difficult to measure. Additionally, screening films without engaged talkbacks or panels, specifically in relationship to documentaries and dramas about Others, can result in a "humanitarian gaze" that "emerges from, reflects and reproduces geopolitical power" (Tascón and Wils, 2017, p. 19). This can cause what Tascón calls "saviour-spectators" who watch "passive victim" characters from a safe distance, perhaps feeling inspired to action or rejuvenated by their own security. Audiences also may see characters from other cultures as "working to become more 'like us'" if the spectator reads the film through their own lens (Tascón and Wils, 2017, p. 26). Furthermore, in their attempts to draw in wide audiences, these festivals often partner with nonprofits, which Winton and Turnin argue "contains" audience responses to films and limits "encounters that hash out the entanglement of politics and aesthetics" (Winton and Turnin, 2017, p. 89). This troubles the idea that "transformation" can take place at all at these festivals, much less without extensive and nuanced discussions that allow for the disruption of comfortable spectator positions. Rewriting mission statements at these festivals to be specifically inclusive of women and other underrepresented filmmakers could broaden these filmmakers' reach, but doing so in ways that do not just reinforce audiences' preexisting worldviews might also require festivals to challenge how they construct audience engagement opportunities and sponsorships.

Since audience festivals that do not incorporate extensive discussions to work through challenging films might actually contradict the goals they aim to achieve, the "activist" elements of their mission statements might be better off including filmmaker-facing initiatives intended to support diversifying the industry itself, even at local levels. The low number of women directors showcased at festivals suggests programmers are complicit in the industry gatekeeping that starts in film schools (when women begin dropping out of the field) and continues to big-budget Hollywood features. For example, although the Festival de Cannes is an industry-facing festival, many audience festivals program Cannes-approved films for their communities. Since mid-tier audience festivals reach the widest cumulative number of spectators, their programmers uphold a system of exclusion. B. Ruby Rich notes, "If status bestows confidence and confidence enhances success, then the overvaluation of male-authored work in film – and art and literature – ensures that women's marginalization is both internalized and externalized" (Rich, "The Confidence Game," 2013, 163). Although she is referencing the film industry's psychological effects on women makers more largely, imparting confidence in filmmakers via festival acceptances (large and small) is one way to begin overcoming this confidence gap. Integrating more films created by a wider variety of people also leads to increased portrayals of diverse populations and stories being told, which should resonate more broadly with audiences. This obviously does not mean all shorts programming blocks will have exactly equal representation by different genders or races of filmmakers all the time, or even could aspire to that, but when the current percentages hold steady over decades and continue privileging straight white men, programmers must consider if they are internalizing gendered and racist aesthetics – stories or styles that privilege films made by cisgendered white men – or how programming films made within an inequitable system reaffirms the status quo even beyond production histories. Altering mission statements of audience film festivals to address biases in film financing, production, and on-screen representation might be one place to begin tackling these inequities if festivals do, indeed, program to meet their stated missions.

Enter the Chicago Feminist Film Festival

Although there is no perfect way to address all of these issues, women's and feminist film festivals by design attempt to work in the service of impact and outreach for all involved – filmmaker communities and local audiences. The hope is that by giving underrepresented filmmakers screening opportunities and allowing audiences to see different types of characters and stories on-screen, the festival opens up new conversations outside of the theater space as well while bolstering filmmakers' careers and confidence. These festivals also tend always to be questioning how to continue supporting filmmakers and leveraging the festival for greater impact. One way this has been achieved is the mere proliferation of feminist film festivals. Former programmers of the Davis Feminist Film Festival, one of the longest-running feminist film festivals in the United States, have created a feminist film festival circuit of sorts throughout the country. The Chicago Feminist Film Festival is one such festival; co-director Michelle Yates graduated from the University of California, Davis, and began her festival work there. In the first year of the Chicago Feminist Film Festival, which took place on the Columbia College Chicago campus and lasted two days, the festival screened one feature (Anna Rose Holmer's *The Fits*, 2015), 42 shorts, and one virtual reality film, *Across the Line* (2015), which simulates crossing a protest line in order to have an abortion. In its second year, the festival expanded to three days of short films and included an opening and closing feature. The horror anthology *XX* (2017) opened the festival, with director Roxanne Benjamin in attendance. Julie Sokolow's documentary *Woman on Fire* (2016), about the first transgender firefighter in the New York Fire Department, closed out the festival. Sokolow and documentary subjects Brooke Guinan and James Baker attended for an extensive talkback with the sold-out audience and continued the conversations at the free-to-the-public closing night party. Current Columbia College Chicago students, faculty, and alumni directed a handful of short films showcased both years, and although several other student films were included, professional filmmakers from around the globe directed the majority of shorts.

The festival programming did not limit itself to a certain gender of director. Instead, the programming process involved looking specifically for a variety of on-screen representations, stories, and filmmaking styles while also getting input from a diversity of pre-screeners, including people of different ages, races, genders, and relationships to filmmaking and feminism. (Many of our pre-screeners do not typically work with film festivals.) We especially looked for stories we had not seen before and made sure to program films from numerous countries. For example, if we were deciding between two similar films, we would take into consideration the gender of the director and the film's country of origin, as we wanted to showcase a number of different filmmaking systems. Over 20 countries were represented in the programming each year, and in the first year, 77% of films programmed were directed or co-directed by female-identified filmmakers. This number jumped to 85% in the second year. Additionally, people of color directed 42% of the films in the first year and 39% in the second. Many films dealt with topics expected from a feminist film festival, like body image, sexuality, gender identity, fertility and pregnancy, breaking into male-dominated professions, and spousal abuse, but films about adoption, disability, mental illness, death with dignity, refugees, and war were also included. Focusing on story and representation may have sidestepped some of the ostensibly "objective" selection criteria utilized at other film festivals that inadvertently leads to eliminating underrepresented filmmakers from selection. To be clear, this is not to say the films we showcased did not have high production values: production values just were not our top consideration. However, the range of pre-screeners involved in the selection process – with their varied backgrounds and interests – also contributed to the multiplicity of programming.

Deliberate submissions processes and requirements also allowed for this breadth of programming, and steps were taken not to exclude filmmakers of various countries, levels, and means. In our first year we did not charge submission fees at all, and in our second year early entrants did not pay a submission fee. The submission fee did increase incrementally after that, resulting in a late fee of $50 (which, frankly, we charged solely to discourage people from submitting at the last minute). For our upcoming year, we are charging $10 for early entries rather than having a free period, because we received so many films that were unrelated to our festival's theme. This increase in unsuitable films from the first year to the second corresponds with our move from accepting submissions through our own website to using Film Freeway and Withoutabox, which increased our visibility substantially – and makes it very easy for filmmakers to submit without ever reading a festival description (though I suspect some filmmakers were trolling us with their submissions). We plan to keep submission fees very low so that they do not present a barrier to entry for any filmmaker. We hope this encourages up-and-coming filmmakers to continue submitting their films so we can continue showcasing a wide range of voices.

One conundrum we face in keeping entry fees low is that it limits our larger budget to bring filmmakers to the festival. It is crucial to us that no filmmakers are priced out of submitting, and yet we also try to offer travel funding for all accepted filmmakers. Often film festivals only invite directors to attend, so when diversity is not considered during the programming process, a proliferation of white men on stage and otherwise taking advantage of film festival benefits results. This contributes to white male access to festival networking while sending a message to audiences that filmmaking is only for certain people. Including a diversity of filmmakers in question-and-answer sessions not only expands responses and topics broached, thus pushing talkbacks into fresh territory, but it also illustrates that opportunities exist in the field for myriad types of people to tell countless kinds of stories. It is especially important for young audience members to see people who resemble them onstage so that the Chicago Feminist Film Festival does not inadvertently reinforce the idea that only certain types of filmmakers find success in the field. In the past two years, we have been able to offer some travel funding, and we have made sure that women filmmakers, LGBTQ filmmakers, and filmmakers of color are all represented on stage – as well as a variety of men – so that discussions will be lively, productive, and challenging.

The intent of the Chicago Feminist Film Festival is to be activist in numerous ways that speak to inequities in industry practices and the aims of feminism more broadly. As part of this, we try to reward risk-taking in programming choices. The feature film *The Fits*, for example, is a profoundly moving tale of girls navigating the oddities of puberty, including its physical changes and social pressures. The film lacks the typical structure and pacing of Hollywood films and refuses to come to definitive conclusions about its characters or their primarily female world – think *Picnic at Hanging Rock* meets *Step Up*. It remains ambiguous in story and objective and is a natural fit for a festival hoping to provoke conversation about film content and production. *The Fits* was written, directed, and produced by a team of three women – Anna Rose Holmer, Saela Davis, and Lisa Kjerulff – who collaborated on dialogue and character development with the girls on the dance team featured in the film. During a talkback session, one audience member, a young Black woman, asked director Holmer, who is white, why a Black woman did not direct this film since it focuses on African-American girls. Holmer thoughtfully explained how creative collaboration worked between the three key women, and why they initially did not know they were making a film about African-American youth, since they did not necessarily plan to cast a whole, real dance team. Holmer did not make excuses but attentively spoke to how race representations allow for a reading back to or on production histories, and how they inform one another.

The relationship between film content, industry trends, practices, and production histories also fostered a mindfulness toward programming films by or about older filmmakers and senior women, who too often disappear from on-screen images and behind-the-scenes filmmaking. (Only 30% of Hollywood representations of women are over the age of 40.) After a short documentary called "Farewell Scenes" (2014), directed by Alina Cyranek, about several women in their eighties and nineties who, through theater classes, take on roles that allow them to bid "farewell" to certain things in life and become active with new ones, one student said she did not understand how the film qualifies as "feminist." This student's comment provided the opportunity to discuss representations of older women on screen and also how aging women become invisible in society. Furthermore, the women at times reflect unflatteringly on their marriages, so simply being interviewed for a film like "Farewell Scenes" might enact feminism in that the women were allowed to be honest and their voices heard uncritically. Older women were also featured as dancers in the film "The Wake" (directed by Oonagh Kearney, 2016), an online psychic in "jazzy@32" (directed by Kara Mulrooney, 2016), a school counselor in "Counsellor" (directed by Venetia Taylor, 2014), the creator and subject of Cecelia Condit's experimental short "Pulling Up Roots" (2015), and the subject of the documentary "Tita Turns 100" (directed by Elio Leturia, 2016). This breadth of representations of older women illustrated a variety of ways women remain active and relevant as they age, and how their actions and histories continue contributing to discussions of feminism, which are at the heart of all screenings and talkback sessions.

By foregrounding the concept of feminism and its relationship to activism as much as possible, the festival space itself may encourage an alternative kind of engagement with film content. In other words, films that might be read differently in the context of other kinds of festivals provoke new conversations in this feminist space. For example, "The Substitute" (2015), a short horror film co-directed by Nathan Hughes-Berry and Madeleine Sims-Fewer, portrays a female teacher's frightful encounter with male students' increasingly threatening behavior at her new school. In the context of a horror film festival, "The Substitute" may be seen as reinforcing male power, since the female teacher ultimately is relegated to the position of submissive student. Screening in the context of the Chicago Feminist Film Festival, however, amplified the gendered power dynamic of classroom spaces and how horrific it can feel for teachers who do not innately embody social and cultural power. The relationship the film creates between female teacher and student, as sexual object of desire for heterosexual male students, allows spectators to interrogate how images of women affect educational spaces and learning. It is not that these conversations could not take place at a horror film festival, but focusing on feminism or feminist intent as a point of reference for discussion encourages audiences to look specifically at the gender dynamics that inform the story. This was the case for a number of films; discussing them in the context of a feminist film festival encouraged thoughtful readings of films and discussions that went beyond questions typically asked at generalist audience film festivals.

In the first year, over 500 people attended the free two-day event, including 25 visiting filmmakers. In its second year, the Chicago Feminist Film Festival attracted over 900 people in three days, again including 25 visiting filmmakers. Students, faculty, and staff helped with the curation process or during the festival, resulting in a community effort to bring film and feminism together. Since a reception space adjoins the theater, free food and drinks were available for all audiences at all times, and community organizations handed out birth control, provided counseling for audiences triggered by films, and provided additional information about topics addressed in certain films. Moreover, filmmakers, academics, and general audiences mingled alongside one another throughout the festival, creating a positive, egalitarian, and inviting sense of feminist community. For 2018, the Chicago Feminist Film Festival will continue with three days of free programming (and snacks) with the aim of growing the number of filmmakers who visit classrooms during the festival. Yates and I also continue mulling the festival's aims and practices. While dream initiatives would bring the industry component of the festival more into the mainstream (e.g., through substantial cash awards, distribution opportunities, and Academy-qualifying status), in the interim the festival plans to continue connecting filmmakers personally. We are also taking up the question of how our mission statement can better embody the Chicago Feminist Film Festival's desire to build meaningful relationships among activism-oriented audiences and film content, a college setting, and the film industry itself. These ongoing discussions include the place or importance of gender and identity politics as they relate to film authorship, exhibition, and this festival specifically. Ideally there will be a day when women's and feminist film festivals become inessential as responses to industrial and sociocultural structures. Looking at the history of women's place in the film industry, as well as fluctuations in waves of feminism, however, makes clear these festival initiatives remain pertinent for bridging gaps between non-traditional films, underrepresented filmmakers, festivals, and the larger film industry in addition to educating, entertaining, and energizing audiences committed to feminism in its many forms.

Notes

1 Quoted in "Women Directors are Everywhere, But Film Festivals Are Still Catching Up – NYFF" by Lauren Du Graf, published October 19, 2016, on www.indiewire.com.

2 Quoted in "Cannes: Thierry Fremaux Interview" by Melanie Goodfellow, published April 15, 2016, on www.screendaily.com.

3 Quoted in "Michael Moore's Traverse City Film Festival 2016: Why Every Movie in Competition Is Directed by a Woman" by Anne Thompson, published July 20, 2016, on www.indiewire.com.

4 This research focuses on the United States, though similar studies are occurring in Europe. See the European Women's Audiovisual Network report, "Where Are the Women Directors" (www.ewawomen.com), or the Directors UK report "Cut Out of the Picture" (www.directors.uk.com).

5 FilmFreeway.com lists over 4,000 festivals, and Withoutabox.com just over 1,000. Combining these results in an overall estimate of 5,000 festivals, though not all film festivals use these submission engines, and some use both. The number of women's and feminist film festivals (approximately 100) comes from Hollywomen.com's "Discover 100+ Women's Film Festivals Worldwide" list, though many of these festivals are inactive. A FilmFreeway.com search for "women" and limited to "Film Festivals with Live Screenings" brings up nearly 200 results, though again, many are inactive or were one-time events. Others show up because a generalist festival has a women's category or uses the word "women" in its festival description. Still, it seems safe to say there are approximately 100 women's or feminist film festivals currently operational worldwide.

6 The International Women's Film Festival of Créteil, founded in 1979, is the longest-running women's film festival in the world. The Rocky Mountain Women's Film Festival, established in 1988, is the longest continuously running women's film festival in the United States. Two other prominent women's film festivals also have been operational since the 1980s: St. John's International Women's Film Festival (1989) and Women's International Film Festival in Seoul (1987).

7 Translations courtesy of Google Translate.

References

"33 Years of Sundance Film Festival." *Sundance Institute.* www.sundance.org/festivalhistory. 15 July 2017.

"About." *Big Sky Documentary Film Festival.* www.bigskyfilmfest.org/festival/about/. 15 June 2016.

"About." *Chicago Feminist Film Festival.* www.chicagofeministfilmfestival.com/ about-2/. 16 July 2017.

"About." *Davis Feminist Film Festival.* www.wrrc.ucdavis.edu/feministfilmfestival.html. 15 June 2016.

"About." *International Women's Film Festival of Créteil.* www.filmsdefemmes.com/fr/a- propos/. 17 July 2017.

"The Berlinale Festival Profile." *Internationale Filmfestspiele Berlin.* www.berlinale.de/en/das_festival/festivalprofil/profil_der_berlinale/index.html. 15 June 2016.

Bernstein, Paula. "Sundance 2015 Infographic: Most Festival Films Will Land Distribution Deals." *Indiewire.com.* 16 January 2015. www.indiewire.com/2015/01/sundance-2015-infographic-most-festival-films-will-land-distribution-deals-66214/. 15 June 2016.

Goodman, Stephanie. "Women Face Long Odds at U.S. Film Festivals, Study Finds." *The New York Times.* 17 May 2017. www.nytimes.com/2017/05/17/movies/women-lack-opportunities-film-festivals-study.html. 29 June 2017.

Lauzen, Martha M. "The Celluloid Ceiling: Behind-the-Scenes Employment of Women on the Top 100, 250, and 500 Films of 2015." In *Center for the Study of Women in Television & Film.* San Diego State University, 2016. www.womenintvfilm.sdsu.edu/files/2015_Celluloid_Ceiling_Report.pdf. 15 June 2016.

———. "Women in Independent Film, 2016–17." In *Center for the Study of Women in Television & Film.* San Diego State University, May 2017. www.womenintvfilm.sdsu.edu/wp-content/uploads/2017/05/2016-17_Women_in_Independent_Film_Report.pdf. 25 June 2017.

Loist, Skadi. "The Film Festival Circuit: Networks, Hierarchies, and Circulation." De Valck, Kredell, and Loist, pp. 49–64, 2016.

"Our Mission." *Rocky Mountain Women's Film Festival.* www.rmwfilminstitute.org/about-us. 15 June 2016.

"Our Mission." *Women's International Film & Arts Festival.* www.womensfilmfest.com/about. 16 July 2017.

"Our Story." *Sundance Institute.* www.sundance.org/about/us. 15 June 2016.

Peranson, Mark. "First You Get the Power, Then You Get the Money: Two Models of Film Festivals." *Dekalog 3: On Film Festivals.* Ed. Richard Porton. Wallflower, 2009, pp. 23–27.

Rich, B. Ruby. *Chick Flicks: Thoughts and Memories of the Feminist Film Movement.* Duke UP, 1998.

———. "The Confidence Game." *Camera Obscura,* vol. 28, no. 1, 2013, pp. 157–165.

Robb, David. "Female Directors Gaining Ground at Major Film Festivals – Study." *Deadline.* 17 May 2017. www.deadline.com/2017/05/female-directors-film-festivals-san-diego-state-study. 29 June 2017.

Smith, Stacy L., Katherine Pieper, Marc Choueiti, and Ariana Case. "Gender & Short Films: Emerging Female Filmmakers and the Barriers Surrounding their Careers." *USC Annenberg School for Communication and Journalism.* 5 October 2015. www.annenberg.usc.edu/pages/~/media/MDSCI/MDSC%20LUNAFEST%20Report%2010515.ashx. 15 June 2016.

Tascón, Sonia. "Watching Others' Troubles: Revisiting 'The Film Act' and Spectatorship in Activist Film Festivals." Tascón and Wils, pp. 21–37.

Tascón, Sonia and Tyson Wils, editors. *Activist Film Festivals: Towards a Political Subject.* Intellect, 2017.

Torchin, Leshu. "Networked for Advocacy: Film Festivals and Activism." In *Film Festival Yearbook 4: Film Festivals and Activism.* Eds. Dina Iordanova and Leshu Torchin, St. Andrews Film Studies, 2012, pp. 1–12.

White, Patricia. "The Last Days of Women's Cinema." *Camera Obscura,* vol. 21, no. 3, 2006, pp. 145–151.

———. *Women's Cinema, World Cinema: Projecting Contemporary Feminisms.* Duke UP, 2015.

Winton, Ezra and Svetla Turin. "The Revolution Will Not Be Festivalized: Documentary Film Festivals and Activism." Tascón and Wils, pp. 81–103, 2017.

Wong, Cindy Hing-Yuk. "Publics and Counterpublics: Rethinking Film Festivals as Public Spheres." De Valck, Kredell, and Loist, pp. 83–99, 2017.

Section IV
Ways of contesting

16

Women organized against sexual harassment

Protesting sexual violence on campus, then and now

Linda Blum and Ethel Mickey

Introduction

In late 1978 a group of undergraduate and graduate women at the University of California, Berkeley organized to protest sexual harassment on campus and press for action on multiple complaints against a faculty member. At the time, Title IX was relatively new, few people had heard of the term "sexual harassment," and even fewer were likely to understand it as a form of sex discrimination or denial of equal educational opportunities for women. The university in 1978, needless to say, had no formal grievance procedure or reporting mechanism to handle such cases. The group – naming itself Women Organized Against Sexual Harassment or WOASH – engaged in intense activity over a two-year period to protest and work to establish such a procedure. Fast-forward to 2014, and a group of women students on the same campus had filed a civil lawsuit against the administration for failing to properly respond to their complaints of sexual assault as a violation of Title IX and their similar rights to equal educational opportunities (Golgowski 2015). Struck by the parallels between these two episodes separated by over 30 years, we have revisited the history of the original group to better understand the local politics of sexual harassment and the linkages between past and present instances of grassroots feminism on campus. Revisiting the history of WOASH also furthers understanding of the complex, decentered character of second-wave feminism.

The role of grassroots campus groups is an important yet often neglected aspect of the fight against sexual harassment. Such local efforts, by targeting a routine expression of male privilege,

*Authors' note: This chapter was accepted for publication in January 2016, when the election of President Donald Trump and the appointment of Betsy DeVos to head the Department of Education were nearly unthinkable. We have made only minor changes, although, amid the larger context of attacking Obama-era policies, DeVos rewrote federal Title IX guidelines, enraging many young feminists. For more discussion of the lessons second-wave feminisms contribute to thinking about current challenges, see Blum and Mickey (2018). For their many insights, we wish to thank the WOASH members who contributed to this project.

contributed much to making sexual harassment a widely recognized term. The major focus, however, of those studying such feminist politics has been on the macro level of national and cross-national arenas. Major studies, most notably those by Abigail Saguy comparing France and the United States (2003) and Kathrin Zippel comparing Germany, the United States, and the European Union (2006), carefully acknowledge the significance of local actors; but they necessarily leave such grassroots activism unexamined while taking on macro-contrasts in national institutional structures and cultural frames. Most other studies of sexual harassment in the United States have focused on the workplace and violations of Title VII – prohibiting employment discrimination – rather than on the campus activism and politics of Title IX. Such studies, for example, gauge the prevalence of harassment across types of occupations and organizations (Gruber 1992; Morgan and Gruber 2011; Welsh, Dawson, and Nierobisz 2002), its relation to actual work requirements in the service sector (Williams 1998), and the turn to diversity training amid fears of organizational liability (Dobbin and Kelly 2007; Kelly and Dobbin 1998).[1] We argue, in contrast, that a closer look at one local Title IX movement from the era of second-wave activism sheds important light on current feminist organizing and campus politics. For as we will discuss, in a sense everything yet nothing has changed.

Background

Under the Obama administration, a movement of young women students against sexual assault took shape at campuses nationwide; such young women assisted each other through Skype, Twitter, and Facebook groups to file complaints of violations of Title IX with the Office of Civil Rights of the Department of Education, with over 100 universities and colleges coming under investigation (Kingkade 2015). Although sexual harassment and sexual assault may appear to be separate issues, with sexual harassment less serious than sexual assault, sexual harassment is an umbrella term that includes more and less severe forms of unwanted sexual attention or "the involuntary eroticization of working [or educational] relationships" (Zippel 2006, x). Most researchers agree that such actions exist on a continuum of gender-based violence from unwanted sexual remarks, touching, demands or threats for sexual favors, to actual physical or sexual assault.[2] The ubiquity of less severe forms of sexual harassment, feminist scholars agree, normalizes more serious forms of violence against women such as sexual assault (Bayard de Volo and Hall 2015; O'Toole, Schiffman, and Edwards 2007; Quina 1990; Wise and Stanley 1987). Indeed, sexual harassment has been described as the "dripping tap" of sexual violence – a constant reminder of the status of women in gendered institutions and the masculine, heteronormative cultures in which they are embedded (Wise and Stanley 1987). Previous literature, moreover, suggests that victims of sexual harassment, even if survivors of its less severe forms, experience similar physical, psychological, and economic consequences to those experiencing other forms of trauma (O'Toole, Schiffman, and Edwards 2007). Sexual harassment and sexual assault on campuses sustain an environment hostile to women and illustrate the persisting weakness in enforcement of Title IX.

WOASH was specifically formed in 1978 when some 30 Berkeley women students came together to demand action on six complaints brought against a faculty member in the sociology department.[3] The group's primary goal was to establish a grievance procedure for handling student complaints of sexual harassment, but the group aimed its outreach efforts to the wider campus community and women employees as well, and pressed the university to take a strong public stance against it.[4] Importantly, after WOASH began its efforts to raise awareness, the number of signed confidential complaints against the professor in question, Elbaki Hermassi, rose to 13. WOASH members knew the problem to be pervasive, at Berkeley and elsewhere,[5] and were inspired by the students suing Yale University; in 1977, the Yale students' was the first lawsuit to allege sexual harassment constituted a violation of Title IX. WOASH members spoke jointly with Yale plaintiff Pamela Price in a 1979 press conference: "it was the example of Pamela Price and those Yale students who supported her which convinced us to form Women Organized Against Sexual Harassment."[6]

WOASH initially attempted to work with faculty and campus administration to address the complaints against Professor Hermassi. When the university took little action after three months of negotiation, WOASH filed a complaint with the federal government's Office of Civil Rights (at that time, part of the federal Department of Health, Education, and Welfare or HEW). In its two years of intense activism surrounding the filing of the Title IX complaint, WOASH members negotiated with campus administration and university attorneys face-to-face and in formal correspondence; held demonstrations and press conferences; drafted and circulated leaflets, pamphlets, newsletters, and petitions; held a campus-wide informational forum and supported complainants while fighting to protect their confidentiality; consulted with sympathetic legal counsel; and researched and debated appropriate grievance mechanisms. In the fall of 1980 Professor Elbaki Hermassi chose to resign, but the fight for appropriate procedures and enforcement of Title IX continued.[7]

Methods

The first author (Blum) was a member of WOASH while a graduate student at Berkeley. Another WOASH member and frequent spokesperson, Ruth Milkman, had saved the group's documentation, eventually creating a (partial) electronic version shared among a small number attending a reunion in 2014, and later donating the entire collection to the Schlesinger Library of the Radcliffe Institute for Advanced Study at Harvard University. Blum's participation in WOASH provided us with insider information, and her retrospective observations and memories, with communication with additional former members, served to fill the gaps in the archives and to answer lingering questions. The other author (Mickey) was a graduate student whose research has focused on gendered organizations. Mickey, as the outside author, provided distance from WOASH to conceptualize the group more broadly within the gendered history of higher education and feminist activism. Our insider-outsider coauthorship served as a check, minimizing bias and encouraging clarification in our interpretation of the archival data (for more, Blum and Mickey 2018; also see Bayard de Volo and Hall 2015).

The archive itself includes documents such as meeting records, newsletters, press packets, media coverage, correspondence with Berkeley administration, petitions, research on other cases, and internal communication among WOASH members. The two authors first engaged extensively with the archives separately and then came together to engage in dialogue over the data, together drawing out conceptual themes and questions. We then analyzed our observations in relation to the literature on the history and politics of sexual harassment, reflecting also on the comparison to current efforts to end campus sexual assault.

Gendered organizations – everything and nothing has changed

Feminist theory has largely taken a structural approach to sexual harassment, examining how the distribution of power and the division of labor in organizations facilitate men's power and women's subordination. Rather than defining sexual harassment as an individual behavior problem among a few deviant men, a gendered organization approach points to features of modern hierarchical organizations that serve to disadvantage women (Acker 1990; Britton 2000; Kanter 1977; Williams 1998). Organizational power in particular tends to facilitate sexual harassment, and women, who tend to be segregated into gender-typed jobs low in status, authority, and pay, often experience harassment by their male superiors or other powerful men (O'Toole, Schiffman, and Edwards 2007). Moreover, when heterosexual display or sexual exploitation become part of the job description, as common in many forms of interactive service work, sexual harassment itself becomes institutionalized (Williams 1998). Women workers with more privilege who are overly visible in male-dominated organizations may also adopt sexualized survival strategies – and these can reproduce the gendered, symbolic boundaries within organizations and invite sexual harassment (Blair-Loy 2001).

Sexual harassment of employees in work organizations drew the attention of policymakers and feminist researchers prior to sexual harassment on campuses being recognized as a pervasive problem. Law and policy rarely recognize the gendered organization perspective, however, and treat discrimination in employment separately from discrimination in education – with sexual harassment in the workplace considered a form of sex discrimination under Title VII of the Civil Rights Act rather than, as in education, under Title IX of the 1972 Education Amendments (with each relegated to their own federal regulatory agencies). Yet members of WOASH, following the Yale case, relied on the legal and intellectual frameworks established by Catharine MacKinnon (1979)[8] and Lin Farley (1978), which focused primarily on workplace sexual harassment. Title VII is relevant to sexual harassment on campus, nonetheless, because colleges and universities are major employers of women and women students. WOASH also made less distinction between women workers and students, drawing frequent parallels in terms of gendered power relations and including women university staff in its outreach efforts. Additionally, many, if not most, WOASH members worked on campus as instructors, teaching and research assistants, or in work-study positions, so the line between student and employee was often blurred.

The demography of higher education has shifted significantly since the 1970s, another gain from second-wave feminism and Title IX. By the start of recent third-wave activism, women had caught up or surpassed men in numbers of students, faculty, and administrators. When WOASH formed in 1978, the number of women earning degrees had markedly increased in the few short years since passage of Title IX – but women still earned less than half of the bachelor's and master's degrees conferred in the US and only 25% of doctoral degrees (see Tables 16.1a and 16.1b). By contrast, in 2013 women earned approximately 60% of bachelor's and master's degrees and over 50% of doctoral degrees (NCES 2015).[9] Yet despite such visible gains, higher education remains a gendered institution resting on the traditionally masculine values of hierarchy, challenge, competition (ostensibly) by individual merit, and independence. Women entering these formerly homosocial spaces tend to experience exclusion and hostility as they threaten male solidarity and privilege (Bystydzienski and Bird 2006; Page, Bailey, and van Delinder 2009; Valian 1998; Yoder 1991). Women students and faculty continue to experience patterns of isolation, inequitable shares of resources, biased evaluation and reward procedures, and incompatibility of work-family arrangements. Moreover, women's clustering in lower, untenured ranks has implications for the politics of sexual harassment: when a campus does acknowledge the problem, it is typically framed as a peripheral "women's issue" rather than a serious institutional concern (AAUP 2014; Dzeich and Weiner 1984; National Academies 2007).

In addition to research on higher education as a gendered institution, much research has focused on the rape culture of college campuses – the set of values, beliefs, and "rape myths" that provide an environment conducive to sexual violence (e.g., Armstrong, Hamilton, and Sweeney 2006; Boswell and Spade 1996). Myths include assumptions about men, women, sexuality, and consent emphasizing that men are naturally sexually aggressive and women naturally passive or "asking for it." The rape culture embedded in academia was perhaps first singled out in research by Dzeich and Weiner as they worked on their book, *The Lecherous Professor*, in the early 1980s; they noticed the "intensity of reactions" from their colleagues, with many threatened and hostile

Table 16.1a Degrees over time by gender

Percentage of women receiving bachelor's, master's, and doctoral degrees in the United States[1]			
	Bachelor's	*Master's*	*Doctoral*
Pre-Title IX			
1970	43.1	38.8	9.6
Post-Title IX			
1978	47.1	47.5	23.9
Present[2]	57.2	59.9	51.4

1 Source: National Center for Education Statistics, Digest of Education Statistics 2015. http://nces.ed.gov/programs/digest/d14/tables/dt14_318.10.asp?current=yes

2 Most recent data from NCES is for the academic year 2012–2013.

Table 16.1b Degrees over time by gender

Women's share of selected professional degrees, 1956–1987 (percentage of total degrees to women)[1]			
	Law	*Medicine*	*MBA*
Pre-Title IX			
1956	5.0	3.5	
1967			2.0
1971–1972	7.3	9.2	
Post-Title IX			
1978–1979	28.5	23	
1986–1987	32	32	33
2011	47.3[2]		
2014		47.5[3]	35.5[4]

1 Adapted from Blum (1991). Original Sources: US Department of Labor, Women's Bureau, 1983, Bulletin 298, table IV-16; 1956 figures from US Bureau of Census, cited in Diamond 1984; 1986 figures for law and medicine cited in Greer 1986; MBA figures from Center for Education Statistics, US Education Department, cited in *Business Week* 1987.

2 Source: American Bar Association, "J.D. and LL.B. Degrees Awarded, 2010–2011 Academic Year."www.americanbar.org/content/dam/aba/administrative/legal_education_and_admissions_to_the_bar/statistics/jd_llb_degrees_awarded.pdf

3 Source: Association of American Medical Colleges, "Total Graduates by U.S. Medical School and Sex, 2010–2014." www.aamc.org/download/321532/data/factstable27-2.pdf.

4 Source: The Association to Advance Collegiate Schools of Business, "Business School Data Guide 2015." www.aacsb.edu/~/media/AACSB/Publications/data-trends-booklet/2015%20Business%20School%20Data%20Guide.ashx

when asked about sexual harassment (1984, 5). One colleague assumed Dzeich and Weiner were out to get men fired, while another approached a dean suggesting their work be monitored to avoid embarrassing the university. Despite the significant influx of women in the ensuing decades, rape culture persists on college campuses and has found its most recent expression in new media forums often connected to Greek systems, such as anonymous campus message boards, blogs, and apps (Press and Tripodi 2014a, 2014b). Sexist and violent language is commonplace in these forums, normalizing cultures of misogyny on campus. This might be exemplified once again through a Title IX case against Yale, where among other incidents of sexual violence, fraternity pledges marched through a central residential quad in October 2010 chanting: "No means yes, yes means anal" (Clark-Flory 2010; Foderaro 2011).

Feminist networks and (old) media strategies

WOASH members were informed by actions against sexual harassment at other universities and among working women's groups, and in this sense were part of a loose feminist network emerging in the late 1970s. Such groups were also gaining increased media visibility – in the "old" pre-internet forms of mass media – a trend well in evidence in the large collection of clippings in the WOASH archive.[10] Most important and attention-getting for women students was the 1977 Yale lawsuit – the first, in an early ruling, to gain the court's affirmation that the lack of a grievance procedure to handle students' sexual harassment complaints constituted sex discrimination and a violation of Title IX. It was a decidedly mixed victory, however: the court dismissed the original class action, and Pamela Price, the remaining individual plaintiff, lost her suit as well as the 1979 appeal in which WOASH had filed an amicus supporting brief – but the preliminary ruling of sex discrimination set a significant precedent and pushed Yale to implement a grievance mechanism. In addition, three of the five original plaintiffs, including Price, went on to accomplished legal careers, and all five were honored by the ACLU for their contributions to the development and enforcement of Title IX.[11]

WOASH's mobilization informed, and was informed by, coverage of nearby actions. At the University of California, San Francisco, a 1979 front-page article in the campus newspaper highlighted the pervasiveness of the problem, with complaints raised by a number of women students and women employees.[12] But events at San Jose State received greater attention: when five women students charged a philosophy professor, Phillip Jacklin, with sexual harassment in May 1979, the university followed its general administrative hearing process – and by early January 1980, announced it had fired him.[13] If the Yale plaintiffs inspired WOASH members to mobilize, and events at UCSF reaffirmed the need, actions at San Jose State served as a strong point of contrast with the recalcitrance at UC Berkeley. The *Berkeley Graduate*, supporting WOASH, noted, "In sharp contrast [to UC Berkeley], the San Jose State administration has resolved a similar case through regular administrative procedures in less than half a year."[14] The *Los Angeles Times*, however, painted the two administrative reactions as similar after UC Berkeley administrators imposed a suspension of one quarter's salary on Elbaki Hermassi and placed a negative report in his personnel record (actions announced just five days after San Jose State made its dismissal of Jacklin public): "In unprecedented actions, one California university professor has been fired and another severely reprimanded." The same article, though, gave visibility to feminist networks and specifically to WOASH:

> The two actions came in the wake of increasingly vocal protests by women's organizations alleging a widespread pattern of sexual harassment of female students on the nation's college campuses . . . leaders of a group called Women Organized Against Sexual Harassment (WOASH) called the action [against Hermassi] "a slap on the wrist."[15]

WOASH in turn drew out contrasts with other schools in its own "WOASH Weekly," circulated widely on the Berkeley campus, though just four times during the heyday period. WOASH Weekly #3 announced in the opening paragraphs that in San Jose, Jacklin had been "dismissed," yet "[t]here were five complainants in that case as opposed to 13 in the Berkeley case." And WOASH Weekly #4 observed more damningly:

> Yale and Harvard have set up grievance procedures, [UC] Santa Cruz and San Jose have held hearings on harassment charges . . . [t]he State of Michigan has set up a special Task Force on Sexual Harassment . . . [the] United Auto Workers won new contract language . . . making

it easier to file grievances involving harassment. And last fall, Mary Heelan won $100,000 from the Johns-Manville Corp.[16]

In fact, WOASH had skillfully garnered media attention, strategically holding press conferences or campus demonstrations at points of impasse to increase pressure on the Berkeley administration. The group's first formal press conference, for example, occurred in February 1979, to announce the filing of the Title IX complaint after three months of fruitless negotiations. One WOASH leader wrote later that the accompanying press release had purposely contained two headlines: while the pervasiveness of sexual harassment and the lack of a grievance procedure was the "real" story, the group realized that the Hermassi scandal was the "bait" and made this its first headline:[17] "I think we all knew that it was the specific case which would attract press interest in the first place . . . we supplied it as 'bait' hoping they'd swallow the 'real' story along with it."[18]

The negative publicity WOASH generated for the university may have had only limited impact, however. UC Berkeley administrators abruptly stopped negotiations with WOASH after the first press conference; but a faculty committee charged with Professor Hermassi's tenure review, perhaps indirectly influenced, refused to move forward unless the administration acted on the allegations. Late that spring, this faculty action provoked administrators (specifically in this case, Vice Chancellor Heyman) to appoint Susan French, a professor of property law at UC Davis Law School, to conduct a confidential investigation of the complaints against Hermassi – and to resume some contact with WOASH.[19]

Professor French submitted her confidential report to Chancellor Bowker in June 1979, and because she could not circulate it, she described her findings to WOASH in a July meeting, recommending an administrative hearing seeking Hermassi's termination with the complaints substantial and serious. After futile months pushing for the report's release, WOASH provoked more negative publicity with a press release and campus protest in October 1979 challenging the cover-up and revealing their knowledge of the findings. "Sex for Grades Cover-Up in Berkeley Case" was the headline in the *San Francisco Examiner*, albeit on page 4;[20] the *Oakland Tribune* similarly proclaimed on page 5, "UC Accused of Cover Up in Sex Harassment Case."[21] Perhaps the best headline went to the campus *Daily Californian* covering the administration's subsequent response – nearly one year since receiving the initial complaints – not with the creation of a grievance procedure or a hearing for Hermassi, but with creation of a half-time faculty assistant position on the status of women:[22] "Women Get Outlet for Gripes."[23]

Another key strategic choice of WOASH to manage media coverage was the decision not to release Hermassi's name. When instead the *Daily Californian* released Hermassi's name, WOASH issued a letter to the editor protesting this decision.[24] Nonetheless, major media outlets blamed WOASH for the public release of his name, with the *San Francisco Chronicle*, for example, writing that "the group has been nipping at the professor's heels since last November" hoping to "try the case in public media," the latter a quote from UC Berkeley Vice Chancellor Heyman.[25] Once Hermassi had been identified, WOASH still refrained from naming him publically. Supportive coverage in the *Berkeley Graduate* in May 1979, for example, reported that "WOASH has been criticized for making this matter public, but members are careful to point out that . . . they did not release the professor's name"; the piece itself refers only to "the professor" or "the defendant."[26] Yet the left-wing *San Francisco Bay Guardian*, like the mainstream *Time* magazine, claimed that "WOASH members leaked his name to the local [campus] newspaper."[27] The *Los Angeles Times* went further, stating that while his accusers remained "anonymous," "nameless and faceless to him and the public," WOASH members had "successfully manipulated" the editor of the campus newspaper to release Hermassi's name, an action he immediately regretted.[28] WOASH meeting notes from April 29, 1979, illustrate the group's frustration: "It would be better if we could define our own issues, but we are stuck with this one for now. Of course, we will continue to point out that this is but one instance of what is a much more widespread problem."[29]

In addition, most articles referring to WOASH rested on repeated use of sexist stereotypes pointing to women as overly emotional and irrational. The *San Francisco Examiner* began an article, "A group of angry women students,"[30] and the *San Francisco Chronicle* in its headline coverage of the next campus demonstration reiterated, "Angry Women Rally at UC," with the first line, "About 100 irate female students."[31] The use of such stereotypes also discredited the complainants while portraying the harasser as victim. For example, the critical April 1979 article from the *San Francisco Bay Guardian* suggested that the complaints could be "hysterical or irresponsible accusations" and that "some feminist students may have acted irresponsibly in their zeal for justice."[32] The *Los Angeles Times* and *Time* magazine both quoted Hermasi plaintively lamenting, "I'm terrified," with the *Los Angeles Times* continuing sympathetically with a further quote from Hermassi, "Every time it comes up it hurts me."[33] More baldly, an editorial in the *Oakland Tribune,* "Trial by Press Conference," condemned WOASH for conducting a "witch hunt."[34] Internal meeting documents indicate that WOASH members were troubled by these distortions, particularly with complainants described as "anonymous accusers" who could cost this "poor, victimized man" his job when in fact each of the 13 complaints was signed, and each complainant willing to come forward, waiting only for the university to call for a hearing.[35]

Perhaps little has changed in this regard over the ensuing decades, as mainstream journalism continues to be insensitive and trivializing when covering gender violence (Gilmore 2017). Saguy also found this to be true in France, particularly turning the individual case into a media sensation and scandal when it involves a high-profile academic or professional man (2003). There are perhaps several indications that this may be changing[36] – however, as WOASH members were aware, "even bad coverage" created visibility for the issue at stake: "Lots of people who saw the [bad] stuff in the straight media . . . did get some insight into the issue, and some understanding of the fact that there is a struggle going on over the issue. And that's important."[37] The success of WOASH's efforts to raise consciousness was perhaps best measured by its coverage in *Time* magazine,[38] the biggest of the big three news weeklies, with readership over 20 million at that time (Macht 2013).

WOASH members, however, relied on more immediate evidence of their successful consciousness-raising. At its second press conference, in August 1979, the group announced that, in response to its February complaint, HEW's Office of Civil Rights would be investigating UC Berkeley for Title IX violations – a tactical victory for the group. But WOASH's statement also described receiving "calls of support and encouragement from working women, students, faculty, parents, and legislators from around the country."[39] The group additionally reported that the local San Francisco office of the Equal Employment Opportunity Commission (for Title VII workplace complaints) and the HEW Office of Civil Rights (for Title IX students' complaints) had each received "a significant increase in inquiries and complaints about sexual harassment" in the "months since WOASH's last public statement" (i.e., its first press conference in February 1979). One WOASH member recalled the thrill of hearing this press conference covered on a local commercial rock radio station,[40] and WOASH later earned statewide coverage on KNBC-TV.[41]

WOASH's success and involvement in feminist networks were further on display at this second (August 1979) press conference with the participation of Yale plaintiff Pamela Price. Price, after graduating from Yale, had moved to attend UC Berkeley's Boalt Hall Law School. She had shared her experiences as one of several speakers in a campus-wide WOASH forum on sexual harassment in March, attended by 300 to 400 and cosponsored by the Berkeley Feminist Alliance and the university office workers in AFSCME Local 1695. At this second press conference,

WOASH also announced its filing of the amicus brief in support of Price's appeal, relying on feminist networks and the pro bono assistance of San Francisco–based Equal Rights Advocates.[42]

Feminist networks continue to be important in the current anti-sexual assault movement, and such networks are arguably more easily created and tapped with new technologies and social media. New technologies have become crucial for allowing millennial activists to communicate across the country in digital spaces such as Facebook groups, Tumblr pages, blogs, and face-to-face over Skype, FaceTime, and the like (Crossley 2017; Milkman 2017). A recent sexual harassment case also demonstrates the effectiveness of social media: UC Berkeley astronomer and Nobel laureate Geoffrey Marcy was pressed to resign in October 2015 after facing multiple student complaints of sexual harassment. The inaction of the UC Berkeley administration echoes its recalcitrance during WOASH's heyday, but students, colleagues, and community members turned to Facebook and Twitter to express their outrage and call for Marcy's dismissal. There was a swift response from the American Astronomical Society as well, with more than 2,500 signing an online petition expressing their support for the complainants (Overbye 2015).

This effectiveness, however, also speaks to the lasting impact of grassroots second-wave groups like WOASH. Although WOASH failed to gain a grievance procedure at UC Berkeley in its two-year heyday, a few women carried on quietly in the years immediately following and finally gained such a mechanism, adopted system-wide in 1986. According to one, Marlene Kim,

> WOASH was just 3 to 5 of us then. But you could say "WOASH" and they [the administration] had this *fear*. You really gave us something. You could say "WOASH" and they'd think it was *all* these women. So that was *good*. The name lived on and inspired fear.[43]

Having an adequate grievance mechanism in place for Marcy's complainants clearly was no panacea, but it did create legitimacy missing for Hermassi's complainants prior to WOASH's mobilization.[44] And the cumulative impact of early campus efforts around the country led to something far larger, the broader awareness capable of sparking outrage.

Internal frictions, feminisms, and race privilege

At a glance, the predominantly white, middle-class members of WOASH may have appeared a homogeneous and privileged student group. Yet friction over the internal group process and strategic choices for specific protest actions divided the group by age, status, and differing strands of feminism. Graduate student women, with a relatively greater investment in the university and hopes for careers in academic research and teaching, were invested in negotiations with the university, with the legal issues at stake and desires for longer-run institutional change. They (or we) also tended to dominate the group, though to be fair, the graduate students were the original founders and went on to make concerted efforts to pair graduate and undergraduate women spokespeople for each action or task. Our political leanings, as graduate students, tended toward the socialist feminism attempting to "marry" the Marxist materialism familiar to us from our studies with insights from radical feminism and its critique of sexual violence (Hartmann 1979, among many). Graduate student members had a range of community political involvements, including with labor union allies, the *Socialist Review* journal collective, and the East Bay Socialist School, but also the Committee to Defend Reproductive Rights, the Berkeley/Oakland Women's Union, and lesbian and gay rights activism. In contrast, many undergraduates in the group tended toward radical feminism and its more singular woman-identified stance, coming from antiviolence and anti-rape politics such as those of the Berkeley Feminist Alliance.[45] These differing perspectives may also have stemmed from (slight but important) age differences or directions of generational-identification: socialist feminism emerged from networks of earlier activists involved in anti-Vietnam war and anti-racist activism, with a greater emphasis on anti-capitalist solidarity and alliance-building (e.g., Breines 2002; also Hansen 1990, among many). For some undergraduate members, our political identification and studies with leftist male faculty may have seemed career-driven compromises,[46] compromises at times leading us to reject the more provocative tactics they favored.[47] One example Blum recalls was a suggestion to seize the campanile, the bell tower in the center of campus.[48] All did agree, however, that the group's meetings should be women-only.[49]

WOASH attempted to operate by consensus and to work against hierarchy among members, practices derived from feminist consciousness-raising groups. Our "constitution," required to become an official campus organization, stated that the only officers would be a chair, with "length of term of office for chairpersons . . . one meeting," and a treasurer to be rotated quarterly "among members of a budget committee"[50] (there were also other committees as needs arose, such as the labor outreach committee, the complaints committee, and the committee researching appropriate procedures).[51] At points of sharp disagreement, however, it was difficult to reach any clear decision with the consensus model. After going slowly around the room on one such occasion (with often some 20 women in attendance), Blum recalls a graduate student finally bursting out, "I don't know *what* we just decided. Couldn't we just vote?!" An archival document signed by two graduate students explained the rationale for the modified, cumbersome process then adopted (late in the spring of WOASH's first year) to handle this friction;[52] it utilized voting only after several attempts to achieve consensus had failed:[53]

> No matter how sensitive or how extensive discussion is, there comes a time when a group has to make a formal decision upon which it will act. It is at this moment that we strongly believe voting to be the most reasonable way of proceeding. . . . However unfortunate it may be, we may not always be able to reach a consensus in the time available.

The archive also contains statements about "skill sharing" indicative of members' concern with the informal hierarchy and the tendency of graduate student women to dominate. A planning document for the group's second academic year (1979–1980) lists with underlining for emphasis:[54] "Devote a reasonable portion of meetings from now on to *skill sharing* . . . making sure that each one of us feels comfortable and competent to do speaking." This is followed by an explanatory note, indicating that attempts at leveling inequalities had been inadequate in the group's first year:

> In the past it has been suggested that we need more attention to internal process. . . . We had hoped that the process of skill sharing in getting ready for more outreach would help make all of us feel more involved, equalize power and resources, etc.[55]

Despite such attempts to address internal tensions, in November 1979 (the fall of WOASH's second year), a surprise radical feminist action defacing university property occurred that had not been subject to the group's deliberation and decision-making. With the university refusing to release the results of the French investigation and still no grievance procedure, WOASH had finally spoken out in protest in an October 1979 press release and campus demonstration.[56] Yet in early November, a group remaining anonymous but most likely sparked by the younger women in WOASH broke into the campus building housing the sociology department, and with red spray paint, "redecorate[d]" the office doors of several senior sociology faculty members, all white men, with "feminist slogans and graphics." The letter of support printed in the campus newspaper which contained this description was signed by 12 men and women, "students and employees of UC Berkeley." Its authors wrote that "this action has sparked a lot of creative debate on sexual harassment and has been very educational in raising people's consciousness about the issue."[57] But a campus leaflet from the Berkeley Feminist Alliance accused the university of silencing this expression of women's "Out Rage" against "[m]ale professors, TA's, students, and bosses [who] objectify and simplify our bodies and ideas." The Alliance's leaflet further castigated the "Old Boy professors" whose office doors were spray painted, maintaining "many" were "harassers themselves." The leaflet continued, "[t]his spraypainted graffiti was literally covered-up within two days as was its sister connection ('A Womyn was Raped Here – ♀Fight Back!') spraypainted on the campanile."[58]

Blum recalls, in addition, the indignation of grad student members caught off-guard and the fear of serious legal repercussions. In the end, none occurred, perhaps because, as a supportive press release from the Office of the Student Advocate indicated, university officials were being closely watched to prevent reprisals. The Student Advocate, an elected ombudsperson position within student government and staffed with additional students on work-study stipends, was staunchly left-wing at the time; and with WOASH's concerted outreach, supportive of its campaign to end sexual harassment.[59] The majority of the student government appears to have been galvanized by that point (November 1979), attesting to the cumulative influence of WOASH's more and less confrontational tactics: in late November, student senators from the People's Anti-nuclear Collective, the Gay People's Union, and the Berkeley Feminist Alliance "stood as the bill [supporting WOASH demands to end the cover-up] was announced and cheered when it passed unanimously."[60]

WOASH also acted effectively as a unified group in a demonstration picketing the central campus two months later, in January 1980 (the middle of year 2), garnering national attention in the *Time* magazine piece.[61] With rumors spreading that the university was secretly negotiating to let Hermassi off with a reprimand (as discussed above), University Chancellor Albert Bowker announced the decision shortly after New Year's to suspend "the Professor" for one quarter without pay while he was already off campus on a year-long salaried sabbatical.[62] To be fair, Bowker considered this a "very severe reprimand" because a copy of the confidential French report would be included in Hermassi's tenure review file, with his tenure to be decided the following fall.[63] To WOASH, however – in addition to the contrast with the firing at San Jose State – Bowker's statement was "an insult."[64] WOASH did not consider the tenure review process Hermassi would face on his return either adequate or appropriate for hearing students' sexual harassment complaints. Tenure hearings were conducted, at that time, primarily by senior male faculty colleagues interested in protecting their shared privilege and the university's reputation. Such a review, even if deciding to sanction Hermassi, would deny the 13 women complainants their rights to due process and possible restitution.[65] Moreover, misconduct actually spanning eight or nine years was described by Bowker as, "occur[ing] during a relatively short period of time while the professor was suffering personal emotional distress," ignoring any emotional distress experienced by the 13 complainants, "ultimately, no complainant suffered direct academic injury."[66] Thus the WOASH January 1980 demonstration occurred just four days after Bowker's announcement (Thursday, January 10), and was attended by about 150 according to the *Daily Californian*.[67]

Although WOASH activism continued through spring 1980, the solidarity between undergraduate and graduate student women had also been frayed by tensions surrounding racial politics. Intriguingly, some feminist scholarship concerned with the gender essentialism in legal theories of sexual violence and its effacing of race divides (e.g., Kent 2007) overlooks the complex awareness of earlier activists such as those in WOASH in the women's liberation branch of the movement (e.g., Reger 2012). Though before terms like "intersectionality" or "white privilege" were common, WOASH members grappled, if imperfectly, with the group's whiteness and consistently acknowledged the disproportionate vulnerability of women of color to sexual harassment and the potential for disproportionate targeting of men of color as perpetrators.

During the two years of WOASH's intense activism, calls for greater ethnoracial diversity on campus, as in feminism as a whole, were growing,[68] and task lists from WOASH meetings mention outreach by core members (Linda Fuller and Margaret (Rivka) Polatnick) with the community-based Third World Women's Alliance.[69] Additionally, in October 1980, WOASH members rallied in support of two Black women employees fired by the university after raising complaints of sexual harassment against their white male supervisor.[70] So perhaps the careful acknowledgment of similarities and differences in the experiences of people of color in WOASH's official ten-page informational pamphlet were not surprising. These were contained in the section, "Who Harasses and Who Is Harassed?" and clarified for example,

> Women of any race, class, and background can be subjected to sexual harassment. However, Third World women and those in lower-level jobs are especially vulnerable to harassment, given their lack of economic security and institutional support (which are magnified by racism).[71]

Yet at least two members (Blum and Press)[72] recalled that the first draft sketches for the pamphlet's cover and other inside pages met with criticism at a meeting for their white features, such as long, straight hair, for example. The drawings were subsequently changed to include features such as curlier, shorter hair, thicker lips, and even a suggestion of a wider nose on the cover.[73]

The lived experience of women of color was made vivid for WOASH members by Yale plaintiff Pamela Price and one of the 13 complainants against Hermassi. Each emphasized the particular vulnerability of Black women to persisting stereotypes of their hypersexual or promiscuous nature. Each also explained that their experiences could not be neatly sorted into separate legal categories of racial versus sexual discrimination (Crenshaw 1989). Price told WOASH: "It's the same old story. Where sex is concerned, black women's accusations are considered lies and white men's denials are believed."[74] She spoke eloquently at the second WOASH press conference:

> By focusing on individuals rather than Title IX, the judge reduced the case to a Black woman's accusation and a white man's denial. . . . Credibility became a code word for the most racist premises: Black women as opposed to white men are not credible. . . . I personally have been called a liar and probably worse in the white halls and chambers of justice.[75]

The Hermassi complainant similarly spoke of racialized and sexualized "intimidati[on]."[76] She wrote that while enrolled in Hermassi's course, he sought her out and proposed sexual experimentation because she was Black:

> He then discussed his personal life and how he had had such bad dealings with white women. He said he didn't know how black women were, but he was willing to try and experiment. In what followed it became clear that he was interested in making me the subject of such an experiment.[77]

In subsequent encounters, she pointed to "offensive" and "inappropriate comments, gestures, and physical advances," concluding: "These incidents took place not only because I am a woman and therefore considered fair game in the eyes of Professor Hermassi, but also because I am a black woman."[78]

WOASH members were also troubled that their own case, against Professor Hermassi, targeted a third-world man. The racial profiling of perpetrators of sexual violence, a social fact that WOASH members were well aware of, is less often mentioned by white feminist scholars of sexual violence.[79] We were well aware that Hermassi was (and is) Tunisian and complexly located in axes of privilege and power: his undergraduate degree was from the Sorbonne and he was lighter skinned, but his research also represented his identification with the third world, specifically with politics and social change in the Maghreb. WOASH routinely set up a noontime informational table along with other student organizations in the major campus thoroughfare, and the first note in a page-long list of tasks and meeting plans indicates our unease with targeting Hermassi: "Woman came to table concerned that this was a 'Zionist' plot: rareness of Arab profs."[80] And Hermassi himself maintained: "I am not an American citizen, and because of my origins, they consider me very easy to victimize" (Dziech and Weiner 1990, 28).

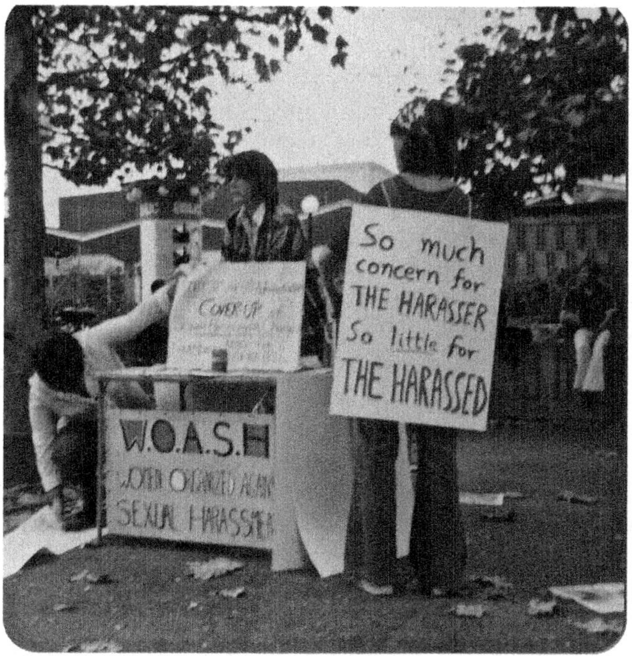

Tabling in Sproul Plaza, 1979–80.

Source: (Photo donated to WOASH archive by M. Rivka Polatnick)

In our formal pamphlet we maintained that "white men are more likely to be in secure positions of authority, and can more often harass women with impunity" – and followed with the campus survey results that the majority of "harassment incidents (62 percent)" involved tenured professors on campus, 94 percent of whom were white.[81] Indeed, many of us were reluctant to target another man of color when the undergraduate members raised a second case for possible action late in the spring of the group's first year. A four-page document denouncing this decision, written by an undergraduate, bears handwritten margin comments from a graduate student leader.[82] These, when taken together, graphically display the friction within the group over our own race privilege. Benson, the undergraduate, clarified first: "Some members of the group wanted to picket the shop of a male employer, incidentally third world, for harassing one of his women employees off the job. I am one of those who advocated action around the case." Milkman, the graduate student, underlined "incidentally" and emphatically penned "no!" in the margin, encapsulating the conflicting perspectives within the group. Benson continued by criticizing the majority: "Pragmatic considerations – looking good in the public eye – or more accurately, redeeming ourselves from allegations of racism, served as the major argument leading eventually to the majority decision to refrain from political action."[83] Benson also chastised the graduate student members for their socialist-feminist politics by painting sensitivity to the group's white privilege and the possibility of alienating women and men of color as an "inevitable contradiction" with,[84] or a "sacrificing" of,[85] women's own interest as a "sex-class"[86] – a radical feminist term denoting the primacy of patriarchy over other forms of oppression. Milkman's margin comments and markings – which expressed the views of many of us – again indicated vigorous disagreement, such as the underline under "inevitable" with a large question mark over it and the word "why," and a bit further down, the query, "Is racism in our interest?"[87]

Benson in fact had begun her document acknowledging this was a conflict between socialist and radical feminist politics, "A recent controversy in WOASH raises the issue of sex-class interest being subverted by Socialist-Feminist concern for the interest of third world people in America."[88] Benson then questioned whether the graduate students in WOASH were too influenced by "a predominantly white male radical professoriate" and too clouded by "ideological ambition" to see that any alliance with third-world people was unrealistic, "an alliance in the sky" against nothing but the "generalized capitalist bogeyman."[89] While we were all young and prone to such impassioned language, Benson's derisive tone hit hard: "This issue has caused great antagonism between members of WOASH which has been expediently and simplistically labeled by those who identify themselves as socialist first and feminist second as Socialist-Feminist vs. Racist-Feminist." To this last accusation, Milkman penned in the margin with obvious exasperation: "No one has introduced labels of any sort but you."[90]

The damage from such a heated exchange, in which terms like "bullshit"[91] and "white girls with rich daddies"[92] were hurled back and forth, might have seemed irreparable. Yet this dense communication occurred in the summer before the second year of intense activity for the group and testified to the reality of another of Milkman's margin notes: "No one's commitment [to ending sexual harassment] has been changed."[93]

To contemporary feminist scholars, it may also appear that WOASH had a gender essentialist definition of sexual harassment, and one that was heterosexist as well. The WOASH pamphlet for example explained: "The kind of sexual harassment that [WOASH] is fighting occurs when men in positions of authority try to use their power in making coercive sexual advances toward women," and these are "situations where the man has institutional power over the woman."[94] WOASH's definition did not stem, however, from a blindness to sexual minority issues as much as to the concern that sexual harassment could be easily domesticated or co-opted, with institutional power removed from its definition. In fact, this has tended to happen when gender-neutral definitions dominate and the problem of harassment becomes one of individual deviance. Policymakers do not, for the most part, recognize the gendered organization perspective of feminist social scientists discussed earlier in this paper. Saguy finds, for example, that in France, framing sexual harassment as a criminal rather than civil offense makes it such an individual-level problem, limiting its ability to challenge the gender system

(2003). Zippel demonstrates (2006), however, that gender-neutral definitions in Germany and the EU attached to notions of dignity allow for a broader range of claims to be brought by men and members of racial or sexual minorities. Again, there can be a cost, though, in individualizing perpetrators with an overly psychological framing rather than focusing on structures of power and privilege – a cost WOASH hoped to avoid.

Also it would be too simplistic to paint WOASH as a heterosexist group. Coming a decade after the Stonewall riots and the emergence of a national gay rights movement, awareness in the greater San Francisco Bay area and on the UC Berkeley campus of the need to combat homophobia was very high. In addition to its lesbian and bisexual members, straight women in WOASH had also just been involved in defeating the Briggs Initiative, 1978's State Proposition 6, which would have banned gays and lesbians from teaching in the state's public schools (defeated in the November 7, 1978, election). Moreover, WOASH members and the entire UC Berkeley community were profoundly shaken by the murders of San Francisco Supervisor and gay rights' activist Harvey Milk and Mayor George Moscone later that same month – particularly with Moscone's eldest daughter a student on campus. Given this dramatic and painful context, it was certainly the case that all WOASH members would have identified feminism as part of a much-needed movement for the rights of sexual minorities.

Conclusion

As many student movement groups, the intense activism of WOASH was short-lived – and by the fall of 1980, when Hermassi resigned after two taxing years, it was sustained by only a remaining handful, Kim and philosophy graduate student Sally Haslanger among them. Universities are billion-dollar enterprises relying on the fact that student activists graduate and leave campus within several years' time. This paper, however, has served to restore the (nearly lost) history and legacy of WOASH and to underscore the significance of local grassroots groups to broader second-wave feminist gains. Even with the short-lived tenure of WOASH and the internal conflicts among members, WOASH contributed to the widespread diffusion of feminism itself (Blum and Mickey 2018). It was a part of the proliferation of second-wave activist groups and women's communities at the end of an era, poised just before the Reagan landslide and the years of conservative backlash that ultimately shifted even UC Berkeley's student government.[95] Although cases on other campuses, particularly Yale, helped to get the term sexual harassment widely recognized, arguably one of the many contributions of WOASH was its carving out space on college campuses for similar feminist activist groups to form.

Another key success of the group was drawing attention to the systemic problem of sexual harassment. Through its press conferences, campus demonstrations, written circulars, outreach to other student groups and community members, and its campus forum, WOASH promoted widespread awareness and changed perceptions of what had been seen as normal or trivial "flirting gone wrong" (Zippel 2006). WOASH members strategically used the specific case of Hermassi to draw attention to the pervasiveness of the problem and the insidious way it denied women access to equal educational opportunities. While the press tended to sensationalize the Hermassi case and, at times, discredit the women complainants and WOASH, most coverage still drew attention to the serious ongoing struggle over the issue.

WOASH also drew attention to the ubiquitous nature of sexual harassment by linking campus and workplace harassment. Although never as fully realized as WOASH members may have wished, the group continued outreach and attempted alliance-building with working women throughout its heyday. Law and government bureaucracy build a sharp distinction between discrimination in education and in employment; however, feminist activists instead may benefit from emphasizing the similarities in gendered organizational structures. Taking a gendered organization approach reveals that sexual harassment continues to be a normative experience for women, as women across divergent institutional locations experience gendered power relations. Yet as policies increasingly frame sexual harassment as an individual-level problem, and research increasingly stems from organizational psychology, the history of WOASH is instructive. WOASH members drew upon the frameworks established in workplace struggles to continually emphasize the institutional context and the need for solidarity with women workers.

In addition to the legacy left by WOASH on the Berkeley community and the feminist movement against sexual harassment, the group also left its mark on its women members. More than a few remain dedicated to feminist issues through their work: in teaching, research, mentorship, and activism, whether in academia, law, or the non-profit or policymaking arena. As mentioned, the legacy of WOASH was nearly lost until 2013, when current Berkeley students involved in their own case and forming the national group, "End Rape on Campus," found inspiration in discovering WOASH in the archives of the *Daily Californian* and tracked down its former leaders.

Much has changed, of course, with the two movements separated by over three decades and targeting seemingly separate issues. At the same time, sadly, far less has changed than we in WOASH might have hoped, and these two instances of grassroots feminism are linked by the continuum of gender violence that persists on college campuses. Students enrolled in colleges across the country continue to protest the inadequate responses of their institutions to complaints of sexual violence, although now the focus has shifted to include peer-to-peer violence and sexual assault, along with newly visible issues such as recognition of transgender students. Several WOASH members have since worked with the anti-sexual assault movement at Berkeley, writing a supporting letter to accompany the current Title IX complaint and speaking on professional panels with leaders of End Rape on Campus. In this sense, the mission and legacy of WOASH continues to unfold, as different generations of feminists, linked by their grassroots efforts, work together to ensure equal opportunities for women and to protest gender violence.

Notes

1 But see Baker 2008, who in addition to emphasizing the original activism of blue-collar women, women of color, and their unions against sexual harassment, also attends to campus activism. Other scholarship on sexual harassment has been primarily in feminist legal theory.

2 As such, in this paper we use the terms "gender-based violence" and "sexual violence" interchangeably. Gender-based violence refers to violence that targets individuals or groups on the basis of their gender or gender expression, and, although not all gender-based violence is sexual in nature, sexual harassment clearly is (see Amnesty International 2004).

3 To Members of the Sociology Faculty, March 15, 1979, Box 1.8. Please note that all such references throughout this paper refer to box and folder location in the WOASH Archive, Schlesinger Library, Radcliffe Institute for Advanced Study, Harvard University, Cambridge, MA.

4 WOASH Brochure 5–6, Box 1.4.

5 WOASH relied from the start on the campus survey conducted by member Donna Benson. She found that, of 269 senior women randomly sampled, nearly 20% had experienced sexual harassment (To Members of the Sociology Faculty, March 15, 1979, Box 1.8; also Benson and Thomson 1979, Box 2.11). Some

archival documents state that the survey was based on 400 responses, but this was the total distributed; 269 were returned, for a 65% response rate. Benson consulted with faculty from the statistics department and African American Studies (ibid., Box 1.8) and later published the survey in the journal *Social Problems* (Benson and Thomson 1982).

6 Statement of WOASH 1, stapled within press packet, August 13, 1979, Box 2.1.

7 Thimann, *Daily Californian* (hereinafter *Daily Cal*) 1, September 9, 1980, Box 1.1.

8 MacKinnon assisted plaintiffs in the Yale case with other members of the New Haven Law Collective, a feminist community-based practice. She was circulating drafts of her pathbreaking book on the issue – but Baker issues a corrective, emphasizing that MacKinnon owes a large debt to women's blue-collar unions (2008, 58, 197).

9 The proportion of women, however, among full-time tenured faculty at research-intensive universities like UC Berkeley remains low. And while women have made major inroads in the humanities, social sciences, and life sciences, they remain underrepresented in mathematics, physics, computer science, and engineering.

10 The WOASH archive includes coverage of the 1977 forum against sexual harassment held by *Ms.* magazine and the founding of the New York-based Working Women United Institute (see Crittenden, *New York Times*, October 25, 1977, Box 1.2); it includes materials from the Michigan Task Force on sexual harassment (Box 2.2), the Vancouver Women's Research Center's report on sexual harassment (Box 2.5), and correspondence with the Cambridge-based Alliance Against Sexual Coercion and a similar group in Madison, Wisconsin (Box 1.2). Clippings include coverage of workplace sexual harassment in the nation's leading newspapers and news magazines (Box 1.2), though only a glimpse of TV coverage (ABC's *World News Tonight*, "Work, Women, and Sexual Harassment," February 12, 1979, Box 1.2).

11 See Box 2.6; Press Packet, August 13, 1979, Box 2.1; Baker 2008, 61–62. On the original plaintiffs, www.aclu.org/title-ix-nine?redirect=womens-rights/title-ix-nine, accessed December 2015, 2015.

12 Stern, *Synapse*, May 5, 1979, Box 1.1.

13 Lehrman, *Daily Cal*, January 1, 1980, Box 1.1.

14 Lerhman, *Berkeley Graduate*, December 1979, Box 1.1.

15 Hager, January 9, 1980, Box 1.1.

16 Box 2.12.

17 WOASH compiled press packets for each press conference, for February 1979 with results from the campus survey and excerpts from the Hermassi complaints and its correspondence with the Berkeley administration (see Box 2.1).

18 Milkman memo to Susan Hansell n.d., Box 1.1.

19 This causal order is outlined in "Agenda Orientation Mtg 10/9/79" (the start of year 2) p. 2, "History," Box 1.15, part of which reads: "Sudden change of heart late spring – we later learned this was due to the tenure decision being held up." This was also confirmed by personal communication, Ruth Milkman, January 2016.

20 October 5, 1979, Box 1.1.

21 Shoemaker, October 6, 1979, Box 1.1.

22 The UC Berkeley administration actually appointed two such half-time faculty assistants during WOASH's two-year heyday, the other the faculty assistant for affirmative action – but to many on campus including WOASH members, these positions for faculty who continued to teach and conduct research were designed to be ineffectual, to give only the appearance of compliance with the law (see Lehrman, October 23, 1979, *Daily Cal*, Box 1.1).

23 Lehrman, October 17, 1979, Box 1.1.

24 To the Editor, *Daily Cal*, February 28, 1979, Box 1.1.

25 "Sex Harassment Charged at UC," February 28, 1979, Box 1.1.

26 Miller, May 1979, "Sexual Politics on Campus," Box 1.1.

27 Reed, *San Francisco Bay Guardian*, April 6, 1979, Box 1.1; *Time*, February 4, 1980, Box 1.1.

28 Hager, April 14, 1979, Box 1.1.

29 Proposal for using the "misconduct" procedures, April 29 [1979], 3, Box 1.8.

30 "Sex-for-grades coverup claimed in Berkeley case," October 5, 1979, Box 1.1.

31 January 11, 1980, Box 1.1; also Shoemaker, *Oakland Tribune*, October 6, 1979, Box 1.1.

32 Reed, April 6, 1979, Box 1.2.

33 Hager, April 14, 1979; *Time*, February 4, 1980, Box 1.1.

34 March 7, 1979, Box 1.1.
35 Proposal for using the "misconduct" procedures, April 29 [1979], 3, Box 1.8.
36 Recent more respectful coverage of the survey findings from the Association of American Universities on sexual violence, and of the resignation of Geoffrey Marcy, a professor of astronomy at UC Berkeley (discussed below), may illustrate a shift in the tone of national media. The AAU survey, based on over 150,000 responses from students at 27 universities, found that 23% of women had been victims of sexual violence (AAU 2015). Saguy also suggests that multiple charges and cases raised against Dominique Strauss-Kahn, though unsuccessful, have shifted the tone in French coverage of sexual violence (2015).
37 Milkman n.d. memo to Susan Hansell, Box 1.1.
38 February 4, 1980, Box 1.1.
39 Statement of WOASH August 13, 1979, 2, Box 2.1; also see letters from individuals in Box 2.9.
40 Milkman personal communication, August 2015.
41 Channel 4's 6 p.m. newscast, May 1, 1980, see letters from individuals, Box 2.9.
42 Box 2.6, Box 2.10.
43 Kim, personal communication, November 2015. Also Sally Haslanger, personal communication, December 2015. Kim and Haslanger worked within student government and in stipended student-employee positions to bring these changes: Kim first in the Student Senate, then in the Student Advocate's Office; Haslanger on the Chancellor's Advisory Committee for Title IX.
44 Kim recalled, for example, that many women came to report sexual harassment when she worked in the Student Advocate's Office, "It was hard! I would cry. A lot came. It was rampant. And they did not want to file charges. It wouldn't have done any good anyway since there was no procedure. But . . . they wanted us to have the information if others came forward" (personal communication, November 2015).
45 Kim, a member of campus NOW, recalled she reached out to all the women's groups on campus while in the Student Senate; of the Berkeley Feminist Alliance she observed, they were "really, really radical" (personal communication, November 2015).
46 Suggested by Benson, "NOTES: The Clash Between . . ." 2, July 20, 1979, Box 1.15: "The radical professoriate . . . appears to be the only academic network accessible to female intellectuals . . . which explains why these women walk the right [*sic*] rope between feminism and male-defined radicalism."
47 Milkman's memo in response to undergraduate member Susan Hansell's essay on WOASH's media coverage, while respectful, also included this rejoinder: "in equating 'present feminists' with 'radical feminists' you ignore . . . the section which identifies not as radical feminists but as socialist feminists . . . WOASH in particular includes many women in the latter category" (Memo to Susan Hansell n.d., Box 1.1).
48 No such motion could be found in the archive, though there is a glimpse in the spray painting incident discussed below.
49 See typed note (Box 1.5): "I did not list men who said they would be interested to be notified about meetings, since our current policy is not to include men in our meetings." During the fall of 1979 (year 2) however, men graduate students in the Sociology department wrote a letter of support for WOASH (November 30, 1979, Box 2.9). WOASH also received support from pro-feminist men in student government and others on campus who attended the March 1979 campus forum (Box 1.5).
50 Addendum to WOASH Archive donated by Blum, December 2015.
51 See handwritten meeting agendas, Box 1.15.
52 Merle [Weiner] and Ruth [Milkman].
53 Dated May 15, 1979, Box 1.15.
54 NOTES ON WOASH FALL PLAN 1, n.d., Box 1.16.
55 Ibid., 3.
56 October 4, 1979 Press Release, Box 2.1; also Box 1.3, correspondence with ASUC; and Box 1.10, Susan French correspondence. This last corroborates that WOASH had fully cooperated with French's investigation, as had the 13 complainants.
57 *Daily Cal*, November 7, 1979, Box 1.1.
58 The spray painting incident, the BFA leaflet noted, was ignored by the campus newspaper, the *Daily Cal*, except for the one letter to the editor (BFA leaflet Box 2.9) – but it received positive coverage in the left-wing *Berkeley Barb* newspaper, quoting African American sociologist of sport Professor Harry Edwards: "It was a beautiful job . . . it should have been framed instead of painted over" (Sharpe, November 1–14, 1979, Box 1.1).

59 E.g., Office of the Student Advocate, FOR IMMEDIATE RELEASE, November 9, 1979, Box 2.9.
60 Lehrman, *Daily Cal*, November 30, 1979, Box 1.1. Ann Merrill, a student senator from the BFA, had stressed to allies several days in advance the "need to be present in force" at the meeting (on Office of the President, ASUC, letterhead, November 19, 1979, Box 1.3; identifying Ann Merrill, campaign leaflet in Box 2.8).
61 February 4, 1980, Box 1.1.
62 Lehrman, *Daily Cal*, January 8, 1980, Box 1.1; Hager, *Los Angeles Times*, January 9, 1980, Box 1.1.
63 Hager, ibid.
64 Kates, *Independent and Gazette*, January 8, 1980, Box 1.1.
65 WOASH Brochure, 6–7, Box 1.4.
66 Bowker in Kates, *Independent*, 1980, ibid.
67 Lehrman, *Daily Cal*, January 11, 1980, Box 1.1.
68 See for example on the campus climate at UC Berkeley, Turner, *New York Times*, January 24, 1980, Box 1.2, on the investigation of UC Berkeley's Boalt Hall Law School. Also Kim, personal communication, November 2015, on sit-in of economics graduate students demanding racial-ethnic diversity in faculty hiring as well as protests by the Graduate Student Assembly with Black, Chicano, and Asian students' associations.
69 June 6 handwritten notes, Box 1.15. Throughout the WOASH archive, the term "Third World" is common, whereas the contemporary preferred term may be "people of color." In contrast to the more restricted usage of "Third World" today, for WOASH it included people of color in residence in the United States, whether of Global South, US, or Global North origin. For example, student government representatives recommended that an appropriate committee to hear students' sexual harassment complaints should include "women and third world representatives" (February 6, 1980, Letterhead ASUC, letter "Dear SBPC . . ." Box 2.10). Polatnick also recalls her outreach to the campus Black Women's and Chicana caucuses, each of which offered WOASH informal support (personal communication, October 2017).
70 Wednesday, October 22 leaflet, and memo closing paragraph "A 'Show of Support' . . ." Box 1.4.
71 Brochure 3, Box 1.4.
72 Co-editor of this volume Andrea L. Press.
73 (Brochure Box 1.4.) Personal communication Blum with Anne Lawrence, Ruth Milkman, and Andrea Press (December 2015).
74 Press Release, 2, August 13, 1979, Box 2.1.
75 Press Release ibid., Price Statement, 2–3, Box 2.1.
76 Letter of Complaint, "Dear Faculty and Staff," 1, November 13, 1978, Box 1.7.
77 Ibid.
78 Ibid., 2.
79 Ignoring this potential, see e.g., Kent (2007); but see Bayard de Volo and Hall (2015, 886 and n. 21). This racist tendency is much discussed by Black feminists, Davis (1981), Richie (2012), among many.
80 Handwritten notes, October 30, Box 2.9.
81 Brochure, 3, Box 1.4.
82 Donna Benson was its undergraduate author and also author of the campus survey ("NOTES: The Clash Between . . ." July 20, 1979, Box 1.15). Ruth Milkman confirmed by personal communication, July 2015, that the margin notes and markings were hers.
83 "NOTES: The Clash Between . . ." 1, July 20, 1979, Box 1.15.
84 Ibid., 3.
85 Ibid., 2.
86 Ibid., 1, 2.
87 Ibid., 3.
88 Ibid., 1.
89 Ibid., 2.
90 Ibid., 3.
91 Ibid., 2.
92 Ibid., 3.
93 Ibid., 3.
94 Brochure 2, Box 1.4.
95 Kim, personal communication, November 2015.

References

Acker, Joan. 1990. "Hierarchies, Jobs, Bodies: A Theory of Gendered Organizations." *Gender & Society* 4(2): 139–158.

American Association of University Professors. 2014. "Survey Report Table 11: Percent of Faculty in Tenure-Track Appointments and Percent of Faculty with Tenure, by Affiliation, Academic Rank, and Gender, 2013–14." *Annual Report on the Economic Status of the Profession.* Retrieved January 5, 2016 (www.aaup.org/sites/default/files/files/2014%20salary%20report/Table11.pdf).

Amnesty International. 2004. "It's In Our Hands: Stop Violence Against Women Summary." London: Amnesty International Publications. Retrieved January 12, 2016 (http://pathssk.org/wp-content/uploads/2011/06/AI-Its-in-Our-hands.pdf).

Armstrong, Elizabeth A., Laura Hamilton, and Brian Sweeney. 2006. "Sexual Assault on Campus: A Multilevel, Integrative Approach to Party Rape." *Social Problems* 53(4): 483–499.

Association of American Universities. 2015. "AAU Campus Survey on Sexual Assault and Sexual Misconduct." Retrieved January 5, 2016 (www.aau.edu/Climate-Survey.aspx?id=16525).

Baker, Carrie N. 2008. *The Women's Movement Against Sexual Harassment.* New York: Cambridge University Press.

Bayard de Volo, Lorraine and Lynn K. Hall. 2015. "'I Wish All the Ladies Were Holes in the Road': The US Air Force Academy and the Gendered Continuum of Violence." *Signs* 40(4): 865–889.

Benson, Donna J. and Gregg E. Thomson. 1982. "Sexual Harassment on a University Campus: The Confluence of Authority Relations, Sexual Interest, and Gender Stratification." *Social Problems* 29(3): 236–251.

Blair-Loy, Mary. 2001. "It's Not Just What You Know, It's Who You Know: Technical Knowledge, Rainmaking, and Gender among Finance Executives." *Research in the Sociology of Work* 10: 51–83.

Blum, Linda M. 1991. *Between Feminism and Labor: The Significance of the Comparable Worth Movement.* Berkeley: University of California Press.

Blum, Linda M. and Ethel L. Mickey. 2018. "Women Organized Against Sexual Harassment: A Grassroots Struggle for Title IX Enforcement, 1978-1980." *Feminist Formations* 30(2): 175–201.

Boswell, Ayres A. and Joan Z. Spade. 1996. "Fraternities and Collegiate Rape Culture: Why Are Some Fraternities More Dangerous Places for Women?" *Gender & Society* 10(2): 133–147.

Breines, Wini. 2002. "What's Love Got to Do with It? White Women, Black Women, and Feminism in the Movement Years." *Signs* 27(4): 1095–1133.

Britton, Dana M. 2000. "The Epistemology of the Gendered Organization." *Gender & Society* 14(3): 418–434.

Bystydzienski, Jill M. and Sharon R. Bird. 2006. *Removing Barriers: Women in Academic Science, Technology, Engineering, and Mathematics.* Bloomington, IN: Indiana University Press.

Clark-Flory, Tracy. 2010. "Yale Fraternity Pledges Chant About Rape." *Salon*, October 15 (www.salon.com/2010/10/15/yale_fraternity_pledges_chant_about_rape/).

Crenshaw, Kimberlé. 1989. "Demarginalizing the Intersection of Race and Sex: A Black Feminist Critique of Antidiscrimination Doctrine, Feminist Theory and Antiracist Policies." *The University of Chicago Legal Forum*: 139–167.

Crossley, Alison Dahl. 2017. *Finding Feminism: Millennial Activists and the Unfinished Gender Revolution.* New York: NYU Press.

Davis, Angela Y. 1981. *Women, Race, and Class.* New York: Random House.

Dobbin, Frank and Erin L. Kelly. 2007. "How to Stop Harassment: Professional Construction of Legal Compliance in Organizations." *American Journal of Sociology* 112(4): 1203–1243.

Dziech, Billie Wright and Linda Weiner. [1984] 1990. *The Lecherous Professor: Sexual Harassment on Campus.* Urbana, IL: University of Illinois Press.

Farley, Lin. 1978. *Sexual Shakedown: The Sexual Harassment of Women on the Job.* New York: McGraw-Hill.

Foderaro, Lisa W. 2011. "At Yale, Sharper Look at Treatment of Women." *The New York Times*, April 7 (www.nytimes.com/2011/04/08/nyregion/08yale.html?_r=0).

Gilmore, Leigh. 2017. *Tainted Witness: Why We Doubt What Women Say About Their Lives.* New York: Columbia University Press.

Golgowski, Nina. 2015. "University of California Berkeley, Regents, Sued by Sexual Assault Survivors." *New York Daily News*, July 1. Retrieved January 5, 2016 (www.nydailynews.com/news/national/uc-berkeley-regents-sued-sexual-assault-survivors-article-1.2277970).

Gruber, James. 1992. "A Typology of Personal and Environmental Sexual Harassment: Research and Policy Implications for the 1990s." *Sex Roles* 26(11–12): 447–464.

Hansen, Karen V. 1990. "Women's Unions and the Search for Political Identity." Pp. 213–238 in *Women, Class and the Feminist Imagination*, edited by Karen V. Hansen and Ilene J. Philipson. Philadelphia: Temple University Press.

Hartmann, Heidi I. 1979. "The Unhappy Marriage of Marxism and Feminism: Towards a More Progressive Union." *Capital & Class* 3(2): 1–33.

Kanter, Rosabeth Moss. 1977. *Men and Women of the Corporation.* New York: BasicBooks.

Kelly, Erin L. and Frank Dobbin. 1998. "How Affirmative Action Became Diversity Management: Employer Response to Anti-discrimination Law, 1961–1996." *American Behavioral Scientist* 41(7): 960–984.

Kent, Tara E. 2007. "The Confluence of Race and Gender in Women's Sexual Harassment Experiences." Pp. 172–180 in *Gender Violence: Interdisciplinary Perspectives* (2nd Edition), edited by L.L. O'Toole, J.R. Schiffman and M.L.K. Edwards. New York: New York University Press.

Kingkade, Tyler. 2015. "106 Colleges Are Under Federal Investigation for Sexual Assault Cases." *The Huffington Post*, April 4. (www.huffingtonpost.com/2015/04/06/colleges-federal-investigation-title-ix-106_n_7011422.html).

Macht, Joshua. 2013. "Running Out of TIME: The Slow, Sad Demise of a Great American Magazine." *The Atlantic*, April 5. Retrieved January 5, 2016 (www.theatlantic.com/business/archive/2013/04/running-out-of-time-the-slow-sad-demise-of-a-great-american-magazine/274713/).

MacKinnon, Catharine A. 1979. *Sexual Harassment of Working Women: A Case of Sex Discrimination.* New Haven, CT: Yale University Press.

Milkman, Ruth. 2017. "A New Political Generation: Millennials and the Post-2008 Wave of Protest." *American Sociological Review* 82(1): 1–31.

Morgan, Phoebe and James E. Gruber. 2011. "Sexual Harassment: Violence against Women at Work and in Schools." Pp. 75–92 in *Sourcebook on Violence against Women* (2nd Edition), edited by C.M. Renzetti, J.L. Edleson and R.K. Bergen. Thousand Oaks, CA: Sage.

National Academies. 2007. *Beyond Bias and Barriers: Fulfilling the Potential of Women in Academic Science and Engineering.* Washington, DC: National Academies Press.

National Center for Education Statistics. 2015. "Digest of Education Statistics: Table 318.10, Degrees Conferred by Postsecondary Institutions, by Level of Degree and Sex of Student: Selected Years 1869–70 Through 2024–25." Retrieved November 3, 2015 (http://nces.ed.gov/programs/digest/d14/tables/dt14_318.10.asp?current=yes).

O'Toole, Laura L., Jessica R. Schiffman and Margie L.K. Edwards. 2007. "Sexual Harassment." Pp. 133–140 in *Gender Violence: Interdisciplinary Perspectives* (2nd Edition), edited by L.L. O'Toole, J.R. Schiffman and M.L.K. Edwards. New York: New York University Press.

Overbye, Dennis. 2015. "Geoffrey Marcy to Resign from Berkeley Astronomy Department." *The New York Times*, October 14. Retrieved November 4, 2015 (www.nytimes.com/2015/10/15/science/geoffrey-marcy-to-resign-from-berkeley-astronomy-department.html).

Page, Melanie C., Lucy E. Bailey and Jean van Delinder. 2009. "The Blue Blazer Club: Masculine Hegemony in Science, Technology, Engineering, and Math Fields." *Forum on Public Policy Online* 2: 23–46.

Press, Andrea and Francesca Tripodi. 2014a. "What We Found While Lurking on an Anonymous College Message Board for Two Years." *Slate*, June 5. Retrieved January 5, 2016 (www.slate.com/blogs/xx_factor/2014/06/05/sexism_on_college_campuses_what_we_found_lurking_on_college_acb_at_a_large.html).

———. 2014b. "The New Misogyny." *The Chronicle of Higher Education*, July 2. Retrieved September 15 (http://chronicle.com/blogs/conversation/2014/07/02/the-new-misogyny/).

Quina, Kathryn. 1990. "The Victimization of Women." Pp. XX in *Ivory Power: Sexual Harassment on Campus*, edited by M.A. Paludi. Albany, NY: State University of New York Press.

Reger, Jo. 2012. *Everywhere and Nowhere: Contemporary Feminism in the United States.* New York: Oxford University Press.

Richie, Beth E. 2012. *Arrested Justice: Black Women, Violence, and America's Prison Nation.* New York: New York University Press.

Saguy, Abigail. 2003. *What Is Sexual Harassment? From Capitol Hill to the Sorbonne.* Berkeley, CA: University of California Press.

———. 2015. "Sexual Harassment in the Social World." Paper in invited session at the Annual Meeting of the American Sociological Association, August 23, Chicago, IL.

Valian, Virgina. 1998. *Why So Slow? The Advancement of Women.* Cambridge, MA: The MIT Press.

Welsh, Sandy, Myrna Dawson and Annette Nierobisz. 2002. "Legal Factors, Extra-Legal Factors, or Changes in the Law? Using Criminal Justice to Understand the Resolution of Sexual Harassment Complaints." *Social Problems* 49(4): 605–623.

Williams, Christine L. 1998. "Sexual Harassment in Organizations: A Critique of Current Research and Policy." *Sexuality & Culture* 1: 19–43.

Wise, Sue and Liz Stanley. 1987. *Georgie Porgie: Sexual Harassment in Everyday Life*. London: Pandora.

Yoder, Janice. 1991. "Rethinking Tokenism: Looking Beyond Numbers." *Gender & Society* 5(2): 178–192.

Zippel, Kathrin. 2006. *The Politics of Sexual Harassment: A Comparative Study of the United States, the European Union, and Germany*. Cambridge, UK: Cambridge University Press.

Appendix

WOASH timeline 1978–1980 and after

First Academic Year 1978–1979	
November 1978	WOASH forms to advocate on behalf of 6 students who have signed complaints against sociology professor Elbaki Hermassi, as well as to raise awareness and establish a grievance procedure for student complaints.
December 1978	WOASH reps meet with sociology department chair and ad hoc faculty committee representative. Hermassi reprimanded at department level.
January 1979	WOASH reps begin a series of 5 meetings with Provost and University Attorney to establish formal grievance procedure.
February 26, 1979	Having reached impasse, WOASH files Title IX complaint. First press conference held in San Francisco to address the university's failure to appoint a Title IX officer or to establish a procedure. WOASH reveals that they have signed complaints against a professor, but they do not release Hermassi's name.
February 27, 1979	*The Daily Cal*, reporting on the WOASH press conference, releases Hermassi's name. The University administration abruptly stops communication or negotiation with WOASH.
March 1, 1979	Campus forum on sexual harassment attracts 300 to 400 hundred students, staff, and community members.
Spring 1979	A faculty committee refuses to move forward with Hermassi's tenure review. Vice Chancellor Heyman appoints Susan French (UC Davis Law School) to "confidentially" investigate 13 signed complaints against Hermassi. WOASH decides to cooperate fully.
June 1979	Susan French submits confidential report to Chancellor Bowker. WOASH cannot see the report.
Late July 1979	French meets with WOASH to describe her findings, including her recommendation for an administrative hearing seeking Hermassi's termination.

July 12, 1979	the Office of Civil Rights determines that sexual harassment constitutes sex discrimination and decides to investigate the complaints filed by WOASH in February.
Summer 1979	The university administration again resumes ongoing meetings with WOASH reps about a formal grievance procedure.
August 13, 1979	Second press conference announcing the Office of Civil Rights' positive (July 12) response to WOASH and WOASH's support for Pamela Price's appeal of the negative decision in her case against Yale.
Second Academic Year 1979–1980	
October 4, 1979	WOASH releases their knowledge of the contents of the still-confidential French report to the press and accuses the administration of making a secret deal with Hermassi.
October 18, 1979	Picketing and sit-in at California Hall to protest the administration's cover up.
Early November 1979	Spray painting of feminist slogans and graphics on the office doors of several senior sociology faculty members.
November 30, 1979	ASUC Berkeley Senate passes resolution demanding the release of French report.
January 7, 1980	Chancellor Bowker releases his decision to suspend Hermassi for one-quarter without pay, and to include the French report in his personnel record. His decision includes no hearing for the complainants.
January 10, 1980	WOASH pickets California Hall to protest Chancellor Bowker's decision. Crowd of 150 reported at demonstration.
February 4, 1980	*Time magazine* publishes its coverage of WOASH and the January demonstration.
Third Academic Year 1980–1981 and Beyond	
September 1980	Ray Colvig, UC Public Affairs Officer, confirms high-level rumor that Hermassi resigned and accepted a position in Tunisia.
October 22, 1980	WOASH rally in support of two Black women employees dismissed by the university after they accused their white male supervisor of sexual harassment.
Later that year AY	University appoints Carol Christ, Professor of English, as its first Title IX officer and the Chancellor's Advisory Committee on Title IX continues to meet (at least through **1984**), but according to informal interview with Marlene Kim (confirmed also by Sally Haslanger), "we butted heads [with the administration] a lot."
Summer 1981	Haslanger works as research assistant for the Chancellor's Advisory Committee on Title IX, reporting on sexual harassment grievance procedures, "I [also] summarized what other policies on gender equity there had been at UCB, what policies other reports had recommended be instituted, and what had come of those recommendations. I recall that most of them had not been implemented" (personal communication December 2015).
March 1986	University of California System-wide policy adopted on Sexual Harassment and Complaint Resolution Procedures covering all employees and students.

17

Online feminism

Global phenomenon, local perspective (on ASPEKT organization and online feminism in Czechoslovak context)

Vanda Černohorská

Introduction

"Thank you for leaving all your good advice at the door." This is a motto one would encounter upon entering the premises of ASPEKT, the oldest feminist organization in Slovakia, founded in 1993 a few years after the fall of the Communist regime. The motto, being half playful and half serious, refers to ASPEKT's early history when the organization's projects and initiatives expanded outside the region and the members started to cooperate with foreign feminist organizations and activists. While most of them approached ASPEKT with open arms and minds aiming toward cooperation and mutual enrichment, some feminists came with ready-made suggestions that were well-intended but didn't really reflect the specific historical and cultural experiences of Slovak and Czech feminism. ASPEKT members' response to such advice was that they too strive for gender equality, but their strategies, projects, and tools are distinctive and unique. In another words, that all those coming should leave their "good advice" at the door. This emphasis on autonomy, uniqueness, and specific context is something ASPEKT cherishes to this day, and it is also deeply embedded in a way the organization approaches digital technologies and new media, a global phenomenon that significantly influenced the way social movements, organizations, and activists operate. This chapter adopts a similar approach and focuses on the relation between two global forces – digital technologies and feminism – through a local and historically specific perspective.

With emerging literature covering the impact of new media and digital technologies on the character of contemporary society, there is a growing concern regarding "how to give voice to small-scale or marginalized groups that tend to be ignored in academic generalization centred on the metropolitan West" (Horst and Miller 2012, 20). Most of the scholars covering the issue of new media activism and digital technologies have been avoiding Central and Eastern Europe, so my aspiration is to bring more academic attention into the region. As I argue, if we aim to understand the role new media play in the present and the future of feminism, it is crucial that we try to do so through exploring the specific local context and its historical development. Such a premise is essential not only when talking about new technologies but also when reflecting on the state of the movement itself. In this chapter I focus on these two global issues – digital technologies and feminism – through an approach locally grounded in the Central European perspective. Drawing on the case study of ASPEKT, one of the most prominent feminist organizations in the region, I aim to illustrate how specific historical and sociopolitical background influences the ways in which they use these new digital tools and media platforms. Subsequently, I argue that only when trying to understand what these tools mean to feminists in different corners of the globe will we fully understand their role in the future of this movement.

First, I provide an overview of sociological and feminist understanding of the role and potential benefits of digital technologies. Next, I examine the recent history of the Central European region and the ASPEKT organization with a focus on the evolution of feminist ideas after the fall of Communism. In the second part of the chapter, I discuss the key topics and themes that emerged within the case study in relation to new media and digital technologies. In the concluding part, I discuss the sustainability of these new forms of online activism. Overall, my goal is to draw attention to the idea that even though digital technologies are a global phenomenon which – organizationally and symbolically speaking – transcend time and space, the way we approach them, and the meaning and potential we ascribe to them, is local and specific. Like feminism itself, digital technologies are aimed not toward homogeneity and linear evolution but to greater plurality and development based on historical and cultural context. In other words, there is no single or right way to approach digital technologies and/or how to be a feminist. Both depend to a large extent on the current sociopolitical conditions and cultural and historical background.

Developing the approach to analysis

With the massive growth in digital technologies over the past decades, scholars are reflecting on the growing importance of these new platforms and technologies for various activists, social movements, and the ways they promote and pursue their shared goals and values (Harcourt 1999; Elliott and Urry 2010; Bredl, Hünninger, and Jensen 2014). While some of the classics from the fields of sociology and media studies express their concerns that digital tools and new media in general increase levels of social isolation or weaken existing communities (Putnam 2001), others highlight their potential to revitalize social relations and the civil sphere (e.g., Rheingold 1993, 2002, 2012; Castells 1996, 1997, 1998, 2001, 2009, 2012). Those authors, who approach the internet and related technologies from a rather optimistic perspective, talk about promotion of democratic involvement among citizens and easier establishing of interest groups and alliances of activists – tendencies that are often put in contrast with declining party membership and electoral turnouts (Webster 2001; Bennett 2008; Chadwick and Howard 2009; Desai 2013). With the growing number of online platforms and the broadening of possibilities for various online activities, there is an increasing amount of scholarly work concerning digital technology–related activism, ranging from the Zapatista movement in Latin America (Burch 2002) to the Occupy movement in the United States (Fuchs 2014) to the protesters in Tahrir Square (Alexander 2011). The scope of interest is far from limited to that of new media as a catalyst for radical protest and social change, but it remains one of the most prevalent types of academic endeavor in recent years (e.g., Fuchs 2014; Gerbaudo 2012).

The ongoing discussion about the role of new media and digital technologies in the life of contemporary social movements and individual organizations is also tightly connected to the debates about the state of contemporary feminism. There are several narratives that have been shaping the public and academic discourse. One of the most widely articulated and repeated is the story about the gradual death of the movement and the ideas it promotes. "Feminism is pronounced 'dead' on a regular basis, especially by anti-feminist commentators eager to ram the final nail into the coffin, but also, sometimes by established feminists" (Redfern and Aune 2010, 1). Such negative backlash is nothing new. Rather it is a recurring phenomenon which has been shaping both the public perception of, and personal attitudes toward, the feminist movement during the past decades (Faludi 2006). Furthermore, there are ongoing voices that constructively question whether the way we conceptualize and think about the feminist movement and ideas is still relevant and valid (Tasker and Negra 2007). While some theorists approach this discussion as a sign that feminism in its traditional sense "is no longer needed, it is a spent force" and therefore will be replaced by a "repertoire of new meanings" (McRobbie 2004, 255), others suggest that the term "need not imply the demise or redundancy of feminism [. . .] [and see] the post as 'coming after,' without necessarily meaning that the earlier versions of feminism have been superseded or killed off" (Robinson 2009, 9).

Clearly, those types of discussions spanning from mainstream media through the academic circles to the public discourses reflect the fact that feminist theory, politics, and the very concrete ways in which the contemporary movement works toward gender equality have been transformed significantly under the influence of changing social, political, and (last but not least) technological circumstances (Nazneen and Sultan 2014). However, it is by no means an indication that feminism would be dead, irrelevant, or obsolete. While briefly overlooking the eruption of voices all over the online sphere, amplifying feminist-conscious ideas in an innovative and creative ways during the past two decades, feminist authors are claiming that the movement is "alive and kicking" (Thornham and Weissmann 2013, 1). Many believe new media and digital technologies have introduced significant changes into civil society and feminist activists are using these new platforms and tools in great numbers (Dobson 2015). "Through different channels and for different reasons, women have harnessed the creative, social, communicative, political, cultural, and economic potential of the Web in many different ways" (Youngs 2007, 6). Those voices and projects are very diverse and in many cases different from what was traditionally labeled as part of the feminist movement, but that does not reduce their range of influence – quite the contrary. Thus the potential benefits of feminist engagement with new digital technologies – or in other words, the question of online feminism – has attracted significant attention among theorists from various corners of the academia (Wolmark 2003). Some theorists go even further and argue that forming new pro-feminist communities within cyberspace could be a successful strategy for utilizing the potential of new technologies in the revitalization of the consciousness-raising tradition. As Gillis, Howie, and Mumford point out:

> the communication technologies of cyberspace are regarded as the opportunity needed to bring about the global feminist movements of the new millennium, the third wave of feminism. The Internet is thus vaunted as the global consciousness-raising tool which the first and second waves lacked.
>
> *(Gillis, Howie, and Mumford 2004, 185)*

Within these theoretical discussions, the potential of digital technologies and new media is seen as a revival of a once vivid practice. The presence of feminist activists within the cyberspace is used as an argument for the movement's currentness and well-being. So in this context, the use of new media by feminist activists is seen not only as a mere reaction to the changing technological environment but also as a chance to disrupt the mainstream anti-feminist discourse that is partially produced by mass media.

In reaction to the growing number of feminist voices in the online sphere, more and more authors are trying to ascertain the specific impact of new media and digital technologies on the lives of women and girls (Harcourt 1999) but also on the feminist and women-oriented organizations across the globe (e.g., Edwards 2004). In most such studies, digital technologies or (broadly said) new media[1] are being treated as a global force, which has the potential to transform things on the transnational but also the local level and affect organizations' politics and matters that are deeply personal to people's lives. In a similar respect, feminism is also a transnational force that influences local policies and personal matters. However, to fully understand its complexity, one has to approach this global issue through its specific local context and histories. As Youngs points out, "[r]ecognition of the materiality of feminism – that is concrete social and geographical attachments and particularities – is implicit in any critical reflection on Western feminist knowledge and principles" (Youngs 1999, 56). The same perspective is necessary when it comes to theorizing digital technologies. Obviously, digital technologies and new media are helping us to overcome geographical distances and reach out to people in different cultural contexts. They create communities, Habermasian public space, and to some extent transform the social movements that are using them (Castells 2012). But how we approach, use, and make sense of them remains (in a similar manner as when we talk about feminism) distinct and unique based on our position in and experience with the social world. Feminism too is a global and uniting concept shared by all those who strive for gender equality across different historical periods and cultural contexts. However, to ignore distinct specificities such as varying goals or strategies deriving from different experiences and contexts as something insignificant in relation to the general concept of feminism would mean to overlook the most crucial aspect of feminism: its diversity and heterogeneity. If we don't account for these differences, we might find ourselves overlooking or even misinterpreting the original, creative, and subversive ways feminists use digital technologies to promote gender equality.

Introducing the ASPEKT organization

The following case study focuses on the Central European region and on one of its oldest and the most well-known feminist organizations, called ASPEKT. As I argue, it helps to demonstrate not only the potential of digital technologies and new media for feminism as a political movement and desirable personal endeavor but also the challenges feminists face in the online sphere. As for the methodology, I keep in mind that "[n]ew digital scenario challenges, in a very radical way, the standard research practices within the social sciences, bringing an unprecedented rate of innovation [. . .] and an exceptional data availability" (Bredl, Hünniger, and Jensen 2014, 6). I therefore combine a qualitative content analysis of the easily accessible archive with published documents, transcribed interviews,[2] articles, annual reports, and the like with a virtual (or digital) ethnography approach (Pink at al. 2016). I believe that the specific ways we approach new media are relevant for the ways we relate to technology, community, and one another. "Ethnography can therefore be used to develop an enriched sense of the meanings of the technology and the cultures which enable it and are enabled by it" (Hine 2000, 8). Rather than approaching new media and digital technologies as mechanical tools, I see it as a cultural artifact or product of culture in itself. With new media and digital technologies having certain interpretative flexibility, I conceptualize the ideas about their sensible use as being developed in a context – in this case, in a feminist, post-socialist, and distinctively Central European context.

ASPEKT was founded in 1993 and was the first feminist organization to form in Slovakia after the Velvet Revolution. It has had significance for the feminist movement in both the Czech Republic and Slovakia during the so-called transition period and has been an active advocate of gender equality for more than two decades. In that time it has organized a number of conferences and educational seminars and has performed analysis and expert consultations in various areas such as gender-sensitive education and the gender pay gap in the region. ASPEKT is also notable for its publications, having issuing more than 100 fiction and nonfiction books by women authors, feminist theory, and educational books. Moreover, in the period 1993–2004 it produced 21 issues of a feminist print journal while covering feminism-related topics and providing its readership with substantial analysis, reports, and comments from the field of women and gender studies. Since ASPEKT started by promoting gender equality in the "offline world" and then expanded into the digital sphere, it provides an opportunity to study the organization in both settings. Notably, ASPEKT explicitly adopts the idea that new media is a potentially subversive arena where one can deconstruct the hegemonic patterns presented in mainstream discourse. As it states on its website:

> Publishing the webzine proves the idea that the Internet is a vital medium for opinions that don't follow the mainstream. [Via new media, one can publish] dramas, fiction, outraged commentaries, interesting news; [. . .] [and draw] attention to good authors and artists and bad advertisements, too."[3]

The organization embraces the idea that digital technologies change the top-down flow of information and emphasizes its organizational advantages, such as the ability to react promptly and flexibly on contemporary issues.

As stated by its founders in 1993, ASPEKT "was and still is one of the constitutive points of the feminist and gender-oriented thinking in Slovakia but also of civil activism and networking of nongovernmental organizations in all the relevant topics regarding the feminist and gender-oriented discourse" (Cviková and Juráňová 2009, 24–25). The historical and geographical circumstances of its origin are more than significant for the character and future development of the organization and its supporters. After the Velvet Revolution in 1989, Slovak (and Czech) society was at the beginning of the so-called transition period, meaning that the region was going through a transition from a communist to democratic political, social, and economic establishment. The most important changes included the opening of the borders, implementation of the free market, changes within the political sphere, and the awakening of the civil society (Berglund, Ekman, Deegan-Krause, and Knutsen 2013). The foundation of the ASPEKT organization was therefore enabled and formed by the actual "changing environment" but it also reacted to the gender relations and inequalities in the pre-1989 society. Theorists focusing on women's position and representation in the so-called Marxist discourse point out that the socialist, pre-1989 worldview, as applied within the Central-Eastern European countries, was a mixture of two components (Saurer, Lanzinger, and Frysak 2006). On the one hand, there was the populist-egalitarian strand, which underlined the equal involvement of women and men in paid work. On the other hand, the communist propaganda played on the nationalist strand that constantly referred to women's sense of loyalty to the nation. As Tatiana Kotzeva puts it: "The image of a socialist woman was elaborated to reinforce the unique mission of woman to sacrifice herself in order to assist in the establishment and further development of the system towards a 'shining future'" (Kotzeva in Corrin 1999, 85). Therefore, one might recognize quite a schizophrenic relationship that the communist party maintained toward its female comrades. While calling for equality, the communist regime attempted to erase gender in the same way it rejected ethnicity or class. Thus, the term "equality" became a hackneyed phrase on handbills, banners, and in official speeches that didn't reflect the actual conditions of everyday women's and men's lives (Kotzeva 1999). But despite the "equality" rhetoric, women also presented a specific object of state policy that, through authorized offices, cared about women's concerns – especially about fulfilling their "natural" role as mothers and caretakers.

Similar sentiment is repeatedly present in *Feminisms for Beginners*[4] (Cviková and Juráňová 2009), a collection of round table discussions between ASPEKT founding members and other important figures related to the feminist movement in Slovakia, part of a project that commemorates the 20th anniversary of the Velvet Revolution. The textual collage, which contains transcribed discussions but also the most significant texts published by the ASPEKT organization in the last two decades, aims to capture the history of the beginnings of feminist and gender discourse in Slovakia. However, it not only summarizes themes that were present in the then public discussion, but it also reveals personal stories and insights that give us a more detailed and rich picture about the transition period in relation to gender and feminist issues.[5] So as mentioned earlier, the very concept of gender and feminist consciousness was rather absent in the public discussion during the communist period. "*Feminism* in general terms (always in the singular and contrary to its actual left-oriented modern history) was presented by official propaganda as 'bourgeois ideology,' which had nothing to say to 'socialist' women" (Šmejkalová 2004, 169, italics in the original). The founders of ASPEKT were well aware of the "heritage" of the communist era and therefore decided to became the first (in the Czechoslovakia region) "interest association of women, who agreed it was time to take the discourse on equality and democracy seriously and apply it to the lived realities of the people of feminine gender in Slovakia."[6]

The trouble with feminism (in post-communist Central Europe)

After 1989, the transition had begun and the trends toward democracy and pluralism affected every single aspect of society and the day-to-day lives of its citizens; though the change was quite different for men and women. The new market-driven system, where the totalitarian party lost its control over the state economy and legacy, required major reforms and the development of new institutions. The former communist countries approached new globalized spheres such as international trade and intercultural arenas and started to cooperate with new political agents like the EU. Many academics analyzing the transition talk about an overall atmosphere of optimism and the high expectations that marked the period (see, e.g., Štulhofer and Sandford 2005; for the non-Czechoslovak context, see Matynia 2010, Sundstrom 2010). The beginnings of the organization were to a large extent influenced by such an enthusiastic climate. The participants and supporters of feminism were (after many years) allowed to openly discuss and express their ideas about the issues of gender equality. But oddly enough, their newfound feminist consciousness was not welcomed with support and understanding (True 2003; Sauer, Lanzinger, and Frysak 2006). After 1989, the public was sometimes compared to the "Sleeping Beauty" character that was just slowly waking up after many years in limbo. In this process of awakening, a few moments were particularly significant for the future development of the society. One of these was the role of mainstream media, namely Czechoslovak television, and its so-called round tables that brought together prominent thinkers, experts, and people that were (until this time) part of the underground opposition. Because of the reach of this type of media, the broader public could get a sense of the new topics and challenges in the post-communist society but also form opinions about the figures involved in these new struggles. These TV series played so prominent a role in this transformation period that it is sometimes called "the television revolution" (Cviková and Juráňová 2009, 16). However, if looking solely at those TV series, women had no leading roles in this spectacle. As ASPEKT founders stress in their discussions after 20 years, not only were most of the round table participants men, but this apparent gender imbalance didn't spark any negative attention. Such a lack of feminist awareness was the very paradoxical heritage of the intense socialist "emancipation" of women.[7] But there were other issues as well. The so-called awakened revolutionary spirit of November 1989 quickly faded away and civil society was dealing with rising intense nationalism, mainly between the years 1993 and 1998. As Ballentine points out, "Slovakia was experiencing difficulty in achieving democratic consolidation, with the government of Vladimír Mečiar increasingly hostile to political and media pluralism" (Ballentine in Mendelson, Glenn 2002, 93). Regrettably, many of those who were actively opposing the nationalist and undemocratic tendencies were at the same time openly unsupportive of the newly founded feminist organization, claiming that they were fragmenting the opposition powers. While feminists around ASPEKT considered themselves part of the anti-nationalist movement, they refused to settle for a concept of democracy that excluded gender equality (Cviková and Juráňová 2009).

In the first years of its existence, the organization focused on the publication of the aforementioned journal but also devoted significant energy to organizing events such as literary evenings, public discussions, and seminars. The diverse and creative mixture of events and meetings was to a large extent enabled by the specific type of funding that ASPEKT received in its early years. Offering long-term-oriented, large but also multidimensional grants whose main goal was to improve networking and cooperation among women's organizations, the Frauenanstiftung organization (associated with the Heinrich Böll Foundation of the German Green Party) was supporting feminist-related endeavors in many post-socialist countries.[8] As James Richter, who has been researching the involvement of Western actors and their assistance to Russian women's organizations during the transition period, claims "[u]nlike most other donors, [. . .] the Frauenanstiftung sponsors conferences and exchanges designed to keep its beneficiaries in touch with each other" and ensures that "its grant recipients feel like partners in a common enterprise" (Richter 2002, 66). Given the fact that the Communist Party supressed any gender equality-related activities that were not orchestrated by the regime and that post-1989 civil society was rather hostile toward newly introduced feminist ideas, ASPEKT members were seeking not only practical experiences and funding but also genuine support, encouragement, and equal partnership. Thanks to the type of assistance they received early on, they were able to carry out projects and events that they personally found meaningful and necessary for the successful development of a fair and just democratic society. So while Richter mentions in his research the importance of Western assistance for overcoming organizational weaknesses, inexperience, and isolation among women's organizations in Russia (Richter 2002, 54–90), ASPEKT members rather talk about the power of trust, independence, and mutually beneficial dialogue that they chose to express. They do this playfully, through the already mentioned motto on the wall in their office: "Thank you for leaving all your good advice at the door." Within the ensuing years of the early 2000s, ASPEKT started to take part in various educational and research projects that were in many cases based on international cooperation between various organizations from different countries.[9] As the organization grew, thanks to international funding, it launched diverse projects that were not limited just to Slovakia and contiguous states but reached far beyond the Central and Eastern European region. Such transnational cooperation requires intense and flexible communication that was to a large extent enabled by digital technologies that were gradually becoming accessible and commonly used by most of the organizations in the nongovernmental sector.

To be (or not to be) remembered

As outlined in the previous section, both the region's and ASPEKT's own history played significant role in the way the organization approaches the issues related to gender equality and strategies it has been using ever since its founding days. Moreover, ASPEKT's affinity to its history and past achievements clearly shapes the way the organization is currently approaching new technological opportunities. While scholars tend to perceive the issue of digital technologies and new media as something future-oriented (Blair, Gajjala, and Tulley 2009), the notion of history and preservation of one's legacy was equally important to most ASPEKT members:

> We are trying to conserve the old web pages like an archive [. . .] and that's really useful for people who would like to come back to it. For example, when students are working on their final papers or other stuff on various topics, they'll find lots of things on ASPEKT's web page [. . .]. Also one can see – through all the invitations and information about certain events – what happened during all those years, which topics were being discussed not only by ASPEKT but also by other organizations as we've always shared other events.
>
> *(Zuzana Maďarová 2015)*[10]

Clearly, there is an explicit perception of new media and digital technologies as a tool that helps organizations to preserve the organization's history more easily and effectively then if they would store it in a physical library. As Zuzana Maďarová, who administers the ASPEKT's website, points out, it is not only about having everything neatly archived; it also needs to be accessible to the broader public. Jana Cviková, one of the founding members of the organization, agrees with her while admitting there is still more work to be done.

> [A]s it turned out, it really is not possible "the paper way" but also, it's not accessible [. . .]. So we did things such as when it was 10 years' anniversary of the ASPEKT, we did [the digitalization] [. . .] but at the end, that there is just a torso of the history on the web [. . .]. There was always so much work to do that we have never had the chance to come back to it.
>
> *(Jana Cviková 2015)*

In the 1990s, ASPEKT was – in terms of writing and publishing – focusing on translation of classic feminist texts, creating original theoretical essays, or elaborate comments that were published either as books or in a monthly journal. But in 2003 they moved from the printed journal to an online webzine. On the one hand, this change was driven by obvious financial circumstances. However, the transition helped the organization to become more open and accessible to potential readers and more inclusive to potential writers as ASPEKT encouraged the younger generation to join in with comments and essays through open online-distributed calls. It also led to a greater diversification of voices and initiatives. The mainstream print industry has been declining over the past decade, but as Zeisler points out, that is not necessarily bad news for feminist media: "Mainstream print outlets [. . .] have contributed a lot to the media landscape, but they have also been, historically, spaces showcasing a limited range of opinion and voices" (Zeisler 2013, 178). Online feminist platforms, therefore, provide space in which alternative voices can be articulated.

The desire to not only be heard but also remembered is, however, about so much more than digitalization and cataloging.

> I think that what is important is the realization that if the organization – or women's activism in general – won't write its own history, no one else will . . . and it is most likely that the others will simply forget about them. That if the activities won't be documented [. . .] then everything that has been done won't become a part of – in quotation marks – mainstream narratives. I think this is something that I have internalized very much.
>
> *(Ľubica Kobová 2015)*[11]

One can argue that the fear of ending up in oblivion exceeds – in the case of ASPEKT organization – mere consideration of one's disappearance from public chronicles. To be or not to be remembered is something deeply feminist in the sense that if women do not actively participate in recording of their own history and promoting of their accomplishments, they can easily end up being left out the history textbooks altogether. Additionally, as the brief overview of the pre 1989 era suggests, those having some firsthand experiences with the communist regime and the ways it molded, erased, and rewrote history on a regular basis are aware of the connection between the notion of memory and power. The distinct heritage of the communist regime together with the feminist character of the organization make for a possible explanation of such specific and – in a sense – even counterintuitively creative use of digital technologies. In other words, they embrace the new technologies in order to preserve the old heritage. Reflecting back on the transition period, it might be easy to forget that one of the ASPEKT's early accomplishments was introducing gender equality to the public discussion in a society where equality becomes a discredited and empty phrase. Through countless lectures, publications, and projects (which are now preserved in the online database), the organization filled the void and set up the cornerstone for following feminist activities in the Czech Republic and Slovakia.

This is what a feminist looks like

Despite striving for a common goal of gender equality, a feminist movement is built on a plurality of ideas and strategies. ASPEKT may be a relatively small organization, yet its members have varying thoughts on the best way how to use new media and digital technologies. While Jana Cviková, a founding figure of the ASPEKT organization, stresses the importance of keeping the high editorial standards when navigating the online sphere, two of the younger respondents I've been talking to launched their own side projects that embody different qualities, mainly currentness, topicality, and immediacy. Ľubica Kobová and Paula Jójart both worked for ASPEKT on positions and projects related to new media and digital technologies such as ASPEKT's webzine or the organization's very first website and were part of the organization's younger generation. But additionally, they decided to launch their own side projects online that allowed them to use new media and digital technologies in a rather different way then while they were working for ASPEKT.

The first one – called simply *Feministky.sk* ("Feminists") – is a community blog or platform where a broader group of young feminists from various fields can express their ideas and comments. Founded by Ľubica Kobová, the site remains one of a very few personal self-described feminist blogs in the Czech and Slovak online sphere. In other words, such sites are not a common or prevalent type of blogging endeavor in the region and they remain a rare effort that usually stays unrecognized by a wider audience. A closer look at an opening letter that Ľubica Kobová sent to potential contributors and fellow bloggers before launching her website shows how this type of project is important for the feminist community in the region.

> Feministky.sk could be blogging space for critical young feminists where they could comment, gloss, analyse what they find important in public sphere (or what they turn into public issue) [. . .]. I consider the name feministky.sk [feminists] itself to be a form of identification, opening the label feminist to broader group of identities than is usually offered to the public and to those who could want to be feminists publicly (but don't work in nongovernmental organizations where they work their way to such label).
>
> *(Ľubica Kobová 2009)*

First, the blogging platform is seen as a space for a young and upcoming generation of feminists whose voices may not have been heard in traditional organizations. For them, projects like this could mean the possibility to engage in critical discussion outside traditional feminist spheres such as the nongovernmental organization (NGO) sector or academia. Second, to be part of such project would mean not only the chance to amplify one's feminist voice but also to publicly declare one's proud affiliation to a feminist tradition.

The second project – called *Hrdzavé klince* ("The Rusty Spikes") – is a single-person-maintained blog where Paula Jójart shares and comments on sexist ads from the local media. In a similar manner to the aforementioned one, it is an example of a personal take on the political issue of sexism in media and public space in general. The blogging platform allows the author to creatively, quickly, and in a straightforward manner reflect on her visual surroundings while potentially addressing audience which don't normally follow feminist NGOs and academics.

> I was just annoyed by sexist advertisements so I started to collect them and I thought I would put them up on the blog together with short comments [. . .]. I kind of missed the fact that we don't have "The Sexist Pig" [contest run by Czech NGO for the most sexist ad of the year] [. . .]. I just liked writing about it. Most of the time, those are just short ironic text, so no big writing.
>
> *(Paula Jójart 2015)*[12]

Those projects are, I argue, very significant especially in the Central and Eastern European region, where calling oneself a "feminist" is uncommon among self-labeling practices. Although available data about self-identification as a feminist refers mainly to Western Europe or to the United States (McCabe 2005), one can get an idea of how the way feminism is being defined in the mainstream public discourse influences individual attitudes.

> This stigmatising of the term "feminism" had its effects. It has led to the development of the phenomenon of the person who states "I'm not a feminist but . . ." where the "but" is followed by endorsement of goals that are usually thought of as feminist, such as equal pay for equal work.
>
> *(Walby 2011, 3)*

In other words, young women may generally share feminist ideas but without labeling them as such (Stacey 1987), which leads to the fact that, especially in the Central and Eastern European region, the term remains reserved or associated with academia and certain types of NGOs and outside of pop culture or broader public discourse. If one combines this with a feminist backlash – which is still very much alive and well in the Czech and Slovak context – digital technologies become one of the only ways to bring feminism into the mainstream. Articles and columns openly criticizing and ridiculing feminist efforts when it comes to issues such as gender-sensitive language in children's textbooks or sexual harassment at universities – to name a few recent debates – create a rather hostile environment for those promoting gender equality and feminist ideas in the public space. In this context, personal blogs and social media serve as an alternative arena for pro-feminist debates and attitudes. While traditional media, organized alongside mainstream patterns, have only limited potential when it comes to disrupting the marginalization and ridicule of feminist (i.e., alternative) actors and voices, digital technologies could actually open those restrictive floodgates and enable greater diversification of the public discourse and reconceptualization of key terms (see, e.g., Couldry and Curran 2003; Downey and Fenton 2003).

The sustainability of online feminism

New media and digital technology–related projects seem to promise a new exciting future for feminist (and other) organizations. However, in reality, many activists and initiatives are facing the issues connected to sustainability, funding, and expertise. Returning to the two aforementioned blogs (*Feministky.sk* and *Hrdzavé klince*), they too face similar challenges. The collective platform "Feminists" hasn't been updated since 2013 and the anti-sexist blog is not being regularly maintained either. Even though they are rather personal and more casual projects that don't necessarily aspire to the same level of professionalism as the famous US-based *feministing.com*[13] or *Jezebel*[14] (which were the original inspiration for these feminist blogs, as their authors stated), they too need to maintain the platform's basic functions.

The ongoing discussions about key advantages and challenges feminist activists face within the online sphere are a frequent part of contemporary academia and the NGO sector. The Barnard Center for Research on Women report (Martin and Valenti 2012), a document following the Online Revolution Convention held in 2012 which summarizes the key advantages and challenges feminist activists face within the online sphere, is an example of such debates. Some of the characteristics could be related to both the ASPEKT organization and the examples of personal online projects. On the one hand, the report appreciates the indisputable influence of online feminism and the role of citizen-produced media when it comes to challenging sexism online, creating safe spaces, and bringing feminist analysis and voices into the mainstream. On the other hand, it criticizes the deprivation and lack of support and resources that the individual bloggers and activists struggle with.

> Online feminism has transformed the way advocacy and action function within the feminist movement. And yet, this amazing innovation in movement organizing is unsustainable. Bloggers and online organizers largely suffer from a psychology of deprivation – a sense that their work will never be rewarded as it deserves to be, that they are in direct competition with one another for the scraps that come from third-party ad companies or other inadequate attempts to bring in revenue.
>
> *(Martin and Valenti 2012, 3)*

One of the possible solutions to these issues could be stronger ties between personal projects and already established feminist organizations that could offer support and expertise to these (often younger) activists. On the other hand, as Ľubica Kobová (founder of *Feministky.sk*) mentioned, launching a project outside the traditional institutional frame and without any funding was precisely the reason for choosing an online platform. Only there, after difficult experiences with overly bureaucratic EU funding, did she feel like she could finally engage in feminist activism free of restrictive boundaries, feminism of her own. So while for some activists, being able to target and engage with the largest audience possible is the aim, for others, the critical voice, valuable content, or independent and alternative status represents the ultimate goal.

Conclusion

Being intrigued by the growing amount of sociological research covering the impact of new media and digital technologies over the character of the feminist movement, I have decided to take a closer look into this fascinating phenomenon. However, I made sure that my research remains local in respect to the chosen subject and its relevant historical, political, and social context. As suggested through the whole chapter, I too recognize the groundbreaking potential of new media over the organizational issues such as easier and faster communication, access to information, and creation of communities, but I also hoped to illustrate that they are much more than yet another efficient tool. For some feminists, digital technologies present a way to make sure that their legacy and achievements will be preserved for future generations. Others use these platforms so they can express their views on feminist topics in creative and personal ways without the binding bureaucratization of external funding. From this perspective, the diversity of approaches to online feminism is as multifarious as the variety of feminism itself, and that is what makes it ultimately such a strong force. As McRobbie reminds us, "what feminism actually means varies, literally, from one self-declared feminist to the next, but this not reduce its field of potential influence, quite the opposite" (McRobbie 2009, 2). The same applies in this case.

My second aim was to show that despite the fact that digital technologies and new media are distinctly global, as they help us to connect over the shared projects and goals regardless of our geographical location, we must try to understand them through a local perspective. Only when attempting to comprehend what they mean to feminists in different corners of the globe will we fully recognize their role in the future of this movement. It is not enough to acknowledge the existence of online feminism outside the Western/Anglophone region. We must also make an attempt to understand how different shades of this phenomenon are influenced by local historical, cultural, and political circumstances. Lastly, I set out to highlight that online feminism does not consist of empowerment and consciousness-raising success stories only. Feminist activists and organizations are facing many serious challenges as they try to make sure that their voices are heard. They must deal with the question of whether digital technologies bring empowerment and give voice to those who have been marginalized within the mainstream media or if they create more burden and hardship than opportunities. They also need to reconcile utilizing the full potential of new media while staying true to their core values, starting up new exciting projects but also making sure that those efforts remain sustainable. While all these obstacles and challenges may be inevitable for online feminism, they also prove one thing: feminism as a movement and as a personal set of beliefs is alive, well, and kicking.

Notes

1 I am using the term "new media" in a broad rather than restrictively narrow sense, referring to Kaplan's definition which includes all web-based services "that build on the ideological and technological foundations of Web 2.0, and that allow the creation and exchange of User Generated Content" (Kaplan and Haenlein 2010, 61). The crucial condition here is the "socialization aspect of Web 2.0 in general" (Hunsinger and Senft 2014), which allows for social interaction, collaborative opportunities, community creation, and horizontal distribution of information.

2 The ASPEKT organization has always been a rather small unit in terms of the number of its core members. My idea was not necessarily to talk to all its current staff but rather to get a diverse group with voices ranging from "post-1989 feminism" to the "younger generation," from long-term stable members to external cooperators. The four interviews were conducted during the summer of 2015 and lasted on average between one and three hours. They were conducted in Czech (interviewer) and Slovak (interviewees) and were later transcribed and coded using the Atlas.ti program, and then translated into English.

3 "ASPEKT's About Page in English," ASPEKT, accessed July 30, 2016, www.aspekt.sk/en/aspekt_english.

4 The term "beginner" is being used here in a deliberate yet playful way as an allusion to the fact that both women who founded the ASPEKT organization and other prominent feminist figures were and to the same extent still are (as they claim in the round table discussions) only getting familiar with the importance of and ways to enforce gender equality in society.

5 As ASPEKT puts it in one of its long-term endeavors, "History of Women": "Within our project, history is not just the summary of important events and figures . . . [. . .], it is also our experience and source of legitimization of the things we do, the things we did" (Cviková and Juráňová 2009, 11).

6 Retrieved February 10, 2016, from http://aspekt.sk/en/aspekt_english.
7 The lack of women in the post-1989 TV and public debates does not, however, mean that there were simply no female members of the anti-regime or dissent structures who would oppose the communist establishment. Besides those publicly known female figures (who were, indeed, in minority compared to their male counterparts), scholars are also starting to recognize women opposing the regime in their private spaces that were – at that time – the only possible place for independent initiatives and civic disobedience (True 2003).
8 Retrieved February 10, 2016, from www.boell.de/en/foundation/organisation-16464.html, www.gwi-boell.de/en/2012/01/10/feminism-heinrich-böll-foundation.
9 To name just a few, the "Pink and Blue World" project, which was carried out from 2005 until 2008, focused on the so-called gender-sensitive approach within the field of primary education. Besides lectures for teachers, workshops, and theater performances for pupils, ASPEKT also invested in an information campaign whose outcomes (educational materials and documents) are available online in both Slovak and English. "ASPEKT's About Page in English," ASPEKT, accessed July 30, 2016, www.aspekt.sk/en/aspekt_english.
10 Zuzana Mad'arová was at the time of the interview a PhD candidate at the Institute of European Studies and International Relations in Bratislava. She was in charge of ASPEKT's web pages and has worked for the organization since 2005.
11 Ľubica Kobová was at the time of the interview a gender studies scholar lecturing at the Charles University in Prague. She has been working in ASPEKT since 1998 (among other things) on international projects and webzine. She now cooperates with the organization externally.
12 Paula Jójart is a LGBTQ activist and co-founder of the Altera organization (an NGO focusing on the rights of lesbian and bisexual women in Slovakia) who cooperates with the ASPEKT organization on an external basis. She has experiences with online-based activism from Macedonia and helped ASPEKT to set up its first web page at the beginning of the 2000s.
13 Feministing, accessed July 30, 2016, http://feministing.com.
14 Jezebel, accessed July 30, 2016, http://jezebel.com.

Bibliography

Alexander, Jeffrey. *Performative Revolution in Egypt: An Essay in Cultural Power.* London and New York: Bloomsbury Academic, 2011.

Ballentine, Karen. "International Assistance and the Development of Independent Mass Media in the Czech and Slovak Republics." In *The Power and Limits of NGOs: A Critical Look at Building Democracy in Eastern Europe and Eurasia*, edited by Sarah E. Mendelson and John K. Glenn, 91–125. New York: Columbia University Press, 2002.

Bennett, Lance W., ed. *Civic Life Online: Learning How Digital Media Can Engage Youth.* London and Cambridge, MA: The MIT Press, 2008.

Berglund, Sten, Joakim Ekman, Kevin Deegan-Krause, and Terje Knutsen, eds. *The Handbook of Political Change in Eastern Europe.* Cheltenham and Northampton, MA: Edward Elgar Publishing, 2013.

Blair, Kristine, Radhika Gajjala, and Christine Tulley. *Webbing Cyberfeminist Practice: Communities, Pedagogies, and Social Action.* Cresskill, NJ: Hampton Press, 2009.

Bredl, Klaus, Julia Hünniger, and Jakob Linaa Jensen, eds. *Methods for Analyzing Social Media.* London and New York: Routledge, 2014.

Burch, Sally. "Latin American Social Movements Take on the Net." *Society for International Development* 45, no. 4 (2002): 35–30.

Castells, Manuel. *The Rise of the Network Society, The Information Age: Economy, Society and Culture Vol. I.* Cambridge, MA and Oxford: Blackwell, 1996.

Castells, Manuel. *The Power of Identity, The Information Age: Economy, Society and Culture Vol. II.* Cambridge, MA and Oxford: Blackwell, 1997.

Castells, Manuel. *End of Millennium, The Information Age: Economy, Society and Culture Vol. III.* Cambridge, MA and Oxford: Blackwell, 1998.

Castells, Manuel. *The Internet Galaxy: Reflections on the Internet, Business and Society.* Oxford: Oxford University Press, 2001.

Castells, Manuel. *Communication Power.* Oxford: Oxford University Press, 2009.

Castells, Manuel. *Networks of Outrage and Hope: Social Movements in the Internet Age.* Cambridge: Polity Press, 2012.

Chadwick, Andrew and Philip N. Howard, eds. *Civic Life Online: Learning How Digital Media Can Engage Youth*. London and New York: Routledge, 2009.
Couldry, Nick and James Curran, eds. *Contesting Media Power: Alternative Media in a Networked World*. New York: Rowman & Littlefield Publisher, 2003.
Cviková, Jana and Jana Juráňová, eds. *Feminizmy pre začiatočníčky. Aspekty zrodu rodového diskurzu na Slovensku*. Bratislava: Aspekt, 2009.
Cviková, Jana. Interview by author. Bratislava, 2015.
Desai, Gaurav. *The Virtual Transformation of the Public Sphere*. New Delhi: Routledge, 2013.
Dobson, Amy Shields. *Postfeminist Digital Cultures: Femininity, Social Media, and Self-Representation*. New York: Palgrave Macmillan, 2015.
Downey, John and Natalie Fenton. "New Media, Counter Publicity and the Public Sphere." *New Media & Society* 5, no. 2 (2003): 185–202.
Edwards, Arthur. "The Dutch Women's Movement Online: Internet and the Organizational Infrastructure of a Social Movement." In *Cyberprotest: New Media, Citizens and Social Movements*, edited by Wim Van De Donk, Brian D. Loader, Paul G. Nixon, and Dieter Rucht, 161–180. London: Routledge, 2004.
Elliott, Anthony and John Urry. *Mobile Lives*. London and New York: Routledge, 2010.
Faludi, Susan. *Backlash: The Undeclared War Against American Women*. New York: Doubleday, 2006.
Fuchs, Christian. *OccupyMedia!: The Occupy Movement and Social Media in Crisis Capitalism*. Hants: Zero Books, 2014.
Gerbaudo, Paolo. *Tweets and the Streets: Social Media and Contemporary Activism*. London: Pluto Press, 2012.
Gillis, Stacy, Gillian Howie, and Rebecca Mumford, eds. *Third Wave Feminism: Critical Exploration*. New York: Palgrave Macmillan, 2004.
Harcourt, Wendy, ed. *Women@Internet: Creating New cultures in Cyberspace*. New York: Zed Books, 1999.
Hine, Christine. *Virtual Ethnography*. London: Sage, 2000.
Horst, Heather A. and Daniel Miller, eds. *Digital Anthropology*. London and New York: Berg, 2012.
Hunsinger, Jeremy and Theresa Senft, eds. *The Social Media Handbook*. New York and London: Routledge, 2014.
Jójart, Paula. Interview by author. Bratislava, 2015.
Kaplan, Andreas M. and Michael Haenlein. "Users of the World, Unite! The Challenges and Opportunities of Social Media." *Business Horizons* 53 (2010): 59–68.
Kobová, Ľubica. Opening email to potential contributors of Feministky.sk blog, 2009.
Kobová, Ľubica. Interview by author. Prague, 2015.
Kotzeva, Tatyana. "Re-imagining Bulgarian Women: The Marxist Legacy and Women's Self-identity." In *Gender and Identity in Central and Eastern Europe*, edited by Chri Corrin, 83–99. London: Frank Cass, 1999.
Maďarová, Zuzana. Interview by author. Bratislava, 2015.
Martin, Courtney E. and Vanessa Valenti, eds. *#FemFuture: Online Revolution*. Barnard Center for Research on Women. 2012, accessed June 30, 2016, http://bcrw.barnard.edu/wp-content/nfs/reports/NFS8-FemFuture-Online-Revolution-Report-April-15-2013.pdf.
Matynia, Elzbieta. "Polish Feminism Between the Local and the Global: A Task of Translation." In *Women's Movements in the Global Era: The Power of Local Feminisms*, edited by Amrita Basu, 193–228. Boulder: Westview Press, 2010.
McCabe, Janice. "What's in a Label? The Relationship Between Feminist Self-Identification and 'Feminist' Attitudes Among U.S. Women and Men." *Gender and Society* 19, no. 4 (2005): 480–505.
McRobbie, Angela. "Post-Feminism and Popular Culture." *Feminist Media Studies* 4, no. 3 (2004): 255–264.
McRobbie, Angela. *The Aftermath of Feminism: Gender, Culture and Social Change*. London: Sage, 2009.
Nazneen, Sohela and Maheen Sultan, eds. *Voicing Demands: Feminist Activism in Transnational Contexts*. New York: Zed Books, 2014.
Pink, Sarah et al., eds. *Digital Ethnography: Principles and Practice*. London and Los Angeles: Sage, 2016.
Putnam, Robert D. *Bowling Alone: The Collapse and Revival of American Community*. New York: Simon & Schuster, 2001.
Redfern, Catharine and Kristin Aune. *Reclaiming the F Word. The New Feminist Movement*. London, New York: Zed Books, 2010.
Rheingold, Howard. *The Virtual Community: Homesteading on the Electronic Frontier*. Readin: Addsion-Wessley, 1993.
Rheingold, Howard. *Smart Mobs: The Next Social Revolution*. Cambridge: Basic Books, 2002.
Rheingold, Howard. *Net Smart: How to Thrive Online*. Cambridge, MA: MIT Press, 2012.

Richter, James. "Evaluating Western Assistance to Russian Women's Organizations." In *The Power and Limits of NGOs: A Critical Look at Building Democracy in Eastern Europe and Eurasia*, edited by S. E. Mendelson and J. K. Glenn, 54–90. New York: Columbia University Press, 2002.

Robinson, Penelope. "No More Waves: Reconceptualising Generation and Postfeminism." *TASA Conference Proceedings, The Future of Sociology*. Australian National University, 2009.

Saurer, Edith, Margareth Lanzinger, and Elisabeth Frysak, eds. *Women's Movements: Networks and Debates in Post-Communist Countries in the 19th and 20th Centuries.* Wien, Köln, and Weimar: Böhlau Verlag, 2006.

Stacey, Judith. "Sexism by a Subtler Name? Postindustrial Conditions and Postfeminist Consciousness in the Silicon Valley." Socialist Review 17, no. 6 (1987): 7–28.

Šmejkalová, Jiřina. "Feminist Sociology in the Czech Republic After 1989 – A Brief Report." *European Societies* 6, no. 2 (2004): 169–180.

Štulhofer, Aleksandar and Theo Sandford, eds. *Sexuality and Gender in Post-Communist Eastern Europe and Russia.* London: Hawthorn Press, 2005.

Sundstrom, Lisa McIntosh. "Russian Women's Activism: Two Steps Forward, One Step Back." In *Women's Movements in the Global Era: The Power of Local Feminisms*, edited by Amrita Basu. 229–254. Boulder: Westview Press, 2010.

Tasker, Yvonne and Diane Negra, eds. *Interrogating Postfeminism: Gender and the Politics of Popular Culture.* Durham and London: Duke University Press, 2007.

Thornham, Helen, Elke Weissmann, eds. *Renewing Feminisms: Radical Narratives, Fantasies and Futures in Media Studies.* New York: Palgrave Macmillian, 2013.

True, Jacqui. *Gender, Globalization, and Postsocialism: The Czech Republic After Communism.* New York: Columbia University Press, 2003.

Walby, Sylvia, ed. *The Future of Feminism.* Cambridge: Polity Press, 2011.

Webster, Frank, ed. *Culture and Politics in the Information Age: A New Politics?* London: Routledge, 2001.

Wolmark, Jenny. "Cyberculture." In *A Concise Companion to Feminist Theory*, edited by Mary Eagleton, 215–236. Oxford: Blackwell Publishing, 2003.

Youngs, Gillian. "Virtual Voices: Real Lives." In *Women@Internet: Creating New Cultures in Cyberspace*, edited by Wendy Harcourt, 55–68. New York: Zed Books, 1999.

Youngs, Gillian. "Making the Virtual Real: Feminist Challenges in the Twenty-First Century." *The Scholar and Feminist Online* 5, no. 2 (2007): unnumbered, accessed November 15, 2011, http://barnard.edu/sfonline/blogs/printgyo.html.

Zeisler, Andi. "New Media, New Feminism: Envolving Feminist Analysis and Activism in Print, on the Web and Beyond." In *Renewing Feminisms: Radical Narratives, Fantasies and Futures in Media Studies*, edited by Helen Thornham and Elke Weissmann, 178–184. New York: Palgrave Macmillian, 2013.

18

Arab women's feminism(s), resistance(s), and activism(s) within and beyond the "Arab Spring"

Potentials, limitations, and future prospects

Sahar Khamis

Unpacking "Arab feminism(s)": three invisibilities, three struggles, and three phases

The underlying faulty assumption that there is only one single form of feminism (i.e., Western feminism) that women have to universally emulate is highly problematic due to its ethnocentric underpinnings, which mask the rich diversities of women's lived realities as well as their competing subjectivities and the multiple feminism(s) they embrace and exhibit on many levels and through different manifestations (Moghadam 1994, 2003; Nazir 2005; Inglehart and Norris 2003).

Negating the notion that there is a single, uniform, and standard type of feminism that can be universally and uncritically applied to women all over the world regardless of their distinctions and variations, this section sheds light on some of the unique particularities of the complex phenomenon of "Arab feminism(s)." It reveals how this complex phenomenon manifested itself in numerous ways and over several stages, which are reflective of Arab women's authentic culture and beliefs as well as their complex political, social, and cultural realities. It discusses how Arab women suffered from three layers of invisibility and participated in three types of struggles, and how their complex process of evolving "feminism(s)" was shaped over three consecutive phases. By doing so, it sheds light on how Arab women's feminism(s), activism(s) a,nd resistance(s) cross-cut different boundaries, binaries, and dichotomies.

Three invisibilities

Arab women have been suffering from three layers of invisibility on three different levels. First, there is invisibility on the socioeconomic level, since many of their important roles, including their economic labor and multiple contributions to their societies, are unnoticed, unappreciated, and unrewarded. This is mainly because many of these women, especially in rural areas and marginalized communities, engage in undocumented, unpaid labor, which is therefore taken for granted and unaccounted for. For example, many women in rural Egypt when asked about their occupation would simply shrug their shoulders and say with embarrassment, "I'm not working! I'm just a housewife!" – thus not acknowledging their backbreaking labor, which extends for many hours both inside and outside the house (Khamis 2004).

Second, there is invisibility on the academic level, where women's issues and gender studies didn't historically receive sufficient attention in academic research until the recent creation of women's studies programs. Yet despite the creation of such programs and the relative increase in academic studies focusing on women's issues in recent years, there is still a shortage in research on Arab and Muslim women, in general, and those who are involved in political activism or who are ideologically driven to join resistance movements and political struggles, in particular (Holt and Jawad 2013). The shortage in such studies by scholars from within the Arab region itself, especially women scholars, who can bring an indigenous, authentic "insider's" perspective on Arab women's lived realities, is even greater. When these studies are found, they are mostly written by, and for, upper-middle-class, elitist, Western-educated women, who are not always representative of their wider societies.

Third, there is invisibility on the media level, where Arab women in general, and Muslim women in particular, are mostly both underrepresented and misrepresented through being overly marginalized and/or overly sexualized. The "Othering" of these women, through adopting mostly Orientalist discourses, leads to the birth of these media (mis)representations (Moghadam 1994, 2003; Nazir 2005; Inglehart and Norris 2003), which are far from flattering because they mostly confine Arab women to the realm of domestication, sexuality, or both. In most cases, they project an image of either a subdued, oppressed, and helpless Arab woman who is confined to the domestic sphere, subjected to male domination, and victimized by societal repression and cultural discrimination; or an image of a highly sexualized Arab woman who is confined to the harem, as strictly an object of male pleasure, such as a belly dancer, for example (Khamis and Mili 2018).

Additionally, the few voices of Arab women who manage to be heard in mainstream media are mostly representative of the 1% elitist, urban, upper-middle-class, Western-educated, and mostly westernized women, leaving out the 99% of women in their respective societies, largely unheard and thus invisible.

These layers of multiple invisibilities, therefore, gave birth to an undesirable phenomenon of Arab women's "tokenism," whereby certain limited categories of elitist, upper-middle-class, Western-educated women are constantly overrepresented, whether in mainstream media coverage, in academic research, or in political representation, at the expense of much broader segments of Arab women. The latter, who are more representative of their respective societies, are therefore largely overlooked and underrepresented, adding to their multiple invisibilities in an ongoing, vicious cycle. These imbalances project largely flawed, skewed, and inaccurate depictions of Arab women's lived realities, roles, and needs (Khamis 2013; Radsch and Khamis 2013).

Fighting these three parallel layers of invisibility requires improving Arab women's lived realities through economic and social development efforts on one hand, as well as paying closer attention to their representation in both academic literature and mediated images on the other hand. The best way to fill this void, overcome these invisibilities, and break away from these predominantly stereotypical depictions and overly simplistic (mis)representations is to unpack their many acts of activism(s), both in the real world and in the virtual world, and their different modes of resistance and heroism in the political, social, and legal spheres simultaneously (Holt and Jawad 2013).

Three struggles

To best understand Arab women's resistance movements, we have to understand what they have been resisting in the first place. This can only be achieved through a better understanding of the many societal constraints and challenges which are imposed on them. These include authoritarian, dictatorial regimes; infrastructural and economic challenges; staggeringly high illiteracy rates coupled with the poor quality of education; and reactionary social forces, patriarchy, and misogyny. Most of these conditions are more pressing in tribal, conservative societies, like Libya and Yemen, but still exist to varying degrees in other Arab countries, even those that have a longer history of women's participation in political and social spheres, such as Egypt, for example (Khamis 2013).

To resist these forces, Arab women engaged in three closely interconnected and intertwined struggles simultaneously, namely: the political struggle against all forms of tyranny, dictatorship and autocracy; the social struggle against all forms of misogyny, patriarchy, and stagnant traditions; and the legal struggle against all laws which could harm women and disadvantage them or deny them their basic rights (Khamis and Mili 2018). We can argue that it is not possible to fight one battle without fighting the others, or to succeed in one battlefield without succeeding in the rest.

Arab women have been determined to merge the parallel struggles for equal citizenship in the legal arena; full participation in the political arena; and greater gender equity in the social arena as part of their quest for justice, freedom, and reform in their newly transforming societies and transitioning states.

In other words, while Arab men have been predominantly fighting one struggle, namely, the political struggle to end dictatorship and authoritarianism and to pave the way for democracy and freedom, Arab women have been fighting parallel, dual struggles, namely, political and social struggles (Al-Malki et al. 2012). As Alamm (2012, 14) points out, "unlike men, women face two battles: the first for political change and the second to obtain a real change of their societal status to become fully equal to their male counterparts." We can, of course, argue that this equality also encompasses the legal struggle, which necessitates adjusting existing laws that could be harmful to women, discriminatory to them, or at least insensitive to their needs, and drafting new gender-sensitive laws instead (Mili 2018).

This compels us to recognize the significance of women's "gender-specific" struggles in the three political, social, and legal spheres in parallel. Politically, Arab women played active roles in resisting external, foreign powers, such as colonization forces in their respective countries, over several historical periods (Moghadam 1994, 2003; Nazir 2005; Inglehart and Norris 2003). More recently, they participated in political movements to end dictatorship, authoritarianism, and autocracy, as witnessed in the Arab uprisings (Holt and Jawad 2013).

Socially, they struggled to create more visibility for women in their respective societies by fighting against negative practices harming women, such as gender discrimination, early marriage, honor killings, and domestic violence (Mili 2018), as well as sexual harassment (Eltantawy 2018). One good and successful example has been the "*Shoft Taharosh*" ("I Saw Harassment") campaign, which was orchestrated and implemented by a group of young Egyptian activists, including women, using a variety of tools, such as social media and graffiti, to resist the epidemic problem of harassment in Egypt (Eltantawy 2018).

Legally, they struggled to draft new laws which are more gender-friendly and which safeguard women's rights and provide them with better protection, such as the groundbreaking law which was issued in Tunisia in July 2017 criminalizing all forms of violence against women (Khamis 2017). The significance of this law is that it extended the definition and scope of violence against women beyond the private, domestic sphere of the home and the family to the public sphere, by criminalizing different forms of violence against women, including physical, sexual, economic, and political violence. It also criminalized all forms of discrimination against women in areas such as employment and elections. Many Tunisian women's rights' groups have been behind the drafting of this significant law, which came as the product of many years of tireless work (Khamis 2017; Mili 2018) and which paved the way for similar laws to be recently adopted in other Arab countries such as Lebanon and Jordan.

It is safe to say that, far from being finished or completed, Arab women's struggles in these three parallel domains exemplify ongoing, cyclical struggles and "unfinished revolutions" (Khamis and Mili 2018), which are simultaneously shaping and reflecting the shifting realities of their transitioning communities.

In their 2013 book, *Women, Islam, and Resistance in the Arab World*, Holt and Jawad (2013) present an overview of different examples of Arab women's activism and heroism both before and during the Arab Spring revolutions. These examples, they argue, provide clear evidence of how women's activism and agency challenge patriarchy and other power structures, in both the social and political domains, in private and public spheres, and both internally and externally. In doing so, they challenge some of the commonly held misconceptions surrounding Arab and Muslim women by revealing that "far from being excluded from the dominant discourse, many Arab women are finding their 'voice' through the modernizing processes of . . . resistance" (p. 7). They argue that this process clearly links "the discourse on gender and national identity with discussions of women's role in national liberation and . . . resistance movements" (p. 8).

An important point worth clarifying is that although the acts of resistance themselves are not new, since they existed in the past against different forces, including colonial powers, for example, and they developed and evolved over several stages, what is new are the various modes of expression and different channels through which such acts are amplified and become more visible.

Three phases

Arab women's struggles in these different domains took varying forms, directions, and levels of intensity over three important and distinct phases. First, there was the early phase of nationalist movements, when Arab women's struggle to achieve more independence and emancipation was intertwined with their own countries' struggle to achieve independence from colonialization and foreign imperialism (Charrad 1997). Most of these movements were initially started by upper-middle-class, Western-educated men, who were joined later on by upper-middle-class, Western-educated women (Mili 2015, 2018).

By joining these early nationalist movements, women were championing the cause of independence both for their nation-states, by striving to free them from the burden of colonization, and for fellow women citizens, by struggling to free them from the burden of stagnant traditions and societal constraints, which impeded their progress. Although these early movements achieved some progress in specific areas, such as creating the first women's organizations and associations in the Arab world and pushing for women's education and voting rights, their impact remained largely limited. They mostly targeted and engaged upper-middle-class, urban women, but didn't trickle down to broader segments of women in their respective societies (Mili 2015, 2018; Charrad 1997).

Second, there was the stage of nation-building, when each country tried to define its own unique and distinct identity as a modern state after earning its independence from colonial, foreign powers by taking further steps on the road to modernization. This stage was mostly characterized by a top-down, state-imposed form of feminism, which was oftentimes championed by the ruler in power and/or the first lady (Mili 2018). A good example illustrating this point is President Habib Bourguiba of Tunisia, who took upon himself the responsibility of modernizing Tunisia after its independence from France by pushing forward a progressive agenda for Tunisian women along secular, Western lines (Mili 2015, 2018). This resulted in big gains for Tunisian women in terms of education, employment, political participation, and public recognition, but it didn't always resonate well with all segments of Tunisian society, some of whom regarded this brand of feminism as Western-imported, state-imposed, and too secular (Khamis and Mili 2018).

This stage also led to the birth of the "first lady syndrome," which refers to the leading role of the first lady, as in the case of Jehan Sadat and Suzanne Mubarak in Egypt, for example, in championing women's issues and drafting new laws which protect their rights. On the one hand, this yielded some gains for women in the political, social, and legal spheres, but on the other hand, it added to the process of "tokenism," whereby women's causes are largely championed by and for limited, elitist, upper-middle-class women.

Therefore, we can safely argue that the two early stages of Arab women's feminist movements, despite their importance and significance, were mostly characterized by being top-down, centralized, elitist, and state-sponsored, and therefore didn't always trickle down sufficiently, or effectively, to wider segments of Arab women.

Third, there was the more contemporary phase of bottom-up, grassroots feminism, which enabled participation by a wide array of Arab women across the board, representing different age groups, socioeconomic backgrounds, religious orientations, ideological affiliations, and geographic areas, as demonstrated in the Arab Spring uprisings and their aftermath (Khamis and Mili 2018; Mili 2015, 2018; Labidi 2014; Charrad and Zarrugh 2014).

Although we cannot and should not limit Arab women's activism and resistance solely to the glorious moment of the Arab Spring uprisings, since their multiple roles and activisms certainly extended before and after this moment, we still have to acknowledge their value, impact, and significance. These sweeping, massive waves of public revolt which shook Arab societies offered women unparalleled opportunities to showcase their multiple forms of activism(s) and resistance(s), both online and offline. This in turn enabled them to better assert their identities and to claim their full rights as equal citizens (Khamis and Mili 2018; Mili 2015, 2018). Most importantly, this third phase enabled grassroots, bottom-up feminist movements and activism(s) to emerge and to exhibit themselves in numerous forms and varied manifestations.

Crosscutting the boundaries and the binaries

The picture emerging from this discussion is that of a complex, rich, and eclectic phenomenon of multiple and parallel struggles, which have been orchestrated by Arab women in many forms and over several stages. Their acts of activism and resistance crosscut the binaries between the old and the new, the traditional and the modern, the private and the public, the internal and the external, the local and the global, the religious and the secular, and the political and the social in a constant, ongoing, cyclical, and interconnected process.

Indeed, it is at the intersections, crossovers, and overlaps between these different binaries and dichotomies that the nuances and intricacies of the complex and multidimensional phenomenon of Arab feminism(s) can be fully comprehended and truly appreciated.

Through negating some of the false dichotomies and binary opposites, such as that between Islamism and feminism or religiosity and modernization, for example, we can equally shake and challenge some of the simplistic, false associations, such as that between "Islam" and "women's oppression." This is especially important since many Arab women activists attribute restrictive practices and control mechanisms in their societies to stagnant, inherited traditions and negative cultural practices emanating from patriarchy and misogyny rather than to Islam itself as a faith and a belief system (Khamis and Mili 2018).

There is also the successful example of women's movements in Tunisia, where members of both secular and Islamist groups, such as the moderate, Islamist Party "Ennahda," collaborated closely across their ideological differences, leading to the unanimous approval and adoption of the groundbreaking law in 2017 which denounced all forms of violence against women (Khamis 2017). This sets a good model to be emulated and adopted elsewhere, and it provides proof that the only way to advance a truly powerful and genuinely liberating agenda for women is through bridging gaps and crosscutting false dichotomies.

The creation of dynamic and evolving stages of Arab feminism(s) has been continuously taking place at the crossroads and intersections between various push and pull mechanisms, and competing forces, including modernization versus conservatism, localization versus globalization, the public sphere versus the private sphere, secularization versus Islamization, and top-down state feminism versus bottom-up grassroots activism (Khamis and Mili 2018).

Understanding how these different aspects of Arab women's activism(s) in the political, social, and legal spheres have historically developed over different phases, as well as how they are interrelated and interconnected to each other, on the one hand, and to international dynamics and regional influences, on the other hand, is crucial to fully unpacking the complexity of the multidimensional phenomenon of Arab feminism(s).

Digital activism within and beyond the Arab Spring: the good, the bad, and the missing

The Arab Spring movements granted Arab citizens, especially youth and women, valuable opportunities to increase their visibility, raise their voices, exercise their leadership, and execute their activism. Much of this was achieved through the deployment of new forms of communication, especially social media, to spread the protesters' multiple messages and to support their varied causes. Taking advantage of the phenomenon of "cyberactivism," which could be best defined as "the use of online communication to advance a cause which is difficult to advance offline" (Howard 2011), Arab women utilized multiple social media venues to assert their will, carve new spaces for themselves in the public sphere, and fight for their social and political causes.

Youth and women were the two most visible demographic groups which undertook leadership roles during the Arab Spring movements. Over 70% of the overall population in the Arab world today is under 30 years of age. Naturally, this is the age group which is most dynamic, passionate about change and reform, capable of organizing and mobilizing, and most technologically savvy (Radsch and Khamis 2013). There is an overlap between these two demographic categories, since many of the heroines and protagonists of the Arab Spring uprisings were young women. This highlights the importance of understanding the role of young Arab women, their activism, and their new expressions of feminism both within and beyond these uprisings.

Arab women played a particularly visible role in instigating, orchestrating, and fueling the Arab Spring movements of 2011, since hundreds of thousands of Arab women throughout the region, including in some of the most traditional, conservative countries, like Yemen and Bahrain, took to the streets alongside men, calling for an end to dictatorship and repression and demanding dignity and freedom (Radsch 2012; Khamis 2011).

In doing so, they were not confining themselves to traditional gender roles, such as nurturing or supporting men in their struggle for freedom. Rather they stepped up to the front lines of resistance, risking their own lives and exposing themselves to the dangers of arrest, assault, harassment, and even rape. The Arab Spring unveiled many examples of brave Arab women who risked not only their reputations but also their physical safety, and the safety of their own families, for the sake of reform, freedom, and democracy (Al-Malki et al. 2012).

By doing so, they became iconic figures and influential public opinion leaders in their respective countries and communities. One good example is Tawakkul Karman, the young Yemeni journalist and human rights activist, who came to be known as "the mother of the revolution in Yemen." In 2011 she was the first Arab woman to be awarded the Nobel Peace Prize, which could be seen as a nod to the Arab Spring movements in general, and to the significant role which Arab women played in them in particular (Khamis 2011).

Another good example was Ayat El Gomizi, the young Bahraini woman who was arrested after publicly reciting a poem against the king and the ruling family of Bahrain – something none of her fellow male citizens dared to do – which won her praise, admiration, and respect by both men and women alike (Radsch and Khamis 2013).

This section sheds light on the most important potentials of digital activism, as exemplified in the multiple opportunities it provided to women, as well as some of the most significant limitations of this process and some of its missing aspects so far.

The potentials of digital activism

Many young Arab women used cyberactivism to participate in the waves of political and social transformations widely known as the Arab Spring, which swept through their respective countries. Most of these activists leveraged social media to enact new forms of leadership, agency, and empowerment, since these online platforms enabled them to express themselves freely and allowed their voices to be heard by the rest of the world, particularly by global media. This resulted in multidimensional personal, social, political, and communicative revolutions, which have been continuously and simultaneously unfolding (Al-Malki et al. 2012; Khamis 2013).

These women represented all ages, socioeconomic backgrounds, religious affiliations, and political ideologies, reflecting the grassroots, across the board, inclusive nature of the Arab Spring movements they were part of. Many of these women emerged as prominent figures in the midst of these uprisings, carving new places for themselves, even in some of the most traditional, conservative communities, like Yemen, Libya, and Bahrain. Thus they became heroines, public opinion leaders, and role models for both men and women alike (Alwadi and Khamis 2018). Many of these young women activists resorted to new media tools, especially social media venues, to advance their struggles and to support their causes.

The multiple forms of activism(s) many of these young women displayed asserted their position as members of a "subaltern counterpublic" (Fraser 1992), who are forming their own resistance communities in political and social domains, both online and offline. By doing so, they are establishing the missing link between private spheres, which have been traditionally categorized as the feminine domain, and public spheres, which have been traditionally categorized as the masculine domain, through increasing the visibility of women's issues and cultivating support for them in the reordering of their transitioning societies (Khamis 2013).

It is helpful to remember that women's mobilization in the Arab revolutions was carried out initially under the name of broader democratic principles, goals, and ambitions, which were equally shared across the board and across the gender divide. However, gendered realities on the ground, such as lack of women's political representation, gender inequity on many levels, and physical violence against women, soon urged women to join forces with organizations that were vested in furthering gender equality against the customs and norms that were well entrenched in the social and political structures of their respective countries.

A good example of this social struggle is the effort exerted by some Arab women activists, many of whom are cyberactivists, to end many forms of physical violence against women, which reached new levels of intensity with the Arab upheavals and women's visible roles as active participants in them, revealing the enduring patriarchal resistance to women's visibility and greater access to the public sphere. These forms of violence against women ranged from sexual harassment on the streets of Cairo to the appalling virginity testing in Tahrir Square, which was performed during the revolution of 2011 to curb women's activism through stigmatizing and intimidating the women who decided to fully participate in the protests. Other horrifying forms of violence included using rape as an ugly weapon against women in Libya and Syira, two of the countries which suffered the most from anarchy, chaos, and lawlessness in the aftermath of the Arab Spring uprisings.

In response to these forms of physical violence, some Egyptian women mobilized to create online and offline communities of protest against sexual harassment, which became epidemic on Egyptian streets. In doing so, they deployed innovative reporting tools, combining social media platforms such as Facebook, Twitter, blogs, and YouTube with on-street protests, different forms of art, including graffiti, and even billboards to send a united, loud scream against the social acceptability of gender injustice, discrimination, and intimidation, as exemplified in the degrading act of sexual harassment (Eltantawy 2018). According to Egyptian-American academic Nahed Eltantawy, "These were golden days for women's activism. Women were out on the streets shouting and chanting to end political repression and humiliation, while also shouting and screaming to end social discrimination, gendered violence, and degradation" (Eltantawy 2017).

Another example was how the prominent Egyptian blogger and activist, Nawara Negm, successfully combined online activism on her popular blog and Twitter accounts with actual activism on the ground, as evidenced in her participation in the protests in Tahrir Square. In doing so, she was also combining activism in the political sphere, through her vocal resistance to all forms of governmental corruption and violations of human rights, with gendered activism, as demonstrated in her pioneering, aggressive campaign against sexual harassment on the streets of Cairo and elsewhere (El Nawawy and Khamis 2013).

These efforts and campaigns resulted in a spillover from the realm of social media to the realm of mainstream media, through raising awareness about different forms of gendered violence, including sexual harassment. This was done through encouraging increased coverage of these issues in mainstream media, resulting in their increased salience, visibility, and prevalence, after being considered "taboo" issues for a long time. Therefore, these young women, through their roles as cyberactivists and citizen journalists, were able to successfully break many of the taboos, both in the political and social domains simultaneously, while reshaping mainstream media's agendas in their respective countries at the same time (El Nawawy and Khamis 2013).

Likewise, the famous Tunisian citizen journalist and blogger, Lina Ben Mehni, reported on the uprisings taking place throughout her country in 2011 via social media, while also paying close attention to gender issues and women's rights, in parallel. Since her country had a few international correspondents and domestic media were tightly controlled, she took upon herself the responsibility of informing the rest of the world about the historical events which were unfolding in Tunisia. By doing so, she and other young women activists in some of the countries where media coverage was either limited or prohibited, such as Libya and Syria, for example, were playing the important role of "acting as bridges to connect their countries with the rest of the world, and providing windows, through which the world can see them and see the unfolding events in their countries," as Syrian journalist Laila Alhussini puts it (Alhussini 2017).

Additionally, Lina Ben Mehni and a number of other young women cyberactivists and citizen journalists throughout the region also addressed women's issues, demands, and concerns through their blogs, Facebook pages, and Twitter accounts to increase awareness about these issues and to rally public support around these causes. The issues they raised included the need for better political representation for women, more inclusion of women in the public sphere, and fighting all forms of discrimination and gendered violence against women (Radsch and Khamis 2013). By doing so, these young Arab women were certainly merging their gender militancy with political militancy in their quest for justice, freedom, and reform.

This is more proof that the Arab Spring movements were not just about political revolutions; they were also about personal, social, and communication revolutions simultaneously, as Arab women activists challenged traditional norms of participation and visibility and brought new issues into the public sphere. By doing so, they started writing a new chapter in the history of their region in general, and the history of Arab women's activism(s) and feminism(s) in particular (Radsch and Khamis 2013).

Arab women's reliance on new media tools to enact their activism and reach their goals is best described as "cyberfeminism," the sister to the process of cyberactivism, defined as "the innovative ways women are using digital technologies to reengineer their lives" (Daniels 2009, 103), to raise awareness about women's issues, and to overcome the challenges confronting them (Khamis 2013). The innovativeness here could be said to stem from both the medium and the message simultaneously, in other words from the new vehicle of transmission in cyberspace as well as from new forms of expression and new mediated messages and representations (Khamis 2016).

While it is important to avoid the (mis)perception that gender is a "unified category and, by implication, that digital technologies mean the same thing to all women across differences of race, class, sexuality" (Daniels 2009, 103), the fact remains that "For many women, including themselves in these new technologies means including themselves in internetworked global feminism" (Daniels 2009, 106). Furthermore, reliance on these new technologies enables "the very people who are excluded from mainstream society . . . to include themselves in these new technologies on their own terms" (Daniels 2009, 106). The outcome of such an inclusion, as Gajjala (2003, 49) puts it, is that "they can see themselves as protagonists of the revolution," a term which best describes Arab women activists, both literally and metaphorically (Khamis 2013).

Through the phenomenon of digital activism, Arab women started redefining the boundaries of private and public spheres, linking political and social domains, connecting national and international audiences, and performing mainstream and citizen journalism all at once (Radsch and Khamis 2013).

For many of these young women, especially those living in traditional, conservative societies, these new media platforms were the only available "windows" which allowed them to see the rest of the world while allowing the rest of the world to see them simultaneously. This was especially true because the use of social media opened new spaces for women to organize and to enact their activism on many levels, both nationally and internationally, and in different forms and modes of expression (Khamis 2013).

Indeed, in some traditional societies, such as certain areas of Libya and Yemen, for example, women have little opportunity to meet and organize because they are often restricted to the home or to controlled public settings. But with access to social media, they were able to organize, network, coordinate, and exchange useful information without breaking social taboos, especially in sex-segregated societies (Radsch and Khamis 2013).

In addition to influencing their fellow citizens to participate in the uprisings, many young women cyberactivists became influential as media outreach coordinators, citizen journalists, and translators, thus acting as "bridges" to the international press, particularly the English-language media worldwide (Radsch and Khamis 2013). This illustrates how citizen journalism

(Bennett 2008) became a particularly powerful form of cyberactivism because of its capacity to shape the public agenda locally as well as public opinion internationally.

Also, social media gave Arab women activists the opportunity to access organizational resources and sources of support from around the world, and to broadcast images from their protest movements to a worldwide audience, in their new roles as citizen journalists. By doing so, they proved that political initiatives and activism cannot be monopolized by the authorities or by their male counterparts. By sharing in this new public space of political protest and participating in all forms of activism, both online and offline, Arab women have risen to positions of prominence, visibility, and heroism while putting the authorities in their respective countries in a defensive position by exposing their transgressions, corruption, and violations of human rights.

Overall, these young women activists relied on social media to achieve three main goals: mobilization, documentation, and education (Khamis 2013). Mobilization refers to the use of social media to help people organize, coordinate, and network, such as using Twitter to orchestrate on-the-ground protests minute by minute, or using Facebook to urge people to unite and rally around a certain cause. A good example is the famous vlog by the young Egyptian activist Asmaa' Mahfouz, who came to be known as "the most brave girl in Egypt" for calling upon fellow Egyptians to go out to the street and protest on January 25, 2011, against the 30-year dictatorial rule of President Hosni Mubarak (Radsch and Khamis 2013).

Another example is how some Libyan and Syrian women activists founded both offline and online groups to raise awareness about the magnitude of the serious problems of rape and harassment, which were brutally used as weapons against women to curb their activism. Many of these activists believed that social media, due to their advantages of anonymity, accessibility, interactivity, immediacy, and broad national and international outreach, were particularly best suited to reach groups of women who were otherwise difficult to reach, such as refugees and victims of rape and violence (Khamis 2013).

The second function of documentation refers to the use of citizen journalism (Bennett 2008), through deploying social media, to provide evidence of governmental corruption and violations of human rights, such as using cell phone cameras to capture incidents of police brutality and harassment of protestors. This included the "eyewitness" accounts, which some of these women journalists and activists captured and uploaded online, while joining many of the protests that took place in their countries. As Egyptian journalist and activist Yasmine El Sayed explains, "many of these women used their cell phone cameras and hand-held devices as 'weapons' to protect themselves, in case they face any assault or harassment by the police or security forces" (El Sayed 2013). Many of these women protestors also captured powerful images of their fellow women protestors being beaten, harassed, or arrested and uploaded them online for the rest of the world to see (Radsch and Khamis 2013). Here again, many of these young women activists hailed the immediacy, availability, accessibility, and wide outreach of these social media tools, which ensured that important events will get instant coverage, both at home and abroad, on a large scale.

The third function of education refers to increasing awareness about current social and political problems, in the hope of resolving them. A good example was brainstorming and deliberating about key issues via blogs. This was evident in the case of prominent bloggers, such as Nawara Negm of Egypt and Lina Ben Mehni of Tunisia, who not only educated the public about political issues, such as governmental corruption and violations of human rights, but also about social issues, such as fighting sexual harassment and gendered violence, and the need for gender equity, both politically and socially (El Nawawy and Khamis 2013).

This function took place on two levels: internal education, which is targeted at a local, domestic audience; and external education, which is targeted at an international audience. A good example of internal education is some of the campaigns which young women activists launched online to combat some of the important challenges facing women, including the unsafe public space created through negative practices, such as rape and sexual harassment, as well as the unsafe private space, which is created through domestic violence and gender discrimination (Eltantawy 2017, 2018).

This reveals how "opportunities to apply considerable . . . pressure for reforms are now available through digital media networks." (Bennett 2008, 20). It is also indicative of the existence of genuine, autonomous e-citizenship among these young Arab women activists, who were able to put forward their own agendas and to make their own voices heard on salient issues of special relevance to them (Khamis 2013).

The function of external education took place through several young Arab women, who used their English language skills and ability to establish successful, symbiotic relations with international media to reach out to a global audience worldwide. A good example was Libyan activist Hana El Hebshi, who was widely recognized for her role in reporting firsthand on the siege of Tripoli. This was especially important since Libya had no independent media outlets, and foreign correspondents were not allowed in the country at that time. She received the International Woman of Courage award from the US State Department for her unique coverage and bold reporting (Radsch and Khamis 2013).

Digital activism: limitations and gaps

Despite the previously discussed potentials of social media, it is also worth investigating some of their limitations and constraints. One of these is the digital divide between the technological haves and have-nots due to a variety of factors, such as technical and technological barriers, economic challenges, infrastructural constraints, as well as educational and literacy barriers in general and digital literacy barriers in particular. All of these are widespread in many parts of the Arab world but are especially more pressing among women, especially those in rural areas (Khamis 2016).

This means that the trickle-down effect of these new communicative practices could be limited and constrained by these factors, and that no matter how powerful and effective these new media technologies may be, the scale of their outreach and influence remains mostly limited to certain segments of society, especially upper-middle-class, educated elites. This in turn resulted in the overrepresentation of these segments of society in both previous academic research as well as in media representations, leading to a skewed, "urban-centric," and "elite-centric" focus (Khamis 2016), as previously discussed.

There is also the danger of "slacktivism" and "clicktivism," which refers to substituting words for actions, or substituting posting, texting, blogging, and tweeting for doing (Khamis 2016). One possible downside to this process of overreliance on new media technologies could be reaching a stage of complete media fatigue due to information overload. This means that people can become saturated with the constant overflow of mediated messages from many sources, which can become an additional barrier between them and taking effective action in the real world.

This last point, coupled with the far from ideal outcomes which unfolded in most of the so-called post-Arab Spring countries, provide an explanation for why some women activists became dismayed and unwilling to continue with their activism today, both online and offline.

The tightening atmosphere of media surveillance, which is part of the overall regression in freedoms in many parts of the Arab world in the post–Arab Spring phase, made social media a double-edged sword. On the one hand, they became powerful tools of resistance to be used by women activists to demand their political and social rights and to fight for their freedom. On the other hand, however, they also became powerful tools for the regimes in power to crush their opponents and to halt their activism in an ongoing, nonstop tug-of-war between both parties.

Many Arab governments today built their cyberactivism learning curves as they started to deploy more effective tools to monitor social media activism and to engage in advanced "cyberwars" against dissidents and opponents. These governments routinely engage in tracing, hacking, and sabotaging the activists' online accounts and websites, making cyberactivism and cyberfeminism highly risky (Khamis 2016).

This resulted in either halting or toning down online activism, resorting to anonymity, or increasing activism from the diaspora, as in the case of many Arab women activists who are carrying out their activism, both online and offline, while being in exile, such as members of the Syrian and Bahraini opposition movements (Khamis 2013). According to Bahraini journalist and activist Nada Alwadi, "Some women activists, including myself, had no option but to flee our home countries and to exercise our activism from abroad, out of fear of regime retaliation and harsh consequences" (Alwadi 2017).

The derailing of the democratic process in a number of Arab Spring countries, some of which witnessed a relapse to military dictatorship (like Egypt), and others which witnessed waves of unrest, sectarian strife, and turmoil (like Libya, Syria, and Yemen), resulted in increasing violations of human rights, including massive military trials and unprecedented escalations in arrests; harsh, unjust sentences; torture incidents; and a crackdown on freedom of the press.

This resulted in many Arab women activists curbing their offline and online activism for fear of arrest and other forms of governmental crackdown, intimidation, or retaliation. According to Egyptian activist and academic Amal Bakry, "Many groups of women activists are either behind bars, in exile, or are simply too worn out, fatigued, depressed, or dismayed to continue their activism" (Bakry 2017).

Other activists decided to continue their activism while relying on pseudonyms and anonymous postings. This anonymity, however, could be a double-edged sword for many of them. On the one hand, the factor of anonymity could provide them with needed protection, not only from political arrests and intimidation but also from social stigmatization. This is especially true in the most conservative, traditional communities in countries like Yemen and Libya, for example, which do not easily accept women's visible involvement in the public sphere, let alone their prominent participation in resistance movements and political opposition. On the other hand, however, this anonymity could decrease the visibility and credibility of these women activists by not allowing them to receive credit and recognition for their activism, since they are not publicly associated with their cyberfeminism efforts and initiatives (Radsch and Khamis 2013). For example, a 20-year-old Libyan activist who refused to be named remarked sadly that her family will only allow her to blog under a pseudonym, which she had mixed feelings about:

> I understand their concerns about my safety and wellbeing, and also the consequences the family could face, both politically and socially, if I blog under my name. But how is this fair to me? CNN and BBC will never find out about me, and they will never interview me!

Another limitation worth highlighting is that no matter how effective social media may be, they cannot substitute for the absence of organized leadership on the ground and cannot fill the power vacuum resulting from the lack of active and organized civic engagement movements and institutions, such as nongovernmental organizations (NGOs) and strong opposition movements (El Nawawy and Khamis 2013). As Amal Bakry puts it, "It is one thing to post, blog and tweet online, but it is another thing to effectively organize and successfully coordinate women's efforts on the ground to bring about actual, positive change in the real world" (Bakry 2017).

This is a lesson that was learned the hard way by many activists who were idealists and visionaries but didn't have other tools to deploy besides social media tools. Many of them, men and women alike, lacked the experience, shrewdness, pragmatism, and maneuver that are needed to succeed in the world of politics. "If you are not at the table, you will be on the menu . . . that's the bitter lesson which many young activists learned in the Arab world today . . . after 7 years of dreaming of a better future" (Alhussini 2017).

Finally, it is important to remember how the role of social media varies, depending on the surrounding political environment and the degree of unity and solidarity, or division and fragmentation, prevailing in it. If there is a moment of unity and uniformity motivated by common goals – such as during the Egyptian revolution of 2011, for example, when all Egyptians across the board chanted the same slogans, "The people want to overthrow the regime" and "Mubarak must go" (Jumet 2017) – social media can be very successful in increasing this unity and solidarity. In this case, they best serve as amplifiers for the voices of protest as well as catalysts, mobilizers, and networking tools, which can aid the process of transformation (Khamis 2016).

However, once this moment of solidarity is replaced by deep divisions, severe polarization, and dangerous fragmentation, as witnessed in many post–Arab Spring countries today, then social media can, to the contrary, widen the gap and increase the tensions and divisions between different groups. Each group can, in this case, use its social media venues as effective weapons to attack its opponents and to defend itself, while refusing to listen to the opponents' views.

This is certainly true in terms of Arab women's online activism today, where the prevailing political divisions and fragmentations in their respective countries resulted in increasingly more fragmented and diametrically opposed movements and groups. This makes it harder to solidify women's efforts in any coordinated manner to achieve significant political, social, economic, and legal gains (Khamis 2016). These women's movements are, after all, both mirrors and molders, which simultaneously reflect and shape the realities in their respective societies.

The only positive exception, so far, has been Tunisia, the cradle of the Arab Spring and the only survivor of its tumultuous waves. A number of civil society organizations in Tunisia, including women's movements, were able to cement their divisions and bridge their differences, contributing to the only successful model of peaceful coalition building among post–Arab Spring countries. These efforts, which were internationally recognized with the Nobel Peace Prize awarded to four civil society groups in Tunisia in 2015, set a positive model for activist groups in the rest of the region in general and for Arab women's activist groups in particular.

A third wave of (Arab) feminism(s)?

The preceding discussion reveals a form of "Arab feminism," which echoes the so-called third wave of feminism in its focus on practices of cultural production (Heywood 2006; Kearney 2006; Schilt and Zobl 2008; Bell 2002), since young Arab women created their own cyberactivist culture, linked by their participation and activism in social media networks. Like other networks of young women linked by their use and creation of content on particular platforms, such as the riot grrrl zine culture or Iranian feminist websites, the specific platform – in this case blogs and social media – "became a central element of the movement" (Bell 2002).

We can argue that the overlap between this third phase of Arab feminism and the so-called third wave of feminism stems from the fact that they are both part of a universal, global movement to build on, and make maximum use of, digital technologies and new media tools to empower laypeople and members of marginalized groups, especially women, at the bottom-up, popular, grassroots level. The goal of these movements is to enable women to make their voices heard and to have their stories told in their own words (Khamis and Mili 2018).

In drawing the comparison between this third stage of Arab feminism and the third wave of feminism in the Western context, therefore, it is certainly useful to highlight the similarities and overlaps between them owing to their participatory tendencies and emancipatory potentials, when it comes to promoting a bottom-up, grassroots model of feminism (Radsch and Khamis 2013).

Yet since each of them is the by-product of its own unique historical, political, and social contexts, it is equally important to highlight some of the discrepancies and differences between them. Most importantly, unlike critiques of grrl zines or other manifestations of third-wave feminism, for focusing too much on a "narrowly construed type of individual expression without drawing out deeper political implication" (Bell 2002), cyberactivism via blogs and social media in the contemporary Arab world proved to be "both individual and political, which ultimately challenges the dichotomy between private and public spheres" (Radsch and Khamis 2013, 887).

In other words, the type of activism enacted by Arab feminists in the midst of these uprisings negates the narrow conceptualization of feminism as referring to the relationship between awareness and action, consciousness-raising, and the importance of autobiographies and the sharing of personal experience that take precedence over generic political and social discourse, including that about a "collective" voice (Armstrong 2004). This is especially important to highlight since Arab women activists

> adopted social media practices that enabled them to articulate their identities in the public sphere and to participate in the uprisings in multiple ways, resulting in a sense of personal empowerment and collective potentiality that was fundamentally linked to the communicative platform.
>
> *(Radsch and Khamis 2013, 887)*

Concluding remarks: future prospects in Arab feminism(s) and activism(s)

This chapter discussed how Arab women's varied forms of activism(s) and resistance(s) both shaped and reflected their shifting identities, changing realities, and new expressions of feminism(s), which in turn shaped and reflected new modes of activism(s), both online and offline. It paid special attention to the complexity of these women's multiple feminism(s), activism(s), and resistance(s) on multiple levels and in different spheres. It also shed light on the positive contributions and advantages of digital activism and the many functions it served to aid Arab women's political and social struggles on the one hand, as well as the constraints and limitations of this phenomenon on the other hand.

Looking ahead, it would be useful to deeply analyze and evaluate both the pros and cons of digital activism, and especially "cyberfeminism," in terms of how it can best contribute to and/or hinder women's multiple forms of activism(s) and varied resistance(s) on numerous levels.

It is important to highlight a number of important findings which emerged out of this analysis of Arab women's activism(s) in the context of the Arab Spring uprisings and their aftermath. First, these findings challenge the false images and stereotypes of Arab and Muslim women as powerless, marginalized, oppressed, and victimized. It pushes back against their overly marginalized, domesticated, and/or sexualized mediated (mis)representations.

Second, in relation to the previous point, instead of simply buying into or superficially negating these commonly held (mis)perceptions of Arab and Muslim women's powerlessness, victimization, and marginalization, it is crucial to unpack their multiple identities and varied contributions as agents of change and active participants in resistance movements. This is best done by giving women a "voice," through interviewing women from different countries, ages, backgrounds, experiences, orientations, and ideologies, to arrive at a rich, deep, varied, and comprehensive understanding of their complex, day-to-day lived realities as women, activists, citizen journalists, and social media users. This is the key to unpacking the complexity of their political, social, and legal struggles to resist different powers and various forms of oppression on multiple levels.

Third, it is equally important to complicate the notions of feminism(s) and resistance(s) by enriching our understanding of their multifaceted, multilayered, and dynamic nature, as manifested in these women's complex roles, identities, lived realities, and various forms of activism(s). This could be best achieved through avoiding the uncritical borrowing of Western notions of feminism and empowerment, which do not take into account the specifics of Arab and Muslim women's sociopolitical lived realities, as well as their cultural and religious contexts (Khamis 2013).

This highlights the need to contextualize the notions of feminism and empowerment within the unique frameworks of Arab women's own societies, which impose different sets of constraints, challenges, and limitations on women. Therefore, it is important to deeply analyze the individual context and the lived realities in each Arab country before, during, and after the Arab Spring uprisings, and their multiple implications on women's rights and their various forms of activism(s), which could be obvious or subtle, direct or indirect, against internal or external forces, and against political or social forces, or both.

Fourth, it is important to remember that no matter how strong, powerful, or helpful social media tools and forms of digital activism are, they remain simply one factor among many others which can influence the outcome of women's activism(s) or, indeed, the outcome of any form of activism. This necessitates adopting a balanced approach of "cyberrealism," which acknowledges that "the new capacities created by the Internet represent a potential that can be tapped under the right circumstance and that do empower more peripheral groups" (Muhlberger 2004, 226), without overestimating or underestimating this potential.

Adopting this informed middle position, therefore, will involve weighing both the pros and cons of digital activism, its strengths and weaknesses, as well as its contributions and limitations, in a realistic manner, which accounts for myriad political, social, and cultural factors simultaneously. After all, these new media technologies can only act as *catalysts* for change, but they cannot be *magical tools* that could make this change happen all by themselves (Khamis 2013). It is always the actors and players on the ground, in this case Arab women activists, who can effectively contribute to bringing about this change if or when they decide to do so.

Fifth, it is crucial to come up with a more inclusive and comprehensive approach, which accounts for different categories of Arab women, when rethinking the notion of "cyberfeminism" and its many related applications. This is particularly important to avoid the "urban-centric," "elite-centric," and "Western-centric" focus which has been prevalent in both media coverage and academic research around this topic so far. This can, in turn, help in overcoming the undesirable phenomenon of "tokenism," which obscures Arab women's multiple realities, as previously discussed.

Adopting such an inclusive approach is especially important with the rising tide of Arab women's activism(s) in the diaspora and in exile, as well as the proliferation of new means of communication in rural areas and in marginalized urban neighborhoods. This proliferation was made possible due to the increasing affordability and accessibility of new communication tools, as well as the growing phenomenon of "secondary internet users," whereby those who are not digitally literate can depend on others to help them navigate the realm of online communication (Khamis 2013, 2016).

The complex realities of Arab women activists and the future of their multiple forms of activism(s) and feminism(s) remain as unchartered and in flux as the complex and shifting realities of their own countries and societies, many of which are currently undergoing drastic changes and significant shifts, in both the political and social landscapes simultaneously. This makes it especially difficult to come up with specific predictions regarding the future of Arab women's activism(s), both online and offline, in the midst of these sweeping waves of change across many parts of the Arab world.

In learning more about Arab women in general, and their involvement in various forms, levels, and manifestations of resistance in particular, it is important to bear in mind that

> the inherited tension between patriarchal patterns of thought and behavior, on the one hand, and freshly articulated . . . norms and principles, on the other hand, looks set to intensify further. The way in which this tension plays out will determine the degree to which women's participation in political struggle will translate into the recognition and institutionalization of women's rights in society.
>
> *(Holt and Jawaad 2013, 181)*

It is both unrealistic and unproductive, therefore, to attempt to divorce women's issues, rights, and activism(s) from the overall, dominant power structures in their respective societies, whether in the political, social, cultural, or legal spheres. At the end of the day, women's rights are, indeed, part and parcel of the prevailing condition of human rights in their respective countries, and the margin of freedom which can be granted to them is closely tied to the overall margin of freedom which can be granted to citizens in their societies. This explains the regression in women's activism(s) and the challenges facing women's movements in many of the ailing post–Arab Spring countries, and the relative improvements in these movements in the only thriving post–Arab Spring country, namely, Tunisia.

The future of Arab women's activism(s) and feminism(s) is, therefore, closely intertwined with the trajectories of their respective nation-states and the progress, or lack thereof, that they will make on the road to democratization, freedom, and reform. We can confidently argue that as the margin of freedom in many of these countries stretches and shrinks, so will the margin of women's rights, freedoms, and activism(s) within each of them. A comparison between the current condition of women's movements in countries like Syria, Libya, Yemen, or even Egypt on one hand, and Tunisia on the other hand, is sufficient to illustrate this point.

However, one thing we can predict with certainty is the continuation of Arab women's struggles to resist all forms of oppression and domination, both in the political and social spheres simultaneously, by continuing to exercise all forms of resistance(s), both online and offline. By so doing, they will also continue to give birth to new forms of activism(s), which will reflect new representations of their identities and multiple manifestations of their feminism(s), in an ongoing, cyclical, and interconnected process.

Although Arab women, just like their own countries, still have a long way to go to consolidate their gains, realize their goals, and achieve tangible victories, we can say with confidence that their journeys toward sociopolitical transformation have already started, and there is no turning back, despite all the obstacles and detours on the road. The new communication tools and technologies, when properly utilized, can serve as useful roadmaps, signs, and lights, which can help them reach their final destinations safely and swiftly.

References

Alamm, Wafa. "Reflections on Women in the Arab Spring: Women's Voices From Around the World." Middle East Program: Woodrow Wilson International Center for Scholars. March, 2012, accessed October 30, 2016 www.wilsoncenter.org/sites/default/files/International%20Women%27s%20Day%20 2012 _4.pdf

Alhussini, Laila. Personal interview with the author, August 2017.

Al-Malki, Amal, David Kaufer, Suguru Ishizaki, and Kira Dreher. *Arab* Women *in Arab News: Old Stereotypes and New Media.* Doha: Bloomsbury Qatar Foundation Publishing, 2012.

Alwadi, Nada. Personal interview with the author, September 2017.

Alwadi, Nada and Sahar Khamis. "Voices Shouting for Reform: The Remaining Battles for Bahraini Women." In *Arab Women's Activism and Socio-Political Transformation: Unfinished Gendered Revolutions*, edited by Sahar Khamis and Amel Mili, 53–72. New York: Palgrave Macmillan, 2018.

Armstrong, Jayne. Web Grrls, Guerilla Tactics: Young Feminisms on the Web. In *Web Studies*, edited by D. Gauntlett and R. Horsely, 92–102. London/Oxford: Arnold/Oxford University Press, 2004.

Bakry, Amal. Personal interview with the author, September 2017.

Bell, Brandi Leighann. Riding the Third Wave: Women-Produced Zines and Feminisms. *Resources for Feminist Research* 29, no. 3/4 (Fall 2002): 187–198.

Bennett, W. Lance. "Changing Citizenship in the Digital Age." In *Civic Life Online: Learning How Digital Media Can Engage Youth*, edited by W. Lance Bennett, 1–24. Cambridge: The MIT Press, 2008.

Charrad, Mounira. *Policy Shifts: State, Islam, and Gender in Tunisia, 1930s–1990s Social Politics*. London: Oxford University Press, 1997.

Charrad, Mounira and Amina Zarrugh. "Equal or Complementary? Women in the New Tunisian Constitution After the Arab Spring." *The Journal of North African Studies* 19, no. 2 (2014): 230–243.

Daniels, Jessie. "Rethinking Cyberfeminism(s): Race, Gender and Embodiment." *Women's Studies Quarterly* 37, no. 1&2 (2009): 101–124.

El Nawawy, Mohammed and Sahar Khamis. *Egyptian Revolution 2.0: Political Blogging, Civic Engagement, and Citizen Journalism.* New York: Palgrave Macmillan, 2013.

El Sayed, Yasmine. Personal interview with the author, April 2013.

Eltantawy, Nahed. Personal interview with the author, September 2017.

Eltantawy, Nahed. "I'm Untouchable! Egyptian Women's War Against Sexual Harassment." In *Arab Women's Activism and Socio-Political Transformation: Unfinished Gendered Revolutions*, edited by Sahar Khamis and Amel Mili, 131–148. New York: Palgrave Macmillan, 2018.

Fraser, Nancy. "Rethinking the Public Sphere." In *Habermas and the Public Sphere*, edited by Craig Calhoun, 109–142. Cambridge, MA: MIT Press, 1992.

Gajjala, Radhika. "South Asian Digital Diasporas and Cyberfeminist Webs: Negotiating Globalization, Nation, Gender, and Information Technology Design." *Contemporary South Asia* 12, no. 1 (2003): 41–56.

Heywood, Leslie L. *The Women's Movement Today: An Encyclopedia of Third-Wave Feminism.* Westport: Greenwood Press, 2006.

Holt, Maria and Haifaa Jawad. *Women, Islam, and Resistance in the Arab World.* Boulder, CO and London: Lynne Rienner Publishers Inc, 2013.

Howard, Philip N. *The Digital Origins of Dictatorship and Democracy: Information Technology and Political Islam.* Oxford: Oxford University Press, 2011.

Inglehart, Ronald and Pippa Norris. *Rising Tide: Gender Equality and Cultural Change Around the World.* Cambridge and New York: Cambridge University Press, 2003.

Jumet, Kira. *Contesting the Repressive State: Why Ordinary Egyptians Protested During the Arab Spring*. London: Oxford University Press, 2017.

Kearney, Mary Celeste. *Girls Make Media.* New York: Taylor & Francis, 2006.

Khamis, Sahar. "Multiple Literacies, Multiple Identities: Egyptian Rural Women's Readings of Televised Literacy Campaigns." In *Women and Media in the Middle East: Power Through Self Expression*, edited by Naomi Sakr, 89–108. London: I. B. Tauris, 2004.

Khamis, Sahar. "The Arab 'Feminist' Spring?" *Feminist Studies* 37, no. 3 (Fall 2011): 692–695.

Khamis, Sahar. "Gendering the Arab Spring: Arab Women Journalists/Activists, 'Cyberfeminism,' and the Socio-Political Revolution." In *The Routledge Companion to Media and Gender*, edited by Cynthia Carter, Linda Steiner, and Lisa McLaughlin, 565–575. London: Routledge, 2013.

Khamis, Sahar. "Five Questions About Arab Women's Activism Five Years After the 'Arab Spring'." *CyberOrient* 10, no. 1 (2016), accessed October 30, 2016 www.cyberorient.net/article.do?articleId=9772

Khamis, Sahar. "A New Tunisian Law Tackles Violence Against Women." A Policy Analysis Report Published by the Arab Center in Washington DC, September 12, 2017. accessed http://arabcenterdc.org/policy_analyses/a-new-tunisian-law-tackles-violence-against-women/

Khamis, Sahar and Amel Mili. "Introductory Themes." In *Arab Women's Activism and Socio-Political Transformation: Unfinished Gendered Revolutions*, edited by Sahar Khamis and Amel Mili, 1–24. New York: Palgrave Macmillan, 2018.

Labidi, Lilia. *Electoral Practice of Tunisian Women in the Context of a Democratic Transition.* Washington, DC: The Wilson Center, 2014.

Mili, Amel. "Political-social Movements: Community Based: Tunisia." In *Encyclopedia of Women & Islamic Cultures*, edited by Suad Joseph, 2015. accessed http://dx.doi.org/10.1163/1872-5309_ewic_COM_002018

Mili, Amel. "Citizenship and Gender Equality in the Cradle of the Arab Spring." In *Arab Women's Activism and Socio-Political Transformation: Unfinished Gendered Revolutions*, edited by Sahar Khamis and Amel Mili, 27–52. New York: Palgrave Macmillan, 2018.

Moghadam, Valentine. *Modernizing Women: Gender and Social Change in the Middle East.* Cairo: American University in Cairo Press, 1994.

Moghadam, Valentine. *Gender and Social Change in the Middle East.* Boulder: Lynne Rienner Publishers, 2003.

Muhlberger, Peter. "Access, Skill, and Motivation in Online Political Discussion: Testing Cyberrealism." In *Democracy Online: The Prospects for Political Renewal Through the Internet*, edited by Peter M. Shane, 225–237. New York: Routledge, 2004.

Nazir, Sameena. *Women's Rights in the Middle East and North Africa.* New York: Freedom House, 2005.

Radsch, Courtney. "Unveiling the Revolutionaries: Cyberactivism and the Role of Women in the Arab Uprisings." James A. Baker III Institute for Public Policy of Rice University, 2012, accessed October 30, 2016 www.bakerinstitute.org/research/unveiling-the-revolutionaries-cyberactivism-and-the-role-of-women-in-the-arab-uprisings/

Radsch, Courtney and Sahar Khamis. "In Their Own Voice: Technologically Mediated Empowerment and Transformation Among Young Arab Women." *Feminist Media Studies* 13, no. 5 (2013): 881–890.

Schilt, Kristen and Elke Zobl. "Connecting the Dots: Riot Grrrls, Ladyfests, and the International Grrrl Zine Network." In *Next Wave Cultures: Feminism, Subcultures, Activism*, edited by A. Harris, 171–192. New York: Taylor & Francis, 2008.

19

Pussy Riot

A feminist band lost in history and translation

Marina Yusupova

On 21 February 2012, five women from the feminist punk rock protest group Pussy Riot entered Moscow's main Orthodox Cathedral and prayed for the Virgin Mary to become a feminist and "chase Putin away."[1] Shortly afterwards, they turned their recording of the performance into a music video entitled "Punk Prayer" and uploaded it onto YouTube.[2] The subsequent reaction from the authorities, the infamous trial of three members of Pussy Riot, and their two-year prison sentence on charges of hooliganism motivated by religious hatred have evoked a huge wave of heated discussion, interpretation, and criticism in Russia and worldwide or, to be more precise, in all Western countries. It is noteworthy that the public reaction and the locus of debates about Pussy Riot in Russia and in the Western countries were vastly different, not to mention diametrically opposed.

The Pussy Riot story was a story the West wanted to hear. Western journalists, politicians, and celebrities seemed to be unanimously inspired by the youthfulness and rebellion of these courageous Russian feminists. The US government and European foreign ministries expressed concern; Amnesty International deemed the women "prisoners of conscience," (Amnesty International 2012); dozens of world celebrities — like Madonna, Bjork, Paul McCartney, and even Danny DeVito — sang, spoke, wrote, and tweeted their support; while many Western journalists and activists hailed them as revolutionaries. Their life realities, experience, and values perfectly resonated with the core of these young women's messages.

But what about Russians? Did anybody in Russia believe that Pussy Riot had started a revolution or identify with the band's ideology? For Russians, even those who share the most liberal values, it is not so evident and simple. Public polls and two years of public debate have shown that virtually everyone in this deeply conservative country has struggled to make sense of the Pussy Riot performance.

According to the Levada Center survey of public opinion (2013), conducted straight after the announcement of the two-year prison sentence for the group members, 68% of Russians stated that they were aware of the trial of Pussy Riot. Forty-four percent considered the trial of Pussy Riot as just, impartial, and objective, while only 17% disagreed with that statement (Levada Analytical Center 2012). Some 78% of people polled in September 2012 believed that the two-year sentence in a general regime penal colony the group members received was an adequate or light

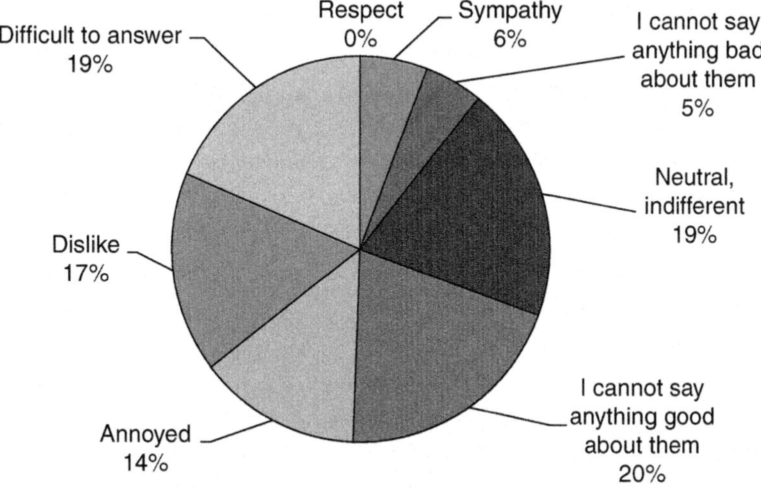

Figure 19.1 What do you feel towards the Pussy Riot Members

Source: Levada Centre, poll taken in August 2012 (2013)

punishment, while only 2% said that such actions should not be criminally punishable (Levada Analytical Center 2013, 123).

The right to riot in Russia, a country where the Western activist phrase "the personal is the political" is a dreadful reminder of Soviet era terror (Baer 2011, 181), is historically and discursively monopolized by men (Elizarov 2012). Women are considered physically and mentally unable to rebel. That is why an image of a woman who "desecrates" a church and enters the taboo space of an altar to make a political statement was so powerful and at the same time tremendously confusing. Therefore, despite the increasing Westernization of the city elites and the rise of anti-Putin sentiments, Russians remain distinctly uncomfortable with these activist women. Notwithstanding that liberal opposition leaders were unanimous in stating that Pussy Riot were held in prison unlawfully, even their response has generated little support for the group's protest itself.

> The performance in the Cathedral of Christ the Saviour is idiotic and there is no room for argument here . . . fools.
>
> *(Delovoy Peterburg 2012)*
> *Alexey Navalny, one of the major opposition figures in Russia*

> I don't like this performance.
>
> *(Novaya Gazeta 2012)*
> *Andrey Loshak, a well-known Russian journalist*

> This performance is a failure.
>
> *(Gosdep-2 2012)*
> *Marat Gelman, the best known Russian art critic*

They should let these chicks go with a slap on the ass.

(Novaya Gazeta 2012)
Boris Nemtsov, a Russian statesman and liberal politician, one of the leaders of the opposition movement "Solidarnost'" and an outspoken critic of Vladimir Putin

15 days of detention and community work for cleaning the churches.

(Gosdep-2 2012)
Kseniya Sobchak, journalist and anti-Putin political activist

So why are the reactions to the Pussy Riot performance so different? Does this mean that the West does not understand Russia and Russia does not understand the West? If so, what is it that Westerners do not understand about Russia? And what is it that Russians, stunned by the massive international support for these young women, do not understand about the West?

Part of the problem stems from an informational vacuum. Russian people still have no idea what feminism is, why it is important, and what problems it aims to solve. According to the FOM public opinion survey, about 40% of Russians have never heard the word "feminism." Twelve percent of those who were aware of feminism expressed negative attitudes toward it. A very small part of the population (8%) positively relates to feminism. It is noteworthy that during the last decade, the percentage of Russians who were indifferent to feminism has doubled (from 14% in 2001 to 29% in 2012). Since 2007, the proportion of people who, if they had a teenage daughter, would wish her commit herself to successful marriage, rather than a good job, has almost doubled (FOM 2012).

For Russia, Pussy Riot, their feminist agenda and so-called guerrilla performance style,[3] is a new and shocking phenomenon that presently fits in well with the Western feminist political movement. In a February 2012 interview with *Vice* magazine (2012), Pussy Riot members named their major feminist influences as Simone de Beauvoir, Andrea Dworkin, Emmeline Pankhurst, Shulamith Firestone, Kate Millett, Rosi Braidotti, and Judith Butler. The unapologetic closing court statements of Maria Alyokhina, Yekaterina Samutsevich, and Nadezhda Tolokonnikova also revealed an intellectual and philosophical rigor inspired by Global North feminist theories (n+1 2012).

Why did the Western theories and activism that inspired Pussy Riot to rebel not have the same effect on other Russian women? Why after more than 20 years of various feminist activities in Russia is there no feminist movement, and why do the overwhelming majority of local people continue to believe that feminism is a Western trend that destroys families? Or in other words, why has one of the most subversive ideologies of the twentieth and twenty-first centuries lost its revolutionary potential in Russia?

Two reasons why feminism has not taken hold in contemporary Russia

In the following part of this paper, I argue that the most recent history of feminism in Russia is a history of profound cultural misunderstanding and outline two reasons for this misunderstanding.[4]

First, Western feminism has been lost in Russian translation. Translated feminist studies into Russian, just like gender and sexuality studies, rely heavily on the method of transliteration. Such terms as for example "conceptualization," "egalitarianism," "essentialism," "femininity," "feminism," "gender," "identification," "marginalization," "masculinity," "narrative," "nomadic subject," "phallocentric discourse," "queer theory," "representation," and "sexism" do not have direct equivalents in the Russian language and were simply transliterated. Therefore, this body of scholarship remains largely un-translated.

The adopted language of Western feminist theories is enormously confusing even for Russian academics, not to mention activists, journalists, and their audience. As a result, the same concepts and ideas that one may find in Russian feminist texts often do not mean the same thing as they do in English.

The name "Pussy Riot" is itself a good example of what happens when we use an English term instead of the native one. Using the name "Pussy Riot" neutralizes the actual meaning. Choosing the English title for a group can be questioned as a "sophisticated but empty gesture," diminishing its association with feminist protest instead of throwing it in one's face (Mizielinska 2006, 89).[5] Accommodation of the English name worked against the aim of the band, masking the powerful message it contains and the very essence of the band's protest.

The reception and discussion of the Pussy Riot performances in Russia might have been different if they had chosen the same name in Russian – "Bunt Pizdy." For many people, this would be a very offensive thing to hear, because in contrast to the word "pussy" which the mainstream audience may not know, everybody in Russia knows what "*pizda*" means. Although the literal translation is very rude, I argue that it would have a bigger potential to attract attention to the issues surrounding women's rights in Russia.[6]

Thus, for Westerners, the use of this name is perceived as a courageous act, whereas for Russians it does not make sense. The transliterated English name masks something important and is partly the reason why people do not understand what Pussy Riot is about, and thus a reason why their feminist agenda did not get sufficient attention (Gapova 2012a). In the Russian language, "Pussy Riot" serves as an empty signifier (Mizielinska 2006, 90).[7] As a result, instead of adopting feminism to the Russian context, they may have strengthened the idea of feminism as a foreign concept, one that has nothing to do with Russia.

This brings us back to the problem of translation in a much broader sense and the second reason why feminist insights currently cannot become a part of Russian reality. In her groundbreaking work *Gender as a Useful Category of Historical Analysis*, American historian Joanne Scott argues that words, just like ideas, have their own histories (1986, 1053). Russia has never had or even heard of the Stonewall riots and the Second Wave feminist movement never happened there. Consequently, the concepts and ideas that these events had given rise to are untranslatable in Russian not only for linguistic but also for historical reasons. This sheds some light on why the postmodern language of Third-Wave feminism that Pussy Riot proudly identifies with sounds like an absurdity in the extreme for people who have never even heard the word "feminism."

> We belong to the third wave of feminism, not to the second. The third wave deconstructs the very idea of sex, so sex discrimination becomes an absurd concept. When you talk about 'gender segregation,' you refer to the initial bipolar model 'man-woman.' We conceive gender differently: There is an infinite quantity of genders that do not align between 'masculine' and 'feminine' poles. (Kiev Report 2012)
>
> *Pussy Riot, 2 February 2012*

Western feminism(s) continues to be imagined as foreign in Russia and did not take root despite the efforts of local feminists and more than 20 years of generous financial and educational support from first world civil rights and feminist organizations. In order to start thinking about the future of feminism in Russia, one has to look back at the history of the post-Soviet feminist initiatives and ask questions such as: how do Western feminist ideas function in the Russian socio-political context? How does translation work in this particular part of the world, and what are the limits of cultural translation? What consequences, advantages, or shortcomings stem from using knowledge developed in Western academia and "international" activist networks in different socio-political contexts?[8]

The insights of post-colonial and transnational feminists studying Third-World countries (Spivak 1988; Mohanty 1991, 2004; Alexander 2006 to name a few) and gender and sexuality scholars working with post-Communist countries (Gal and Kligman 2000a, 2000b; Johnson and Robinson 2007; Baer 2011; Kulpa and Mizielinska 2011) show that the Western version of feminism cannot be universally applied elsewhere. To understand the reasons for the failure of in Russia, one has to turn to the insights of transnational feminism – a contemporary paradigm that critiques Western mainstream feminism for using itself as a reference for all the various communities, resists utopic ideas about "global sisterhood," and seeks to lay the ground for more productive and equitable social relations across borders and cultural contexts.

Transnational feminists and queer scholars argue that "American [and European] activists must not be self-congratulatory about the apparent globalization of their [gender] and sexual politics" (Patton 2002 in Mizielinska 2006, 92). The idea that the Anglo-American version of feminism (I, along with the aforementioned authors, argue that this is a version, and not the universal standard) can be transferred to a completely different socio-political context undermines the need for local research (Mizielinska 2006, 96) and more importantly, as Mohanty (1991) argues, is a form of "discursive colonization."

The idea of discursive colonization or cultural imperialism ("the assumption that every country will go through exactly the same stages of 'development'" gradually approaching gender equality and freedom of sexual expression) (Mizielinska 2006, 99–100) gives us a lens through which to see the reasons for the profound cultural misunderstandings that characterize the most recent history of feminism in Russia. The failure of Russian feminism – that largely relied on Western theories and practices along with Black and Post-colonial feminisms – poses a challenge "to some of the organizing premises of Western feminist thought" (Ahmed et al. 2000, 111).

Building on the work of the aforementioned authors, I argue that when conducting a feminist protest, one has to take local history, culture, and socio-political context seriously. Notions of universalism may in fact have very conservative and reactionary consequences affecting millions of people.[9]

To put it simply, although "it is definitely encouraging to think that we are part of a big global movement," the political and strategic decisions of local movements should always be local. The solutions, strategies, and tactics that Russian feminists are using or planning to use should be constructed upon local traditions, social structures, and practices (a Finnish queer scholar in Mizielinska's research) (Mizielinska 2006, 98). In a long-term perspective "by importing Western identities [and ideas] into different cultural contexts without acknowledging differences, one can do more harm than good" (Mizielinska 2006, 98).

The failure of Russian feminism should be closely researched and discussed. This analysis and emphasis on awareness of the local can become the most significant source of inspiration for feminist researchers and activists in the future. A feminist campaign can be very inspiring for local people if the organizers know something about the culture and do not just blindly adopt Western strategies (e.g. protesting and parading) (Mizielinska 2006; Kulpa and Mizielinska 2011). The primary aim of feminist activists and researchers must be to engage in self-conscious discourse and activism, which empowers Russian people to speak, recognize their histories and different approach to gender and sexuality in order to create conditions for their voices to be heard. I can envision Pussy Riot and Russian feminists engaged in a struggle for justice and equality and using the Russian language, which is clear to everybody.

Acknowledgments

I express my gratitude to my adviser Dr Adi Kuntsman for her support and insightful remarks and my colleague Ravi Hensman for his helpful suggestions. In particular, I thank all the organizers, speakers, and participants of the "Gender, Sexuality, and Power" OSI-HESP Regional Seminar for Excellence in Teaching Project (2011–2014) for their invaluable contribution to my professional and personal growth and inspiration for writing this paper.

Notes

1 Pussy Riot performance at Christ the Savior Cathedral (original video) www.youtube.com/watch?v=grEBLskpDWQ
2 Punk Prayer 'Mother of God, Chase Putin Away' www.youtube.com/watch?v=GCasuaAczKY
3 Guerrilla performance refers to a type of ad hoc concert arranged very quickly and without advance ticket sales. It takes place in an unusual, sometimes unannounced setting not designed to accommodate live music (e.g., public transport, parking lot, roof of a building).
4 This paper does not consider the Kremlin's recent turn toward conservative values traditional gender roles, and a general patriarchal renaissance in Russia, which among other things has conditioned and reinforced the expulsion of women's rights and civil rights discourses from the public sphere. Although I am fully aware of the crucial importance of the contemporary political dimension of this problem, I consider it to be a separate topic for analysis, which is outside the scope of this paper.
5 Mizielinska applies this argument to the translation of the word "queer" into Finnish and Polish. She argues that the term is largely untranslatable in these languages and is mainly retained in the original English, which in her view, "worked against the aim of queer theory, masking its associations with non-normative sexuality instead of throwing sexuality in one's face" (2006, 89).
6 This point could be contested because, as Elena Gapova argues, "the women's question" is not even formulated in Russia, where feminist activists mainly speak about gender-related problems that emerged in Western context(s) (see Gapova 2012a, 2012b).
7 Here again I use the argument and wording from Mizielinska (2006).
8 Mizielinska (2006), Kupla and Mizielinska (2011), and Baer (2011) raise similar questions in relation to Queer theory and sexualities studies.
9 An illustrative example here may be the recent neo-conservative and discriminatory anti-gay law adopted in Russia.

References

Ahmed, Sara, Jane Kilby, Celia Lury, and Maureen McNeil. 2000. "Introduction." In *Transformations: Thinking Through Feminism*, edited by Sara Ahmed, Jane Kilby, Celia Lury, and Maureen McNeil, 1–24. London: Routledge.

Alexander, M. Jacquie. 2006. *Pedagogies of Crossing: Mediations on Feminism, Sexual Politics, Memory, and the Sacred.* Durham, NC: Duke University Press.

Amnesty International. 2012. "Russian Federation: Release Punk Singers Held After Performance in Church." www.amnesty.org/en/library/asset/EUR46/014/2012/en/c9edb950-30b6-4b90-a4d3-ddf8b97bc4c3/eur460142012en.html

Baer, Brian James. 2011. "Queer in Russia: Othering the Other of the West." In *Queer in Europe*, edited by Lisa Downing and Robert Gillet, 173–188. London: Ashgate.

Delovoy Peterburg. 2012. "Navalny zastupilsia za Pussy Riot." [Navalny Comes for the Defense of Pussy Riot.] *Sergey Gurkin*, March 7. www.dp.ru/a/2012/03/07/Navalnij_zastupilsja_za_P/

Elizarov, Nikita. 2012. "Simptom Pussy Riot. Bunt Pizdy protiv Khuya." [Symptom Pussy Riot. Riot of Pussy against Dick.] http://old.looo.ch/2012-04/762-pussy_riot_symptom

FOM (Fond Obshchestvennoe Mnenie). 2012. "'Zhenshchina toze chelovek': predstavleniia rossiian o feminisme." ['A Woman Is Also a Human Being': Russians About Feminism.] *Public Poll "FOMnibus,"* August 26. http://fom.ru/obshchestvo/10611

Gal, Susan, and Gail Kligman. 2000a. *The Politics of Gender After Socialism: A Comparative-Historical Essay.* Princeton, NJ: Princeton University Press.

Gal, Susan, and Gail Kligman, eds. 2000b. *Reproducing Gender: Politics, Publics, and Everyday Life After Socialism.* Princeton, NJ: Princeton University Press.

Gapova, Elena. 2012a. Delo "Pussy Riot": feministskiy protest v kontekste klassovoy bor'by. [Pussy Riot Case: Feminist Protest in the Context of Class Struggle.] *Neprikosnovenniy zapas* 5 (85). http://magazines.russ.ru/nz/2012/5/g2.html

Gapova, Elena. 2012b. Interview About Pussy Riot. www.youtube.com/watch?v=FNw_azv1eZI

Gosdep-2. 2012. Programma Ksenii Sobchak: Pussy Riot, March 17. www.youtube.com/watch?v=QFhPV_FiDRk

Johnson, Janet E., and Jean C. Robinson, eds. 2007. *Living Gender After Communism.* Bloomington: Indiana University Press.

Kiev Report. 2012. "Pussy Riot: Gendernoe ravenstvo vigodno vsem!" [Pussy Riot: Gender Equality Is Good for Everybody.] February 2. http://kievreport.com/arts/436

Kulpa, Robert, and Joanna Mizielinska, eds. 2011. *De-Centring Western Sexualities.* London: Ashgate.

Levada Analytical Center. 2012. "Tret' Rossiian verit v chestnyi sud nad Pussy Riot." [One Third of Russians Believe in Fair Trial of Pussy Riot.] www.levada.ru/17-08-2012/tret-rossiyan-verit-v-chestnyi-sud-nad-pussy-riot

Levada Analytical Center. 2013. "From Opinion Towards Understanding." *Russian Public Opinion 2012–2013.* Annual. Moscow: Levada Center. www.levada.ru/books/obshchestvennoe-mnenie-2012-eng

Mizielinska, Joanna. 2006. "Queering Moominland: The Problems of Translating Queer Theory Into a Non-American Context." *SQS Journal* 1 (1): 87–104. www.helsinki.fi/jarj/sqs/SQSMizielinska.pdf

Mohanty, Chandra T. 1991. "Under Western Eyes: Feminist Scholarship and Colonial Discourse." In *Third World Women and the Politics of Feminism*, edited by Chandra T. Mohanty, Ann Russo & Lourdes Torres, 51–80. Bloomington: Indiana University Press.

Mohanty, Chandra T. 2004. *Feminism Without Borders.* Durham, NC: Duke University Press.

n+1. 2012. "Pussy Riot Closing Statements." https://nplusonemag.com/online-only/online-only/pussy-riot-closing-statements/

Novaya Gazeta. 2012. "V Khamovnicheskom sude zavershen pervyi den slushanii po delu Pussy Riot." [Khamovniki District Court Has Finished the First Day of Hearing of the Pussy Riot Case.] Kostyuchenko, Elena, July 30. www.novayagazeta.ru/news/58666.html?p=6

Scott, Joan W. 1986. "Gender: A Useful Category of Historical Analysis." *The American Historical Review*, 91 (5): 1053–1075.

Spivak, Gayatri. 1988. "Can the Subaltern Speak?" In *Marxism and the Interpretation of Culture*, edited by Cary Nelson and Lawrence Grossbergm, 271–313. London: MacMillan.

Vice. 2012. "Meeting Pussy Riot." March 12. www.vice.com/read/A-Russian-Pussy-Riot

20

None of this is new (media)

Feminisms in the social media age

Alice E. Marwick

Do you consider yourself a third-wave feminist?

I don't much like the terminology, because it never seems very accurate to me. I know people who are considered third-wave feminists who are 20 years older than me.

Maybe we're onto the fourth wave now.

Maybe the fourth wave is online.

—*Jessica Valenti, founder of Feministing.org (Solomon 2009)*

The need for unity is often misnamed as a need for homogeneity.

—*Audre Lorde*

Introduction

Feminism is enjoying a moment in the pop culture spotlight. Pop musicians Beyoncé and Taylor Swift openly identify as feminists, comedians Mindy Kaling and Amy Schumer helm explicitly feminist television shows, terms like "rape culture" and "slut-shaming" are mainstream, and acts of feminist activism, from Slutwalk to Pussy Riot, make headlines around the world. While just a few years ago older feminists bemoaned the lack of action by younger women, today's feminism is youth-centric, often brash and confrontational, and largely coordinated online (Evans 2014; Keller, Mendes, and Ringrose 2016). On social media sites like Twitter, Tumblr, and YouTube, young feminists voice opinions, debate transgender identity and police brutality, spread memes and jokes, and share activist strategies. The tools that young feminists use today look different from those of the past. The petition, the protest march, the flyer, and the newsletter have their online equivalents, but social media brings with it similar social dynamics leveraged across a different set of media technologies and, thus, possibilities. Tracing the history of feminism and internet communication demonstrates that many of these tensions are intrinsic to feminist activism, yet the scope and scale of modern digital communication brings some into sharper relief.

Social media is an umbrella term for a diverse set of technologies, websites, mobile apps, and protocols that facilitate the creation, annotation, and sharing of digital media. While broadcast media like television and radio limited content creation to professionals, social media makes it possible for ordinary people to create and spread their own media to wide audiences; Henry Jenkins calls this blurring of the line between media producers and consumers *participatory culture* (2006). While social media applications differ in functionality, danah boyd identifies four common characteristics of user-generated content: digital media is *replicable, scalable, persistent,* and *searchable* (boyd 2010). Content created by individuals is replicable as it can easily be copied and spread; it is scalable because it can be potentially seen by millions; it is persistent since it leaves digital footprints in archives and search engines; and it is searchable, often instantly (Marwick and Ellison 2012). These material functionalities allow users to perform certain actions, such as combing through archives, annotating tweets and blog posts, commenting on videos, and otherwise remixing and drawing from vast digital histories. Despite these new possibilities, we should avoid fetishizing digital technologies; as new media scholar Nancy Baym writes, "Any medium that allows people to make meaning together is social. There is nothing more 'social' about 'social media' than there is about postcards, landline telephones, television shows, newspapers, books, or cuneiform" (2015). As Baym points out, media artifacts and communication technologies of all kinds inspire and facilitate discussion and connection.

For many years, scholars have documented women's online activities (Baym 2000; Bury 2005; Shade 2002), but there are fewer historically informed accounts of *feminist* internet activity. In this chapter, I conduct a literature review of early social technologies to trace a rough history of online feminism, from early computer-mediated technologies (1980s through mid-1990s), to personal homepages and e-zines popular during the late 1990s to mid-2000s, to the blogging wave of the mid- to late 2000s. While these periods are blurry, imprecise, and necessarily overlapping, they are distinguished by the specifics of available technologies (which in turn affect what users can do) and the demographics of the user base. I then turn to the contemporary technologial landscape and explore feminist practice on sites like Twitter and Tumblr. Using two case studies, Gamergate and the debate over intersectionality, I show that while social media facilitates connection and collaboration, it also highlights conflict, not only between feminists and their detractors but also within feminism itself.

While excavating these hidden histories, several themes came to light. There is a prominent and persistent tension between the fantasy of online community as collaborative and collective – the cyber-utopian narrative of digital exceptionalism that Nancy Baym urges us to abandon – and the reality of "feminism" as an enormously diverse group of people with varying opinions, what might more accurately be called *feminisms.* For instance, women of color have recognized the normative whiteness of online feminist activism for more than 25 years, calling for more intersectional and global perspectives (Kolko 2000; Nakamura 1999). Feminist participation, both on- and offline, is consistently framed in ways that privilege adult activism and push out young women's activities and experiences (Harris 2008). And unfortunately, men have harassed female users of social technologies since such technologies existed, since misogyny and sexism do not disappear once socializing moves online. The narrative of "social media" as open and democratic allows for feminist education, networked activism, and camaraderie, but it also opens participants to conflict and cruelty online. Social media can be simultaneously feminist and misogynist; like all media, it is subject to the structural power relations that exist between those who use it.

As this volume shows, defining "feminism" is easier said than done. Whenever possible, I keep to accounts of self-defined feminist communities, whether they are the cyberfeminist theorists of the 1990s or the young feminist blog Fbomb in the 2000s. However, it is important to note that this essay centers on US internet use; while I use examples from other contexts, many of the technologies and practices highlighted here originate in North America.

Excavating a feminist prehistory of social media

Although the internet and the World Wide Web did not drift into public consciousness until the mid-1990s, an expansive network of digital communication existed for years before that. Independently run bulletin board systems (BBSs) and commercial dial-up networks like Prodigy, CompuServe, and Delphi existed alongside early internet services including LISTSERVs (electronic mailing lists devoted to particular topics) and Usenet groups (topically organized discussion forums), which were primarily available to those affiliated with large Western universities. While these spaces and groups looked nothing like the social media of today – they were entirely textual and required a substantial amount of specialized knowledge to use and access – they are one of the earliest examples of computer-mediated communication and user-generated content. Users shared thoughts and opinions on popular culture, politics, their personal lives, and a vast array of specialized interests. And much like the social media of today, women in general and feminists in particular faced an array of difficulties participating in early electronic spaces.

For one thing, the participants in these spaces were remarkably alike by modern standards. The vast majority of electronic communication well into the early 1990s was heavily dominated by white, educated North American men, and the presence of any women at all was often a curiosity (Shade 2002). One 1992 study estimated that 95% of internet users were men (Herring 2003). As a result, simply asserting the existence of women in cyberspace became a political issue. For instance, in 1983, CompuServe user Pamela Bowen submitted a proposal to create a women's forum, as women were getting together regularly to talk but were frustrated by interruptions and chat requests from men. Her suggestion was rejected because there "were not enough women online to justify it" (Balka 1993). The women who did exist in these spaces tended to be, like their male equivalents, highly educated professionals, primarily affiliated with the technology industry and the sciences.[1]

Despite their elite status, women in early electronic communities faced a number of obstacles to full participation, including harassment and conversational monopolization by men. Ellen Balka summarizes:

> women users of other computer networks frequently complain about attacks upon their views by men, their continuous struggle to keep the "conversation" focused upon women, and their boredom with debates about fundamental assumptions (that men should help change diapers, that daycare should be more accessible).
>
> *(1993)*

Cheris Kramarae and H. Jeannie Taylor, members of the University of Illinois's influential Women, Information Technology, and Scholarship working group, elaborated on these points. They noted that women face "obscenities, racial slurs and vicious personal attacks" online "from people who might not say such things in face-to-face interaction," that virtually all open forums, even those dedicated ostensibly to women's issues such as the Usenet groups soc.women and soc.feminism, are "overrun by men." They also remarked upon the increasing presence of sexual harassment in groups devoted to academic and professional concerns, such as sexist or sexual jokes and limericks, which women were often afraid to criticize for fear of jeopardizing their own careers (Kramarae and Taylor 1993). Laurel Sutton's analysis of the alt.feminism Usenet group similarly found that 67% of posters were male, with 74% of posts coming from men, who were overwhelmingly likely to adopt hostile, aggressive, or adversarial posting styles and to dominate conversation for weeks at a time, which was likely to alienate interested women

(1994; Herring 1993). Thus, even spaces that were set up for discussion of feminism and women's issues were often hostile to women themselves.

Despite this, women did participate in early electronic communities, often in explicitly feminist ways. Many set up women-only networks, groups, and LISTSERVs as a way to combat harassment, flaming, and trolling from men. Soc.women, originally called net.women, was so frustrating for its participants that they created the mail-feminist mailing list as a response to what they saw as "boring, endless" conversations and "women's opinions . . . treated as dumb, stupid, or ignorant by men" (Balka 1993). Others in the late 1980s and early 1990s created computer networks specifically to address broader social concerns. The Women's Bulletin Board System (WBBS) was established in the mid-1980s by social justice activists for women's groups to facilitate feminist organizing (Balka 1993).[2] Women's centers used the Big Sky Telegraph network, created to connect small rural classrooms in Montana, to connect and share resources (Uncapher 1999).

Cyberfeminism

While today it seems unsurprising that women online faced harassment and sexism, to many early scholars of cyberculture, one of the primary virtues of textual online spaces was that they made it possible for people to communicate without corporeal cues like appearance or voice (Stone 1996; Turkle 1995). In its less progressive version, such disembodiment was a fantasy of mind/body dualism in which people could disconnect from their "meat-space" identities and meet as pure intellect. This was present in cyberpunk fiction such as William Gibson's *Neuromancer* and Neal Stephenson's *Snow Crash* and echoed in celebratory accounts of early online community such as Howard Rheingold's *Virtual Community* (2000). To many feminist scholars influenced by Judith Butler's work on performativity (1990), the *disembodiment hypothesis* held that internet users, liberated from the constraints of the flesh, could actively choose which gender or sexuality to "be," perhaps creating alternate identities nothing like their own (Wynn and Katz 1997). By making it possible for users to self-consciously adopt and play with different gender identities, online communities would reveal the choices involved in the production of gender, breaking down binaries and encouraging fluidity in sexuality and gender expression. Sherry Turkle wrote, "like transgressive gender practices in real life, by breaking the conventions, [online gender play] dramatizes our attachment to them" (1995, 212).

In the early 1990s, with the gradual opening of the internet to more diverse populations, a new *cyberfeminist* movement emerged to combat the male technophile culture which alienated women. "Cyber" being a popular signifier during this time period to describe a wide variety of online and computer-generated experiences, the term surfaced in multiple locations (Paasonen 2011; Reynolds 2013). The Australian artist collective VNS Matrix published "A Cyberfeminist Manifesto for the 21st Century" in 1991, which drew from French feminist theory, futurism, and cunt art[3] to claim a space for feminism within cyberpunk. British cultural theorist Sadie Plant popularized the term in her own cyberfeminist manifesto, in which she positioned digitalization and networks as a tools "that will eventually overturn the phallogocentric hegemony" (Paasonen 2011, 338; Plant 1996). From these origins, cyberfeminism spread rapidly, but the term was always slippery. As Kate Reynolds writes, many cyberfeminists were brought together at the First Cyberfeminist International at the Documenta X conference in Germany:

> During the conference, the women collaboratively constructed a definition of Cyberfeminism called the "100 Anti-Theses." This document lists one hundred things that cyberfeminism is not, and is composed of statements in four separate languages. The decision not

> to [define] Cyberfeminism has allowed the term a versatility that many previous types of feminism lacked, though it is perhaps this lack of solidity that allowed the Cyberfeminist movement to drift into obscurity.
>
> *(Reynolds 2013)*

Over the years, cyberfeminism came to mean, variously:

> - Feminist analysis of relationships between humans and machines
> - Drawing from Donna Haraway (1985), critical interrogation of technologies and practices
> - Research on gendered online cultures and technology uses, and how technology reinforces hierarchies and divisions.
>
> *(Paasonen 2011, 340)*

Often playful, satirical, and ironic, cyberfeminism sometimes veered into an essentialist view of male and female capabilities. Most cyberfeminists maintained that technology was not intrinsically masculine, and that in theory, computer networks ought to be consistent with the democratic, decentralized, participatory structures of women's organizations dedicated to feminist social change (Balka 1993; Wajcman 2007), but others portrayed women as inherently good at such community-building and nurturing (Van Zoonen 2001). For instance, Susan Hawthorne and Renate Klein explained that cyberfeminism aimed not only to counter the power differentials between men and women online, but in a way coherent with the essentialist philosophy that was present in one faction of second-wave feminism:

> Connectivity is at the heart of feminism. In the 1970s we rallied around the concept of sisterhood, and challenged the patriarchal ideology of women as enemies of each other. We connected the personal to the political. We talked in consciousness-raising (CR) groups, connecting through understanding our similarities and our differences. And despite the fragmenting forces of postmodernism, economic rationalism and globalization, women around the world have continued to explore those issues which we have in common, while recognizing our diversity. As we have come to understand, focusing on difference alone, fragments us, separates us and disenfranchises us politically.
>
> *(Hawthorne and Klein 1999, 5–6)*

As this quote's admonition to avoid "focusing on difference" illustrates, however, cyberfeminism in the 1990s remained the realm of elite white women, with most of its participants being academics, artists, and the highly educated – because the internet at that time was largely populated by such people. Radhika Gajjala and Annapurna Mamidipudi explained that "cyberfeminists share the belief that women should take control of and appropriate the use of Internet technologies in an attempt to empower themselves" (1999, 8) which ignored the fact that it may not be possible for women in the Global South – or even Western minority women – to use Western technologies in an authentically "empowering" way. Gajjala and Mamidipudi also voiced suspicion of cyberfeminism's frame of the internet as intrinsically democratic, which implied that solving the "digital divide," or the difference in access amongst different populations (women/men, rural/urban, Global North/Global South) would increase democracy, rather than potentially re-creating colonial power dynamics (1999).

A significant amount of empirical work demonstrating the falsity of the disembodiment hypothesis affirmed this critique (Bury 2005). Women's personal experiences online showed that gender did not disappear in "virtual" spaces, and critical feminist and cyberculture scholars pointed out that anonymity and persistent pseudonymity established a white, male, able-bodied, straight, English-speaking, educated subject as normative (Stone 1996; Kramarae and Taylor 1993).[4] When someone marked themselves as varying from this subject position – perhaps by stating their race, or by using non-American forms of English, for instance – they were often subject to harassment and racism, or accused of "playing the race card" (Gajjala 2000; Nakamura 1999; Kolko 2000). Cyberfeminism, for many women of color and non-Western women, provided a critique of male dominance but did not sufficiently address intersectional issues.

Personal homepages, e-zines, and cybergrrrls

In 1993, the National Center for Supercomputing Applications at the University of Illinois Urbana-Champaign released a free graphical web browser called Mosaic. While clunky and limited by today's standards, Mosaic made it easy for people with internet access to browse through pages created by others. While the number of web users was still very small, many users' imaginations were sparked by the ability to make web pagespages that anyone else with web access could see. Personal homepages might consist of a dry curriculum vitae and headshot, a webcam monitoring a department's coffee maker, a rant about President Clinton, a list of the owner's CD collection, bad adolescent poetry, a fan page for the *X-Files*, or virtually anything else the proprietor could think of. Gradually, personal homepages became a genre unto themselves, following a fairly well-trodden rhetorical path of self-presentation: first-person voice, links representing interests (hobbies, musical taste), direct expression of personality traits, and affiliation with online web communities (Papacharissi 2002; Dominick 1999). These pages increased in popularity with the advent of free hosting services such as Geocities, which provided would-be homepagers with tools for easier page creation and editing.

While women's online participation grew rapidly during this time, from 15% in 1995 to 38.5% in 1997 (Warnick 1999), homepages were still primarily the domain of men, with a 1999 study estimating that 87% of homepage authors were male (Dominick 1999, 650).[5] Despite this, feminist personal homepagers did exist and frequently found each other, forging online communities and connections. Some of these pages were feminist in the "personal as political" sense, drawing from zine culture, riot grrrls, and the clip-art ethos of punk rock and do-it-yourself culture to focus on self-expression and first-person narrative (Comstock 2001; Scott 1998).

Zines, or homemade magazines created using paper, ink, tape, and copy machines and traded through the mail, were a significant site of young feminist activism and identity during the 1990s (Piepmeier 2009; Radway 2016). Zines were a truly participatory media, encouraging even young women with limited resources to create and spread ideas using low-budget, accessible technologies (Duncombe 1997). Young women shared deeply personal experiences in their zines, using zine trading, letters, conventions, and rock shows to knit together communities of support and affiliation (Comstock 2001; Radway 2011). While many zine writers, or zinesters, were early adopters of the web, many more were suspicious of the increasing commercialization of these new technologies as the dot-com boom loomed large (Marwick 2013a). Some zinesters used the web to promote, distribute, or even reproduce their paper zines – popular blog *BoingBoing* began as a paper zine – but even for those who did not, their influence was such that "ezine" became a catch-all term for an online magazine, co-authored website, or even a large personal homepage. The ethos of "riot grrrl," a movement countering sexism in the punk rock scene[6] with a significant zine component, was depoliticized as webmistresses and commercial organizations refashioned "grrrl" into a marker of postfeminist cyber-edginess (Comstock 2001). Barbara Warnick explains that the authors of many of the grrrl ezines and sites "emphasized artistic expression (in writing and graphics), social support relevant to concerns of site visitors, music and film reviews, and gripes about coverage of women's issues in the popular press" rather than explicit activist or social justice politics (1999, 14).

Some of the most successful grrrl homepages and e-zines joined webrings, or linked collections of websites organized around a particular theme. While most webrings were purely amateur, the two best known grrrl networks functioned as startups, or as they were known at the time, "dot-coms": Chickclick and Estronet (the two merged in 1999). While each member site was independently published, often by individual women, these networks attempted to create revenue sharing and business models so that creators could profit from their work (Swanson n.d.). Typically shying away from explicit feminist identification, grrrl networks framed themselves primarily as alternatives to the limited content for women found in the mainstream media (Marwick 2013a; Warnick 1999). The founder of ChickClick, Heidi Swanson, explained:

> Most women's on-line sites assume women just want their horoscopes, recipes and tips on losing weight and getting a boyfriend. But that's not reality. Women between 13 and 35 are hungry for information about what really impacts their lives – getting jobs, music, dating, even snowboarding.
>
> *(Ganahl 1998)*

Many of the more radical homepages by, for example, women of color, queer women, and self-identified feminists were absent from these networks in favor of those closer to Swanson's idea of what we might call a postfeminist e-zine (see Figure 20.1: ChickClick Homepage 1999).

Personal homepages were social media in the sense that the individual creating them was creating and broadcasting content via the web, but they generally lacked the ability for the audience to participate beyond signing a guestbook or emailing the owner. Swanson explains that ChickClick attempted to scaffold levels of participation for young women who, unlike the early adopter creators of ChickClick's sites, might be reluctant to fully embrace technology:

> If we could get a visitor to the front door of ChickClick we would then provide different layers of involvement. Let people test the waters and whatnot, and ease into whatever they were comfortable with. You could just read the articles, sister sites, other member posts if you wanted. On the more active side, we rolled out ChickPages, and bulletin boards. Thousands of homepages were built, and millions of thoughts and opinions were logged on the bulletin boards – which in turn was inspirational to all the new users who were/are just stumbling onto ChickClick that day for the first time.
>
> *(Swanson n.d.)*

ChickClick's homepage hosting and bulletin boards allowed young women to participate not only by consuming content but by creating and contributing their own.

Explicitly feminist activist sites existed during this time period, but not all of them were what we might consider *social. Ms.* magazine's website included a lively bulletin board. The "Pro-Choice Webring" brought together women actively working on expanding reproductive rights (Arreola 2013; Ladd 2001). A 2001 survey of 50 different US-based feminist activist organizations showed that they used web pages and email to disseminate information, lobby politicians, and organize local events but found that these tools did not support interpersonal interaction or strengthen personal relationships and might exclude economically underprivileged women (Vogt and Chen 2001). A different survey of global feminist organizations found widespread support for using LISTSERVs and the web to mobilize other women and gather information cheaply and

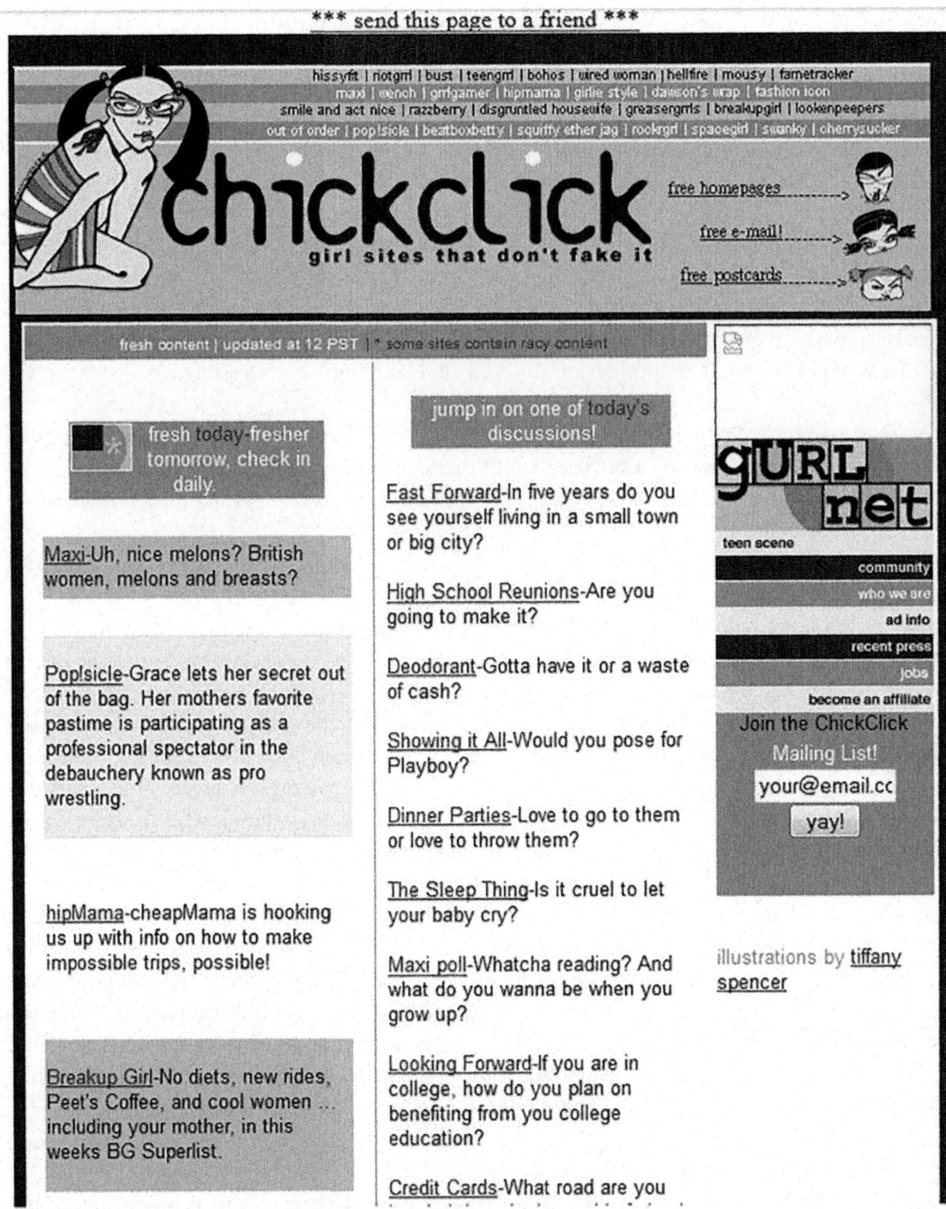

Figure 20.1 ChickClick homepage, 1999

easily, but these uses were limited to the elite, educated populations in most countries (Harcourt 2000). For the most part, these were professional activists using the internet as a new way to disseminate information, rather than the participatory ideal of social media.

Internet use increased somewhat in diversity by the late 1990s; 44.4% of all Americans, 16.1% of Hispanics, and 18.9% of African Americans had home internet access as of August 2000 (Rohde and Shapiro 2000). While many online communities of color existed, the media (and academia) paid scant attention to them, preferring instead to focus on digital divide rhetoric (Everett 2002). Dara N. Byrne argues that, given the importance of Black social networks to racial identity and community development, African Americans were more likely to participate in black-centered online communities such as BlackPlanet, The Drum, or NetNoir than predominantly white networks (2007). Many of these ethnic online communities, however, including MiGente and AsianAvenue, focused on "general cultural information," market segmentation, and profit rather than facilitating feminist or activist work (McLaine 2003). Of course, women did use the internet for such purposes. For instance, black women activists used the internet to spread information throughout their communities during the 1997 Million Women March (MWM) by printing out MWM websites, photocopying them, and disseminating them throughout their neighborhoods (Everett 2002). Such creative appropriation of internet technology used preexisting social networks to combine "traditional" activist techniques like newsletters and protest marches with the increased scale of information dissemination brought about by the internet.

Both traditional feminist activism and the experiences of women of color were largely absent from the popular grrrl networks. One of Estronet's member sites was *HUES* magazine (Hear Us Emerging Sisters), a magazine for multicultural women. While not explicitly feminist, founder Ophira Edut explains that *HUES* allowed for a range of identifications: "Since some women of color have historically felt excluded by the label, we let each writer define herself: womynist, womanist, feminist, girl-powered, humanist, unlabeled – whatever allowed her most authentic self-expression" (Jewish Women's Archive 2015). Also left out was much of the critical element of riot grrrl culture found in zines like *Slant, Evolution of a Race Riot*, and *Bamboo Girl*, which critiqued the predominantly white riot grrrl narrative as well as punk masculinity (Piano 2002). Doreen Piano argues that it was in compilation zines written by "women of color, transgender, queer, working-class women, and race-conscious anglos" that "critical feminist interventions take place and where the work of second-wave women of color such as bell hooks, Cherrie Moraga, Chela Sandoval, and Patricia Hill Collins is being continued" (2002, p. 20). These interventions did not necessarily extend to the Hello Kitty, pinup girl aesthetic of feminist e-zines and online networks.[7]

Feminist blogging

The dot-com bust had vast effects on the commercial development of the web but did not stop independent web publishing. In fact, the early 2000s saw a rise in easy-to-use tools like Geocities, Blogger, and LiveJournal which made it possible for people to create homepages, blogs, and online journals without advanced technical knowledge (Nardi, Schiano, and Gumbrecht 2004; Rettberg 2013). Blogs are frequently updated personal publications, which range in format from lists of links with minimal description, to collections of long essays, to diaries, to blogs that post photographs or songs, to group blogs run by multiple people first-person style, to sites containing breaking news and political commentary. Blogs became immensely popular in the early 21st century, to the point that "blog" was Merriam-Webster's word of the year in 2004 (Rettberg 2013). Much was written about the political significance of blogs, especially those about the Iraq War or mainstream politics. But to a certain extent, blogging was simply an extension of the earlier personal homepages and journals that proliferated online.

This distinction was gendered. Blog stereotypes of the mid-2000s fell into two categories: the highly professionalized pundit blog written by an adult man, or the angsty teenage girl writing a digital diary on LiveJournal (Gregg 2006). Susan Herring argues that many of the pioneers of personal web publishing were women and girls, but online journals and personal homepages were considered insignificant by the mainstream media and tech press when compared to political blogs or tech blogs, which were primarily written by men (Herring et al. 2004). Studies focusing on political blogs found that most bloggers were men, while those examining personal blogs found the opposite (Harp and Tremayne 2006; Nowson and Oberlander 2006). This dichotomy reified a particular sense of politics which excluded the personal as political perspective taken up by feminists since the second wave (Gregg 2006). But women were very active in the blogosphere, not only writing personal essays about their experiences, but writing explicitly about a wide range of public issues, including feminism.

The feminist blogosphere is and was large and sprawling, and can roughly be divided into two types of blogs. The first is the highly professionalized, popular feminist blog such as *Feministing, Racialicious, Pandagon, Feministe,* and *Jezebel.* While most of these started as volunteer efforts, in their heyday each was known for frequent updates, audiences in the hundreds of thousands, and quick responses to developments in political news and popular culture. *Feministing*, at its peak, was the most popular feminist publication in the world, with half a million hits per month (Solomon 2009). Several of these blogs have shut down or are shadows of their former selves, due primarily to the enormous amount of labor required, lack of funding, or blogger burnout (Martin and Valenti 2013), but others are still thriving and popular today. For instance, Amanda Marcotte's *Pandagon* shut down in 2015, and Amanda became a full-time political writer for *Salon.* Jessica Valenti left *Feministing* to write a number of best-selling books on feminism (the site still exists and is maintained by a rotating collective of young feminists). *Jezebel* is still very active but has shifted its focus somewhat to popular culture and mainstream politics.

The second type consists of personal blogs written by feminist women and girls focused on their individual thoughts and experiences. Jessalyn Keller interviewed a number of feminist girl bloggers, who stated that their blogs existed to expose and educate their peers about feminism, as a form of activism in themselves, and as community participation (Keller 2016a, 2016b). Girls framed blogging as a way to contribute to a cause they deeply believed in, since they were often cut off from adult forms of feminist activism like protest marches and events due to lack of financial resources or geographic isolation. Crucially, interacting with readers and other bloggers was a key part of feminist blogging – the most popular blogs had extensive comment sections and often forums and opportunities for readers to publish on the site. For many young bloggers, reading other women's blogs, responding to comments, and guest blogging was a core part of their blogging practice. Moreover, personal blogs provided important spaces "to reflect experiences that have been trivialized, denigrated or ignored in the past, particularly the views of women and younger members of society" (Gregg 2006). Anita Harris frames these sites as counterpublics and points out that while they may be less focused on political outcomes than "traditional," adult-centric activism, their importance is in their existence as forums and places for debate. Young women's blogs and, today, social media presences focus more on individual strategies and tactics for dealing with everyday sexism, media representation, and the culture industry. She argues that for many young people, the media, rather than the government, is the site of power (2008). Young feminist blogs allow girls to participate in ways appropriate to their circumstances rather than following a model set by adults or political elites. For instance, *FBomb*, which describes itself as "a blog/community created for teenage girls who care about their rights as women and want to be heard," had, on the day I visited, front-page articles on Gamergate, intergenerational activism, inequality in mental healthcare, the burkini ban, and indie rock feminism (Zeilinger 2016).

To some extent, blogs have been superceded by social media like Twitter, Tumblr, and Instagram, which allow for personal publishing with even less overhead. But while blogs are not as popular as they were, many still exist as important sites for identity development and information dissemination. Professionally run blogs abound, but personal blogs still remain influential in many areas, such as fashion (*Fashiontoast, The Blonde Salad*), parenting (*A Cup of Jo, The Bloggess*), food

(*Smitten Kitchen, The Pioneer Woman*), and personal finance (*Mr. Money Mustache, Money Saving Mom*), to name but a few.

Contemporary social media: tweets and Tumblrs

Before moving on to present-day social media, I must acknowledge the vastness of the contemporary feminist internet. Women all over the world, in a variety of contexts, harness the power of digital participatory technologies from SMS messages to YouTube vlogs to Twitter memes to spread feminist ideals and create community. Rather than singling out a particular technology, Keller et al. argue that "digital feminist activism" as a networked whole enables *affective solidarity*, Clare Hemmings's theory that emotional connections and shared anger are a necessary precursor to feminist activism (Keller, Mendes, and Ringrose 2016; Hemmings 2012). Rather than solidifying around any single site or grouping of sites, feminist affect exists within a network of digital connections that enable women to share their experiences and co-experience rage, frustration, and anger with sexism and intersectional oppression. Social media resembles an overlapping ecosystem more than a series of individual spaces, which is reflected in the way that users create, disseminate, and comment on content. The technologies that facilitate this change rapidly; today's Instagram and Snapchat are tomorrow's obsolete MySpace and LiveJournal.

The dynamics found on feminist girl blogs described in the last section resemble those on contemporary social media platforms like Tumblr, Twitter, and Facebook. Feminist participation in these spaces often resembles a series of elaborate in-jokes, with memes, nuggets of news, cultural criticism, pop culture, and hashtags spreading rapidly and seamlessly throughout online communities and across websites. Notably, much of this content is graphical, in contrast to the lengthy text posts found on blogs. Tumblr, a micro-blogging platform which affords lightweight "reblogging" and "liking" other users' posts, has become a significant community of practice for young feminist world-building (Connelly 2015; Thelandersson 2013). A visitor to the Daily Feminist on Tumblr (http://the-daily-feminist.tumblr.com/), for instance, is greeted with dozens of overlapping animated gifs, graphics, and text posts, which on a random day included:

- The text "REBLOG IF YOU THINK TRANS WOMEN BELONG IN FEMALE AND LESBIAN SPACES"
- A list of victims of the anti-LGBTQ Orlando shooting
- A GIF of Trevor Noah of the Daily Show criticizing media portrayals of Hillary Clinton and Elizabeth Warren
- Graphic reading "I support people who have abortions"
- Screenshots of Twitter posts discussing rape culture
- An orange graphic reading "Virginity Is a Social Construct"
- A cartoon about the validity of women dressing in different ways (Figure 20.2)
- A comic about Native American women and sexual assault (Figure 20.3)
- A graphic about sexual assault (Figure 20.4).

Such images, ideas, and snippets circulate and disseminate across platforms and places. A young woman uses a graphics app on her smartphone to add a feminist tagline to an animated GIF of a Disney princess she found via Google Images and posts it to her Tumblr; the GIF might be reblogged by 15 other feminist Tumblrs, posted on Facebook, tweeted, and posted to a feminist forum on Reddit, where it receives an additional 50 comments. In her undergraduate thesis on feminist social media, Scripps student Taryn Riera describes part of her morning routine checking Reddit, Facebook, and Tumblr:

Figure 20.2 Cartoon by Moga reblogged 4,200 times on Tumblr (http://artbymoga.tumblr.com/)

> I stop to reblog another photo on Tumblr, this one of a ballet dancer who wrote that she was always told her "black girl hips" would keep her from ever being successful in ballet, before returning to Facebook to like my friend's link and comment on how insightful the article was. I yawn, frowning at the sunlight pouring through my window and directly into my eyes, then get out of bed to start my day. Already, in the half hour it takes me to check my feeds and interact across various platforms, I have been validated in my anger to a sexist joke, educated about a topic I might not have encountered, and visited spaces that make intersectional feminist ideas the norm.
>
> *(Riera 2015, 5)*

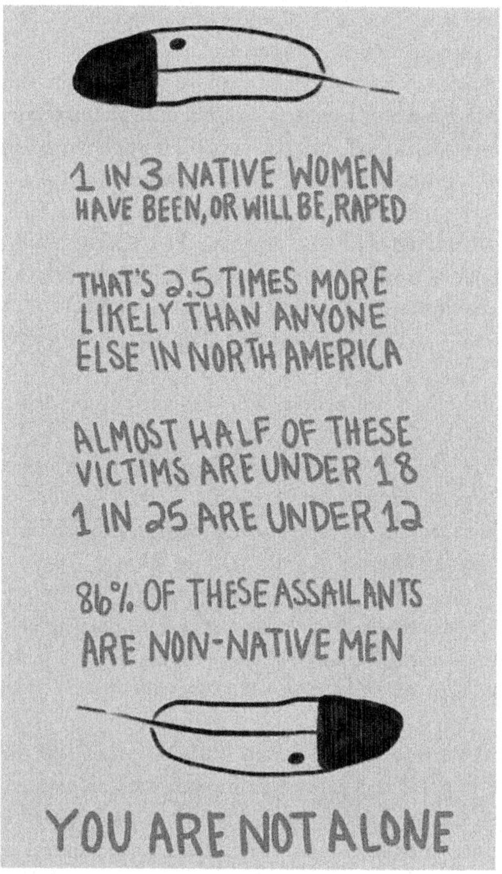

Figure 20.3 Part of a comic by AngelMilk09 (Angel Smith). Reblogged 4,500 times on Tumblr

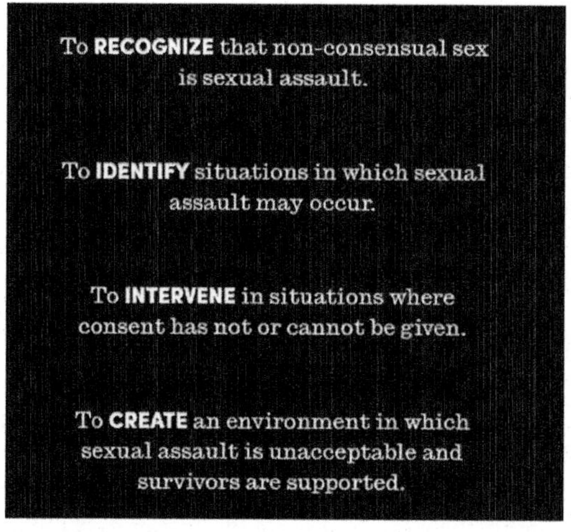

Figure 20.4 Graphic reblogged 664 times on Tumblr (author unknown)

The proliferation of such feminist spaces online normalizes a feminist gaze on the world, and allows young women to participate in ways appropriate to their comfort level, access, and technical knowledge. Of course, not only young feminists use social media. But social media has indubitably contributed to the grassroots resurgence of interest in feminism among young women.

Contemporary feminist social media practice is so diverse that it is impossible to describe in a single chapter. To provide another example, I will briefly discuss "hashtag feminism" and how its use of both humor and critique contributes to building affective ties and what Carrie Rentschler calls "a culture of support and response" (2014, 76). "Hashtag feminism" is the use of hashtags on Twitter to create participatory commentary on current events or controversial issues, often hilarious, pointed, or absurd. For instance, #safetytipsforladies satirized anti-rape strategies presented to women (watch your drink, don't walk by yourself after dark) with such gems as:

@CaptKimothy: Most rapists are people, so consider only befriending animals and ghosts #safetytipsforladies
@hilaryjfb: If you hide your forearms in your sleeves, the rapist will mistake you for a T-Rex and carry on his way #safetytipsforladies
@gimmepanda – The majority of rapists are known to the victim. Consider not knowing any men. #safetytipsforladies

Hashtags allow dozens, hundreds, or thousands of people to participate in a group conversation and see what others have written. While they have a myriad of uses, hashtag feminism frequently uses humor or irony to create affective responses (Rentschler 2015). Carrie Rentschler argues:

> The humor of #safetytipsforladies explains both its spread and the memetic remaking of feminist jokes that respond to victim blaming attitudes and slut shaming rhetoric. In the process, #safetytipsforladies helped change the terms of feminist debate about sexual violence, drawing broader media attention to feminist rape prevention discourse through the derisive laughter that energizes current feminisms. The hashtag activism of #safetytipsforladies illustrates how humor nurtures a politics of joy and resilience in the face of rape culture and its apologists.
>
> *(2015, 355)*

Shared humor can create a feeling of intimate community and belonging. Hashtag feminism can also be a way for women to see that experiences they thought of as individual are universal. For example, the #everydaysexism hashtag brought together thousands of women across the world sharing experiences of street harassment. Ryan Bowles Eagle writes, "The effect of reading so many similar stories in such sheer numbers, different voices testifying to similar experiences from diverse places, serves as powerful evidence for the pervasiveness of violence against women – evidence that cannot be easily silenced" (2015, 352).

However, hashtag feminism is often limited in its ability to address complexity. Shenila Khoja-Moolji discusses the #bringbackourgirls hashtag, designed to bring attention to the kidnapping of hundreds of Nigerian schoolgirls by radical group Boko Haram, and Lauren Berlandt's concept of *intimate publics* (2015). Khoja-Moolji demonstrates how the widespread use of the hashtag created affective bonds between strangers, but that the ability to form these bonds depends on a shared history or sensibility. She points out that #bringbackourgirls fits into a Western narrative of Islam as an oppressive threat to women, and flattens many of the complex histories and differences in the news story. Hashtag feminism, then, can be a simplistic answer to complicated problems.

None of this is new: feminisms in conflict

Despite the positive possibilities of social media, social media's affordances illuminate two ongoing problems with feminist activism. The first is male harassment of feminist women, which is more prevalent than ever, in part due to the same technical functionality that feminists take advantage of to build online community. Social features like forums, Twitter, hashtags, digital video, and the like are used by individuals and a variety of groups (including the alt-right, men's rights activists and Gamergate supporters) to systemically shut down feminist discourse online, as are tactics like "doxxing," or publicizing personal, private information; "dogpiling," or coordinating attacks, and social shaming. The second involves the continued presence of white normativity in feminist spaces online. When women of color criticize racist comments or point out absence, they are frequently accused of "toxic feminism" and of creating division where there need be none – a long-standing tactic to privilege white middle-class voices. In this section I use two case studies to demonstrate how social media makes these conflicts visible far beyond individual participants.

Harassment and Gamergate

The long-documented harassment of women online has increased in both frequency and severity in the last few years as feminist activism has flourished online (Citron 2014). Caroline Criado-Perez campaigned to add a woman to the British banknote and was subject to threats of death and sexual abuse on Twitter (Hattenstone 2013). Developer Adria Richards complained about conference attendees making sexual jokes and was met with a barrage of threatening messages, including a photoshopped picture of a naked, bound, decapitated woman (Marwick 2013b). *Jezebel* writer Lindy West wrote about rape jokes in comedy; in addition to threats of rape and violence, a reader created a Twitter account in the name of her deceased father and tweeted that he was disappointed in her (West 2015). The frequency of such attacks on platforms like Twitter – and the lack of built-in tools to deal with them – as well as the frequency of sexist speech on communities like Reddit, raises questions around the limits of online free speech and why, exactly, such racist and misogynist speech has become so common (Citron 2014; O'Leary 2012). Speaking out about sexism comes with a price. Many successful and visible online feminists, like Amanda Marcotte of *Pandagon*, Jamia Wilson of Women, Action and the Media, and Jill Filipovic, former editor of *Feministe*, have either pulled back from the public eye or pondered quitting. Jessica Valenti says that it's "not just the physical safety concerns but the emotional ramifications" of constant, daily threats, and abuse (Goldberg 2015). The possible effects of harassment include a chilling effect on women's online participation, long-term emotional and professional difficulty for the women harassed, and an increase in sexual stereotyping and discrimination both off- and online.

The online harassment of women is both individual and systemic. While a variety of people with a spectrum of political positions engage in harassing behavior, feminists (especially women of color and queer women) are often targeted for harassment which is coordinated through chat rooms, image boards, and subreddits. While those involved in such attacks may be self-identified trolls, members of the alt-right, white nationalists, anti-Semites, and so forth, it is "men's rights" groups who have been targeting feminists online for years (Dragiewicz 2011). Founded in the 1970s to lobby against domestic violence and child custody laws, modern men's rights groups focus on a host of issues under a general umbrella of anti-feminism. Reddit has become notorious as a clearinghouse for men's rights activists (MRA). The two best-known MRA subreddits are /r/MensRights and r/TheRedPill, the latter a reference to the character Neo finding enlightenment in the film *The Matrix*. As Adrienne Massanari writes, while the most virulent anti-feminism is found in these two communities, "the misogynistic views of TRP and MR do not simply stay put in those subreddits; they become part of the larger Reddit culture – informing the ways in which women are discussed and treated on the rest of the site" (2015, 138). The vocabulary and beliefs of men's rights activists, such as "misandry" (hatred of men by women) and "SJWs" (social justice warriors, a pejorative term), have infiltrated many internet spaces, especially those seen as key to geek masculinity. Geek masculinity is a type of middle-class white masculinity that privileges technical expertise and command of pop-cultural knowledge, while narrowly circumscribing proper "geek" identity within a raced and gendered framework (Massanari 2015, 128–9).

The best known, best-coordinated attack against feminists of the last few years is Gamergate, a movement purporting to be about "ethics in game journalism" which was strategically planned and executed by members of the anonymous bulletin board 4chan, a notorious hub of troll culture. Gamergate began as an organized brigade on independent game developer Zoe Quinn, who was accused by an ex-boyfriend of sleeping with a reviewer to garner positive coverage of her game *Depression Quest*. Ms. Quinn was inundated with thousands of hateful messages. Her attackers disseminated nude photos of her as well as personal information including her address and social security number – which she was accused of fabricating. Gamergaters called her parents, called her phone at all hours of the night, and openly discussed raping her, her weight, and the smell of her vagina. As the harassment escalated, Anita Sarkeesian, a feminist media critic and favorite target of anti-feminist gamers for several years, was doxxed and forced to cancel an appearance at the University of Utah due to a death threat. Another game developer, Brianna Wu, posted anti-Gamergate memes on Tumblr and Twitter and received death threats. Actress Felicia Day, a long-time gaming advocate, wrote an emotional blog post about the effects that Gamergate was having on her ability to trust male gamers and was promptly doxxed for her trouble. What Quinn, Sarkeesian, Wu, and Day had in common was a feminist sensibility and the audacity to criticize video game culture. While Sarkeesian's videos cataloging tropes of women in videogames might seem mild to feminist media studies scholars, they represent an attack on a popular culture dominated by masculine gender norms and thus threaten the hegemony of geek masculinity.

Whitney Philips, who studies trolling, or the act of trying to "disrupt or upset as many people as possible, using whatever linguistic or behavioral tools are available," (2015, 2) writes that trolling rhetoric "is predicated on highly-gendered notions of victory and domination, and . . . is used to silence, punish, and correct 'soft' or otherwise feminized speech" (2015, 167). While there is a clear difference between subcultural trolling, online harassment, and the actions of "haters" or cyberbullies, there are commonalities as well. Internet communities like 4chan and Reddit share a strong belief in "free speech" and regulation of online participation as censorship (Reagle 2015). These classic liberal values of the internet often, in practice, privilege combative or openly biased community members over the comfort of female members, leading to male domination even in high-minded online communities like Wikipedia (Reagle 2012). Members of online communities, particularly those framed as *open* or *participatory*, often explain gender gaps in membership as a matter of individual choice rather than systemic bias. Thus aggressive online speech, whether practiced in the profanity and pornography-laced environment of 4chan or the loftier venues of newspaper comments sections, often frames sexism as an issue of freedom of expression and normalizes sexist, anti-feminist language.

Intersectionality and "toxic feminism"

In her review of 2013 feminist activism, Kira Cochrane writes that the feminists she spoke with primarily defined themselves as *intersectional feminists*, who view oppression as multiple and overlapping rather than simply about gender. She writes:

> Today's feminists generally seem to see it as an attempt to elevate and make space for the voices and issues of those who are marginalized, and a framework for recognizing how class, race, age, ability, sexuality, gender and other issues combine to affect women's experience of discrimination.
>
> *(2013)*

Indeed, feminist social media includes the voices of women of color, queer women, transgender people, working-class women, and women with disabilities. However, the ideal of intersectionality is often overshadowed in practice by the concerns of what disability blogger Rachel Cohen-Rottenberg calls "cis-gendered, able-bodied, normatively sized, middle-class, white Anglo-Saxon Protestant women" (Cohen-Rottenberg 2013). Indeed, Jessie Daniels points out that "what remains unquestioned . . . is the dominance of white women as architects and defenders of a framework of feminism in the digital era" (2016). She cites Sheryl Sandberg's *Lean In* and #banbossy campaign as examples of mainstream feminist activism which primarily address the need to increase female leadership in corporate America, which concerns a very small number of privileged women. Similarly, a *Feministing* essay by Syreeta McFadden criticizes media discussions of stay-at-home-moms versus working moms for excluding the voices of working-class women, who are most affected by the lack of childcare and labor protections in the United States (McFadden 2013). As feminist discussions move beyond individual blogs or Twitter into the mainstream, they are often stripped of this type of nuance and reframed as issues of most interest to wealthy target markets. Moreover, the media often points to white female bloggers as the visible figureheads of "digital feminism" while ignoring their more diverse counterparts.

These conflicts came into stark relief with the release of the #femfuture report in 2013, authored by Feministing bloggers Courtney Martin and Vanessa Valenti. In this report, a sort of "State of the Union" of feminist blogging, Martin and Valenti argued that blogging was crucial to sustaining feminist activism, but that a lack of financial support for feminist blogs and affective support for bloggers risked "blogger burnout." The report was based on a 2012 meeting of a diverse community of feminist bloggers, but both Martin and Valenti fit the mold of the professional white middle-class feminist. They were immediately criticized for focusing on solutions most appropriate for professional non-profit organizations, for releasing the report without asking for community input, and ignoring the contributions of radical women of color (Risam 2015). These critiques were compounded by a 2014 article by *Nation* writer Michelle Goldberg, who labeled the Twitter debate around #femfuture as "toxic" and created largely by women of color. As Roopika Risam writes, "in doing so, she [instantiated] a notion of toxic femininity, positioning women of color feminists as the disruptive bodies that transgress fictive, ideal feminist spaces on Twitter" (2015). In other words, "toxic feminism" idealizes a homogenous, civil, pleasant feminist space which is normatively white and middle class, and further marginalizes the voices of feminists who do not fit this model (Daniels 2016; Risam 2015).

The "toxic feminism" discourse also marginalizes the very real concerns of women of color and other excluded groups. In 2013, Mikki Kendall started the #solidarityisforwhitewomen to highlight the marginalization of women of color in white feminist movements. The tipping point for Kendall was Hugo Schwyzer, a professor with a long history of drug abuse, sleeping with students, and intimate partner violence who was consistently given a platform on sites like *Feministe* and *Jezebel* as a sort of celebrity male feminist (Gable 2014). Schwyzer was also known to frequently argue with feminists of color. Tope Fadiran writes:

> [Schwyzer's whiteness] points to broader issues with racism and white privilege in mainstream feminism that women of color have spoken to for decades. In Schwyzer's case, women of color have been raising objections about his history, and his dismissive and hostile behavior towards women of color, for many years, with little success in getting white feminists in his circle to hold him, or themselves, accountable.
>
> *(Fadiran 2012)*

Frustrated with what she saw as a lack of accountability on the part of mainstream digital feminists, Kendall began a series of historically informed tweets:

> #SolidarityIsForWhiteWomen when you ignore the culpability of white women in lynching, Jim Crow, & in modern day racism
>
> #SolidarityIsForWhiteWomen when you idolize Susan B. Anthony & claim her racism didn't matter
>
> #SolidarityIsForWhiteWomen when feminist discussions of misogyny in music ignore the lyrics of [the Rolling Stones song] Brown Sugar

The hashtag quickly caught on, and feminists of color added their own contributions:

> @RBraceySherman: #SolidarityIsForWhiteWomen = fighting for #reprorights but saying nothing ab shackling of pregnant & forced sterilization incarcerated WOC
>
> @zblay: #solidarityisforwhitewomen when pink hair, tattoos, and piercings are "quirky" or "alt" on a white woman but "ghetto" on a black one.
>
> @Blackamazon: #SolidarityIsForWhiteWomen calls Hillary the first viable women's candidate even though Shirley was the first and only nominee

These tweets and thousands of others point to significant conflicts between the ideal of intersectional feminism versus the material, oppressive histories of white-normative feminism.

These concerns have not disappeared in the digital age; indeed, technologies like Twitter make them more visible. Roopika Risam writes, "online feminists fearing toxicity are struggling with the argument that intersectional feminists have been making all along: there isn't a single, common cause within feminist movements. Indeed, the proliferation of intersectional feminist hashtags, demonstrates that online feminism is labyrinthine" (2015). Ideally, the ability of different feminisms to interact online would lead to greater understanding and a displacement of the white-normative narrative. Despite the "toxic" backlash described above, the ability to quickly and actively call out racism, classism, transphobia, or ableism (etc.) within feminist movements and find solidarity with others is a strength of today's fast-moving social media landscape.

Indeed, much online feminist activism is intersectional and inclusive. In 2014, for instance, the Association for Progressive Communications organized a Gender, Sexuality, and the Internet Meeting in Malaysia, where 50 attendees – gender and women's rights activists, queer organizations, human rights advocates, and technology activists – collectively created a document outlining the "Feminist Principles of the Internet" (revised in 2015) (Association for Progressive Communications 2015). The 17 principles, which include statements on access, resistance, movement building, privacy, and violence, aim to not only challenge sexism but also to recognize the full realities of women, girls, and queer people's lives:

> A feminist internet works towards empowering more women and queer persons – in all our diversities – to fully enjoy our rights, engage in pleasure and play, and dismantle patriarchy. This integrates our different realities, contexts and specificities – including age, disabilities, sexualities, gender identities and expressions, socioeconomic locations, political and religious beliefs, ethnic origins, and racial markers.
>
> *(Association for Progressive Communications 2016)*

The #ImagineAFeministInternet movement involves women from all over the world; it incorporates a sophisticated critique of neoliberal techno-capitalism and global surveillance; it acknowledges the severity of online harassment and positions it within a larger context of violence toward women and girls; and it involves a range of other issues that affect women globally (Nagarajan 2016). The activists working toward making this feminist internet possible demonstrate the potential of the internet – especially when combined with face-to-face meetings and on-the-ground coordination – to address both the diversity of women's lives and the power of collective organizing.

Conclusion

The affordances and dynamics of social media, and internet technologies more generally, both allow for feminists to connect and form communities while simultaneously opening them to both internal and external criticism. After years in which feminism was largely absent from youth and popular culture, the strong resurgence in grassroots feminist activism, art, politics, and culture, especially among young women is, frankly, quite heartening to this middle-aged feminist. Social media allows feminists of all ages to tell personal stories, affectively engage with the experiences of others, collectively organize, and mobilize politically. However, social technologies – both in terms of functionality and cultural discourses and narratives – are not intrinsically feminist. While they might facilitate certain types of feminist community-building, they also lack tools for combating harassment and backlash. These platforms on which young feminist activists depend are also firmly situated in a Silicon Valley geek culture itself plagued by sexism, causing intrinsic conflicts between the ideals of feminism and those who would seek to combat it. Ultimately, the strengths and possibilities of feminism flourish online, but online feminists – especially young women, women of color, queer women, and women in the Global South – are often subject to the worst abuses of technology. Rather than presuming that we can fiat technical solutions to such problems, feminist social media participation requires support and community from feminists of all ages, nationalities, and political orientations.

Notes

1 A mid-1980s effort to create a CompuServe-like service for professional women, the Amazon Line, failed partially because the creators "found that many of the women they had hoped to attract did not do their own typing, but rather had secretaries who typed for them" (Balka 1993).

2 It was shut down in 1990 after the building that hosted it was struck by lightning.

3 Cunt art, which originated with feminist artist Judy Chicago and a group of women at the Fresno State College Feminist Art Program, explicitly references vaginal imagery and takes "female sexuality as a vital and multivalent aspect of female experience" (Meyer 2006, 322; Meyer and Wilding 2010). The VNS

Matrix manifesto read, in part, "We are the modern cunt . . . we are the virus of the new world disorder/ rupturing the symbolic from within/saboteurs of the big daddy mainframe/the clitoris is a direct line to the matrix" (VNS Matrix 1991).

4 Lisa Nakamura points out that the fantasy of the disembodied subject who sidesteps discrimination coincides with the neoliberal ideal of colorblindness and "fair competition" in the market, both prominent in the 1990s (2008, 5).

5 Dominick summarizes: "In sum, the typical author of a personal page is a young, single male who is either a student or has a white-collar job that is associated with computer technology" (1999, 650).

6 The relationship between riot grrrl and race is very complicated. From its origins, riot grrrl was criticized not only because it was primarily composed of white women, but because many of these white women reproduced racist discourses and attitudes. There is a parallel history of extensive creative expression by young people of color during this time period, particularly in zines. Therefore, to tell the history of zine-related feminism and activism as that of riot grrrl makes invisible the contributions of women of color – and queer women (Radway 2016; Nguyen 2012).

7 This ethos was often at explicit odds with cyberfeminism. Faith Wilding, one of the Fresno State College feminist artists, wrote in a 1998 essay that so-called cybergrrls "often uncritically recirculate and re-present sexist and stereotyped images of women from popular media – the buxom gun moll; the supersexed cyborg femme; the 50's tupperware cartoon women, are favorites – without any analysis or critical recontextualization" (1998, 8). She instead called for women on the web to create and circulate female imagery which did not rely on gender binaries.

References

Arreola, Veronica. 2013. "Back to the #FemFuture." *Viva La Feminista*, April 16. www.vivalafeminista.com/2013/04/back-to-femfuture.html.

Association for Progressive Communications. 2015. "Feminist Principles of the Internet." *Imagine a Feminist Internet*, July 22–24, Port Dickson, Malaysia. http://feministinternet.net/sites/default/files/Feminist-PrinciplesoftheInternetv2.0_0.pdf.

———. 2016. "Feminist Principles of the Internet." *Feminist Principles of the Internet*, August. http://feministinternet.net/.

Balka, Ellen. 1993. "Women's Access to On-Line Discussions About Feminism." *The Electronic Journal of Communication/La Revue Electronique de Communication* 3 (1). www.cios.org/EJCPUBLIC/003/1/00311.HTML.

Baym, Nancy. K. 2000. *Tune in, Log on: Soaps, Fandom, and Online Community*. London: Sage.

———. 2015. "Social Media and the Struggle for Society." *Social Media + Society* 1 (1): 1–2.

boyd, d. 2010. "Social Network Sites as Networked Publics: Affordances, Dynamics, and Implications." In *A Networked Self: Identity, Community, and Culture on Social Network Sites*, edited by Z. Papacharissi, 39–58. New York: Routledge.

Bury, Rhiannon. 2005. *Cyberspaces of Their Own: Female Fandoms Online*. New York: Peter Lang.

Butler, Judith. 1990. *Gender Trouble: Feminism and the Subversion of Identity*. New York: Routledge.

Byrne, Dara N. 2007. "Public Discourse, Community Concerns, and Civic Engagement: Exploring Black Social Networking Traditions on BlackPlanet. Com." *Journal of Computer-Mediated Communication* 13 (1): 319–40.

Citron, Danielle. 2014. *Hate Crimes in Cyberspace*. Cambridge, MA: Harvard University Press.

Cochrane, Kira. 2013. "The Fourth Wave of Feminism: Meet the Rebel Women." *The Guardian*, December 10. www.theguardian.com/world/2013/dec/10/fourth-wave-feminism-rebel-women.

Cohen-Rottenberg, Rachel. 2013. "Why This Disabled Woman No Longer Identifies as a Feminist." *Disability and Representation | Changing the Cultural Conversation*, July 30. www.disabilityandrepresentation.com/2013/07/30/why-this-disabled-woman/.

Comstock, Michelle. 2001. "Grrrl Zine Networks: Re-Composing Spaces of Authority, Gender, and Culture." *Journal of Advanced Composition* 21 (2): 383–410.

Connelly, Sarah M. 2015. "'Welcome to the FEMINIST CULT': Building a Feminist Community of Practice on Tumblr." Undergraduate Senior Thesis, Gettysburg, PA: Gettysburg College. http://cupola.gettysburg.edu/student_scholarship/328/.

Daniels, Jessie. 2016. "The Trouble with White Feminism: Whiteness, Digital Feminism and the Intersectional Internet." In *The Intersectional Internet: Race, Sex, Class, and Culture Online*, edited by S. U. Noble and B. M. Tynes, 40–60. New York: Peter Lang.

Dominick, Joseph R. 1999. "Who Do You Think You Are? Personal Home Pages and Self-Presentation on the World Wide Web." *Journalism & Mass Communication Quarterly* 76 (4): 646–58.

Dragiewicz, Molly. 2011. *Equality With a Vengeance: Men's Rights Groups, Battered Women, and Antifeminist Backlash.* Lebanon, NH: Northeastern University Press.

Duncombe, Stephen. 1997. *Notes From Underground: Zines and the Politics of Alternative Culture.* New York: Verso Books.

Eagle, Ryan Bowles. 2015. "Loitering, Lingering, Hashtagging: Women Reclaiming Public Space Via #BoardtheBus, #StopStreetHarassment, and the #EverydaySexism Project." *Feminist Media Studies* 15 (2): 350–3.

Evans, Elizabeth. 2014. *The Politics of Third Wave Feminisms.* New York: Springer.

Everett, Anna. 2002. "The Revolution Will Be Digitized: Afrocentricity and the Digital Public Sphere." *Social Text* 20 (2): 125–46.

Fadiran, Tope. 2012. "Why Do Some Feminist Spaces Tolerate Male Abusers?" *GlobalComment*, January 25. http://globalcomment.com/why-do-some-feminist-spaces-tolerate-male-abusers/.

Gable, Mona. 2014. "The Hugo Problem." *Los Angeles Magazine*, March 26. www.lamag.com/longform/the-hugo-problem/.

Gajjala, Radhika. 2000. "Internet Constructs of Identity and Ignorance: 'Third-World' Contexts and Cyberfeminism." *The Future of Narrative Discourse: Internet Constructs of Literacy and Identity*, 33–6.

Gajjala, Radhika, and Annapurna Mamidipudi. 1999. "Cyberfeminism, Technology, and International 'Development'." *Gender and Development* 7 (2): 8–16.

Ganahl, Jane. 1998. "The Chief Chick of ChickClick: Spinning a Web for the Anti-Cosmo-Girl." *San Francisco Chronicle*, December 24. www.sfgate.com/cgi-bin/article.cgi?f=/e/a/1998/12/24/STYLE8833.dtl.

Goldberg, Michelle. 2015. "Feminist Writers Are So Besieged by Online Abuse That Some Have Begun to Retire." *The Washington Post*, February 19. www.washingtonpost.com/opinions/online-feminists-increasingly-ask-are-the-psychic-costs-too-much-to-bear/2015/02/19/3dc4ca6c-b7dd-11e4-a200-c008a01a6692_story.html.

Gregg, Melissa. C. 2006. "Posting With Passion: Blogs and the Politics of Gender." In *Uses of Blogs*, edited by A. Bruns and J. Jacobs, 151–60. New York: Peter Lang. http://espace.library.uq.edu.au/view/UQ:72839.

Haraway, Donna. 1985. "A Manifesto for Cyborgs: Science, Technology, and Socialist Feminism in the 1980's." *Socialist Review* 80: 65–108.

Harcourt, Wendy. 2000. "The Personal and the Political: Women Using the Internet." *CyberPsychology & Behavior* 3 (5): 693–7.

Harp, Dustin, and Mark Tremayne. 2006. "The Gendered Blogosphere: Examining Inequality Using Network and Feminist Theory." *Journalism & Mass Communication Quarterly* 83 (2): 247–64.

Harris, Anita. 2008. "Young Women, Late Modern Politics, and the Participatory Possibilities of Online Cultures." *Journal of Youth Studies* 11 (5): 481–95.

Hattenstone, Simon. 2013. "Caroline Criado-Perez: 'Twitter Has Enabled People to Behave in a Way They Wouldn't Face to Face'." *The Guardian*, August 23. www.theguardian.com/lifeandstyle/2013/aug/04/caroline-criado-perez-twitter-rape-threats.

Hawthorne, Susan, and Renate Klein. 1999. *Cyberfeminism: Connectivity, Critique and Creativity.* North Melbourne: Spinifex Press.

Hemmings, Clare. 2012. "Affective Solidarity: Feminist Reflexivity and Political Transformation." *Feminist Theory* 13 (2): 147–61.

Herring, Susan. C. 1993. "Men's Language: A Study of the Discourse of the LINGUIST List." In *Proceedings of the XVth International Congress of Linguists* 3: 347–50.

———. 2003. "Gender and Power in Online Communication." In *The Handbook of Language and Gender*, edited by Janet Holmes and Miriam Meyerhoff, 202–28. Malden, MA: Blackwell.

Herring, S. C., I. Kouper, L. A. Scheidt, and E. L. Wright. 2004. "Women and Children Last: The Discursive Construction of Weblogs." In *Into the Blogosphere: Rhetoric, Community, and Culture of Weblogs*, edited by L. J. Gurak, S. Antonijevic, L. Johnson, C. Ratliff, and J. Reyman. http://blog.lib.umn.edu/blogosphere/women_and_children.html.

Jenkins, H. 2006. *Fans, Bloggers, and Gamers: Exploring Participatory Culture.* New York: New York University Press.

Jewish Women's Archive. 2015. "Ophira Edut." *Jewish Women's Archive.* Accessed July 5. http://jwa.org/feminism/edut-ophira.

Keller, Jessalynn. 2016a. *Girls' Feminist Blogging in a Postfeminist Age*. New York: Routledge.

———. 2016b. "Making Activism Accessible: Exploring Girls' Blogs as Sites of Contemporary Feminist Activism." In *Girlhood Studies and the Politics of Place: Contemporary Paradigms for Research*, edited by C. Mitchell and Carrie Rentschler. New York: Berghahn Books.

Keller, Jessalynn, Kaitlynn D. Mendes, and Jessica Ringrose. 2018. "Speaking 'Unspeakable Things': Documenting Digital Feminist Responses to Rape Culture." *Journal of Gender Studies* 27 (1): 22–36.

Khoja-Moolji, Shenila. 2015. "Becoming an 'Intimate Publics': Exploring the Affective Intensities of Hashtag Feminism." *Feminist Media Studies* 15 (2): 347–50.

Kolko, B. E. 2000. "Erasing@ Race: Going White in the (Inter) Face." In *Race in Cyberspace*, edited by B. E. Kolko, L. Nakamura, and G. B. Rodman, 213–32. London: Routledge.

Kramarae, Cheris, and H. Jeannie Taylor. 1993. "Men and Women on Electronic Networks: A Conversation or a Monologue?" In *Women, Information Technology, and Scholarship*, edited by H. Jeannie Taylor, Cheris Kramarae, and Maureen Ebben. Urbana: University of Illinois, Center for Advanced Study.

Ladd, Donna. 2001. "Click for Choice." *The Village Voice*, February 6.

Martin, Courtney, and Vanessa Valenti. 2013. "#FemFuture: Online Revolution." 8. *New Feminist Solutions*. New York, NY: Barnard Center for Research on Women.

Marwick, Alice. 2013a. *Status Update: Celebrity, Publicity, and Branding in the Social Media Age*. New Haven, CT: Yale University Press.

——— . 2013b. "Donglegate: Why the Tech Community Hates Feminists." *Wired Opinion*, March 29. www.wired.com/opinion/2013/03/richards-affair-and-misogyny-in-tech/.

Marwick, A., and Nicole B. Ellison. 2012. "'There Isn't Wifi in Heaven!' Negotiating Visibility on Facebook Memorial Pages." *Journal of Broadcasting & Electronic Media* 56 (3): 378–400.

Massanari, Adrienne Lynne. 2015. *Participatory Culture, Community, and Play: Learning From Reddit*. New York: Peter Lang Publishing.

McFadden, Syreeta. 2013. "What We Don't Talk About When We Talk About Mommy Wars." *Feministing*, July 11. http://feministing.com/2013/07/11/what-we-dont-talk-about-when-we-talk-about-mommy-wars/.

McLaine, Steven. 2003. "Ethnic Online Communities: Between Profit and Purpose." In *Cyberactivism: Online Activism in Theory and Practice*, edited by Martha McCaughey and Michael D. Ayers. New York: Routledge.

Meyer, Laura. 2006. "Power and Pleasure: Feminist Art Practice and Theory in the United States and Britain." In *A Companion to Contemporary Art Since 1945*, edited by Amelia Jones, 317–42. Malden, MA: Blackwell Publishing.

Meyer, Laura, and Faith Wilding. 2010. "Collaboration and Conflict in the Fresno Feminist Art Program: An Experiment in Feminist Pedagogy." *N. Paradoxa: International Feminist Art Journal* 26 (July): 40–51.

Nagarajan, Chitra. 2016. "What Does a Feminist Internet Look Like?" *The Guardian*, September 12, sec. Opinion. www.theguardian.com/commentisfree/2016/sep/12/feminist-internet-empowering-online-harassment.

Nakamura, Lisa. 1999. "Race In/For Cyberspace: Identity Tourism and Racial Passing on the Internet." In *Cyberreader*, edited by Victor Vitanza. Boston: Allyn and Bacon.

———. 2008. *Digitizing Race: Visual Cultures of the Internet*. Minneapolis: University of Minnesota Press.

Nardi, Bonnie A., Diane J. Schiano, and Michelle Gumbrecht. 2004. "Blogging as Social Activity, Or, Would You Let 900 Million People Read Your Diary?" In *Proceedings of the 2004 ACM Conference on Computer Supported Cooperative Work*, 222–31. ACM. http://dl.acm.org/citation.cfm?id=1031643.

Nguyen, Mimi Thi. 2012. "Riot Grrrl, Race, and Revival." *Women & Performance: A Journal of Feminist Theory* 22 (2–3): 173–96.

Nowson, Scott, and Jon Oberlander. 2006. "The Identity of Bloggers: Openness and Gender in Personal Weblogs." *AAAI Spring Symposium: Computational Approaches to Analyzing Weblogs*, 163–7. www.aaai.org/Papers/Symposia/Spring/2006/SS-06-03/SS06-03-032.pdf.

O'Leary, Amy. 2012. "Sexual Harassment in Online Gaming Stirs Anger." *The New York Times*, August 1, sec. U.S. www.nytimes.com/2012/08/02/us/sexual-harassment-in-online-gaming-stirs-anger.html.

Paasonen, Susanna. 2011. "Revisiting Cyberfeminism." *Communications* 36 (3): 335–52.

Papacharissi, Zizi. 2002. "The Presentation of Self in Virtual Life: Characteristics of Personal Home Pages." *Journalism and Mass Communication Quarterly* 79 (3): 643–60.

Phillips, Whitney. 2015. *This Is Why We Can't Have Nice Things: Mapping the Relationship Between Online Trolling and Mainstream Culture*. Cambridge, MA: MIT Press.

Piano, Doreen. 2002. "Congregating Women: Reading 3rd Wave Feminist Practices in Subcultural Production." *Rhizomes* 4. www.rhizomes.net/issue4/piano.html.

Piepmeier, Alison. 2009. *Girl Zines: Making Media, Doing Feminism*. First Edition. New York: New York University Press.
Plant, Sadie. 1996. "On the Matrix: Cyberfeminist Simulations." In *Cultures of Internet: Virtual Spaces, Real Histories, Living Bodies*, edited by R. Shields, 170–83. London: Sage.
Radway, Janice. 2011. "Zines, Half-Lives, and Afterlives: On the Temporalities of Social and Political Change." *PMLA* 126 (1): 140–50.
———. 2016. "Girl Zine Networks, Underground Itineraries, and Riot Grrrl History: Making Sense of the Struggle for New Social Forms in the 1990s and Beyond." *Journal of American Studies* 50 (1): 1–31.
Reagle, Joseph M. 2012. "'Free as in Sexist?' Free Culture and the Gender Gap." *First Monday* 18 (1). http://journals.uic.edu/ojs/index.php/fm/article/view/4291.
———. 2015. *Reading the Comments: Likers, Haters, and Manipulators at the Bottom of the Web*. Cambridge, MA: MIT Press.
Rentschler, Carrie. 2014. "Rape Culture and the Feminist Politics of Social Media." *Girlhood Studies* 7 (1): 65–82.
———. 2015. "#Safetytipsforladies: Feminist Twitter Takedowns of Victim Blaming." *Feminist Media Studies* 15 (2): 353–6.
Rettberg, Jill Walker. 2013. *Blogging*. New York: Polity.
Reynolds, Kate. 2013. "History of Cyberfeminism." Electronic document. *History of Cyberfeminism*, April 15. https://historyofcyberfeminism.wordpress.com/history-of-cyberfeminism/.
Rheingold, Howard. 2000. *The Virtual Community: Homesteading on the Electronic Frontier*. Cambridge, MA: MIT Press.
Riera, Taryn. 2015. "Online Feminisms: Feminist Community Building and Activism in a Digital Age." Senior Thesis, Claremont, CA: Scripps College. http://scholarship.claremont.edu/cgi/viewcontent.cgi?article=1699&context=scripps_theses.
Risam, Roopika. 2015. "Toxic Femininity 4.0." *First Monday* 20 (4). www.firstmonday.dk/ojs/index.php/fm/article/view/5896.
Rohde, Gregory L., and Robert Shapiro. 2000. *Falling Through the Net: Toward Digital Inclusion*. Washington, DC: US Department of Commerce, Economics and Statistics Administration, National Telecommunications and Information Administration. www.ntia.doc.gov/legacy/ntiahome/fttn00/falling.htm.
Scott, Krista. 1998. "'Girls Need Modems!' Cyberculture and Women's Ezines." *Master of Arts, Women's Studies*. Toronto, Canada: York University. www.stumptuous.com/mrp.html.
Shade, Leslie Regan. 2002. *Gender and Community in the Social Construction of the Internet*. New York: Peter Lang.
Solomon, Deborah. 2009. "Fourth-Wave Feminism." *The New York Times*, November 15, sec. Magazine. www.nytimes.com/2009/11/15/magazine/15fob-q4-t.html.
Stone, Allucquère Rosanne. 1996. *The War of Desire and Technology at the Close of the Mechanical Age*. Cambridge, MA: MIT Press.
Sutton, Laurel A. 1994. "Using Usenet: Gender, Power, and Silence in Electronic Discourse." In *Proceedings of the 20th Annual Meeting of the Berkeley Linguistics Society*, 506–20. Berkeley, CA: Berkeley Linguistics Society.
Swanson, Heidi. n.d. "Project: ChickClick." *101cookbooks.com*. www.101cookbooks.com/heidiswanson/html/ccframeset.html.
Thelandersson, Fredrika. 2013. "Tumblr Feminism: Third-Wave Subjectivities in Practice." MA Thesis, Department of Media, Culture & Communication, New York: New York University.
Turkle, Sherry. 1995. *Life on the Screen: Identity in the Age of the Internet*. New York: Simon & Schuster.
Uncapher, Willard. 1999. "Electronic Homesteading on the Rural Frontier." In *Communities in Cyberspace*, edited by Marc A. Smith and Peter Kollock. New York: Routledge, 264–89.
Van Zoonen, Liesbet. 2001. "Feminist Internet Studies." *Feminist Media Studies* 1 (1): 67–72.
VNS Matrix. 1991. "Cyberfeminist Manifesto for the 21st Century." http://obn.org/reading_room/manifestos/html/cyberfeminist.html.
Vogt, Christina, and Peiying Chen. 2001. "Feminisms and the Internet." *Peace Review* 13 (3): 371–4.
Wajcman, Judy. 2007. "From Women and Technology to Gendered Technoscience." *Information, Communication & Society* 10 (3): 287–98.
Warnick, Barbara. 1999. "Masculinizing the Feminine: Inviting Women on Line." *Critical Studies in Mass Communication* 16 (1): 1–19.
West, Lindy. 2015. "What Happened When I Confronted My Cruellest Troll." *The Guardian*, February 2. www.theguardian.com/society/2015/feb/02/what-happened-confronted-cruellest-troll-lindy-west.

Wilding, Faith. 1998. "Where Is Feminism in Cyberfeminism?" *N. Paradoxa,: International Feminist Art Journal* 1 (2): 6–13.

Wynn, Eleanor, and James E Katz. 1997. "Hyperbole over Cyberspace: Self-Presentation and Social Boundaries in Internet Home Pages and Discourse." *The Information Society* 13 (4): 297–327.

Zeilinger, Julie. 2016. "Feminist Blog About Womens Rights for Teenage Girls | Fbomb." Blog. *Thefbomb.org*. http://thefbomb.org/.

Section V
Coda conversation

A conversation with Tressie McMillan Cottom, Jack Halberstam, and Sherry Ortner

Tasha: *We've been framing this book around uses of feminism, as an approach to the work we do across disciplines and ways of connecting academic feminism and activism, politics and policy. We want to have a conversation about your use of, and relationship to, feminism in your own work and in general – its present state, and challenges for the future. Let's start with your personal trajectory, and your scholarly relationship to feminism: how has it changed over time?*

Sherry: I feel like it's gone up and down in all different kinds of cycles. I actually still remember when Shelly Rosaldo, may she rest in peace, said, "We're going to do a panel on feminism, or gender, or women, or something at the AAA" [Ed. Note: American Anthropological Association], in 19 . . . I hate to say it . . . like '72. And then Shelly and Louise [Lamphere] called us, lots of people – just friends – and said, "This is what we want to do." And we all said, "Well, we don't know anything about women or gender or feminism or anything like that, we do other stuff." And then Shelly said, "Well, you have to." . . . So we all said, "Okay," and we did it. That is how *Is Female to Male as Nature Is to Culture* came out. I guess I feel like, over time, two things. One is that feminist politics has gone in cycles and I'm very happy, as probably everyone is, thrilled, excited, kind of apprehensive about the current cycle where feminism is back. But then there's been all these periods where it has not been here and very much in the background. And it would fade away in my own work, too, and then I would sort of wake up and say, "Wait a minute. I haven't talked about this for a while. I really have to get back to this." So it seems to me more like that, back and forth with other kinds of work rather than a consistent stream of work that has carried through everything I've been doing.

Andrea: *The nature of doing it changed dramatically – I mean it must have, right?*

Sherry: Yeah. But in so many different ways, different kinds of sources – I wouldn't write *Is Female to Male as Nature Is to Culture* today – I don't think. I mean, who's doing structuralism? . . . So it changes in terms of topicality, frameworks, and so forth in all these different ways, referencing or engaging with other scholars differently over time. But also, the kinds of things I began to look at, like film, which I wasn't looking at when I started out.

Jack: I think Sherry really captures the ups and downs of a relationship to any political orientation. It doesn't stay constant because the world that we live in shifts and changes. So I'm sure we all have a kind of on-again, off-again sense of urgency around feminism in our lives. I know that basically when I was a young person, feminism came to me like a lifeline, really, because I grew up in England in a really sexist environment and getting this kind of ideological structure or discourse through which to understand the world that I grew up in was really, really important to me. . . . It wasn't my first sense of political consciousness by any means but it was a very important one. But the problem is that by my late twenties, feminism felt like an obstacle because, by about the late '80s, early '90s, some of what we called feminism was a very moralistic discourse – especially white feminism is what I'm really talking about. White feminism really felt like a policing discourse. It was a way in which the category of womanhood was being patrolled in very particular ways and I felt very alienated by that as a butch person, as somebody with a transgender orientation. It was tough for me to stay engaged with feminism. I would say that.

Intellectually, however, I feel like I've stuck with feminism. Like, it's always been important to me. Somebody who has to bring feminism to bear upon queer studies and queer studies to bear upon feminism. And, in that respect, it was just as important to me to critique white gay men as it was to critique police versions of white feminism and white male heterosexuality. So I feel that I can't do without feminism in the thinking that I do now. That said, I think that we have reached a bit of an impasse with feminism. I'm dismayed to always be teaching classes to young, often mostly white, women who come in already knowing what they think the terrain of feminism is. They have sort of knee-jerk reactions around race and class issues and I really, really wish that we were teaching more men. And so I wonder whether feminism has reached a kind of limit – what is feminism right now? It's these sorts of convulsive responses to this extremely predictable toxic masculinity that we're surrounded by, that we've all known about. This is not a revelation to us in any way, shape or form. And I guess I'm looking for logical political structures to tether my operation to . . . I'd like to find bigger categories through which to think about solidarity, and which doesn't mean I give up on feminism, but I still feel like I'm somewhat at odds with feminism at times.

Tressie: I think I could echo a lot of what Jack just said, my personal trajectory is going to be just a little different than Jack and Sherry because of how I come to it, that's kind of the whole point. My personal project with feminism is greatly influenced by (where) I come from . . . my mother was very much a revolutionary in her day. She had been an organizer and a Black Panther and so for us feminism was always part of this project of freedom, action and really grounded in our ideas of being black and women at the same time. And we're also US southern, I mean coming from that very traditional trajectory of black people in the United States. And so, my understanding was always grounded in a pragmatism; this was not theory for me. I actually didn't have any exposure to feminist theory as we understand it within academic feminism until my personal reading after undergrad and then into graduate school and this, again, because of my trajectory. So, I go to historically black college and undergrad where we don't even have a gender studies program. There's no women's studies – it's still actually common for black colleges in the US because so much of that curriculum was sort of embedded across disciplines, alongside race scholarships. We consider that the canon and so we didn't break it out as feminist, except we were so often being taught by black feminist professors. So, I didn't know it as separate from canonical thinking. I thought that was just like the Great Books liberal arts curriculum, which was black women interpreting the world for me – I didn't understand that as feminism or feminist theory.

Then, I end up going to Emory, which is probably the exact opposite of a historically black college, for graduate school, and this was my first time experiencing both formal white academic feminism and seeing black women and non-white women and queer women, especially queer women of color at Emory, organizing a feminist theory sort of in opposition to it (while) for me those things had not ever been separate before.

So, I'm at Emory at the same time the Crunk Feminist Collective is working and writing, these were young academic women of color, many of them queer, who had just created the space at Emory, mostly because, at a university that had this really historic women's studies program, the curriculum had been overwhelmingly white and overwhelmingly classist/elitist.

And so my introduction to what that discourse looked like was really watching the Crunk Feminist Collective respond to and engage with the women's studies program there at Emory, and then in sociology who considered both of those conversations irrelevant. So, the way that I start to try to reconcile that . . . was to just always stay grounded in my pragmatic philosophy of black feminism. I mean that's what I think I keep returning to. One reason for that, of course, is probably because of comfort and familiarity but also because as an intellectual project, it's been about the only thing that, for me, resolves some of the conflicts and tensions of the theoretical wars . . . the sort of pragmatic discourse that shaped black feminism, especially of a radical left black feminist discourse . . . there's a theory of change and there's a theory of action that just appeals to me as an intellectual project.

. . . (but) I'm not sure that feminism has to be my primary research objective as much as it is primary to the way I approach *doing* research . . . the fact that my research design is almost always centering and understanding of feminists – my data, my theory, my research project, where I'm doing the research, what questions I'm asking – are almost always embedded in what is happening for the women who are excluded from all of those dominant narratives.

The fact that I'm grounded in orienting my critical response to who had been missing from research (is) absolutely about the fact that I come from a black feminist tradition.

Sherry: . . . I hate being the oldest person in the room. [laughter]

What everybody was saying and feeling kind of echoes in my own experience but also not. I guess one of the things I was picking up that I think might be interesting for all of us, because we're all professors in universities, is the kind of feedback that comes from teaching students, mostly young women, about anything, including feminism, but especially anything political and how they just haven't hit the real world yet somehow. I find that I take cues from them and then that was sort of the basis of [the] paper I wrote about post feminism. I was really upset about the idea of post feminism. I thought, "What do you mean postfeminism?" Are you kidding? I mean, "look at the world. What are we talking about?" But the students are like: "That's over." And I just realized that it's the experience gap. It's a kind of privilege, not just of class, and there's a lot of that, and race, it's a lot of that. But also . . . youth and inexperience. A kind of privilege of not having to deal with the big, bad world yet. I just sometimes think to myself, "Honey, wait until you get out there, then you're going to find out."

So I think we get a different kind of message about what's happening with feminism as a movement when we look at and interact with our students from the way in which we interact with the world. . . . Anyone have thoughts about that?

Jack: That's really interesting, Sherry, what you're saying, I think one area that in the classroom we have to push more and more is in relationship to an historical arc for many of the arguments that we're having nowadays because things happen so quickly in an era of social media and digital platforms, that it feels to them, I think, as if since last Thursday, a million things have happened in the world, you know? [. . .] I think when it comes to either the ancient past or a couple of hundred years, [students are] willing to see that things were really different at the end of the 18th century, for example. When you push students or young people to understand that things were really different in the 1970s, for example, that's harder . . .

And then, you know, Sherry, thinking about some of your recent work on dark anthropology, it's super interesting to me to see these various turns that people are making to use some of the tools in feminism but using them in really different ways. Like, I think that category where you have an anthropology of the difficult, the imperiled, the precarious, that can't just simply be lumped under a feminist project because there are plenty of feminist projects now that are about the corporate, the wealthy, the successful, the . . . governance feminism. So I'm always looking for those kinds of categories, . . . I feel like we need to be super inventive about the kinds of tools that we use, not just to bring into the classroom, but to approach a rapidly shifting social scene.

Tressie: . . . Sherry, yeah. This whole thing about postfeminism. The way I hope that conversation gets flipped is, you know, I'll talk to you about a postfeminism when we can talk seriously about a post–white patriarchy. That's, you know, it's the same thing about post-racial. Well, I'll talk to you about that after post-racism . . . I'm kind of like Jack. I did not get into this job to teach history and I talk to my colleagues all the time about how I end up having to because – especially with a sociological project – there's nothing we can talk about if you don't know the historical context.

One of the fascinating things is how sophisticated students [are] with the discourse – if not of feminist theory, especially queer theory and post-colonial theory. This misled me initially because while they had a sophistication with the language, the language had been totally disconnected from the conversations that had produced those theories. I call it a tumblerization of theory . . . they knew the words but [those] concepts had not been anchored to a broader conversation for them. We had such success, I think, with feminist language, especially in the internet age, in the digital age, it is a seductive language. It feels really good when you learn these words that help you describe why you're the only weirdo in your high school. Right? And for millions of kids, that's what they are, and they get these words that help them explain that. "Oh my God, yeah. Okay. Intersectionality? Oh, awesome. I am queer. This is so great. There is a label and a word to describe how I feel." And they were getting that from popular culture discourse, especially popular culture discourse that that had been remixed for them on these social media platforms. They had no idea where the words came from, however.

I think that is actually indicative of a lot of what happens in the crossover. In many ways I think the contemporary feminist discourse might be a victim of the success of some academic feminist discourse, that the things that have crossed over to popular discussion do so first by divorcing (themselves) from the peoples and the groups and the conflicts that have produced them.

I do like the democratic appeal of online, digitally mediated, internet-based discussion that breaks academic feminism out of the academy because that was supposed to be our political project. Right? I like the democratic potential but I am trying to think about how we can retain that while also retaining the context of the critique in democratic ways. I don't have an answer for it but do think that is a challenge for contemporary feminism.

Andrea: Can I intervene there because this does lead into one of the questions we had which is about the current moment – a much more interesting moment than we thought it was going to be when we started this book. As I follow all the discussions about sexual harassments and assaults, I'm struck exactly by what Tressie is talking about, that (journalists) seem to not have a sense of history. Maybe it's a structural analysis that we're lacking. There's something they need to learn, I think, from academic feminism but we're not able to communicate with them. And what about #MeToo?

Sherry: I may be at one end of a spectrum here, but I feel like this whole unfolding of (accounts of) sexual harassment, rape, you know, Harvey Weinstein and everything after that is kind of thrilling to me. Now I know people are already moving into a critical mode about it and, I'm like, "Don't get too critical too fast." You know. "Enjoy it." I feel like this is what a revolution could begin with and I'm very excited about it. But – to go to your point about privileged and underprivileged kinds of figures within the narrative – one of the things I've been tracking and I think really is important to keep highlighting, is all this stuff about hotel maids. I mean, that there seems to be a site, a particular kind of site, in which this happens specifically – well, the workplace in general but hotels for specific reasons in particular where this kind of issue really has been completely kept under wraps and the problems of the employees were particularly acute because they couldn't afford to lose the job. It's different from a Hollywood actress who is afraid of Harvey Weinstein, yes, but she is not going be unable to feed her children. So it's important to get some focus within this unfolding about sexual harassment and rape; that's one of the ways I've been trying to focus on the issues where I feel they can get, sort of, blurry. Movie stars and so forth, they're very high visibility, but it's important to recognize the ways in which this really does cross the class lines and the race lines and so forth in terms of victimization, and the cost of victimization. The cost of being unable to come out and talk about it, unable to report it and so forth.

Jack: It is an interesting moment. I might be a little bit less optimistic than Sherry about it partly because we seem to be focused on very privileged men. You know, we're bringing down the Weinsteins. But we're not talking in a structural way about white masculinity per se and the way in which it is cultivated and constructed in our society, and the way in which it is allotted so much space and so many opportunities for wrong doing without punishment. And we're also not talking about heterosexuality as the training ground, not simply for male predation, but also for female submission, because a lot of these stories suggest, especially with the #MeToo campaign, that a lot of people have had the exact same experience from these exact same people for a very, very long time without that becoming even a tiny little thorn in the side of heteronormativity.

I really think that we have to have a national conversation about what is going wrong in terms of the raising of white boys . . . we seem to have granted white masculinity a kind of impunity that no other subject in the society has and that white men sort of nudge each other and say – as we saw Trump doing in the tape that was played during his campaign saying: "Hey, you know, you can do this. You can get away with that."

And I don't know why people don't want to talk about heterosexuality, I guess, and I think it's because it implicates, particularly white women, in some of these structures that we're so excited to be finally debating publicly. Let's not forget that 50% of white women voted for Trump and that recent election of Moore versus Cummings, right? Again, white people came out for a goddamn pedophile. So there's something deeper here. Like, Sherry, I really hope this is one of those sparks that's going to lead to a moment of cultural reckoning. But the reckoning has to be about the right things. It can't be that there's a kind of group of bad apples that we need to chastise and publicly critique. What we need here is an extension of what we're calling feminism and an understanding that class, race, and gender are colluding as discourses in the society that we live in to create a massive cushion for a group of people against the kinds of charges that are regularly brought against, for example, men of color.

And, by the way, a lot of this sexual harassment legislation on campuses is being used against queer people . . . [and] people who are teaching sexuality are becoming very vulnerable. And if we don't have a bigger conversation about this, it might be a runaway train that we're too late to put the brakes on.

Tressie: . . . while we didn't want to get off on #MeToo . . . I've been thinking a lot [of] Jack's point about not wanting to implicate heterosexuality . . . which I'm close to thinking about as being so deeply embedded in the patriarchal thing . . . and the race class and gender implications embedded in that and it brought to mind the case of Terry Crews. So he's this actor, black male actor who embodies, I think . . . the racist perverse ideas of black male sexuality as being both deviant and highly desirable. And he talks about being sexually abused at work by a white gay male. And how his case complicated the entire narrative, but in a way that could have been a moment for us to think that "Is it about being women or is it about power?"Yeah? And so that was always supposed to be like the structural critique that I think everybody is noting. Right? That is we focused on what the power relationship was, there was a way to have a contemporary feminism that would both allow us to critique Harvey Weinstein, think about the often invisible bodies of poor minorities, especially immigrant women who do hotel service work, for example, and allow us to critique what has happened to Terry Crews, and that is supposed to be the potential, I think, of integrative feminist critique that can be both structural and about agency and also about the context in which those things play out. And so much of that is missing in our contemporary discourse.

Which leads me to my second point about the media or the public discourse . . . where people use the language without necessarily understanding where the language comes from . . . I don't have an answer except that I do know that in a digital economy, attention is almost everything. So how can we amplify that kind of discourse and show it as a model for what a substantive critique of patriarchy would look like for contemporary feminism and popular discourse? So assuming that that is the goal or at least one of the aims of academic feminism: to exert some influence on popular discourse and to also learn from popular discourse. I think about: How can you produce or support or build a tribe around [that] kind of work [and] broader level [of] structural analyses?

You know, we are in this moment, I think, where we can't undersell, too; one of the reasons why we even know about a Harvey Weinstein, there's a structural piece about what has happened to women's economic potential that has made it possible for them to have this moment, but we're also in a media moment that made it possible for us to have a story about Harvey Weinstein that would not have happened previously. What we do not have is a political moment to capitalize on those other two things.

So what this suggests to me is that we have done a better job at building some sort of apparatus of social change in media and popular culture, and that we have done a somewhat effective job of thinking about that celebrity culture, and have not done a very good job of that politically.

So what's the political apparatus that's going to pick up #MeToo and translate that into political change? And not just political change for women who lean in, but political change for poor queer women of color. Right? How do we translate that? How do we do that?

And there, we have not done as good a job. And so I wonder what the jump is between popular culture and politics right now and that seems to me to be the site for contemporary feminism to pick up the ball and run.

Tasha: So we've got the academics; we've got popular culture, but we have all this rage in the political realm . . . and you've suggested that feminism faces a very serious challenge in jumping those levels. That in a sense – to use, Tressie, your thought of being victims of our own success, and of teaching the language but dropping off the context – not being able to operationalize feminisms on a political level. What can feminists in the academy contribute to moving that forward, to making structural changes?

Andrea: Can I just also echo Sherry's excitement because I do think that such a broad discussion, which is what we are having, fraught with dangers as Jack is bringing up, is still an unusual moment and maybe a moment for political mobilization, but how to make the interconnections: academic, feminism, media event . . . really effective politically?

Sherry: I have two little thoughts there. One is that there was an enormous apparatus that organized the 2017 Women's March in January. I mean, there was a huge organizing structure, somewhat loosely organized, but it's out there. I'd be really interested to find out what a lot of the folks who were involved in that are doing now because – this is my little optimistic thing – I think things are going to happen and I think people are organizing . . . it didn't just happen by accident. There were a lot of people who worked very hard on that. So I think that's important.

The other thing – and I know, this is all very embarrassing and like "liberal" – but I'm interested in women elected officials in terms of making something happen with some kind of lasting impact. Again, I feel like that's where I'm trying to find some kind of leverage in my utter despair and complete misery about the entire Trump phenomenon. The only thing where, in fact, something does seem to be happening is with women, and it can be women across a fairly wide spectrum. Again, elected women tend to be highly educated and more right than not. But not entirely. I feel like I want to find those areas that are already happening and support those things. So that's on the political end.

Then I just want to throw in, since I have the floor for one second, I just want to throw in one point getting back to the structural issues or patriarchy . . . I agree with everything that Jack said and Tressie said about really finding the sites in which patriarchy is basically made and re-made on a day-to-day basis, whether it's in the entire structure of heterosexuality, whether it's the daily practices of race and class and all that. But I also want to talk about capitalism because I feel that capitalism is so fundamentally patriarchal. I mean, even though it's about something else nominally, well, not just nominally, practically, but its fundamental structure is a patriarchal structure. And I feel like we have to look at all the different levels. So it's not just the kind of everyday, although that's hugely important, and it's not raising children, which I think, again, is hugely important in terms of sexual identities and so forth, but I also think that you get a kind of situation where, on the ground, a lot more equality in certain areas tends to be being made or being experienced. But when you look up at the top, at the big macro-structure of corporations, the military, the big nasty, big mega-structural stuff, it's just totally and absolutely patriarchal from top to bottom. It's hierarchies of men in this hyper-masculine mode. It's the organizing principle, in a sense, of capitalist action.

Tressie: Listen, it's hard bringing a feminist gun to a gunfight. The problem is, the guns they bring to those fights are just so much bigger than anything usually a feminist has. It is stunning to me to feel the weight of something like a military industrial complex or a corporatocracy. Or we're starting to think of interlocking corporate analyses. I mean, truly what they bring to that fight, which is capital and military power, which are one in the same thing – you know – you get to be rich by who you can kill. So, bringing a feminist analysis to that – or a feminist practice, not analysis, we can do analysis, we've got that all day long. So a feminist practice to that? I don't even know what that looks like politically in practical terms. I know what it looks like in ideological terms and that has always been one of the great big challenges I think for doing feminist work as opposed to thinking and writing it.

I was thinking about – Sherry was talking about capitalism . . . the stuff that gives me a sense of hope, however fragile, and a deep pleasure [is] I've seen working-class women coalitions, so I think about Fight for 15, who, for example, are probably the most direct political apparatus for the kinds of women that we're talking about in service work because so much of their precarity is wrapped up, of course, in their low economic returns to their labor. And it's about the role of service work in a financialized capitalistic system, which is where we now are, and a system of global capital where women move about the global system of patriarchy which is, itself, also, again, implicated deeply in a global hierarchy of race that says that brown immigrant women's bodies, by the time they get to the "first world" are always destined to be in second world labor even in the first world. That's where we are. That's why nobody cares about hotel maids, quite frankly.

And so thinking about the new feminism of watching, sort of, on the ground women, do maybe feminists practice without really delving into the feminist ideology, which I actually think is fine. You know. We've had those sort of grass roots political moments historically and I think it's fine. I don't think we need to necessarily bring ideology and worry about the fact that they are not doing the theoretical work of feminism, even if they're doing the practical work of feminism. But that one of the things that maybe academic feminism can contribute to those moments is translating what that work is to those other audiences in a way which that they understand. Right?

Politically, I was thinking about – one of the good things that I think is coming out of the last election and one of the reasons why we had a fairly good midterm is there were movements – I'm not sure if they're organizations – but there were, I don't know, networks encouraging women to run. I think *Elle* and *Cosmo* also had a version of this, you know, reaching out to women who maybe never had considered running for politics, and encouraging them to do so. And I think about one of the outcomes of that is that Atlanta elected a black woman mayor . . . and she's already being called a neoliberal stooge. And . . . this is the challenge, right? The problem is, that when you are in the political system, you are by default defending a capitalist political enterprise and you are responsible for defending, to some extent, a neoliberal ideology.

At the same time, the kind of work that you can probably do locally to actually improve the lives of women is probably far greater than what many academic feminists will ever be able to achieve. And I just always wonder if there cannot be – if we can call a truce on deciding who is or who is not, in the short term, a neoliberal stooge to allow for the fact that all of these things probably have to happen at the same time. That's my idealism speaking. It may not be possible. But if I had a great hope for contemporary feminism, it would be – if not to resolve that – to at least make peace with the fact that you're going to have activists, you're going to have politicians, and then you're going to have philosophers. And those things are sometimes going to have different short-term aims but should share a long-term aim. And is there a way for us to have a, sort of, integrative way of thinking about that?

Jack: I feel like there are a lot of different questions on the table here about: Can feminism really have an impact on the political status quo? What are our hopes moving forward? Those kinds of things would you say? Is that where we're at with this? I think that one of the things that we can do, even though we began this conversation by complaining a little bit about the disconnect in the classroom that I'm sure many people are having. At the same time, I do think that it is in the teaching that something has to be conveyed and exchanges need to happen between what we learn from students, what they learn from the university, that will have some kind of impact on the discourse moving forward. And I do think it's going to be a discourse that is bigger than feminism. I think Sherry's counsel there to be looking at the larger framework of capitalism is so important because, at either end of the scale it comes to the way in which women – "women" in its broadest sense – function within capitalism.

At one end of the scale, you've got, basically poor people, are women with children, often women of color with children who, because we're tearing away at welfare and entitlements and any kind of social services, means that they are much more affected by this particular current climate. But at the other end of the scale, you also have women who are benefiting greatly from the current policy of giving everything to the very wealthy and giving nothing to the very poor. So we have to reckon with that, and I don't think that feminism, as a project that is about uniting women, can actually manage that. You know, the fact that "lean in" feminism is so appealing to so many people means that, even as we've won some battles, we've lost a lot of other battles. And that does mean that we have to think much more capaciously about who we are politically and about how little this current political system does to address the kinds of political concerns that many people who might loosely consider themselves to be on the left have.

This might be the moment, certainly a revolutionary moment as Sherry said, but not necessarily around the sexual harassment stuff. I think the sexual harassment stuff, along with all of these incidents of lone male shooters, along with the massive homeless encampments that we're seeing in most major cities around the country, particularly places like L.A. and San Francisco, I mean, that should tell us that the political system we have, democratically elected or not, is not working. And I don't think that feminism is going to be our way out. I think that it's very, very easy to absorb feminism into a structure that continues to distribute goodies to people at the top by taking from people at the bottom.

So it's not the moment to let go of feminism because we are living an historical switch point around certain forms of behavior, particularly between men and women. But at the same time, we need new political vocabularies, which are being seen throughout this conversation, and I think we need to think about what we do as teachers. We need a different understanding of pedagogy. It might be a lot about creating two-way conversations rather than one-way and then complaining about how the students don't get what we're saying. We really have a lot to learn from younger people who are often on the political frontlines of many of these issues and who, I think, are super angry at older people because of the massive debt that they're being handed for an education that older people did not pay for, because they will never buy a home or because they've been sold a crock of shit about what it actually means to own a home, that because the environment's ruined. Because the political system, that's supposed to be made up of checks and balances, proves not to be.

I think if I was 18, I'd be pretty pissed off and distrustful of anyone over the age of, what was it, 35 that you're supposed to distrust?

Tressie: Anyone over 30, yes.

Jack: That's about 30, right. Because this is a generational divide. Older people who have done well from a housing market and free education have not passed that on to younger people. Those kinds of divisions have been a big deal in feminism all along but I think that they have a different kind of inflection right now.

Andrea: Well, our last question was going to be about the future of feminism . . . I do see a youth movement. I'm not sure I see it coming out of the sexual harassment . . . there's something going on around the legal aspect: how can we legislate nondiscriminatory practices under capitalism? Can we make headway by working through the legal system? And I think sex harassment activists for decades have not made this headway. You know, it's been very difficult but maybe we are in a moment where that's one place to start attacking some of the foundations of patriarchal capitalism.

Jack: Well, can I just say something about that? I mean, I just don't think that's the way to go and I think it's sort of horrifying that people are being fired because people sense that somebody is sexist. You know? I mean, this is not what we want. And I think as soon as you bring in the law. . . . The problem is that, in the past, the law has been used in universities to make sure that the university isn't liable for anything that happens under its roof. So that's why they brought in Title IX is because when the university investigated itself, guess what? It never found that it did anything wrong. Nobody in the university ever did anything wrong. You know, "Wow." What a big revelation, right?

So now Title IX comes in, but now it tips in the other direction where you have a kind of jealous prosecution, not of universities, however, or the way in which universities might institutionalize inequality. You're just picking people off. And that's not going to be good for anyone because one day it's a sexist guy, the next day, it's someone who teaches sexuality where something triggered someone in their classroom and then a bunch of other people said, "Yeah, I didn't like the way that was discussed either." Or a joke was made. The law is unfortunately not nuanced and not settled enough and not a tool that has been set up to make the kinds of distinctions that I think we would like to see made between various forms of behavior. That's also part of a kind of culture. I mean, you were asking about culture. This is also about the culture of places that needs to shift and change, you cannot legislate culture. What has to happen is that's part of what we're doing in the university is introducing people to complex cultural texts and conversations in order to produce people who will make distinctions and be able to calculate several moves ahead on any given decision they make, who will think critically about political conundrums, not just a "yes," "no," "like," "don't like," "accuse," "guilty," "innocent." . . . The law is too blunt of an instrument for the kinds of shifts and changes that we're looking for.

Tressie: What the law can do well, and what it seems to do best, is define who is a citizen, who has a voice in the body politic. That's what the inclusion of African Americans has been about. It's what the inclusion of immigrants continues to be about. It's what the inclusion of queer people, especially trans people, continues to be about right now. Inclusion in the body politic, meaning, "I want an equal say in the republic" or what the normative assumptions about what and who the law is supposed to protect. I want that. After that, law, to Jack's point, becomes a very blunt instrument for the institutionalization of norms. That is because law fundamentally is about protecting property and so when you're fundamentally about defining what is property and what ownership is, you're almost always going to side with property owner, the owners of capital. You're always going to side with capital because your goal is to defend capital and property.

It's why we see the adoptions of – among the examples that Jack gave is one that I was very cautious about – when many of my colleagues, many of them critical scholars, wanted to adopt institutional rules that required things like trigger warnings on syllabi, and I said to them, "You understand that the only problematic discourse in the corporate university that is going to be considered a problem is going to be exactly the discipline where we critique power and capitalism." Right? It's only a matter of time where the rule that you want to institute to defend the vulnerable disciplines like women's studies and feminists' studies and African-American studies and black studies and Latino studies are almost automatically then going to be turned into white male students saying, "A feminist studies class triggered me."

That what we're never going to have is a trigger warning on the econ syllabus where the econ syllabus is, quite frankly, the most oppressive syllabus in the whole university. Right? That was never going to happen. Macro is the most violent syllabus in any contemporary university.

[But] I cannot consider the context of those things because it's not what law is for. It's not for context. Law is to decide what to do once context has failed, once culture has failed. Right? That's the project. . . . And so I also get very weary when people want legal code to do that kind of work in the institution.

Having said that, nothing changes attitudes as effectively as changes in people's material conditions. As it turns out, people's hearts and minds tend to follow their behinds – meaning once they feel either economically vulnerable or economically safe, from there they act backwards to decide what they believe in and what their attitudes are. So, to bring it back to our first question of the hope of feminism, my hope really does rest mostly with socialist feminism right now, broadly defined.

[Feminism that] understands that you've got to build coalitions that change people's material conditions because it's one of the best ways to shift culture. And, in fact, I think that's a lesson from #Metoo, right? That what really ended up happening is that even a minute structural change in who was in charge of studios, a tipping point in the understanding of who had some material power of editorial boards, and a critical mass of women journalists and feminist writers, sort of moved the needle on what was acceptable to assume was okay. And so if anything, I think maybe that . . . should be the hope of feminism is to integrate those two things [and] maybe deemphasizes the legal project, which is a lesson from my abolitionist feminist friends, who talk about [how] we cannot continue to support carceral feminism because it is just fundamentally at odds with anything that wants to upend capitalism. Because capitalism depends on imprisonment in the way that liberalism depends on institutions, and the way that the law depends on negating social context and culture. So that's my hope.

Andrea: So, what changes the culture, Sherry?

Sherry: This is such an amazing conversation . . . I agree with everything everybody says [but] I want to go back to Jack saying that we need this bigger vocabulary, and I think that's absolutely true; you mentioned the dark anthropology paper, which is very dear to my heart right now. But, at the same time, I realized after I published it that I never said one word about patriarchy or gender or sexuality or men or women or anything. It was entirely institutional and structural and so forth in this completely unfeminist kind of way.

This is a paper about recent trends in anthropological theory with the key point being that anthropological theory since the '70s or the '80s has focused increasingly on the more and more brutal aspects of social life, of capitalism, of precarity, of the way in which people are just – pardon the expression – feeling fucked: depression, anxiety. I mean, you know, the other side of that. So then, in the following issue of [the same] journal, there was a forum of other papers commenting on the original article and I wrote a response to the responses. [In it] I expressed my regret about having not talked about anything related to feminist issues: of power, of sexuality, intersectionality . . . the whole thing. I mean . . . I don't think I used the word "apologize," but that was what I was feeling like. So, I guess what I'm feeling like – and this goes all the way back to my original comment – is I often find myself very schizophrenic between these two discourses and between these two ways of trying to think about the world. I think socialists' lives are one of the places where, of course, they do try to put that together. But it's really hard. I think that's where I'm at with that.

Jack: It's hard but it's a different project. That's why, like naming the particular institutional forms that have been instrumental in patriarchy [and] have marginalized women; White supremacy has brutalized people of color, and so on. That's one piece of an intellectual project. But that dark anthropology where we actually do an ethnography of the impact of those institutional structures on the communities that are intended [to] be affected and are affected, is another kind of project that I think points to the violence of what people are calling "inclusion," neoliberal inclusion. It's not exclusion that is simply the place of oppression. It is, in fact, the way in which people have folded into corrective structures that are the issues.

And I think . . . dark anthropology can reveal that, which is why it's such interesting work. And I think that the reason that feminism becomes such an easy target is because it looks like we're sitting in the same place year after year, decade after decade, continuing to rail against man and patriarchy when, in fact, feminisms are many, many different things and probably need to be registered as such. It's a tiny little word for all the different things that we have even talked about in the last hour and a half and I really think that it is counterproductive sometimes to use these words that then have a trans-historical resonance and seem to lump together all kinds of different social justice and political projects.

And what happens is you end up with a compromised position that is a kind of lean-in governance feminism or cultural feminism or worse. That's the reason I came to that essay . . . or why I would read the Crunk Collective, because I am looking for other kinds of narrative frameworks, especially to teach with because the students think they know what feminism is. They already have their critiques. They already have their position on it. And those people can't be taught. So we need some defamiliarizing languages for what we're talking about so that people don't just default all the time to the same kind of mechanisms. I think that that's, in the end, what the future has to be.

I actually think in the future we need to get rid of gender, sexuality, feminist programs and we need to replace them with much more capacious categories in order to do the work beyond the 17 eager-beaver undergraduate women who are already signed on to our project.

Tasha: What would that be called? How would you organize that?

Jack: Even just like, you know, replacing a gender and sexuality studies program with something . . . maybe [this] is too Foucauldian but a, kind of, histories of bodies, desire and power. You know? You can do everything that you need to do around queer studies under that heading. But people coming in don't already know what it is that you want to do with bodies, power, history, desire. But also that you would teach a class on dark anthropology or you would teach a class on Crunk Feminism or on diverse collectivities.

Part of our problem is that the disciplines have already determined what constitutes the proper area of study. That's why we all love the Foucauldian idea of subjugated knowledges, because subjugated knowledges are not knowledge that's being suppressed. It's knowledge that has been rendered unthinkable by the particular regimes of knowing that we all inhabit. And I think that if we take that seriously, then we need to change the rubrics in which we think. I don't want to keep walking into classrooms and showing amazing films like *Born in Flames* or a lost classic like *Times Square* and have students tell me that the films are romanticizing poverty or are racist, you know, on some weird scale that they have of racism – *Born in Flames* is racist. Why? Because it's about white women resisting some of the suggestions that black women in the film make, which is – in 1979 when the film was made – was referencing real struggles that were being talked about between white women and black women.

But under the heading of gender sexuality feminism – even visualizing disagreement between white women and black women – is now seen by a younger generation as racist.

Andrea: Tressie, one of the really brave things I see in your work is addressing how black feminism can actually speak to other feminisms – you're often confronting that issue and that difficulty of language.

Tressie: Yeah. So I agree with Jack [but] I'll be coming from a slightly different perspective; I'm also really attracted to defamiliarizing what we think we know. My belief is this: you cannot teach them until people are in what I call a student posture, and I mean that both institutionally, meaning a formal student, but I also mean that just in everyday life. I think it works for intimate relationships; I think it works at the grocery store. The idea that you can't go around and drop your narrative into people – that's not how that works. People have to come into a space where they are suitably uncomfortable and unfamiliar enough that they would seek learning. Right? Then until that space is created, there's nothing you can really do. And so I think Jack's point is very provocative in the sense that we may have reached . . . in academic feminism anyway, the end of the utility of a formal institutional discipline or department's ability to do that with students. [But] this seems super unfair though, because there's almost nothing that's ever going to be lobbed at something like, again, the economics department or the math department.

This is the problem I think with our discipline to the extent that we think of academic feminism as disciplinary. It is a problem that is just always embedded in marginalized people: our need to constantly reinvent our discourses in a way that dominant knowledges just don't have to do.

My hope continues to be embedded in black feminism, and something I derive from a lot of young feminists is to think of that feminism in plural; because of the mutual subjectivity of race and class and gender that happen at the intersections of black feminism, I think we have done a better job than big tent feminism welcoming exactly the types of subjectivities that keep us constantly in that space. Black feminism was dealing with queerness, for example, way before white feminism ever was. We were dealing with capitalism almost from our inception because we were thinking about our enslavement, which was a capitalist arrangement. So . . . under black feminism we are constantly in the student posture because we are almost defamiliarized in that way. We are persistently, almost definitionally, outside of those other hegemonic structures.

This is the reason why, I think, the Black Lives movement – a youth led movement that emerged almost entirely out of queer youth of color – can become normalized and accepted and, you know, celebrated under the umbrella of black feminisms – that's the space we're always occupying.

And this analysis [is also] the counterpoint to the problem that Jack presents us with . . . which is the utility of formal discourse of feminism, even feminisms, right now to have that sort of radical potential, precisely because of all of the work that goes into making those formal institutions.

And I'll tell you, so the young black feminists, especially young queer feminists that I talk to, they're mad! They're mad as hell and they are extremely radical – and sometimes have become victims of the tumblerization theory – but I'll tell you what I do think they've got right . . . they're more comfortable with unknowing than I think the feminists that have come before them were. They are very comfortable with the fact that they don't know where their next form of solidarity is coming from and it's because, I think, this generation is so comfortable with precarity. This is the generation born into the precarious moment. They're like, "I can't trust a job. I can't trust marriage. I can't trust a man. Like, none of those things are predicted to ever exist for me in five to ten years." And while that may be a horrible place to live for your individual psyche, what it has given them, I think, is a collective framework for organizing and theorizing their lives and building a movement around it. It's extremely powerful and maybe a lesson for the rest of us.

Index

Note: Page numbers in *italic* indicate a figure and page numbers in **bold** indicate a table on the corresponding page.